Grand Prix de
MONACO

CIRCUIT DE MONACO
=3180 M.

Rainer W. Schlegelmilch
Hartmut Lehbrink

Grand Prix de
MONACO

PROFILE OF A LEGEND

KÖNEMANN

I wish to express my particular gratitude to the Automobile Club of Monaco and the Daimler-Benz Classic Archiv.
They made a considerable contribution to the quality and completeness of this volume with their photos from the early years
of the Monaco Grand Prix.
I also wish to thank my former colleagues Günter Molter, Michael Hewett and Bernard Cahier for their excellent photo material.
Equally, my thanks go to Adriano Cimarosti and Norbert Michel for their committed collaboration, and Hartmut Lehbrink for his brilliant texts.
My friends Bernard Asset, Paul-Henri Cahier and Alois Rottensteiner made valuable additions to my photography with their best "Monaco shots".
A big thank you to them and, last but not least, also to the always prepared and hard-working Könemann team.

Meinen ganz besonderen Dank möchte ich dem Automobilclub von Monaco und dem Daimler-Benz Classic Archiv aussprechen.
Mit ihren Bildern aus den Anfangsjahren des Grand Prix von Monaco haben sie einen großen Beitrag zur Qualität und Vollständigkeit
dieses Werkes beigetragen.
Ich danke auch meinen früheren Kollegen Günter Molter, Michael Hewett und Bernard Cahier für ihr ausgezeichnetes Bildmaterial.
Ebenso Adriano Cimarosti und Norbert Michel für ihre engagierte Mitarbeit und Hartmut Lehbrink für seine brillanten Texte.
Meine Freunde Bernard Asset, Paul-Henri Cahier und Alois Rottensteiner bereicherten meine Fotografie mit ihren besten »Monaco-Shots«.
Ihnen ein großes Dankeschön und last not least auch dem immer einsatzfähigen und fleißigen Könemann-Team.

Je tiens à remercier tout particulièrement l'Automobile-Club de Monaco et les Daimler-Benz Classic Archiv.
Avec leurs clichés des toutes premières années du Grand Prix de Monaco, ils ont fourni une contribution déterminante à la qualité
et à l'intégralité du présent ouvrage.
Je remercie également mes anciens collègues Günter Molter, Michael Hewett et Bernard Cahier pour leurs remarquables photographies.
Merci également à Adriano Cimarosti et à Norbert Michel pour leur concours de tous les instants et à Hartmut Lehbrink pour ses textes brillants.
Mes amis Bernard Asset, Paul-Henri Cahier et Alois Rottensteiner ont enrichi mes photographies de leurs meilleurs « Monaco-Shots ».
A eux tous un grand merci et, last but not least, également à l'équipe de Könemann toujours présente et débordante de zèle.

Rainer W. Schlegelmilch

Photography: Rainer W. Schlegelmilch
Text: Hartmut Lehbrink
Statistics: Norbert Michel & Pierre Abeillon

Art direction and design: Peter Feierabend
Managing editor: Sally Bald
Layout and typography: Oliver Hessmann
Assistant: Thomas Lindner
Translation into English: Christian von Arnim & Paul Motley
Translation into French: Jean-Luc Lesouëf
Production manager: Detlev Schaper
Assistant: Nicola Leurs
Production: Mark Voges
Reproductions: Omniascanners, Milan
Printing and binding: Neue Stalling, Oldenburg
Printed in Germany

ISBN 3-8290-0658-6
10 9 8 7 6 5 4 3 2 1

CONTENTS · INHALT · SOMMAIRE

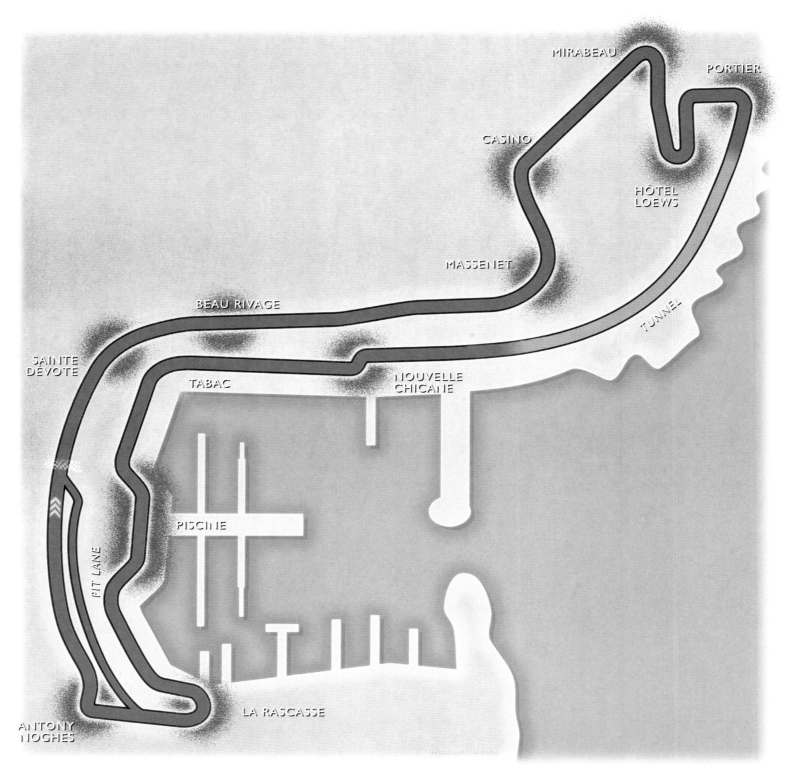

Map labels: MIRABEAU, PORTIER, CASINO, HÔTEL LOEWS, MASSENET, BEAU RIVAGE, TUNNEL, SAINTE DÉVOTE, TABAC, NOUVELLE CHICANE, PISCINE, PIT LANE, LA RASCASSE, ANTONY NOGHES

SAINTE DÉVOTE church alongside the track, dating from 1870, with a beautiful 18th century altar; BEAU RIVAGE once the site of a palace hotel of this name; MASSENET square near the Casino, named after the French composer Jules Massenet (1842–1912). He was a friend of Prince Albert I and frequently liked to visit Monaco; CASINO Monte Carlo casino was started in 1878 by the architect of the Paris Opera, Charles Garnier, and completed in 1910; MIRABEAU luxury hotel with 99 rooms; LOEWS luxury hotel with 600 rooms; PORTIER small harbor, reserved for fishing boats; TABAC originally a tobacconist between two flights of stairs at the quay, today there is a tunnel with a small tobacconist on this site; LA RASCASSE restaurant and bar, built in 1972; ANTONY NOGHES named in honor of the spiritual father of the Monaco Grand Prix and subsequent president of the ACM from 1940 until 1953.

SAINTE DÉVOTE 1870 erbautes Gotteshaus nahe der Strecke, mit schönem Altar aus dem 18. Jahrhundert; BEAU RIVAGE Hier stand einst ein Palasthotel dieses Namens; MASSENET Platz in der Nähe des Casinos, benannt nach dem französischen Komponisten Jules Massenet (1842–1912). Er war ein Freund des Fürsten Albert I und kam häufig und gerne nach Monaco; CASINO Das Casino von Monte Carlo wurde 1878 vom Erbauer der Pariser Oper Charles Garnier geschaffen und 1910 vollendet; MIRABEAU Hotel der Luxusklasse mit 99 Zimmern; LOEWS Hotel der Luxusklasse mit 600 Zimmern; PORTIER kleiner Hafen, für Fischerboote reserviert; TABAC Ursprünglich gab es dort ein Tabakgeschäft zwischen zwei Treppen am Kai. Heute findet sich an dieser Stelle ein Tunnel mit einem kleinen Tabakladen; LA RASCASSE Restaurant und Bar, 1972 gebaut; ANTONY NOGHES so genannt zu Ehren des geistigen Vaters des Grand Prix Automobile de Monaco und späteren Präsidenten des ACM von 1940 bis 1953.

SAINTE DÉVOTE chapelle construite en 1870 près du circuit et qui renferme un magnifique autel du 18e siècle ; BEAU RIVAGE ici se trouvait jadis un palace portant ce nom ; MASSENET place proche du Casino, baptisée du nom du compositeur français Jules Massenet (1842–1912). C'était un ami du prince Albert Ier qui se rendait fréquemment et avec plaisir à Monaco ; CASINO le Casino de Monte-Carlo a été construit en 1878 par Charles Garnier, auteur de l'Opéra de Paris du même nom, et achevé en 1910 ; MIRABEAU hôtel de grand luxe avec 99 chambres ; LOEWS hôtel de grand luxe avec 600 chambres ; PORTIER petit port réservé aux bateaux de pêche ; TABAC initialement se trouvait ici un bureau de tabac entre deux escaliers montant du quai. Aujourd'hui s'y trouve un tunnel avec de nouveau un petit bureau de tabac ; LA RASCASSE bar-restaurant construit en 1972 ; ANTONY NOGHES ainsi nommé en l'honneur du père spirituel du Grand Prix Automobile de Monaco et futur président de l'ACM de 1940 à 1953.

FOREWORD by Alain Prost

Monaco is the circuit I know the best and where I've contested more races than anywhere else. My best memory has got to be 1986. It was a fantastic racing weekend, a dream: pole position, fastest lap ever and then victory… It's the atmosphere and feeling you find in Monaco: the driver and his car must become one and that does not happen very often in one's career. This Grand Prix is mythical, incredible: it seems totally unreasonable to let Formula 1 cars race through Monaco; however, whether driver, team boss, mechanic or above all sponsor, everyone loves to come and participate. This exceptional race has changed quite a lot through the years, especially regarding safety requirements. Though it may appear technically less interesting than other races, it is the most impressive and prestigious race of the year. Monaco is also a race for drivers: the greatest drivers are almost always present in this event. Of course speed is vital – but then so are concentration, finesse and tactics. Winning in Monaco has always been a sort of mini World Championship. It is an important stage in the racing calendar. If there is one Grand Prix that every team boss must win just once, it is Monaco.

Monaco ist die Rennstrecke, die ich am besten kenne und auf der ich die meisten Rennen meiner Laufbahn bestritten habe. Die schönsten Erinnerungen verbinde ich mit dem Jahr 1986. Es war ein fantastisches Rennwochenende, fast wie im Traum: Pole Position, die schnellste Runde und Sieg… Das sind die Atmosphäre und das Feeling, die man in Monaco braucht: Man muß mit seinem Auto vollkommen verschmelzen – ein Gefühl, das ein Rennfahrer in seiner Laufbahn nicht sehr häufig verspürt. Monaco ist ein mit Mythen behafteter, faszinierender Grand Prix, mystisch und unfaßbar: Unter dem Gesichtspunkt der Vernunft betrachtet, sollten hier eigentlich keine Formel-1-Rennen ausgetragen werden, aber die Fahrer, Rennstallchefs, Mechaniker und ganz besonders die Sponsoren kommen gerne nach Monaco. Es ist eine besondere Rennstrecke, die sich im Laufe der Jahre sehr verändert hat, vor allem durch die Sicherheitsanforderungen. Auch wenn andere Strecken in technischer Hinsicht vielleicht interessanter sind, ist Monaco dennoch die eindrucksvollste Veranstaltung mit dem größten Prestige im ganzen Rennkalender. Es ist darüber hinaus eine klassische Fahrerstrecke: Es gibt nur wenige große Piloten, die hier nicht ihr Können unter Beweis gestellt haben. Natürlich muß man schnell sein, um sich durchsetzen zu können, aber die Strecke erfordert auch Konzentration, Finesse und Taktik. Ein Sieg in Monaco kam schon immer einem Mini-Weltmeistertitel gleich. Das Rennen ist eine wichtige Etappe im Rennkalender, und wenn es für die Rennstallchefs einen Grand Prix gibt, den man unbedingt einmal gewinnen muß, so ist es dieser.

Monaco est le circuit que je connais le mieux, c'est celui sur lequel j'ai couru le plus souvent dans ma carrière. Mon meilleur souvenir, c'est 1986. C'était un week-end de course fantastique, c'était comme dans un rêve, une pole position, un record du tour et la victoire… C'est le genre d'atmosphère et de feeling qu'il faut trouver à Monaco : il faut faire complètement corps avec sa voiture et ça n'arrive que rarement dans la carrière d'un pilote. C'est un Grand Prix mythique, incroyable : normalement, la raison voudrait qu'on ne coure pas à Monaco avec des Formule 1, mais qu'on soit pilote, chef d'écurie, mécanicien, ou surtout sponsor, tout le monde aime y aller. C'est un circuit spécial, qui a beaucoup évolué au fil des ans, en particulier pour des impératifs de sécurité. Bien qu'il soit peut-être moins intéressant que d'autres sur le plan technique, c'est le plus impressionnant et le plus prestigieux de l'année. Monaco est aussi un circuit de pilote : rares sont les grands pilotes qui ne s'y soient pas illustrés. Il exige bien entendu des qualités de rapidité, mais aussi de concentration, de finesse et de tactique. Gagner à Monaco a toujours été une sorte de mini championnat du monde. C'est une étape très importante, et en tant que patron d'écurie, s'il y a un Grand Prix que l'on doit absolument gagner un jour, c'est bien celui-là !

BIRTH OF A LEGEND

GEBURT EINER LEGENDE · NAISSANCE D'UNE LÉGENDE

You can see it in his face: Antony Noghes, self-assured citizen of the Principality of Monaco and a passionate disciple of the motor car, is a man of action – a man whose alert gaze is focused firmly on the future, with such firm determination in fact that he might strike you as being unbendingly obstinate. What the thirty-five year old had in mind on an October day in 1925 was that the Automobile Club de Monaco (ACM), of which he was General Commissioner, should join the AIACR (Association Internationale des Automobile Clubs Reconnus) which was, in some respects, the mother of the FIA (Fédération Internationale de l'Automobile), another organization based in Paris. This was by no means an easy mission: the august gentlemen grouped around their President, Baron de Zuylen, were renowned for being unwelcoming and brittle whenever they were faced with an applicant wishing to join their hallowed circle of approved members.

The ACM had not been known by this name for very long at this time. Indeed, the name originated as a derivation of the names of the clubs which had preceded it. While the motor car

Man sieht es seinem Gesicht an: Antony Noghes, selbstbewußter Bürger des Fürstentums Monaco und leidenschaftlicher Apostel des Automobils, ist ein Mann der Tat, den wachen Blick unbeirrt in die Zukunft gerichtet, ja stur bis hin zur Unbeugsamkeit. Was sich der 35jährige an jenem Oktobertag des Jahres 1925 in den schmalen Kopf gesetzt hat, ist dies: Der Automobile Club de Monaco (ACM), dessen Generalkommissar er ist, soll Mitglied der AIACR (Association Internationale des Automobile Clubs Reconnus) werden, der Mutter der FIA (Fédération Internationale de l'Automobile) gewissermaßen und wie diese in Paris angesiedelt. Die Mission wird nicht einfach sein: Die hohen Herren unter ihrem Präsidenten Baron de Zuylen sind bekannt sperrig und spröde sowie jemand um Aufnahme in die erlauchte Loge der bereits zugelassenen Mitglieder ersucht.

Der ACM heißt noch nicht lange so, und sein Name ist programmatisch wie die Namen der Clubs, aus denen er hervorgegangen ist. Als das Auto in den Windeln liegt, ist der Stadtstaat eine Domäne der Radfahrer. Das Veloziped spielt eine erfreuliche Doppelrolle: Es dient zugleich elementarer

Son visage ne trompe pas : Antony Noghes, citoyen de la Principauté de Monaco conscient de son statut et prophète passionné de l'automobile, est un homme d'action, le regard vif tourné résolument vers l'avenir, parfois têtu à en être intraitable. Ce que, ce jour d'octobre 1925, cet homme de 35 ans s'est mis en tête est rien moins que cela : faire de l'Automobile Club de Monaco (ACM), dont il est le commissaire général, un membre de l'AIACR (Association Internationale des Automobile-Clubs Reconnus), qui est en quelque sorte l'organe suprême de la FIA, la Fédération Internationale de l'Automobile, et, comme celle-ci, a son siège à Paris. Sa mission ne sera pas simple : les dignitaires regroupés autour de leur président, le baron de Zuylen, sont connus pour leur froideur et leur arrogance dès que quelqu'un demande à être admis dans l'illustre loge des membres déjà affiliés.

Il n'y a pas longtemps que l'ACM porte ce nom, un nom à caractère de programme tout comme celui des clubs dont il est l'émanation. A cette époque où l'automobile en est encore à ses balbutiements, la ville-Etat est le domaine des cyclistes.

was still in its early infancy, the city state was firmly in the hands of the cycling fraternity. The bicycle – or velocipede as it was then known – had a mutually enhancing dual role in life: it provided an elementary form of personal transport on the one hand, and it was an excellent means of physical self-improvement on the other. For as soon as you leave the immediate vicinity of the Monte Carlo harbor, you encounter uphill gradients, some of them very steep indeed – always, of course, offering the tempting prospect of a rewarding run downhill. In September 1890, these cycling devotees among the subjects of Prince Albert I formed the *Sport* Vélocipédique Monégasque (SVM).

In 1907, imbued with the spirit of a new age, the SVM was renamed the SAVM (Sport Automobile et Vélocipédique de Monaco). On 31 October 1909, Antony's equally dynamic father, Alexandre Noghes, was elected to serve as its President. In a memorable speech on 1 December that year, he went on to expound a daring idea. Everyone was aware of the long-standing tradition of rivalry with the neighboring town of Nice. It was time to set a new tone, by establishing a rally based

Fortbewegung und der körperlichen Ertüchtigung. Denn sowie man den unmittelbaren Einzugsbereich des Hafens von Monte Carlo verläßt, gilt es zum Teil erhebliche Steigungen zu überwinden, während andererseits lustvolle Abfahrten als Lohn winken. Im September 1890 schließen sich die bekennenden Radler unter den Untertanen des Fürsten Albert I. im Sport Vélocipédique Monégasque (SVM) zusammen.

1907 wird der SVM, durchweht vom Geist der neuen Zeit, umbenannt zum SAVM, Sport Automobile et Vélocipédique de Monaco. Als Präsident wählt man am 31. Oktober 1909 Antonys gleichfalls dynamischen Vater Alexandre Noghes. In einer denkwürdigen Rede vom 1. Dezember des gleichen Jahres entwickelt dieser eine kühne Idee. Immer, das wisse man ja, schwele die Rivalität mit dem Nachbarn Nizza. Da müsse man einen Akzent setzen, mit einer Rallye für Automobile nach dem Vorbild der italienischen Convegni Ciclisti. Bei denen gehe es darum, möglichst viele Radfahrer von möglichst vielen Plätzen an einem Punkt zusammenkommen zu lassen. Man werde die Zweiräder einfach durch Autos ersetzen.

Le vélocipède joue un double rôle, réjouissant : moyen de locomotion élémentaire, il est aussi un instrument d'éducation physique. En effet, dès que l'on quitte les abords immédiats du port de Monte Carlo, il faut grimper des côtes parfois escarpées qui récompensent en contrepartie le courageux cycliste par une descente échevelée. En septembre 1890, les cyclistes pratiquants parmi les sujets du Prince Albert I se regroupent au sein du Sport Vélocipédique Monégasque (SVM).

En 1907, le SVM, touché par l'esprit des temps nouveaux, est rebaptisé en SAVM, Sport Automobile et Vélocipédique de Monaco. Le 31 octobre 1909, ses membres élisent comme président Alexandre Noghes, le père, tout aussi dynamique, d'Antony. Dans son mémorable discours du 1er décembre de la même année, le père déclare avoir eu une idée audacieuse. Nul n'ignore, en effet, la rivalité qui couve à l'égard de la ville voisine, Nice. Il voulait donc faire sensation, en organisant un rallye pour automobiles calqué sur les Convegni Ciclisti italiennes. L'objectif de celles-ci est de faire converger le plus grand nombre de cyclistes possible partis du plus grand nombre de villes possible vers un seul et même point. Mais à

The Principality in 1901: on the right is the Rocher and the old town Monaco situated 60 meters above the sea; on the left is the newer part Monte Carlo; in the center is La Condamine with its shops and harbor.

Das Fürstentum im Jahre 1901: rechts der Rocher mit der Altstadt Monaco, 60 m über dem Meer gelegen, links der neue Stadtteil Monte Carlo, in der Mitte das Geschäfts-und Hafenviertel La Condamine.

La Principauté en 1901 : à droite le Rocher avec la vieille ville de Monaco, située à 60 mètres-au-dessus de la mer, à gauche le nouveau quartier Monte Carlo, au milieu le quartier des affaires et le port La Condamine.

on the model of the Italian Convegni Ciclisti. In this event, the aim was to bring together in one place as many cyclists as possible, after starting from as many different locations as possible. This time, however, the idea would be to substitute motor cars for bicycles.

In late January 1911, the first Rallye Automobile Monaco took place with drivers setting out from Paris, Berlin, Brussels, Boulogne, Vienna and Geneva. The winner was a driver called Henri Rougier who, at the wheel of a 25 horsepower Turcat-Méry, achieved an average speed of 13.8 kph (8.6 mph). Mind you, the event prompted many loud voices to vent their discontent. The 23 participants and the organizers fell out mightily about the finer points of the race rules, which stressed the importance of the aesthetic appeal and comfort of the contending vehicles whereas, some argued, the emphasis should have been placed firmly on sports performance.

The inexorable rise of the automobile meant that by the Twenties cyclists were no longer such a common sight in Monaco. After an extraordinary general meeting on 29 March 1925, the words Sport Vélocipédique disappeared completely from the name of the club, a change behind which Alexandre Noghes had thrown his weight with his usual smooth persuasiveness. The SAVM mutated into the ACM, which required the blessing of the AIACR in order to avoid it dwindling into a pale shadow of a local club.

This is what went through Antony Noghes' mind on the way to Paris, where he was duly greeted with scepticism on his arrival. Each applicant had to provide evidence of a certain number of registered motor vehicles, he was told, and, moreover, of an important national motor sport event. For that, the Principality was no doubt too small, his interlocutors added. The Rallye Monte Carlo did not count because it was staged over the whole of Europe. Noghes was filled with anger as he took his leave, indicating pointedly that Monaco was going to become the venue of an event which would be the talk

Ende Januar 1911 geht die erste Rallye Automobile Monaco über die Bühne, mit Paris, Berlin, Brüssel, Boulogne, Wien und Genf als Ausgangsorten. Sieger wird Henri Rougier am Lenkrad eines Turcat-Méry 25 PS mit einem Stundenmittel von 13,8 km. Die Sache geht nicht ohne schrille Töne ab. Die 23 Teilnehmer und die Organisatoren kriegen sich nämlich über die Feinheiten des Reglements in die Wolle, welches der Schönheit und dem Komfort des Fahrzeugs einen zu hohen Stellenwert beimesse, wo es doch in erster Linie um die sportliche Leistung gehe.

Mit dem unaufhaltsamen Vormarsch des Automobils in den Zwanzigern werden die Radfahrer im Stadtbild von Monaco rarer. Nach einer außerordentlichen Generalversammlung am 29. März 1925 verschwindet der Sport Vélocipédique ersatzlos aus dem Namen des Clubs, wofür sich Alexandre Noghes mit der ihm eigenen geschmeidigen Beredsamkeit stark gemacht hat. Der SAVM mutiert zum ACM, und der bedarf des Segens der AIACR, damit er nicht als blasses lokales Pflänzchen verkümmert.

Dies ist es, was Antony Noghes auf dem Wege nach Paris durch den Kopf geht. Dort begegnet man ihm in der Tat mit Skepsis. Jeder Bewerber müsse eine gewisse Anzahl von zugelassenen Kraftfahrzeugen nachweisen und überdies eine bedeutende nationale Motorsportveranstaltung. Zu dergleichen sei das Fürstentum ja wohl zu klein. Die Rallye Monte Carlo zähle nicht als Fleißkärtchen, da im Grunde ganz Europa der Austragungsort sei. Noghes verabschiedet sich voller dumpfen Zorns. Man plane, kündigt er noch rasch forsch an, Monaco zum Schauplatz eines Ereignisses zu machen, von dem die ganze Welt sprechen werde. Was genau das sein wird, weiß er selbst noch nicht. Aber während der Zugfahrt zurück an die Côte nimmt ein Plan Gestalt an, vage zunächst, dann immer konkreter. Ein paar Tage später erkundet er längst vertrautes Terrain unter einem neuen Aspekt, zu Fuß, um Muße zu haben für eine Vision. Seine Begehung

cette différence près que l'on remplacerait tout simplement les deux roues par des voitures.

Fin janvier 1911, les pilotes du premier Rallye Automobile Monaco prennent donc la route, avec Paris, Berlin, Bruxelles, Boulogne, Vienne et Genève comme villes de départ. Le premier vainqueur est Henri Rougier, au volant d'une Turcat-Méry 25 ch, à une moyenne de 13,8 km/h. Mais tout ne va pas sans couacs. Les 23 participants et les organisateurs ont, en effet, maille à partir sur des détails du règlement, qui accorde une trop grande importance à la beauté et au confort des véhicules alors qu'il s'agit en première ligne d'un événement sportif.

Face aux progrès irrésistibles de l'automobile, les cyclistes disparaissent peu à peu du paysage urbain de Monaco dans les années vingt. A l'issue de l'Assemblée générale extraordinaire du 29 mars 1925, Sport Vélocipédique est supprimé tout simplement du nom du club selon le plaidoyer, comme toujours enflammé et convaincant, d'Alexandre Noghes. Le SAVM se mue en ACM, mais il lui faut la bénédiction de l'AIACR s'il ne veut pas végéter telle une fragile petite plante régionale.

Et c'est ce qui préoccupe Antony Noghes, en route vers Paris, où il ne récoltera que scepticisme. Tout candidat doit pouvoir se prévaloir d'un certain nombre de véhicules automobiles immatriculés et, en outre, être l'organisateur d'une importante manifestation nationale de compétition automobile. Or, la Principauté est incontestablement trop petite pour cela, lui rétorque-t-on. Quant au Rallye de Monte-Carlo, on ne pouvait le considérer comme telle puisque, dans le fond, il était organisé dans l'Europe entière, ajoute-t-on. Alexandre Noghes s'en alla, furieux, déclarant haut et clair que Monaco deviendrait bientôt le théâtre d'un événement dont parlerait le monde entier. Quant à savoir ce que cela serait exactement, lui-même ne le savait pas encore. Mais, dans le train qui le ramenait vers la Côte d'Azur, un plan commençait à prendre forme dans son esprit, vague tout d'abord, puis de

of the world. What exactly that was going to be, he did not yet know himself. A plan began to take shape during the train journey back to the Riviera, indistinct at first, becoming increasingly concrete. A few days later he began to investigate long-familiar territory but this time he looked at it with new eyes, and on foot in order to develop and refine his vision. His walk started at the Boulevard Albert I. Then he climbed the considerable incline to Casino square, walked down to Monte Carlo station, then turned right at Portier on to the coast road, through the tunnel to the Quai des Etats-Unis, and continued his way along the Quai Albert I to the gasometer before returning finally to Boulevard Albert I.

What the visionary on his lonely walk did not realize, despite all his self-assurance, was that he had just invented the most famous – and the most controversial – Grand Prix circuit of all time. Initially, cobbles and tram tracks were reminders of its everyday use. For two years he nursed the project. Then he obtained a prominent supporter in Louis Chiron, 28, one of the most successful racing drivers of his time and a native of the town, like Noghes himself. Chiron did not stint on the superlatives and thus Noghes sought an audience with Prince Pierre. He, too, was considerably taken with the project; after all, the plan would serve the greater glory of the Principality and the House of Grimaldi, as well as representing a clever move against rival Nice. On 13 October 1928, the ACM was duly recognized by the AIACR and came under its umbrella. On 14 April 1929, Pierre drove a lap of honor of the circuit on the occasion of the Premier Grand Prix Automobile de Monaco. The race organizer, Charles Faroux, a hard-bitten old hand in the business who knew all the tricks, was at the wheel. But even he admitted that his heart had leapt with the same enthusiasm as it would have done in his youth. And he added what a superb idea it was to have a Grand Prix through the streets of the town.

beginnt auf dem Boulevard Albert I. Dann erklimmt er den beträchtlichen Anstieg zum Casinoplatz, steigt ab zum Bahnhof von Monte Carlo, wendet sich bei Portier nach rechts auf die Küstenstraße, durchquert den Tunnel des Taubenschießens zum Quai des Etats-Unis, setzt seinen Weg fort über den Quai Albert I bis zum Gasometer und biegt schließlich wieder in den Boulevard Albert I ein.

plus en plus concret. Quelques jours plus tard, il part inspecter un terrain qu'il connaît bien, en essayant de l'observer sous un angle différent ; il parcourt ce chemin à pied pour avoir le temps de modeler sa vision. Sa promenade commence sur le Boulevard Albert I. Puis il couvre la longue montée jusqu'à la Place du Casino avant de redescendre vers la gare de Monte-Carlo, de s'engager à droite, au virage du Portier, en direction de la route du littoral et de traverser le Tunnel du Tir au pigeon vers le Quai des Etats-Unis et de poursuivre son chemin le long du Quai Albert I jusqu'au Gazomètre et de revenir enfin sur le Boulevard Albert I.

Ce qu'ignore encore ce visionnaire et promeneur solitaire malgré sa confiance à déplacer des montagnes, c'est qu'il vient d'inventer le circuit de Grand Prix le plus célèbre de tous les temps – mais aussi le plus controversé. Au début, des pavés et des rails de tramway rappellent même sa raison d'être, dans la vie quotidienne. Pendant deux ans, il porte en lui son projet. Puis il se procure un célèbre allié, en la personne de Louis Chiron, 28 ans, l'un des pilotes de course les plus prestigieux de son époque et, comme Noghes lui-même, enfant de la ville. Chiron ne tarit pas de superlatifs, ce qui incite Antony Noghes à demander une audience auprès du Prince Pierre. Lui aussi est immédiatement enthousiasmé par le projet, d'autant plus que celui-ci ne pourrait qu'accroître la gloire de la Principauté et de la dynastie des Grimaldi, tout en étant un camouflet à la face de sa concurrente, la ville de Nice. Le 13 octobre 1928, l'ACM obtient protection et est officiellement admise dans le giron de l'AIACR. Le 14 avril 1929 à l'occasion du premier Grand Prix automobile de Monaco, Pierre couvre un tour d'honneur sur le circuit. Charles Faroux, ce vieil habitué de l'automobile qui connaît toutes les ficelles du métier, est au volant de la voisin. Ce qui n'a pas empêché son cœur de battre avec le même enthousiasme que dans sa jeunesse, déclare-t-il. Et d'ajouter qu'organiser ce Grand Prix dans les rues de la ville était une idée magnifique !

1

3

Past beauty: Sainte Dévote, (1) in 1930 with the palace hotel Beau Rivage on the hill to the Casino and (3) with the Hotel Renaissance in 1932, (2) the Bas Moulins, 1932 and (5) Tir aux Pigeons, 1932. (4) Premiere: 1929 poster with the list of entrants.

Verblichene Pracht: Sainte Dévote, (1) 1930 mit dem Hotelpalast Beau Rivage an der Steigung zum Casino und (3) mit dem Hotel Renaissance, 1932, (2) die Passagen Bas Moulins, 1932 und (5) Tir aux Pigeons, 1932. (4) Premiere: Poster von 1929 mit der Liste der Teilnehmer.

Magnificence passée : Sainte Dévote, (1) 1930 avec le Palace Beau Rivage situé dans la montée du Casino et (3) l'Hôtel Renaissance 1932, (2) les passages Bas Moulins, 1932 et (5) Tir aux Pigeons, 1932. (4) Première : tableau de 1929 avec la liste des participants.

2

Was der einsam wandernde Visionär trotz strotzender Zuversicht nicht weiß: Er hat soeben die berühmteste Grand-Prix-Piste aller Zeiten erfunden – und die umstrittenste. Anfänglich erinnern sogar Kopfsteinpflaster und Straßenbahnschienen an ihren alltäglich-zivilen Verwendungszweck. Zwei Jahre trägt er das Projekt mit sich herum. Dann verschafft er sich prominente Schützenhilfe, Louis Chiron, 28, einen der erfolgreichsten Rennfahrer seiner Zeit und Sohn der Stadt wie Noghes selbst. Chiron spart nicht mit Superlativen, und so ersucht Antony Noghes um Audienz bei Fürst Pierre. Auch der ist ungemein angetan, dient doch der Plan dem höheren Ruhme des Fürstentums und des Hauses Grimaldi und ist zugleich ein cleverer Schachzug gegen den Konkurrenten Nizza. Am 13. Oktober 1928 findet der ACM Schutz und Anerkennung unter dem Dach der AIACR. Am 14. April 1929 aber dreht Pierre anläßlich des Premier Grand Prix Automobile de Monaco eine Ehrenrunde über den Circuit. Am Lenkrad des Voisin sitzt Rennleiter Charles Faroux, ein alter Hase im Geschäft, abgebrüht und mit allen Wassern gewaschen. Gleichwohl: Sein Herz habe mit der gleichen Begeisterung geschlagen wie in seiner Jugend, sagt er. Und: Was für eine tolle Idee das sei, dieser Grand Prix durch die Straßen der Stadt.

5

1929

In an indefinable way, William Grover, who had been born in 1903 to an English father and a French mother, was surrounded by secrecy, a mystery man, or at the very least a character who could not easily be pinned down. For a time he drove the wealthy Irish painter Sir William Orpen from one end of Europe to the other in his Rolls-Royce. He went underground when France fell in 1940, was captured by the Gestapo in 1943 and was tortured to death. His racing appearances were rare. But Grover displayed flashes of brilliance, which he tried to hide behind the somewhat transparent pseudonym of "Williams".

Perhaps his greatest success was his victory at the first Grand Prix Automobile de Monaco, which was started punctually at 1.30 pm on 14 April 1929 and covered 100 laps of the circuit to give a total race length of 318 kilometers (197.6 miles). Wearing his baseball cap in mid-Nineties style, with the peak jauntily turned to the back, "Williams" was at the wheel of a green Bugatti 35 B – with a 2,262 cc engine producing 130 bhp at 5,500 rpm, it was one of the most powerful cars of its type, just arrived from the high-quality production facility of the Molsheim magician. The 16 participants were at the start, partly by invitation, partly because they had applied to take part; nine went through to the finish. Eight of the cars were Ettore Bugatti's creations, of which six completed the race. The Principality did not stint with the prizes: 100,000 francs awaited the winner, 30,000, 20,000, 15,000 and 10,000 francs for the next in line, 3,000 for the fastest lap and 1,000 for the leader at the end of each ten laps. The starting positions were decided by ballot, as they would be until as late as 1932, so chance played its mischievous game.

On pole position, its right wheels between the tramlines, lurked the Bugatti 35 of Philippe Etancelin, "Williams" was in the middle of the row behind, but way back in last-but-one place was Rudolf Caracciola in his Mercedes SSK. Surrounded by the nimble swarm of blue Bugattis, and squeezed by the narrow, winding route of the town circuit, the white giant of the German was as much at home here as a hawk in a cage of budgerigars. During training on the rainy Friday – Thursday was for a first reconnaissance and Saturday was a day off for the drivers – Caracciola did not feel the need to cut in the compressor except on the rise to the Casino. Nevertheless, he worked his way up to "Williams" and even managed to take the lead on two occasions, until a four-and-a-half minute tyre change during lap 51, under the staring eyes of race organizer Charles Faroux, decisively threw him back to third place.

Unfortunately, Louis Chiron, the local hero and a world-class driver, was conspicuous by his absence as he was racing at Indianapolis for Delage. The timing of this important American event frequently clashed with the Monaco Grand Prix and would continue to cause problems for many drivers.

Irgendwie ist William Grover, 1903 als Sohn eines Engländers und einer Französin geboren, von Geheimnis umfächelt, ein Mystery Man, zumindest aber ein schillernder Charakter. Eine Zeitlang chauffiert er den wohlhabenden irischen Maler Sir William Orpen in dessen Rolls-Royce kreuz und quer durch Europa. 1940 geht er mit dem Fall Frankreichs in den Untergrund, wird von der Gestapo 1943 aufgegriffen und zu Tode gefoltert. Seine Gastspiele im Rennsport sind rar. Aber Brillanz blitzt auf, die Grover hinter dem eher transparenten Pseudonym »Williams« zu verhüllen sucht.

Vielleicht sein größter Erfolg: Der Sieg beim ersten Grand Prix Automobile de Monaco, am 14. April 1929 über 100 Runden des Circuits mit einer Gesamtlänge von 318 Kilometern pünktlich um 13.30 Uhr in die Wege geleitet. Den Schirm seiner Schlägermütze im Stil der Mittneunziger keß nach hinten gedreht, lenkt »Williams« einen grünen Bugatti 35 B, mit 2262 cm³ und 130 PS bei 5500/min der stärkste unter seinesgleichen und just aus der Edel-Manufaktur des Zauberers von Molsheim angekommen. 16 Teilnehmer sind am Start, teils auf Einladung, teils weil sie sich beworben haben, neun erreichen das Ziel. Acht Wagen sind Geschöpfe Ettore Bugattis, davon kommen sechs in die Wertung. Das Fürstentum läßt sich nicht lumpen: 100 000 Francs winken dem ersten, 30 000, 20 000, 15 000 und 10 000 Francs den folgenden, 3000 für die schnellste Runde, 1000 für die Führenden im Zehn-Runden-Takt. Noch bis 1932 einschließlich werden die Startpositionen per Los ermittelt, spielt der Regisseur Zufall sein schelmisches Spiel.

Auf der Pole Position lauert, die rechten Räder zwischen Straßenbahnschienen, der Bugatti 35 von Philippe Etancelin, »Williams« in der Mitte der Reihe dahinter, erst im vorletzten Glied Rudolf Caracciola auf seinem Mercedes SSK. Umspielt vom flinken Schwarm der blauen Bugatti und eingeklemmt vom engen Geschlängel des Stadtkurses ist der weiße Riese des Deutschen zu Hause wie ein Sperber in einem Käfig für Wellensittiche. Im verregneten Freitagstraining – der Donnerstag diente einer ersten Erkundung, am Samstag haben die Piloten dienstfrei – mag Caracciola den Kompressor nur auf dem Anstieg zum Casino zuschalten. Gleichwohl arbeitet er sich immer wieder an »Williams« heran, führt auch zweimal, bis ihn ein viereinhalb Minuten andauernder Wechsel der Hinterreifen in der 51. Runde unter dem gestrengen Blick von Rennleiter Charles Faroux endgültig auf Rang drei zurückwirft.

Louis Chiron aber, *local hero* und Weltklassemann, glänzt durch Abwesenheit. Er startet in Indianapolis für Delage. Daß das amerikanische Super-Ereignis häufig zeitgleich mit dem Grand Prix de Monaco stattfindet, wird in Zukunft noch vielen Fahrern zu schaffen machen.

Bizarrement, ce William Grover, né en 1903 de père anglais et de mère française, est nimbé d'une espèce de mystère, homme énigmatique ou, tout au moins, personnage chatoyant. Pendant un certain temps, il a sillonné l'Europe comme chauffeur du riche peintre irlandais Sir William Orpen, au volant de sa Rolls-Royce. En 1940, lorsque la France capitule, il entre dans la clandestinité, est arrêté par la Gestapo en 1943 et torturé à mort. Ses apparitions en compétition automobile sont rares. Mais son intelligence de la course transparaît, une intelligence que Grover cherche à dissimuler sous son pseudonyme, vite percé à jour, de « Williams ».

Sans doute son plus grand succès : sa victoire lors du premier Grand Prix Automobile de Monaco, le 14 avril 1929, sur cent tours du circuit représentant une longueur totale de 318 kilomètres, mis en scène ponctuellement à 13 heures 30. Dans le plus pur style « grunge » du milieu des années quatre-vingt-dix, la visière de sa casquette sur la nuque, « Williams » pilote une Bugatti 35 B verte de 2262 cm³ de cylindrée développant 130 ch à 5500 tr/mn. La voiture la plus puissante du plateau et qui vient de lui être livrée par la prestigieuse manufacture du « sorcier » de Molsheim. Seize concurrents prennent le départ, certains invités, d'autres parce qu'ils se sont qualifiés, neuf franchissant le drapeau à damier. Huit voitures parmi les six classées sont des créations d'Ettore Bugatti. La Principauté n'est pas pingre : le vainqueur reçoit 100 000 francs, les autres prix étant respectivement de 30 000, 20 000, 15 000 et 10 000 francs, le meilleur tour en course étant récompensé de 3000 francs et le leader de tous les dixièmes tours, de 1000 francs. Jusqu'en 1932 compris, les positions au départ sont tirées au sort, jeu auquel le destin ne s'avère pas toujours équitable.

Piaffant en pole position, les roues de droite entre des rails de tramway, la Bugatti 35 de Philippe Etancelin, « Williams » au centre de la deuxième ligne et, en avant-dernière ligne seulement, Rudolf Caracciola, au volant de sa Mercedes SSK. Entouré par l'armada des virevoltantes Bugatti bleues et empêtré dans les étroits virages du circuit urbain, le dinosaure blanc de l'Allemand est aussi à l'aise ici qu'un épervier dans une cage de perruches. Lors des essais du vendredi sous la pluie – le jeudi a été réservé à une première exploration du circuit et, le samedi, les pilotes avaient journée libre – Caracciola n'a pu faire hurler son compresseur que dans la montée du Casino. Et pourtant, il se rapproche régulièrement de « Williams », prend même deux fois la tête avant qu'un changement de roue arrière qui le pénalisera de quatre minutes et demie au 51ᵉ tour ne le repousse définitivement au troisième rang sous le regard perçant du directeur de course Charles Faroux.

Malheureusement le régional de l'étape et pilote de classe mondiale Louis Chiron brille par son absence puisqu'à Indianapolis il prend le départ pour Delage. La méga-compétition américaine sera, par la suite, fréquemment organisée en même temps que le Grand Prix de Monaco, coïncidence qui, à l'avenir, créera encore bien des maux de tête à de nombreux pilotes.

Land of smiles: these two friendly gentlemen are the real protagonists of the first Monaco Grand Prix: Caracciola (left) and "Williams".

Land des Lächelns: Diese beiden freundlichen Herren sind die eigentlichen Protagonisten des ersten Grand Prix de Monaco, Caracciola (links) und »Williams«.

Le pays de la bonne humeur : ces deux hommes souriants sont en réalité les deux grands rivaux du premier Grand Prix de Monaco, Caracciola (à gauche) et « Williams ».

N°	DRIVERS		ENTRANTS	CARS	ENGINES	RACE RESULTS
12	**"Williams"**	**GB**	**William Grover**	**Bugatti 35B**	**8L 2262 cc + C**	**1st: 3h56'11"0**
18	Georges Bouriano	B	Barette	Bugatti 35C	8L 1991 cc + C	2nd: 3h57'28"8
34	Rudolf Caracciola	D	Rudolf Caracciola	Mercedes-Benz SSK	6L 7069 cc + C	3rd: 3h58'33"6
14	Philippe de Rothschild	F	Philippe de Rothschild	Bugatti 35C	8L 1991 cc + C	4th: 99 laps
28	René Dreyfus	F	René Dreyfus	Bugatti 37A	4L 1496 cc + C	5th: 97 laps
4	Philippe Etancelin	F	Philippe Etancelin	Bugatti 35C	8L 1991 cc + C	6th: 96 laps
30	Mario Lepori	CH	Mario Lepori	Bugatti 35B	8L 2262 cc + C	7th: 94 laps
32	Michel Doré	F	Michel Doré	La Licorne	6L 1493 cc	8th: 89 laps
24	Louis Rigal	F	Louis Rigal	Alfa Romeo 6C-1750	6L 1752 cc + C	9th: 87 laps
22	Raoul de Rovin	F	Raoul de Rovin	Delage 15S8	8L 1487 cc + C	R
16	Goffredo Zehender	I	Goffredo Zehender	Alfa Romeo 6C-1750	6L 1752 cc + C	R
6	Christian Dauvergne	F	Christian Dauvergne	Bugatti 35C	8L 1991 cc + C	R
10	Guglielmo Sandri	I	Guglielmo Sandri	Maserati 26	8L 1493 cc + C	R
36	Albert Perrot	F	Albert Perrot	Alfa Romeo 6C-1500	6L 1487 cc + C	R
26	Diego de Sterlich	I	Diego de Sterlich	Maserati 26B	8L 1979 cc + C	R
8	Marcel Lehoux	F	Marcel Lehoux	Bugatti 35C	8L 1991 cc + C	R

(1) White elephant: Rudolf Caracciola, here at Station Hairpin, has his hands full with the powerful Mercedes SSK. (2) Lehoux, Dauvergne and Etancelin (all Bugattis) in the first row of the grid. (3) Good team: René Dreyfus (Bugatti) with Jerry the mechanic.

(1) Weißer Elefant: Rudolf Caracciola, hier in der Bahnhofskurve, hat mit dem mächtigen Mercedes SSK alle Hände voll zu tun. (2) Lehoux, Dauvergne und Etancelin (alle Bugatti) in der ersten Reihe. (3) Gutes Team: René Dreyfus (Bugatti) mit Mechaniker Jerry.

(1) L'éléphant blanc : Rudolf Caracciola, dans le virage de la Gare, a fort à faire avec l'imposante Mercedes SSK. (2) Lehoux, Dauvergne et Etancelin (tous sur Bugatti) en première ligne. (3) Bonne équipe : René Dreyfus (Bugatti) avec son mécanicien Jerry.

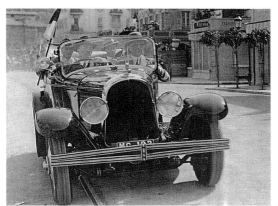

(4) "Williams" (Bugatti) overtakes de Rovin (Delage). (5) De Rovin,
de Rothschild (Bugatti) and Etancelin at the gasometer. (6) Before
the storm: Prince Pierre of Monaco in the Voisin closes the circuit.
(Following double page) Lost time: Caracciola during a pit stop
which holds him up for four-and-a-half valuable minutes.

(4) »Williams« (Bugatti) überholt de Rovin (Delage). (5) De Rovin,
de Rothschild (Bugatti) und Etancelin am Gasometer. (6) Vor dem
Sturm: Fürst Pierre de Monaco in einem Voisin schließt den Circuit.
(Folgende Doppelseite) Verlorene Zeit: Caracciola bei einem
Boxenstopp, der ihn viereinhalb kostbare Minuten aufhält.

(4) « Williams » (Bugatti) double de Rovin (Delage). (5) De Rovin,
de Rothschild (Bugatti) et Etancelin au virage du Gazomètre. (6) Le
calme avant la tempête : le prince Pierre de Monaco, dans une Voisin,
ferme le circuit. (Double page suivante) Temps perdu : Caracciola lors
d'un arrêt qui lui coûtera quatre minutes trente précieuses.

1930

The second Monaco Grand Prix ended with the total triumph of the blue cars from Molsheim: Bugattis filled places one to six in a monopoly of a marque, establishing a record which was to remain unchallenged at any future Grand Prix. Rudolf Caracciola, third in the previous year and long afterwards a star in Germany, was not allowed to enter – his Mercedes-Benz SSK was apparently deemed unsuitable for the course. Curious, this, as a second German with an SSK, Count Max d'Arco, was allowed to the starting grid, although he did not survive the first lap after his goggles were smashed by flying stones. Another prominent German was also left shamefully behind: the mountain king Hans Stuck, whose Austro Daimler six-cylinder machine was plagued by brake problems.

11 of the 18 participants who turned up for training on Thursday were new to Monaco; and for the Englishman Bobby Bowes with his Frazer Nash it was not only his first, but also his last time. Elegantly dressed, he reported for duty in collar and tie, but quickly concluded that perhaps this was not the thing for him after all!

The race began, and at the front a duel between René Dreyfus and Louis Chiron soon flared up. The prestige of the pearls of the Côte d'Azur was at stake: Chiron lived in Monaco, and Dreyfus resided in Nice. The Monégasque kept the lead with almost playful ease until the 83rd lap. But then a pit stop cost him more than a minute as the spark plugs also had to be changed and later the accelerator pedal jammed. Dreyfus, who at first was content to keep him in his sights, overtook him on lap 90, to the great consternation of the highly partisan Monégasque crowd, and had almost a minute's lead as he crossed the finishing line. His patron, Friderich, who had acquired Dreyfus' Bugatti 35 B for 160,000 francs, had good reason to laugh all the way to the bank, for the prize money for the winner was once again 100,000 francs. Those who bet on Dreyfus could also take mischievous pleasure in his victory – the odds were 6:1.

At this early stage it was already evident that the Monaco Grand Prix sometimes proceeded with a sovereign disregard for justice. "Williams", the victor the previous year, never really managed to get a grip on the race and failed to complete it. As for the rest, the list of starters included a number of future stars: as well as Stuck, the party included Arcangeli, Borzacchini and Etancelin.

In 1980, 50 years after his success, René Dreyfus revealed a small secret. In 1930, the fuel mixture had been freed from control in Monaco, which had automatically led to greater consumption. A few nights before the race a voice had advised him in a dream to use an additional tank. He had done so, and had thus managed to do the 100 laps without a pit stop…

Der zweite Grand Prix de Monaco endet mit einem totalen Triumph der Blauen aus Molsheim: Bugatti auf den Rängen eins bis sechs, Monokultur einer Marke und Rekord, der bei keinem zukünftigen Grand Prix angetastet werden wird. Der Vorjahresdritte Rudolf Caracciola, in Deutschland längst ein Star, wird nicht zugelassen, sein Mercedes-Benz SSK sei für die Strecke nicht geeignet. Verwunderlich, daß ein weiterer Deutscher mit einem SSK an den Start gehen darf, Graf Max d'Arco: Er übersteht die erste Runde nicht, nachdem seine Brille durch Steinschlag zersplittert ist. Auch andere deutsche Prominenz bleibt schmählich auf der Strecke: der Bergkönig Hans Stuck, dessen Austro Daimler Sechszylinder von Problemen mit den Bremsen heimgesucht wird.

11 der 18 Teilnehmer, die sich zum Training am Donnerstag einstellen, sind in Monaco zum erstenmal dabei, der Engländer Bobby Bowes mit seinem Frazer Nash auch zum letztenmal. Er meldet sich zwar in gepflegter Eleganz mit Hemdkragen und Krawatte zum Dienst, gelangt dann aber zu der Einsicht, dieses Metier sei doch nicht ganz das Rechte für ihn.

Das Rennen beginnt, und ganz vorn entbrennt sogleich ein Duell zwischen René Dreyfus und Louis Chiron. Das Prestige der Perlen der Côte d'Azur steht auf dem Spiel: Chiron ist Einwohner von Monaco, Dreyfus residiert in Nizza. Bis zur 83. Runde führt der Monegasse geradezu spielerisch. Doch dann kostet ihn ein Boxenstopp über eine Minute, da auch die Zündkerzen gewechselt werden müssen. Später klemmt das Gaspedal. Dreyfus, der zunächst in Sichtweite gefolgt ist, überholt Chiron zur Bestürzung der höchst parteilichen Monegassen in der 90. Runde und führt bei der Zieldurchfahrt mit fast einer Minute Vorsprung. Ins Fäustchen lacht sich sein Mäzen Friderich, der Dreyfus' Bugatti 35 B für 160 000 Francs angeschafft hat, denn das Preisgeld für den ersten Rang beträgt wieder 100 000 Francs. Und auch wer auf Dreyfus gewettet hat, hat Anlaß zu diebischem Vergnügen – die Quote betrug 6:1.

Schon jetzt zeigt sich, daß der Grand Prix de Monaco manchmal mit souveräner Ungerechtigkeit verfährt. »Williams«, im Jahr zuvor noch sicherer Sieger, vermag sich nie so recht in Szene zu setzen und scheidet vorzeitig aus. Im übrigen liest sich die Starterliste wie ein Brevier künftiger Größen: Neben Stuck sind zum Beispiel Arcangeli, Borzacchini und Etancelin mit von der Partie.

1980, 50 Jahre nach seinem Erfolg, gibt René Dreyfus ein kleines Geheimnis preis. 1930 sei in Monaco die Treibstoffmixtur freigestellt worden, was automatisch zu mehr Verbrauch geführt habe. Ein paar Nächte zuvor habe ihm eine Stimme im Traum geraten, einen Zusatztank zu verwenden. Dies habe er getan und sei deshalb ohne Boxenstopp über die 100 Runden gekommen…

Le second Grand Prix de Monaco se termine par un triomphe absolu des bolides bleus de Molsheim : Bugatti monopolise les six premières places, monoculture d'une marque, établissant un record qui ne sera jamais plus battu lors d'un Grand Prix à l'avenir. Le troisième de l'édition précédente, Rudolf Caracciola, depuis lors un demi-dieu en Allemagne, n'est pas admis au départ sous prétexte que sa Mercedes-Benz SSK n'était pas appropriée pour le circuit. Bizarre, tout de même, qu'un autre Allemand, le comte Max d'Arco, puisse prendre le départ avec une SSK : mais il ne terminera même pas le premier tour, ses lunettes ayant été perforées par des gravillons. Une autre grande vedette allemande doit aussi jeter prématurément l'éponge : le « roi de la montagne », Hans Stuck, dont l'Austro-Daimler à six-cylindres est handicapée par des problèmes de freins.

Onze des dix-huit participants qui ont pris part aux essais du jeudi s'alignent à Monaco pour la première fois. Pour l'Anglais Bobby Bowes, avec sa Frazer Nash, ce sera aussi la dernière. Elégamment vêtu d'une chemise à col relevé avec cravate, il prend place sur la grille du départ, mais se rend rapidement compte qu'il n'a sans doute pas l'étoffe pour un tel métier.

Les pilotes prennent le départ et, aux avant-postes, René Dreyfus et Louis Chiron se livrent bientôt un duel à couteaux tirés. Le prestige des deux villes rivales de la Côte d'Azur est en jeu : Chiron est un enfant de Monaco et Dreyfus réside à Nice. Jusqu'au 83ᵉ tour, le Monégasque le domine de la tête et des épaules. Mais un arrêt aux stands lui coûte plus d'une minute, car il doit aussi remplacer les bougies. Plus tard, c'est l'accélérateur qui fait des siennes. Dreyfus, qui n'a tout d'abord cessé de le talonner, double Chiron pour le plus grand effroi des Monégasques très chauvins, lors du 90ᵉ tour, et franchit la ligne d'arrivée avec près d'une minute d'avance. Un homme content de son coup est bien son mécène Friderich, qui a acquis la Bugatti 35 B de Dreyfus pour 160 000 francs, car la prime pour la première place est, cette année aussi, de 100 000 francs. Et, si quelqu'un a parié sur Dreyfus, lui aussi a tout motif de se réjouir : la cote était de 6 pour 1.

Dès maintenant, il s'avère que le Grand Prix de Monaco fait parfois preuve d'une injustice souveraine. « Williams », le vainqueur de l'année précédente, ne semble jamais vraiment à l'aise et abandonne prématurément. Pour le reste, la liste des concurrents recèle nombre de grandes vedettes à venir : outre Hans Stuck, on y trouve par exemple Arcangeli, Borzacchini et Etancelin.

En 1980, 50 ans après son succès mémorable, René Dreyfus révèle un petit secret. En 1930, dit-il, la composition du carburant à Monaco était libre, ce qui entraînait automatiquement un surcroît de consommation. Quelques nuits auparavant, ajoute-t-il, une voix lui aurait conseillé en rêve d'utiliser un réservoir supplémentaire. Chose dite, chose faite, raison pour laquelle il a pu couvrir les 100 tours sans devoir ravitailler…

N°	DRIVERS		ENTRANTS	CARS	ENGINES	RACE RESULTS
22	**René Dreyfus**	**F**	**René Dreyfus**	**Bugatti 35B**	**8L 2262 cc + C**	**1st: 3h41'02"6**
18	Louis Chiron	F	Automobiles Bugatti	Bugatti 35C	8L 1991 cc + C	2nd: 3h41'24"4
16	Guy Bouriat	F	Automobiles Bugatti	Bugatti 35C	8L 1991 cc + C	3rd: 3h49'20"4
42	Goffredo Zehender	I	Goffredo Zehender	Bugatti 35B	8L 2262 cc + C	4th: 3h51'39"0
20	Michel Doré	F	Michel Doré	Bugatti 37A	4L 1496 cc + C	5th: 4h12'06"0
46	Hans Stuber	CH	Hans Stuber	Bugatti 35C	8L 1991 cc + C	6th: 94 laps
14	Juan Zanelli	RCH	Juan Zanelli	Bugatti 35B	8L 2262 cc + C	R
6	Ernst Burggaller	D	Ernst Burggaller	Bugatti 35C	8L 1991 cc + C	R
24	Philippe Etancelin	F	Philippe Etancelin	Bugatti 35C	8L 1991 cc + C	R
26	Marcel Lehoux	F	Marcel Lehoux	Bugatti 35B	8L 2262 cc + C	R
8	Hans Stuck	A	Hans Stuck	Austro Daimler	6L 3614 cc	R
32	Luigi Arcangeli	I	Officine Alfieri Maserati S.A.	Maserati 26B	8L 1980 cc + C	R
28	"Williams"	GB	Automobiles Bugatti	Bugatti 35C	8L 1991 cc + C	R
36	Clemente Biondetti	I	Scuderia Materassi	Talbot 700	8L 1485 cc + C	R
12	Georges Bouriano	B	Emile Bouriano	Bugatti 35B	8L 2262 cc + C	R
34	Baconin Borzacchini	I	Officine Alfieri Maserati S.A.	Maserati 26B	8L 1980 cc + C	R
2	Comte Max d'Arco	D	Comte Arco-Zinneberg	Mercedes-Benz SSK	6L 7069 cc + C	R

1

2

3

4

5

(1) Blue riders: the Team Bugatti (number 18: Louis Chiron). (2) Goffredo Zehender (Bugatti) turns round to check on his rivals at Tobacconist's Corner. (3) French racing blue ahead of German racing white: Bouriat and Burggaller (both Bugattis). (4) Etancelin (Bugatti) with cap turned back to front Nineties style; (5) Arcangeli at the gasometer. (6) Dreyfus (with dust cap), his patron Friderich (with hat), and Jerry the mechanic (with cap).

(1) Blaue Reiter: das Aufgebot der Equipe Bugatti (Nummer 18: Louis Chiron), (2) Goffredo Zehender (Bugatti) schaut sich ausgangs der Tabakskurve nach seinen Konkurrenten um. (3) Französisches Rennblau vor deutschem Rennweiß: Bouriat und Burggaller (beide Bugatti), (4) Etancelin (Bugatti) mit umgedrehter Kappe im Stil der neunziger Jahre, (5) Arcangeli am Gasometer, (6) gut behütet: Dreyfus (mit Staubkappe), Mäzen Friderich (mit Hut) und Mechaniker Jerry (mit Mütze).

(1) Les cavaliers bleus : l'armada de l'écurie Bugatti (numéro 18 : Louis Chiron). (2) Goffredo Zehender (Bugatti) jette un coup d'œil sur ses concurrents à la sortie du virage du Bureau de Tabac. (3) Le bleu de l'écurie française face au blanc germanique : Bouriat et Burggaller (tous les deux sur Bugatti). (4) Etancelin (Bugatti) avec sa casquette à l'envers dans le style des années 90. (5) Arcangeli au Gazomètre. (6) Bien chapeautés : Dreyfus (avec casque), le mécène Friderich (avec chapeau) et le mécanicien Jerry (avec casquette).

1931

It would only have taken a little more for the 1931 Monaco Grand Prix to turn into a manufacturer's cup: 23 cars were lined up on the starting grid, 16 of them Bugattis. Four of them were Type 51 factory cars for the Monégasque Louis Chiron, the Italian Achille Varzi, and the Frenchmen Albert Divo and Guy Bouriat. The only real resistance was offered by the three Maserati 8 C 2500s, entered under the sign of the trident for the Frenchman René Dreyfus and the two Italians Luigi Fagioli and Clemente Biondetti. The private Maserati belonging to Carlo Pedrazzini was simply window dressing, hardly worth a mention, as were a Peugeot and an Alfa Romeo. And finally, fighting a losing battle, Rudolf Caracciola with his Mercedes-Benz SSKL (Super Sport Kurz Leicht, or Super Sport Short Light), which was by no means as compact and light as the abbreviation suggested. Even the strategic skills of his team manager Alfred Neubauer, on his way to becoming a legend, like Caracciola himself, were of no use here: the roller-coaster which was Monaco was governed by its own laws, and they decreed on this occasion that the race should be conducted between the blue cars from Molsheim and the red ones from Modena.

And so it turned out. After the start, Dreyfus led on the rise behind Sainte Dévote, but was then overtaken by "Williams". However, a broken valve spring put the winner of 1929 out of contention in lap five. Varzi and Caracciola chased Dreyfus until lap seven, then Varzi took the lead while the SSKL began to show signs of trouble – the clutch, which was to give up the ghost completely on lap 53. In the meantime, Chiron worked his way to the front, equalling the lap record from 1930, as did Fagioli and, on the last lap, Achille Varzi.

But it was Louis Chiron – native of the town, who as a child had raced down the steep streets of the Principality on his bicycle out of sheer pleasure at the speed – who drove towards a victory which was challenged by no-one, and then put in an extra lap at full throttle, just in case. His lead was almost five minutes at the end, and Jean Bugatti, the eldest son of the "Patron" Ettore Bugatti, vaulted over the pit wall in a show of delight. Sweet revenge for 1930 – Dreyfus' Maserati had been silenced long before with a defective engine. Chiron, in the meantime, was revelling in the cheers of his compatriots, clutching the cup which the Association of Monégasque Hoteliers had donated. They were proud of one another. This was also confirmed by the silver cigarette case which Alexandre Noghes, President of the ACM, presented to him a few days later, which carried an inscription engraved on it which said (in French, of course): Let it bear witness to the goodwill of all his comrades in the ACM in commemoration of his magnificent victory.

Rudolf Caracciola, meanwhile, preferred to remember the weekend before: that was when he had won the Mille Miglia with his SSKL.

Nicht viel würde fehlen, und der Grand Prix de Monaco 1931 geriete zum Markenpokalrennen: 23 Autos stehen am Start, 16 davon Bugatti. Vier sind Werkswagen vom Typ 51 für den Monegassen Louis Chiron, den Italiener Achille Varzi, die Franzosen Albert Divo und Guy Bouriat. Wirkliche Gegenwehr droht von den drei Maserati 8 C 2500, im Zeichen des Dreizacks gemeldet für den Franzosen René Dreyfus und die beiden Italiener Luigi Fagioli und Clemente Biondetti. Der private Maserati von Carlo Pedrazzini: nur Staffage, und kaum der Rede wert auch jeweils ein Peugeot und ein Alfa Romeo. Auf verlorenem Posten schließlich: Rudolf Caracciola mit dem Mercedes-Benz SSKL (Super Sport Kurz Leicht), der keineswegs so kompakt und so schwerelos ist, wie das Kürzel behauptet. Da hilft auch das strategische Geschick seines Rennleiters Alfred Neubauer nichts, wie Caracciola selbst auf dem Saumpfad in die Legende: Die Achterbahn von Monaco hat ihre eigenen Gesetze. Und die schreiben diesmal fest, das Rennen werde zwischen den Blauen aus Molsheim und den Roten aus Modena ausgetragen.

In der Tat: Nach dem Start führt Dreyfus auf dem Anstieg hinter Sainte Dévote, wird aber dann von »Williams« überholt. Eine gebrochene Ventilfeder wirft den Sieger von 1929 in der fünften Runde aus dem Gefecht. Varzi und Caracciola jagen Dreyfus bis Runde sieben. Dann führt Varzi, während der SSKL zu kränkeln beginnt – die Kupplung, die im 53. Durchgang endgültig den Dienst verweigern wird. Nach vorn arbeitet sich unterdessen Chiron, der den Rundenrekord von 1930 ebenso einstellt wie Fagioli und, noch im letzten Durchgang, Achille Varzi.

Louis Chiron jedoch, der Sohn der Stadt, der schon als Kind mit dem Fahrrad aus schierer Freude am Tempo die steil abfallenden Straßen des Fürstentums hinunterraste, fährt einem durch nichts und niemand gefährdeten Sieg entgegen, leistet sich gar noch eine zusätzliche Vollgas-Runde, für alle Fälle. Fast fünf Minuten beträgt sein Vorsprung am Ende, und Jean Bugatti, der älteste Sohn des »Patrons« Ettore Bugatti, flankt vor lauter Glück über die Boxenmauer. Süße Rache für 1930 – längst ist der Maserati von Dreyfus mit defekter Maschine verstummt. Chiron indes schwelgt im Jubel seiner Landsleute, im Arm den Pokal, den die Vereinigung der monegassischen Hoteliers gestiftet hat. Man ist stolz aufeinander. Davon zeugt auch das silberne Zigarettenetui, das ihm Alexandre Noghes, Präsident des ACM, ein paar Tage später überreicht: es möge Louis Chiron als Zeugnis der Sympathie seiner Kameraden im ACM zum Andenken an seinen prächtigen Sieg gelten, steht darauf eingraviert.

Rudolf Caracciola jedoch denkt lieber an das Wochenende zuvor zurück: Da hat er mit dem SSKL die Mille Miglia gewonnen.

Cette année-là, il s'en est fallu de peu que le Grand Prix de Monaco ne prenne des allures de course monomarque : 23 voitures sont au départ, dont 16 Bugatti. Quatre sont des voitures d'usine, des 51, pour le Monégasque Louis Chiron, l'Italien Achille Varzi ainsi que les Français Albert Divo et Guy Bouriat. La seule véritable opposition provient des trois Maserati 8 C 2500, inscrites sous l'emblème du trident pour le Français René Dreyfus et les deux Italiens Luigi Fagioli et Clemente Biondetti. La Maserati privée de Carlo Pedrazzini ne fait que de la figuration, ce qui est aussi le cas de la seule Peugeot et de l'unique Alfa Romeo. Et, enfin, sans la moindre chance, Rudolf Caracciola avec la Mercedes-Benz SSKL (Super Sport Courte Légère), qui n'est absolument pas aussi compacte ni aussi légère que le prétend l'abréviation. Même le sens de la stratégie légendaire de son directeur de course, Alfred Neubauer, qui, comme Caracciola lui-même, s'engage à grands pas dans la légende, restera vain : les montagnes russes de Monaco ont leurs propres lois. Et elles proclament cette fois que la victoire sera disputée entre les Bleus de Molsheim et les Rouges de Modène.

Et, de fait, après le départ, c'est Dreyfus qui attaque en tête la montée derrière Sainte Dévote avant d'être doublé par « Williams ». Mais la rupture d'un ressort de soupape contraint le vainqueur de 1929 à déposer les armes au cinquième tour, Varzi et Caracciola prennent Dreyfus en chasse jusqu'au septième tour. Varzi prend alors la tête pendant que la SSKL commence avoir des problèmes : l'embrayage refusera définitivement tout service au 53ᵉ tour. Pendant ce temps, Chiron regagne peu à peu du terrain et bat le record du tour de 1930, imité en cela par Fagioli et, dans l'ultime boucle, par Achille Varzi.

Louis Chiron, le fils de la ville, qui, dès sa plus tendre enfance, dévalait par pur goût de la vitesse les rues escarpées de la Principauté au guidon de son vélo, s'apprête, quant à lui, à remporter une victoire dont rien ni personne ne pourra le priver et il se permet même un tour supplémentaire, accélérateur collé au plancher, par mesure de précaution. A l'arrivée, il a près de cinq minutes d'avance et Jean Bugatti, le fils aîné du « Patron » Ettore Bugatti, ne peut contenir sa joie et franchit d'un bond la murette des stands. Délicieuse revanche pour 1930 – il y a longtemps que la Maserati de Dreyfus s'est tue sur panne de moteur. Chiron, lui, laisse déferler sur lui l'allégresse de ses compatriotes, portant dans les bras la coupe que l'association des hôteliers monégasques lui a offerte. Chacun est fier de soi. Ce qu'atteste l'étui à cigarettes en argent que le président de l'ACM, Alexandre Noghes, lui remet quelques jours plus tard et sur lequel sont gravés ces mots : « A Louis Chiron, comme témoignage de sympathie de ses camarades de l'ACM, en souvenir de sa victoire mémorable ».

Rudolf Caracciola, lui, préfère se rappeler le week-end précédent : il a en effet gagné les Mille Miglia avec la SSKL.

N°	DRIVERS		ENTRANTS	CARS	ENGINES	RACE RESULTS
22	**Louis Chiron**	**F**	**Automobiles Bugatti**	**Bugatti 51**	**8L 2262 cc + C**	**1st: 3h39'09"2**
52	Luigi Fagioli	I	Officine Alfieri Maserati S.A.	Maserati 8C-2500	8L 2495 cc + C	2nd: 3h43'04"4
26	Achille Varzi	I	Automobiles Bugatti	Bugatti 51	8L 2262 cc + C	3rd: 3h43'13"0
20	Guy Bouriat	F	Automobiles Bugatti	Bugatti 51	8L 2262 cc + C	4th: 98 laps
46	Goffredo Zehender	I	Goffredo Zehender	Alfa Romeo 6C-1750	6L 1752 cc + C	5th: 97 laps
38	André Boillot	F	André Boillot	Peugeot 174S	4L 3990 cc	6th: 96 laps
48	Clemente Biondetti	I	Officine Alfieri Maserati S.A.	Maserati 26M	8L 2495 cc + C	7th: 91 laps
12	Clifton Penn-Hughes	GB	Clifton Penn-Hughes	Bugatti 35C	8L 1991 cc + C	8th: 89 laps
30	Comte Stanislaus Czaikowski	PL	Comte Stanislaus Czaikowski	Bugatti 35C	8L 1991 cc + C	9th: 85 laps
50	René Dreyfus	F	Officine Alfieri Maserati S.A.	Maserati 26M	8L 2495 cc + C	R
24	Albert Divo	F	Automobiles Bugatti	Bugatti 51	8L 2262 cc + C	R
10	Earl Edward Richard Howe	GB	Earl Howe	Bugatti 51	8L 2262 cc + C	R
56	Hans Stuber	CH	Hans Stuber	Bugatti 35C	8L 1991 cc + C	R
16	Bernhard Ackerl	A	Bernhard Ackerl	Bugatti 37A	4L 1496 cc + C	R
8	Rudolf Caracciola	D	Rudolf Caracciola	Mercedes-Benz SSKL	6L 7069 cc + C	R
18	Juan Zanellli	RCH	Juan Zanelli	Bugatti 35B	8L 2262 cc + C	R
4	Hermann zu Leiningen	D	Hermann zu Leiningen	Bugatti 35C	8L 1991 cc + C	R
6	Heinrich-Joachim von Morgen	D	Heinrich-Joachim von Morgen	Bugatti 35B	8L 2262 cc + C	R
2	Ernst Burggaller	D	Ernst Burggaller	Bugatti 35C	8L 1991 cc + C	R
32	Marcel Lehoux	F	Marcel Lehoux	Bugatti 35B	8L 2262 cc + C	R
54	Carlo Pedrazzini	CH	Carlo Pedrazzini	Maserati 26B	8L 1980 cc + C	R
28	Philippe Etancelin	F	Philippe Etancelin	Bugatti 35C	8L 1991 cc + C	R
34	"Williams"	GB	William Grover	Bugatti 35C	8L 1991 cc + C	R

(1) Caracciola in his white Mercedes (number 8) has just overtaken Lehoux (Bugatti) on the approach to the gasometer. (2) Tram tracks still dissect the home straight. (3) Dreyfus (Maserati), who has to retire towards the end with engine trouble. (4) Chiron laps Burggaller at the chicane (both in Bugattis). (5) Chiron's car after victory.

(1) Caracciola im weißen Mercedes (Nummer 8) hat vor dem Gasometer gerade Lehoux (Bugatti) überholt. (2) Noch durchfurchen Straßenbahnschienen die Zielgerade. (3) Dreyfus (Maserati), der gegen Ende mit Motorschaden ausfällt. (4) Chiron überrundet Burggaller hinter der Schikane (beide auf Bugatti). (5) Der Wagen des Siegers Chiron.

(1) Caracciola (Mercedes blanche numéro 8) vient de doubler Lehoux (Bugatti) avant le virage du Gazomètre. (2) Les rails de tramway entaillent encore la ligne droite de l'arrivée. (3) Dreyfus (Maserati) abandonnera sur panne de moteur peu avant la fin de la course. (4) Chiron prend un tour d'avance sur Burggaller à la sortie de la chicane (tous les deux sur Bugatti). (5) La voiture du vainqueur, Chiron.

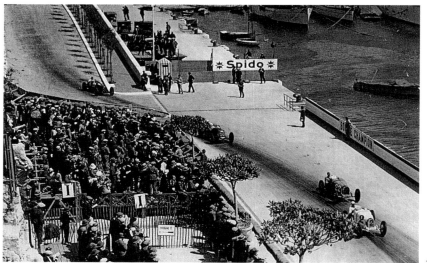

(1) The German drivers Burggaller and zu Leiningen look out rather morosely from under their racing whites. (2) After passing the finishing line, Chiron drives another lap just to be on the safe side. (3) In victory pose: Rudi Caracciola; (4) in victory mood: Chiron and his mechanic Wurmser.

(1) Die deutschen Piloten Burggaller und zu Leiningen schauen eher verdrießlich aus der weißen Rennwäsche. (2) Nach der Zieldurchfahrt begibt sich Chiron vorsichtshalber in eine weitere Runde im Renntempo. (3) In Siegerpose: Rudi Caracciola, (4) in Siegerlaune: Chiron und sein Rennmechaniker Wurmser.

(1) Les pilotes allemands Burggaller et zu Leiningen ont l'air plutôt désappointé dans leurs combinaisons blanches. (2) Après avoir franchi la ligne d'arrivée, Chiron couvre par précaution un tour supplémentaire à pleine vitesse. (3) Le vainqueur rayonnant : Rudi Caracciola. (4) La bonne humeur des gagnants : Chiron et son mécanicien Wurmser.

1932

Following the start of the season in Tunis on 3 April, the European Grand Prix season opened with the race in Monaco on 17 April. The town was prepared. The route had been almost completely resurfaced, the absurdity of dangerous tramlines having been removed from the track, and the tunnel had been provided with lighting a year earlier. Three training days – Thursday, Friday, and half an hour on Saturday morning at an ungodly hour – had also been adopted since 1931. The 12,000 seats in the stands offered a welcome opportunity to sit down – the race was, after all, three-and-a-half hours long.

In the war of blue against red, of the Gitanes-blue Bugattis against the Italians in the color of passion, red was on the advance, numerically too. Four Type 51 cars were registered by Team Bugatti for local star Louis Chiron, the Frenchmen Guy Bouriat and Albert Divo and the Italian Achille Varzi. The Officine Alfieri Maserati was represented by René Dreyfus (France) as well as Luigi Fagioli and Amedeo Ruggeri (Italy) with 8C 2800s. Tazio Nuvolari, Giuseppe Campari and Baconin Borzacchini were starting for Alfa Corse with Monza models. Their cars were painted Alfa red, but a separate Monza for Rudolf Caracciola was white; he was taking a holiday from Mercedes before going on to greater things there. There was no love lost between them: for all their usual rivalry, the three Italian musketeers stuck together against the German.

For the last time, the ballot, and thus the capricious goddess of luck, decided the starting line-up. That may have been unjust, but it ensured an entertaining race: 17 cars rolled up, all of them with eight cylinders, with Fagioli in the last row, Caracciola and Divo in the last but one, Nuvolari in the third last and Chiron, who drove the fastest training lap at 2'04", in the second row.

After the land speed record-breaking driver Malcolm Campbell opened the track at the wheel of his Rolls-Royce, it was the three Bugatti 51s of Chiron, "Williams" and Marcel Lehoux, who at the start had all been positioned on the outside right, which initially took the lead, followed by Ruggeri's Maserati. Pressure from behind encouraged Chiron into another lap record in the sixth lap, while Varzi worked his way forward into third place and, in turn, set the fastest lap time of the day.

Caracciola had already overtaken six competitors by Beau Rivage on the opening lap, but he was not too bothered by the onslaught of Nuvolari, the "flyer from Mantua" and allowed him to pass. The Italian followed Chiron in second place like a shadow until the Monégasque made an error in lap 29: his Bugatti smashed into the sandbags at the chicane and turned over. The driver was thrown clear and he was not injured. Fagioli then took third place and a nice fourth place emerged for the English privateer, Earl Francis Curzon Howe, in his Bugatti. He was in green – the British racing color, and the color of hope.

Nach dem Saisonbeginn in Tunis am 3. April wird mit dem Lauf in Monaco am 17. April der Reigen der europäischen Grand-Prix-Saison eröffnet. Die Stadt ist gerüstet, der Streckenbelag fast ganz erneuert, die Absurdität der Straßenbahnschienen als bedrohliche Intarsien in der Fahrbahn beseitigt, der Tunnel seit einem Jahr beleuchtet. Ebenfalls seit 1931 die Norm: drei Trainingstage, Donnerstag, Freitag sowie eine halbe Stunde am Samstag, in aller Herrgottsfrühe. 12 000 Tribünenplätze bieten willkommene Sitzgelegenheiten – immerhin dauert das Rennen dreieinhalb Stunden.

Im Planspiel blau gegen rot, der gitanesblauen Bugatti gegen die Italiener in der Farbe der Leidenschaft, ist rot auf dem Vormarsch, auch numerisch. Vier Wagen vom Typ 51 hat die Equipe Bugatti gemeldet, für Lokalmatador Louis Chiron, die Franzosen Guy Bouriat und Albert Divo und den Italiener Achille Varzi. Die Officine Alfieri Maserati ist durch René Dreyfus (Frankreich) sowie Luigi Fagioli und Amedeo Ruggeri (Italien) mit dem 8C 2800 vertreten. Für Alfa Corse starten Tazio Nuvolari, Giuseppe Campari und Baconin Borzacchini auf dem Modell Monza. Ihre Wagen sind alfarot, weiß ein weiterer Monza für Rudolf Caracciola, der Urlaub von Mercedes macht, bevor dort größere Dinge auf ihn warten. Grün ist man einander nicht: Bei aller Rivalität halten die drei italienischen Musketiere wie Pech und Schwefel gegen den Deutschen zusammen.

Zum letztenmal entscheidet das Los und damit die launische Göttin Fortuna über die Startaufstellung. Das ist ungerecht, sorgt aber für Unterhaltung: 17 Wagen rollen an, alles Achtzylinder, mit Fagioli in der letzten, Caracciola und Divo in der vorletzten, Nuvolari in der drittletzten und Chiron, der mit 2'04" die schnellste Trainingszeit markiert hat, in der zweiten Reihe.

Nachdem Rekordfahrer Malcolm Campbell am Lenkrad eines Rolls-Royce die Strecke freigegeben hat, führen zunächst die drei Bugatti 51 von Chiron, »Williams« und Marcel Lehoux, die am Start rechts außen hintereinander gestanden haben, dahinter Ruggeris Maserati. Druck von hinten ermuntert Chiron zu einem neuen Rundenrekord im sechsten Durchgang, während sich Varzi auf Platz drei vorarbeitet und seinerseits die schnellste Zeit des Tages fährt.

Caracciola hat in der Startrunde bis Beau Rivage schon sechs Konkurrenten überholt, läßt indessen den nach vorn stürmenden »fliegenden Mantuaner« Nuvolari gelassen passieren. Der folgt Chiron an zweiter Stelle wie ein Schatten, bis der Monegasse in der 29. Runde einen Fehler macht: Sein Bugatti prallt auf die Sandsäcke an der Schikane und überschlägt sich. Chiron wird aus dem Wagen geschleudert, verletzt sich aber nicht. Fagioli wird Dritter, und ein schöner vierter Platz springt für den englischen Privatfahrer Earl Francis Curzon Howe auf seinem Bugatti heraus. Der ist grün – die britische Rennfarbe und die Farbe der Hoffnung.

Après le lever de rideau à Tunis, le 3 avril, la manche de Monaco inaugure la série des Grands Prix européens, le 17 avril. La ville a fourbi ses armes, le revêtement à été presque totalement refait, l'absurdité des rails de tramway comme dangereuse marqueterie dans le revêtement a été éliminée et le tunnel est éclairé depuis un an. Sont aussi devenus la norme depuis 1931 : trois jours d'essai, le jeudi, le vendredi ainsi qu'une demi-heure le samedi aux toutes premières heures du jour. Les 12 000 places sur les gradins offrent des sièges accueillants – la course durant en effet trois heures et demie.

Dans le duel bleus contre rouges, des Bugatti bleues de France contre les Italiens arborant la couleur de la passion, le rouge est en passe de prendre l'avantage, aussi sur le plan numérique. L'équipe Bugatti a inscrit quatre 51, pour le régional de l'étape, Louis Chiron, les Français Guy Bouriat et Albert Divo ainsi que l'Italien Achille Varzi. René Dreyfus (France), Luigi Fagioli et Amedeo Ruggeri (Italie) défendent les couleurs de l'Officine Alfieri Maserati avec la 8C 2800. Tazio Nuvolari, Giuseppe Campari et Baconin Borzacchini, au volant de Monza, ont endossé la casaque d'Alfa Corse. Leurs voitures arborent le rouge alfa tandis qu'une autre Monza blanche est pilotée par Rudof Caracciola, provisoirement libéré par Mercedes où va bientôt l'attendre la consécration. Si ce n'est pas vraiment l'entente cordiale, en dépit de leur rivalité traditionnelle, les trois mousquetaires italiens sont pourtant de solides alliés face à l'Allemand.

Pour l'ultime fois, c'est la loterie et, par conséquent, l'imprévisible roue de la fortune qui décident de la composition de la grille de départ. Aussi injuste cette procédure soit-elle, elle a au moins le mérite de donner du piment. 17 voitures sont sous les ordres du starter, uniquement des huit-cylindres, avec Fagioli en dernière ligne, Caracciola et Divo en avant-dernière ligne, Nuvolari juste devant et Chiron, qui a obtenu le meilleur temps aux essais avec 2,04 minutes, au second rang.

Après que Malcolm Campbell, le champion absolu de la vitesse, eut couvert le tour de lancement au volant d'une Rolls-Royce, ce sont tout d'abord les trois Bugatti 51 de Chiron, « Williams » et Marcel Lehoux, l'une derrière l'autre à l'extérieur au moment du départ, qui prennent la tête, suivies par la Maserati de Ruggeri. Chiron sent le souffle de ses poursuivants et signe un nouveau record du tour au sixième passage tandis que Varzi remonte jusqu'à la troisième place et signe, de son côté, le tour le plus rapide du jour.

Au cours du premier tour, Caracciola a déjà doublé six concurrents avant d'atteindre Beau Rivage, mais laisse volontairement passer le Mantouan volant Nuvolari, qui se précipite sur le peloton de tête. Au deuxième rang, les Italiens le suivront comme son ombre jusqu'à ce que le Monégasque commette une erreur au 29e tour. Sa Bugatti percute les sacs de sable à la chicane et part en tonneau. Le pilote est éjecté, mais se relève sans la moindre blessure. Fagioli termine troisième tandis que le pilote privé anglais Earl Francis Curzon Howe obtient une magnifique quatrième place avec sa Bugatti. Elle est de couleur verte – la couleur de la Grande-Bretagne, mais aussi celle de l'espoir.

Record-breaking driver Malcolm Campbell films his racing colleagues for posterity, his lower half protected by sandbags.

Rekordfahrer Malcolm Campbell filmt seine rasenden Kollegen zur bleibenden Erinnerung, die untere Körperhälfte durch Sandsäcke geschützt.

Le pilote de record Malcolm Campbell immortalise ses collègues de circuit, bien protégé derrière une rangée de sacs de sable.

N°	DRIVERS		ENTRANTS	CARS	ENGINES	RACE RESULTS
28	**Tazio Nuvolari**	**I**	**Alfa Corse**	**Alfa Romeo 8C-2300**	**8L 2336 cc + C**	**1st: 3h32'25"3**
2	Rudolf Caracciola	D	Rudolf Caracciola	Alfa Romeo 8C-2300	8L 2336 cc + C	2nd: 3h32'28"0
36	Luigi Fagioli	I	Officine Alfieri Maserati S.A.	Maserati 8C-2800	8L 2812 cc + C	3rd: 3h34'43"0
4	Earl Edward Richard Howe	GB	Earl Howe	Bugatti 51	8L 2262 cc + C	4th: 98 laps
32	Goffredo Zehender	I	Goffredo Zehender	Alfa Romeo 8C-2300	8L 2336 cc + C	5th: 96 laps
20	Marcel Lehoux	F	Marcel Lehoux	Bugatti 51	8L 2262 cc + C	6th: 95 laps
22	"Williams"	GB	William Grover	Bugatti 51	8L 2262 cc + C	7th: 95 laps
10	Guy Bouriat	F	Automobiles Bugatti	Bugatti 51	8L 2262 cc + C	8th: 93 laps
14	Albert Divo	F	Automobiles Bugatti	Bugatti 51	8L 2262 cc + C	9th: 91 laps
26	Giuseppe Campari	I	Alfa Corse	Alfa Romeo 8C-2300	8L 2336 cc + C	10th: 86 laps
24	Baconin Borzacchini	I	Alfa Corse	Alfa Romeo 8C-2300	8L 2336 cc + C	R
34	René Dreyfus	F	Officine Alfieri Maserati S.A.	Maserati 8C-2800	8L 2812 cc + C	R
16	Achille Varzi	I	Automobiles Bugatti	Bugatti 51	8L 2262 cc + C	R
30	Philippe Etancelin	F	Philippe Etancelin	Alfa Romeo 8C-2300	8L 2336 cc + C	R
18	Comte Stanislaus Czaikowski	PL	Comte Stanislaus Czaikowski	Bugatti 51	8L 2262 cc + C	R
12	Louis Chiron	F	Automobiles Bugatti	Bugatti 51	8L 2262 cc + C	R
38	Amedeo Ruggeri	I	Officine Alfieri Maserati S.A.	Maserati 8C-2800	8L 2812 cc + C	R

(1) Borzacchini (Alfa Romeo) laps "Williams" (Bugatti), the winner of 1929. (2) Chiron (Bugatti) leading "Williams", Ruggeri (Maserati) and Lehoux (Bugatti) at Station Hairpin. (3) Caracciola in his white Alfa Romeo with red racing numbers.

(1) Borzacchini (Alfa Romeo) überrundet »Williams« (Bugatti), den Sieger von 1929. (2) Chiron (Bugatti) vor »Williams«, Ruggeri (Maserati) und Lehoux (Bugatti) in der Bahnhofskurve. (3) Caracciola im weißen Alfa Romeo mit roten Startnummern.

(1) Borzacchini (Alfa Romeo) double « Williams » (Bugatti), le vainqueur de 1929. (2) Chiron (Bugatti) devant « Williams », Ruggeri (Maserati) et Lehoux (Bugatti) au virage de la Gare. (3) Caracciola au volant de son Alfa Romeo blanche, avec les numéros rouges.

(1) Unequal team-mates:
Nuvolari and Caracciola after
the victory honors. (2) In happy
harmony: Ernesto
Maserati between his drivers
Ruggeri, Dreyfus and Fagioli.
(3) Tire change for
Nuvolari's Alfa Romeo.

(1) Ungleiche Teamgefährten:
Nuvolari und Caracciola nach
der Siegerehrung. (2) In
schöner Eintracht: Ernesto
Maserati zwischen seinen
Piloten Ruggeri, Dreyfus und
Fagioli. (3) Reifenwechsel an
Nuvolaris Alfa Romeo.

(1) Coéquipiers mais pas
comparables : Nuvolari et
Caracciola après la remise
des coupes. (2) Bonne
entente : Ernesto Maserati
entre ses pilotes Ruggeri,
Dreyfus et Fagioli.
(3) Changement de pneus sur
l'Alfa Romeo de Nuvolari.

LITTLE RED RIDING HOOD

ROTKÄPPCHEN · LE PETIT CHAPERON ROUGE

In the Thirties, Tazio Nuvolari with his electrifying charisma is a popular hero in Italy.

In den dreißiger Jahren ist Tazio Nuvolari in Italien ein Volksheld von elektrisierender Ausstrahlung.

Dans les années 30, Tazio Nuvolari est, en Italie, un héros populaire au charisme qui donne la chair de poule.

Tazio Georgio Nuvolari, rumor had it, had made a pact with the devil – and that at a time when a hotline to hell was at least as important as a first-class sponsor connection is today.

The subterranean party to the contract did not, however, conform to his mythical stereotype: 17 times, "Nivola", as everyone called him affectionately, dug his way out of the remains of his vehicle, or he was pulled out with more or less gory injuries. The old Nuvolari would have been a gift to any anatomical department: there was not a bone in his body which he had not broken at least once. In the end, his close friend Diavolo clawed the "Flying Mantuan" out of bed when everyone would have much preferred a beautiful Faustian exit with lightning, thunder and the smell of sulphur.

Nuvolari was obsessed, racing was his message to humankind, down to his body language. He sat proud and upright, wearing a yellow sweater, a red leather helmet on his head, the hairy arms long and relaxed, and the eternal chin arrogantly turned into the wind. Sometimes he could not contain himself. Then he would put back his head and let out a shout of happiness, drumming with his fists on the sides of his Bugatti or Alfa Romeo or Auto Union. Or he bared his yellow teeth like a terrier when someone overtook him, becoming particularly enraged when it was his arch enemy Achille Varzi. His driving style gave the impression of a permanent accident. But "Nivola" was delicate, and made the cars work for him, as once did the dainty lady from Prague, Elisabeth Junek.

At his last Mille Miglia, in 1948 in a Ferrari, he was spitting blood – tuberculosis. Tazio Nuvolari died silently in a coma on a hot August day. There was absolutely no doubt about one thing in the immense group of mourners: "Nivola" was the greatest.

Tazio Georgio Nuvolari, munkelt man, habe einen Pakt mit dem Teufel – und das zu einer Zeit, in der ein heißer Draht zur Hölle mindestens genauso wichtig war wie heute eine erstklassige Sponsor-Connection.

Der subterrane Vertragspartner verhält sich gleichwohl nicht mythenkonform: 17 Male rappelt sich »Nivola«, wie ihn alle zärtlich nennen, aus den armen Resten seiner Fahrzeuge, oder er wird herausgeklaubt, mehr oder minder blutig blessiert. Der alte Nuvolari wäre ein Glücksfall für jede Anatomie: kein Knochen, den er sich nicht schon einmal gebrochen hat. Am Ende krallt sich Duzfreund Diavolo den »fliegenden Mantuaner« aus dem Bett, wo sich doch alle einen schönen faustischen Abgang mit Blitz, Donner und Schwefelgestank gewünscht hätten.

Nuvolari ist ein Besessener, Rennen zu fahren die Botschaft, die er der Menschheit zu machen hat, fast schon Teil seiner Körpersprache. Im gelben Sweater, einen roten Lederhelm auf dem Schädel, die haarigen Arme lässig lang und das ewige Kinn arrogant in den Fahrtwind gereckt, sitzt er stolz und aufrecht. Manchmal übermannt es ihn. Dann legt er den Kopf zurück, heult einen Lustschrei heraus und trommelt mit den Fäusten auf die Flanken seines Bugatti oder Alfa Romeo oder Auto Union. Oder er bleckt wie ein Terrier die Zähne, wenn ihn einer überholt, vollends rasend vor Zorn, wenn es sich um seinen Intimfeind Achille Varzi handelt. Sein Fahrstil wirkt wie ein permanenter Unfall: »Nivola« ist zierlich und läßt deshalb die Autos für sich arbeiten wie einst die grazile Pragerin Elisabeth Junek.

Bei seiner letzten Mille Miglia, 1948 im Ferrari, spuckt er Blut – die Tuberkulose. Tazio Nuvolari stirbt sprachlos im Koma, an einem heißen Augusttag. Über eines gibt es überhaupt keinen Zweifel in der schier unübersehbaren Trauergemeinde: »Nivola« war der Größte.

Tazio Georgio Nuvolari, dit-on, aurait passé un pacte avec le diable – et ce, à une époque où entretenir de bonnes relations avec l'enfer était au moins tout aussi important que d'avoir, aujourd'hui, avoir de bonnes connections avec un sponsor de toute première qualité.

Mais son infernal partenaire ne se comporte pas obligatoirement en conformité avec son mythe : à dix-sept reprises, « Nivola », comme on le surnommait tendrement, s'extrait ou se fait extraire des vestiges fumants de sa voiture, blessé et plus ou moins sanguinolent. Le vieux Nuvolari aurait été un exemple de choix pour tout étudiant en anatomie : il n'avait pas d'os qu'il ne s'était brisé au moins une fois. En fin de compte, c'est pourtant dans son lit que son ami intime il Diavolo ira chercher le « Mantouais volant » alors que tous auraient souhaité une magnifique disparition à la Faust avec éclairs, tonnerre et odeur de soufre.

Nuvolari est un obsédé ; piloter en course, le message qu'il doit transmettre à l'humanité, fait quasiment partie de sa langue gestuelle. Dans son sweater jaune, avec son serre-tête de cuir rouge sur le crâne, les bras poilus interminablement longs et son manteau en galoche dressé avec arrogance contre le vent, il est assis, fier et le port altier. Parfois, il se laisse aller. Il renverse alors la tête en arrière, pousse un grognement de plaisir et tambourine des poings sur les flancs de sa Bugatti, de son Alfa Romeo ou de son Auto Union. Ou, tel un terrier, il montre ses dents jaunes lorsque quelqu'un le double, fou furieux de colère quand il s'agit de son ennemi intime, Achille Varzi. Par son style de conduite, il semble vouloir causer en permanence un accident, mais « Nivola » a une stature de jockey et laisse donc travailler les voitures pour lui comme le faisait jadis la Praguoise à la silhouette gracile, Elisabeth Junek.

Lors de ses dernières Mille Miglia, en 1948 sur Ferrari, il crache le sang – il est tuberculeux. Tazio Nuvolari meurt sans dire un mot, dans le coma, par une chaude journée du mois d'août. Une opinion ne prête absolument pas à contestation dans la foule des personnes assistant à l'enterrement : « Nivola » était le plus grand.

1933

The 1933 Monaco Grand Prix, third race of the season, was the last to be carried out in accordance with the previously open formula. But for the first time all the drivers came under time pressure from the beginning: they had to earn their place in the starting line-up by their best qualifying time, following the example of Indianapolis.

The new arrangement immediately resulted in a prominent victim. Towards the end of the first session, on the Thursday, Rudolf Caracciola's brakes failed at the chicane. With lightning speed he changed down through the gears, but could not in the end prevent the rear of his car smashing into the barrier. As he attempted to walk, he collapsed with a piercing pain and had to be carried away on a chair. The diagnosis: a complicated fracture of the femur. The doctors in Bologna performed a near-miracle, but there was a high price to pay for their delicate medical balancing act. The German emerged from the operation with a right leg which was five centimeters shorter.

With his friend Louis Chiron, Caracciola had formed the Scuderia CC. His white Alfa Romeo 8C 2300 Monza carried blue piping along the bonnet, Chiron's blue counterpart had white piping, and they appeared to be well equipped for the battle against the factory teams. Team Bugatti entered the Italian Achille Varzi, the Frenchman René Dreyfus and the Briton William Grover ("Williams") in Type 51s. The all-Italian team of Tazio Nuvolari, Baconin Borzacchini, Carlo Felice Trossi and Eugenio Siena started for the Scuderia Ferrari, representing Alfa Romeo's interests, in 8 C 2600 and 2300 Monzas. The main driver for Officine Alfieri Maserati was Luigi Fagioli in a lone 8 C 3000.

18 cars were assembled on the starting grid, overlooked by an enormous crowd, and the 18 drivers finally lifted their arms as a signal that their engines were running. Everything which followed dimmed into insignificance in the face of the duel which developed between Varzi, in pole position, and Nuvolari. Indeed, a principle was at stake, for the two protagonists could not have been more different. Nuvolari displayed a manic compulsion behind the wheel, snarling and with rolling eyes, obsessed seemingly to the point of madness. Varzi, in contrast, was the elegant stylist, who hid his ambition behind an impassive mask, always dressed to the nines and the idol of his fans, as was Nuvolari of his. Nuvolari led for 66 laps across the timing line, Varzi for 34. But that did not mean a thing. For they were constantly at loggerheads, frequently driving side-by-side, watching each other out of the corner of their eyes, and often their cars touched. Eventually Varzi won, but not before being chased to a new track record on lap 99. At the same time the red devil from Mantua simply demanded too much from his Alfa. A piston broke, and to top it all, he was disqualified for receiving external assistance. He accepted the verdict with a dangerous calm. Meanwhile, buddies they were not.

Der Grand Prix de Monaco 1933, dritter Lauf der Saison, ist der letzte, der nach der bisher gültigen freien Formel ausgetragen wird. Zum erstenmal jedoch gerät jedermann von vornherein unter Zeitdruck: Seine Position in der Startaufstellung verdient man sich nach dem Vorbild von Indianapolis durch die schnellste Runde im Training.

Die neue Regelung fordert umgehend ein prominentes Opfer. Gegen Ende der ersten Sitzung am Donnerstag wird Rudolf Caracciola an der Schikane von seinen Bremsen im Stich gelassen. Blitzschnell schaltet er durch die Gänge, kann aber nicht verhindern, daß sein Wagen am Ende mit dem Heck in die Barriere knallt. Beim Versuch zu laufen knickt er unter stechenden Schmerzen ein und wird auf einem Stuhl fortgetragen. Diagnose: komplizierter Bruch eines Oberschenkelknochens. Die Ärzte in Bologna wirken wahre Wunder. Aber der Preis für ihren heiklen medizinischen Kompromiß ist hoch, da der Deutsche mit einem um fünf Zentimeter verkürzten rechten Bein aus der Operation hervorgeht.

Caracciola hatte sich mit seinem Freund Louis Chiron zur Scuderia CC zusammengefunden. Sein weißer Alfa Romeo 8C 2300 Monza trägt eine blaue Paspellierung längs der Motorhaube, Chirons blaues Pendant eine weiße. Für den Kampf gegen die Werksteams ist man bestens gewappnet. Die Equipe Bugatti hat den Italiener Achille Varzi, den Franzosen René Dreyfus und den Briten William Grover (»Williams«) auf dem Typ 51 gemeldet. Für die Scuderia Ferrari, welche die Interessen von Alfa Romeo wahrnimmt, startet die allitalienische Riege Tazio Nuvolari, Baconin Borzacchini, Carlo Felice Trossi und Eugenio Siena mit dem 8C 2600 und 2300 Monza. Im Namen des Officine Alfieri Maserati tritt vor allem Luigi Fagioli auf einem einsamen 8C 3000 an.

Gesäumt von einer schier unübersehbaren Menge stehen 18 Wagen am Start, und 18 Piloten heben am Ende den Arm als Zeichen, daß ihre Motoren laufen. Alles, was dann folgt, verblaßt zur Bedeutungslosigkeit angesichts des Duells zwischen Varzi und Nuvolari an der Spitze. Es geht auch ums Prinzip: Verschiedener könnten die Protagonisten nicht sein. Nuvolari ist der Triebtäter am Volant, augenrollend und zähnefletschend, besessen bis hin zur Manie, Varzi der elegante Stilist, der seinen Ehrgeiz mit einem Pokergesicht maskiert, immer wie aus dem Ei gepellt, der Abgott seiner Fangemeinde wie Nuvolari das Idol der seinigen. 66 Runden führt Nuvolari auf der Höhe der Zeitnahme, 34 Varzi. Aber das hat nichts zu sagen. Denn überall hat man sich in der Wolle, fährt oft nebeneinander, den anderen aus den Augenwinkeln belauernd. Häufig berühren sich die Wagen. Varzi siegt und wird in Runde 99 noch zu einem neuen Streckenrekord gehetzt. Zugleich mutet der rote Teufel aus Mantua der Maschine seines Alfa zuviel zu. Ein Kolben reißt ab. Zu allem Überdruß wird er wegen Inanspruchnahme fremder Hilfe aus der Wertung genommen, erträgt das Verdikt mit gefährlicher Ruhe. Indes: Zum Werden einer Männerfreundschaft hat all das nicht beigetragen.

Le Grand Prix de Monaco de 1933, troisième manche de la saison, est le dernier à être organisé selon la formule libre en vigueur jusque-là. C'est la première fois, pourtant, que quelqu'un voit le temps lui échapper d'emblée : à l'exemple d'Indianapolis, on prend place sur la ligne de départ en fonction du meilleur temps réalisé au cours des essais.

Le nouveau règlement fait immédiatement une victime fameuse. A la fin de la première séance, le jeudi, Rudolf Caracciola est lâché par ses freins à l'entrée de la chicane. A la vitesse de l'éclair, il rétrograde plusieurs fois successivement, mais ne peut empêcher sa voiture de percuter les fascines de l'arrière à la sortie de la chicane. Après avoir mis pied à terre, il s'effondre sous des douleurs atroces et est évacué sur une chaise. Diagnostic : fracture complexe d'un os de la cuisse. Les médecins de Bologne font des miracles. Mais le prix de leur scabreux compromis médical est lourd, car l'Allemand quitte la salle d'opération avec une jambe droite raccourcie de cinq centimètres.

Caracciola avait rejoint son ami Louis Chiron au sein de la Scuderia CC. Son Alfa Romeo blanche 8C 2300 Monza porte une rayure bleue le long de son capot moteur et celle de Chiron, une blanche. Leurs armes sont optimales pour la lutte contre les écuries d'usine. L'équipe Bugatti a recruté l'Italien Achille Varzi, le Français René Dreyfus et le Britannique William Grover (« Williams ») sur les 51. La Scuderia Ferrari, qui défend les couleurs d'Alfa Romeo, s'aligne avec un quatuor d'Italiens : Tazio Nuvolari, Baconin Borzacchini, Carlo Felice Trossi et Eugenio Siena avec des 8C 2600 et 2300 Monza. Luigi Fagioli, sur une 8C 3000 bien isolée, est le principal héros de l'Officine Alfieri Maserati.

Devant une foule immense, 18 voitures sont au départ et les 18 pilotes lèvent alors le bras pour indiquer que leur moteur tourne. Tout ce qui se passe ensuite sombre dans le plus vif désintérêt, compte tenu du duel acharné que se livrent en tête Varzi en pole position et Nuvolari. C'est aussi une question de principe : les deux protagonistes ne pourraient être plus différents. Nuvolari est un fanatique au volant, roulant les yeux et montrant les dents, apparemment obsédé jusqu'à en être malade. Varzi est le styliste élégant qui dissimule son ambition derrière un masque de joueur de poker, toujours tiré à quatre épingles, un véritable dieu pour sa chapelle de fans comme Nuvolari est l'idole des siens. Pendant 66 tours, Nuvolari passe en tête devant le poste de chronométrage et Varzi, pendant 34 tours. Mais cela ne veut rien dire. En effet, les deux hommes ne se quittent pas d'une roue, roulent fréquemment l'un à côté de l'autre, s'épiant du coin de l'œil. Les voitures se touchent même de temps à autre. Finalement Varzi est sacré vainqueur, mais il lui fallut encore signer un nouveau record du tour lors de la 99e boucle. Le diable rouge de Mantoue, quant à lui, a trop présumé du moteur de son Alfa Romeo. Un piston lâche et, par dessus le marché, il est déclassé pour avoir recouru à une aide extérieure et prend connaissance du verdict dans un trompeur calme olympien. Quoi qu'il en soit, tout cela n'a pas suffi pour instaurer entre les deux hommes une amitié virile.

Right turn: Falchetto (Bugatti) and Fagioli (Maserati) at Portier; both retire early.

Rechtsabbieger: Falchetto (Bugatti) und Fagioli (Maserati) bei Portier. Beide scheiden vorzeitig aus.

Virage à droite : Falchetto (Bugatti) et Fagioli (Maserati) au virage du Portier. Tous les deux abandonneront prématurément.

N°	DRIVERS		ENTRANTS	CARS	ENGINES	PRACTICE RESULTS	RACE RESULTS
10	*Achille Varzi*	*I*	*Automobiles Ettore Bugatti*	*Bugatti 51*	*8L 2262 cc + C*	*1st: 2'02"*	*1st: 3h27'49"4*
26	Baconin Borzacchini	I	Scuderia Ferrari	Alfa Romeo 8C-2600 Monza	8L 2556 cc + C	2nd(3): 2'03"	2nd: 3h29'49"4
8	René Dreyfus	F	Automobiles Ettore Bugatti	Bugatti 51	8L 2262 cc + C	6th: 2'05"	3rd: 99 laps
16	Louis Chiron	F	Scuderia CC	Alfa Romeo 8C-2300 Monza	8L 2336 cc + C	2nd: 2'03"	4th: 97 laps
32	Carlo Felice Trossi	I	Scuderia Ferrari	Alfa Romeo 8C-2300 Monza	8L 2336 cc + C	10th: 2'08"	5th: 97 laps
38	Goffredo Zehender	I	Goffredo Zehender	Maserati 8CM	8L 2991 cc + C	10th(11): 2'08"	6th: 94 laps
12	"Williams"	GB	Automobiles Ettore Bugatti	Bugatti 51	8L 2262 cc + C	14th: 2'11"	7th: 90 laps
24	Laszlo Hartmann	H	Laszlo Hartmann	Bugatti 51	8L 2262 cc + C	18th: 2'22"	8th: 86 laps
28	Tazio Nuvolari	I	Scuderia Ferrari	Alfa Romeo 8C-2300 Monza	8L 2556 cc + C	4th: 2'04"	disqualified
14	Benoit Falchetto	F	Benoit Falchetto	Bugatti 51	8L 2262 cc + C	12th: 2'09"	R
18	Philippe Etancelin	F	Philippe Etancelin	Alfa Romeo 8C-2300 Monza	8L 2336 cc + C	4th(5): 2'04"	R
34	Luigi Fagioli	I	Officine Alfieri Maserati S.A.	Maserati 8C-3000	8L 2991 cc + C	7th: 2'06"	R
6	Earl Edward Richard Howe	GB	Earl Howe	Bugatti 51	8L 2262 cc + C	12th(13): 2'09"	R
22	Jean-Pierre Wimille	F	Jean-Pierre Wimille	Alfa Romeo 8C-2300 Monza	8L 2336 cc + C	7th(8): 2'06"	R
20	Marcel Lehoux	F	Marcel Lehoux	Bugatti 51	8L 2262 cc + C	9th: 2'07"	R
36	Raymond Sommer	F	Raymond Sommer	Maserati 8CM	8L 2991 cc + C	17th: 2'15"	R
4	Tim Birkin	GB	Sir Henry Birkin	Alfa Romeo 8C-2300 Monza	8L 2336 cc + C	14th(15): 2'11"	R
30	Eugenio Siena	I	Scuderia Ferrari	Alfa Romeo 8C-2300 Monza	8L 2336 cc + C	16th: 2'13"	R

(1) Here we go: Varzi (Bugatti), Chiron (Alfa Romeo) and
Borzacchini (Alfa Romeo) at the start. (2) Racing shadow: the
camera is the only thing that manages to catch Varzi. (3) Nuvolari
(Alfa Romeo) and Varzi at Sainte Dévote. (4) The perfect line: Count
Trossi (Alfa Romeo) in front of Hartmann and Howe (Bugattis).
(5) The end for the "Flying Mantuan" — after 99 laps.

(1) Aufbruchstimmung: Varzi (Bugatti), Chiron (Alfa Romeo) und
Borzacchini (Alfa Romeo) beim Start. (2) Huschender Schatten: Nur
der Kamera entkommt Varzi nicht. (3) Nuvolari (Alfa Romeo) und
Varzi bei Sainte Dévote. (4) Auf der Ideallinie: Graf Trossi (Alfa
Romeo) vor Hartmann und Howe (beide Bugatti). (5) Aus für den
»fliegenden Mantuaner« — nach 99 Runden.

(1) Impatience : Varzi (Bugatti), Chiron (Alfa Romeo) et Borzacchini
(Alfa Romeo) au départ. (2) Ombre chinoise : il n'y a qu'à l'appareil
photo que Varzi n'échappe pas. (3) Nuvolari (Alfa Romeo) et Varzi à
Sainte-Dévote. (4) Trajectoire idéale : le Comte Trossi (Alfa Romeo)
devant Hartmann et Howe (tous les deux sur Bugatti). (5) Abandon
pour le « Mantouais volant » — au bout de 99 tours.

(1) Long disappeared from the scene: Hotel Terminus and the old station.

(1) Längst von der Bildfläche verschwunden: Hotel Terminus und der alte Bahnhof.

(1) Longtemps disparus du paysage : l'Hôtel Terminus et la Vieille Gare.

(2) René Dreyfus (Bugatti) reports back to the pit, while (3) Chiron no longer hides his liking for a certain tire manufacturer. (4) In his customary casual clothes: Tazio Nuvolari. (5) Varzi, never without his cigarette, even at his moment of triumph.

(2) René Dreyfus (Bugatti) berichtet an der Box, während (3) Chiron aus seiner Sympathie für eine bestimmte Reifenmarke keinen Hehl macht. (4) In der üblichen legeren Kleidung: Tazio Nuvolari. (5) Im Augenblick des Triumphs darf bei Varzi die Zigarette nicht fehlen.

(2) René Dreyfus (Bugatti) fait son rapport aux stands, tandis que (3) Chiron ne cache pas sa sympathie pour une certaine marque de pneumatiques. (4) Comme d'habitude, en tenue décontractée : Tazio Nuvolari. (5) Même au moment du triomphe, Varzi ne renonce jamais à sa cigarette.

1934

Nineteen thirty-four was the year when the AIACR, motor sport's governing body, cut back on the uncontrolled growth of free and semi-free formulas. A minimum weight of 750 kilograms was announced for a Formula 1 monoposto, without oil, water, petrol, tyres and the driver. A minimum length of 500 kilometers remained the prescribed race length, but the small kingdom of the Grimaldis was allowed to preserve its long-established special status. Through its narrow streets 318 kilometers were deemed to be sufficient.

The new regulations were premiered in Monaco, where the race was set for Easter Monday, 2 April, and thus was unusually early. For safety reasons, only 16 participants were invited. The silver arrows still remained in the quiver: the Auto Unions were to have their debut on 27 May in Berlin, the Mercedes at the Eifel race on 3 June. Thus the Monaco Grand Prix turned into a race between three marques: six Alfas, five Maseratis and five Bugattis appeared on the list of competitors. The Scuderia Ferrari, the semi-official Alfa Romeo team, provided Type P3s for the two Algerians Guy Moll and Marcel Lehoux, the Monégasque Louis Chiron, as well as the two Italians Carlo Felice Trossi and Achille Varzi; Bugatti supplied Type 59s for René Dreyfus, Jean-Pierre Wimille and Robert Benoist; and the Officine Alfieri Maserati had a single factory car, the Tipo 4 C 2500, for the young Roman Piero Taruffi, a man who, as it turned out, had a great future ahead of him. Tazio Nuvolari, on the other hand, joined the private drivers on this occasion in a Bugatti 51 and was as fast in training as the fastest factory driver, René Dreyfus.

The event which only five years earlier had put out its first tentative shoots had by now blossomed into the top event of the season. Well over 100,000 spectators filled every nook and cranny, clung to the hill under the old town, or peered out of or round every building with a view of the track. An estimated 35,000 cars were parked within the town. Countless warships and yachts bobbed up and down in the harbor, and the royal box was full to bursting with prominent figures. As well as the ruling family itself, which was always well aware of its duty to be present, royal guests including the kings of Sweden and Spain also joined the assembly.

Of course, everyone supported their popular compatriot Chiron and was, initially, well rewarded. He overcame Dreyfus with his Bugatti as early as the first lap and retained the lead until lap 97. Victory had appeared certain, but then the Alfa skidded into the sandbags by the Station Hairpin — either because of oil on the track or because Chiron lost his concentration for a second: no-one knows. He got out of the car and heaved it back on to the track while Guy Moll slipped past, putting a minute between himself and the Monégasque. In the end, the race was marked by several firsts and records: a double success for the Scuderia Ferrari, first place – the first in his Grand Prix career – for the prodigy Guy Moll (born 1910). The Monaco Grand Prix has still not been won by a younger person. Previous race records, however, remained unchallenged.

Neunzehnhundertvierunddreißig: Da hat die amtierende Motorsport-Legislative AIACR den Wildwuchs freier und halbfreier Formeln beschnitten. 750 Kilogramm Mindestgewicht sind für einen Formel-1-Monoposto angesagt, ohne Öl, Wasser, Benzin, Reifen und den Fahrer. 500 Kilometer Minimallänge für einen Grand Prix bleiben vorgeschrieben. Das kleine Reich der Grimaldis bewahrt sich allerdings seinen längst eingewurzelten Sonderstatus. In der Enge seiner Häuserschluchten tun es auch 318 Kilometer.

In Monaco feiert die neue Regelung Premiere. Das Rennen ist für den Ostermontag angesetzt, am 2. April und damit ungewöhnlich früh. Nur 16 Teilnehmer sind eingeladen, aus Gründen der Sicherheit. Noch bleiben die Silberpfeile im Köcher: Die Auto Union werden am 27. auf der Berliner Avus debütieren, die Mercedes beim Eifelrennen am 3. Juni. So gerät der Grand Prix von Monaco zum Drei-Marken-Rennen: Sechs Alfa, fünf Maserati und fünf Bugatti finden sich auf der Liste der Konkurrenten. Die Scuderia Ferrari, das halb-offizielle Alfa Romeo-Team, setzt den Typ P3 für die zwei Algerier Guy Moll und Marcel Lehoux, den Monegassen Louis Chiron sowie die beiden Italiener Carlo Felice Trossi und Achille Varzi ein, Bugatti den Typ 59 für René Dreyfus, Jean-Pierre Wimille und Robert Benoist, die Officine Alfieri Maserati einen einzigen Werkswagen Tipo 4 C 2500 für den jungen Römer Piero Taruffi, einen Mann mit Zukunft, wie sich erweisen wird. Tazio Nuvolari indes ist für dieses Mal unter die Privatfahrer gegangen, auf dem Bugatti 51, und im Training ebenso schnell wie der schnellste Werkspilot René Dreyfus.

Längst ist, was fünf Jahre zuvor zögerlich knospte, zum Top-Ereignis der Saison erblüht. Weit über 100 000 Zuschauer füllen jeden Winkel, hängen im Berg unterhalb der Altstadt, lugen um jede Häuserecke mit Blick auf die Piste. An die 35 000 Autos sind im Stadtgebiet geparkt. Im Hafen dümpeln zahlreiche Kriegsschiffe und Yachten. Prallvoll mit Prominenz ist auch die Fürstenloge: Neben der Regentenfamilie, die eine Art Präsenzpflicht bei der Stange hält, hat sich auch Royalty wie die Könige von Schweden und Spanien ein Stelldichein gegeben.

Natürlich ergreift man Partei für den populären Mitbürger Chiron und kommt zunächst auch auf seine Kosten: Der kämpft den Bugattisten Dreyfus aus dem benachbarten Nizza noch in der ersten Runde nieder und führt bis zur 97. Runde. Der Sieg scheint sicher. Doch dann rutscht der Alfa vor der Bahnhofskurve in die Sandsäcke, auf einer Ölspur oder weil Chiron sich einen Augenblick nicht konzentriert hat — man weiß es nicht. Er verläßt den Wagen und wuchtet ihn zurück in die Fahrrinne, während Guy Moll vorbeischlüpft und eine Minute Abstand zwischen sich und den Monegassen legt. Am Ende sind lauter Novitäten und Rekorde zu verzeichnen: Doppelerfolg für die Scuderia Ferrari, Rang eins – der erste in seiner Grand-Prix-Karriere – für das Wunderkind Guy Moll (Jahrgang 1910). Bis heute hat kein Jüngerer den Großen Preis von Monaco gewonnen. Die bestehenden Bestwerte allerdings blieben unangetastet.

Dix-neuf cent trente-quatre : l'autorité suprême de la compétition automobile, l'AIACR, a mis de l'ordre dans l'anarchie des formules libres et semi-libres. Le règlement est précis : poids minimum de 750 kilos pour une monoplace Formule 1, sans huile, eau, essence, pneus ni pilote. Le circuit du Grand Prix doit obligatoirement recouvrir une longueur minimum de 500 kilomètres, mais le petit royaume des Grimaldi continue toutefois de cultiver sa spécificité depuis longtemps ancrée dans la tradition. Dans le dédale de béton, 318 kilomètres suffisent.

Le nouveau règlement fête sa première à Monaco. La course figure au calendrier pour le lundi de Pâques, le 2 avril, soit une date inhabituellement précoce. Pour des motifs de sécurité, seize participants seulement ont été invités. Les Flèches d'argent n'ont pas encore quitté leur carquois : les Auto-Union feront leurs débuts le 27 mai, sur le circuit berlinois de l'Avus, et les Mercedes, lors de la course de l'Eifel, le 3 juin. Le Grand Prix de Monaco sera donc disputé entre trois marques : six Alfa Romeo, cinq Maserati et cinq Bugatti composent la liste des concurrents. La Scuderia Ferrari, l'écurie semi-officielle d'Alfa Romeo, engage des P3 pour les deux Algériens Guy Moll et Marcel Lehoux, le Monégasque Louis Chiron ainsi que les deux Italiens Carlo Felice Trossi et Achille Varzi ; Bugatti aligne des 59 pour René Dreyfus, Jean-Pierre Wimille et Robert Benoist, tandis que l'Officine Alfieri Maserati a préparé une seule voiture d'usine, une Tipo 4 C 2500, pour le jeune Romain Piero Taruffi, homme plein d'avenir comme on le constatera plus tard. Tazio Nuvolari figure cette fois-ci parmi les pilotes privés, sur une Bugatti 51, ce qui ne l'empêche pas d'être aussi rapide, aux essais, que le meilleur des pilotes d'usine, René Dreyfus.

Il y a longtemps que ce qui ne s'était épanoui qu'avec hésitation juste cinq ans auparavant est devenu l'événement le plus mondain de la saison. Largement plus de 100 000 spectateurs envahissent chaque recoin de rue, s'accrochent sur les pentes du Rocher aux pieds de la Vieille Ville, se réfugient à chaque angle de maison pour jeter un coup d'œil sur la piste. Près de 35 000 voitures sont garées dans les rues de la ville. De nombreux bateaux de guerre flottent dans le port et la loge princière regorge de hautes personnalités : outre la famille du régent, pour laquelle il est de son devoir de faire acte de présence, des têtes couronnées se sont aussi donné rendez-vous, tels le roi de Suède et l'ex-roi d'Espagne.

La foule prend naturellement parti pour son populaire concitoyen, Louis Chiron, et n'est d'ailleurs pas déçue par le début de la course : dès le premier tour, il prend le dessus sur le pilote de Bugatti et citoyen de la ville voisine de Nice qu'est Dreyfus, gardant la tête jusqu'au 97e tour. La victoire lui semble assurée. Mais l'Alfa dérape et percute les sacs de sable à l'entrée du virage de la Gare. A cause d'une trace d'huile ou parce que Chiron s'est déconcentré quelques secondes ? On ne le saura jamais. Il descend de voiture et, furieux, la repousse sur la piste au moment même où Guy Moll passe en le frôlant et gagne la course avec une minute d'avance sur le Monégasque. A l'issue de la course, les nouveautés et records sont légion : doublé pour la Scuderia Ferrari, première victoire – la première dans sa carrière de pilote de Grand Prix – pour l'enfant prodige Guy Moll (né en 1910). Jusqu'à aujourd'hui, il est resté le plus jeune pilote à avoir remporté le Grand Prix de Monaco. Mais les records de course existants n'ont toutefois pas été battus.

Politics of strength: four of the five Alfa Romeos of the Scuderia Ferrari for Lehoux, Trossi, Chiron and Moll.

Politik der Stärke: vier der fünf Alfa Romeo der Scuderia Ferrari für Lehoux, Trossi, Chiron und Moll.

La loi du plus fort : quatre des cinq Alfa Romeo de la Scuderia Ferrari pour Lehoux, Trossi, Chiron et Moll.

N°	DRIVERS		ENTRANTS	CARS	ENGINES	PRACTICE RESULTS	RACE RESULTS
20	**Guy Moll**	**F**	**Scuderia Ferrari**	**Alfa Romeo B (P3)**	**8L 2905 cc + C**	**6th(7): 2'00"**	**1st: 3h31'31"4**
16	Louis Chiron	F	Scuderia Ferrari	Alfa Romeo B (P3)	8L 2905 cc + C	6th: 2'00"	2nd: 3h32'33"4
8	*René Dreyfus*	*F*	*Usines Bugatti*	*Bugatti 59*	*8L 2821 cc + C*	*1st(3): 1'59"*	*3rd: 99 laps*
18	Marcel Lehoux	F	Scuderia Ferrari	Alfa Romeo B (P3)	8L 2905 cc + C	6th(10): 2'00"	4th: 99 laps
28	*Tazio Nuvolari*	*I*	*Tazio Nuvolari*	*Bugatti 59*	*8L 2821 cc + C*	*1st(5): 1'59"*	*5th: 98 laps*
24	*Achille Varzi*	*I*	*Scuderia Ferrari*	*Alfa Romeo B (P3)*	*8L 2905 cc + C*	*1st(4): 1'59"*	*6th: 98 laps*
4	Whitney Straight	USA	Stable Whitney Straight	Maserati 8CM	8L 2991 cc + C	11th: 2'02"	7th: 96 laps
30	Eugenio Siena	I	Scuderia Siena	Maserati 8C-3000	8L 2991 cc + C	12th: 2'05"	8th: 96 laps
12	Pierre Veyron	F	Pierre Veyron	Bugatti 51	8L 2262 cc + C	14th: 2'06"	9th: 95 laps
2	Earl Edward Richard Howe	GB	Earl Howe	Maserati 8CM	8L 2991 cc + C	15th: 2'08"	10th: 85 laps
22	*Carlo Felice Trossi*	*I*	*Scuderia Ferrari*	*Alfa Romeo B (P3)*	*8L 2905 cc + C*	*1st: 1'59"*	*R*
32	Piero Taruffi	I	Officine Alfieri Maserati S.A.	Maserati 4C-2500	4L 2482 cc + C	6th(8): 2'00"	R
14	*Philippe Etancelin*	*F*	*Philippe Etancelin*	*Maserati 8CM*	*8L 2991 cc + C*	*1st(2): 1'59"*	*R*
26	Renato Balestrero	I	Gruppo San Giorgio	Alfa Romeo 8C-2300	8L 2556 cc + C	12th(13): 2'05"	R
10	Jean-Pierre Wimille	F	Usines Bugatti	Bugatti 59	8L 2821 cc + C	6th(9): 2'00"	R

(5) In contrast to today's practice, the drivers raise their arm once the engine is running; Lehoux in front (Alfa Romeo), number 12: Earl Howe (Maserati). (6) Friends: Caracciola (in the foreground with hat) and Louis Chiron. Still convalescing after his serious accident in the previous year, the German attends the Grand Prix as a spectator. (7) Victory cup: honors for Guy Moll.
(Following double page) At the end of the first lap, Louis Chiron (Alfa Romeo) is in the lead.

(5) Im Gegensatz zur heutigen Praxis heben die Fahrer den Arm, wenn der Motor läuft, vorn Lehoux (Alfa Romeo), Nummer 12: Earl Howe (Maserati). (6) Freunde: Caracciola (im Vordergrund mit Hut) und Louis Chiron. Noch Rekonvaleszent nach seinem schweren Unfall im Jahr zuvor, wohnt der Deutsche dem Grand Prix als Zuschauer bei. (7) Pokal-Sieg: Ehrung für Guy Moll.
(Folgende Doppelseite) Am Ende der ersten Runde führt Louis Chiron (Alfa Romeo).

(5) Au contraire d'aujourd'hui, les pilotes lèvent le bras lorsque le moteur tourne. Au premier plan, Lehoux (Alfa Romeo), numéro 12 : le Comte Howe (Maserati). (6) Amis: Caracciola (au premier plan avec chapeau) et Louis Chiron. Encore en convalescence après son grave accident de l'année précédente, l'Allemand assiste au Grand Prix en spectateur. (7) Il remporte la coupe : distinction pour Guy Moll.
(Double page suivante) Louis Chiron (Alfa Romeo) termine le premier tour en tête.

(1) Moll (Alfa Romeo) about to enter Tobacconist's Corner.
(2) Pushing: Etancelin in his Maserati. (3) Team-mates: Count Trossi and Chiron in the Alfa Romeos managed by Enzo Ferrari.
(4) Sermon: race organizer Charles Faroux calls on the drivers to drive with discretion.

(1) Moll (Alfa Romeo) eingangs der Tabakskurve. (2) Schiebung: Etancelin im Maserati. (3) Unter Brüdern: Graf Trossi und Chiron in den Alfa Romeo, deren Einsatz Enzo Ferrari leitet. (4) Moralpredigt: Rennleiter Charles Faroux fordert zu defensivem Fahren auf.

(1) Moll (Alfa Romeo) à l'entrée du virage du Bureau de Tabac.
(2) A la poussette : Etancelin sur Maserati. (3) Entre frères : le comte Trossi et Chiron sur Alfa Romeo, sous la direction d'Enzo Ferrari. (4) Sermon : le directeur de course Charles Faroux invite les pilotes à faire preuve de fair-play.

1935

It was painful, but the Monaco Grand Prix was not included in the series of races which made up the European Championship, announced by the AIACR for the first time in 1935. These took place only in Belgium, Germany, Switzerland, Italy and Spain.

Once again the Monaco Grand Prix was held on Easter Monday, and this year the chicane was new – and a little slower. The starting line-up of 3/2/3/2/3/2 was also new – and a little safer. The presence of only a single French car, driven by a Briton and painted British racing green – the Bugatti 59 of Earl Francis Curzon Howe – was a great disappointment to the patriotic crowd.

New, above all, however, was the presence of three Mercedes Type W 25 factory cars for Rudolf Caracciola, Manfred von Brauchitsch and Luigi Fagioli, under the leadership of the powerfully-voiced team manager Alfred Neubauer. Auto Union sent regards and apologies, but the circuit was considered to be not suitable for its cars. Team Bugatti, too, was missing – the blue cars from Molsheim were becoming a rarer sight by this time. As if to make up for that, the Scuderia Ferrari had registered four P3s on behalf of Alfa Romeo for Tazio Nuvolari, who had fallen from grace in the interim, and his compatriot Antonio Brivio, as well as for Louis Chiron and René Dreyfus. Maserati, too, waged war by proxy. A 6 C 34 for Philippe Etancelin and the 8 CM for Goffredo Zehender displayed the badge of the Turin Scuderia Subalpina, founded two years earlier by Count Luigi della Chiesa, but they could only qualify for the fourth row. The first row of the starting grid was occupied by the three silver Mercedes, screaming through the streets of the town with elemental power; behind them came five Alfa Romeos.

But the expected walkover of the three W 25s did not materialize. True, Luigi Fagioli drove to victory, which never seemed in doubt from the moment he left the starting grid, the first such occurrence in the history of the race. But his teammates were not smiled upon so favorably by Lady Luck, who so often ruled the race track at Monaco so arbitrarily. At the end of the first lap Manfred von Brauchitsch returned slowly to the pits with transmission trouble. Caracciola was tormented by terrible pains in his right leg and hip, the result of his crash during training in 1933. On lap 49, Etancelin overtook the German on the inside at the gasometer bend and managed to stay ahead of the Mercedes for a further six laps, but then fell back again with brake problems. Caracciola, in the meantime, was eliminated on lap 65. Stinging smoke rose from his engine, a valve spring having broken at the very least. Alfred Neubauer showed his concern and signalled to Fagioli for restraint. Immediately the latter's lap times fell by up to six seconds, which was not usual. In his autobiography, "Men, Women and Engines", Neubauer accused the Italian of a lack of discipline. However, on this occasion, with victory in sight he could afford to relax a little.

Es schmerzt, aber der Grand Prix de Monaco zählt nicht zum Zyklus der Läufe um die Europameisterschaft, die 1935 von der AIACR zum erstenmal ausgeschrieben wird. Sie gastiert lediglich in Belgien, Deutschland, der Schweiz, Italien und Spanien.

Wieder findet er am Ostermontag statt. Neu – und etwas langsamer – ist die Streckenführung an der Schikane. Neu – und etwas sicherer – ist die Startaufstellung im Rhythmus 3/2/3/2/3/2. Neu – und dies sehr zum Leidwesen der patriotisch gesonnenen Menge – ist die Anwesenheit von nur einem einzigen französischen Auto, dazu von einem Briten gefahren und in British Racing Green lackiert – des Bugatti 59 von Earl Francis Curzon Howe.

Neu ist vor allem die Präsenz von drei Mercedes Werkswagen vom Typ W 25 für Rudolf Caracciola, Manfred von Brauchitsch und Luigi Fagioli, unter der Stabführung des stimmgewaltigen Rennleiters Alfred Neubauer. Die Auto Union läßt grüßen und sich entschuldigen, die Strecke sei nicht geeignet für ihre Fahrzeuge. Und auch die Equipe Bugatti fehlt – die Blauen aus Molsheim beginnen sich rar zu machen in jenen Jahren. Dafür hat die Scuderia Ferrari im Namen und im Auftrag von Alfa Romeo vier P3 gemeldet für Tazio Nuvolari, der zwischenzeitlich in Ungnade gefallen war, seinen Landsmann Antonio Brivio, Louis Chiron und René Dreyfus. Auch Maserati läßt einen Stellvertreter-Krieg führen. Ein 6 C 34 für Philippe Etancelin und der 8 CM für Goffredo Zehender tragen das Wappen der Turiner Scuderia Subalpina, zwei Jahre zuvor durch den Grafen Luigi della Chiesa gegründet. Im Training gerät man entschieden ins Hintertreffen. Die erste Startreihe ist für die silbernen Mercedes reserviert, die mit schierer Urgewalt durch die Straßen der Stadt schrillen, dahinter folgen fünf Alfa Romeo.

Die erwartete Prozession der drei W 25 bleibt hingegen aus. Gewiß fährt Luigi Fagioli einem nie gefährdeten Start-Ziel-Sieg entgegen, dem ersten in der Geschichte des Rennens. Seinen Teamgefährten aber spielt die Fortuna der Pisten, die in Monaco häufig mit ausgesuchter Willkür waltet, übel mit. Aus der ersten Runde kehrt Manfred von Brauchitsch in langsamer Fahrt zu den Boxen zurück – Getriebeschaden. Caracciola wird gepeinigt von furchtbaren Schmerzen im rechten Bein und in der Hüfte, Folge seines Trainingssturzes 1933. In der 49. Runde überholt Etancelin den Deutschen innen in der Gasometerkurve, hält sich sechs Durchgänge lang vor dem Mercedes und fällt dann wieder zurück – Probleme mit den Bremsen. Caracciola indessen fällt in der 65. Runde aus. Beißender Qualm erhebt sich über dem Triebwerk, mindestens eine Ventilfeder ist gebrochen. Alfred Neubauer zeigt sich besorgt, signalisiert Fagioli, er möge sich zurückhalten. Prompt sinken dessen Rundenzeiten um bis zu sechs Sekunden. Das ist untypisch: In seiner Autobiographie »Männer, Frauen und Motoren« bezichtigt Neubauer den Italiener der Disziplinlosigkeit. Indes: Den sicheren Sieg vor Augen kann man schon mal ein Auge zudrücken.

La décision est douloureuse, mais le Grand Prix de Monaco ne figure pas au calendrier du Championnat d'Europe que l'AIACR organise pour la première fois en 1935. Il n'a retenu que la Belgique, l'Allemagne, la Suisse, l'Italie et l'Espagne. Le Grand Prix a de nouveau lieu le lundi de Pâques. Cette année, le tracé est nouveau – et un peu plus lent – à cause d'une chicane redessinée. De même la composition de la grille de départ selon le schéma 3/2/3/2/3/2 est nouvelle – et, aussi, un peu plus sûre. La présence d'une seule et unique voiture française, qui plus est, conduite par un Britannique et peinte aux couleurs British Racing Green – la Bugatti 59 de Earl Francis Curzon Howe est une autre nouveauté – pour le plus grand dépit d'une foule à la fibre naturelle patriotique.

Nouvelle est, surtout, la présence de trois Mercedes d'usine, des W 25, pour Rudolf Caracciola, Manfred von Brauchitsch et Luigi Fagioli, sous la houlette du corpulent directeur de course à la voix de tribun, Alfred Neubauer. Auto Union se rappelle au bon souvenir de tous, mais objecte que le circuit n'est pas approprié pour ses voitures. Quant à l'équipe Bugatti, elle brille par son absence – les voitures bleues de Molsheim commencent à se faire rares ces années-là. En revanche, la Scuderia Ferrari, qui court pour le compte d'Alfa Romeo, a inscrit quatre P3 pour Tazio Nuvolari, qui était entre-temps tombé dans le discrédit, pour son compatriote Antonio Brivio ainsi que Louis Chiron et René Dreyfus. Maserati aussi participe à la guerre par personne interposée. Une 6 C 34 pour Philippe Etancelin et la 8 CM pour Goffredo Zehender arborent le blason de la Scuderia Subalpina de Turin, fondée deux ans auparavant par le comte Luigi della Chiesa, mais n'atteinnent que la quatrième place. Les Mercedes argentées monopolisent la première ligne de départ – leur bruit strident qui résonne dans les rues de la ville donnant une idée de leur puissance prolifique – suivies par cinq Alfa Romeo.

Mais la victoire tant attendue des trois W 25 reste chimère. Certes, Luigi Fagioli conserve la tête du départ à l'arrivée sans jamais avoir été en danger, ce qui est une première dans l'histoire de l'automobile. Mais la fortune des circuits, qui s'est si fréquemment distinguée, à Monaco, par son arbitraire flagrant, joue un jeu cruel avec ses coéquipiers. Manfred von Brauchitsch regagne les stands pratiquement au ralenti à l'issue du premier tour – panne de boîte de vitesses. Caracciola est torturé par d'atroces douleurs dans la jambe droite et la hanche, séquelles de son accident aux essais de 1933. Au 49e tour, Etancelin fait l'intérieur à l'Allemand dans le virage du Gazomètre et reste devant la Mercedes pendant six tours avant de devoir le laisser passer à nouveau – problèmes de freins. Mais la chance n'est pas aux côtés de Caracciola, qui doit abandonner au 65e tour. Une fumée piquante s'échappe du moteur et au moins un ressort de soupape est brisé. Alfred Neubauer ne cache pas sa préoccupation et donne à Fagioli le signal de lever le pied. Immédiatement, ses temps au tour s'allongent de jusqu'à six secondes. Chose qui n'a rien de typique : dans son autobiographie « Hommes, Femmes et Moteurs », Neubauer reproche à l'Italien son absence de discipline. Quoi qu'il en soit : la victoire assurée à portée de la main, on peut en l'occurrence faire preuve d'un peu de tolérance.

The qualifying results are announced on a huge board. Howe (Bugatti) and Dusio (Maserati) did not take part in the third session on Sunday.

Auf einer großen Tafel werden die Trainingsresultate kundgetan. An der dritten Sitzung am Sonntag haben Howe (Bugatti) und Dusio (Maserati) nicht teilgenommen.

Les résultats des essais sont affichés sur un grand tableau. Howe (Bugatti) et Dusio (Maserati) n'ont pas participé à la troisième séance du dimanche.

N°	DRIVERS		ENTRANTS	CARS	ENGINES	PRACTICE RESULTS	RACE RESULTS
4	**Luigi Fagioli**	**I**	**Daimler-Benz AG**	**Mercedes-Benz W25B**	**8L 3992 cc + C**	**3rd: 1'57"3**	**1st: 3h23'49"8**
18	René Dreyfus	F	Scuderia Ferrari	Alfa Romeo B (P3)	8L 3165 cc + C	4th: 1'59"0	2nd: 3h24'21"3
22	Antonio Brivio	I	Scuderia Ferrari	Alfa Romeo B (P3)	8L 2905 cc + C	6th: 2'01"0	3rd: 3h24'56"2
24	Philippe Etancelin	F	Scuderia Subalpina	Maserati 6C-34	6L 3724 cc + C	9th: 2'02"2	4th: 99 laps
16	Louis Chiron	F	Scuderia Ferrari	Alfa Romeo B (P3)	8L 2905 cc + C	7th: 2'01"8	5th: 97 laps
14	Raymond Sommer	F	Raymond Sommer	Alfa Romeo B (P3)	8L 2905 cc + C	8th: 2'02"0	6th: 94 laps
26	Goffredo Zehender	I	Scuderia Subalpina	Maserati 8CM-3000	8L 2991 cc + C	10th: 2'04"0	7th: 93 laps
32	Luigi Soffietti	I	Luigi Soffietti	Maserati 8CM-3000	8L 2991 cc + C	134th: 2'05"1	8th: 91 laps
10	J. de Villapadierna	E	Count Villapadierna	Maserati 8CM	8L 2991 cc + C	15th: 2'07"3	R
2	*Rudolf Caracciola*	*D*	*Daimler-Benz AG*	*Mercedes-Benz W25B*	*8L 3992 cc + C*	*1st: 1'56"6*	*R*
20	Tazio Nuvolari	I	Scuderia Ferrari	Alfa Romeo B (P3)	8L 3165 cc + C	5th: 1'59"4	R
8	Earl Edward Richard Howe	GB	Earl Howe	Bugatti 59	8L 3255 cc + C	10th(12): 2'04"0	R
30	Giuseppe Farina	I	Gino Rovere	Maserati 6C-34	6L 3724 cc + C	10th(11): 2'04"0	R
28	Piero Dusio	I	Scuderia Subalpina	Maserati 8CM-3000	8L 2991 cc + C	14th: 2'06"0	R
6	Manfred von Brauchitsch	D	Daimler-Benz AG	Mercedes-Benz W25B	8L 3992 cc + C	2nd: 1'57"0	R

(1) Race organizer Charles Faroux (foreground, with hat) faces the three Mercedes-Benz on the first row of the grid. (2) Shadow-play: Manfred von Brauchitsch (Mercedes-Benz) at the harbor. Runners-up: the Alfa Romeos of the Scuderia Ferrari – (3) Dreyfus (number 18) and (4) Brivio – finished second and third. (5) The winner, Fagioli (Mercedes-Benz) laps Soffietti (Maserati).

(1) Rennleiter Charles Faroux (vorn links mit Hut) stellt sich den drei Mercedes-Benz in der ersten Reihe. (2) Schatten-Spiel: Manfred von Brauchitsch (Mercedes-Benz) am Hafen. Ferner liefen: Die Alfa Romeo der Scuderia Ferrari – (3) Dreyfus (Nummer 18) und (4) Brivio – landen nur auf den Plätzen. (5) Der Sieger Fagioli (Mercedes-Benz) überrundet Soffietti (Maserati).

(1) Le directeur de course Charles Faroux (au premier plan à gauche avec chapeau) fait face aux trois Mercedes-Benz en première ligne. (2) Jeux d'ombres : Manfred von Brauchitsch (Mercedes-Benz) au port. Loin derrière : les Alfa Romeo de la Scuderia Ferrari – (3) Dreyfus (numéro 18) et (4) Brivio – termineront dans le peloton. (5) Le vainqueur Fagioli (Mercedes-Benz) l'emporte d'un tour sur Soffietti (Maserati).

4

5

Pit work at Mercedes-Benz: (1) the tireless W 25 of Fagioli, (2) preparing the lap indicators, (4) team boss Alfred Neubauer in imperial pose. (3) The in-line eight-cylinder engine of an Alfa Romeo B3. (5) Quiet pleasure: the winner, Luigi Fagioli, (6) Zehender (Maserati), who came seventh, (7) Giuseppe Farina in his Maserati.

Boxenarbeit bei Mercedes-Benz: (1) der unbesohlte W 25 von Fagioli, (2) Vorbereitung der Rundenanzeige, (4) Rennleiter Alfred Neubauer in imperialer Pose. (3) Der Reihenachtzylinder eines Alfa Romeo B3. (5) Stille Freude: der Sieger Luigi Fagioli, (6) Zehender (Maserati), der Platz sieben belegt, (7) Giuseppe Farina im Maserati.

Travail aux stands chez Mercedes-Benz : (1) la W 25 de Fagioli sans pneus, (2) préparation du panneautage, (4) le directeur de course Alfred Neubauer en pose d'empereur. (3) Le huit-cylindres en ligne d'une Alfa Romeo B3. (5) Joie discrète : le vainqueur Luigi Fagioli, (6) Zehender (Maserati), qui termine septième et (7) Giuseppe Farina sur Maserati.

1936

Panta rhei, Heraclitus taught us – all is flux. The Monaco Grand Prix was no exception. And thus the eighth time that this event took place, on 13 April 1936, there were well-measured innovations and several planned and unplanned firsts. The preliminary event for racing cars up to 1,500 cc on Saturday afternoon established a tradition around the Prince Rainier Cup, which gave rise to the later Formula 3 races as part of the supporting programme. The main event – on Easter Monday as in the previous two years – had now become part of the exclusive series of Grands Prix through which the European Championship was fought out.

In the feud between the silver arrows, Auto Union thus faced up to its rival, Mercedes-Benz, with the most recent version of its powerful V16 engine, with 6,005 cc and 520 bhp at 5,000 rpm, on what was conceivably the most unsuitable terrain of the hilly and tortuous town circuit. Sports manager was Dr Karl Feuereissen, and his driving team consisted of the experienced "mountain king" Hans Stuck, the impetuous whizz-kid Bernd Rosemeyer and the cool Italian gentleman Achille Varzi. Mercedes-Benz, in crisis that year, faced up to this squad with its W 25 E, with a 4,740 cc engine producing 494 bhp at 5,800 rpm. Its four drivers were Rudolf Caracciola, Manfred von Brauchitsch, Luigi Fagioli and Louis Chiron, who one might almost say was giving a guest performance on his home stage. The Monégasque showed his gratitude by claiming pole position in 1'53"2 and was thus the first to break the 100 kph barrier. Strong opposition was to be expected from the Scuderia Ferrari, which had entered four Alfa Romeo 8 Cs with their 3,822 cc engines delivering 330 bhp at 5,400 rpm; Antonio Brivio, Giuseppe Farina, Mario Tadini and Tazio Nuvolari were at the wheel.

On race day it was raining, a further novelty. There was also a curious symmetry among the German cars in the starting line-up. Chiron and Caracciola were positioned outside right and left on the first row, with Nuvolari between them; Stuck and Rosemeyer were on the second row; Varzi on the third between Farina and Jean-Pierre Wimille (Bugatti 59); and von Brauchitsch and Fagioli were on the fourth. But Chiron's glory lasted no longer than five minutes. On the second lap Tadini's engine had dripped oil at the chicane, which turned into a lethal film on the track as it came into contact with the rain water. Chiron skidded on it, as did von Brauchitsch, Tadini and Eugenio Siena (Maserati). When Fagioli's W 25 went into a spin after the chicane on the tenth lap because an inattentive track marshal had shovelled sand into the driver's face, three Mercedes had been eliminated.

But one driver managed to make it, the "rain king" Rudi Caracciola, although he had to give way to Nuvolari for a time. Rosemeyer backed the long tail of his Auto Union into a balustrade in front of the Casino on lap 13, while Varzi and Stuck in second and third places carefully felt their way through the infernal rain. Three German cars in the first three places – that too was new. In 1937, however, things would get even better.

Panta rhei, lehrt Heraklit, alles fließt. Der Grand Prix de Monaco macht da keine Ausnahme. Und so wartet die achte Auflage am 13. April 1936 mit wohldosierter Innovation sowie etlichen geplanten und ungeplanten Premieren auf. Mit einem Lauf für Rennwagen bis 1500 cm³ am Samstag nachmittag um den Coupe de Prince Rainier wird eine Tradition verankert, die zu den späteren Formel-3-Rennen im Rahmenprogramm führt. Das Hauptereignis – wie in den vergangenen beiden Jahren am Ostermontag – gehört nun zum handverlesenen Zirkel der Großen Preise, in denen die Europameisterschaft ausgefochten wird.

Im Bruderkampf der Silberpfeile stellt sich die Auto Union dem Rivalen Mercedes deshalb auch auf dem denkbar ungeeignetsten Terrain des gebirgigen Stadtkurses, mit der jüngsten Evolutionsstufe ihrer mächtigen V16 mit 6005 cm³ und 520 PS bei 5000/min. Sportlicher Leiter ist Dr. Karl Feuereissen. Die Riege der Piloten besteht aus dem routinierten »Bergkönig« Hans Stuck, dem ungestümen Senkrechtstarter Bernd Rosemeyer und dem kühlen italienischen Gentleman Achille Varzi. Mercedes-Benz, in jenem Jahr in die Krise geraten, setzt diesem Aufgebot den W 25 E entgegen, mit 4740 cm³ und 494 PS bei 5800/min. Die vier Fahrer sind Rudolf Caracciola, Manfred von Brauchitsch, Luigi Fagioli und Louis Chiron, der gewissermaßen ein Gastspiel auf eigener Bühne gibt. Der Monegasse dankt mit der Pole Position von 1'53"2 und springt damit als erster über die Hürde von 100 Stundenkilometern. Energische Opposition ist von der Scuderia Ferrari zu erwarten, die vier Alfa Romeo 8 C mit 3822 cm³ und 330 PS bei 5400/min gemeldet hat, am Volant Antonio Brivio, Giuseppe Farina, Mario Tadini und Tazio Nuvolari.

Am Renntag regnet es, ein weiteres Novum. In der Startaufstellung finden sich die deutschen Wagen zu merkwürdiger Symmetrie zusammen. Chiron und Caracciola stehen in der ersten Reihe links und rechts außen, zwischen ihnen Nuvolari, Rosemeyer und Stuck in der zweiten, Varzi in der dritten zwischen Jean-Pierre Wimille (Bugatti 59) und Farina, von Brauchitsch und Fagioli in der vierten. Chirons Glorie währt keine fünf Minuten. In der zweiten Runde hat Tadinis Triebwerk in der Schikane eine Ölspur gelegt, die sich mit dem Regenwasser zu einem tückischen Film verquickt. Chiron gleitet darauf aus, mit ihm von Brauchitsch, Tadini und Eugenio Siena (Maserati). Als Fagiolis W 25 in der zehnten Runde hinter der Schikane ins Schleudern gerät, weil ein unachtsamer Streckenposten dem Piloten Sand ins Gesicht schaufelt, sind drei Mercedes eliminiert.

Einer indes kommt durch, der »Regenkönig« Rudi Caracciola, auch wenn er Nuvolari ein Zeitlang den Vortritt lassen muß. Rosemeyer staucht das lange Heck seines Auto Union in der 13. Runde rücklings in eine Balustrade vor dem Casino, während sich Varzi und Stuck auf den Rängen zwei und drei behutsam durch das Regeninferno tasten. Drei deutsche Wagen auf den ersten drei Rängen – auch das ist neu. Aber 1937 kommt es noch besser.

Panta rhei, nous apprend Héraclès, tout coule de source. Le Grand Prix de Monaco n'échappe pas à cette règle. Et c'est ainsi que la huitième édition, le 13 avril 1936, se distingue par une bonne dose d'innovation ainsi que par de nombreuses premières, prévues et imprévues. Avec une première manche pour voitures de course de moins de 1500 cm³, le samedi après-midi, pour la Coupe du Prince Rainier, on crée une tradition qui figure de nos jours encore au programme avec les courses de Formule 3. L'événement majeur – le lundi de Pâques, comme les deux années précédentes – fait désormais partie des Grands Prix triés sur le volet au cours desquels on se dispute le titre de champion d'Europe.

Dans la lutte fratricide des Flèches d'argent, Auto Union relève donc le gant face à sa rivale Mercedes même sur le circuit urbain escarpé, qui leur est pourtant bien peu approprié, avec la dernière évolution de sa puissante V16 de 6005 cm³ et 520 ch à 5000 tr/mn. Le directeur sportif est Karl Feuereissen. Le trio de pilotes se compose du « roi de la montagne », l'expérimenté Hans Stuck, de la téméraire « shooting star » Bernd Rosemeyer et du froid gentleman italien Achille Varzi. Ballottée par les crises cette année-là, Mercedes-Benz réplique avec la W 25 E, de 4740 cm³ et 494 ch à 5800 tr/mn. Les quatre pilotes sont Rudolf Caracciola, Manfred von Brauchitsch, Luigi Fagioli et Louis Chiron, qui donne donc un intermède sur une scène qui lui est familière. Le Monégasque exprime sa gratitude avec la pole position en 1'53"2, étant, par la même occasion, le premier à franchir le seuil des 100 km/h au tour. On est en droit de s'attendre à une opposition énergique de la part de la Scuderia Ferrari, qui a inscrit quatre Alfa Romeo 8 C de 3822 cm³ et 330 ch à 5400 tr/mn, pilotées par Antonio Brivio, Giuseppe Farina, Mario Tadini et Tazio Nuvolari.

Le jour de la course, fait sans précédent, il pleut. Sur la grille du départ, les voitures allemandes forment une bizarre symétrie. Chiron et Caracciola occupent la gauche et l'extrême droite en première ligne avec, entre eux, Nuvolari ; Rosemeyer et Stuck en seconde ligne, Varzi en troisième entre Jean-Pierre Wimille (Bugatti 59) et Farina, von Brauchitsch et Fagioli sont en quatrième. L'épopée de Chiron ne durera pas cinq minutes. Au deuxième tour, le moteur de Tadini, a laissé à la chicane une trace d'huile qui se mélange avec l'eau de pluie en un piège incontournable. Chiron dérape, suivi comme son ombre par Brauchitsch, Tadini et Eugenio Siena (Maserati). Lorsque la W 25 de Fagioli part en dérapage, au dixième tour, à la sortie de la chicane parce qu'un commissaire de piste distrait envoie du sable dans le visage du pilote, trois Mercedes sont éliminées.

L'un, par contre, arrivera au bout, le « Roi de la Pluie » Rudi Caracciola, qui aura toutefois dû laisser la primauté à Nuvolari pendant un certain temps. Rosemeyer cabosse la longue poupe de son Auto Union en percutant de l'arrière une balustrade devant le Casino, au 13e tour, tandis que Varzi et Stuck survivent au terrible orage aux deuxième et troisième places. Trois voitures allemandes aux trois premiers rangs – cela, aussi, est nouveau. Mais 1937 réserve encore bien des surprises.

Chiron (Mercedes-Benz) in front of Rosemeyer (Auto Union) at Tobacconist's Corner. Both will retire early.

Chiron (Mercedes-Benz) vor Rosemeyer (Auto Union) in der Tabakskurve. Beide werden das Rennen vorzeitig beenden müssen.

Chiron (Mercedes-Benz) devant Rosemeyer (Auto Union) au virage du Bureau de Tabac. Tous deux devront abandonner la course prématurément.

N°	DRIVERS		ENTRANTS	CARS	ENGINES	PRACTICE RESULTS	RACE RESULTS
8	**Rudolf Caracciola**	**D**	**Daimler-Benz AG**	**Mercedes-Benz W25E**	**8L 4740 cc + C**	**3rd: 1'54"0**	**1st: 3h49'20"4**
4	Achille Varzi	I	Auto Union AG	Auto Union Typ C	V16 6005 cc + C	7th: 1'56"1	2nd: 3h51'09"5
2	Hans Stuck	A	Auto Union AG	Auto Union Typ C	V16 6005 cc + C	4th: 1'54"3	3rd: 99 laps
24	Tazio Nuvolari	I	Scuderia Ferrari	Alfa Romeo 8C-1935	8L 3822 cc + C	2nd: 1'53"7	4th: 99 laps
26	Antonio Brivio	I	Scuderia Ferrari	Alfa Romeo 8C-1935	8L 3822 cc + C	11th: 1'58"0	5th: 97 laps
16	Jean-Pierre Wimille	F	Automobiles Bugatti	Bugatti 59	8L 3251 cc + C	8th: 1'56"6	6th: 97 laps
22	Raymond Sommer	F	Raymond Sommer	Alfa Romeo B	8L 2905 cc + C	14th: 2'03"3	7th: 94 laps
38	Piero Ghersi	I	Scuderia Torino	Maserati 6C-34	6L 3724 cc + C	17th: 2'08"7	8th: 87 laps
18	"Williams"	GB	Automobiles Bugatti	Bugatti 59	8L 3251 cc + C	16th: 2'05"0	9th: 84 laps
20	Philippe Etancelin	F	Philippe Etancelin	Maserati V8RI	V8 4788 cc + C	15th: 2'04"0	R
32	Carlo Felice Trossi	I	Scuderia Torino	Maserati V8RI	V8 4788 cc + C	12th: 1'59"0	R
6	Bernd Rosemeyer	D	Auto Union AG	Auto Union Typ C	V16 6005 cc + C	5th: 1'55"2	R
12	Luigi Fagioli	I	Daimler-Benz AG	Mercedes-Benz W25E	8L 4740 cc + C	10th: 1'57"4	R
36	Eugenio Siena	I	Scuderia Torino	Maserati 6C-34	6L 3725 cc + C	18th: 2'11"2	R
14	Manfred von Brauchitsch	D	Daimler-Benz AG	Mercedes-Benz W25E	8L 4740 cc + C	9th: 1'56"7	R
30	Giuseppe Farina	I	Scuderia Ferrari	Alfa Romeo 8C-1935	8L 3822 cc + C	6th: 1'55"6	R
10	*Louis Chiron*	*F*	*Daimler-Benz AG*	*Mercedes-Benz W25E*	*8L 4740 cc + C*	*1st: 1'53"2*	*R*
28	Mario Tadini	I	Scuderia Ferrari	Alfa Romeo 8C-1935	8L 3822 cc + C	13th: 1'20"0	R

(1) Accident for von Delius (Auto Union) beyond the chicane in the last qualifying session; (2) a slide into retirement at the same spot for Fagioli (Mercedes-Benz) in the race itself. (3) Early exit: from lap 13 Rosemeyer's Auto Union is wedged in the parapet at Massenet – driver error.
(4, 5) Pirouettes on oil: scenes from the mass pile-up in the second lap, number 10: Chiron, 6: Rosemeyer, 30: Farina (Alfa Romeo), 14: von Brauchitsch (Mercedes-Benz).

(1) Unfall für von Delius (Auto Union) im letzten Training hinter der Schikane, (2) Ausrutscher und Ausfall für Fagioli (Mercedes-Benz) im Rennen an der gleichen Stelle, (3) Heck-Schleuder: Ab Runde 13 steckt Rosemeyers Auto Union bei Massenet rückwärts in der Brüstung, Fehler des Fahrers. (4, 5) Pirouetten in Öl: Szenen des Massensturzes in der zweiten Runde, Nummer 10: Chiron, 6: Rosemeyer, 30: Farina (Alfa Romeo), 14: von Brauchitsch (Mercedes-Benz).

(1) Accident pour von Delius (Auto Union), lors des derniers essais, à la sortie de la chicane. (2) Dérapage et abandon pour Fagioli (Mercedes-Benz) en course au même endroit. (3) Dérapage incontrôlé : au 13e tour, l'Auto Union de Rosemeyer percute en marche arrière les fascines à Massenet, erreur du pilote. (4, 5) Pirouettes sur l'huile : scènes du carambolage monstre au deuxième tour. Numéro 10 : Chiron, 6 : Rosemeyer, 30 : Farina (Alfa Romeo), 14 : von Brauchitsch (Mercedes-Benz).

PILOTES ENGAGÉS
dans le VIIIme Grand Prix Automobile de Monaco

SCUDERIA FERRARI : de gauche à droite :
TADINI, BRIVIO, NUVOLARI, PINTACUDA et FARINA.

EQUIPE AUTO-UNION, de gauche à droite : VARZI, STUCK, ROSEMEYER.

PILOTES ENGAGÉS
dans le VIIIme Grand Prix Automobile de Monaco

De haut en bas et de gauche à droite :
WIMILLE et WILLIAMS sur «Bugatti» - TROSSI, SIENA et ETANCELIN sur «Maserati»

(1) The protagonists of the 8th Monaco Grand Prix are presented in the program. Some of them will be laughing on the other side of their faces by the end of race day. (2) The correct line: Ghersi (Maserati) in front of Caracciola (Mercedes-Benz), Nuvolari (Alfa Romeo) and Etancelin (Maserati) at the gasometer. (3) Climax of a career: Chiron, who promptly places his Mercedes-Benz in pole position.

(1) Die Protagonisten des 8. Grand Prix de Monaco werden im Programm vorgestellt. Einigen von ihnen wird am Sonntag das Lächeln vergehen. (2) Die Linie stimmt: Ghersi (Maserati) vor Caracciola (Mercedes-Benz), Nuvolari (Alfa Romeo) und Etancelin (Maserati) am Gasometer. (3) Höhepunkt einer Karriere: Chiron, der seinen Mercedes-Benz prompt auf die Pole Position stellt.

(1) Présentation des protagonistes du 8e Grand Prix de Monaco dans le programme. Quelques-uns ne riront plus le dimanche. (2) La trajectoire est bonne : Ghersi (Maserati) devant Caracciola (Mercedes-Benz), Nuvolari (Alfa Romeo) et Etancelin (Maserati) au Gazomètre. (3) Temps fort d'une carrière : Chiron, qui place immédiatement sa Mercedes-Benz en pole position.

A GERMAN HERO

EIN DEUTSCHER HELD · UN HÉROS ALLEMAND

Strange", the former Grand-Prix driver Innes Ireland once said, "how important it is what someone is called. Alan Jones, for example – quickly forgotten. And the man was, after all, World Champion in 1980." Then he allowed his own name to melt on his tongue, like a precious composition of sound and rhythm, pleasurably chanted "Stirling Moss" and, in a fit of nostalgia, added "Caracciola" – with a faint English accent.

The aura of Rudolf Caracciola, however, would shine through from the semi-darkness of the pre-war years even without his melodic four syllables, indivisibly combined and linked with the might of Mercedes. The German vernacular, in any case, had already trimmed it to fit Teutonic expression as "der Karratsch", something which went as far as to become common usage in verbal and even written reporting about him; just as later the same was to happen to the convenient abbreviation "Schumi" for Michael Schumacher from the generation of racing offspring. Trace elements of Sicilian origins somewhere in the depths of the family history came to expression in his looks. His parents were well-off hoteliers in Remagen, on the left bank of the Rhine, which became famous through this great son of the town and through its bridges – both of them film material, although for different reasons. Even today a few Caracciolas can still be found in the telephone books of the region.

The skill of this calm Rhinelander in his chosen profession is also archetypally German – in the sense of a convenient preconceived label – quality, high-class work, "made in Germany". In April 1923, Rudolf Caracciola won his first race in Berlin – in a borrowed EGO. This EGO trip had consequences. During the next 30 years, rudely interrupted by the Second World War, his successes populate the results lists like a marathon of statistics; 225 wins, three European Championships, speed records on Adolf Hitler's showpiece autobahn. "Der Karratsch" himself was also such a prestige object of the ruling caste, a pampered and cosseted figurehead of the Reich, with the difference that in contrast to Hans Stuck, for example, he tore himself out of the sticky embrace of the system and finally sought and was given appropriate asylum in Ticino, with a Swiss passport.

Caracciola was no raging daredevil, not one for storm and stress. Rarely was he responsible for the fastest lap or a lap record. He drove as fast as was necessary, and seldom as fast as he could – as in Bern 1937, where he deemed it advisable to stay on the first row of the grid. Where Tazio Nuvolari, for example, appeared to operate beyond good and evil, brutally punishing his racing cars, and giving rise to the suspicion that here was someone permanently on the verge of disaster, "Karratsch" caressed his cars, turned them into friends and partners through good treatment. Such abundance of delicate feeling in fingers and toes predestined him to become a specialist of the wet track, a rare and valuable art at the wheel of the hp-monsters of the 1930s. He was, indeed, called the "rain master". Even the all-powerful Mercedes team boss and dictator of the race track, Alfred Neubauer, knew to honor that. The "fat one", as he was respectfully abused behind his back, was in any case linked by an

Merkwürdig«, sagt der frühere Grand-Prix-Fahrer Innes Ireland einmal, »es ist so ungeheuer wichtig, wie jemand heißt. Alan Jones zum Beispiel – das ist rasch vergessen. Dabei war der Mann immerhin Weltmeister 1980.« Und dann läßt er sich seinen eigenen Namen auf der Zunge zergehen wie eine kostbare Komposition aus Klang und Rhythmus, skandiert lustvoll »Stirling Moss« und fügt in einem nostalgischen Ausflug »Caracciola« an – mit einem kleinen englischen Akzent.

Der Mythos Rudolf Caracciola würde indes auch ohne Schützenhilfe durch diesen melodischen Viersilber aus dem Halbdunkel der Vorkriegsjahre herüberleuchten, untrennbar verquickt und verwoben mit dem Mythos Mercedes. Die deutsche Volksseele hat ihn sich ohnehin zurechtgeschnitzt zu einem teutonisch-mundgerechten »der Karratsch«, das vordringt bis in die mündliche und sogar die schriftliche Berichterstattung von seinen Taten und Leiden wie später das kommode Kürzel Schumi für Michael Schumacher aus der Generation der rasenden Urenkel. Spurenelemente sizilianischen Geblüts irgendwo in den Tiefen der Familienchronik schlagen sich allenfalls nieder in seinem Aussehen. Seine Eltern sind wohlhabende Hoteliers im linksrheinischen Remagen, das berühmt wird durch diesen großen Sohn der Stadt und durch seine Brücke, beides Filmstoffe, wenn auch aus ganz unterschiedlichen Gründen. Noch heute finden sich ein paar Caracciolas in den Telefonbüchern der Region.

Urdeutsch – im Sinne des plakativ-bequemen Vorurteils – ist auch das, was dieser gelassene Rheinländer im Vollgas-Metier zu bieten hat, Wertarbeit »made in Germany« gewissermaßen vom Edelsten. Im April 1923 gewinnt Rudolf Caracciola in Berlin sein erstes Rennen – mit einem geliehenen EGO. Der EGO-Trip zeitigt Folgen. In den nächsten 30 Jahren, rüde unterbrochen von den Kampfhandlungen des Zweiten Weltkriegs, tummeln sich seine Erfolge über die Ergebnislisten wie ein statistischer Volkslauf, 225 Siege, drei Europameisterschaften, Geschwindigkeitsrekorde auf Adolf Hitlers Paradestück Autobahn. Auch »der Karratsch« selber ist so ein Prestigeobjekt der herrschenden Kaste, eine verhätschelte und gepäppelte Galionsfigur des Reichs, nur daß er sich im Gegensatz etwa zu Hans Stuck dem Älteren aus der schleimigen Umarmung durch das System losreißt und schließlich mit einem Schweizer Paß im Tessin ein angemessenes Asyl sucht und erhält.

Caracciola ist kein blindwütiger Draufgänger, kein Stürmer und Dränger. Selten geht eine schnellste Runde oder ein Rundenrekord auf sein Konto. Er fährt so schnell, wie er muß, selten so schnell, wie er kann – wie in Bern 1937, wo ihm der Aufenthalt in der ersten Startreihe empfehlenswert erscheint. Wo etwa Tazio Nuvolari jenseits von Gut und Böse zu verkehren scheint, seine Rennwagen brutal knüppelt und knechtet und den Verdacht aufkeimen läßt, hier entkomme jemand mit knapper Not einer permanenten Katastrophe, streichelt der »Karratsch« seine Autos förmlich, macht sie sich zu Freunden und Partnern durch gute Behandlung. Soviel delikates Finger- und Fußspitzengefühl prädestiniert ihn zum Spezialisten auf feuchter Strecke, eine rare und kostbare Kunst am

C'est bizarre, dit un jour l'ancien pilote de Grand Prix Innes Ireland, comme le nom que l'on porte peut avoir de l'importance. Alan Jones, par exemple, a vite sombré dans l'oubli. Et pourtant, l'homme a tout de même été champion du monde en 1980. » Et il fait alors rouler avec délice sur sa langue son propre nom, comme un précieux cocktail de sons et de rythmes, scande sur un ton de gourmet « Stirling Moss » et ajoute dans un envol de nostalgie « Caracciola » avec un accent anglais presque imperceptible.

Le mythe Rudolf Caracciola continuerait de vivre aujourd'hui depuis la semi-obscurité des années de l'avant-guerre encore, même sans l'aide bienvenue de ces quatre syllabes mélodieuses, indissolublement lié à l'empire Mercedes. Le bon peuple allemand, l'a, de toute façon, ré-écrit d'une façon plus conforme à la langue parlée teutonne, « le Karratsch », qui pénètre jusque dans les reportages oraux et même écrits de son talent et de ses souffrances comme, plus tard, le fera le bien pratique diminutif Schumi pour Michael Schumacher de la génération de leurs petits-fils dédiés au culte de la vitesse. Les gènes de son sang sicilien remontant quelque part jusqu'aux profondeurs de la chronique familiale se répercutent, dans le meilleur des cas, dans sa physionomie. Ses parents sont des hôteliers aisés de Remagen, petite ville sur la rive gauche du Rhin, près de Cologne, qui deviendra célèbre plus tard grâce à son prestigieux fils et à son fameux pont, qui auront tout deux fourni matière à des films, bien que pour des raisons tout à fait différentes. Aujourd'hui encore, on trouve quelques Caracciola dans les annuaires téléphoniques de la région.

Typiquement allemand est aussi – chose qui n'a rien d'un cliché ni d'un préjugé - ce qui a fait la force de ce Rhénan décontracté parmi les spécialistes du pied au plancher : un travail de précision « made in Germany », mais de la plus grande des qualités. En avril 1923, Rudolf Caracciola gagne sa première course à Berlin – sur une EGO d'emprunt. Son ego s'en ressent et cela aura des conséquences. Au cours des trente années qui suivront, interrompues par la césure brutale du conflit de la Seconde Guerre mondiale, ses succès émailleront les listes de résultats comme les noms des participants à un marathon, 225 victoires et trois titres de champion d'Europe, records de vitesse sur l'autoroute de prestige d'Adolf Hitler à la clef. « Le Karratsch » lui-même est ainsi devenu un objet de prestige de la caste au pouvoir, une figure de proue chérie et dorlotée du Troisième Reich, à cette différence près que, contrairement à Hans Stuck père, par exemple, il résiste aux embrassades gluantes du système et, enfin doté d'un passeport suisse, il demande et obtient un asile digne de lui dans le Tessin.

Caracciola n'est pas un fanatique de la vitesse que la colère rend aveugle, il n'est pas de ceux qui jouent des coudes et bousculent tout sur leur passage. Il est rare qu'il inscrive un tour le plus rapide ou un record en course à son palmarès. Il conduit aussi vite qu'il le doit, rarement aussi vite qu'il le peut – comme à Berne en 1937, où il lui semble recommandé de figurer sur la première ligne au départ. Là où un Tazio Nuvolari, par exemple, pilote à la limite de la sortie de route, brutalisant et cravachant sans égards ses voitures de course, faisant tout de suite poindre le soupçon que quelqu'un échappe de justesse à une catastrophe permanente, « le Karratsch » caresse littéralement ses voitures, s'en fait des amies et des partenaires grâce à ses bons traitements. Tant de doigté et de délicatesse le prédestinent comme spécialiste des courses sous la pluie,

Good hunting: Rudolf Caracciola wearing a hunting hat and with his dachshund Moritz, half mascot and half member of the family.

Waidmanns Heil: Rudolf Caracciola mit jagdlichem Hut und Dackel Moritz, halb Maskottchen, halb Mitglied der Familie.

Le chasseur amateur : Rudolf Caracciola avec son chapeau de chasse et son Dackel Moritz, à moitié mascotte, à moitié membre de la famille.

intimate elective and soul affinity with his star and model pupil. He was sometimes accused of favoring Caracciola like a teacher who has been led astray by a petite blonde, and his powerfully angry response showed that he felt caught in the act.

This sport, however, which lifted him from the warm stench of mediocrity and placed him among the immortals, like his boxing contemporary Max Schmeling, also treated Rudi Caracciola, the lead-footed icon, with incomprehensible brutality. Not once did he have to climb out of a burning wreck, and he rarely ended up off the track. Yet three accidents wore him down, even if he did master the great lesson of smiling through the pain in many small victories over adversity. He would never recover from his accident during qualifying on that April Thursday in Monaco in 1933. From then onwards he no longer had the joint on his right femur, and "der Karratsch" had to battle against such disparate competitors as Stuck, Rosemeyer, Nuvolari, the clock and the pain. The second station of his cross: an accident in the Indianapolis 500 in 1946, once again during qualifying, fractured his skull.

His third crash finished him off completely. On the 13th lap of a race in Bern, on 18 May 1952, his Mercedes 300 SL for once lost its way and felled a tree. The driver was rescued, but sustained a complicated fracture, this time to the left femur in a macabre symmetry of suffering. The remaining years of his life were spent in a peculiarly semi-conscious state in the cultivated seclusion of his villa in Ruvigliana. His black Mercedes 220 was seldom seen in the neighbouring elegant city of Lugano. Its registration number: TI 4444.

For Caracciola still stuck to tradition. As early as the Roaring Twenties the distinctive set of fours on his powerful Nürburg model Mercedes-Benz Cabriolet, revealed that "der Karratsch" was coming.

Volant der PS-Ungeheuer der Dreißiger. In der Tat nennen sie ihn den »Regenmeister«. Auch der allgewaltige Mercedes-Rennleiter und Pisten-Diktator Alfred Neubauer weiß das zu würdigen. Den »Dicken«, wie man ihn hinter seinem Rücken respektvoll schmäht, verbindet sowieso eine innige Wahl- und Seelen-verwandtschaft mit seinem Star und Musterschüler. Manchmal macht man ihm den Vorwurf, er ziehe Caracciola vor wie ein irregeleiteter Studienrat eine niedliche Blondine, und sein mächtig ausbrechender Zorn verrät dann, daß er sich ertappt fühlt.

Nur: Dieser Sport, der ihn hochhebt aus dem warmen Mief der Gewöhnlichen und der Gewöhnlich-keit und in den Olymp der Unsterblichen versetzt wie seinen boxenden Zeitgenossen Max Schmeling, vergeht sich zugleich mit einer unfaßlichen Rohheit an der Bleifuß-Ikone Rudi Caracciola. Nicht ein einziges Mal entsteigt er einem brennenden Wrack, und kaum je landet er abseits der Piste. Gleichwohl machen drei Unfälle ihn fertig, wenn er auch die hohe Schule des Lächelns im Schmerz beherrscht in lauter kleinen Siegen des Trotzdem. Schon von seinem Trainingsunfall an jenem Aprildonnerstag des Jahres 1933 in Monaco wird er sich nie erholen. Denn seitdem fehlt die Gelenkkugel an seinem rechten Oberschenkel, und »der Karratsch« kämpft gegen solche disparaten Konkurrenten wie Stuck, Rosemeyer, Nuvolari, die Uhr und die Qual. Die zweite Station auf seinem Leidensweg: Unfall in Indy 1946, wieder im Training, Schädelbruch.

Sein dritter Crash bringt ihn endgültig zur Strecke. In der 13. Runde eines Sportwagenrennens in Bern am 18. Mai 1952 kommt sein Mercedes 300 SL nun doch vom rechten Wege ab und fällt einen Baum. Der Fahrer wird geborgen mit einer komplizierten Fraktur, diesmal im linken Oberschenkel in einer makabren Symmetrie des Leidens. Die verbleibenden Jahre seines Lebens verbringt er in einem eigentümlichen Dämmerzustand in der gepflegten Klausur seiner Villa zu Ruvigliana. Nur selten sieht man seinen schwarzen Mercedes 220 in der benachbarten eleganten Weltstadt Lugano. Sein Kennzeichen: TI 4444.

Denn noch immer hält Caracciola auf Tradition. Die markante Vierernummer verriet nämlich schon in den Roaring Twenties an seinem mächtigen Mercedes-Benz-Cabriolet vom Typ Nürburg, daß da »der Karratsch« daherkam.

un don rare et précieux au volant des dinosaures débordants de chevaux des années trente. Ce n'est d'ailleurs pas le fait du hasard si on le surnomme « le roi de la pluie ». Alfred Neubauer, le plantureux et tout-puissant directeur de course de Mercedes et dictateur des pistes, sait apprécier cela à sa juste valeur. « Der Dicke » (le Gros), comme on le surnomme non sans respect dans son dos, ressent de toute façon une affinité d'élection et une proximité intellectuelle intime avec sa vedette et son élève préféré. On lui reproche parfois de donner la préférence à Caracciola comme un vieux professeur sur le retour le ferait pour une jolie petite blonde et le violent accès de colère que cela déclenche immédiatement trahit bel et bien qu'il s'estime pris en flagrant délit.

Mais ce sport qu'il extrait de la tiédeur fade du banal et du coutumier pour le transcender dans l'Olympe de l'immortalité comme son contemporain le boxeur Max Schmeling, se venge simultanément avec une incroyable brutalité sur le Mozart de l'accélérateur qu'est Rudi Caracciola. Il ne sera pas extrait une seule fois d'une épave en flammes et il ne commettra pratiquement aucune sortie de route. Et pourtant, trois accidents l'achèvent, même s'il maîtrise toujours la grande école du sourire dans la douleur à travers les nombreuses petites victoires conquises sur le défi. Il ne se remettra plus jamais de son accident subi lors des essais un jeudi d'avril 1933 à Monaco. En effet, depuis, il lui manque l'articulation du fémur droit et « le Karratsch » se bat contre des concurrents aussi disparates que Stuck, Rosemeyer ou Nuvolari, que le chronomètre ou la douleur. Seconde station sur son calvaire : son accident aux 500 miles d'Indianapolis, en 1946, de nouveau aux essais, qui se solde par une fracture du crâne.

Sa troisième collision lui brisera la nuque… au figuré : au 13e tour d'une course pour voitures de sport à Berne, le 18 mai 1952, sa Mercedes 300 SL quitte brutalement la piste et sectionne un arbre. Le pilote en réchappe mais en garde une fracture compliquée. Il s'agit cette fois-ci de la cuisse gauche dans une macabre symétrie de la souffrance. Il passera les dernières années de sa vie dans une espèce d'étrange état semi-comateux dans le luxueux huis-clos de sa villa de Ruvigliana. On ne verra que rarement sa Mercedes 220 noire sillonner l'élégante villégiature voisine, Lugano. Sa plaque minéralogique arbore la combinaison TI 4444.

En effet, Caracciola a encore le sens de la tradition. Ce caractéristique triple quatre trahissait en effet, durant les Années folles déjà, que, quand survenait un imposant cabriolet Mercedes-Benz Nürburg, c'était « le Karratsch » qui faisait son arrivée.

1937

A new date, 8 August, was chosen for the last Monaco Grand Prix before the War in order to escape the vagaries of the April weather. And so it happened; a reliably blue sky appeared for the whole of the weekend and Mediterranean summer heat permeated the tiny feudal state on the Riviera. During race week it became a German colony; the common language in the pits was German, and the tone on the race track was set by the archetypal roar of Mercedes-Benz and Auto Union. The color silver dominated as the racing cars zipped by, for motor racing under the swastika was a continuation of politics by other means.

The most powerful machines came from Mercedes-Benz. From their 5,660 cc eight-cylinder engines the model W 125 cars drew a sturdy 580 bhp at 5,800 rpm. They required one liter of fuel per kilometer to keep them happy, a real devil's brew which consisted of methyl alcohol, acetone and trace elements of other substances. These frenzied Molotov cocktails were driven by Rudolf Caracciola, Manfred von Brauchitsch, the Swiss Christian Kautz and the Italian Goffredo Zehender. In contrast, Auto Union, from whose voluminous 6,005 cc V16 mid-mounted engines their designer Ferdinand Porsche had managed to extract 540 bhp at 5,000 rpm, was struggling. Their inferiority was apparent despite brilliant drivers such as Bernd Rosemeyer and Hans Stuck, who were joined by Rudolf Hasse, from Saxony. Totally outclassed, however, was the Scuderia Ferrari with three 1936 Alfa Romeo Tipo 12 Cs (4,064 cc, 370 bhp at 5,800 rpm) for Giuseppe Farina, Antonio Brivio and Carlo Pintacuda. Nuvolari, the only one who might have succeeded in breaking the dominance of the Germans, did not even bother to appear. He was negotiating, it was whispered, with Auto Union. But the cars of this team were to suffer a black weekend.

Hasse drove into the wall in the tunnel on lap two, and Rosemeyer came to a halt at the gasometer on lap 20 with jammed steering and later took over Stuck's car – much to the latter's disgust. Right at the front, however, the duel between Caracciola and von Brauchitsch grew hotter so that in the end even the all-powerful Mercedes team manager, Alfred Neubauer, was no longer able to control it. After ten laps Caracciola was four seconds ahead, after 20, seven. Then the W 125 with start number 8 lost more than two minutes in the pits: a change of spark plugs. Von Brauchitsch then led with a one-lap advantage, but his illustrious stablemate responded with a new fastest lap time, finally made up the missing lap and followed von Brauchitsch like a shadow after his pit stop. Von Brauchitsch was furious – the mechanics had taken longer than necessary on purpose – but when Caracciola had to top up with water, von Brauchitsch's victory was no longer at risk.

Behind a bend, Neubauer wrote, a gentleman in an elegant double-breasted suit had signalled to him his distance from his pursuer – Louis Chiron. The reason was a private matter: Caracciola had stolen his wife Baby …

Für den letzten Grand Prix de Monaco vor dem Krieg hat man mit dem 8. August einen neuen Termin gewählt, um den Schikanen des Aprilwetters zu entgehen. Und in der Tat: Verläßlicher Blauhimmel stellt sich über das ganze Wochenende ein, und mediterrane Sommerhitze durchglüht den winzigen Feudalstaat an der Côte. In diesen Tagen wird er zur teutonischen Kolonie. Die Verkehrssprache an den Boxen ist Deutsch. Für den guten Ton auf der Piste sorgt der Urschrei der Mercedes und der Auto Union. Beim Vorbeiwischen der Rennwagen dominiert die Farbe Silber. Denn Motorsport im Zeichen des Hakenkreuzes ist Fortsetzung der Politik mit anderen Mitteln.

Die stärksten Stücke stammen von Mercedes. Aus 5660 cm³ schöpfen die Achtzylinder des Modells W 125 stämmige 580 PS bei 5800/min. Sie wollen pro Kilometer mit einem Liter Treibstoff bei Laune gehalten werden, wahren Elixieren des Teufels aus Methylakohol, Aceton und Spurenelementen anderer Substanzen. Pilotiert werden diese rasenden Molotowcocktails von Rudolf Caracciola, Manfred von Brauchitsch, dem Schweizer Christian Kautz und dem Italiener Goffredo Zehender. Die Auto Union, deren voluminösen V16-Mittelmotoren von 6005 cm³ ihr Schöpfer Ferdinand Porsche 540 PS bei 5000/min entlockt hat, tun sich dagegen schwer. Sie sind unterlegen trotz brillanter Fahrer wie Bernd Rosemeyer und Hans Stuck, denen sich der Sachse Rudolf Hasse zugesellt hat. Gänzlich auf verlorenem Posten aber steht das Aufgebot der Scuderia Ferrari, drei Alfa Romeo Tipo 12 C Jahrgang 1936 (4064 cm³, 370 PS bei 5800/min) für Giuseppe Farina, Antonio Brivio und Carlo Pintacuda. Nuvolari, der einzige, der in die Dominanz der Deutschen einbrechen könnte, läßt sich erst gar nicht sehen. Er verhandele aber, so wispert man, mit der Auto Union. Deren Wagen werden gebeutelt von einem schwarzen Wochenende.

Hasse fährt in der zweiten Runde im Tunnel gegen die Mauer. Rosemeyer kommt in der 20. am Gasometer mit blockierter Lenkung zum Stillstand und übernimmt später das Fahrzeug von Stuck – sehr zu dessen Ingrimm. Ganz vorn aber entbrennt der Zweikampf zwischen Caracciola und von Brauchitsch, entzieht sich schließlich selbst der Kontrolle des allgewaltigen Mercedes-Rennleiters Alfred Neubauer. Nach zehn Runden hat Caracciola vier Sekunden Vorsprung, nach 20 sieben. Dann verliert der W 125 mit der Startnummer 8 über zwei Minuten an der Box: Zündkerzenwechsel. Von Brauchitsch führt mit einer Runde Vorsprung. Sein illustrer Stallgefährte antwortet mit einer neuen Bestzeit, entrundet sich schließlich, folgt von Brauchitsch nach dessen Boxenhalt wie ein Schatten. Der schäumt – die Mechaniker hätten ihn absichtlich langsam abgefertigt. Als Caracciola Wasser nachfassen muß, ist der Sieg des anderen nicht länger gefährdet.

Hinter einer Kurve, schreibt Neubauer, habe ihm ein Herr im eleganten Zweireiher die Abstände zu seinem Verfolger signalisiert – Louis Chiron. Die Ursachen liegen im privaten Bereich: Caracciola hat ihm seine Frau Baby ausgespannt …

Pour ce qui allait être le dernier Grand Prix de Monaco de l'avant-guerre, on avait choisi le 8 août comme nouvelle date pour échapper aux aléas de la météorologie printanière. Et ce fut une réussite : un ciel bleu sans nuages perdure pendant tout le week-end et une canicule méditerranéenne baigne le minuscule Etat princier de la Côte d'Azur. Pour tout le temps de la course il se mue en une colonie teutonne ; la langue officielle dans les stands est l'allemand. Sur la piste, les Mercedes et les Auto Union font entendre leurs barrissements à la ronde. Dans le défilé flou des voitures de course, c'est la couleur argent qui prédomine, car sous le signe de la croix gammée, la compétition automobile est la poursuite de la politique avec d'autres armes.

Les plus affûtées sont celles de Mercedes. D'une cylindrée de 5660 cm³, les huit cylindres de la W 125 développent 580 ch à 5800 tr/mn. Mais il faut un litre de carburant au kilomètre pour les maintenir en vie, d'authentiques élixirs diaboliques se composant d'alcool de méthyle, d'acétone et d'éléments de traces d'autres substances. Ces cocktails Molotov à quatre roues sont pilotés par Rudolf Caracciola, Manfred von Brauchitsch, le Suisse Christian Kautz et l'Italien Goffredo Zehender. Les Auto Union avec leur singulier et encombrant V16 de 6005 cm³ en position centrale, des entrailles desquelles leur créateur Ferdinand Porsche extrait 540 ch à 5000 tr/mn, ont par contre la tâche plus difficile. Malgré des pilotes aussi brillants que Bernd Rosemeyer et Hans Stuck, qui ont été rejoints par le Saxon Rudolf Hasse, elles restent inférieures. La Scuderia Ferrari semble condamnée d'avance avec ses trois Alfa Romeo Tipo 12 C de 1936 (4064 cm³, 370 ch à 5800 tr/mn) pour Guiseppe Farina, Antonio Brivio et Carlo Pintacuda. Nuvolari, le seul qui aurait encore pu croiser le fer avec les Allemands, ne s'est même pas déplacé. Selon la rumeur, il négocierait avec Auto Union, dont les voitures ne connaîtront que des difficultés durant tout le week-end.

Au cours du second tour, Hasse percute le mur dans le tunnel. Au 20e tour, Rosemeyer doit s'arrêter au Gazomètre, direction bloquée, et reprend plus tard la voiture de Stuck – à la plus grande fureur de celui-ci. Mais, aux avant-postes, le duel fait rage entre Caracciola et von Brauchitsch, échappant même finalement au contrôle du tout-puissant directeur de course de Mercedes, Alfred Neubauer. Au bout de dix tours, Caracciola a quatre secondes d'avance et sept au 20e tour. Puis la W 125 avec le numéro 8 perd plus de deux minutes aux stands : changement de bougies. Von Brauchitsch a alors un tour d'avance, mais son illustre coéquipier réplique avec un nouveau record du tour, finit par le rattraper et, après l'arrêt de von Brauchitsch aux stands, suit celui-ci comme son ombre. Il écume de rage – les mécaniciens, pense-t-il, ont volontairement traîné en longueur. Lorsque Caracciola doit refaire son plein d'eau, la victoire de von Brauchitsch n'est plus en péril.

Derrière un virage, écrivit Neubauer, un homme vêtu d'un élégant costume croisé lui communiquait l'écart par rapport à son poursuivant – il s'agissait de Louis Chiron. La raison en était de nature privée : Caracciola lui avait « piqué » sa femme Baby …

Signalling success: the figures indicate that after 69 laps the three Mercedes-Benz of Manfred von Brauchitsch, Caracciola and Zehender are in the lead.

Tafel-Freuden: Die Schilder zeigen an, daß nach 69 Runden die drei Mercedes-Benz von Manfred von Brauchitsch, Caracciola und Zehender an der Spitze liegen.

Panneaux de la joie : les numéros indiquent que, au bout de 69 tours, les trois Mercedes-Benz de Manfred von Brauchitsch, Caracciola et Zehender sont en tête.

N°	DRIVERS		ENTRANTS	CARS	ENGINES	PRACTICE RESULTS	RACE RESULTS
10	**Manfred von Brauchitsch**	**D**	**Daimler-Benz AG**	**Mercedes-Benz W125**	**8L 5660 cc + C**	**2nd: 1'48"4**	**1st: 3h07'23"9**
8	Rudolf Caracciola	D	Daimler-Benz AG	Mercedes-Benz W125	8L 5660 cc + C	1st: 1'47"5	2nd: 3h08'49"2
12	Christian Kautz	CH	Daimler-Benz AG	Mercedes-Benz W125	8L 5660 cc + C	5th: 1'49"7	3rd: 98 laps
4	Hans Stuck	A	Auto Union AG	Auto Union Typ C	V16 6005 cc + C	4th: 1'49"2	4th: 97 laps (with Rosemeyer)
14	Goffredo Zehender	I	Daimler-Benz AG	Mercedes-Benz W125	8L 5660 cc + C	7th: 1'53"3	5th: 97 laps
24	Giuseppe Farina	I	Scuderia Ferrari	Alfa Romeo 12C-1937	V12 4064 cc + C	8th: 1'53"4	6th: 97 laps
18	Raymond Sommer	F	Raymond Sommer	Alfa Romeo 8C-1935	8L 3822 cc + C	12th: 1'57"6	7th: 95 laps
32	Hans Ruesch	CH	Hans Ruesch	Alfa Romeo 8C-1935	8L 3822 cc + C	10th: 1'55"8	8th: 92 laps
26	Carlo Pintacuda	I	Scuderia Ferrari	Alfa Romeo 12C-1937	V12 4064 cc + C	9th: 1'55"6	9th: 87 laps (with Trossi)
20	Laszlo Hartmann	H	Laszlo Hartmann	Maserati 8CM	V8 2991 cc + C	13th: 2'03"2	R
28	Clemente Biondetti	I	Scuderia Torino	Maserati 6C-34	6L 3724 cc + C	15th: 2'10"4	R
22	Antonio Brivio	I	Scuderia Ferrari	Alfa Romeo 12C-1937	V12 4064 cc + C	11th: 1'56"7	R
2	Bernd Rosemeyer	D	Auto Union AG	Auto Union Typ C	V16 6005 cc + C	3rd: 1'49"0	R
30	Luigi Soffietti	I	Scuderia Torino	Maserati 6C-34	V8 3724 cc + C	14th: 2'04"9	R
6	Rudolf Hasse	D	Auto Union AG	Auto Union Typ C	V16 6005 cc + C	6th: 1'51"6	R

(1) Zehender in front of Farina (Alfa Romeo). (2) Caracciola leading von Brauchitsch and the rest. (3) Hard work for the "Mountain King" Hans Stuck. (4) Full employment: change of sparkplugs for the four Mercedes-Benz. (5) Power station: the mighty sixteen-cylinder engine in the rear of the Auto Union provided approximately 540 bhp. The driver turns lion tamer here. (6) Happy faces for von Brauchitsch and Caracciola. But there's tension between the two.

(1) Zehender vor Farina (Alfa Romeo). (2) Caracciola vor von Brauchitsch und dem Rest. (3) Harte Arbeit für den »Bergkönig« Hans Stuck. (4) Voll-Beschäftigung: Kerzenwechsel an den vier Mercedes-Benz. (5) Kraft-Werk: der riesige Sechzehnzylinder des Auto Union gibt ungefähr 540 PS ab. Da wird der Pilot zum Dompteur. (6) Fröhliche Mienen bei von Brauchitsch und Caracciola. Dennoch knistert es zwischen den beiden.

(1) Zehender devant Farina (Alfa Romeo). (2) Caracciola devant von Brauchitsch et le reste. (3) Travail dur pour le « roi de la montagne » Hans Stuck. (4) Plein emploi : changement de bougies sur les quatre Mercedes-Benz. (5) Pilote ou dompteur ? Le gigantesque seize-cylindres de l'Auto Union développe environ 540 ch. (6) Mines réjouies chez von Brauchitsch et Caracciola. Et pourtant, le torchon brûle entre les deux hommes.

1948

Eleven years had passed since the last Monaco Grand Prix, and the glamorous state of the Grimaldis had emerged from the inferno of the Second World War unscathed. The driving force behind the renaissance of the Grand Prix was the same man who had once brought it into being: Antony Noghes, President of the ACM. A few other faces, though marked by the decade just passed, also appeared strangely familiar. There was Louis Chiron, the victor of 1931, now almost 50, and Tazio Nuvolari, who won in 1932, but now an elderly gentleman of 55. Or the doctor of economics, Giuseppe Farina, who was born in 1906. He had made his debut in Monaco in 1935, but the climax of his racing career still lay ahead of him.

Participating for the first time were stars of tomorrow such as Alberto Ascari, Maurice Trintignant, Luigi Villoresi, Piero Taruffi or the Siamese Prince Birabongse Bhanudej Bhanubandh, or Bira for short, for obvious reasons. Five of the seven marques on the starting grid were new: Cisitalia, Delahaye, ERA (English Racing Automobiles), Ferrari and Simca-Gordini. The team of the enterprising and multi-talented Amédée Gordini had entered four cars for Jean-Pierre Wimille, Bira, Trintignant and Raymond Sommer, lightweights with 1,430 cc engines, but highly manoeuvrable and thus threatening. The Russian Prince Igor Troubetskoy had a Ferrari 166 (V12, 1,995 cc), and there were two ERAs with 1,488 cc six-cylinder in-line engines with compressors for Reg Parnell and Cuth Harrison. Delahaye was not considered to have any chance, neither were the two from Cisitalia for Nuvolari and Taruffi. The small circle of favorites was made up of Maserati drivers, above all Villoresi, Ascari and Farina in the 4CL and CLT with 16-valve four-cylinder supercharged engines of 1,490 cc and producing 260 bhp at 7,000 rpm.

And it was, indeed, Farina who received the victory cup from the hand of Princess Ghyslaine, the wife of the Regent Louis II. Pole position and fastest lap, too, went to the man from Turin. True, Wimille with the Simca-Gordini surprised him at the start and led on the rise to the Casino. It was also true that Villoresi overtook him past Portier bend and basked for five minutes in the glow of being the race leader before his Maserati developed transmission problems. But then Farina, putting an ever greater distance between himself and the rest, had lapped all the others by the half-way point of the race and was even able to allow himself a 90-second pit stop without losing the lead.

In the meantime, Louis Chiron, in his heavy Talbot Lago (six-cylinder in-line engine of 4,485 cc) had worked his way up from twelfth to second place and then defended it fiercely against all comers. The old fire had still burnt, he said later. And anyway, he knew every inch of the track, be it in a race or at rush-hour.

Die kleine Ewigkeit von elf Jahren ist seit dem letzten Großen Preis von Monaco verstrichen, der Glamour-staat der Grimaldis aus dem Inferno des Zweiten Weltkriegs ungeschoren hervorgegangen. Motor hinter der Renaissance des Grand Prix ist derselbe Mann, der ihn einst ins Leben gerufen hat: Antony Noghes, Präsident des ACM. Auch ein paar andere Gesichter, von der vergangenen Dekade gezeichnet, sind seltsam vertraut. Da ist Louis Chiron, der Sieger von 1931, mittlerweilen fast 50. Oder Tazio Nuvolari, der 1932 gewann, inzwischen ein älterer Herr von 55 Jahren. Oder der Doktor der Volkswirtschaft Giuseppe Farina, Jahrgang 1906. Er debütierte 1935 in Monaco, hat aber die Krönung seiner Rennfahrerlaufbahn noch vor sich.

Zum erstenmal mit von der Partie: Stars von morgen wie Alberto Ascari, Maurice Trintignant, Luigi Villoresi, Piero Taruffi oder der siamesische Prinz Birabongse Bhanudej Bhanubandh, aus verständlichen Gründen kurz Bira genannt. Neu sind fünf der sieben Marken am Start, Cisitalia, Delahaye, ERA (English Racing Automobiles), Ferrari und Simca-Gordini. Die Equipe des rührigen Multitalents Amédée Gordini hat vier Wagen gemeldet für Jean-Pierre Wimille, Bira, Trintignant und Raymond Sommer, Leichtgewichte von 1430 cm³ Motorvolumen, aber wendig und damit gefährlich. Der russische Fürst Igor Troubetskoy setzt einen Ferrari 166 ein (V12, 1995 cm³), zwei Wagen mit Reihensechszylindern von 1488 cm³ und Kompressor für Reg Parnell und Cuth Harrison die britische Manufaktur ERA. Keine Chance gibt man dem Delahaye sowie den beiden Cisitalia von Nuvolari und Taruffi. Der kleine Kreis der Favoriten hingegen rekrutiert sich aus Maserati-Piloten, vor allem Villoresi, Ascari und Farina auf den 4CL und CLT, Vierzylindern mit 16 Ventilen, 1490 cm³ und Kompressor, Leistung bei 7000/min 260 PS.

Und tatsächlich ist es Farina, der den Pokal für den Sieg aus der Hand von Prinzessin Ghyslaine entgegennimmt, der Gattin des Regenten Louis II. Auch Pole Position und schnellste Runde gehen auf das Konto des Turiners. Zwar hat ihn Wimille mit dem Simca-Gordini beim Start überrumpelt, führt auch den Anstieg zum Casino hinauf. Zwar überholt ihn Villoresi hinter der Portierskurve und sonnt sich fünf Minuten lang im Glanz des Spitzenreiters, bevor sein Maserati von Problemen mit dem Getriebe heimgesucht wird. Doch dann setzt sich Farina immer mehr ab, hat bei Halbzeit alle anderen überrundet und kann sich sogar einen Boxenstopp von 90 Sekunden gönnen, ohne den ersten Platz einzubüßen.

Unterdessen hat sich Louis Chiron auf seinem klobigen Talbot Lago (Reihensechszylinder, 4485 cm³) vom zwölften auf den zweiten Platz vorgearbeitet und verteidigt diesen wütend nach hinten. Das alte Feuer habe immer noch gelodert, sagt er später. Und überdies kennt er ja jeden Zentimeter der Strecke, im Renntempo wie in der Rush-hour.

Onze ans se sont écoulés depuis le dernier Grand Prix de Monaco et l'Etat d'opérette des Grimaldi avec ses paillettes et son luxe a survécu sain et sauf à l'enfer de la Seconde Guerre mondiale. Le moteur de la renaissance du Grand Prix est cet homme même qui, jadis, lui a donné vie, Antony Noghes, le président de l'ACM. Quelques autres visages, bien que marqués par les aléas de la décennie écoulée, sont bizarrement familiers. Il y a là Louis Chiron, le vainqueur de 1931, entre-temps âgé de près de 50 ans, et Tazio Nuvolari, qui a gagné en 1932, un homme de déjà 55 ans. Ou encore le docteur en économie Giuseppe Farina, millésime 1906. Il a fait ses débuts à Monaco en 1935, mais a encore devant lui l'apogée de sa carrière de pilote de course.

Pour la première fois de la partie : des vedettes de demain comme Alberto Ascari, Maurice Trintignant, Luigi Villoresi, Piero Taruffi ou le Prince siamois Birabongse Bhanubandh, surnommé Bira pour une raison aisément compréhensible. Cinq des sept marques au départ sont : Cisitalia, Delahaye, ERA (English Racing Automobiles), Ferrari et Simca-Gordini. L'équipe du « sorcier » Amédée Gordini a inscrit quatre voitures pour Jean-Pierre Wimille, Bira, Trintignant et Raymond Sommer, des poids plumes avec un moteur de 1430 cm³ de cylindrée, mais maniables et, donc dangereuses. Le Prince russe Igor Troubetskoy engage une Ferrari 166 (V12, 1995 cm³), et les pilotes Reg Parnell et Cuth Harrison représentent la manufacture britannique ERA disposent de deux voitures à six-cylindres en ligne de 1488 cm³ et compresseur. On ne donne pas cher des chances de la Delahaye et des deux Cisitalia de Nuvolari et Taruffi. Le nombre réduit des favoris se recrute par contre parmi les pilotes de Maserati, notamment Villoresi, Ascari et Farina sur les 4CL et CLT, des quatre-cylindres à 16 soupapes, 1490 cm³ et compresseur, d'une puissance de 260 ch à 7000 tr/mn.

Et, de fait, c'est Farina qui se voit remettre la coupe de la victoire des mains de la Princesse Ghyslaine, l'épouse du régent Louis II. Le Turinois signe également la pole position et le tour le plus rapide en course. Certes, Wimille, sur Simca-Gordini, l'a surpris au départ, s'élançant en tête dans la montée du Casino. Certes, Villoresi le double à la sortie du virage du Portier et peut, cinq minutes, briller dans le rôle de leader avant que sa Maserati ne commence à rencontrer des problèmes de boîte de vitesses. Mais, ensuite, Farina se détache de plus en plus irrésistiblement, a doublé tous les autres à la mi-temps et peut même se payer le luxe d'un arrêt de quatre-vingt-dix secondes aux stands sans devoir céder sa première place.

Pendant ce temps, Louis Chiron, sur son encombrante Talbot Lago (six-cylindres en ligne, 4485 cm³) a gagné place après place, de la douzième à la deuxième, qu'il défend bec et ongles devant ses concurrents. Le feu sacré brûlait toujours en lui, déclara-t-il plus tard. De plus, il connaît chaque centimètre du circuit, en course comme dans les embouteillages.

Prince Rainier of Monaco closes the track before the start in a Cisitalia Type 202. Antony Noghes, President of the Automobile Club de Monaco between 1940 and 1953, holds the flag.

Prinz Rainier von Monaco schließt die Strecke vor dem Start in einem Cisitalia Typ 202. Die Fahne hält Antony Noghes, Präsident des Automobile Club de Monaco zwischen 1940 und 1953.

Le Prince Rainier de Monaco ferme le circuit avant le départ dans une Cisitalia Type 202. Antony Noghes, Président de l'Automobile Club de Monaco de 1940 à 1953, tient le drapeau.

N°	DRIVERS		ENTRANTS	CARS	ENGINES	PRACTICE RESULTS	RACE RESULTS
30	*Giuseppe Farina*	*I*	*Giuseppe Farina*	*Maserati 4CLT*	*4L 1490 cc + C*	*1st: 1'53"8*	*1st: 3h18'26"9*
38	Louis Chiron	F	Ecurie France	Talbot-Lago MC	6L 4482 cc	11th: 2'00"4	2nd: 3h19'03"1
42	Emmanuel de Graffenried	CH	Enrico Plate	Maserati 4CL	4L 1491 cc + C	7th: 1'58"1	3rd: 98 laps
16	Maurice Trintignant	F	Equipe Gordini	Simca Gordini T15	4L 1433 cc	13th: 2'00"8	4th: 98 laps
24	Luigi Villoresi	I	Scuderia Ambrosiana	Maserati 4CL	4L 1491 cc + C	3rd: 1'54"3	5th: 97 laps (with Ascari)
4	Yves Giraud-Cabantous	F	Ecurie France	Talbot-Lago MD	6L 4482 cc	12th: 2'00"6	6th: 95 laps
10	Eùgene Chaboud	F	Ecurie Lutecia	Delahaye Monoplace	6L 3557 cc	19th: NC	7th: 88 laps
2	Clemar Bucci	RA	Scuderia Milan	Maserati 6CM/4CL	4L 1491 cc + C	8th: 1'59"7	8th: 65 laps
32	Piero Taruffi	I	Squadra Piero Dusio	Cisitalia D46	4L 1489 cc	4th: 1'55"7	R
28	Nello Pagani	I	Enrico Plate	Maserati 4CL	4L 1491 cc + C	9th: 1'59"8	R
26	Alberto Ascari	I	Scuderia Ambrosiana	Maserati 4CL	4L 1491 cc + C	6th: 1'55"9	R
12	Jean-Pierre Wimille	F	Equipe Gordini	Simca Gordini T11	4L 1433 cc	2nd: 1'54"2	R
36	Igor Troubetskoy	F	Scuderia Inter	Ferrari 166I	V12 1995 cc	16th: 2'05"0	R
22	Cuth Harrison	GB	Cuthbert Harrison	ERA B/C	6L 1488 cc + C	17th: 2'06"0	R
20	Reg Parnell	GB	Reginald Parnell	ERA E	6L 1488 cc + C	18th: 2'08"0	R
34	Tazio Nuvolari	I	Squadra Piero Dusio	Cisitalia D46	4L 1089 cc	15th: 2'01"8	R
8	Louis Rosier	F	Louis Rosier	Talbot-Lago T26C	6L 4482 cc	14th: 2'01"0	R
14	Raymond Sommer	F	Equipe Gordini	Simca Gordini T15	4L 1433 cc	5th: 1'55"8	R
40	Prince "Bira"	THA	Equipe Gordini	Simca Gordini T15	4L 1433 cc	10th: 2'00"4	R

(1) Wimille in the speedy Simca-Gordini races away fleet of foot from his colleagues on the first row of the grid. (2) Villoresi in his Maserati at the harbor. (3) Pole position, fastest lap and victory for "Nino" Farina (Maserati). (4) Kiss of honor: Chiron greets his second wife. (5) Rosier in a Talbot-Lago. (6) The victors' smile: Farina and Chiron with Antony Noghes in the middle. (7) Royal reception: Princess Ghyslaine and Prince Rainier.

(1) Wimille im flinken Simca-Gordini enteilt seinen Kollegen aus der ersten Reihe bereits leichtfüßig. (2) Villoresi im Maserati am Hafen. (3) Pole Position, schnellste Runde und Sieg für »Nino« Farina (Maserati). (4) Küßchen in Ehren: Chiron begrüßt seine zweite Frau. (5) Rosier im Talbot-Lago. (6) Siegerlächeln: Farina und Chiron, in der Mitte Antony Noghes. (7) Fürstlicher Empfang durch Prinzessin Ghyslaine und Prinz Rainier.

(1) Wimille sur sa rapide Simca-Gordini s'échappe déjà aisément loin devant ses collègues de la première ligne. (2) Villoresi sur Maserati au Port. (3) Pole position, tour le plus rapide en course et victoire pour « Nino » Farina (Maserati). (4) Un baiser en tout honneur : Chiron et sa seconde épouse. (5) Rosier sur Talbot-Lago. (6) Le sourire du vainqueur : Farina et Chiron avec, au centre, Antony Noghes. (7) Réception princière : la Princesse Ghyslaine et le Prince Rainier.

1950

Normally the proximity of the Mediterranean, be it wildly thrashing or lazily calm, contributed enormously to the attractiveness and special atmosphere of the Monaco Grand Prix. On 21 May 1950, however, it intervened out of the blue – not at the start, but early in the course of events. This is how it happened:

The Grand Prix was the second race in the history of the Formula 1 World Championship. The mixed formula which the CSI (Commission Sportive Internationale) had earlier prescribed for Formula 1 – an engine capacity of 1.5 liters with compressor or 4.5 liters without – still applied. Alfa Romeo had entered three Alfetta 158s, with supercharged engines producing 350 bhp at 8,500 rpm, for the three "Big Fs" – Juan Manuel Fangio, Giuseppe Farina and Luigi Fagioli – and without doubt they were the favorites.

The Scuderia Ferrari also made use of supercharged engines, but with only 280 bhp at 8,000 rpm, the V12s in the 125/F1s of Alberto Ascari and Luigi Villoresi were clearly less powerful than the eight-cylinder in-line engines of the Alfas. The ageing Maserati 4 CLT/48s for Louis Chiron and Franco Rol were, by comparison, just padding. Nevertheless, the fearless Argentinian Froilan Gonzalez did manage to fight his way up to third place on the starting grid with his 4 CLT/50, next to Farina and Fangio, who had taken 2.6 seconds off his team-mate during his pole-position lap during the first qualifying session.

Farina led the race initially, but as early as the Tabac bend Fangio had taken command. But disaster was not far off: a wave had spilled over the sea wall onto the race track. Fangio somehow managed to get through, while Farina's Alfa bounced from one wall to the other, finally turning itself into a kind of barrier, along with Fagioli's Alfa, against the flow of following cars. A pile-up of nine cars occurred in the end, turning the track into one of the largest vehicle graveyards in the history of Formula 1.

Nevertheless, Fangio and the remaining competitors found a way through the wreckage on the second lap. The Argentinian said later that he had suddenly recognized from the movement of the spectators before the bend that something was wrong up ahead. On the same eventful lap, Gonzalez's Maserati caught fire, as did the driver, who jumped out of the car at the gasometer bend and extinguished his flaming clothes against the wall. The two Ferraris initially challenged Fangio's Alfetta, but Villoresi's race ended on lap 64 with damage to the rear axle. Ascari also had problems: the gears kept jumping out and the brakes began to fade so eventually he was lapped, like all the others. Although Fangio's drive was magnificent, the records established by Mercedes-Benz in 1937 were to remain intact until 1955. Meanwhile, the Formula 3 race supporting the Grand Prix was won by a young Englishman of whom much more would be heard in the future: Stirling Moss.

Normalerweise trägt die Nähe des Mittelmeers, ob wild bewegt oder träge gewellt, ungemein zur Attraktivität und besonderem Ambiente des Großen Preises von Monaco bei. Am 21. Mai 1950 indes greift es gewissermaßen aus heiterem Himmel ein, wenn schon nicht in den Ausgang, so doch in den Gang der Dinge. Und das kommt so:

Das Rennen ist der zweite Lauf in der Geschichte der modernen Grand Prix. Noch gilt die Mischformel, welche die CSI (Commission Sportive Internationale) der Formel 1 verordnet hat: Eine Hubraumbegrenzung auf 1,5 Liter mit Kompressor oder 4,5 Liter ohne. Alfa Romeo hat drei Alfetta 158 gemeldet, mit aufgeladenen Maschinen von 350 PS bei 8500/min, für die drei »Großen F« Juan Manuel Fangio, Giuseppe Farina und Luigi Fagioli. Sie sind zweifellos die Favoriten.

Auf zwangsbeatmete Triebwerke greift auch die Scuderia Ferrari zurück – noch. 280 PS bei 8000/min, deutlich weniger als die Achtzylinder-Reihenmotoren der Alfa, leisten die V12 der 125/F1 für Alberto Ascari und Luigi Villoresi. Nur Staffage hingegen: die alternden Maserati 4 CLT/48 für Louis Chiron und Franco Rol. Der unerschrockene Argentinier Froilan Gonzalez kämpft sich allerdings mit einem 4 CLT/50 auf den dritten Startplatz vor, neben Farina und Fangio, der seinem Teamgefährten während seiner Pole-Position-Runde im ersten Training 2,6 Sekunden abgeknöpft hat.

Farina führt kurz, aber schon vor der Tabakskurve hat Fangio das Kommando übernommen. Dort lauert Unheil: Eine Welle ist über die Brüstung auf die Piste geschwappt. Irgendwie mogelt sich Fangio durch, während die Alfa des Italieners zwischen den Mauern hin- und hergeworfen wird und sich schließlich zusammen mit dem Wagen von Fagioli wie eine Barriere gegen den Strom der Nachfolgenden stemmt. Am Ende verkeilen sich neun Autos zu einem der größten Autofriedhöfe in der Historie der Formel 1.

Gleichwohl finden Fangio und die verbleibenden Konkurrenten in der zweiten Runde einen Pfad durch das Inferno. Er habe, gibt der Argentinier später zu Protokoll, am Verhalten der Zuschauer vor der Kurve schon frühzeitig erkannt, daß da vorne irgendetwas nicht in Ordnung sei. Im gleichen Durchgang brennt der Maserati von Gonzalez ein wenig und auch der Fahrer, der an der Gasometerkurve aus dem Fahrzeug springt und die Flammen an seiner Kleidung gegen eine Wand erstickt. Gegenwehr gegen Fangios Alfetta leisten anfänglich die beiden Ferrari, bis Villoresi in der 64. Runde mit einem Hinterachsschaden aus dem Rennen geworfen wird. Auch Ascari hat Sorgen: Die Gänge springen heraus, die Bremsen lassen nach, so daß er überrundet wird wie alle anderen. Fangios Fahrt mag grandios gewesen sein – die Rekorde der Mercedes von 1937 bleiben unangetastet bis 1955. Das Formel-3-Rennen im Rahmenprogramm aber gewinnt ein junger Engländer, von dem man noch viel hören wird: Stirling Moss.

Normalement, la proximité de la Méditerranée, qu'elle soit en colère ou assoupie, contribue incomparablement à l'attrait et à l'ambiance particuliers à des Grands Prix de Monaco. Le 21 mai 1950, par contre, elle joue un rôle qui n'était pas prévu au programme, et, si elle n'influe pas sur l'issue de l'action, elle en trouble néanmoins le déroulement. En voici l'explication :

La course est la seconde manche dans l'histoire des Grands Prix modernes. La formule en vigueur est encore la formule mixte imposée par la CSI (Commission Sportive Internationale) à la Formule 1 : 1,5 l avec compresseur ou 4,5 l sans compresseur. Alfa Romeo a inscrit trois Alfetta 158 à moteur suralimenté de 350 ch à 8500 tr/mn pour les trois « Grands F » : Juan Manuel Fangio, Giuseppe Farina et Luigi Fagioli. Ils sont les favoris incontestés.

Les moteurs suralimentés sont aussi l'option choisie par la Scuderia Ferrari – provisoirement. Mais les V12 des 125/F1 d'Alberto Ascari et Luigi Villoresi développent seulement 280 ch à 8000 tr/mn, nettement moins, donc, que les huit-cylindres en ligne des Alfa. Condamnées à faire de la figuration : les vieillissantes Maserati 4 CLT/48 de Louis Chiron et Franco Rol. Le téméraire Argentin Froilan Gonzalez obtient toutefois de haute lutte une troisième place sur la grille de départ avec sa 4 CLT/50, aux côtés de Farina et Fangio, qui a distancé son coéquipier de 2,6 secondes lors du tour qui lui a valu la pole position aux premiers essais.

Farina mène brièvement, mais avant le virage du Bureau de Tabac, Fangio a repris le commandement. Là, le danger menace : une vague a déferlé sur la piste par-dessus le parapet. Comme par miracle, Fangio parvient à s'en tirer tandis que l'Alfa de Farina virevolte entre les murs et, finalement, conjointement avec la voiture de Fagioli, forme une barrière contre le fleuve des poursuivants. A la fin, neuf bolides sont enchevêtrés, l'un des plus grands cimetières de voitures dans l'histoire de la Formule 1.

Cela n'empêche pas Fangio ni les concurrents survivants de se faufiler à travers les décombres durant le deuxième tour. Le comportement des spectateurs avant le virage lui avait donné à temps le sentiment que quelque chose de bizarre s'était produit, déclarera plus tard l'Argentin en guise de commentaire. Durant ce même tour riche en rebondissements, la Maserati de Gonzalez prend feu et enflamme son pilote qui bondit de sa voiture au virage du Gazomètre et éteint les flammes de sa combinaison contre un mur. Au début, les deux Ferrari font opposition face à l'Alfetta de Fangio jusqu'à ce qu'une rupture de freins arrière contraigne Villoresi à jeter l'éponge au 64e tour, mais Ascari a, lui aussi, des soucis : les vitesses sautent, les freins sont à l'agonie, tant et si bien qu'il finit par être doublé comme tous les autres aussi. La course de Fangio aura peut-être été épique – les records atteint par Mercedes en 1937 resteront inégalés jusqu'en 1955. Pendant ce temps, un jeune Anglais dont on entendra encore beaucoup parler, gagne à la course de Formule 3 en marge du programme : Stirling Moss.

Successful start: Fangio in the Alfa Romeo is already out of sight. Tobacconist's Corner (left) is still empty and dry.

Gelungener Start: Fangio im Alfa Romeo ist bereits außer Sicht. Noch ist die Tabakskurve (links) leer und trocken.

Départ réussi : Fangio, sur Alfa Romeo, est déjà hors de vue. Le virage du Bureau de Tabac (à gauche) est encore vide et sec.

N°	DRIVERS		ENTRANTS	CARS	ENGINES	PRACTICE RESULTS	RACE RESULTS
34	**Juan Manuel Fangio**	**RA**	**Alfa Corse**	**Alfa Romeo 158**	**Alfa Romeo 8L 1497 cc + C**	**1st: 1'50"2**	**1st: 3h13'18"7**
40	Alberto Ascari	I	Scuderia Ferrari	Ferrari 125	Ferrari V12 1497 cc + C	7th: 1'53"8	2nd: 99 laps
48	Louis Chiron	F	Officine Alfieri Maserati S.A.	Maserati 4CLT/48	Maserati 4L 1491 cc + C	8th: 1'56"3	3rd: 98 laps
42	Raymond Sommer	F	Scuderia Ferrari	Ferrari 125	Ferrari V12 1497 cc + C	9th: 1'56"6	4th: 97 laps
50	Prince "Bira"	THA	Enrico Plate	Maserati 4CLT/48	Maserati 4L 1491 cc + C	15th: 2'02"2	5th: 95 laps
26	F. R. Gerard	GB	F. R. Gerard	ERA A/B	ERA 6L 1488 cc + C	16th: 2'03"4	6th: 94 laps
6	Johnny Claes	B	Ecurie Belge	Talbot-Lago T26C	Talbot 6L 4483 cc	18th: 2'12"0	7th: 94 laps
38	Luigi Villoresi	I	Scuderia Ferrari	Ferrari 125	Ferrari V12 1497 cc + C	6th: 1' 52"3	R
14	Philippe Etancelin	F	Philippe Etancelin	Talbot-Lago T26C	Talbot 6L 4483 cc	4th: 1'54"1	R
2	Jose Froilan Gonzalez	RA	Scuderia A. Varzi	Maserati 4CLT/50	Maserati 4L 1489 cc + C	3rd: 1'53"7	R
8	Harry Schell	USA	Horschell Racing Corporation	Cooper T12	JAP V2 1095 cc	19th: NC	R
10	Robert Manzon	F	Equipe Gordini	Simca Gordini T15	Gordini 4L 1491 cc + C	11th: 2'00"4	R
52	Emmanuel de Graffenried	CH	Enrico Plate	Maserati 4CLT/48	Maserati 4L 1491 cc + C	12th: 2'00"7	R
44	Franco Rol	I	Officine Alfieri Maserati S.A.	Maserati 4CLT/48	Maserati 4L 1491 cc + C	17th: 2'04"5	R
12	Maurice Trintignant	F	Equipe Gordini	Simca Gordini T15	Gordini 4L 1491 cc + C	13th: 2'01"4	R
32	Giuseppe Farina	I	Alfa Corse	Alfa Romeo 158	Alfa Romeo 8L 1497 cc + C	2nd: 1'52"8	R
16	Louis Rosier	F	Ecurie Rosier	Talbot-Lago T26C	Talbot 6L 4483 cc	10th: 1'57"7	R
36	Luigi Fagioli	F	Alfa Corse	Alfa Romeo 158	Alfa Romeo 8L 1497 cc + C	5th: 1'54"2	R
24	Cuth Harrison	GB	Cuthbert Harrison	ERA B/C	ERA 6L 1488 cc + C	14th: 2'01"6	R

(1, 2) Wet grave: after three-quarters of a lap the track becomes a scrap yard as the ocean interferes in the course of events. Nine cars are destroyed or damaged. The drivers remain unscathed. (3) Angry aristocrat: the Thai Prince Birabongse argues with an official.

(1, 2) Nasses Grab: Nach einer Dreiviertelrunde wird die Piste zum Schrottplatz, als der Ozean in den Gang der Dinge eingreift. Neun Wagen werden zerstört oder ramponiert. Die Piloten bleiben ungeschoren. (3) Zorniger Exot: Der thailändische Prinz Birabongse streitet mit einem Offiziellen.

(1, 2) D'où est venue toute cette eau ? Après trois-quarts de tours, la piste est transformée en un cimetière de voitures lorsque l'océan intervient dans le cours des choses. Neuf voitures sont détruites ou endommagées. Les pilotes s'en sortent sains et saufs. (3) Altesse en colère : algarade du prince thaïlandais Birabongse avec un fonctionnaire.

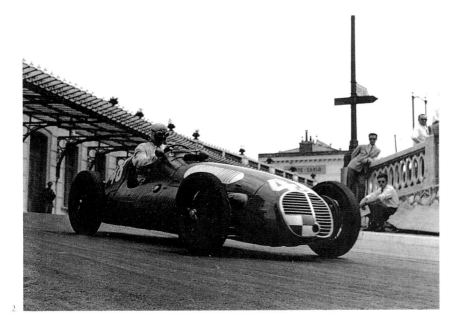

(1) Alberto Ascari in front of "Gigi" Villoresi (both Ferraris) at the Station Hairpin. (2, 3) The old and the new stars: Chiron in a Maserati and Fangio. (4) Two champions: Ascari is interviewed. Fangio listens sympathetically.

(1) Alberto Ascari vor »Gigi« Villoresi (beide Ferrari) in der Bahnhofskurve. (2, 3) Der alte und der neue Star: Chiron auf Maserati und Fangio. (4) Zwei Champions: Ascari wird interviewt. Fangio hört voller Sympathie zu.

(1) Alberto Ascari devant « Gigi » Villoresi (tous les deux sur Ferrari) au virage de la Gare. (2, 3) L'ancienne et la nouvelle star : Chiron sur Maserati et Fangio. (4) Deux champions : interview d'Ascari, que Fangio écoute sans dissimuler sa sympathie.

SIMPLY THE BEST

SIMPLY THE BEST · TOUT SIMPLEMENT LE MEILLEUR

An achievement, we say, when someone has made something of their life. The whole of Juan Manuel Fangio's life is an achievement. Everything falls into place to produce perfection and becomes a parable of what a person can achieve. Everything is a fresh start and a return to the beginning, only this time at a higher level, concentric circles, a pattern with meaning. How strange: born on 24 June 1911, one of six children to Herminia and Don Loreto Fangio, in Balcarce, 250 miles south of Buenos Aires, Juan Manuel Fangio was buried in Balcarce in July 1995 for eternal rest after his retirement, mourned by his large family, the nation and, respectfully, the whole world.

Thirty-seven years after his birth, he drove his first Grand Prix in Reims in 1948, his last one in 1958, 37 years before his death, once again in Reims. In the intervening decade he built his own memorial, made up of a whole lot of statistical one-offs: 24 wins in 51 Grands Prix between 1950 and 1958, five World Championships in Alfa Romeos, Mercedes, Ferraris and Maseratis, permanently surrounded by the aura of invincibility and that incomprehensible feature we call personality.

What gave him his superiority? He himself made a valiant, almost touching effort to help clarify the Fangio phenomenon, patiently seeking to dispel the childish notion that he took wonder pills before races. Anyone who wanted anything from him had to speak the familiar Spanish or Italian. For as he was Fangio he could afford to ignore the racing language, which is English. His purpose had been to achieve the greatest success with a minimum of effort, he said. Also, on the evening before a race he would drive a lap or two in his hire car in order to see in the light of the headlights where a tiny bit of improvement to the ideal line might still be squeezed out of the strip at the side of the track. Also, he always asked the mechanics at which speed the engine delivered the best torque. In this way he could prevent uselessly taking the engine up to the red.

Rhythm and precision were the characteristic features of his style, as Stirling Moss observed, whose own dreams of secular greatness and honor as maestro failed because of Fangio, and who was therefore left no option but to honor his achievement, to love him and chase along behind the Maestro in a ringside seat, as it were. The Briton saw himself as the victim of merciless accuracy in terms of both space and time: Fangio always took the same line, and his lap times varied only minimally, even at the Nürburgring. And Moss was willing to acknowledge that sixth sense; for example, the way Fangio threaded his car between skidding cars and flying pieces of wreck in Pierre Levegh's devastating accident at Le Mans in 1955, which killed him and 86 spectators, had come close to magic.

When Fangio and Moss had their first encounter in 1949, the Londoner was just half the Argentinian's age. A generational conflict was being fought here as well, of course, unrelenting and hard, and the victor was certain from the beginning. "Youth strikes against Fangio", was the motto for the 1956 German Grand Prix. But though youth generally struck in vain, be it called Castellotti, Musso, Collins, Hawthorn or Moss, it was never quite

Eine runde Sache, sagt man, wenn einer etwas hingestellt hat im Leben. Das ganze Leben des Juan Manuel Fangio ist so eine runde Sache. Da fügt und glättet sich alles zur Perfektion, wird zur Parabel dafür, wie weit es ein Mann bringen kann. Da ist alles Aufbruch und Rückkehr zum Ursprünglichen, nur um soviel reicher, konzentrische Kreise, ein Muster, das Sinn macht. Wie merkwürdig: Am 24. Juni 1911 als eines von sechs Kindern der Eheleute Herminia und Don Loreto Fangio zu Balcarce 400 Kilometer südlich von Buenos Aires geboren, wird Juan Manuel Fangio in Balcarce im Juli 1995 zur bleibenden Ruhe nach dem Ruhestand gebettet, beweint von seiner großen Familie, zum Leidwesen seiner Nation, respektvoll beklagt von der ganzen Welt.

In Reims fährt er 1948, 37 Jahre nach seiner Geburt, seinen ersten Grand Prix, zu seinem letzten startet er 37 Jahre vor seinem Tod, 1958, wieder in Reims. In der Dekade dazwischen zimmert er sein eigenes Denkmal aus lauter statistischen Einmaligkeiten: 24 Siege in 51 Großen Preisen zwischen 1950 und 1958, fünf Weltmeisterschaften auf Alfa Romeo, Mercedes, Ferrari und Maserati, dauerhaft verfugt durch den Nimbus der Unbesiegbarkeit und das Unfaßbare, das man Persönlichkeit nennt.

Was macht ihn so überlegen? Er selber müht sich ja redlich, fast schon rührend, bei der Aufklärung des Phänomens Fangio behilflich zu sein, zerstreut sogar geduldig die kindische Unterstellung, er verzehre vor Rennen eine Wunderpille. Wer etwas von ihm will, muß ihm schon im vertrauten Spanisch oder auf italienisch kommen. Denn weil er Fangio ist, kann er es sich leisten, die Rennsprache Englisch einfach links liegen zu lassen. Sein Prinzip sei es, mit geringstem Aufwand den größten Erfolg zu erzielen, sagt er dann. Und: Am Abend vor einem Rennen fahre er noch einmal mit seinem Mietwagen eine oder zwei Runden, um im Scheinwerferlicht auszumachen, wo sich dem Grenzstreifen neben der Piste noch ein Fetzen Ideallinie abgewinnen lasse. Und: Er erkundige sich stets bei den Mechanikern, bei welcher Drehzahl eine Maschine das beste Drehmoment liefere. Also müsse er sie nicht nutzlos bis an den roten Bereich schinden.

Rhythmus und Präzision prägten seinen Stil, beobachtet Stirling Moss, dessen eigene Blütenträume von säkularer Größe und Meisterwürden an Fangio scheitern und dem deshalb nichts übrigbleibt als zu ehren, zu lieben und dem Maestro gewissermaßen auf einem rasenden Logenplatz hinterherzujagen. Der Brite sieht sich als Opfer einer erbarmungslosen Akkuratesse im räumlichen wie im zeitlichen Sinne: Immer bewege Fangio sich auf dem gleichen Strich, und nur minimal streuten seine Rundenzeiten, selbst am Nürburgring. Und bescheinigt ihm diesen sechsten Sinn: Wie Fangio 1955 in Le Mans bei dem verheerenden Unfall von Pierre Levegh, der diesem und 86 Zuschauern das Leben kostete, seinen Weg durch das Chaos gefädelt habe, zwischen schleudernden Wagen und schwirrenden Wrackteilen, das habe schon an Magie herangereicht.

Als Fangio und Moss 1949 zum ersten Mal aufeinandertreffen, ist der Londoner gerade mal halb so alt wie der Argentinier. Natürlich wird da auch ein

C'est une « chose ronde », dit-on en allemand, quand quelqu'un a réussi quelque chose de bien dans sa vie. Or toute la vie de Juan Manuel Fangio est bel et bien une « chose ronde ». Tous les éléments s'insèrent à la perfection et sans césure, telle une espèce de parabole de ce dont un homme est capable. Tout est révolution et retour aux sources, mais avec beaucoup plus de richesse, de cercles concentriques, avec un schéma qui donne un sens. Etonnant parallèle : né le 24 juin 1911 à Balcarce, à 400 kilomètres au sud de Buenos Aires, Juan Manuel Fangio est l'un des six enfants des époux Herminia et Don Loreto Fangio ; il sera également inhumé à Balcarce en juillet 1995 où il trouvera le repos éternel après une retraite bien méritée, pleuré par toute sa grande famille, pour le plus grand désarroi d'une nation, et regretté respectueusement par le monde entier.

Il participe à son premier Grand Prix à Reims en 1948, à l'âge de 37 ans, et s'engagera aussi pour son dernier en 1958, 37 ans avant sa mort, de nouveau à Reims. Durant les dix années séparant ces deux dates, il élève peu à peu son propre mémorial se composant d'une myriade de statistiques uniques : 24 victoires en 51 Grands Prix entre 1950 et 1958, cinq championnats du monde sur Alfa Romeo, Mercedes, Ferrari et Maserati, nappé pour l'éternité de l'aura de l'invincibilité et de l'insaisissable que l'on appelle la personnalité.

Mais qu'est-ce qui lui donne une telle suprématie ? Lui-même s'efforce infiniment, au point qu'il en est presque émouvant, de venir en aide pour expliquer le phénomène Fangio ; il dissipe même patiemment le préjugé infantile selon lequel il avalerait un comprimé miracle avant la course. Quiconque veut apprendre quelque chose de lui, doit déjà s'adresser à lui dans la langue qui lui est familière, l'espagnol, ou lui parler en italien. En effet, s'agissant de Fangio, on peut se permettre de laisser tout simplement de côté cet esperanto de la compétition automobile qu'est l'anglais. Son principe consiste, dit-il, à obtenir le plus grand succès possible avec un minimum d'efforts. Et, la veille d'une course, il accomplit encore un ou deux tours avec sa voiture de location pour, à la lueur des phares, chercher où il est encore possible d'arracher de haute lutte un fragment de trajectoire idéal aux bordures qui délimitent la piste. Et il se renseigne toujours auprès des mécaniciens, ajoute-t-il, pour savoir à quel régime un moteur délivre le meilleur couple. Ainsi, il n'a pas besoin de le cravacher inutilement jusque dans la zone rouge.

Rythme et précision caractérisent son style, a observé un jour Stirling Moss, dont les propres rêves de couronnes de laurier, d'immortalité et de titres de champion du monde ont achoppé sur Fangio et qui n'a, par conséquent, eu d'autre alternative que d'honorer et d'aimer, de talonner en quelque sorte le maestro depuis la meilleure place imaginable, à une longueur de capot. Le Britannique se considère comme victime d'un savoir-faire sans pitié tant dans l'espace que dans le temps : Fangio s'est toujours déplacé sur la même ligne et ses temps au tour n'ont toujours divergé que de très peu, même au Nürburgring. Et il lui atteste un sixième sens : par exemple au Mans en 1955, lors de la catastrophe causée par la collision de Lance Macklin et Pierre Levegh, dans laquelle ce dernier et 86 spectateurs trouvent la mort, l'adresse avec laquelle Fangio réussit à se faufiler à travers le chaos, entre les

JUAN MANUEL FANGIO 1911—1995

as much wounded in its professional honor as one year later at the Nürburgring, when Fangio, in his mid-forties, drove the greatest race of his career.

The master carried on racing until he stopped for the only reason he was willing to acknowledge: he did not want to do it any more – burnout syndrome, which overcame him on the long straights in Reims, where there is much time for contemplation, and coupled, perhaps, with the certainty that he really was no longer the youngest.

From that moment on he devoted his attention to his Daimler-Benz dealership, from which from 1951 had been fed the gruff and indestructible 170 Diesel into the armada of taxis swarming through the streets of Buenos Aires. And he took good care of his reputation, which over the years turned into the stuff of legend.

His five championships set an indestructible standard which everyone else challenged in vain, even Senna, even Prost, who in the process did their best to destroy each other's chances. "When Fangio enters the room", the alert Frenchman said at a celebration of the old master's 80th birthday in the Dorchester Hotel, in London, in 1991, "you know that someone is here", and his voice became quite rough with respect. He was called bandy legs, and it is true that he was no model of an athlete. But Fangio was fit; he did not need torturous muscle building equipment and fitness studios, but during the European winter he knocked the ball about with the boys on Balcarce beach, until they ran out of puff. That is how he won the 1955 Argentinian Grand Prix in the burning heat, the hot frame of his Mercedes burning a mark on his skin in lasting memory while the others flaked out.

But in December 1970 he suffered his first heart attack, a second in 1981 as he was driving the 300 SLR in Dubai during an historic race, the old fire in his heart and soul – he was, after all, Fangio. Barely a year later the Argentinian specialist Dr Favaloro did his first bypass, like on Fangio's brother Toto. He had been under anaesthetic for three days and nights, Fangio reported, using images from the subject of which he knew best, and had then woken up with a new engine. But the kidneys, too, were beginning to cause trouble. Increasingly frequently he had to undergo dialysis until no-one could help him any longer – not even the best doctors in the world, who were always at Juan Manuel Fangio's disposal.

Generationenkonflikt ausgefochten, unerbittlich und mit aller Härte, und der Sieger steht von vornherein fest. »Jugend stürmt gegen Fangio« hat man als Motto über dem Großen Preis von Deutschland 1956 ausgegeben. Aber die Jungen stürmen stets vergeblich, ob sie nun Castellotti, Musso, Collins, Hawthorn oder Moss heißen, nie indessen in ihrer Berufsehre so gekränkt und gepiesackt als ein Jahr später auf dem Nürburgring, als dieser Mittvierziger das größte Rennen seiner Karriere fährt.

Bis es dem Meister beliebt, aus dem einzigen Grunde aufzuhören, den er selber anerkennt: weil er keine Lust mehr hat – ein Burnout-Syndrom, das ihn auf den langen Geraden von Reims übermannt, wo man viel Muße zum Nachdenken hat, vielleicht auch gepaart mit der Gewißheit, er sei nun wirklich nicht mehr der Jüngste.

Von nun an widmet er sich seiner Daimler-Benz-Niederlassung, die schon 1951 den knorrigen und unverwüstlichen 170 Diesel in die Armada von Taxis eingespeist hat, die durch die Straßen von Buenos Aires wimmelt. Und er verwaltet klug seinen Ruhm, der sich über die Jahre zur Legende verdichtet.

Seine fünf Championate, wie es scheint, haben einen schier unverrückbaren Standard gesetzt, gegen den alle vergeblich anrennen, selbst Senna, selbst Prost, die einander dabei auch noch wütend behindern. »Wenn Fangio den Raum betritt«, sagt der alerte Franzose, als man 1991 im Londoner Dorchester Hotel des alten Meisters 80. Geburtstag würdigt, »dann spürt man, daß einer drin ist«, und die Stimme wird ganz spröde vor lauter Ehrfurcht. Sie nennen ihn den Krummbeinigen, und wie ein Modellathlet sieht er wirklich nicht aus. Aber Fangio ist fit, braucht dazu kein muskelschwellendes Martergerät und kein Stärkestudio, sondern bolzt während des europäischen Winters mit den Bengels auf dem heißen Strand von Balcarce, bis denen die Puste ausgeht. So übersteht er den Großen Preis von Argentinien 1955 bei sengender Hitze als Sieger, während der glühende Rohrrahmen des Mercedes ein Brandzeichen in seine Haut eingräbt zum bleibenden Gedenken und die anderen schlappmachen.

Im Dezember 1970 aber ereilt ihn sein erster Herzinfarkt, 1981 ein zweiter, als er in Dubai den 300 SLR bei einem historischen Rennen fährt, das alte Feuer im Herzen und in der Seele, denn er ist Fangio. Ein knappes Jahr später legt ihm der argentinische Spezialist Dr. Favaloro seinen ersten Bypass wie schon seinem Bruder Toto. Er habe, berichtet Fangio und bemüht dabei eine Bildsprache aus dem Gebiet, in dem er sich am besten auskennt, drei Tage und Nächte in Narkose gelegen und sei dann mit einem neuen Motor aufgewacht.

Aber auch die Nieren beginnen Schwierigkeiten zu machen. Immer häufiger muß er sich der Dialyse unterziehen, bis ihm niemand mehr helfen kann – nicht einmal die besten Ärzte der Welt, die Juan Manuel Fangio immer zur Verfügung gestanden haben.

bolides en dérapage et les morceaux d'épaves dissimulés sur la piste avait quelque chose de magique.

Lorsque Fangio et Moss se rencontrent pour la première fois, en 1949, le Londonien est pratiquement deux fois plus jeune que l'Argentin. Naturellement, les deux hommes liquident par là aussi un conflit de génération, sans pitié et avec dureté, et le nom du vainqueur est connu d'avance. « La jeunesse s'attaque à Fangio », a-t-on choisi comme devise pour le Grand Prix d'Allemagne de 1956. Mais les jeunes attaquent toujours en vain, qu'ils s'appellent Castellotti, Musso, Collins, Hawthorn ou Moss, plus gravement blessés dans leur honneur professionnel et plus humiliés que jamais quand, un an plus tard, au Nürburgring, ce quadragénaire signe la meilleure course de sa carrière.

Jusqu'à ce qu'il soit du bon plaisir du champion de raccrocher son casque pour le seul motif qu'il admet lui-même : parce qu'il n'a plus envie – un syndrome de « burn-out » qui l'accable un jour sur les longues lignes droites de Reims, où l'on a tant de temps pour réfléchir, mais peut-être aussi à cause de la certitude qu'il n'est maintenant plus vraiment à sa place ici à cause de son âge.

A partir de cet instant-là, il se consacre à sa concession Daimler-Benz, grâce à laquelle, dès 1951, la frustre mais inusable 170 Diesel est venue rejoindre l'armada de taxis qui sillonnent les rues de Buenos Aires. Et il commercialise avec intelligence sa célébrité qu'il transforme en légende au fil des ans.

Ses cinq titres de champion du monde ont, semble-t-il, posé un jalon qui paraît inaccessible et contre lequel tous courent en vain, même Senna, même Prost, lesquels, qui plus est, se jettent encore mutuellement des bâtons dans les roues. « Quand Fangio pénètre dans une pièce, déclare le célèbre petit Français, invité, en 1991, au quatre-vingtième anniversaire du grand champion, célébré à l'hôtel Dorchester de Londres, on sent que quelqu'un est là », et sa voix tremble d'une admiration difficilement contenue. On le surnomme l'homme aux jambes en O et il n'a vraiment rien d'un athlète modèle. Mais Fangio est en forme, il n'a pas besoin pour cela d'appareils de culture physique ni de clubs de musculation ; pendant l'hiver européen, il joue au contraire au football avec de jeunes Brésiliens, sur le sable chaud de la plage de Balcarce, jusqu'à ce qu'ils en aient la respiration coupée. Ainsi termine-t-il le Grand Prix d'Argentine de 1955 en vainqueur par une chaleur torride, à tel point que le châssis tubulaire porté au rouge de sa Mercedes le marque au feu, souvenir indélébile, et que les autres jettent l'éponge l'un après l'autre.

Mais, en décembre 1970, il est victime de son premier infarctus, d'un deuxième en 1981 lorsqu'il conduit à Dubaï une 300 SLR lors d'une course pour voitures historiques, toujours le feu sacré brûlant au coeur et dans l'âme, car on n'est pas Fangio pour rien. A peine un an plus tard, un spécialiste argentin, le Dr Favaloro, réalise un premier pontage coronarien, comme précédemment sur son frère Toto. Il est resté, déclare Fangio en guise de commentaires – en s'efforçant d'utiliser la langue du domaine qu'il connaît le mieux – anesthésié pendant trois jours et trois nuits avant de se réveiller alors avec un nouveau moteur. Mais les reins, eux aussi, commencent à lui causer des difficultés. Il doit de plus en plus fréquemment se soumettre à la dialyse jusqu'à ce que personne ne puisse plus l'aider – pas même les meilleurs médecins du monde, que Juan Manuel Fangio a toujours eus à sa disposition.

Every inch the champion: Juan Manuel Fangio.

Jeder Zoll ein Champion: Juan Manuel Fangio.

Champion jusqu'au bout des ongles : Juan Manuel Fangio.

1952

On Whit Monday 1952, the Monaco Grand Prix was transformed into a race for sports cars with engines larger than 2 liters, competing over the usual 100 laps, with the exception that the track had been modified at Sainte Dévote and shortened by 35 meters. The Grand Prix single-seaters being raced elsewhere during this and the following year – Formula 2 cars with 2-liter engines – were simply refused entry to Monaco.

As with the motorcycle race in the programme supporting the 1948 Grand Prix, the experiment failed for the time being, for the simple reason that the bodywork blocked the drivers' view of the kerbs. In any case, the weekend was burdened by a gloomy omen: during training for the Prix de Monaco (for sports cars up to 2 liters) Luigi Fagioli, 54, was seriously injured in his Lancia Aurelia B 20 at the tunnel exit and he died on 26 June.

Although the Mercedes 300 SLs were missing, the main race was well attended. Aston Martin sent three DB 3s for Reg Parnell, Peter Collins and Lance Macklin, all with six-cylinder engines of 2,922 cc producing 145 bhp at 5,000 rpm; Jaguar Cars sent an XK 120 C (3,442 cc, 200 bhp at 5,800 rpm) for Stirling Moss. As the fifth place earned during qualifying by Robert Manzon and his Gordini T 15 S showed, Team Gordini, with its six-cylinder 2.3-liter engines, was well able to keep up. Enzo Ferrari did not enter a factory team, but was honorably represented by private teams, including that of the brothers Vittorio, Paolo, Umberto and Giannino of the Marzotto industrial dynasty, who entered a Spider Vignale 225 S (2,715 cc, 210 bhp at 7,200 rpm) for Vittorio and a Barchetta 340 (4,101 cc, 260 bhp at 6,500 rpm) for Piero Carini. Then there was the Scuderia della Guastalla with two 225 S cars for Eugenio Castellotti and Antonio Stagnoli and the 3-liter 250 S of Giovanni Bracco, who had just won the Mille Miglia. Seven of the 18 cars in the field came from the noble house of Ferrari, including the first five – all of them with 12-cylinder engines.

Initially, however, Moss and Manzon were engaged in a nail-biting duel at the head of the race. On lap 24, the Gordini overtook the Jaguar in front of the Casino gardens, but already there was a warning sign. Behind Sainte Dévote, flames shot out of Reg Parnell's car. They were quickly extinguished, but the Aston Martin was parked right in the middle of the track and in the sights of the two leaders, who were unable to take evasive action. A short while later, the Allard of the Briton Anthony Hume smashed backwards into the pile-up.

That meant that the hour of the men from the middle of the field had suddenly come. The remainder of the race turned into a duel between Castellotti (from start position 10) and Marzotto (who had started the race from position 11). The final result was decided not least by the work of the pit crews – as would be the case in the Grands Prix of the late Nineties…

Am Pfingstmontag 1952 kommt es an historischer Stätte zur Koexistenz des völlig Unvereinbaren: ein Rennen für Sportwagen von mehr als zwei Litern um den Grand Prix de Monaco über die üblichen hundert Runden, nur daß die Strecke bei Sainte Dévote modifiziert und 35 Meter kürzer geworden ist. Den Grand-Prix-Monoposti jenes und des folgenden Jahres, Formel-2-Autos mit zwei Litern Hubraum, verweigert man kurzerhand das Gastrecht.

Wie der Motorradlauf im Rahmenprogramm des Großen Preises von 1948 scheitert das Experiment, schon weil die Karosserien den Blick der Piloten auf den Kantstein versperren. Ohnehin lastet ein düsteres Omen über dem Wochenende: Beim Training zum Prix de Monaco (bis zwei Liter) verletzt sich Luigi Fagioli, 54, am Tunnelausgang in seinem Lancia Aurelia B 20 schwer und stirbt am 26. Juni.

Obwohl die Mercedes 300 SL fehlen, ist das Hauptrennen gut besetzt. Die Aston Martin Ltd. hat für Reg Parnell, Peter Collins und Lance Macklin drei DB 3 geschickt, Sechszylinder mit 2922 cm³ und 145 PS bei 5000/min, die Jaguar Cars Ltd. einen XK 120 C (3442 cm³, 200 PS bei 5800/min) für Stirling Moss. Wie bereits der fünfte Rang im Training für Robert Manzons Gordini T 15 S zeigt, kann die Equipe Gordini mit ihrem Sechszylinder von 2,3 Litern durchaus mithalten. Enzo Ferrari verzichtet auf eine Werksbeteiligung und läßt sich durch private Teams würdig vertreten. Da ist das Aufgebot der Gebrüder Vittorio, Paolo, Umberto und Giannino aus der Industriellen-Dynastie Marzotto, ein Spider Vignale 225 S (2715 cm³, 210 PS bei 7200/min) für Vittorio Marzotto und ein Barchetta 340 (4101 cm³, 260 PS bei 6500/min) für Piero Carini. Da ist die Scuderia della Guastalla mit zwei 225 S für Eugenio Castellotti und Antonio Stagnoli und dem Dreiliter 250 S von Giovanni Bracco, der just die Mille Miglia gewonnen hat. Aus dem noblen Hause Ferrari stammen sieben der 18 Wagen des Felds, unter ihnen die ersten fünf – allesamt Zwölfzylinder.

Zunächst indessen fechten Moss und Manzon ein mitreißendes Duell an der Spitze aus. In der 24. Runde überholt der Gordini den Jaguar vor den Gärten des Casinos. Doch schon bahnt sich ein Menetekel an: Hinter Sainte Dévote schlagen Flammen aus dem Wagen von Reg Parnell. Sie werden rasch gelöscht. Aber der Aston Martin parkt mitten in der Fahrspur und im Fadenkreuz der beiden Spitzenreiter, die ihm nicht ausweichen können. Kurz darauf schlägt der Allard des Briten Anthony Hume rückwärts in die Havaristen ein.

Damit hat unversehens die Stunde der Männer aus dem dritten Glied geschlagen: Der Rest des Rennens wird zum Zweikampf zwischen Castellotti (Startplatz 10) und Marzotto, der das Rennen aus der elften Position angegangen ist. Über den Ausgang entscheidet nicht zuletzt die Arbeit der Boxencrews – wie in den Grand Prix der späten Neunziger…

Le lundi de la Pentecôte 1952, le Grand Prix de Monaco devient une course de voitures de sport de plus de deux litres sur les traditionnels cent tours, à cette différence près que la piste a été modifiée à Sainte Dévote et que sa longueur a été raccourcie de 35 mètres. Les monoplaces de Grand Prix de cette année-là et de l'année suivante, les voitures de Formule 2 de deux litres de cylindrée, se sont vu refuser le droit de séjour.

Comme pour la course de moto en marge du Grand Prix de 1948, l'expérience se solde cette fois par un échec, ne serait-ce que parce que la carrosserie empêche le pilote de viser les bordures de trottoir. La chance n'est de toute façon pas du côté des organisateurs durant tout le week-end : lors des essais du Grand Prix de Monaco jusqu'à deux litres, Luigi Fagioli, 54 ans, se blesse grièvement à la sortie du tunnel, avec sa Lancia Aurelia B 20, et décède le 26 juin.

Malgré l'absence des Mercedes 300 SL, le plateau est très relevé. Aston Martin a envoyé trois DB 3 pour Reg Parnell, Peter Collins et Lance Macklin, des six-cylindres de 2922 cm³ et 145 ch à 5000 tr/mn, Jaguar a dépêché une XK 120 C (3442 cm³, 200 ch à 5800 tr/mn) pour Stirling Moss. Comme le prouve déjà le cinquième rang aux essais pour Robert Manzon et sa Gordini T 15 S, l'équipe Gordini est parfaitement dans le coup avec sa six-cylindres de 2,3 litres. Enzo Ferrari renonce à une participation officielle se fait représenter par des écuries privées, y compris celle des frères Vittorio, Paolo, Umberto et Giannino de la dynastie industrielle des Marzotto, une Spider Vignale 225 S (2715 cm³, 210 ch à 7200 tr/mn) pour Vittorio Marzotto et une Barchetta 340 (4101 cm³, 260 ch à 6500 tr/mn) pour Piero Carini. Il y a là la Scuderia della Guastalla avec une 225 S pour Eugenio Castellotti et Antonio Stagnoli et la trois-litres 250 S de Giovanni Bracco, qui vient de remporter les Mille Miglia. Sept des dix-huit voitures de la grille proviennent de la fameuse manufacture Ferrari, parmi elles les cinq premières – toutes des douze-cylindres.

Au début, Moss et Manzon se livrent un duel à couper le souffle en tête de la course. Au 24ᵉ tour, la Gordini double la Jaguar devant les jardins du Casino. Mais la débâcle s'annonce : derrière Sainte Dévote, des flammes s'échappent de la voiture de Reg Parnell. Elles sont rapidement éteintes. Mais l'Aston Martin est garée au beau milieu de la trajectoire et dans le collimateur des deux leaders, qui ne parviennent pas à l'éviter. Quelques instants plus tard, l'Allard du Britannique Anthony Hume percute les épaves en marche arrière.

Ainsi sonne, contre toute attente, l'heure des troisièmes couteaux : le reste de la course se mue en un duel entre Castellotti, parti de la dixième place, et Marzotto, qui s'est élancé depuis la onzième. Et c'est finalement la célérité des mécaniciens des stands qui décide de l'issue de la course – comme lors des Grands Prix de la fin des années 90 …

During the second qualifying session for sports cars up to two liters, Luigi Fagioli has a serious accident in his Lancia Aurelia at the exit to the tunnel. The reason remains unknown. The winner of the 1935 Monaco Grand Prix dies eighteen days later. He is only 54.

Beim zweiten Training für Sportwagen bis zwei Liter hat Luigi Fagioli in seinem Lancia Aurelia ausgangs des Tunnels einen schweren Unfall. Der Grund bleibt im dunkeln. 18 Tage später stirbt der Sieger des monegassischen Grand Prix von 1935. Er ist nur 54 Jahre alt geworden.

Lors des seconds essais pour voitures de sport jusqu'à deux litres, Luigi Fagioli, dans sa Lancia Aurelia, est victime d'un grave accident à la sortie du tunnel. On ne saura jamais pourquoi. 18 jours plus tard, le vainqueur du Grand Prix de Monaco de 1935 succombe à ses blessures, âgé seulement de 54 ans.

N°	DRIVERS		ENTRANTS	CARS	ENGINES	PRACTICE RESULTS	RACE RESULTS
94	**Comte Vittorio Marzotto**	**I**	**Scuderia Marzotto**	**Ferrari 225S**	**Ferrari V12 2715 cc**	**11th: 2'03"2**	**1st: 3h21'28"7**
92	Eugenio Castellotti	I	Scuderia della Guastalla	Ferrari 225S	Ferrari V12 2715 cc	10th: 2'02"9	2nd: 3h21'43"9
90	Antonio Stagnoli/Clemente Biondetti	I	Scuderia della Guastalla	Ferrari 225S	Ferrari V12 2715 cc	3rd: 2'00"7	3rd: 98 laps
58	Jean Lucas/André Simon	F	Luigi Chinetti	Ferrari 225S	Ferrari V12 2715 cc	15th: 2'06"9	4th: 96 laps
60	"Pagnibon"	F	Pagnibon	Ferrari 225S	Ferrari V12 2715 cc	8th: 2'02"2	5th: 95 laps
82	Tom Wisdom	GB	T. H. Wisdom	Jaguar C-Type	Jaguar 6L 3442 cc	16th: 2'09"0	6th: 94 laps
74	Peter Collins	GB	Aston Martin	Aston-Martin DB3	Aston Martin 6L 2922 cc	12th: 2'03"5	7th: 92 laps
62	René Cotton	F	René Cotton	Delahaye 135S	Delahaye 6L 3575 cc	18th: 2'10"2	8th: 85 laps
76	Lance Macklin	GB	Aston Martin	Aston-Martin DB3	Aston Martin 6L 2922 cc	5th(6): 2'01"1	R
100	Francesco Mascarenhas	P	F. Mascarenhas	Allard J2	Chrysler V8 5434 cc	17th: 2'09"5	R
78	*Stirling Moss*	*GB*	*Jaguar Cars*	*Jaguar C-Type*	*Jaguar 6L 3442 cc*	*1st(2): 2'00"2*	R
96	Piero Carini	I	Scuderia Marzotto	Ferrari 340	Ferrari V12 4102 cc	12th(13): 2'03"5	R
64	Louis Rosier	F	Ecurie Rosier	Talbot-Lago T26GS	Talbot 6L 4483 cc	7th: 2'01"9	R
56	Robert Manzon	F	Equipe Gordini	Gordini 15S	Gordini 6L 2262 cc	5th: 2'01"1	R
84	Anthony Hume	GB	A. H. Bryde	Allard J2	Chrysler V8 5434 cc	14th: 2'03"6	R
72	Reg Parnell	GB	Aston Martin	Aston-Martin DB3	Aston Martin 6L 2922 cc	4th: 2'00"8	R
88	Giovanni Bracco	I	Scuderia della Guastalla	Ferrari 250S	Ferrari V12 2953 cc	9th: 2'02"8	R
68	*Pierre Levegh*	*F*	*Pierre Levegh*	*Talbot-Lago T26GS*	*Talbot 6L 4483 cc*	*1st: 2'00"2*	R

(1) Moss leads in the Jaguar immediately after the start. (2) Aptly named: the subsequent winner Vittorio Marzotto (Ferrari). (3) Behind Moss, Levegh (Talbot) has to fight off an attack from Carini (Ferrari). (4) Moss approaching Sainte Dévote; (5) Macklin (Aston Martin) overtakes Lucas (Ferrari). (6) Prince Rainier congratulates the winner.

(1) Unmittelbar nach dem Start führt Moss im Jaguar. (2) Nomen est omen: der spätere Sieger Vittorio Marzotto (Ferrari). (3) Hinter Moss muß sich Levegh (Talbot) der Attacken von Carini (Ferrari) erwehren. (4) Moss vor Sainte Dévote. (5) Macklin (Aston Martin) überholt Lucas (Ferrari). (6) Prinz Rainier gratuliert zum Sieg.

(1) Dès le départ, Moss passe en tête sur Jaguar. (2) Nomen est omen : le futur vainqueur Vittorio Marzotto (Ferrari). (3) Derrière Moss, Levegh (Talbot) repousse les attaques de Carini (Ferrari). (4) Moss à l'entrée de Sainte Dévote. (5) Macklin (Aston Martin) double Lucas (Ferrari). (6) Le Prince Rainier félicite le vainqueur.

(1-8) The heavy sports cars with their enveloping bodywork turn out to be little suited to the narrow circuit and partly eliminate one another in a chain-reaction of horror.

(1-8) Die schweren Sportwagen erweisen sich mit ihren umgreifenden Karosserien als ungeeignet für den engen Circuit und eliminieren einander teilweise in einer Kettenreaktion des Schreckens.

(1-8) Avec leur carrosserie enveloppante, les lourdes voitures de sport sont totalement déplacées sur cet étroit circuit et s'éliminent en partie mutuellement lors d'une effrayante réaction en chaîne.

(9) Moss' damaged Jaguar is prepared for being transported away. (10) The Ferrari of Antonio Stagnoli, who drove the fastest lap.

(9) Moss' ramponierter Jaguar wird zum Abtransport vorbereitet. (10) Der Ferrari von Antonio Stagnoli, der die schnellste Runde fährt.

(9) La Jaguar endommagée de Moss en cours de préparation pour son évacuation. (10) La Ferrari d'Antonio Stagnoli, qui signe le tour le plus rapide en course.

1955

On the eve of the 13th Monaco Grand Prix, which carried the honorary title of Grand Prix d'Europe, a number of drivers took another saunter around the track. With great attention they eyed the chicane, that notorious weak point of the course. There was no disagreement: anyone who drove into the barriers here would head straight for the Mediterranean. The superstitious Alberto Ascari touched wood – just in case.

1955, this was the second year of the new 2.5-liter formula. Everything was back in order and from now on the Monaco Grand Prix would have its firm place in the Formula 1 schedule. One thing had changed: the start was now directly alongside the harbor, a few hundred meters from the gasometer bend.

Together with the old fighter Luigi Villoresi and the young hope Eugenio Castellotti, Ascari now belonged to the team of Gianni Lancia, driving a D 50 which designer Vittorio Jano had produced in five months. In a noble gesture, a fourth car was entrusted to the 56-year-old local boy Louis Chiron. He had already achieved first, second, third, fourth and fifth places in Monaco. By accident, design or fate, he was to take sixth place on this occasion. Giuseppe Farina and Maurice Trintignant started in Ferraris (625/F1), as did Piero Taruffi and the American Harry Schell (555 Super Squalo); the Frenchman Jean Behra, the Italian Luigi Musso and the Argentinian Roberto Mieres were driving for Officine Alfieri Maserati in Tipo 250Fs.

But the favorites were the Mercedes W 196s, which had already made their mark on the 1954 season and were being driven by Juan Manuel Fangio, Stirling Moss and Hans Herrmann. But this formidable fighting force was decimated as early as the first training session. At the Massenet section before the Casino, Herrmann crashed and trapped his car under the barriers, missed being decapitated by a hair's breadth, but managed to escape with a broken leg. The Frenchman André Simon replaced him after being informed of his luck by telephone in the Hotel Mirabeau. As so often, this most exceptional among the Grands Prix had an unusual script.

Fangio led until half-time, followed by Moss – a common sight that year – but then Moss appeared on his own, pointing behind him to where Fangio's Mercedes was just being pushed aside at the Station Hairpin with a faulty rear axle. Moss maintained his lead for 20 laps, but then his W 196 rolled out of the tunnel in a cloud of steam and he just managed to make the pits to retire with engine trouble.

Steam was also produced on the same lap by Ascari's Lancia, but for a very different reason. His car plunged into the harbor at the chicane due either to faulty brakes or perhaps oil on the track. But Ascari came to the surface and swam strongly to a rescue boat, only to die a few days later while testing a sports car at Monza. The lead was now taken by a somewhat surprised Trintignant, who was a wine grower by trade and the mayor of Vergèze, in the neighbouring département of Gard. Eugenio Castellotti tried hard to close the gap, but his attack came too late to change the finishing order.

Am Vorabend des 13. Großen Preises von Monaco, der honoris causa den Titel Grand Prix d'Europe trägt, bummeln einige der Piloten noch einmal um die Strecke. Aufmerksam nimmt man die Schikane in Augenschein, diesen notorischen Schwachpunkt des Kurses. Und alle sind sich einig: Wer hier gegen die Brüstung fährt, fliegt ins Mittelmeer. Der abergläubische Alberto Ascari klopft auf Holz – für alle Fälle.

Man schreibt 1955, das zweite Jahr der neuen 2,5-Liter-Formel. Alles hat wieder seine Ordnung, und der Grand Prix de Monaco wird von nun an seinen festen Platz im Terminkalender einnehmen. Eines hat sich geändert: Man wird unmittelbar neben dem Hafen starten, ein paar hundert Meter vor der Gasometerkurve.

Wie der alte Kämpe Luigi Villoresi und der junge Hoffnungsträger Eugenio Castellotti gehört Ascari zum Aufgebot von Gianni Lancia, auf dem D 50, den Konstrukteur Vittorio Jano in fünf Monaten in die Welt gesetzt hat. Einen vierten Wagen vertraut man in einer noblen Geste dem 56jährigen Einheimischen Louis Chiron an. Er hat es in Monaco schon auf je einen ersten, zweiten, dritten, vierten und fünften Platz gebracht. Zufall oder planendes Schicksal: Der sechste folgt dieses Mal. Auf Ferrari starten Giuseppe Farina und Maurice Trintignant (625/F1) sowie Piero Taruffi und der Amerikaner Harry Schell (555 Super Squalo), für die Officine Alfieri Maserati auf dem Tipo 250F der Franzose Jean Behra, der Italiener Luigi Musso und der Argentinier Roberto Mieres.

Favoriten aber sind die Mercedes W 196, die bereits der Saison 1954 nachdrücklich ihren Stempel aufgedrückt haben, für Juan Manuel Fangio, Stirling Moss und Hans Herrmann. Diese Streitmacht wird bereits beim ersten Training am Donnerstag dezimiert. Am Streckenabschnitt Massenet klemmt Herrmann seinen Wagen unter die Brüstung, wird um ein Haar enthauptet, kommt aber mit einem Beinbruch davon. An seiner Statt fährt der Franzose André Simon, im Hotel Mirabeau telefonisch von seinem Glück in Kenntnis gesetzt. Und auch sonst schreibt der Ungewöhnlichste unter den Grand Prix wie üblich sein eigenes Drehbuch.

Gewiß führt Fangio bis zur Halbzeit, dicht gefolgt von Moss – ein Bild, das sich einschleift in jenen Jahren. Doch dann erscheint der Brite allein auf der Bildfläche, deutet nach hinten, wo Fangios Mercedes just an der Bahnhofskurve mit defekter Hinterachse beiseite geschoben wird. Seine eigene Führung währt 20 Runden. Dann rollt der W 196 von Dampf umwabert aus dem Tunnel, schafft es gerade noch bis an die Box: Motorschaden.

Dampf erzeugt im gleichen Durchgang auch Ascaris Lancia, aus ganz anderen Gründen. Er stürzt an der Schikane ins Wasser, nachlassende Bremsen, vielleicht auch Öl auf der Piste. Der Pilot rettet sich mit rüstigen Stößen in ein Boot. Einige Tage später jedoch starb er dann bei der Testfahrt eines Sportwagens in Monza. In Führung findet sich nun der verblüffte Trintignant, im Zivilberuf Winzer und Bürgermeister zu Vergèze im benachbarten Département Gard. Daran ändern auch späte Attacken von Eugenio Castellotti nichts mehr.

La veille du 13e Grand Prix de Monaco qui porte « honoris causa » le titre de Grand Prix d'Europe, quelques pilotes vont encore une fois se promener le long du circuit. Ils inspectent attentivement la chicane, qui est le talon d'Achille notoire du circuit. Mais tous sont unanimes : celui qui percute ici le parapet plonge dans la Méditerranée. Le superstitieux Alberto Ascari touche du bois – on ne sait jamais !

Nous sommes en 1955, seconde année de la nouvelle formule 2,5 litres. Tout est de nouveau bien orchestré et le Grand Prix de Monaco reprend désormais sa place incontournable au programme des courses de Formule 1. Une chose a changé : le départ est donné directement près du port, quelques centaines de mètres avant le virage du Gazomètre.

Comme le vieux renard Luigi Villoresi et le jeune espoir Eugenio Castellotti, Ascari est désormais l'un des mercenaires de Gianni Lancia, sur la D 50, que l'ingénieur Vittorio Jano a mis au monde en cinq mois. Une quatrième voiture est confiée par noblesse à l'autochtone Louis Chiron, âgé de 56 ans. A Monaco, il a déjà terminé premier, deuxième, troisième, quatrième et cinquième. Hasard ou coup de pouce du destin ? Cette fois-ci, il terminera sixième. Sur Ferrari, on trouve Giuseppe Farina et Maurice Trintignant (625/F1) ainsi que Piero Taruffi et l'Américain Harry Schell (555 Super Squalo), pour l'Officine Alfieri Maserati, avec des Tipo 250 F, ce sont les Français Jean Behra, l'Italien Luigi Musso et l'Argentin Roberto Mieres qui prennent le départ.

Mais les favorites sont les Mercedes W 196, qui ont déjà marqué de leur sceau la saison 1954, conduites par Juan Manuel Fangio, Stirling Moss et Hans Herrmann. Les trois mousquetaires sont décimés lors des essais du jeudi. A Massenet, devant le Casino, Herrmann coince sa voiture sous le garde-fou, manquant d'être décapité, mais s'en tire avec une fracture de la jambe. Il sera remplacé au pied levé par le Français André Simon, que l'on informe de sa chance par téléphone à l'hôtel Mirabeau. A maints égards, ce Grand Prix devait apporter des rebondissements inattendus.

Tout d'abord, Fangio mène jusqu'à la mi-temps, talonné par Moss – un cas de figure qui se répétera souvent ces années-là. Puis, soudain, le Britannique apparaît seul en tête, faisant comprendre d'un geste que la Mercedes de Fangio a été poussée au bord de la piste juste dans le virage de la Gare avec un essieu arrière défectueux. Il préserve son propre leadership pendant vingt tours. Puis la W 196 sort du tunnel dans un nuage de vapeur et parvient tout juste à regagner les stands : panne de moteur.

Vapeur que produit aussi la Lancia d'Ascari durant le même tour, mais pour une tout autre raison. A la chicane, son véhicule plonge dans le port. Freins fatigués ou, peut-être, une trace d'huile sur la piste ? Le pilote atteint un bateau de sauvetage au prix d'un crawl énergique, avant de mourir quelques jours plus tard dans une voiture d'essai à Monza. C'est maintenant Trintignant qui se retrouve en tête pour son plus grand étonnement, lui qui est dans le civil vigneron et maire de Vergèze, dans le département, tout proche, du Gard. Et ce ne sont pas non plus les attaques tardives d'Eugenio Castellotti qui le priveront de la victoire.

Life in the fast lane: under the bonnet of the transporter which is bringing Herrmann's crashed W196 back, the engine of the 300 SL allows a top speed of over 100 mph.

Doppeltes Flottchen: Unter der Haube des Transporters, der Herrmanns havarierten W196 zurückbringt, lauert das Triebwerk des 300 SL und sorgt für 160 Stundenkilometer Spitze.

Ne pas se fier aux apparences : sous le capot du camion qui ramène la W196 accidentée de Herrmann rugit un moteur de 300 SL qui permet d'atteindre 160 km/h.

N°	DRIVERS		ENTRANTS	CARS	ENGINES	PRACTICE RESULTS	RACE RESULTS
44	**Maurice Trintignant**	**F**	**Scuderia Ferrari**	**Ferrari 625**	**Ferrari 4L 2498 cc**	**9th: 1'44"4**	**1st: 2h58'09"7**
30	Eugenio Castellotti	I	Scuderia Lancia	Lancia D50	Lancia V8 2488 cc	4th: 1'42"0	2nd: 2h58'30"0
34	Jean Behra	F	Officine Alfieri Maserati S.A.	Maserati 250F	Maserati 6L 2494 cc	5th: 1'42"6	3rd: 99 laps (with Perdisa)
42	Giuseppe Farina	I	Scuderia Ferrari	Ferrari 625	Ferrari 4L 2498 cc	13th(14): 1'46"0	4th: 99 laps
28	Luigi Villoresi	I	Scuderia Lancia	Lancia D50	Lancia V8 2488 cc	6th(7): 1'43"7	5th: 99 laps
32	Louis Chiron	F	Scuderia Lancia	Lancia D50	Lancia V8 2488 cc	19th: 1'47"3	6th: 95 laps
10	Jacky Pollet	F	Equipe Gordini	Gordini 16	Gordini 6L 2473 cc	20th: 1'49"4	7th: 91 laps
48	Piero Taruffi	I	Scuderia Ferrari	Ferrari 555	Ferrari 4L 2498 cc	13th(15): 1'46"0	8th: 86 laps (with Frere)
6	Stirling Moss	GB	Daimler-Benz AG	Mercedes-Benz W196	Mercedes 8L 2496 cc	3rd: 1'41"2	9th: 81 laps
40	Cesare Perdisa	I	Officine Alfieri Maserati S.A.	Maserati 250F	Maserati 6L 2494 cc	11th: 1'45"6	R (with Behra)
26	Alberto Ascari	I	Scuderia Lancia	Lancia D50	Lancia V8 2488 cc	1st(2): 1'41"1	R
46	Harry Schell	USA	Scuderia Ferrari	Ferrari 555	Ferrari 4L 2498 cc	18th: 1'46"8	R
36	Roberto Mieres	RA	Officine Alfieri Maserati S.A.	Maserati 250F	Maserati 6L 2494 cc	6th: 1'43"7	R
12	Elie Bayol	F	Equipe Gordini	Gordini 16	Gordini 6L 2473 cc	16th: 1'46"5	R
2	Juan Manuel Fangio	RA	Daimler-Benz AG	Mercedes-Benz W196	Mercedes 8L 2496 cc	1st: 1'41"1	R
8	Robert Manzon	F	Equipe Gordini	Gordini 16	Gordini 6L 2473 cc	13th: 1'46"0	R
4	André Simon	F	Daimler-Benz AG	Mercedes-Benz W196	Mercedes 8L 2496 cc	10th: 1'45"5	R
18	Mike Hawthorn	GB	Vandervell Products	Vanwall VW1	Vanwall 4L 2490 cc	11th(12): 1'45"6	R
14	Louis Rosier	F	Ecurie Rosier	Maserati 250F	Maserati 6L 2494 cc	17th: 1'46"7	R
38	Luigi Musso	I	Officine Alfieri Maserati S.A.	Maserati 250F	Maserati 6L 2494 cc	8th: 1'44"3	R

(1) At the start Ascari's Lancia is sandwiched between the two Mercedes of Fangio and Moss. (2) Schell (Ferrari) and Villoresi (Lancia) in front of the crowded steep face of the Rocher. (3) Behra (Maserati) at Tobacconist's Corner. (4) Castellotti in a Lancia stays in front of Moss for a short time only, with Ascari following. (5) First place for Trintignant in a Ferrari, 18 seconds ahead of Castellotti.

(1) Beim Start steckt Ascaris Lancia im Sandwich der beiden Mercedes von Fangio und Moss. (2) Schell (Ferrari) und Villoresi (Lancia) vor der vollbesetzten Steilwand des Rocher. (3) Behra (Maserati) in der Tabakskurve. (4) Castellotti im Lancia kann sich nur kurz vor Moss halten. Ascari folgt. (5) Platz eins für Trintignant auf Ferrari, 18 Sekunden vor Castellotti.

(1) Au départ, la Lancia d'Ascari est prise en sandwich entre les deux Mercedes de Fangio et Moss. (2) Schell (Ferrari) et Villoresi (Lancia) devant la foule agglutinée sur la paroi du Rocher. (3) Behra (Maserati) au virage du Bureau de Tabac. (4) Castellotti sur Lancia ne résistera pas longtemps à Moss. Ascari s'engouffre dans la brèche. (5) Première place pour Trintignant sur Ferrari, avec 18 secondes d'avance sur Castellotti.

(1) Kindling: traces of Ascari's descent into the harbor and
(2) recovery of the dripping Lancia. (3) Smoke signals: Moss comes
to a halt with one of the rare engine failures of the W 196.
(4) Intensive contact: after Hans Herrmann's accident in qualifying,
his Mercedes-Benz is stuck under the balustrade at Massenet.

(1) Kleinholz: Spuren von Ascaris Abgang in den Hafen und
(2) Bergung des Lancia aus dem nassen Element. (3) Rauchzeichen:
Moss rollt aus mit einem der seltenen Motorschäden des W 196.
(4) Intensiver Kontakt: Nach dem Trainingsunfall von Hans
Herrmann steckt sein Mercedes-Benz bei Massenet in der
Balustrade.

(1) Débris : les traces du plongeon d'Ascari dans le port et (2) sa
Lancia repêchée de l'eau. (3) Signes de fumée : Moss est trahi par sa
W 196, dont c'est l'une des rares pannes de moteur. (4) Contact
intime : après son accident aux essais, Hans Herrmann percute les
balustrades avec sa Mercedes-Benz à Massenet.

3

4

1956

Undoubtedly, 13 May 1956 was not Juan Manuel Fangio's day, in fact it was a date which he would dearly like to have forgotten. One thing cannot be denied, however, with regard to the great Argentinian's appearance at the 14th Monaco Grand Prix: he provided high entertainment value.

This season, Fangio was driving under the sign of the *cavallino rampante*. His car was the latest version of the Ferrari-Lancia, and his stablemates, who were obliged to support him solidly from the beginning, were Luigi Musso, Eugenio Castellotti and Peter Collins. Stirling Moss, his partner at Mercedes-Benz the previous year, had become the leader of the Maserati team, and the rivalry between these two friends had the effect of pouring fuel on the fire of the Italian feud between the racing stable from Modena and the Scuderia from Maranello.

In addition to Moss, Jean Behra and Cesare Perdisa were at the wheel of Maserati 250Fs. Amédée Gordini, who had almost been brought to his knees by chronic money worries, gave his swansong with cars for Hernando da Silva Ramos, Elie Bayol, André Pilette and Robert Manzon. Four cars carried the livery of British racing green, two Vanwalls for Harry Schell and Maurice Trintignant and the two BRMs belonging to the Owen Racing Organisation for Tony Brooks and Mike Hawthorn. But the BRMs disappeared back into their transporters after practice, the men from Bourne being unable to come to grips with their engine problems, which left just 14 cars to line up at the start. Only 16 had been admitted to the race for safety reasons after the crashes of the previous years. The chicane had been narrowed for the same reason, which cost about two seconds per lap.

Yet the race still started with a crash. It was caused by Fangio, whose car swung wildly out of control after Sainte Dévote. His victims were Musso and Schell, who landed in the straw bales, while Castellotti, Collins and Behra managed to slip past unharmed. Now back in fifth place, Fangio took up the chase of Moss, who was in the lead, and he had moved up into second place by lap 32 when he banged his car again near the Tabac bend and bent a wheel. The number 20 Ferrari limped into the pits on lap 40, the driver got out and he could not be found for a while. Meanwhile, team manager Eraldo Sculati had the car repaired as best he could and gave it to Castellotti, whose own car had been forced to withdraw due to transmission problems. When Fangio reappeared, Sculati flagged Collins in and told him to vacate his seat for the Argentinian, who had regained his strength and composure and was soon back driving with his customary greatness. But Stirling Moss drove as if by magic that day and was in a class of his own, even if he did become embroiled in a collision with Perdisa towards the end. In the meantime, Fangio continued to race through the town with all his power and skill unleashed, coming ever closer to Moss during the remaining 46 laps until he was only six seconds behind him at the finish, after setting the best time of the day on his last lap. The aura of being the greatest is fed, too, by events such as these.

Der 13. Mai 1956 ist gewiß nicht der Tag des Juan Manuel Fangio, ein Datum, das er gerne vergessen würde wie das ganze Jahr, obwohl es ihm seine vierte Weltmeisterschaft beschert. Eines indessen kann man dem Auftritt des großen Argentiniers beim 14. Grand Prix de Monaco nicht absprechen: einen hohen Unterhaltungswert.

Fangio fährt in dieser Saison im Zeichen des *cavallino rampante*. Sein Arbeitsgerät: die neueste Version des Ferrari-Lancia, seine Stallgefährten, von vorneherein zu Solidarität verpflichtet: Luigi Musso, Eugenio Castellotti und Peter Collins. Stirling Moss, sein Partner bei Mercedes im Jahr zuvor, ist mittlerweile die Nummer eins bei Maserati. Die Rivalität der beiden befreundeten Gegner wirkt wie Benzin im Feuer des italienischen Bruderzwists zwischen dem Rennstall aus Modena und der Scuderia aus Maranello.

Im Maserati 250 F sitzen außer Moss Jean Behra und Cesare Perdisa. Amédée Gordini, von chronischen Geldsorgen fast schon in die Knie gezwungen, gibt seine Abschiedsvorstellung mit Wagen für Hernando da Silva Ramos, Elie Bayol, André Pilette und Robert Manzon. Vier Fahrzeuge sind in englischem Renngrün livriert, zwei Vanwall für Harry Schell und Maurice Trintignant und die beiden BRM der Owen Racing Organization von Tony Brooks und Mike Hawthorn. Sie verschwinden nach dem Training wieder im Transporter, da die Männer aus Bourne ihre Motorenprobleme nicht in den Griff bekommen. So stehen ganze 14 Wagen am Start. Nur 16 waren zugelassen, sicherheitshalber nach den Unfällen der vergangenen Jahre. Aus dem gleichen Grunde hat man die Schikane verengt, was pro Runde ungefähr zwei Sekunden kostet.

Dennoch beginnt das Rennen wieder mit einem Unfall. Täter ist Fangio mit einem wilden Schlenker hinter Sainte Dévote, die Opfer sind Musso und Schell, die in den Strohballen landen, während Castellotti, Collins und Behra ungeschoren vorbeischlüpfen. In Position fünf nimmt Fangio die Verfolgung des führenden Moss auf, liegt an zweiter Stelle, als er in der 32. Runde hinter der Tabakskurve erneut aneckt und ein Rad verbiegt. In der 40. Runde humpelt der Ferrari mit der Nummer 20 an die Box. Der Pilot steigt aus, ist eine Zeitlang unauffindbar. Rennleiter Eraldo Sculati läßt das Auto notdürftig herrichten und vertraut es Castellotti an, dessen eigener Wagen mit Getriebeschaden ausgefallen ist. Als Fangio wieder auftaucht, winkt Sculati Collins herein, der seinen Sitz für den Argentinier räumen muß. Der hat sich irgendwie regeneriert und zu seiner üblichen Größe zurückgefunden. Stirling Moss fährt vorn wie entrückt, eine Klasse für sich, auch wenn er gegen Ende noch in eine Kollision mit Perdisa verwickelt wird. Unterdessen tobt Fangio wie entfesselt durch die Stadt, nähert sich dem Briten in 46 Durchgängen bis auf sechs Sekunden, fährt in der letzten Runde noch die beste Zeit des Tages. Der Mythos, der Größte zu sein, lebt auch von solchen Pointen.

Le 13 mai 1956 n'est assurément pas le jour de Juan Manuel Fangio, une date qu'il oublierait tout aussi volontiers que l'année entière bien que celle-ci lui ait valu son quatrième titre de champion du monde. Il est en tout cas une chose que l'on ne peut pas contester à la prestation du grand Argentin lors du 14ᵉ Grand Prix de Monaco : il aura bien amusé la galerie.

Cette saison-là, Fangio conduit sous le signe du *cavallino rampante*. Sa monture est la toute dernière version de la Ferrari-Lancia et il a pour coéquipiers, contraints par contrat à faire preuve de solidarité, Luigi Musso, Eugenio Castellotti et Peter Collins. Stirling Moss, son partenaire chez Mercedes l'année précédente, a été promu numéro 1 chez Maserati. La rivalité entre les deux adversaires et pourtant amis est comme de l'essence jetée dans le feu de la lutte fratricide italienne entre l'écurie de Modène et la Scuderia de Maranello.

Egalement aux commandes d'une Maserati 250 F, outre Moss, Jean Behra et Cesare Perdisa. Amédée Gordini, en permanence handicapé par l'étiage chronique dans sa trésorerie, donne sa représentation d'adieu avec des voitures confiées à Hernando da Silva Ramos, Elie Bayol, André Pilette et Robert Manzon. Quatre bolides arborent la livrée British Racing Green, deux Vanwall pour Harry Schell et Maurice Trintignant et les deux BRM de la Owen Racing Organization confiées à Tony Brooks et Mike Hawthorn. Après les essais, elles disparaissent immédiatement dans les camions, car les hommes de Bourne n'ont pas réussi à solutionner leurs problèmes de moteur. Ainsi ne voit-on s'aligner que quatorze voitures au départ. Seize seulement avaient été admises à la course, par mesure de sécurité, après les accidents des années précédentes. Pour le même motif, la chicane a été rendue plus étroite, ce qui coûte environ deux secondes au tour.

Et pourtant, la course débute de nouveau par un accident. Le coupable est Fangio, auteur d'un sauvage dérapage à la sortie de Sainte Dévote, et les victimes sont Musso et Schell, qui atterrissent dans les bottes de paille tandis que Castellotti, Collins et Behra parviennent à se faufiler sains et saufs. De la cinquième place, Fangio repart à la poursuite de Moss passé en tête et est lui-même deuxième lorsque, au trente-deuxième tour, à la sortie du virage du Bureau de Tabac, il tape à nouveau et voile une roue. Au quarantième tour, la Ferrari numéro 20 arrive aux stands en boitant. Le pilote descend et disparaît comme s'il s'était évaporé. Entretemps, le directeur de course, Eraldo Sculati, fait réparer tant bien que mal la voiture, qu'il confie à Castellotti, dont le propre bolide avait dû abandonner sur panne de boîte de vitesses. Lorsque Fangio réapparaît, Sculati ordonne à Collins de rentrer aux stands et de restituer son siège à l'Argentin. Celui-ci s'est régénéré on ne sait trop comment et se remet bientôt au volant avec son panache habituel. Cependant, Stirling Moss fait une course à part, dominant ses concurrents de la tête et des épaules, bien que, vers la fin, il soit encore impliqué dans une collision avec Perdisa. Pendant ce temps, Fangio, pilote déchaîné à travers la ville, se rapproche jusqu'à six secondes du Britannique en quarante-six tours, signant encore le meilleur temps du jour au dernier tour. Le mythe du plus grand vit également de telles performances.

Musical cars: in the second half of the race, Castellotti in Fangio's car is leading Fangio in Collins' car.

Vexierspiel: Hier liegt in der zweiten Hälfte des Rennens Castellotti im Ferrari Fangios vor Fangio im Ferrari von Collins.

Chaises musicales : ici, durant la seconde moitié de la course, Castellotti dans la Ferrari de Fangio mène devant Fangio dans la Ferrari de Collins.

N°	DRIVERS		ENTRANTS	CARS	ENGINES	PRACTICE RESULTS	RACE RESULTS
28	**Stirling Moss**	**GB**	**Officine Alfieri Maserati S.A.**	**Maserati 250F**	**Maserati 6L 2494 cc**	**2nd: 1'44"6**	**1st: 3h00'32"9**
26	Peter Collins	GB	Scuderia Ferrari	Ferrari-Lancia D50	Lancia V8 2488 cc	9th: 1'47"0	2nd: 3h00'39"0 (with Fangio)
30	Jean Behra	F	Officine Alfieri Maserati S.A.	Maserati 250F	Maserati 6L 2494 cc	4th: 1'45"3	3rd: 99 laps
20	*Juan Manuel Fangio*	*RA*	*Scuderia Ferrari*	*Ferrari-Lancia D50*	*Lancia V8 2488 cc*	*1st: 1'44"0*	*4th: 94 laps (with Castellotti)*
6	"Nano" da Silva Ramos	BR	Equipe Gordini	Gordini T16	Gordini 6L 2473 cc	10th: 1'50"0	5th: 93 laps
4	Elie Bayol	F	Equipe Gordini	Gordini T32	Gordini 8L 2474 cc	10th(11): 1'50"0	6th: 88 laps (with Pilette)
32	Cesare Perdisa	I	Officine Alfieri Maserati S.A.	Maserati 250F	Maserati 6L 2494 cc	7th: 1'46"0	7th: 86 laps
18	Horace H. Gould	GB	Goulds' Garage	Maserati 250F	Maserati 6L 2494 cc	14th: 1'51"7	8th: 85 laps
2	Robert Manzon	F	Equipe Gordini	Gordini T16	Gordini 6L 2473 cc	12th: 1'50"3	R
8	Louis Rosier	F	Ecurie Rosier	Maserati 250F	Maserati 6L 2494 cc	13th: 1'51"6	R
22	Eugenio Castellotti	I	Scuderia Ferrari	Ferrari-Lancia D50	Lancia V8 2488 cc	3rd: 1'44"9	R
14	Maurice Trintignant	F	Vandervell Products	Vanwall VW2	Vanwall 4L 2490 cc	5th(6): 1'45"6	R
24	Luigi Musso	I	Scuderia Ferrari	Ferrari-Lancia D50	Lancia V8 2488 cc	8th: 1'46"8	R
16	Harry Schell	USA	Vandervell Products	Vanwall VW1	Vanwall 4L 2490 cc	5th: 1'45"6	R

(1) In good company: at the start Moss (Maserati) is flanked by the two Ferraris with Fangio and Castellotti at the wheel. (2) Black day for the champion: Fangio in his damaged car. (3, 4) Mature performance: six years after his success in the Formula 3 race, Stirling Moss wins the Monaco Grand Prix. The Maserati also reveals traces of combat. (5) Chiron does not qualify but he enjoys the champagne just the same.

(1) Gute Nachbarschaft: Beim Start wird Moss (Maserati) flankiert von den beiden Ferrari mit Fangio und Castellotti am Lenkrad. (2) Schwarzer Tag für den Champion: Fangio in seinem lädierten Auto. (3, 4) Reife Leistung: Sechs Jahre nach seinem Erfolg im Rahmenrennen der Formel 3 siegt Moss beim Großen Preis von Monaco. Auch der Maserati trägt Kampfspuren. (5) Chiron kann sich nicht qualifizieren. Aber den Champagner genießt er noch immer.

(1) Bon voisinage : au départ, Moss (Maserati) est escorté par les deux Ferrari de Fangio et Castellotti. (2) Journée noire pour le champion : Fangio dans sa voiture endommagée. (3, 4) Belle prestation : six ans après son succès à la course de Formule 3 en levée de rideau, Moss remporte le Grand Prix de Monaco. La Maserati porte aussi des traces de lutte. (5) Chiron ne parvient pas à se qualifier, mais il n'en apprécie pas moins le champagne.

2

1957

Exceptionally, the 15th edition of the Monaco Grand Prix, on 19 May 1957, was run over 105 laps to ensure that the race really would take three hours. Once again some minor changes had been made to the chicane, but it remained what it had previously been – a pressure point and a natural stage for drama and tragi-comedy. The protagonists were the same as in the previous year, but the script was radically rewritten, if only because the merry-go-round of drivers had revolved in the interim.

Fangio was now driving for the Officine Alfieri Maserati in his final season, still every inch a superstar, in whose shadow his team colleagues Harry Schell, Carlos Menditeguy and Giorgio Scarlatti were in another class. The simple designation 801 represented the most recent metamorphosis of the former Lancia D 50, which had now been taken completely into the Ferrari family. The Scuderia entered four cars, for Peter Collins, Mike Hawthorn, Maurice Trintignant and Count Wolfgang von Trips. Further strengthened and eminently suited for the battle for the lead were the Vanwalls for Stirling Moss and the speeding dentist Tony Brooks.

A small sensation was caused by the Cooper T 43, which the British racing stable owner and private entrant Rob Walker had entered for the rising Australian Jack Brabham. It was a delicate little mid-engined car, although this was not the first time that such a layout had been seen in Grand Prix racing – 20 years previously the enormous 16-cylinder engines of Auto Union had performed their task mounted right behind the driver.

At the start of the race, Fangio and Moss thrust through the gasometer bend, still side-by-side with Collins, all three of them having started from the front row. Moss, showing little respect, overtook the World Champion on the inside at Sainte Dévote, and one lap later Collins, too, passed him on the rise to the Casino. On the fourth lap Moss was too fast in his approach to the chicane and sand bags and barriers flew in all directions. It was too late for Collins, who was right on his heels, and his car crashed into the left barrier. Fangio, guided once again by his sixth sense, managed to get through, but Brooks braked sharply when he saw the wreckage and Mike Hawthorn, behind him, could not take evasive action and touched the Vanwall. His Ferrari was driven like a wedge into the small gap between Collins' car and the harbor, while his severed front wheel splashed into the water.

Tony Brooks continued his drive behind Fangio in second position, which he kept to the end. Fangio, however, did what he liked best, controlling the race from the front. Nor was he wrong-footed when he was no longer able to change into second gear from lap 85 onwards. The slowest time, approximately ten minutes, was recorded by Brabham, who pushed his Cooper from the tunnel all the way to the finishing line with a faulty fuel pump. This gallant effort was sufficient for him to claim sixth place as a down payment on a great future.

Die 15. Auflage des Grand Prix de Monaco am 19. Mai 1957 geht über 105 Runden, ausnahmsweise, damit die Show auch wirklich drei Stunden währt. Wieder hat man ein wenig an der Schikane retuschiert. Sie bleibt trotzdem, was sie ist: Ein neuralgischer Punkt, wie geschaffen zur Schaubühne für Drama und Tragikomödie. Die Protagonisten sind dieselben wie im Jahr zuvor, das Skript hingegen wurde radikal umgeschrieben, schon weil sich in der Zwischenzeit das Fahrerkarussell gedreht hat.

Fangio startet für die Officine Alfieri Maserati, jeder Zoll ein Superstar, in dessen Schatten seine Teamkollegen Harry Schell, Carlos Menditeguy und Giorgio Scarlatti zu bloßen Wasserträgern verkümmern. Auf den schlichten Namen 801 hört die letzte Metamorphose des Lancia D 50, der nun endgültig in die Ferrari-Familie aufgenommen ist. Vier Exemplare setzt die Scuderia ein, für Peter Collins, Mike Hawthorn, Maurice Trintignant und Graf Berghe von Trips. Weiter erstarkt und durchaus geeignet für den Kampf um die Spitze: die Vanwall für Stirling Moss und den rasenden Zahnarzt Tony Brooks.

Eine kleine Sensation rührt der Cooper T 43 auf, den der britische Rennstallbesitzer und Berufs-Gentleman Rob Walker für den aufstrebenden Australier Jack Brabham gemeldet hat, ein zierliches Wägelchen mit Mittelmotor. Sein Erscheinen ist gleichwohl keine Premiere – bereits die riesigen Sechzehnzylinder der Auto Union 20 Jahre zuvor verrichteten ihre Arbeit im Rücken des Piloten.

Durch die Gasometerkurve drängen sich Fangio und Moss, mit Collins aus der ersten Reihe gestartet, noch Seite an Seite. Der Brite überholt den Weltmeister respektlos innen in Sainte Dévote, und einen Durchgang später geht auch Collins auf der Steigung zum Casino an ihm vorbei. In der vierten Runde trifft Moss zu schnell an der Schikane ein. Sandsäcke und lange Balken fliegen in alle Richtungen. Zu spät für Collins, der ihm auf dem Fuße folgt: Sein Wagen knallt in die Barriere links der Fahrbahn. Fangio, wie von einem siebten Sinn geleitet, kommt durch. Brooks aber bremst beim Anblick des Trümmerfelds vor ihm scharf. Hinter ihm kann Mike Hawthorn nicht ausweichen und touchiert den Vanwall. Sein Ferrari wird wie ein Keil in die schmale Lücke zwischen dem Fahrzeug von Collins und das Hafenbecken getrieben, während das rechte Vorderrad in das aufspritzende Wasser klatscht.

Tony Brooks setzt seine Fahrt fort, hinter Fangio an zweiter Position, die er bis zum Ende hält. Der jedoch tut, was er am liebsten tut: Er kontrolliert das Rennen von der Spitze her und läßt sich auch nicht aus dem Tritt bringen, als sich ab Runde 85 der zweite Gang nicht mehr einlegen läßt. Die langsamste Zeit, ungefähr zehn Minuten, geht auf das Konto von Brabham, der seinen Cooper mit defekter Benzinpumpe vom Tunnel bis zur Ziellinie schiebt. Dennoch: Es reicht zu einem sechsten Rang, als Anzahlung auf Größeres in Zukunft.

La 15ᵉ édition du Grand Prix de Monaco, le 19 mai 1957, est programmée sur 105 tours, à titre exceptionnel, pour que le show dure vraiment trois heures. Une fois de plus, on a un peu retouché la chicane. Elle reste malgré tout ce qu'elle est : un point névralgique taillé sur mesure comme scène de drames et de tragi-comédies. Les protagonistes sont les mêmes que l'année précédente, mais le scénario, lui, a été réécrit de fond en comble, ne serait-ce que parce que, entre-temps, le manège des pilotes a continué de tourner.

Superstar jusqu'au bout des ongles, Fangio court à présent sa dernière saison pour l'Officine Alfieri Maserati, avec, dans son ombre, ses coéquipiers Harry Schell, Carlos Menditeguy et Giorgio Scarlatti réduits aux rôles de simples seconds couteaux. La dernière métamorphose de l'ancienne Lancia D 50, désormais adoptée définitivement dans la famille Ferrari, a reçu le sobre nom de baptême 801. La Scuderia en engage quatre exemplaires, pour Peter Collins, Mike Hawthorn, Maurice Trintignant et le comte Wolfgang von Trips. De nouveau plus puissantes et tout à fait aptes à se battre pour la lutte en tête : les Vanwall de Stirling Moss et du dentiste le plus rapide du monde, Tony Brooks.

Une petite sensation est la Cooper T 43 que le propriétaire d'écurie et gentleman driver britannique Rob Walker a inscrite pour un Australien en pleine ascension, Jack Brabham : une minuscule petite voiture à moteur central. Cette architecture n'est pourtant pas révolutionnaire : les gigantesques seize-cylindres d'Auto Union tournaient déjà, vingt ans auparavant, derrière la nuque de leur pilote.

Dans le virage du Gazomètre, Fangio et Moss, partis en première ligne avec Collins, sont encore côte à côte. Sans le moindre respect, le Britannique fait l'intérieur au champion du monde à Sainte Dévote et, un tour plus tard, Collins aussi le double dans la montée du Casino. Au quatrième tour, Moss entre trop vite dans la chicane. Des sacs de sable et des poutres volent à travers les airs. Trop tard pour Collins qui le talonnait : sa voiture percute de plein fouet la barrière à gauche de la piste. Fangio, comme guidé par un pressentiment, se faufile. Mais, à la vue du champ de ruines devant lui, Brooks écrase la pédale de freins. Derrière lui, Mike Hawthorn ne peut plus l'éviter et touche la Vanwall. Sa Ferrari est poussée comme un coin dans le mince trou entre la voiture de Collins et le bassin du port tandis la roue avant droite amputée plonge dans l'eau dans de grandes éclaboussures.

Tony Brooks poursuit sa course échevelée, deuxième derrière Fangio, position qu'il détiendra jusqu'au drapeau à damier. Son adversaire fait cependant ce qui lui convient le mieux : il contrôle la course depuis la tête et ne se départit pas non plus de son calme même lorsque la seconde ne se laisse plus passer à partir du 85ᵉ tour. Le tour le plus lent, d'une dizaine de minutes, est à inscrire au passif de Brabham, qui pousse sa Cooper en panne de pompe à essence du tunnel jusqu'à la ligne d'arrivée. Cette noble endurance lui vaut une sixième place, acompte sur les résultats brillants que lui réserve l'avenir.

N°	DRIVERS		ENTRANTS	CARS	ENGINES	PRACTICE RESULTS	RACE RESULTS
32	*Juan Manuel Fangio*	*RA*	*Officine Alfieri Maserati S.A.*	*Maserati 250F*	*Maserati 6L 2494 cc*	*1st: 1'42"7*	*1st: 3h10'12"8*
20	Tony Brooks	GB	Vandervell Products	Vanwall VW7/V1	Vanwall 4L 2490 cc	4th: 1'44"4	2nd: 3h10'38"0
2	Masten Gregory	USA	Scuderia Centro Sud	Maserati 250F	Maserati 6L 2494 cc	10th: 1'48"4	3rd: 103 laps
10	Stuart Lewis-Evans	GB	Connaught Engineering	Connaught B	Alta GP 4L 2472 cc	14th: 1'49"1	4th: 102 laps
30	Maurice Trintignant	F	Scuderia Ferrari	Ferrari 801	Lancia V8 2495 cc	6th: 1'46"7	5th: 100 laps
14	Jack Brabham	AUS	Cooper Car Co.	Cooper T43	Climax FPF 4L 1967 cc	13th: 1'48"8	6th: 100 laps
24	Wolfgang von Trips	D	Scuderia Ferrari	Ferrari 801	Lancia V8 2495 cc	9th: 1'48"2	R (with Hawthorn)
34	Giorgio Scarlatti	I	Officine Alfieri Maserati S.A.	Maserati 250F	Maserati 6L 2494 cc	15th: 1'49"4	R (with Schell)
6	Ron Flockhart	GB	Owen Racing Organisation	BRM P25	BRM 4L 2491 cc	11th: 1'48"6	R
36	Carlos Menditeguy	RA	Officine Alfieri Maserati S.A.	Maserati 250F	Maserati 6L 2494 cc	6th(7): 1'46"7	R
12	Ivor Bueb	GB	Connaught Engineering	Connaught B	Alta GP 4L 2472 cc	16th: 1'49"4	R
38	Harry Schell	USA	Officine Alfieri Maserati S.A.	Maserati 250F	Maserati 6L 2494 cc	8th: 1'47"3	R
22	Horace H. Gould	GB	Goulds' Garage	Maserati 250F	Maserati 6L 2494 cc	12th: 1'48"7	R
28	Mike Hawthorn	GB	Scuderia Ferrari	Ferrari-Lancia D50	Lancia V8 2495 cc	5th: 1'46"4	R
26	Peter Collins	GB	Scuderia Ferrari	Ferrari 801	Lancia V8 2495 cc	2nd: 1'43"3	R
18	Stirling Moss	GB	Vandervell Products	Vanwall VW3/V4	Vanwall 4L 2490 cc	3rd: 1'43"6	R

(1) Masten at Massenet: the American Masten Gregory in the Maserati in front of the Casino. (2) Traffic jam at the gasometer: at the front, Fangio (Maserati) and Moss (Vanwall) are already powering away. (3) During qualifying only, Fangio tries out a Maserati with a twelve-cylinder engine. He is more than six seconds faster in the six-cylinder. (4) Sideways glance: slight drift for Fangio. (5) Rearing to go: Jack Brabham at the Monaco debut of the rear-engined Cooper-Climax.

(1) Masten im Maserati eingangs Massenet: der Amerikaner Gregory vor dem Casino. (2) Getümmel am Gasometer: Vorn pfeilen bereits Fangio (Maserati) und Moss (Vanwall) davon. (3) Nur im Training versucht Fangio sein Heil in einem Maserati mit zwölf Zylindern. Mit dem Sechszylinder ist er über drei Sekunden schneller. (4) Seitenblick: Fangio in leichtem Drift. (5) Mit Eifer bei der Sache: Jack Brabham beim Monaco-Debüt des Cooper-Climax mit Heckmotor.

(1) Masten, sur Maserati, à l'entrée de Massenet : l'Américain Gregory devant le Casino. (2) Embouteillage au Gazomètre : en tête, Fangio (Maserati) et Moss (Vanwall) s'échappent déjà. (3) Il n'y a qu'aux essais que Fangio pilotera la Maserati douze-cylindres. Avec la six-cylindres, il est plus rapide de trois secondes. (4) Coup d'œil de côté : Fangio en léger dérapage. (5) Concentré au travail : Jack Brabham lors des débuts à Monaco de la Cooper-Climax à moteur-arrière.

(1) Fraternally united: the Ferraris of Hawthorn (number 28) and Collins rest motionless in the barriers while Trintignant's is still very much mobile. (2) Fangio and his friend Harry Schell. (3) Casual clothes: the Britons Hawthorn, Brooks and Moss. (4) Unwrapped and ready for action: the Ferrari-Lancia 801 to be driven by Count Berghe von Trips. (5) Garaged cars: the two Maseratis of Menditeguy and Scarlatti.

(1) Brüderlich vereint: Die Ferrari von Hawthorn (Nummer 28) und Collins ruhen reglos im Gebälk, während das Exemplar von Trintignant noch sehr mobil ist. (2) Fangio und sein Freund Harry Schell. (3) Liberale Kleiderordnung: die drei Briten Hawthorn, Brooks und Moss. (4) Ausgepackt und angepackt: der Ferrari-Lancia 801, den Graf Trips pilotieren wird. (5) Garagenwagen: die beiden Maserati von Menditeguy und Scarlatti.

(1) Unies dans l'adversité : les Ferrari de Hawthorn (numéro 28) et Collins réduites au chômage se font doubler par celle de Trintignant. (2) Fangio et son ami Harry Schell. (3) Tenue décontractée : les trois Britanniques Hawthorn, Brooks et Moss. (4) Déballage : la Ferrari-Lancia 801 que va piloter le Comte von Trips. (5) Pour une fois au garage : les deux Maserati de Menditeguy et Scarlatti.

1958

The face of Formula 1 changed at the end of the Fifties. Apart from the impressive Mercedes-Benz interlude in the middle of the decade, it was the Alfa Romeos, the Ferraris and the Maseratis in their various interpretations of Italian racing red which set the tone. But now English became the *lingua franca* in the pits, exported to the Grand Prix tracks by marques such as Vanwall, BRM, Lotus, Connaught and Cooper. At the same time the rear-engine revolution started by Britain's John Cooper shook deeply-rooted structures.

The first race of the 1958 season, on 18 January in Buenos Aires, was won by Stirling Moss with the Cooper of the racing stable owner Rob Walker, painted in his distinctive colors of dark blue with a white ring on the nose. The starting line-up and the results list for the Monaco Grand Prix on 18 May were an accurate reflection of the comparative strengths in the current season. Ten of the 16 participants came from the British Isles, including the five fastest in qualifying. The engine was placed behind the driver in the three Coopers, and four of the five cars in the points positions were made in the British factories at which Enzo Ferrari turned up his nose so pointedly.

At the wheel of his Dino 246s, with their potent V6 engines, were Mike Hawthorn, Peter Collins, Luigi Musso and Wolfgang von Trips. The Vanwalls, specially adapted with their short noses for combat at close quarters along the boulevards and avenues, were driven by Moss, Tony Brooks and Stuart Lewis-Evans. The Cooper Car Company entered Jack Brabham and Roy Salvadori, whose passport in the future was to show him to have become a citizen of Monaco. Maurice Trintignant sat at the wheel of the winning car from Argentina, Jean Behra and Harry Schell started for BRM, and Cliff Allison for Lotus, together with a certain Graham Hill, who had managed to make the social promotion from mechanic to driver.

The usual chaos at the start resulted in Salvadori's Cooper rushing to the front and arriving too fast at the gasometer bend, where it briefly deviated from the ideal line by heading towards Nice and playing no further part thereafter. Behra led for 25 laps until his BRM was forced into the pits with chronic brake problems. Three laps later the Frenchman with the plastic ear – a reminder of an earlier accident – had to give up. This meant that Mike Hawthorn's hour had come, after he had moved irresistibly from the sixth place on the starting grid into the lead. But earlier, another driver had been doing even better: Moss, to whom Hawthorn had had to give way between laps 32 and 38, before defective valves stranded the Vanwall on the track. But the writing was soon on the wall for Hawthorn as well. Shortly before half-distance the Ferrari rolled to a halt with its fuel pump dangling loose. Now the wheel of fortune pointed at starting number 20, the blue Cooper of Maurice Trintignant. In a case of *déjà vu,* the small Frenchman was able to transform the bad luck of others into his own good luck for the second time since 1955 to become, after Fangio, the second man to have won the Monaco Grand Prix twice.

Ende der Fünfziger hat sich das Antlitz der Formel 1 gewandelt. Abgesehen von dem furiosen Mercedes-Intermezzo Mitte des Jahrzehnts haben die Alfa Romeo, die Ferrari und die Maserati mit ihren unterschiedlichen Interpretationen von italienischem Rennrot den Ton angegeben. Nun aber wird Englisch zur *lingua franca* der Boxengasse, an die Grand-Prix-Pisten exportiert von Marken wie Vanwall, BRM, Lotus, Connaught und Cooper. Zugleich erschüttert die Heckmotor-Revolution, die der Brite John Cooper angezettelt hat, tief eingewurzelte Strukturen.

Das erste Rennen der Saison 1958 am 18. Januar in Buenos Aires gewinnt Stirling Moss mit dem Cooper des Rennstalleigners Rob Walker in dessen markanten Farben, dunkelblau mit einem weißen Nasenring. Startaufstellung und Ergebnisliste des Grand Prix de Monaco am 18. Mai bilden die neuen Kräfteverhältnisse getreulich ab. Zehn der 16 Teilnehmer sind Produkte von der Insel, darunter die fünf Trainingsschnellsten. In den drei Cooper siedelt das Triebwerk im Rücken des Fahrers. Vier von den fünf Fahrzeugen in den Punkterängen sind in den englischen Manufakturen entstanden, über die Enzo Ferrari so hartnäckig die Nase rümpft.

Seine Dino 246 mit ihren potenten V6-Motoren werden gelenkt von Mike Hawthorn, Peter Collins, Luigi Musso und Graf Berghe von Trips. Die Vanwall, mit kurzen Nasen speziell auf den Nahkampf auf Boulevards und Avenuen abgerichtet, fahren Moss, Tony Brooks und Stuart Lewis-Evans. Die Cooper Car Company meldet Jack Brabham und Roy Salvadori, den sein Paß später einmal als Bürger von Monaco ausweisen wird. Maurice Trintignant sitzt am Volant des Siegerwagens von Argentinien. Für BRM starten Jean Behra und Harry Schell, für Lotus Cliff Allison und ein gewisser Graham Hill, dem der soziale Aufstieg vom Mechaniker zum Piloten gelungen ist.

Das übliche Chaos nach dem Start spült Salvadoris Cooper nach vorn, der sich an der Gasometerkurve mit überschüssigem Tempo kurz Richtung Nizza von der Ideallinie absetzt, und später keine Rolle mehr spielt. 25 Runden lang führt Behra, bis den BRM seine chronischen Probleme mit den Bremsen an die Box zwingen. Drei Durchgänge später scheidet der Franzose mit der Ohrprothese aus. Damit schlägt die Stunde des Mike Hawthorn, der sich vom sechsten Startplatz aus schier unwiderstehlich den Platz an der Spitze erobert hat. Einer kann's noch besser: Moss, den der Dino-Pilot zwischen der 32. und der 38. Runde vorbeilassen muß, bis defekte Ventile den Vanwall auf der Strecke stranden lassen. Doch auch für Hawthorn erscheint die Schrift an der Wand: Acht Minuten vor Halbzeit rollt der Ferrari mit baumelnder Benzinpumpe aus. Damit zeigt das Rad der Fortuna auf die Startnummer 20, den blauen Cooper von Maurice Trintignant. Wie sich die Bilder gleichen: Zum zweiten Mal nach 1955 vermag der kleine Franzose mit dem Menjoubärtchen das Pech der anderen in sein eigenes Glück umzumünzen, nach Fangio der zweite Doppelsieger in der Chronik des Rennens.

A la fin des années Cinquante, la face de la Formule 1 s'est métamorphosée. Abstraction faite du furieux intermède des Mercedes dès le milieu de la décennie, ce sont les Alfa Romeo, les Ferrari et les Maserati qui ont donné le ton avec leurs interprétations différentes du rouge course italien. Désormais, l'anglais devient la *lingua franca* dans la voie des stands, exporté sur les pistes de Grands Prix par des marques comme Vanwall, BRM, Lotus, Connaught et Cooper. Simultanément, la révolution du moteur arrière déclenchée par le Britannique John Cooper rompt des structures profondément enracinées.

La première course de la saison 1958, le 18 janvier à Buenos Aires, est le butin de Stirling Moss, avec la Cooper du propriétaire d'écurie Rob Walker dans ses couleurs significatives, bleu foncé avec un museau blanc. La grille de départ et le classement du Grand Prix de Monaco, le 18 mai, reflètent fidèlement les nouveaux rapports de force. Dix des seize participants sont de purs produits de la fière Albion, dont les cinq plus rapides aux essais. Dans les trois Cooper, le moteur est placé dans le dos du pilote. Quatre des cinq voitures qui terminent dans les points sont la création de ceux qu'Enzo Ferrari qualifie, non sans une certaine condescendance, de « garagistes » anglais.

Ses Dino 246 avec leur puissant moteur V6 sont pilotées par des hommes de la trempe d'un Mike Hawthorn, Peter Collins, Luigi Musso et du comte Berghe von Trips. Les Vanwall, que leurs nez tronqués prédestinent pour la lutte rapprochée sur les boulevards et les avenues, sont confiées à Stirling Moss, Tony Brooks et Stuart Lewis-Evans. La Cooper Car Company a inscrit Jack Brabham et Roy Salvadori, dont le passeport le légitimera plus tard comme citoyen de Monaco. Maurice Trintignant est au volant de la voiture victorieuse en Argentine. Jean Behra et Harry Schell défendent les couleurs de BRM comme le font, pour Lotus, Cliff Allison et un certain Graham Hill qui a réussi une promotion sociale de mécanicien à pilote.

Le chaos traditionnel du départ voit la Cooper de Salvadori partir en tête avant de faire des infidélités à la trajectoire, prenant brièvement la direction de Nice, pour avoir abordé trop vite le virage du Gazomètre. Il ne jouera dès lors plus aucun rôle. Pendant 25 tours, Jean Behra est en tête jusqu'à ce que les problèmes chroniques de fin contraignent le BRM à rejoindre les stands. Trois tours plus tard, le Français à l'oreille en plastique, reliquat d'un précédent accident, jette l'éponge. C'est alors que sonne l'heure de Mike Hawthorn, qui a gagné place par place et grimpe irrésistiblement de la sixième à la première. Mais un autre adversaire est encore meilleur : Moss, auquel le pilote de la Dino doit laisser le leadership du 32e au 38e tour avant qu'une rupture de soupape n'oblige la Vanwall à s'arrêter au bord du circuit. Mais le destin ne réserve pas un meilleur sort non plus à Mike Hawthorn : huit minutes avant mi-course, la Ferrari termine sa démonstration avec une pompe à essence desserrée. La roue de la fortune s'arrête alors sur le numéro 20, la Cooper bleue de Maurice Trintignant. Comme l'histoire bégaie : pour la deuxième fois depuis 1955, le petit Français à la fine moustache profite du malheur des autres pour forger son propre bonheur et devenir, après Fangio, le second double vainqueur dans la chronique de la course.

N°	DRIVERS		ENTRANTS	CARS	ENGINES	PRACTICE RESULTS	RACE RESULTS
20	**Maurice Trintignant**	**F**	**RRC Walker Racing Team**	**Cooper T45**	**Climax FPF 4L 2015 cc**	**5th: 1'41"1**	**1st: 2h52'27"9**
34	Luigi Musso	I	Scuderia Ferrari	Ferrari Dino 246	Ferrari 6L 2417 cc	10th: 1'42"6	2nd: 2h52'48"1
36	Peter Collins	GB	Scuderia Ferrari	Ferrari Dino 246	Ferrari 6L 2417 cc	9th: 1'42"4	3rd: 2h53'06"7
16	Jack Brabham	AUS	Cooper Car Co.	Cooper T45	Climax FPF 4L 2207 cc	3rd: 1'41"0	4th: 97 laps
8	Harry Schell	USA	Owen Racing Organisation	BRM P25	BRM 4L 2497 cc	12th: 1'43"8	5th: 91 laps
24	Cliff Allison	GB	Team Lotus	Lotus 12	Climax FPF 4L 1960 cc	13th: 1'44"6	6th: 87 laps
40	Wolfgang von Trips	D	Scuderia Ferrari	Ferrari Dino 246	Ferrari 6L 2417 cc	11th: 1'43"7	R
58	Joakim Bonnier	S	Joakim Bonnier	Maserati 250F	Maserati 6L 2494 cc	16th: 1'45"0	R
26	Graham Hill	GB	Team Lotus	Lotus 12	Climax FPF 4L 1960 cc	15th: 1'45"0	R
18	Roy Salvadori	GB	Cooper Car Co.	Cooper T45	Climax FPF 4L 2015 cc	4th: 1'41"0	R
38	Mike Hawthorn	GB	Scuderia Ferrari	Ferrari Dino 246	Ferrari 6L 2417 cc	6th: 1'41"5	R
28	Stirling Moss	GB	Vandervell Products	Vanwall VW7	Vanwall 4L 2490 cc	8th: 1'42"3	R
6	Jean Behra	F	Owen Racing Organisation	BRM P25	BRM 4L 2497 cc	2nd: 1'40"8	R
46	Giorgio Scarlatti	I	Giorgio Scarlatti	Maserati 250F	Maserati 6L 2494 cc	14th: 1'44"7	R
30	*Tony Brooks*	*GB*	*Vandervell Products*	*Vanwall VW10*	*Vanwall 4L 2490 cc*	*1st: 1'39"8*	*R*
32	Stuart Lewis-Evans	GB	Vandervell Products	Vanwall VW5	Vanwall 4L 2490 cc	7th: 1'41"8	R

(1) At the start Jean Behra (BRM) is still a shade ahead of Brabham (Cooper number 16). (2) Today ahead of yesterday: the Vanwall of Lewis-Evans following behind the nimble Cooper of Trintignant looks clumsy by comparison. (3) Only sixth in practice, Hawthorn drives the fastest lap in the race. (4) Starting last: Bonnier in a private Maserati. (5) On the way to fourth place: Brabham in the factory Cooper.

(1) Noch liegt beim Start Jean Behra (BRM) vorn, eine Idee vor Brabham (Cooper Nummer 16). (2) Heute führt vor Gestern: Gegenüber dem wieselflinken Cooper von Trintignant wirkt der folgende Vanwall von Lewis-Evans klobig. (3) Nur sechster im Training, fährt Hawthorn (Ferrari) die schnellste Runde im Rennen. (4) Vom letzten Platz gestartet: Bonnier im privaten Maserati. (5) Auf dem Weg zu Rang vier: Brabham im Werks-Cooper.

(1) Juste après le départ, Jean Behra (BRM) est encore en tête, un soupçon devant Brabham (Cooper numéro 16). (2) Le présent devance le passé : par rapport à la minuscule Cooper de Trintignant, la Vanwall de Lewis-Evans qui le suit ressemble à un dinosaure. (3) Sixième seulement aux essais, Hawthorn (Ferrari) signe le tour le plus rapide en course. (4) Parti de la dernière place : Bonnier, sur une Maserati privée. (5) En route vers la quatrième place : Brabham au volant de la Cooper d'usine.

(1) As in 1955, luck lends a helping hand in Trintignant's victory. (2) Photo opportunity with cup and garland and (3) a moment of reflection during the anthem in front of the royal box.

(1) Wie 1955 hilft das Glück beim Sieg Trintignants etwas nach. (2) Fototermin mit Pokal und Kranz und (3) Andacht vor der Fürstenloge während der Marseillaise.

(1) Comme en 1955, la chance donne un coup de pouce à Trintignant pour la victoire. (2) Pose pour les photographes avec coupe et couronne de lauriers et (3) concentration devant la loge princière pendant que résonne la Marseillaise.

1959

Since the traditional race within the framework of the Argentinian Temporada had been removed from the schedule, the curtain on the 1959 Formula 1 World Championship season rose for the first time on 10 May: the 17th Monaco Grand Prix. The occasion was a time to reflect on recent losses. Within two years, Ferrari had lost their drivers de Portago, Castellotti, Musso and Collins, all of whom had died on the race track, while Mike Hawthorn, the new World Champion, had lost his life on 22 January 1959 after overtaking the racing stable owner Rob Walker on a wet road and crashing into a tree.

Jean Behra, Phil Hill and Tony Brooks were now driving Dino 246s revamped by Carlo Chiti for the red Scuderia and Cliff Allison was also driving for the Ferrari team in a 156/F2. Vanwall, having won the first World Championship for Constructors in 1958, had withdrawn because sadness at the loss of his driver Stuart Lewis-Evans in the Moroccan Grand Prix, on top of commercial pressures, had undermined the health of Tony Vanderwell, the company's sensitive owner.

Nevertheless, the British were strongly represented. There was the most recent evolution of the BRM P 25 for Harry Schell, Jo Bonnier and Ron Flockhart. There was the Lotus 16, nicknamed the mini-Vanwall, for Graham Hill. There were the factory Cooper T 51s of Jack Brabham, Bruce McLaren and Masten Gregory, as well as the private model of the Walker team for Stirling Moss. The genealogy of their in-line four-cylinder engines from Coventry Climax was a curious one in that they originated from a Second World War fire pump.

The situation in qualifying was not dissimilar to that on the labour market in the Nineties: 24 applicants fought for 16 places. A lady, the combative Italian Maria Teresa de Filippis, was among those who fell through the qualifying sieve, for the second time in two attempts. And as in the previous year, Jean Behra took the lead at the start and managed to keep it, as in 1958, for a quarter of the distance until his Ferrari would no longer play ball: it was retired with engine trouble. As early as lap 21 Moss found a way past him, followed a short while later by Jack Brabham, while Brooks and Schell were fighting for third place. There were no spectacular events on this occasion with the exception of a shunt at the exit from Sainte Dévote on the second lap, which eliminated the three Formula 2 cars which had qualified – the Porsche of von Trips, the Ferrari of Allison and the Lotus of Bruce Halford.

But the man of the meeting was Stirling Moss, as so often in Monaco. By lap 30 his lead over Brabham was 30 seconds, at half-time it was 40 seconds, and on the eightieth lap it was more than a minute. But then the Cooper began to vibrate, and Moss was left standing on the following lap with a damaged rear axle. The 33-year-old Jack Brabham, in the meantime, not to be outdone, set a new lap record on lap 83 before calmly finishing the race.

Prince Rainier and his wife, Princess Grace, presented the "quiet Australian" with a blossom-shaped cup. Being a frugal and economical person, he did not spill a single drop of the victory champagne for the first of his 14 Grand Prix wins.

Da der traditionelle Lauf im Rahmen der argentinischen Temporada aus dem Terminkalender gestrichen worden ist, hebt sich der Vorhang zur Saison 1959 erst vor dem 17. Grand Prix de Monaco am 10. Mai. Er wird in mancherlei Hinsicht von Verlusten geprägt. Ferrari hat im Schachspiel ohne Bedenkzeit gegen den Renntod binnen zwei Jahren die Piloten de Portago, Castellotti, Musso und Collins verloren. Mike Hawthorn, der neue Weltmeister, ist am 22. Januar 1959 bei einem mutwilligen Straßen-Duell gegen den Rennstallchef Rob Walker auf nasser Fahrbahn ums Leben gekommen.

Für die rote Scuderia fahren Jean Behra, Phil Hill und Tony Brooks in dem von Carlo Chiti überarbeiteten Dino 246 sowie Cliff Allison im 156/F2. Vanwall, immerhin Weltmeister der Konstrukteure 1958, hat sich zurückgezogen, weil Trauer über den Verlust seines Fahrers Stuart Lewis-Evans beim marokkanischen Grand Prix und Leistungsdruck die Gesundheit des sensiblen Firmeneigners Tony Vanderwell unterhöhlt haben.

Gleichwohl sind die Briten stark vertreten. Da ist die jüngste Evolutionsstufe des BRM P 25 für Harry Schell, Jo Bonnier und Ron Flockhart. Da ist der Lotus 16, genannt der Mini-Vanwall, für Graham Hill. Da sind die Werks-Cooper T 51 von Jack Brabham, Bruce McLaren und Masten Gregory sowie das private Exemplar des Walker-Teams von Stirling Moss. Die Genealogie ihrer Reihenvierzylinder von Coventry Climax liest sich kurios: Sie stammen ab von einer Feuerspritze des Zweiten Weltkriegs.

Die Situation im Training gleicht der Lage am Arbeitsmarkt der neunziger Jahre: 24 Aspiranten streiten sich um 16 Plätze. Durchs Schüttelrost der Qualifikation fällt unter anderen eine Dame, die wehrhafte Italienerin Maria Teresa de Filippis, zum zweiten Mal in zwei Anläufen. Und wie im Vorjahr übernimmt Jean Behra anfänglich die Spitze, hält diese wie 1958 über ein Viertel der Distanz, bis sein Ferrari nicht mehr mitmacht: Motordefekt. Bereits in der 21. Runde hat Moss einen Weg an ihm vorbeigefunden, bald darauf auch Jack Brabham, während sich Brooks und Schell um Rang drei streiten. Spektakuläre Begebenheiten bleiben diesmal aus, bis auf einen Auffahrunfall hinter Sainte Dévote im zweiten Durchgang, der die drei Formel-2-Wagen eliminiert, den Porsche von Graf Trips, den Ferrari von Allison, den Lotus von Bruce Halford.

Der Mann des Meetings aber heißt Stirling Moss, wie so oft in Monaco. In der 30. Runde beträgt sein Vorsprung vor Brabham 30 Sekunden, bei Halbzeit 40 Sekunden, in der 80. Runde über eine Minute. Doch dann beginnen Vibrationen den Cooper zu beuteln, der nach der folgenden Runde auf der Strecke bleibt: Schaden an der Hinterachse. Der 33jährige Jack Brabham indes läßt sich nicht lumpen, fährt im 83. Durchgang neuen Rundenrekord und das Rennen selbst in aller Ruhe zuende.

Prinz Rainier und Landesmutter Gracia Patricia überreichen dem »stillen Australier« einen blütenförmigen Pokal. Vom Champagner für seinen Sieg indessen, den ersten von insgesamt 14, vergießt er als haushälterischer und sparsamer Mensch keinen Tropfen.

Comme la manche traditionnelle dans le cadre de la Temporada argentine a été rayée du calendrier, le rideau pour la saison 1959 se lèvera pour la première fois sur le 17e Grand Prix de Monaco, le 10 mai. Un Grand Prix qui fait prendre conscience de nombreuses pertes. Ferrari a perdu en deux ans ses pilotes de Portago, Castellotti, Musso et Collins morts sur le circuit. Mike Hawthorn, nouveau champion du monde, s'est tué, le 22 Janvier 1959, en livrant un duel au chef d'écurie Rob Walker après avoir percuté un arbre sur une route glissante.

Pour la Scuderia rouge, Jean Behra et Tony Brooks pilotent la Dino 246 retravaillée par Carlo Chiti et Cliff Allison prend le volant d'une 156/F2. Vanwall, pourtant champion du monde des courses Constructeurs 1958, s'est retiré parce que la tristesse causée par la mort de son pilote Stuart Lewis-Evans au Grand Prix du Maroc ainsi que la pression commerciale avaient mis à mal la santé du sensible propriétaire de la firme, Tony Vanderwell.

La phalange des Britanniques est néanmoins des plus fortes. On y trouve l'évolution la plus récente de la BRM P 25 pour Harry Schell, Jo Bonnier et Ron Flockhart. Il y a aussi la Lotus 16, surnommée la mini-Vanwall, pour Graham Hill. Il y a enfin les Cooper d'usine T 51 Jack Brabham, Bruce McLaren et Masten Gregory ainsi que celle de l'écurie privée de Rob Walker avec Stirling Moss. La généalogie de leurs quatre-cylindres en ligne Coventry-Climax est pour le moins bizarre : ils descendent en droite ligne d'un camion de pompiers de la Seconde Guerre mondiale.

La sélection naturelle est des plus rudes lors des essais : 24 candidats se disputent les 16 places sur la grille. Une dame, notamment, tombera à travers le tamis des qualifications : la pugnace Italienne, Maria Teresa de Filippis, pour la deuxième fois en deux tentatives. Et, comme l'année précédente, Jean Behra occupe tout d'abord la tête, qu'il détient, comme en 1958, pendant plus d'un quart de la distance avant que sa Ferrari ne soit trahie par sa fiabilité : panne de moteur. Dès le 21e tour, Moss réussit à le doubler, ce que fait aussi Jack Brabham, tandis que Brooks et Schell se battent pour la troisième place. Les événements spectaculaires se font rares cette année-là, si ce n'est le carambolage derrière Sainte Dévote, au deuxième tour, qui élimine les trois voitures de Formule 2, la Porsche du comte von Trips, la Ferrari d'Allison et la Lotus de Bruce Halford.

L'homme du jour a pour nom Stirling Moss, comme si souvent à Monaco. Au 30e tour, son avance sur Brabham est de 30 secondes, et de 40 secondes à la mi-course et de plus d'une minute au 80e tour. Mais des vibrations commencent alors à ébranler la Cooper, qui ne termine même pas le tour suivant : panne de l'essieu arrière. Avec ses 33 ans, Jack Brabham ne se laisse pas impressionner, établit un nouveau record au 83e tour et termine la course elle-même dans le plus grand calme.

Le Prince Rainier et la First Lady Gracia Patricia remettent à l'« Australien taciturne » une coupe en forme de fleur. Connu pour sa parcimonie et son sens de l'économie, il ne perd pas une seule goutte du champagne de sa première victoire, la première d'une longue série de 14.

Magnificent background: Phil Hill in his Ferrari Dino; three laps behind, he will come fourth.

Vor großer Kulisse: Phil Hill im Ferrari Dino, der mit drei Runden Rückstand Platz vier belegen wird.

Panorama impressionnant : Phil Hill sur Ferrari Dino, qui terminera quatrième avec trois tours de retard.

N°	DRIVERS		ENTRANTS	CARS	ENGINES	PRACTICE RESULTS	RACE RESULTS
24	**Jack Brabham**	**AUS**	**Cooper Car Co.**	**Cooper T51**	**Climax FPF 4L 2495 cc**	**3rd: 1'40"1**	**1st: 2h55'51"3**
50	Tony Brooks	GB	Scuderia Ferrari	Ferrari Dino 246	Ferrari 6L 2417 cc	4th: 1'41"0	2nd: 2h56'11"7
32	Maurice Trintignant	F	RRC Walker Racing Team	Cooper T51	Climax FPF 4L 2495 cc	6th: 1'41"7	3rd: 98 laps
48	Phil Hill	USA	Scuderia Ferrari	Ferrari Dino 246	Ferrari 6L 2417 cc	5th: 1'41"3	4th: 97 laps
22	Bruce McLaren	NZ	Cooper Car Co.	Cooper T51	Climax FPF 4L 2207 cc	13th: 1'43"9	5th: 96 laps
38	Roy Salvadori	GB	High Efficiency Motors	Cooper T45	Maserati 4L 2494 cc	8th: 1'42"4	R
30	*Stirling Moss*	*GB*	*RRC Walker Racing Team*	*Cooper T51*	*Climax FPF 4L 2495 cc*	*1st: 1'39"6*	*R*
20	Ron Flockhart	GB	Owen Racing Organisation	BRM P25	BRM 4L 2497 cc	10th: 1'43"1	R
16	Harry Schell	USA	Owen Racing Organisation	BRM P25	BRM 4L 2497 cc	9th: 1'43"0	R
18	Joakim Bonnier	S	Owen Racing Organisation	BRM P25	BRM 4L 2497 cc	7th: 1'42"3	R
46	Jean Behra	F	Scuderia Ferrari	Ferrari Dino 246	Ferrari 6L 2417 cc	2nd: 1'40"0	R
40	Graham Hill	GB	Team Lotus	Lotus 16	Climax FPF 4L 2495 cc	14th: 1'43"9	R
26	Masten Gregory	USA	Cooper Car Co.	Cooper T45	Climax FPF 4L 2495 cc	11th: 1'43"2	R
44	Bruce Halford	GB	John Fisher	Lotus 16	Climax FPF 4L 1460 cc	16th: 1'44"8	R
52	Cliff Allison	GB	Scuderia Ferrari	Ferrari Dino 156	Ferrari V6 1489 cc	15th: 1'44"4	R
6	Wolfgang von Trips	D	Dr. Ing. hc. F. Porsche KG	Porsche F2-718	Porsche 4F 1498 cc	12th: 1'43"8	R

Jack Brabham (Cooper)

Tony Brooks (Ferrari)

Maurice Trintignant (Cooper)

Stirling Moss (Cooper)

Jean Behra (Ferrari)

Wolfgang von Trips (Porsche)

Joakim Bonnier (BRM)

(1) Third, but not for long: Schell (BRM) in front of Brooks at the station. (2) Hairy moment: Behra tries to keep his nose in front of Moss.

(1) Dritter, aber nicht für lange: Schell (BRM) vor Brooks am Bahnhof. (2) Schräg-Sekunde: Behra bemüht sich, die Spitze vor Moss zu halten.

(1) Troisième, mais pas pour longtemps : Schell (BRM) devant Brooks à la Gare. (2) Duel à couteaux tirés : Behra se défend bec et ongles contre Moss.

(1) The end for Graham Hill's Lotus (fire) and Schell's BRM (encounter with straw bales) in the same place. (2) Crumple zone: exit of the Formula 2 cars at Sainte Dévote. (3) Meeting of the old masters: Fangio, Farina, Etancelin and Taruffi. (4) Risk-taking at the side of the road: Monaco has not yet armored itself against its Grand Prix. (5) Under the eyes of the law: the Ferrari force…

(1) Ausfall für Graham Hills Lotus (Feuerchen) und Schells BRM (gegen die Strohballen verbogen) an der gleichen Stelle. (2) Knautsch-Zone: Exitus der Formel-2-Brigade bei Sainte Dévote. (3) Meeting der alten Meister: Fangio, Farina, Etancelin und Taruffi. (4) Vabanque am Wegessaum: Noch hat sich Monaco nicht gegen seinen Grand Prix gepanzert. (5) Unter den Augen des Gesetzes: die Ferrari-Streitmacht…

(1) Abandon pour la Lotus de Graham Hill (incendie) et la BRM de Schell (qui a percuté les bottes de paille) au même endroit. (2) Cimetière de voitures : quelques Formule 2 font leur sortie à Sainte Dévote. (3) Rencontre de grands champions : Fangio, Farina, Etancelin et Taruffi. (4) Inconscients du risque : Monaco ne s'est pas encore blindée contre son Grand Prix. (5) Sous les yeux de la loi : l'armada Ferrari…

3

4

2

5

1960

At the 18th Monaco Grand Prix, the last based on the 2.5-liter formula, 24 competitors were fighting for 16 places, as in the previous year, and by the late afternoon of 29 May only four serious contenders were left. The first casualty had occurred early in the meeting. Changing down while approaching the chicane during the hectic first training session, Cliff Allison accidentally changed from fifth into second gear. The rear wheels locked and the driver was catapulted out of the Ferrari and seriously injured as he landed on the concrete.

When, in the final stages of the Grand Prix, the points for fifth and sixth places beckoned, everything which could still move in any way at all limped, hobbled and bumped over the track. Joakim Bonnier (BRM) and Richie Ginther (Ferrari) won the "Grand Prix of the wounded", 17 and 30 laps respectively behind the victor Moss, their cars spread around the track like mobile chicanes.

But the period between these events also passed with the speed and ups and downs of a slapstick comedy. The cast included Phil Hill and Wolfgang von Trips with the Dino 246s for Ferrari; Ginther drove the 246 P (for posteriore), an interim model with the engine behind the driver. For Lotus: John Surtees, Alan Stacey and Innes Ireland in the new Type 18, which appeared very small. So keen was Moss on Colin Chapman's brilliant interpretation of the mid-engine principle that he persuaded his patron Rob Walker also to acquire a Lotus 18. Jack Brabham and Bruce McLaren started for Cooper with the T 53s, Bonnier, Graham Hill and Dan Gurney for BRM with the P 48s. There was one brief and unusual interloper: the Scarab of the American millionaire heir Lance Reventlow, who came, looked, failed to qualify, and was never seen again.

A lightning start from the second row put Bonnier in the lead. Behind him, Moss overtook Brabham on the fifth lap. Bonnier then used hand signals repeatedly to indicate to Moss that he should pass, but Stirling ignored him coolly until lap 17. Then, after quarter-distance, a rain shower made the track very slippery, creating exactly the right sort of conditions for Moss. But it was Brabham who went ahead from lap 34, although he spun into the wall near Sainte Dévote seven laps later, so once again the Englishman was in the lead. His car, however, required a 25-second pit stop after lap 60. The engine was misfiring and a spark plug lead had to be tightened. Moss needed eight laps before catching the escaping Swede again while braking at the approach to the chicane. And when the BRM entered the pits soon afterwards with broken rear suspension, the dark blue Lotus became unstoppable, Moss winning with a 52-seconds lead over Bruce McLaren and his Cooper.

Beim 18. Großen Preis von Monaco, dem letzten nach der Zweieinhalbliterformel, kämpfen wie im Jahr zuvor 24 Konkurrenten um 16 Startplätze, und am späten Nachmittag des 29. Mai sind nur noch vier Wagen wirklich im Rennen. Das birgt seine Gefahren und zeitigt seine Folgen. Beim Herunterschalten vor der Schikane in der Hektik schon des ersten Trainings geht der Brite Cliff Allison versehentlich vom fünften in den zweiten Gang. Die Hinterräder blockieren, der Pilot fliegt in hohem Bogen aus dem Ferrari und verletzt sich schwer beim Aufprall auf den Beton.

Als in der Endphase des Grand Prix die Punkte für den fünften und den sechsten Rang winken, hinkt, humpelt und holpert plötzlich alles wieder über den Kurs, was sich noch irgendwie bewegen kann. Joakim Bonnier (BRM) und Richie Ginther (Ferrari) gewinnen den Grand Prix der Defekten 17 beziehungsweise 30 Runden hinter dem Sieger Moss, gleichwohl als mobile Schikanen über die Strecke verstreut.

Aber auch die Zeit zwischen diesen Ereignissen läuft ab mit dem Tempo und den Turbulenzen einer Slapstickkomödie. Die Darsteller: für Ferrari Phil Hill und Graf Berghe von Trips mit dem Dino 246. Ginther fährt den 246 P (für posteriore), ein Interimsmodell mit dem Triebwerk hinter dem Fahrer. Für Lotus: John Surtees, Alan Stacey und Innes Ireland auf dem neuen, winzig wirkenden Typ 18. So angetan ist Moss von Colin Chapmans genialer Auslegung des Mittelmotor-Prinzips, daß er seinen Patron und Gönner Rob Walker dazu bewegt hat, ebenfalls einen Lotus 18 anzuschaffen. Für Cooper starten Jack Brabham und Bruce McLaren auf dem T 53, für BRM mit dem P 48 Bonnier, Graham Hill und Dan Gurney. Eine exotische Erscheinung: der Scarab des amerikanischen Millionenerben Lance Reventlow. Er kommt, sieht, qualifiziert sich nicht und läßt sich nie wieder blicken.

Mit einem Blitzstart aus der zweiten Reihe setzt sich Bonnier an die Spitze. Hinter ihm überholt Moss Brabham im fünften Durchgang. Immer wieder gibt Bonnier dem Briten durch Handzeichen zu verstehen, er könne vorbeifahren. Moss ignoriert sie kühl – bis zur 17. Runde. Nach einem Viertel der Distanz macht ein Schauer die Strecke schmierig, eigentlich Moss-Wetter. Ab Runde 34 führt indes Brabham, dreht sich sieben Durchgänge später bei Sainte Dévote in die Mauer. Wieder ist der Engländer vorn. Sein Auto bedarf allerdings nach dem 60. Durchgang für 25 Sekunden ambulanter Behandlung. Das Triebwerk hustet, ein Zündkabel muß befestigt werden. Acht Runden benötigt Moss, bis er sich den flüchtigen Schweden erneut geschnappt hat, beim Anbremsen der Schikane. Und während die BRM fürs erste mit gebrochener Hinterradaufhängung die Box anläuft, ist der dunkelblaue Lotus nicht zu bremsen, Stirling Moss siegt mit 52 Sekunden Vorsprung vor Bruce McLarens Cooper.

Lors du 18ᵉ Grand Prix de Monaco, le dernier organisé selon la formule 2,5 litres, 24 concurrents se sont, comme l'année précédente, disputé les seize places au départ et, en fin d'après-midi, le 29 mai, quatre voitures seulement sont encore réellement en course. Cela n'est pas sans danger et les conséquences se font attendre. En rétrogradant à l'entrée de la chicane dans la nervosité des premiers essais déjà, le Britannique Cliff Allison passe par mégarde de la cinquième à la deuxième. Les roues arrière se bloquent, le pilote sort de sa Ferrari en vol plané et atterrit, grièvement blessé, sur la piste en béton.

Lorsque, durant la phase terminale du Grand Prix, et que les points de la cinquième et de la sixième place sont à portée de la main, tout ce qui peut encore se mouvoir, d'une façon ou d'une autre, rampe, cahote, sautille et boitille soudain de nouveau sur le circuit. Joakim Bonnier (BRM) et Richie Ginther (Ferrari) gagnent ce Grand Prix des pannes avec, respectivement, 17 et 30 tours de retard derrière le vainqueur Moss, leurs voitures s'échelonnant sur le circuit telles des chicanes mobiles.

Mais le temps entre ces événements s'écoule avec la vitesse et le burlesque d'un film du cinéma muet. Quels sont les acteurs : pour Ferrari, Phil Hill et le comte Berghe von Trips avec la Dino 246. Ginther pilote la 246 P (pour posteriore), un modèle intérimaire avec le moteur placé derrière le pilote. Pour Lotus, John Surtees, Alan Stacey et Innes Ireland sur la 18 toute nouvelle qui semble vraiment minuscule. Stirling Moss est tellement séduit par la géniale interprétation du principe du moteur central selon Colin Chapman qu'il a convaincu son patron et mécène Rob Walker d'acheter également une Lotus 18. Jack Brabham et Bruce McLaren, sur une T 53, défendent les couleurs de Cooper, BRM étant représentée avec des P 48 confiées à Bonnier, Graham Hill et Dan Gurney. Une brève et originale apparition : la Scarab de l'héritier et milliardaire américain Lance Reventlow qui vient, voit, ne se qualifie pas et repart pour ne plus jamais donner de nouvelles.

Parti comme une fusée de la seconde ligne, Bonnier prend immédiatement la tête. Derrière lui, Moss double Brabham au cinquième tour. Jo Bonnier ne cesse alors de faire signe au Britannique pour l'inviter à le doubler. Moss ne réagit pas — jusqu'au 17ᵉ tour. Puis, après un quart de la course, une ondée rend la piste glissante, offrant à Moss des conditions idéales. Mais, à partir du 34ᵉ tour, c'est Brabham qui est en tête avant de faire un tête-à-queue, sept tours plus tard, et de percuter le mur à Sainte Dévote. L'Anglais est de nouveau en tête. Après le 60ᵉ tour, sa voiture doit toutefois se faire rafraîchir pendant 25 secondes. Le moteur tousse, un câble d'allumage doit être refixé. Il faut huit tours à Moss avant d'avoir rattrapé le Suédois entre-temps en tête, au freinage de la chicane. Et, tandis que la BRM regagne une première fois les stands avec une suspension arrière rompue, la Lotus bleu foncé devient irrattrapable et Moss gagne avec 52 secondes d'avance sur la Cooper de Bruce McLaren.

Downhill all the way: beset by mechanical problems, Innes Ireland pushes his Lotus half a lap to reach the finishing line. The slope between the Casino and the sea provides help.

Von nun an geht's bergab: Von mechanischen Problemen heimgesucht, schiebt Innes Ireland seinen Lotus ins Ziel – eine halbe Runde lang. Die Gefällestrecke zwischen dem Casino und dem Meer erweist sich als hilfreich.

Maintenant, il n'y a plus que des descentes : victime de problèmes mécaniques, Innes Ireland pousse sa Lotus vers la ligne d'arrivée – pendant un demi-tour. Il profite des descentes entre le Casino et la mer.

N°	DRIVERS		ENTRANTS	CARS	ENGINES	PRACTICE RESULTS	RACE RESULTS
28	*Stirling Moss*	*GB*	*RRC Walker Racing Team*	*Lotus 18*	*Climax FPF 4L 2495 cc*	*1st: 1'36"3*	*1st: 2h53'45"5*
10	Bruce McLaren	NZ	Cooper Car Co.	Cooper T53	Climax FPF 4L 2495 cc	9th(11): 1'38"6	2nd: 2h54'37"6
36	Phil Hill	USA	SEFAC Ferrari S.p.A.	Ferrari Dino 246	Ferrari 6L 2417 cc	9th(10): 1'38"6	3th: 2h54'47"4
18	Tony Brooks	GB	Yeoman Credit Bank Racing Team	Cooper T51	Climax FPF 4L 2495 cc	3rd: 1'37"7	4th: 99 laps
2	Joakim Bonnier	S	Owen Racing Organisation	BRM P48	BRM 4L 2497 cc	3rd(5): 1'37"7	5th: 83 laps
34	Richie Ginther	USA	SEFAC Ferrari S.p.A.	Ferrari Dino 246	Ferrari 6L 2417 cc	9th: 1'38"6	6th: 70 laps (R)
6	Graham Hill	GB	Owen Racing Organisation	BRM P48	BRM 4L 2497 cc	6th: 1'38"0	7th: 66 laps (R)
38	Wolfgang von Trips	D	SEFAC Ferrari S.p.A.	Ferrari Dino 246	Ferrari 6L 2417 cc	8th: 1'38"3	8th: 61 laps
22	Innes Ireland	GB	Team Lotus	Lotus 18	Climax FPF 4L 2495 cc	7th: 1'38"2	9th: 56 laps (R)
4	Dan Gurney	USA	Owen Racing Organisation	BRM P48	BRM 4L 2497 cc	14th: 1'38"9	R
8	Jack Brabham	AUS	Cooper Car Co.	Cooper T53	Climax FPF 4L 2495 cc	2nd: 1'37"3	disqualified
14	Roy Salvadori	GB	High Efficiency Motors	Cooper T51	Maserati 4L 2495 cc	12th: 1'38"7	R
24	Alan Stacey	GB	Team Lotus	Lotus 18	Climax FPF 4L 2495 cc	13th: 1'38"9	R
26	John Surtees	GB	Team Lotus	Lotus 18	Climax FPF 4L 2495 cc	15th: 1'39"0	R
16	Chris Bristow	GB	Yeoman Credit Bank Racing Team	Cooper T51	Climax FPF 4L 2495 cc	3rd(4): 1'37"7	R
44	Maurice Trintignant	F	Scuderia Centro Sud	Cooper T51	Maserati 4L 2494 cc	16th: 1'39"1	R

1

(1) Uncomfortably close after the start, in the foreground Count von Trips in a Ferrari and Salvadori in a Cooper. (2) Just a brief guest performance: Lance Reventlow in the Scarab. (3) Winner in the box listening to the British national anthem with a soldierly bearing. (4) Ante Portas: Phil Hill in the Ferrari. (5) As the track begins to dry, Moss (Lotus) is looking for damp patches to protect his Dunlop tires.

(1) Ungemütliches Zusammensein nach dem Start, im Vordergrund Graf Trips im Ferrari und Roy Salvadori auf Cooper. (2) Kurzes Gastspiel: Lance Reventlow im Scarab. (3) Logen-Platz: Der Sieger lauscht in soldatischer Haltung der englischen Hymne. (4) Ante portas: Phil Hill auf Ferrari. (5) Als die Piste zu trocknen beginnt, sucht Moss (Lotus) feuchte Stellen auf, um seine Dunlop-Reifen zu schonen.

(1) La place est disputée après le départ : au premier plan, le comte von Trips sur Ferrari et Roy Salvadori sur Cooper. (2) Bref intermède : Lance Reventlow sur Scarab. (3) Place de loge : le vainqueur au garde-à-vous pendant l'hymne britannique. (4) Ante portas : Phil Hill sur Ferrari. (5) Lorsque la piste commence à sécher, Moss (Lotus) recherche les endroits encore humides pour ménager ses pneus Dunlop.

2

Various views: (1) Brabham
(Cooper), (2) Moss (Lotus)
and (3) McLaren (Cooper).

Verschiedene Blick-Winkel:
(1) Brabham (Cooper),
(2) Moss (Lotus) und
(3) McLaren (Cooper).

Façons de voir : (1) Brabham
(Cooper), (2) Moss (Lotus)
et (3) McLaren (Cooper).

LUCKLESS GENIUS

GENIE OHNE FORTÜNE · GÉNIE SANS FORTUNE

Of one thing I am certain", Stirling Moss used to say. "If someone wants something badly enough, he will do it. If you live for nothing else and concentrate on it without fail, you can even walk on water." The declared aim of the stocky Londoner was to be Formula 1 champion. There can be no doubt that he had the will and the perseverance. Yet he never succeeded in either thing. The bit with the water he only tried on skis, and the dream of the World Championship burst like a bubble.

For fate, acting in accordance with unknown laws and often appearing unjust, had sent this genius on wheels a driver who was even more blessed, Juan Manuel Fangio, against whom his ambition broke like breakers against a rock. Three times the great Argentinean deprived him of the World Championship at the height of his powers and sent him to second place, although not into mediocrity. The fourth time, in 1958, the same thing happened to him again through his compatriot Mike Hawthorn, a less bright star in the Grand Prix firmament. During that time one point made all the difference between splendour and misery.

But he could also be pompous and he made mistakes, and suffered bad luck. At some point, Enzo Ferrari had wounded his ego. Moss never forgave such things, and from that time onwards he never discussed Maranello again. He was proud to be British, preferred racing cars from Britain – an inexcusable fad for a top driver. For at that time the first floor of racing was certainly not furnished in British Racing Green. The tone was set by others, primarily in Ferrari and Maserati red.

Sometimes his only chance with inferior material was if luck smiled on him and the weather god made rain, as happened at Monaco in 1960 or at the Nürburgring in 1961. For then, Moss could indeed walk on water, and then what Count Wolfgang Berghe von Trips, in ungrudging admiration, called the Moss-factor came into play: "On a wet track, Stirling is good for a second per lap." Tired of the constantly repeated cliche, and angry because he had become a monument in his own lifetime, he would occasionally surprise his interviewer with the confession that he hated rain. Another cliche: that Stirling Moss could perform true miracles in cars which were little more than scrap. He never threw in the towel and instead forced his will even on fatally wounded or totally overtaxed cars.

Moss was absolutely of world class in sports cars, a category in which Fangio only returned lacklustre performances. In the two-seaters the balding Briton won everything worth winning; the 1955 Mille Miglia, for example, and the Targa Florio in a Mercedes in the same year, as well as various 1,000-kilometer races at the Nürburgring – 1956 and 1960 in a Maserati, 1958 and 1959 in an Aston Martin – all events which separate the men from the boys. The only thing that persistently eluded him like a *fata morgana* was a victory at Le Mans.

Some years Moss was racing somewhere on almost every weekend and, God knows, not simply for the love of it by the standards of the time. His income was estimated at 45 to 50,000 dollars as early as the mid-fifties, when his father, Alfred, cleverly managed and

Von einem bin ich fest überzeugt«, pflegt Stirling Moss zu sagen. »Wenn jemand etwas wirklich will, dann schafft er es auch. Wer ausschließlich dafür lebt und sich unbeirrbar darauf konzentriert, kann sogar auf dem Wasser laufen.« Des untersetzten Londoners erklärtes Ziel: Champion zu sein in der Formel 1. Kein Zweifel – den Willen hat er und auch das Stehvermögen. Gleichwohl klappt beides nicht. Die Sache mit dem Wasser versucht er nur auf Skiern, und der Traum vom Weltmeister platzt wie eine Seifenblase, die schon allzu lange durch den Raum geschwebt ist.

Denn das Schicksal, das nach unerforschlichen Gesetzen handelt und uns oft ungerecht erscheint, hat diesem Genius auf Rädern einen noch begnadeteren Autofahrer über den Weg geschickt und vor die Nase gesetzt, den Mann Juan Manuel Fangio, an dem seine Ambition zerschellt wie der Brecher am Felsen. Dreimal nimmt ihm der große Argentinier in der Blüte seiner Jahre die Weltmeisterschaft weg und verweist ihn auf Rang zwei, wenn auch nicht in die Zweitrangigkeit. Das vierte Mal, 1958, widerfährt ihm ein Gleiches durch seinen Landsmann Mike Hawthorn, einen viel trüberen Stern am Grand-Prix-Himmel. Auf einen Punkt Rückstand beläuft sich damals die Differenz zwischen Glanz und Elend.

Aber er ist auch ehrpusselig, macht Fehler und hat Pech. Irgendwann einmal hat Enzo Ferrari seinem Ego eine Blessur zugefügt. Sowas verzeiht Moss nie, und seitdem ist Maranello für ihn kein Thema mehr. Er ist bekennender Brite, bevorzugt Rennautos von der Insel, eine schier unverzeihliche Marotte für einen Spitzenfahrer. Denn damals ist die Beletage des Rennsports noch keineswegs in British Racing Green tapeziert. Den Ton geben andere an, vorwiegend in ferrari- und maseratirot.

Manchmal hat er mit unterlegenem Material nur dann eine Chance, wenn die Gunst der Stunde über ihm lächelt und der Wettergott es regnen läßt wie in Monaco 1960 oder 1961 am Nürburgring. Dann nämlich wandelt Moss eben doch auf den Wassern, und dann vor allem kommt zum Tragen, was Wolfgang Graf Berghe von Trips in neidloser Bewunderung den Moss-Faktor nennt: »Auf nasser Strecke ist Stirling eine Sekunde pro Runde gut.« Ermüdet durch das tausendmal wiederholte Klischee und genervt, weil er schon zu Lebzeiten zum eigenen Denkmal geworden ist, wird er seine Gesprächspartner später gelegentlich mit dem Bekenntnis verblüffen, er habe Regen gehaßt. Ein anderes Klischee: daß Stirling Moss selbst auf kaum noch flottem Schrott wahre Wunder wirken kann. Niemals wirft er das Handtuch, zwingt selbst einem waidwunden oder sonst restlos überforderten Fahrzeug noch seinen Willen auf.

Absolute Weltklasse ist Moss im Sportwagen, eine Sparte, in der Fangio nur lustlose Pflichtübungen abliefert. Im Zweisitzer gewinnt der kahlköpfige Brite alles, was Rang und Namen hat, die Mille Miglia 1955 zum Beispiel und die Targa Florio im gleichen Jahr im Mercedes ebenso wie diverse 1000-Kilometer-Rennen auf dem Nürburgring, 1956 und 1960 auf Maserati, 1958 und 1959 auf Aston Martin, alles Veranstaltungen, die die Knaben von den Männern absondern. Nur ein Sieg in Le Mans entzieht sich ihm hartnäckig wie eine Fata Morgana.

Il est une chose dont je suis intimement convaincu, a coutume de dire Stirling Moss : quand quelqu'un veut vraiment quelque chose, il l'obtient. Si l'on ne vit que pour une grande chose, en mobilisant toute son énergie, alors on peut marcher sur les eaux. » Objectif déclaré du Londonien aux cheveux éclaircis : devenir champion du monde de Formule 1. Il n'y a pas de doute – la volonté, il l'a, et la résistance aussi. Et pourtant, il sortira désillusionné : la chose avec l'eau, il ne la tente que sur des skis ; et le rêve de devenir champion du monde s'évanouit comme une bulle de savon qui a trop longtemps voleté dans les airs.

En effet, le destin qui obéit à des impondérables et nous semble souvent injuste a fait croiser la route de ce génie du volant avec celle d'un conducteur encore plus doué, un homme qui a pour nom Juan Manuel Fangio et sur lequel son ambition achoppera comme une lame de fond contre la falaise. A trois reprises, le grand Argentin au faîte de son art lui chipera le titre de champion du monde, faisant de lui son dauphin sans en faire pour autant un champion de seconde classe. La quatrième fois, en 1958, la même chose lui arrivera face à son compatriote Mike Hawthorn, une étoile plus pâle au firmament des Grands Prix. Un seul point marque, à cette époque, la différence entre la lumière et l'obscurité.

Mais il est aussi susceptible, commet des erreurs et n'a pas toujours la baraka. Un jour, Enzo Ferrari l'a blessé au plus profond de lui-même. Moss ne pardonne jamais une telle chose et, depuis, Maranello ne l'intéresse plus. Il est Britannique jusqu'au bout des ongles et donne la préférence aux voitures de course anglaises, une marotte absolument impardonnable pour un très grand pilote. En effet, à cette époque, le panthéon de la compétition automobile est encore loin d'être tapissé en British Racing Green. Ce sont d'autres qui donnent le ton, essentiellement avec une carrosserie en rouge Ferrari, au rouge Maserati.

Parfois, doté d'un matériel de moindre qualité, sa seule chance est que la fortune lui sourit et que Dieu ouvre ses écluses comme c'est le cas à Monaco en 1960 ou au Nürburgring en 1961. Alors, en effet, Moss sait bel et bien marcher sur l'eau et c'est ainsi que l'on comprend ce qu'avait voulu dire le comte Berghe von Trips quand, dans une franche admiration, il parlait du facteur Moss. « Sur le mouillé, Stirling Moss vaut une bonne seconde au tour. » Fatigué par ce cliché mille fois répété et énervé d'entendre dire qu'il est déjà devenu son propre monument de son vivant, Moss avouera occasionnellement, plus tard, à ses interlocuteurs stupéfaits qu'il haïssait la pluie. Autre cliché : Stirling Moss lui-même est capable de faire de véritables miracles même quand sa voiture n'est plus qu'une épave. Il ne jette jamais l'éponge et, au contraire, impose encore sa volonté à une voiture blessée à mort ou pratiquement au bout du rouleau.

Moss est un virtuose incontesté au volant d'une voiture de sport, une discipline à laquelle Fangio ne s'est jamais prêté avec un grand enthousiasme. Au volant d'une biplace, le Britannique aux cheveux rares gagne tout ce qui brille d'une lueur particulière dans le calendrier de la compétition automobile, les Mille Miglia de 1955 par exemple, et la Targa Florio de la même année, sur Mercedes, de même que, à diverses reprises, la course des 1000 Kilomètres du Nürburgring, en 1956 et 1960

marketed his son. But in the end providence stopped him with two shots across the bows. It is a true miracle that Stirling Moss is still among us.

At the fated Belgian Grand Prix of 1960, at Spa-Francorchamps, a race which claimed the lives of his friends Chris Bristow and Alan Stacey, his Lotus left the track at the end of an enormously long skid mark on the notoriously endless right-hand bend at Burnenville, crashed down a slope and landed among grazing cows. Moss broke both his legs, but he was already back in action again in mid-August in Oporto, Portugal, against the advice of his doctor and contrary to all reason. He had to leave his crutches as he got in his car. He won the US Grand Prix in Riverside in November, whilst still convalescing.

But 1962 had something even more dreadful in store for him. On Easter Monday, Moss started in the pale green Lotus of the UDT racing stable for the 100-mile race at Goodwood. During the 35th lap he arrived much too fast at the right-left combination with the biblically innocent name of St Mary's Corner. No-one knows why, no-one will ever know. The car ploughed a 150-yard long furrow in the grass and burst apart as it hit an earth bank. The driver's recovery was in doubt for a long time. The left half of his body was partly paralysed. The worst injuries, those to the head, were invisible. Yet Moss recovered, helped by his iron

Manchmal ist Moss an fast jedem Wochenende irgendwo im Renntempo unterwegs, und beileibe nicht um Gotteslohn nach den Maßstäben jener Zeit. Auf 80 bis 100 000 Mark schätzt man sein Einkommen bereits in den Mittfünfzigern, als sein Vater Alfred seinen driftenden Filius klug managt und vermarktet. Doch am Ende stoppt ihn die Vorsehung mit zwei Schüssen vor den Bug. Ein wirkliches Wunder ist auch, daß Stirling Moss noch unter uns weilt. Bei jenem fatalen Grand Prix von Belgien 1960 in Spa, als der gefräßige Renntod die Leben seiner Kameraden Chris Bristow und Alan Stacey fordert, kommt er mit seinem Lotus in der berüchtigten endlosen Rechtsbiegung Burnenville am Ende einer enormen Radierspur von der Strecke ab, stürzt einen Abhang hinunter mitten zwischen weidende Kühe und bricht sich beide Beine. Im portugiesischen Oporto Mitte August ist Moss schon wieder mit von der Partie, gegen den Willen des Arztes und gegen jede Vernunft. Er muß die Krücken ablegen, bevor er in den Wagen steigt. Den Großen Preis der USA in Riverside im November gewinnt er, noch immer Rekonvaleszent.

1962 wartet Schlimmeres auf ihn. Am Ostermontag startet Moss auf dem blaßgrünen Lotus des UDT-Renn-stalls beim 100-Meilen-Rennen zu Goodwood. In der 35. Runde trifft er an der Rechts-Links-Kombination mit dem biblisch-unverfänglichen Namen St. Mary's Corner

sur Maserati, en 1958 et 1959 sur Aston Martin, rien que des courses qui séparent l'ivraie du bon grain. Il n'y a que la victoire au Mans qui lui échappera toujours avec entêtement, comme un mirage.

Pendant quelques années Moss se retrouve au volant d'une voiture de course presque chaque week-end et ce, vraiment pas pour le seul amour de l'art selon les critères de son temps. On estime déjà ses revenus à 80 000 ou 100 000 Marks au milieu des années 50 lorsque son père Alfred manage et gère intelligemment son champion du volant de fils. Mais, à la fin, la prémonition obtient raison avec deux coups de semonce. C'est d'ailleurs un véritable miracle que Stirling Moss soit encore parmi nous aujourd'hui. Lors du fatal Grand Prix de Belgique de 1960 à Spa, course qui coûtera la vie à ses amis Chris Bristow et Alan Stacey, sa Lotus quitte la piste dans le redoutable et interminable virage à droite de Burnenville, en laissant une interminable trace de pneus sur la piste, dévale une pente et atterrit entre des vaches ruminant dans un pâturage. Moss se brise les deux jambes, mais, à la mi-août, plein d'élan, il se place à nouveau sur la ligne de départ d'Oporto, au Portugal, contre la volonté de ses médecins et contre toute raison. Il doit se déplacer avec des béquilles pour aller se glisser dans le cockpit de sa voiture. Il gagne ensuite le Grand Prix des Etats-Unis, à Riverside, en novembre, bien que toujours convalescent.

Never champion and yet one of the greatest in his sport: Stirling Moss. His name alone promises a dynamic approach.

Nie Champion und dennoch einer der Größten in seinem Sport: Stirling Moss. Schon sein bloßer Name verspricht Dynamik.

Jamais champion et, pourtant, l'un des plus grands de son sport : Stirling Moss. Son nom, déjà, est synonyme de dynamique.

constitution. He kept the broken steering wheel of the Lotus as a souvenir of that dark hour.

On 1 May 1963 he returned to Goodwood for a private test, drove a few laps over the deserted and damp course and got out of the car: "Sorry, that's it." His lightning reflexes had gone. He had had to think about each tiny action at the wheel. There was no longer any point.

Since that time, Stirling Moss has rushed through life, a Jack of all trades and a multi-talented untiring ambassador of his sport. Thus he continues to serve, as patron of his own Scuderia called Smart (for Stirling Moss Automobile Racing Team), as manager of a CanAm racing stable, as reporter, and simply as the slowly weathering monument called Stirling Moss. He drives in historic races or demonstrates historic racing cars. And when he puts on his helmet, celebrating his appearances, a murmur still goes through the crowd, particularly when, from a distance, he looks as he once used to under his white protective headgear.

Numerous anecdotes are told about him, such as when the Isetta was being launched in London, the local BMW dealer invited Moss to take a run in the bubble car. "You can easily drive a bit faster", the representative of the Bavarian company said after a bend. "Fine", Moss responded calmly, and left the next bend centrifugally in a sideways role. He was constantly having his licence withdrawn, and then he navigated the reefs and cliffs of the London rush-hour on a racing bike.

For a time he bought houses in the elegant parts of the English metropolis, refurbished them with a team of helpers and either rented them or sold them at a useful profit. His own house in the shadow of the London Hilton is stuffed full of electronic bits and pieces, which all serve the purpose of making life more comfortable for their owner. A little fountain splashes into a goldfish pond in a grotto, like a Wagner opera.

viel zu schnell ein. Niemand weiß warum, keiner wird es je erfahren. Der Wagen pflügt eine 50 Meter lange Furche in den Rasen und zerplatzt dann an einem Erdwall. An der Genesung des Piloten wird lange gezweifelt. Seine linke Körperhälfte ist teilweise paralysiert. Die schlimmsten Verletzungen sieht man nicht, die im Kopf. Dennoch rappelt sich Moss wieder auf, wobei ihm seine stählerne Kondition zugute kommt. Das zerknautschte Lenkrad des Lotus bewahrt er sich als Souvenir an jene dunkle Stunde auf.

Am 1. Mai 1963 kehrt er zum Lokaltermin nach Goodwood zurück, dreht einige Runden über den verlassenen und feuchten Kurs und steigt dann aus: »Sorry, das war's.« Seine gedankenschnellen Reflexe seien ihm verlorengegangen. Über jede winzige Handlung am Volant habe er nachdenken müssen. So mache alles keinen Sinn mehr.

Seitdem vagabundiert Stirling Moss durchs Leben, ein Hansdampf in vielen Gassen, zugleich ein Multitalent und nimmermüder Botschafter seines Sports. Dem bleibt er erhalten, als Patron einer eigenen Scuderia namens Smart (Stirling Moss Automobile Racing Team), als leitender Angestellter eines CanAm-Rennstalls, als Berichterstatter und einfach als das allmählich verwitternde Monument Stirling Moss. Er fährt auf historischen Rennen oder demonstriert historische Rennwagen. Und wenn er, seine Auftritte zelebrierend, seinen Helm aufsetzt, geht noch immer ein Raunen durch die Menge, zumal er unter seinem weißen Kopfschutz, von weitem gesehen, ausschaut wie einst.

Unzählige Anekdoten kursieren über ihn wie diese: Als in London die Isetta vorgestellt wird, lädt der lokale BMW-Händler auch Moss zu einer kleinen Spritztour mit dem kugeligen Mobil ein. »Sie können ruhig schneller fahren«, sagt der Statthalter der Bayern hinter einer Kurve. »Geht in Ordnung«, erwidert Moss gleichmütig, und man verläßt die nächste Ecke zentrifugal in einer seitlichen Rolle. Immer wieder entzieht man ihm den Führerschein, und dann umschifft Stirling Moss die Riffs und Klippen der Londoner Rush-hour auf einem Rennrad.

Eine Zeitlang kauft er Häuser in den eleganteren Vierteln der englischen Metropole, krempelt mit einem Team von Helfershelfern das Unterste zuoberst und vermietet oder verkauft sie wieder äußerst gewinnbringend. Sein eigenes Heim im Schatten des London Hilton ist vollgestopft mit elektronischem Schnickschnack, der vor allem einem Zweck dient, seinem Besitzer das Leben kommod zu erleichtern. In einer Grotte wie aus einer Wagneroper plätschert ein Brünnlein auf ein Goldfischbecken herab.

Mais c'est en 1962 que le pire se produira. Le lundi de Pâques, au volant de la Lotus de l'écurie UDT, Moss s'aligne au départ de la course des 100 Miles de Goodwood. Lors du 35e tour, il entre beaucoup trop vite dans la combinaison droite-gauche au nom biblique et innocent de St. Mary's Corner. Nul ne sait pourquoi, on l'ignorera toujours. La voiture laboure une trace de 50 mètres dans le gazon et se désintègre contre un remblai de terre. On met longtemps en doute que le pilote puisse survivre. La moitié gauche de son corps est partiellement paralysée. On ne voit pas les blessures les plus graves, celles qui ont touché la tête. Et pourtant, Moss se rétablit, à l'occasion de quoi sa condition d'athlète lui aura été bénéfique. Depuis, il conserve le volant tordu de la Lotus comme souvenir de cette heure sombre.

Le 1er mai 1963, il revient à Goodwood pour tester sa condition, couvre quelques tours sur le circuit abandonné de tous et humide, puis descend de voiture : « Désolé, c'est terminé ! » Il a perdu ses réflexes éclairs, explique-t-il. Il lui a fallu réfléchir avant de faire la moindre action au volant. Dans de telles conditions, cela n'a plus aucun sens.

Depuis, Stirling Moss vagabonde à travers la vie, farceur invétéré, à la fois un talent universel et ambassadeur infatigable de son sport. Sport auquel il reste d'ailleurs fidèle, comme patron d'une propre écurie baptisée Smart (pour Stirling Moss Automobile Racing Team), comme cadre de l'écurie de CanAm, comme reporter et, tout simplement aussi comme le monument du nom de Stirling Moss qui s'écaille peu à peu. Il participe à des courses de voitures historiques ou fait des démonstrations d'antiques voitures de collection. Et quand, célébrant sa présence, il enfile son casque, une rumeur d'autant plus forte se fait encore entendre dans la foule que, sous sa cagoule blanche, il ressemble de loin au Stirling Moss de jadis.

On se raconte d'innombrables anecdotes à son sujet, notamment celle-ci : lors de la présentation, à Londres, de l'Isetta, le concessionnaire BMW du lieu invite aussi Moss à l'accompagner et à prendre le volant de cette espèce de pot de yaourt à quatre roues. « N'hésitez pas à rouler plus vite, si vous voulez », lui dit l'« ambassadeur » des Bavarois à Londres. « Pas de problème », lui répond Moss sans sourciller, et les deux hommes sortent du prochain virage en une magnifique série de tonneaux sous l'effet de la force centrifuge. Il se fait régulièrement confisquer son permis de conduire, mais ce n'est pas un handicap pour Stirling Moss qui défie les risques et les périls de la rush hour londonienne au guidon d'un vélo de course.

Pendant un certain temps, il a fait l'acquisition de maisons dans les quartiers les plus chics de la métropole anglaise, les rénove avec une équipe de copains pour les louer ou les revendre à un prix lucratif. Son propre domicile à l'ombre du Hilton de Londres est truffé de gadgets électroniques qui ont surtout un objectif : faciliter le plus possible la vie de leur propriétaire. Dans une grotte ressemblant à un opéra wagnérien, un petit jet d'eau babille au-dessus d'un aquarium où s'ébattent des poissons rouges.

1961

In 1961, the Ferrari myth looked to be in excellent shape. The men in Maranello had done their homework much more thoroughly in advance of the new Formula 1 – 1.5 liters maximum, 450 kilograms minimum – than their British opponents, who were still dreaming to some extent about past glories. Time, then, to storm the bastion of Monaco, time for the revenge of the reds for the three humiliating defeats in a row by the products of the tiny British manufacturers Cooper and Lotus. Worse still, the winning cars from 1958 to 1960 had been privately owned, the property of the patron and enthusiast Rob Walker, who owned a stately home in Frome, in the south-west of England.

Would the revenge be successful? That was a question which would be answered in a great moment of motor sport. Ferrari had entered the lists with three 156/F1s, two older versions, the cylinder banks of whose V6 engines were still angled at 65 degrees, for Phil Hill and Wolfgang von Trips, and the latest version, with cylinder banks at an angle of 120 degrees, for Richie Ginther. With over 180 bhp they were at least 30 bhp more powerful than the best Coventry Climax engines of the British teams. Jim Clark and Innes Ireland drove for Team Lotus in Type 21s, but Rob Walker's star driver Moss had to be satisfied with the Type 18 from the previous year. Bruce McLaren and Jack Brabham each had a substantially slimmed-down Cooper T 55, Brabham's car earning the last starting position when he drove it in the first practice session. The World Champion of 1959 and 1960 then left to catch a plane to America in order to qualify for the Indianapolis 500 race. Graham Hill and Tony Brooks drove the BRM P48/57, while Porsche optimistically fielded a team of three four-cylinder cars for Jo Bonnier, Dan Gurney and Hans Herrmann; it would be a vain effort. This was to prove Stirling Moss' weekend, the maestro lightly disregarding the laws of aerodynamics by having the side panels of his Lotus removed to improve cockpit ventilation, and by doing so making his semi-reclined work visible to everyone as he was cooled by fresh air.

Although starting from pole position, he was initially taken by surprise by Ginther, who for 14 laps gave him the opportunity to study a Ferrari from the rear. Bonnier then moved uncomfortably close from behind, so Moss slipped past into the lead, with the Swedish Porsche driver still in his slipstream. But the latter soon succumbed to the pressure of the two Ferraris behind him. By lap 26 Phil Hill had moved into second position, with Ginther filling his rear-view mirrors. At the half-way point of the race Moss was separated from his pursuers by four-and-a-half seconds, which was slightly more than his mentor Rob Walker deemed appropriate. But the gap changed little, even when Ginther launched an attack on lap 84 and set the best time of the day. The balding Englishman calmly adjusted to the new circumstances and drove on to win the Monaco Grand Prix for third time. It was victory for Stirling Moss, the superior human being, over a Ferrari 156, the superior machine.

"Stirling alone", Count Wolfgang Berghe von Trips said in ungrudging admiration, "is worth a second per lap."

Im Jahr 1961 boomt der Ferrari-Mythos. Im Vorfeld der neuen Formel 1, anderthalb Liter maximal, 450 Kilogramm minimal, haben die Männer in Maranello ihre Hausaufgaben einfach viel besser gemacht als die britische Konkurrenz, die noch ein bißchen vergangener Glorie nachträumt. Zeit also auch für einen Sturm auf die Bastion Monaco, Rache der Roten für drei schmähliche Niederlagen in Folge durch Erzeugnisse der britischen Mini-Manufakturen Cooper und Lotus. Schlimmer noch: Die Siegerwagen der Jahre 1958 bis 1960 stammten aus Privatbesitz, Eigentum des Mäzens und Enthusiasten Rob Walker, Schloßbesitzer zu Frome im Südwesten Englands.

Ob die Revanche gelingt oder nicht, diese Frage wird in einer Sternstunde des Motorsports beantwortet. Ferrari tritt mit drei 156/F1 an, zwei älteren, deren V6 sich noch um 65 Grad spreizen, für Phil Hill und Graf Trips, und der neuesten Version mit Zylinderbänken im Winkel von 120 Grad für Richie Ginther. Mit über 180 PS sind sie mindestens 30 PS stärker als die besten Climax-Maschinen der britischen Teams. Für Lotus fahren Jim Clark und Innes Ireland auf dem Typ 21. Rob Walkers Starpilot Moss muß sich mit dem Modell 18 vom letzten Jahr begnügen. Im deutlich verschlankten Cooper T 55 sitzen Bruce McLaren und Jack Brabham, welcher sich in vier Runden beim ersten Training den letzten Startplatz sichert: Der Weltmeister von 1959 und 1960 verreist zwischendurch mal kurz, um sich für Indianapolis zu qualifizieren. Graham Hill und Tony Brooks fahren den BRM P48/57, während Porsche eine Streitmacht von drei rundlichen Vierzylindern für Jo Bonnier, Dan Gurney und Hans Herrmann ins Feld führt. Vergebliche Liebesmüh – es ist das Wochenende des Stirling Moss, der sich locker über die Gesetze der Aerodynamik hinwegsetzt und die anderen verhöhnt, indem er die seitlichen Planken seines Lotus wegen der Hitze herausnehmen läßt und seine halb liegende Tätigkeit für jedermann sichtbar frischluftgekühlt verrichtet.

Obwohl er aus der Pole Position startet, wird er zunächst von Ginther überrumpelt, der ihm 14 Runden lang Gelegenheit gibt, die Heckansicht des Ferrari zu studieren. Von hinten rückt Bonnier ungemütlich nahe, so daß Moss vorbeischlüpft, den schwedischen Porsche-Piloten in seinem Kielwasser. Doch der erliegt bald dem Druck der beiden Ferrari hinter ihm. Im 26. Durchgang ist Phil Hill auf Position zwei angelangt, Ginther formatfüllend im Rückspiegel. Bei Halbzeit des Rennens trennen Moss viereinhalb Sekunden von seinen Verfolgern, eine Idee mehr, als Mentor Rob Walker als angemessene Distanz empfohlen hat. Dabei bleibt es auch, als Ginther in der 84. Runde eine Attacke lanciert und die Bestzeit des Tages fährt. Der kahlköpfige Engländer stellt sie gleich darauf gelassen ein und gewinnt den Grand Prix de Monaco zum dritten Mal, der Sieg des überlegenen Mannes Stirling Moss gegen die überlegene Maschine Ferrari 156.

»Stirling allein«, sagt Wolfgang Graf Berghe von Trips in neidloser Bewunderung, »ist eine Sekunde pro Runde wert.«

En 1961, le mythe Ferrari est à son apogée. Avant l'avènement de la nouvelle Formule 1 – cylindrée maximum de 1,5 litre, poids minimum de 450 kilogrammes – les hommes de Maranello ont, tout simplement, bien mieux fait leurs devoirs que leurs concurrents britanniques qui se sont laissé bercer dans leur gloire passée. Rendez-vous est donc pris pour partir à l'assaut du bastion de Monaco, revanche des Rouges pour trois humiliantes défaites infligées successivement par les petits « garagistes » anglais Cooper et Lotus. Plus grave encore : les voitures victorieuses de 1958 à 1960 appartenaient à une écurie privée, la propriété du mécène et fanatique Rob Walker, châtelain de Frome, dans le sud-ouest de l'Angleterre.

La revanche va-t-elle réussir ou non ? C'est en lettres de feu que la compétition automobile répond à cette question. Ferrari descend dans l'arène avec trois 156/F1, deux plus toutes fraîches, dont le V6 décrit encore un angle de 65 degrés pour Phil Hill et le comte von Trips, et la toute dernière version avec des bancs de cylindres à 120 degrés pour Richie Ginther. Avec plus de 180 chevaux, elles en ont au minimum trente de plus que les meilleurs moteurs Climax des Britanniques. Pour Lotus, Jim Clark et Innes Ireland sont au volant d'une 21. Stirling Moss, le pilote vedette de Rob Walker, doit se contenter d'une 18 de l'année précédente. Dans les Cooper T 55 considérablement amincies ont pris place Bruce McLaren et Jack Brabham, qui s'assure la dernière place sur la grille de départ en quatre tours dès les premiers essais : le champion du monde de 1959 et 1960 s'éclipse brièvement entre-temps afin de prendre l'avion pour l'Amérique et de se qualifier pour les 500 Miles d'Indianapolis. Graham Hill et Tony Brooks conduisent la BRM P48/57 tandis que Porsche, avec beaucoup d'optimisme, a envoyé ses trois rondelettes quatre-cylindres pour Jo Bonnier, Dan Gurney et Hans Herrmann. Ce sera peine perdue – c'est le week-end de Stirling Moss qui, dans un royal mépris de l'aérodynamique et en faisant démonter les panneaux latéraux de sa Lotus pour améliorer la ventilation et permet ainsi à chacun de l'observer, à demi allongé, exercer son art, bien rafraîchi, comme il se doit, par le vent de la course.

Bien que parti de la pole position, il est surpris tout d'abord par Ginther, qui lui donne pendant quatorze tours, l'occasion d'étudier attentivement la croupe de sa Ferrari. De l'arrière, Bonnier fait sentir alors son haleine menaçante, si bien que Moss se décide à doubler, entraînant dans son sillage le pilote suédois de la Porsche. Mais celui-ci ne peut, bientôt, plus résister aux assauts des deux Ferrari qui le talonnent. Au 26e tour, Phil Hill se retrouve deuxième, avec Ginther remplissant ses rétroviseurs. A la mi-course, quatre secondes et demie séparent Moss de ses poursuivants, un soupçon de plus que son mentor Rob Walker lui recommande comme distance appropriée. Mais il y eut peu de changement même lorsque Ginther, au 84e tour, tente une attaque et signe le meilleur temps du jour. L'Anglais à la chevelure clairsemée en fait autant dans la foulée et gagne le Grand Prix de Monaco pour la troisième fois, victoire d'un homme, Stirling Moss, au volant d'une machine qui a dominé de la tête et des épaules, la Ferrari 156.

« Stirling à lui seul », déclare le comte Wolfgang Berghe von Trips sincèrement admiratif, « vaut une seconde au tour. »

The shortest distance between two points is a straight line: Brooks (BRM), McLaren (Cooper), Phil Hill (Ferrari), Graham Hill (BRM) and Count von Trips (Ferrari) approaching Station Hairpin.

Die kürzeste Linie zwischen zwei Punkten ist die Gerade: Brooks (BRM), McLaren (Cooper), Phil Hill (Ferrari), Graham Hill (BRM) und Graf Trips (Ferrari) vor der Bahnhofskurve.

Le plus court pour aller de A à B est la ligne droite : Brooks (BRM), McLaren (Cooper), Phil Hill (Ferrari), Graham Hill (BRM) et le comte von Trips (Ferrari) devant le virage de la Gare.

N°	DRIVERS		ENTRANTS	CARS	ENGINES	PRACTICE RESULTS	RACE RESULTS
20	**Stirling Moss**	**GB**	**RRC Walker Racing Team**	**Lotus 18**	**Climax 4L 1496 cc**	**1st: 1'39"1**	**1st: 2h45'50"1**
36	Richie Ginther	USA	SEFAC Ferrari S.p.A.	Ferrari 156	Ferrari V6 1484 cc	2nd: 1'39"3	2nd: 2h45'53"7
38	Phil Hill	USA	SEFAC Ferrari S.p.A.	Ferrari 156	Ferrari V6 1484 cc	5th: 1'39"8	3rd: 2h46'31"4
40	Wolfgang von Trips	D	SEFAC Ferrari S.p.A.	Ferrari 156	Ferrari V6 1484 cc	5th(6): 1'39"8	4th: 98 laps
4	Dan Gurney	USA	Porsche System Engineering	Porsche F2-718	Porsche 4F 1498 cc	10th: 1'40"6	5th: 98 laps
26	Bruce McLaren	NZ	Cooper Car Co.	Cooper T55	Climax 4L 1496 cc	5th(7): 1'39"8	6th: 95 laps
42	Maurice Trintignant	F	Scuderia Serenissima	Cooper T51	Maserati 4L 1484 cc	15th: 1'42"4	7th: 95 laps
32	Cliff Allison	GB	UDT Laystall Racing Team	Lotus 18	Climax 4L 1496 cc	14th: 1'42"3	8th: 93 laps
6	Hans Herrmann	D	Porsche System Engineering	Porsche F2-718	Porsche 4F 1498 cc	11th(12): 1'41"1	9th: 91 laps
28	Jim Clark	GB	Team Lotus	Lotus 21	Climax 4L 1496 cc	3rd: 1'39"6	10th: 89 laps
22	John Surtees	GB	Yeoman Credit Racing Team	Cooper T53	Climax 4L 1496 cc	11th: 1'41"1	11th: 68 laps (R)
2	Joakim Bonnier	S	Porsche System Engineering	Porsche F2-787	Porsche 4F 1498 cc	9th: 1'40"3	12th: 59 laps (R)
16	Tony Brooks	GB	Owen Racing Organisation	BRM P48/57	Climax 4L 1496 cc	8th: 1'40"1	R
8	Michael May	CH	Scuderia Colonia	Lotus 18	Climax 4L 1496 cc	13th: 1'42"0	R
24	Jack Brabham	AUS	Cooper Car Co.	Cooper T55	Climax 4L 1496 cc	16th: 1'44"0	R
18	Graham Hill	GB	Owen Racing Organisation	BRM P48/57	Climax 4L 1496 cc	3rd(4): 1'39"6	R

(1) Beautiful backs: Brooks, McLaren, Phil Hill and Graham Hill at Tobacconist's Corner. (2) Moss (Lotus) with the two Porsches of Gurney and Bonnier in his rear-view mirror. (3) Ginther (Ferrari) passes the station where Surtees (Cooper) has just parked. (4, 5) Nothing fits: the remains of Innes Ireland's Lotus after his accident in the third practice session.

(1) Schöne Rücken: Brooks, McLaren, Phil Hill und Graham Hill in der Tabakskurve. (2) Moss (Lotus) mit den beiden Porsche von Gurney und Bonnier im Rückspiegel. (3) Ginther (Ferrari) passiert den Bahnhof, vor dem Surtees (Cooper) gerade geparkt hat. (4, 5) Alles krumm und schief: Die Reste von Innes Irelands Lotus nach seinem Unfall während des dritten Trainings.

(1) Belles perspectives : Brooks, McLaren, Phil Hill et Graham Hill au virage du Bureau de Tabac. (2) Moss (Lotus) avec les deux Porsche de Gurney et Bonnier dans son rétroviseur. (3) Ginther (Ferrari) longe la Gare, devant laquelle Surtees (Cooper) vient de garer sa voiture. (4, 5) Tout est tordu : l'épave de la Lotus d'Innes Ireland après son accident lors de la troisième séance d'essais.

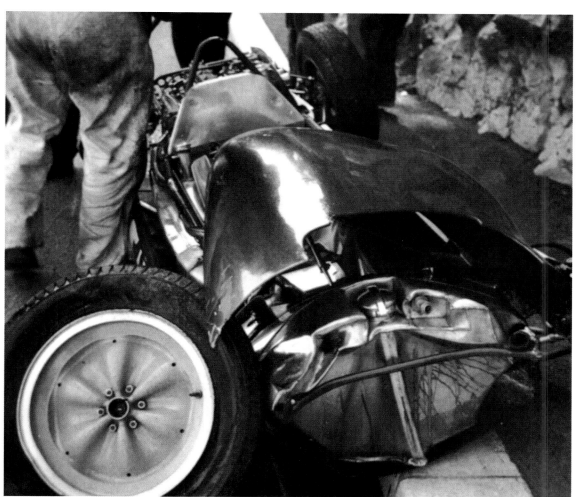

Setting the tone: (1) the V6 engine of the Ferrari 156/F1 and (2) the car itself. (3) Fat pipe: rear view of one of the Porsche four-cylinders. (4) Pause for reflection: an introverted Phil Hill, World Champion in 1961. (5) Under-powered: Moss on a moped. (6) A man sees red: race organizer Louis Chiron in anger.

Tonangebend: (1) der V6 des Ferrari 156/1 und (2) der Wagen selbst. (3) Dickes Rohr: Heckansicht eines der Porsche-Vierzylinder. (4) Denk-Pause: Phil Hill, Weltmeister 1961, ganz introvertiert. (5) Untermotorisiert: Moss auf einem Kleinkraftrad. (6) Ein Mann sieht rot: Rennleiter Louis Chiron im Zorn.

Donnant le ton : (1) le V6 de la Ferrari 156/1 et (2) la voiture elle-même. (3) L'arrière d'une Porsche quatre-cylindres. (4) Concentré : Phil Hill, champion du monde 1961, totalement introverti. (5) Sous-motorisé : Moss sur une mini-moto. (6) Un homme voit rouge : le directeur de course Louis Chiron en colère.

4

5

6

1962

Early on, the roaring St Vitus' dance around the Casino had become an unquenchable source of imagery for its reporters. Three factors, above all, contributed in 1962 to their truism that a new game brought new luck. A serious accident at Goodwood on Easter Monday that year had effectively ended the career of that Mozart with the lead foot, Stirling Moss. Tony Brooks had retired at the tender age of 30. Coventry Climax and BRM had developed powerful and solid V8 engines and had thus restored the balance of forces. Moreover, Ferrari had been visibly weakened by the exodus of angry key members of staff at the end of the previous season.

Phil Hill, Lorenzo Bandini and the wild Belgian Willy Mairesse were driving Tipo 156/F1s which progress had passed by almost without a trace. Lotus driver Jim Clark, on the way to becoming the Formula 1 icon of the mid-Sixties, drove Colin Chapman's sophisticated Lotus 25, of forward-looking monocoque construction, while Innes Ireland and Trevor Taylor still had to make do with the spaceframe-chassis Type 24. The BRM P57s of the Owen Racing Organisation were entrusted to Graham Hill and Richie Ginther, while the newest Cooper T60 was reserved for Bruce McLaren. The South African Tony Maggs, in contrast, made his debut in a T55 with the four-cylinder Coventry Climax FPF engine from the previous year. The other person who had to rely on an "antique" was Jo Bonnier, with a Porsche 718 in the colors of the Scuderia Venezia. Dan Gurney was at the wheel of the new eight-cylinder car from Stuttgart. The Bowmaker team registered two Lola Mk 4s for John Surtees and Roy Salvadori.

Seconds after the start, chaos broke out at the gasometer bend. The car of Mairesse, who had smuggled his way through between Graham Hill and Clark from the second row in an over-ambitious manoeuvre, was approaching much too fast. While the driver was attempting to bring the Ferrari back on to the right course, Ginther, Trintignant, Ireland, Taylor and Gurney collided in a chain reaction, and Ginther's right rear wheel was severed and struck and killed a track marshal. Bruce McLaren, in the meantime, had escaped at the front, but had to give way to Graham Hill on the seventh lap. Clark kept on attacking, setting the best time of the day on lap 42, but he had to struggle with a faulty clutch and the absence of several gears and eventually returned to the pits on foot after lap 55. At the same time, Hill had managed to build a safety cushion of seven seconds between McLaren and himself, which increased to one minute before rapidly decreasing again. On lap 93, the BRM rolled to a halt on the slope at the Station Hairpin with several sheared connecting rods. McLaren took the lead again and held on to it, even if Phil Hill's Ferrari moved threateningly close to the Cooper in the final stages.

Schon früh wird der tosende Veitstanz um das Casino zum schier unversiegbaren Quell für die Bildsprache seiner Berichterstatter. Zu deren Binsenweisheit, neues Spiel bedeute neues Glück, tragen 1962 vor allem drei Faktoren bei. Ein schwerer Unfall in Goodwood am Ostermontag jenes Jahres hat die Karriere des Bleifuß-Mozarts Stirling Moss faktisch beendet. Tony Brooks zog sich im zarten Alter von 30 Jahren in den Ruhestand zurück. Coventry Climax und BRM haben potente und standfeste V8-Triebwerke entwickelt und damit das Gleichgewicht der Kräfte wieder hergestellt. Überdies zeigt sich Ferrari sichtlich geschwächt vom Exodus von wütendem Schlüsselpersonal am Ende der vorigen Saison.

Phil Hill, Lorenzo Bandini und der wilde Belgier Willy Mairesse lenken den Tipo 156/F1, an dem der Fortschritt fast spurlos vorübergegangen ist. Lotus-Pilot Jim Clark, auf dem Weg zur Formel-1-Ikone der Mittsechziger, fährt Colin Chapmans raffiniertes Opus 25 in zukunftsträchtiger Monocoque-Bauweise, während Innes Ireland und Trevor Taylor noch mit dem Modell 24 abgespeist werden. Die BRM P 57 der Owen Racing Organisation sind Graham Hill und Richie Ginther anvertraut. Der neueste Cooper T 60 bleibt Bruce McLaren vorbehalten. Der Südafrikaner Tony Maggs debütiert hingegen im T 55 mit dem Vierzylinder Coventry Climax FPF vom Vorjahr. Ebenfalls auf eine Antiquität angewiesen ist Jo Bonnier mit einem Porsche 718 in den Farben der Scuderia Venezia. Am Volant des neuen Achtzylinders der Stuttgarter sitzt Dan Gurney. Zwei Lola Mk 4 hat das Bowmaker Team gemeldet, für John Surtees und Roy Salvadori.

Sekunden nach dem Start brechen an der Gasometerkurve Chaos und Tohuwabohu aus. Viel zu schnell trifft der Wagen von Mairesse ein, der sich in einem wüsten Manöver aus der zweiten Reihe zwischen Graham Hill und Clark durchgemogelt hat. Während sich der Pilot bemüht, den Ferrari wieder in die vorgeschriebene Richtung zu zwingen, kollidieren in einer krachenden Kettenreaktion Ginther, Trintignant, Ireland, Taylor und Gurney. Ginthers rechtes Hinterrad reißt ab und tötet einen Streckenposten. Unterdessen enteilt an der Spitze Bruce McLaren, muß aber Graham Hill in der siebten Runde passieren lassen. Clark attackiert unentwegt. Er fährt im 42. Durchgang die beste Zeit des Tages, laboriert aber an einer defekten Kupplung und dem Ausstand mehrerer Gänge und kehrt nach der 55. Runde zu Fuß an die Box zurück. Zur gleichen Zeit hat sich Hill ein Sicherheitspolster von sieben Sekunden auf McLaren erarbeitet, das bis zu einer Minute anschwillt und dann rapide abnimmt. In der 93. Runde rollt der BRM mit etlichen abgerissenen Pleueln auf dem Gefälle an der Bahnhofskurve aus. McLaren führt erneut, und dabei bleibt es, auch wenn Phil Hills Ferrari dem Cooper in der Endphase bedrohlich naherückt.

Très vite, le ballet des monoplaces virevoltant autour du Casino va devenir une source d'inspiration intarissable pour la grandiloquence de ses reporters. En 1962, trois facteurs, notamment, contribuent à étayer le bien-fondé de la devise : « Nouvelle donne, nouvelle chance ! » Un grave accident survenu à Goodwood le lundi de Pâques de cette année-là a, de facto, mis un terme prématuré à la carrière du Mozart de l'accélérateur, Stirling Moss. A l'âge tendre de 30 ans, Tony Brooks est parti pour une retraite précoce. Coventry Climax et BRM ont mis au point de puissants et fiables moteurs V8 et, ainsi, rééquilibré les rapports de forces. De plus, Ferrari est manifestement exsangue depuis l'exode de ses cerveaux, à la fin de la saison précédente.

Phil Hill, Lorenzo Bandini et le téméraire Belge Willy Mairesse pilotent une Tipo 156/F1 sur laquelle le progrès n'a pratiquement pas laissé de traces. Jim Clark, le pilote Lotus de Formule 1 en passe de devenir la superstar du milieu des années 60, conduit la filigrane œuvre d'art de Colin Chapman, la 25 monocoque qui est une véritable révolution, tandis que Innes Ireland et Trevor Taylor doivent encore se contenter d'une 24. Les BRM P 57 de la Owen Racing Organisation ont été confiées à Graham Hill et Richie Ginther alors que la toute dernière Cooper T 60 reste l'apanage de Bruce McLaren. Le Sud-Africain Tony Maggs, par contre, débute sur la T 55 avec le Coventry Climax FPF à quatre cylindres de l'année précédente. Jo Bonnier doit également se contenter d'une antiquité avec la Porsche 718 aux couleurs de la Scuderia Venezia. Dan Gurney a pris le volant de la nouvelle huit-cylindres de la firme de Stuttgart. L'écurie Bowmaker, quant à elle, a inscrit deux Lola Mk 4 pour John Surtees et Roy Salvadori.

Quelques secondes après le départ, c'est le chaos le plus complet au virage du Gazomètre. La voiture de Mairesse, qui s'est faufilée entre Graham Hill et Clark depuis la deuxième ligne au prix d'une manœuvre trop ambitieuse, et entre beaucoup trop vite. Alors que son pilote s'efforce de faire reprendre la bonne trajectoire à sa Ferrari, dans une dramatique réaction en chaîne, Ginther, Trintignant, Ireland, Taylor et Gurney se télescopent. La roue arrière droite de la Porsche de Ginther, arrachée, percute et tue un commissaire de piste. Pendant ce temps, Bruce McLaren s'échappe en tête, mais doit laisser passer Graham Hill au septième tour. Jim Clark attaque comme un forcené. Au 42e tour, il signe le meilleur temps du jour, mais a des problèmes d'embrayage et, après la défection de plusieurs rapports, rentre à pied aux stands, durant le 55e tour. Pendant ce temps-là, Hill a accumulé une avance confortable de sept secondes sur McLaren, avance qui augmentera jusqu'à une minute avant de décroître à nouveau rapidement. Au 93e tour, la BRM descend lentement la côte du virage de la Gare avec plusieurs bielles rompues. McLaren reprend la tête et y reste même si la Ferrari de Phil Hill vient flairer le pot d'échappement de la Cooper en fin de course.

Moment of joy: victory number three in the short career of New Zealander Bruce McLaren (Cooper).

Eitel Freude: Sieg Nummer drei in der kurzen Karriere des Neuseeländers Bruce McLaren (Cooper).

Allégresse : victoire numéro trois dans la courte carrière du Néo-Zélandais Bruce McLaren (Cooper).

N°	DRIVERS		ENTRANTS	CARS	ENGINES	PRACTICE RESULTS	RACE RESULTS
14	**Bruce McLaren**	NZ	Cooper Car Co.	Cooper T60	Climax V8 1496 cc	3rd: 1'36"4	1st: 2h46'29"7
36	Phil Hill	USA	SEFAC Ferrari S.p.A.	Ferrari 156	Ferrari V6 1477 cc	9th: 1'37"1	2nd: 2h46'31"0
38	Lorenzo Bandini	I	SEFAC Ferrari S.p.A.	Ferrari 156	Ferrari V6 1477 cc	10th: 1'37"2	3rd: 2h47'53"8
28	John Surtees	GB	Bowmaker Racing Team	Lola Mk4	Climax V8 1496 cc	11th: 1'37"9	4th: 99 laps
2	Joakim Bonnier	S	Porsche System Engineering	Porsche F2-718	Porsche F4 1498 cc	15th: 1'42"4	5th: 93 laps
10	Graham Hill	GB	Owen Racing Organisation	BRM P57	BRM V8 1498 cc	2nd: 1'35"8	6th: 92 laps (R)
40	Willy Mairesse	B	SEFAC Ferrari S.p.A.	Ferrari 156	Ferrari V6 1477 cc	3rd(4): 1'36"4	7th: 90 laps (R)
22	Jack Brabham	AUS	Brabham Racing Organisation	Lotus 24	Climax V8 1496 cc	6th: 1'36"5	8th: 77 laps (R)
34	Innes Ireland	GB	UDT Laystall Racing Team	Lotus 24	Climax V8 1496 cc	8th: 1'37"0	R
18	*Jim Clark*	GB	*Team Lotus*	*Lotus 25*	*Climax V8 1496 cc*	*1st: 1'35"4*	R
26	Roy Salvadori	GB	Bowmaker Racing Team	Lola Mk4	Climax V8 1496 cc	12th: 1'38"5	R
16	Tony Maggs	RSA	Cooper Car Co.	Cooper T55	Climax 4L 1496 cc	16th: 1'42"7	R
20	Trevor Taylor	GB	Team Lotus	Lotus 24	Climax V8 1496 cc	14th: 1'40"0	R
8	Richie Ginther	GB	Owen Racing Organisation	BRM P48/57	BRM V8 1498 cc	13th: 1'39"0	R
4	Dan Gurney	USA	Porsche System Engineering	Porsche F1-804	Porsche F8 1494 cc	3rd(5): 1'36"4	R
30	Maurice Trintignant	F	RRC Walker Racing Team	Lotus 24	Climax V8 1496 cc	7th: 1'36"8	R

(1) Confusion at the gasometer: the right rear wheel of Ginther's BRM (number 8) will kill a marshal. (2) John Cooper signals to McLaren the extent to which he is lagging behind Graham Hill. (3) Phil Hill (standing in the car) and Dan Gurney. (4) While the field sets off on the first lap, Trevor Taylor's Lotus pitifully points its nose into the air. (5) "Kamikaze-Willy" Mairesse (Ferrari) only comes seventh. (6) Pole position and fastest lap for Clark (Lotus). (7) Graham Hill comes sixth.

(1) Wirrwarr am Gasometer: Das rechte Hinterrad von Ginthers BRM (Nummer 8) wird einen Strecken-posten erschlagen. (2) John Cooper signalisiert McLaren seinen Rückstand auf Graham Hill. (3) Phil Hill (stehend im Wagen) und Dan Gurney. (4) Während das Feld in die erste Runde aufbricht, reckt Taylors Lotus kläglich die Nase in die Luft. (5) »Kamikaze-Willy« Mairesse (Ferrari) wird nur siebter. (6) Pole Position und schnellste Runde für Clark (Lotus). (7) Graham Hill wird sechster.

(1) Panique au Gazomètre : la roue arrière droite de la BRM de Ginther (numéro 8) va tuer un commissaire de piste. (2) John Cooper signale à McLaren son retard sur Graham Hill. (3) Phil Hill (debout dans sa voiture) et Dan Gurney. (4) Pendant que le peloton entame son premier tour, la Lotus de Taylor voit son capot s'envoler. (5) Willy « le kamikaze » Mairesse (Ferrari) sera septième. (6) Pole position et tour le plus rapide en course pour Clark (Lotus). (7) Graham Hill sera sixième.

1963

Monaco and safety – that has always been a delicate subject. Spectacular accidents which in the end turned out not to be too serious were almost amongst the attractions of the Grand Prix – preferably around the chicane, but also at the gasometer bend and Sainte Dévote. It was between these last two points of the town's race traffic that the start and finish lines were placed in 1963, in their proper place as it were, for this area had always been used except during the "harbor interlude" from 1955 to 1962. The completely new element, however, was that the competitors started in rows of two, each row slightly offset so that each driver had enough elbow room for manoeuvre between the pavements of the Boulevard Albert I.

With its 21st race, the Monaco Grand Prix had reached adulthood and this time it marked the start of the season as a European Grand Prix. But an assured place on the starting grid below the Grimaldi palace was the privilege of just five drivers on this occasion: only the previous race winners – Bruce McLaren and Maurice Trintignant – and the three World Champions – Jack Brabham, Phil Hill and Graham Hill – were guaranteed starting positions.

John Surtees and Willy Mairesse drove the latest injection version of the Ferrari 156, Jim Clark and Trevor Taylor had Lotus 25s, Graham Hill and Richie Ginther BRM P 57s and Bruce McLaren and Tony Maggs Cooper T 66s. The Brabham factory had only recently been founded so Jack Brabham had bought and entered a Lotus 25 for himself, but there was already a Brabham BT 7, manufactured by his factory, for Dan Gurney.

At the start, the fastest driver in qualifying, Jim Clark, fell back behind the two BRMs, and the Scot required 18 laps in order to wrestle the lead from Hill. He then extended it persistently and constantly until seven seconds separated the two on lap 40, and 15 seconds at the three-quarter point of the race. Meanwhile, Hill got increasingly into trouble. On lap 28 Surtees appeared behind him and attached himself to the rear of the BRM like a terrier and pushed him up to third place on lap 57, after Sainte Dévote. However, two things were causing problems for Big John: fluctuating oil pressure in the six-cylinder engine, and a greasy oil film on his racing goggles, which meant he was driving almost blind in the relative darkness of the tunnel. But while Jim Clark's Lotus came to a halt on lap 79 at the gasometer with locked transmission after spinning the car, the view ahead had become clearer again for Surtees and he was able to use the Ferrari to the full once more, culminating in his best time being set during the last lap. This took him very close to Bruce McLaren in third place.

At this point Graham Hill had already firmly built the first step to his throne as the first real king of Monaco. Jim Clark, in contrast, who would become the 1963 World Champion, was left empty-handed – as always in the Principality.

Monaco und die Sicherheit – das ist seit jeher ein delikates Thema. Der spektakuläre, aber meist glimpflich sich abwickelnde Unfall gehört fast schon zu den Attraktionen des Grand Prix – vorzugsweise im Umfeld der Schikane, aber auch an der Gasometerkurve und bei Sainte Dévote. Zwischen diesen beiden Knotenpunkten des rasenden Stadtverkehrs wird 1963 der Start- und Zielbereich angesiedelt, gewissermaßen an seinem angestammten Platz. Denn vakant war dieser nur während des Hafen-Intermezzos zwischen 1955 und 1962. Ganz neu hingegen: daß die Konkurrenten in Zweierreihen antreten, leicht versetzt, damit jedermann genug Ellbogenfreiheit hat zwischen den Bordsteinkanten des Boulevard Albert I.

Mit seiner 21. Auflage ist der Grand Prix de Monaco volljährig geworden nach altem Recht und markiert als Großer Preis von Europa den Beginn der Saison. Der sichere Arbeitsplatz im Schatten der Grimaldi-Paläste ist diesmal ein Privileg von fünf Piloten: Lediglich den früheren Siegern Bruce McLaren und Maurice Trintignant sowie den drei Weltmeistern Jack Brabham, Phil Hill und Graham Hill wird der Start garantiert.

Die neueste Version des Ferrari 156 mit Einspritzung fahren John Surtees und Willy Mairesse, den Lotus 25 Jim Clark und Trevor Taylor, den BRM P 57 Graham Hill und Richie Ginther, den Cooper T 66 Bruce McLaren und Tony Maggs. Die Gründerjahre der Brabham-Manufaktur sind just angebrochen, so daß Jack Brabham für sich selbst noch das Fremdfabrikat Lotus 25, für Dan Gurney hingegen bereits einen BT 7 aus eigener Fertigung gemeldet hat.

Beim Start fällt der Trainingsschnellste Jim Clark hinter die beiden BRM zurück. 18 Runden benötigt der Schotte, um Hill die Führung abzuringen. Er baut sie zäh und kontinuierlich aus: Sieben Sekunden beträgt der Abstand zwischen den beiden in Runde 40, 15 Sekunden bei drei Vierteln des Rennens. Unterdessen gerät Hill zunehmend in Bedrängnis. Im 28. Durchgang erscheint Surtees hinter ihm, verbeißt sich wie ein Terrier im Heck des BRM, verweist ihn in Runde 57 hinter Sainte Dévote auf Rang drei. Zwei Dinge machen Big John zu schaffen, schwankender Öldruck im Sechszylinder, ein schmieriger Ölfilm auf der Rennbrille, der ihn in der relativen Finsternis des Tunnels fast erblinden läßt. Während jedoch Jim Clarks Lotus in Runde 79 am Gasometer mit blockierendem Getriebe nach einem Dreher zum Stillstand kommt, hat Surtees an Durchblick gewonnen und kann wieder auf die volle Unterstützung des Ferrari zählen, kulminierend in seiner Bestzeit in der letzten Runde. Sie trägt ihn ganz nahe an den Drittplazierten Bruce McLaren heran.

Da hat Graham Hill bereits die unterste Stufe zu seinem Thron als erster wirklicher König von Monaco im Boden verankert. Jim Clark hingegen, Weltmeister des Jahres 1963, ging leer aus – wie immer im Fürstentum.

Monaco et la sécurité – depuis toujours un thème scabreux ici. L'accident spectaculaire, mais le plus souvent sans conséquences graves fait pratiquement partie des attractions du Grand Prix – le plus souvent aux alentours de la chicane, ou encore dans le virage du Gazomètre ou à Sainte Dévote. Entre ces deux derniers pôles de la circulation urbaine à la vitesse grand V se trouve traditionnellement, depuis 1963, la ligne de départ et d'arrivée, tradition à laquelle il n'a, en effet, été dérogé que durant l'intermède des quais du port, de 1955 à 1962. Une chose est, par contre, complètement nouvelle : les concurrents s'alignent deux par deux, légèrement décalés, pour que chacun ait suffisamment de liberté de mouvement entre les bordures de trottoirs du Boulevard Albert I.

Avec sa 21e édition, le Grand Prix de Monaco est devenu majeur selon le droit établi et, avec le label de Grand Prix d'Europe, il marque le début de la saison. Un poste de travail sûr sur la ligne de départ à l'ombre du palais des Grimaldi, est cette année-là, un privilège réservé exclusivement à cinq pilotes : seuls les anciens vainqueurs, Bruce McLaren et Maurice Trintignant, ainsi que les trois champions du monde, Jack Brabham, Phil Hill et Graham Hill, ont une place au départ garantie.

La nouvelle version de la Ferrari 156 à injection est pilotée par John Surtees et Willy Mairesse : les Lotus 25, par Jim Clark et Trevor Taylor, les BRM P 57, par Graham Hill et Richie Ginther, les Cooper T 66, par Bruce McLaren et Tony Maggs. La création de l'écurie Brabham est encore toute récente, à tel point que Jack Brabham doit même s'aligner au volant d'un modèle, une Lotus 25, alors que Dan Gurney dispose déjà d'une BT 7 sortie des ateliers de l'Australien.

Au départ, le plus rapide des essais, Jim Clark, se laisse surprendre par les deux BRM et l'Ecossais a besoin de 18 tours pour reprendre le dessus sur Hill. Il accentue son avance avec âpreté et persévérance : elle atteint sept secondes au 40e tour, et de 15 secondes aux trois-quarts de la course. Pendant ce temps, Hill a de plus en plus de difficulté à contenir ses poursuivants. Au 28e tour, Surtees le talonne tel un terrier rageur dans les basques de la BRM et le relègue à la troisième place au 57e tour, à la sortie de Sainte Dévote. Mais « Big John » a deux graves problèmes : une pression d'huile vacillante dans son six-cylindres et un film d'huile sur sa visière qui le contraint à conduire à l'aveuglette dans l'obscurité presque complète du tunnel. Au moment même où la Lotus de Jim Clark s'immobilise au Gazomètre, boîte de vitesses bloquée, au 79e tour, après un tête-à-queue, Surtees y voit plus clair et peut à nouveau compter sur l'appui total de sa Ferrari, ce qui se traduit immédiatement par le meilleur temps atteint en course au dernier tour. Cela le met à la portée immédiate du troisième, Bruce McLaren.

Mais Graham Hill est déjà monté sur la première marche de son trône de véritable roi de Monaco. Jim Clark, par contre, futur champion du monde 1963, fait chou blanc – comme toujours dans la Principauté.

Buses will run again on Monday: Innes Ireland.

Der Bus verkehrt erst Montag wieder: Innes Ireland.

Le bus ne reprendra son service que lundi : Innes Ireland.

N°	DRIVERS		ENTRANTS	CARS	ENGINES	PRACTICE RESULTS	RACE RESULTS
6	**Graham Hill**	**GB**	**Owen Racing Organisation**	**BRM P57**	**BRM V8 1498 cc**	**2nd: 1'35"0**	**1st: 2h41'49"7**
5	Richie Ginther	USA	Owen Racing Organisation	BRM P57	BRM V8 1498 cc	3rd(4): 1'35"2	2nd: 2h41'54"3
7	Bruce McLaren	NZ	Cooper Car Co.	Cooper T66	Climax V8 1495 cc	8th: 1'36"0	3rd: 2h42'02"5
21	John Surtees	GB	SEFAC Ferrari S.p.A.	Ferrari 156	Ferrari V6 1476 cc	3rd: 1'35"2	4th: 2h42'03"8
8	Tony Maggs	RSA	Cooper Car Co.	Cooper T66	Climax V8 1495 cc	10th: 1'37"9	5th: 98 laps
10	Trevor Taylor	GB	Team Lotus	Lotus 25	Climax V8 1495 cc	9th: 1'37"2	6th: 98 laps
11	Joakim Bonnier	S	RRC Walker Racing Team	Cooper T60	Climax V8 1495 cc	11th: 1'38"6	7th: 94 laps
9	*Jim Clark*	*GB*	*Team Lotus*	*Lotus 25*	*Climax V8 1495 cc*	*1st: 1'34"3*	*8th: 78 laps (R)*
3	Jack Brabham	AUS	Brabham Racing Organisation	Lotus 25	Climax V8 1495 cc	15th: 1'44"7	9th: 77 laps
14	Innes Ireland	GB	British Racing Partnership	Lotus 24	BRM V8 1498 cc	5th: 1'35"5	R
20	Willy Mairesse	B	SEFAC Ferrari S.p.A.	Ferrari 156	Ferrari V6 1476 cc	7th: 1'35"9	R
17	Maurice Trintignant	F	Reg Parnell Racing	Lola Mk4A	Climax V8 1495 cc	14th: 1'41"0	R
4	Dan Gurney	USA	Brabham Racing Organisation	Brabham BT7	Climax V8 1495 cc	6th: 1'35"8	R
12	Jim Hall	USA	British Racing Partnership	Lotus 24	BRM V8 1498 cc	13th: 1'41"0	R
25	Joseph Siffert	CH	Siffert Racing Team	Lotus 24	BRM V8 1498 cc	12th: 1'39"4	R

1

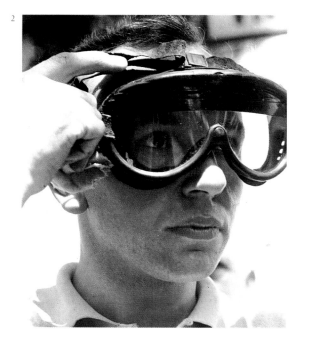

2

3

Portraits of the Sixties: (1) Graham Hill, Trintignant, McLaren, Hall, Trevor Taylor, Ireland; (2) Surtees; (3) Siffert and (4) Brabham. Five of them are still around to tell of the 21st Monaco Grand Prix in May 1963.

Portraits of the Sixties: (1) Graham Hill, Trintignant, McLaren, Hall, Trevor Taylor, Ireland, (2) Surtees, (3) Siffert und (4) Brabham. Fünf von ihnen können heute noch erzählen vom 21. Grand Prix de Monaco im Mai 1963.

Portraits des années soixante : (1) Graham Hill, Trintignant, McLaren, Hall, Trevor Taylor, Ireland, (2) Surtees, (3) Siffert et (4) Brabham. Cinq d'entre eux peuvent aujourd'hui encore parler du 21ᵉ Grand Prix de Monaco de mai 1963.

The ancestors: (1) former driver Franco Cortese was with Ferrari from the beginning. (2) Gianni Lancia and Dr. "Nino" Farina. (3) Past heroes of the Monaco Grand Prix in go-karts on the newly reclaimed land of Fontvieille.

Die Ahnen: (1) Alt-Pilot Franco Cortese war bei Ferrari Mann der ersten Stunde. (2) Gianni Lancia und Dr. »Nino« Farina. (3) Einstige Helden des monegassischen Grand Prix im Go-Kart auf dem frisch aufgeschütteten Landgewinn Fontvieille.

Les ancêtres : (1) le vieux pilote Franco Cortese a été l'homme de la première heure chez Ferrari. (2) Gianni Lancia et « Nino » Farina. (3) D'anciens héros du Grand Prix de Monaco en kart à Fontvieille, tout fraîchement gagné sur la mer.

(1) Should there be an accident, there is no one to help but God and a few straw bales. (2) Graham Hill and (3) Ginther (BRM), (4) McLaren (Cooper), (5) Surtees (Ferrari). (6) Taylor's Lotus is a nose ahead of Maggs' Cooper.

(1) Bei einem Unfall helfen nur Gott und ein paar Strohballen. (2) Graham Hill und (3) Ginther (BRM), (4) McLaren (Cooper), (5) Surtees (Ferrari). (6) Taylors Lotus hat die Nase vorn vor dem Cooper von Maggs.

(1) En cas d'accident, on ne peut se fier qu'à Dieu et à quelques bottes de paille. (2) Graham Hill et (3) Ginther (BRM), (4) McLaren (Cooper), (5) Surtees (Ferrari). (6) La Lotus de Taylor a pris l'avantage sur la Cooper de Maggs.

1

2

Measure for measure: while Jim Clark (1–3) has to retire once again, Hill (3, 4) wins in Monaco for the first time. The Scotsman nevertheless becomes World Champion in 1963.

Zweierlei Maß: Während Jim Clark (1–3) wieder ausfällt, wird Hill (3, 4) zum ersten Mal Sieger in Monaco. Weltmeister 1963 ist am Ende dennoch der Schotte.

Deux poids, deux mesures : alors que Jim Clark (1–3) abandonne de nouveau, Hill (3, 4) signe sa première victoire à Monaco. Mais, à la fin du compte, ce sera pourtant l'Ecossais qui sera champion du monde en 1963.

3

4

1964

The 1964 Monaco Grand Prix was surrounded by a sense of *déjà-vu,* rather like a film which one has seen before. As in the previous year, it ended with a BRM double victory for Graham Hill and Richie Ginther. As in 1963, too, Jim Clark was in pole position, setting the pace for quite some time, but finally had to drop out due to a mechanical defect. And as in 1961, Innes Ireland was lifted out of his wrecked Lotus by concerned helpers during the first training session after an accident near the chicane.

But despite these surprising similarities in the details, the Monégasque May show followed its own script, as did every Grand Prix. Stable partnerships had been preserved at BRM (Graham Hill and Richie Ginther in P261s) and Brabham (Jack Brabham and Dan Gurney with BT7s). However, several positions were filled with new faces: John Surtees in a Tipo 158 and Lorenzo Bandini in a six-cylinder "Aero" were driving for Ferrari, for example, Phil Hill and Bruce McLaren in T73s for the Cooper Car Company, and Jim Clark and Peter Arundell in Lotus 25s. That old warrior, Maurice Trintignant, gave his final performance in a BRM P57 being run by the private team owner Rob Walker, while the multiple motorcycle champion Mike Hailwood took his first tentative steps into Formula 1 with a Lotus-BRM 25.

The Monaco Grand Prix created legends as no other race. The inevitable décor of the pits included the cult figures of Moss and Fangio on this occasion, and they became witnesses to another innovation. The 16 participants initially rolled to a position which was 100 meters behind of the actual start in order to make a final check on the health and functioning of their vehicles. This time Clark left no doubt right from the beginning as to who ruled the roost. When the Scot braked for the first time at the sharp bend at the gasometer, he had already put a time gap of three seconds between himself and his nearest pursuer, Jack Brabham, and after one third of the race he led Hill by ten seconds.

This was all the more remarkable as the Lotus felt rather woolly. In the heat of battle, Clark had drifted into the straw bales at the chicane during the first lap and had damaged the rear anti-roll bar. When flying sparks indicated that the matter was becoming more urgent, Colin Chapman ordered his star into the pits where the defective strut was removed. This happened after lap 36 and Clark subsequently had to take his place behind Gurney and Hill.

At half-distance, the trio were moving around the track as if the cars were tied together, less than two seconds separating the first and third car. But Gurney was already having to cope with transmission problems, and on lap 53 he was overtaken by Hill before the Station Hairpin and lap 62 spelled the end for the American. In the meantime, Clark, fighting with fluctuating oil pressure, made a short stop after lap 92 and returned to the pits on foot four laps later, an onlooker as the two BRMs completed their triumphal laps. John Surtees, the 1964 World Champion, had dropped out a long time earlier. The results in Monaco are seldom predictable.

Den Großen Preis von Monaco 1964 umfächelt ein Hauch von Déjà-vu, so, als hätte man einen Film schon einmal gesehen. Wie im Jahr zuvor endet er mit einem BRM-Doppelsieg für Graham Hill und Richie Ginther. Wie 1963 steht Jim Clark auf der Pole Position, gibt lange den Ton an und muß schließlich mit einem mechanischen Defekt die Segel streichen. Und wie 1961 wird Innes Ireland während der ersten Trainingssitzung nach einem Unfall in der Nähe der Schikane von besorgten Helfern aus einem verstümmelten Lotus gehievt.

Trotz frappierender Ähnlichkeiten im Detail folgt das monegassische Mai-Spektakel jedoch wie jeder Grand Prix seiner eigenen Dramaturgie. Stabile Partnerschaften haben sich erhalten bei BRM (Graham Hill und Richie Ginther auf dem P261) und Brabham (Jack Brabham und Dan Gurney mit dem BT7). Etliche Planstellen sind neu besetzt: Für Ferrari zum Beispiel fahren John Surtees auf dem Tipo 158 und Lorenzo Bandini auf dem Sechszylinder »Aero«, für die Cooper Car Company Phil Hill und Bruce McLaren mit dem T73, für Lotus Jim Clark und Peter Arundell (Lotus 25). Der alte Kämpe Maurice Trintignant gibt seine Abschiedsvorstellung im BRM P57 des privaten Teameigners Rob Walker, während der mehrfache Motorradchampion Mike Hailwood mit einem Lotus-BRM 25 erste zaghafte Schrittchen in die Formel 1 unternimmt.

Wie kein zweiter eignet sich der Grand Prix von Monaco zur Wiederaufbereitung von Legenden: Zum unvermeidlichen Dekor der Boxengasse zählen diesmal die Kultfiguren Moss und Fangio. Sie werden zu Augenzeugen einer Novität: Die sechzehn Teilnehmer rollen zunächst an eine Position 100 Meter vor dem eigentlichen Start, um die organische Gesundheit und Funktionsfähigkeit ihrer Fahrzeuge abzuklären. Diesmal läßt Clark von Beginn an keinen Zweifel daran, wer der eigentliche Herr im Hause ist. Als der Schotte zum ersten Mal die Spitzkehre am Gasometer anbremst, hat er sich bereits drei Sekunden von seinem nächsten Verfolger Jack Brabham abgesetzt, führt nach einem Drittel des Rennens zehn Sekunden vor Hill.

Das ist um so bemerkenswerter, als sich der Lotus schwammig anfühlt. In der Hitze des Gefechts ist Clark in der ersten Runde an der Schikane bis in die Strohballen gedriftet und hat den hinteren Stabilisator beschädigt. Als Funkenflug verrät, daß die Sache dringlich wird, ordert Colin Chapman seinen Star an die Box, wo die defekte Strebe entfernt wird. Dies geschieht nach der 36. Runde, und Clark muß sich anschließend hinter Gurney und Hill einreihen.

Bei Halbzeit zirkuliert das Trio, als seien die Wagen mit Abschleppseilen verbunden: Knapp zwei Sekunden trennen den ersten und den dritten. Aber Gurney wird bereits von Problemen mit dem Getriebe heimgesucht. In der 53. Runde überholt ihn Hill vor der Bahnhofskurve, nach der 62. kommt das Aus für den Amerikaner. Unterdes kämpft Clark mit schwankendem Öldruck, legt nach dem 92. Durchgang einen Boxenstopp ein, kehrt während des 96. zu Fuß an die Box zurück und wird Zaungast der Triumphfahrt der beiden BRM. John Surtees, der Weltmeister von 1964, ist längst ausgeschieden: Die Ergebnisse von Monaco lassen sich selten hochrechnen.

Le Grand Prix de Monaco 1964 a un goût de déjà vu, comme ces films que l'on regarde pour la seconde fois. Comme l'année précédente, il se termine par un doublé BRM avec Graham Hill et Richie Ginther. Comme en 1963, Jim Clark se trouve en pole position, fait longtemps régner sa loi en tête avant d'abandonner finalement sur panne mécanique. Et, comme en 1961, Innes Ireland est dégagé de l'épave de sa Lotus par des secouristes soucieux à la suite d'un accident durant la première séance d'essais, à proximité de la chicane.

Malgré cette similitude frappante sur les détails, le spectacle du mois de mai donné sur la scène monégasque suit sa propre dramaturgie comme chaque Grand Prix auparavant. De solides alliances se sont forgées chez BRM (entre Graham Hill et Richie Ginther avec la P261) et Brabham (Jack Brabham et Dan Gurney avec la BT7). Mais le jeu des chaises musicales a continué de fonctionner : chez Ferrari, par exemple, on trouve John Surtees au volant de la Tipo 158 et Lorenzo Bandini à celui de la six-cylindres « Aero » ; pour la Cooper Car Company, ce sont Phil Hill et Bruce McLaren qui prennent le volant de la T73, ceux des Lotus, des 25, étant confiés à Jim Clark et Peter Arundell. Maurice Trintignant, le vieux renard de la course, donne sa représentation d'adieu dans la BRM P57 de l'écurie privée de Rob Walker tandis que le multiple champion du monde de moto, Mike Hailwood, fait des premiers pas hésitants en Formule 1 dans le baquet d'une Lotus-BRM 25.

Plus que toute autre course, le Grand Prix de Monaco est de nature à faire resurgir les légendes : dans l'incontournable décorum de la voie des stands, on voit défiler cette année des personnages mythiques tels Stirling Moss et Juan Manuel Fangio. Ils seront les témoins d'une innovation : les seize concurrents se déploient tout d'abord à cent mètres de la ligne de départ proprement dite afin de bien vérifier la santé organique et la fiabilité de leurs bolides. Cette fois-ci, d'emblée, Clark ne laisse poindre aucun doute : c'est lui le maître des lieux. Lorsque l'Ecossais freine pour la première fois à l'épingle du Gazomètre, il s'est déjà assuré trois secondes d'avance sur son poursuivant immédiat, Jack Brabham, et à dix secondes d'avance sur Hill au premier tiers de la course.

Chose d'autant plus remarquable que la Lotus a un comportement plutôt flou. Dans l'ardeur du combat, Clark a frôlé les bottes de paille en dérapant et a endommagé sa barre antiroulis arrière, dans le premier tour, à la chicane. Des étincelles trahissent que la cause est grave et Colin Chapman donne à son pilote vedette l'ordre de rentrer aux stands, où le stabilisateur défectueux est démonté. On est au 36e tour et Clark doit alors reprendre la course derrière Gurney et Hill.

A la mi-temps, les trois hommes sont dans un mouchoir, deux secondes à peine séparant le premier et le troisième. Mais Gurney commence déjà à ressentir des problèmes de boîte de vitesses. Au 53e tour, Hill le double dans le virage de la Gare et l'Américain abandonne au 62e tour. Pendant ce temps, Clark voit sa pression d'huile fluctuer, fait un bref arrêt aux stands au 92e tour, mais rentre à pied. Au 96e, il est le témoin involontaire de l'arrivée triomphale des deux BRM. John Surtees, le champion du monde de 1964, a depuis longtemps déjà rangé sa combinaison : l'issue du Grand Prix de Monaco est presque toujours imprévisible.

For the first time in the history of the race the cars roll to a prestart. Siffert (Lotus-BRM number 24) still has to drive a whole lap.

Zum ersten Mal in der Geschichte des Rennens werden die Wagen zum Vorstart aufgestellt. Siffert (Lotus-BRM Nummer 24) muß noch eine komplette Runde fahren.

Pour la première fois dans l'histoire de la course, les voitures prennent place sur la prégrille. Siffert (Lotus-BRM numéro 24) doit encore faire un tour complet.

N°	DRIVERS		ENTRANTS	CARS	ENGINES	PRACTICE RESULTS	RACE RESULTS
8	**Graham Hill**	**GB**	**Owen Racing Organisation**	**BRM P261**	**BRM V8 1498 cc**	**3rd: 1'34"5**	**1st: 2h41'19"5**
7	Richie Ginther	USA	Owen Racing Organisation	BRM P261	BRM V8 1498 cc	8th: 1'35"9	2nd: 99 laps
11	Peter Arundell	GB	Team Lotus	Lotus 25	Climax V8 1497 cc	6th: 1'35"5	3rd: 97 laps
12	Jim Clark	GB	Team Lotus	Lotus 25	Climax V8 1497 cc	1st: 1'34"0	4th: 96 laps (R)
19	Joakim Bonnier	S	RRC Walker Racing Team	Cooper T66	Climax V8 1497 cc	11th: 1'37"4	5th: 96 laps
18	Mike Hailwood	GB	Reg Parnell Racing	Lotus 25	BRM V8 1498 cc	15th: 1'38"5	6th: 96 laps
16	Bob Anderson	GB	DW Racing Enterprises	Brabham BT11	Climax V8 1497 cc	12th: 1'38"0	7th: 86 laps (R)
24	Joseph Siffert	CH	Siffert Racing Team	Lotus 24	BRM V8 1498 cc	16th: 1'38"7	8th: 78 laps
9	Phil Hill	USA	Cooper Car Co.	Cooper T73	Climax V8 1497 cc	8th(9): 1'35"9	9th: 70 laps (R)
20	Lorenzo Bandini	I	SEFAC Ferrari S.p.A.	Ferrari 156	Ferrari V6 1476 cc	6th(7): 1'35"5	10th: 68 laps (R)
6	Dan Gurney	USA	Brabham Racing Organisation	Brabham BT7	Climax V8 1497 cc	5th: 1'34"7	R
4	Maurice Trintignant	F	Maurice Trintignant	BRM P57	BRM V8 1498 cc	13th: 1'38"1	R
5	Jack Brabham	AUS	Brabham Racing Organisation	Brabham BT7	Climax V8 1497 cc	2nd: 1'34"1	R
10	Bruce McLaren	NZ	Cooper Car Co.	Cooper T66	Climax V8 1497 cc	10th: 1'36"6	R
21	John Surtees	GB	SEFAC Ferrari S.p.A.	Ferrari 158	Ferrari V8 1489 cc	3rd(4): 1'34"4	R
15	Trevor Taylor	GB	British Racing Partnership	BRP Mk1	BRM V8 1498 cc	13th(14): 1'38"1	R

(1) The third man: first Clark, then Gurney, then Hill in the lead. (2) Racing goodbye: Trintignant (BRM) takes his leave from the Monaco Grand Prix in 1964. (3) Under palms: Hill in the evening sun. (4) Phil Hill (Cooper) will cross the finishing line together with the winner Graham Hill, although 30 laps behind: his suspension is defective. (5) Dan Gurney (Brabham), who has to retire after 62 laps with a damaged transmission, at the station.

(1) Der dritte Mann: Erst führt Clark, später Gurney, schließlich Hill. (2) Rasendes Adieu: Trintignant (BRM) verabschiedet sich 1964 vom Grand Prix de Monaco. (3) Unter Palmen: Hill in der Abendsonne. (4) Phil Hill (Cooper) wird zusammen mit Graham Hill die Ziellinie überqueren, allerdings mit 30 Runden Rückstand: Die Aufhängung ist defekt. (5) Dan Gurney, dessen Brabham nach 62 Runden mit Getriebeschaden ausfällt, am Bahnhof.

(1) Le troisième homme : c'est d'abord Clark qui mène, puis Gurney et enfin Hill. (2) Adieu à toute vitesse : Trintignant (BRM) fait ses adieux au Grand Prix de Monaco en 1964. (3) Sous les palmiers : Hill sous le soleil de l'après-midi. (4) Phil Hill (Cooper) va franchir la ligne d'arrivée en même temps que Graham Hill, mais avec 30 tours de retard, à cause d'une panne de suspension. (5) Dan Gurney à la Gare. Sa Brabham abandonnera au bout de 62 tours sur panne de boîte de vitesse.

5

Jim Clark comes fourth. But this placing hides a drama. On one occasion the Scot enters the pits to have a loose roll-bar removed. On another he has already left the car because of lack of oil pressure when Lotus boss Colin Chapman persuades him to carry on.

Jim Clark wird vierter. Aber hinter dieser Plazierung verbirgt sich ein Drama. Einmal läuft der Schotte die Box an, um den lockeren hinteren Stabilisator entfernen zu lassen. Ein zweites Mal ist er ohne Öldruck bereits ausgestiegen, da überredet ihn Lotus-Chef Colin Chapman dazu, weiterzumachen.

Jim Clark termine quatrième, un résultat qui est le synonyme de tout un drame. Une première fois, l'Ecossais rejoint les stands pour faire enlever une barre stabilisatrice arrière desserrée. Une deuxième fois, il a déjà quitté sa voiture sans pression d'huile, lorsque le chef de Lotus, Colin Chapman, le persuade de repartir.

1

2

10 MAC LAREN Bruce

(1) Preparing to leave: royalty leaves its box to depart, the way its status demands. (2) Bruce McLaren and his wife Patty. The spelling is not quite right yet. (3, 4) Graham Hill's tension visibly recedes after Louis Chiron has shown the moustache the black and white checkered flag.

(1) Fertigmachen zum Aufsitzen: Die Hoheiten verlassen ihre Loge, um sich standesgemäß zu entfernen. (2) Bruce McLaren und Gattin Patty. Mit der Rechtschreibung hapert es noch. (3, 4) Die Anspannung bei Graham Hill läßt sichtbar nach, nachdem Louis Chiron dem Schnauzbart die schwarzweißkarierte Flagge gezeigt hat.

(1) Prêts à partir : Leurs Altesses quittent leur loge pour rentrer au palais dans leurs limousines. (2) Bruce McLaren et son épouse Patty. On a encore du mal à écrire son nom. (3, 4) La tension retombe visiblement chez Graham Hill, après que Louis Chiron a brandi le drapeau à damier devant le barbu.

1965

In the mid-Sixties, Graham Hill made life easy for the betting fraternity and minimized their winnings at the same time: pole position, fastest lap and third victory in that order at the 23rd Monaco Grand Prix. In doing so, the moustachioed Briton did not always follow the straight and narrow, and went 50 meters on foot.

Jim Clark, top of the class in the World Championship that year, was absent on this occasion and so was Team Lotus: their priority was Indianapolis on the day after Monaco, and their gamble paid off; the Scot won the American 500-mile marathon at the third attempt. Dan Gurney, too, gave precedence to the home game, and in his place Denny Hulme made his debut in the Brabham BT 7, while Jack Brabham himself was at the wheel of a BT 11. Hill and Jackie Stewart, winner of the Monaco Formula 3 race the previous year, were in the two BRM P 261s. The Cooper Car Company had entered Type T 77s for Bruce McLaren and Jochen Rindt. Ferrari, in the meantime, was still trying to regain its composure and was wrestling with the question of into how many combustion units could 1.5 liters best be divided. John Surtees drove the V8 Tipo 158, and Lorenzo Bandini the 12-cylinder car with the irritating model designation 512. Ronnie Bucknum and Richie Ginther, in the two screaming Honda RA 272s with their transverse V12 engines, only managed to take the last positions on the starting grid.

Hill and Stewart took off at speed from the first row, much to the pleasure of their team patron Louis Stanley, and were followed by the two Ferraris, which in turn had the Brabhams breathing down their necks. When Graham Hill shot out of the tunnel at about 120 mph on lap 25, a good eye for distances and clever judgment were much in need, for the chicane was blocked by Bob Anderson's Brabham, rolling along in a leisurely fashion. Hill chose the escape route and drove into the emergency exit, then immediately got out of the stationary BRM in order to heave it back on to the track. After this half-athletic, half-choreographic interlude, he found himself back in fifth position. On lap 26 Brabham overtook Surtees, then went past Bandini at the gasometer in lap 34 and took over the race lead, for on lap 30 a spin on oil near Sainte Dévote had thrown Jackie Stewart back by two places. But the Australian's pleasure was to be short-lived because on lap 42 his Brabham's Climax engine expired.

In the meantime, Hill was driving as if possessed, lapping two seconds per lap faster than anyone else and catching Surtees on lap 53 on the slope towards Mirabeau, then Bandini at the same place on lap 65. The Italian then made life difficult for his team-mate taking his time in allowing him to overtake in order to launch his counter-attack on Hill. But it was all in vain, and Big John had to push his Ferrari across the finishing line with a dead engine.

By this time the Lotus driver Paul Hawkins was back in dry clothing, having safely survived his descent into the harbor, like Alberto Ascari ten years earlier.

Mitte der Sechziger macht Graham Hill den Wettlustigen die Entscheidung beim Buchmacher leicht und minimiert zugleich deren Gewinne: Pole Position, schnellste Runde und dritter Sieg in Folge beim 23. Grand Prix de Monaco. Dabei gerät der schnauzbärtige Brite zwischendurch auf Abwege und legt 50 Meter als Fußgänger zurück.

Jim Clark, Klassen-Primus im Welt-Championat jenes Jahres, fehlt diesmal und mit ihm Team Lotus: Priorität hat Indy am Tag nach Monaco. Das Vabanquespiel lohnt sich: Der Schotte gewinnt das amerikanische 500-Meilen-Marathon beim dritten Anlauf. Auch Dan Gurney gibt dem Heimspiel den Vorzug. An seiner Statt debütiert Denny Hulme im Brabham BT 7, während Jack Brabham selbst einen BT 11 lenkt. In den beiden BRM P 261 sitzen Hill und Jackie Stewart, der Sieger des monegassischen Formel-3-Laufs im Jahr zuvor. Die Cooper Car Company hat den Typ T 77 für Bruce McLaren und Jochen Rindt gemeldet. Ferrari indessen ringt am Ende der aktuellen Formel 1 noch immer um Fassung und die Antwort auf die Frage, auf wieviele Verbrennungseinheiten man anderthalb Liter am besten aufteilt. Den V8 Tipo 158 fährt John Surtees, den Zwölfzylinder mit der irritierenden Modellbezeichnung 512 Lorenzo Bandini. Für Ronnie Bucknum und Richie Ginther in den beiden kreischenden Honda RA 272 mit ihren quer installierten V12 reicht es nur zu Plätzen in der letzten Startreihe.

Aus der ersten setzen sich Hill und Stewart sehr zur Erbauung ihres Team-Patrons Louis Stanley zügig ab, gefolgt von den beiden Ferrari, denen Brabham zäh im Nacken hängt. Als Graham Hill in der 25. Runde mit Tempo 190 aus dem Tunnel schießt, sind Augenmaß und eine kluge Entscheidung gefragt, denn die Schikane wird verstopft von Bob Andersons gemächlich dahinrollendem Brabham. Hill wählt die Notbremsung in den Notausgang und verläßt gleich darauf den stationären BRM, um ihn auf die Piste zurückzuwuchten. Nach dieser halb athletischen, halb choreographischen Einlage findet er sich auf Rang fünf wieder. Im 26. Durchgang überholt Brabham Surtees, bremst im 34. auch Bandini am Gasometer aus und führt das Rennen an. Denn in der 30. Runde hat ein Dreher auf Öl bei Sainte Dévote Jackie Stewart um zwei Plätze zurückgeworfen. Lange währt des Australiers Freude nicht: Nach der 42. Runde bewegt sich in der Climax-Maschine des Brabham nichts mehr.

Unterdessen fährt Hill wie ein Besessener, zwei Sekunden pro Runde schneller als irgendjemand sonst, schnappt sich in der 53. auf dem Gefälle Richtung Mirabeau Surtees, in der 65. an der gleichen Stelle auch Bandini. Der Italiener macht seinem Teamgefährten mit dem klingenden Namen das Leben schwer, läßt ihn erst spät passieren und seinen Angriff auf Hill vortragen. Umsonst: Über die Ziellinie muß Big John den Ferrari mit abgestorbenem Motor schieben.

Zu diesem Zeitpunkt ist Lotus-Pilot Paul Hawkins schon wieder in trockene Kleidung geschlüpft: Wie Alberto Ascari zehn Jahre zuvor hat der kernige Australier einen Abflug in den Hafen unversehrt überstanden.

Vers le milieu des années 60, Graham Hill facilite considérablement la tâche aux parieurs, mais, par la même occasion, diminue sensiblement leurs gains : pole position, tour le plus rapide en course et troisième victoire consécutive au 23e Grand Prix de Monaco. Et ce, bien que, entre-temps, le Britannique à la typique petite moustache ait connu des problèmes et dû couvrir 50 mètres à pieds.

Jim Clark, l'homme à battre au championnat de cette année, brille par son absence et, avec lui, le Team Lotus : priorité a été donnée à Indy, qui doit avoir lieu le lendemain de Monaco. Le coup de poker se solde par un succès : l'Ecossais gagne les 500 Miles d'Indianapolis aux Etats-Unis, à sa troisième tentative. Dan Gurney, lui aussi, donne la préférence à un match à domicile. Sa place est comblée par Denny Hulme, qui fait ses débuts au volant de la Brabham BT 7 tandis que Jack Brabham lui-même conduit une BT 11. Dans les deux BRM P 261, on voit Hill et Jackie Stewart, le vainqueur du Grand Prix de Formule 3 de Monaco de l'année précédente. La Cooper Car Company a inscrit deux T 77 pour Bruce McLaren et Jochen Rindt. Ferrari, de son côté, est encore indécis, à la fin de l'actuelle Formule 1, et n'a toujours pas répondu à la question du nombre de cylindres optimal pour 1500 cm^3. La V8 Tipo 158 est pilotée par John Surtees et la douze-cylindres à la dénomination bizarre 512, par Lorenzo Bandini. Ronnie Bucknum et Richie Ginther, avec leurs deux stridentes Honda RA 272 à moteur douze-cylindres transversal devront se contenter des deux dernières places au départ.

De la première, ce sont Hill et Stewart qui jaillissent le plus rapidement, pour le plus grand ravissement de leur patron, Louis Stanley, suivis des deux Ferrari talonnées par Brabham. Lorsque Graham Hill jaillit du tunnel à 190 km/h, au 25e tour, il lui faut un bon coup d'œil et un coup de chance, car la chicane est bloquée par la Brabham de Bob Anderson qui roule au ralenti. Hill choisit de freiner en catastrophe en direction de l'échappatoire, puis bondit immédiatement de sa Brabham arrêtée pour la repousser sur la piste. Après cet intermède athlétique digne d'un chorégraphe, il se retrouve au 5e rang. Au 26e tour, Brabham double Surtees, pique aussi Bandini au freinage du 34e tour, au Gazomètre, et prend la tête. En effet, au 30e tour, Jackie Stewart qui a fait un tête-à-queue sur une flaque d'huile à Sainte Dévote, est retombé de deux places. Mais la joie de l'Australien ne durera pas longtemps : au 42e tour, le moteur Climax de la Brabham rend l'âme.

Pendant ce temps, Hill, déchaîné, prend deux secondes au tour à tous ses adversaires et double Surtees dans la descente de Mirabeau au 53e tour puis Bandini au même endroit, au 65e. L'Italien ne facilite pas la tâche à son coéquipier au nom strident et ne le laisse doubler que très tard pour qu'il puisse porter une attaque contre Hill. Mais son effort est vain. « Big John » doit pousser jusqu'à la ligne d'arrivée sa Ferrari au moteur qui s'est tu.

A ce moment-là, Paul Hawkins, pilote de Lotus, a déjà de nouveau endossé des vêtements secs : comme Alberto Ascari dix ans auparavant, l'Australien a survécu sans mal à un plongeon dans le port.

Beautiful vista: the gallery above Tobacconist's Corner, a natural platform, provides a clear view of the fast-approaching cars.

Schöne Aussichten: Die Empore oberhalb der Tabakskurve vermittelt gleichsam als Naturtribüne einen unverbaubaren Blick auf die heraneilenden Wagen.

Vue imprenable : le balcon au-dessus du virage du Bureau de Tabac, tribune naturelle, offre une vue incomparable sur les voitures qui déboulent.

N°	DRIVERS		ENTRANTS	CARS	ENGINES	PRACTICE RESULTS	RACE RESULTS
3	**Graham Hill**	**GB**	**Owen Racing Organisation**	**BRM P261**	**BRM V8 1498 cc**	**1st: 1'32"5**	**1st: 2h37'39"6**
17	Lorenzo Bandini	I	SEFAC Ferrari S.p.A.	Ferrari 512	Ferrari V12 1490 cc	4th: 1'33"0	2nd: 2h38'43"6
4	Jackie Stewart	GB	Owen Racing Organisation	BRM P261	BRM V8 1498 cc	3rd: 1'32"9	3rd: 2h39'21"5
18	John Surtees	GB	SEFAC Ferrari S.p.A.	Ferrari 158	Ferrari V8 1489 cc	5th: 1'33"2	4th: 99 laps (R)
7	Bruce McLaren	NZ	Cooper Car Co.	Cooper T77	Climax V8 1497 cc	7th: 1'34"3	5th: 98 laps
14	Joseph Siffert	CH	RRC Walker Racing Team	Brabham BT11	BRM V8 1498 cc	10th: 1'36"0	6th: 98 laps
12	Joakim Bonnier	S	RRC Walker Racing Team	Brabham BT7	Climax V8 1497 cc	12th(13): 1'36"5	7th: 97 laps
2	Denis Hulme	NZ	Brabham Racing Organisation	Brabham BT7	Climax V8 1497 cc	8th: 1'34"5	8th: 92 laps
9	Bob Anderson	GB	DW Racing Enterprises	Brabham BT11	Climax V8 1497 cc	9th: 1'35"5	9th: 85 laps
10	Paul Hawkins	AUS	DW Racing Enterprises	Lotus 33	Climax V8 1497 cc	14th: 1'37"0	10th: 79 laps (R)
15	Richard Attwood	GB	Reg Parnell Racing	Lotus 25	BRM V8 1498 cc	6th: 1'33"9	R
1	Jack Brabham	AUS	Brabham Racing Organisation	Brabham BT11	Climax V8 1497 cc	2nd: 1'32"8	R
19	Ronnie Bucknum	USA	Honda R & D Co.	Honda RA 272	Honda V12 1495 cc	14th(15): 1'37"0	R
11	Frank Gardner	AUS	John Willment Automobiles	Brabham BT11	BRM V8 1498 cc	10th(11): 1'36"0	R
16	Mike Hailwood	GB	Reg Parnell Racing	Lotus 25	BRM V8 1498 cc	12th: 1'36"5	R
20	Richie Ginther	USA	Honda R & D Co.	Honda RA 272	Honda V12 1495 cc	16th: 1'39"7	R

4

5

6

Ready to jump: (1) Stewart (BRM) and (2) Bandini (Ferrari) on the brow of the hill before the drop down to Mirabeau. (3) Pressure point: for twelve laps Bandini (Ferrari) resists the attacks of the eventual winner Graham Hill (BRM). (4) Divided as one: internal team duels are also fought as hard as they come; here Hill is in front of Stewart (both BRMs). (5) First Grand Prix for Denis Hulme (Brabham), eighth place, eight laps behind. (6) The former racing driver Louis Chiron lives dangerously even in retirement, as does the policeman in the foreground.

Bereit zum Sprung: (1) Stewart (BRM) und (2) Bandini (Ferrari) auf dem Buckel vor dem Gefälle nach Mirabeau. (3) Druck-Sache: Zwölf Runden lang widersteht Bandini (Ferrari) den Attacken des späteren Siegers Graham Hill (BRM). (4) Vereinte Zwietracht: Auch teaminterne Duelle werden mit aller Härte ausgetragen, hier Hill vor Stewart (beide BRM). (5) Erster Grand Prix für Denis Hulme (Brabham), achter Rang, acht Runden zurück. (6) Selbst im Ruhestand lebt der ehemalige Rennfahrer Louis Chiron gefährlich, wie auch der dienstlich tätige Ordnungshüter links im Bild.

Prêts à bondir : (1) Stewart (BRM) et (2) Bandini (Ferrari) sur la bosse qui annonce la descente vers Mirabeau. (3) Talonné : pendant douze tours, Bandini (Ferrari) résiste aux attaques du futur vainqueur, Graham Hill (BRM). (4) Guerre intestine : les duels entre coéquipiers ne connaissent aucun égard, ici, Hill devant Stewart (tous les deux sur BRM). (5) Premier Grand Prix pour Denis Hulme (Brabham), huitième rang, huit tours de retard. (6) Même à la retraite, l'ancien pilote de course Louis Chiron vit dangereusement, de même que le policier à gauche sur la photo.

3

4

In the fifth and final year of the 1½-liter formula, the engines have matured, are reliable and deliver up to 220 bhp: (1, 4) the transverse Honda V12, (2) Climax V8, (3) Ferrari V8.

Im fünften und letzten Jahr der Anderthalbliterformel sind die Motoren ausgereift, standfest und bis zu 220 PS stark geworden: (1, 4) der quer eingebaute Honda-V12, (2) Climax-V8, (3) Ferrari-V8.

Pour la cinquième et dernière année de la Formule 1,5 litre, les moteurs bien au point et fiables développent jusqu'à 220 ch : (1, 4) le Honda V12 monté en position transversale, (2) le Climax V8, (3) le Ferrari V8.

4

5

6

Stars of the screen and cockpit: (1) Steve McQueen with Ronnie Bucknum, (2) Graham Hill and Jo Bonnier, (3) Phil Hill in conversation with Stewart, (4) Bandini and (5) the Australian Paul Hawkins, who (6) is being made fun of by his colleagues at the German Grand Prix because of his harbor bath.

Stars aus Kino und Cockpit: (1) Steve McQueen mit Ronnie Bucknum, (2) Graham Hill und Jo Bonnier, (3) Phil Hill im Gespräch mit Stewart, (4) Bandini und (5) der Australier Paul Hawkins, der (6) wegen seines Bades im Hafen von seinen Kollegen beim Großen Preis von Deutschland verspottet wird.

Vedettes de l'écran et du cockpit : (1) Steve McQueen avec Ronnie Bucknum, (2) Graham Hill et Jo Bonnier, (3) Phil Hill conversant avec Stewart, (4) Bandini et (5) l'Australien Paul Hawkins que ses collègues raillent, (6) lors du Grand Prix d'Allemagne, à cause de son bain dans le port.

Club des anciens pilotes: (1) Louis Chiron in the Bugatti 35 leading Fangio in his Mercedes-Benz W 196. (2) Fangio in his Alfetta. (3) Stirling Moss with the Lotus 18 and (4) Chiron as the Prince's co-driver in a 1910 Renault, behind him Prince Bernhard of the Netherlands.

Club des anciens pilotes: (1) Louis Chiron im Bugatti 35 vor Fangio im Mercedes-Benz W 196, (2) Fangio im Alfetta, (3) Stirling Moss mit dem Lotus 18 und (4) Chiron als Copilot des Fürsten in einem Renault von 1910, hinter ihm Prinz Bernhard der Niederlande.

Club des anciens pilotes : (1) Louis Chiron sur Bugatti 35 devant Fangio sur Mercedes-Benz W 196, (2) Fangio sur Alfetta, (3) Stirling Moss avec la Lotus 18 et (4) Chiron comme copilote du Prince au volant d'une Renault de 1910 ; derrière lui, le Prince Bernhard des Pays-Bas.

UNCROWNED KING

KÖNIG OHNE KRONE · LE ROI SANS COURONNE

Like the career of many a great master, Norman Graham Hill's also fell into two phases, which might roughly be described with the over-used phrase "the rise and fall". He reached the watershed between the two almost exactly at the age of 40.

Anyone who wants to find out about the early Graham Hill need do no more than look at a photo from the first half of the 1960s: thin lips, accurately trimmed moustache, carefully combed hair. He sits at the wheel, collected and yet with stoical calm. His body language and face express that persistent and disciplined fanaticism which can take you far in life.

But Hill also had humour, from scurrilous to black, very British, like the man himself. "I know that I'm sitting in a Lotus when I get overtaken by a wheel from my car", was his sarcastic homage to the brilliant Lotus boss and technical visionary Colin Chapman, with whom Hill once started as a mechanic, and to whom he presented his second World Championship in 1968. That saying became proverbial among the racing fraternity, a relaxed linguistic way of describing the hair-raising situations into which he and others were plunged by the fragility of Chapman's creations.

Another example: in John Frankenheimer's racing epic film *Grand Prix* the actors playing the racing drivers celebrate an unfettered victory party, roaring with false joy after the 1966 Belgian Grand Prix. The true heroes are allowed to be there as extras, Joakim Bonnier, for example, and Graham Hill. The latter's expression speaks volumes of his amusing superiority, and above all when a misplaced spray of champagne hits him in the eye, a masterpiece of mimicry equal to that of any professional actor.

A third example: during qualifying for the 1962 German Grand Prix, at the Nürburgring, the film camera fell off the Porsche of the Dutch Count Godin de Beaufort at the lower dead center of the Fuchsröhre part of the track, where it was at its fastest. De Beaufort did not even notice his loss, but Hill did. His BRM hit the object on the track at 140 mph, was slit open from below, started to slide on its own oil and finally came to rest in a ditch after endless spins, a wreck of steel, aluminium and rubber. The driver was unhurt – a miracle. As Hill arrived back at the start and finish, driven by a marshal, he had the software of the camera draped about him like Laocoön, the snakes. His appearance expressed two things: theatrical accusation, but also conscious situation comedy. He won the race on the following Sunday and his first World Championship at the end of the year.

Hill simply had to live with the accidents, and he coped with them unmoved, like a hard-bitten schoolboy with an "E" in mathematics. In Watkins Glen, in early October 1969, he was braking to enter a section of the track called The Loop, lost control of his car, smashed into an earth bank, and rolled over several times. Hill fell out, since he was not properly strapped in after a pit-stop, and he broke both legs with complicated fractures. The doctors did their best in a four-and-a-half hour operation. But they were having to deal with an obsessive. He would be back for the South African Grand Prix on 7 March 1970, Hill announced. By December he was in a wheelchair. In January he was

Wie die Karriere so manches großen Meisters zerfällt auch die des Norman Graham Hill in zwei Phasen, die mit den abgegriffenen Vokabeln Aufstieg und Fall grob umrissen sind. Die Wasserscheide zwischen den beiden erreicht er im Alter von genau 40 Jahren.

Wer etwas über den frühen Graham Hill erfahren möchte, braucht sich lediglich ein Foto aus der ersten Hälfte der Sechziger anzuschauen und ist schon im Bilde: schmale Lippen, akkurat gestutzter Schnäuzer, gepflegte Haartracht. Am Lenkrad sitzt er gesammelt und dennoch mit stoischer Gelassenheit. In Körpersprache und Antlitz drückt sich jener hartnäckige und disziplinierte Fanatismus aus, mit dem man es weit bringen kann im Leben.

Aber Hill hat auch Humor, skurril bis schwarz, *very British* wie der ganze Mann. »Immer, wenn mich ein Rad meines eigenen Wagens überholt, weiß ich, daß ich in einem Lotus sitze«, lautet seine sarkastische Hommage an den genialischen Lotus-Chef und technischen Visionär Colin Chapman, bei dem Hill einst als Mechaniker anfing und dem er 1968 seine zweite Weltmeisterschaft beschert. Der Satz wird sprichwörtlich in der Branche, eine lockere sprachliche Aufbereitung der haarsträubenden Situationen, in die die Zerbrechlichkeit von Chapmans Kreationen ihn und andere gestürzt hat.

Ein anderes Beispiel: In John Frankenheimers Vollgas-Epos *Grand Prix* feiern die falschen Film-Rennfahrer in geheuchelter Glückseligkeit grölend eine zügellose Siegesparty nach dem Grand Prix von Belgien 1966. Die echten Heroen dürfen als Komparsen dabeisein, Joakim Bonnier zum Beispiel und Graham Hill. Aber dessen Miene spricht Bände in seiner drolligen Distanz, vor allem als ihn ein verirrter Schuß Champagner ins Auge trifft, eine mimische Meisterleistung wie die eines Bühnen-Profis.

Ein drittes: Beim ersten Training zum Großen Preis von Deutschland 1962 auf dem Nürburgring schüttelt der Porsche des holländischen Grafen Godin de Beaufort eine mitgeführte Filmkamera ab, in der Senke des Streckenteils Fuchsröhre, da, wo man am schnellsten ist. De Beaufort bemerkt den Verlust gar nicht, aber Hill. Sein BRM trifft das Objekt auf der Fahrbahn mit Tempo 230, wird von unten aufgeschlitzt, rutscht auf dem eigenen Öl aus und kommt nach einer endlosen Schleuderpartie im Graben zur Ruhe, ein armes Knäuel aus Stahl, Aluminium und Gummi. Der Fahrer ist unverletzt, ein Wunder. Als Hill, von einem Streckenposten chauffiert, wieder bei Start und Ziel eintrifft, wird er von der Software der Kamera umringelt wie Laokoon von den Schlangen. Sein Anblick drückt zweierlei aus, theatralische Anklage, aber auch bewußt ausgespielte Situationskomik. Das Rennen am folgenden Sonntag gewinnt er ebenso wie sein erstes Championat im gleichen Jahr.

Mit Unfällen muß Hill halt leben und steckt sie ungerührt weg wie ein hartgesottener Pennäler eine Fünf in Mathematik. Watkins Glen Anfang Oktober 1969: Da bremst sein Lotus den Streckenabschnitt The Loop an, gerät außer Kontrolle, knallt gegen einen Erdwall, überschlägt sich etliche Male. Hill wird herausgeschleudert, da er nicht angeschnallt ist, bricht sich beide Beine in komplizierten Frakturen. In einer

Comme la carrière de tant d'autres grandes personnalités, celle de Norman Graham Hill se déroule en deux phases que l'on peut décrire grossièrement avec les vocables, usés jusqu'à la corde, d'essor et de décadence. La ligne de séparation des eaux entre ces deux époques se trouve aux alentours de la quarantaine. Quiconque veut apprendre quelque chose au sujet de Graham Hill le jeune n'a pas besoin de grand-chose, il suffit de regarder une photo de lui remontant à la première moitié des années 60 et l'on est déjà informé : des lèvres minces, une mince moustache taillée avec élégance, une chevelure soignée ; au volant, il est assis de façon concentrée et, pourtant, avec une décontraction stoïque. Dans sa langue gestuelle et son allure transparaît ce fanatisme intraitable et discipliné qui permet à un homme d'aller loin dans la vie.

Mais Hill a aussi de l'humour, passant du bizarre au noir, très « british », comme l'homme lui-même. « A chaque fois qu'une roue de ma voiture me double, je sais que je suis assis dans une Lotus », déclare-t-il en hommage sarcastique à son génial chef, le constructeur des Lotus et visionnaire de la mécanique qu'était Colin Chapman, auprès duquel Graham Hill a jadis commencé comme mécanicien et auquel il a rapporté, en 1968, son deuxième championnat du monde. La phrase prend valeur de proverbe dans la branche, métaphore ironique des situations à vous faire dresser les cheveux sur la tête, dans lesquelles la fragilité des créations de Colin Chapman l'a précipité, lui et bien d'autres encore.

Autre exemple : dans *Grand Prix*, le film culte de la compétition automobile tourné par John Frankenheimer, les faux pilotes de course du cinéma fêtent dans une gaieté feinte, de façon bruyante et licencieuse, une victoire au Grand Prix de Belgique de 1966. Les véritables héros ont été invités à y participer en tant que figurants avec, notamment, Joakim Bonnier et Graham Hill. Mais son visage dit plus que mille mots dans sa distance ironique, surtout lorsqu'un verre de champagne égaré le touche à l'œil, avec une mimique qui est un chef-d'œuvre digne d'un professionnel de l'écran.

Troisième exemple : lors des premiers essais de qualification pour le Grand Prix d'Allemagne en 1962 sur le Nürburgring, la Porsche du comte hollandais Godin de Beaufort qui le précède perd une caméra de cinéma fixée sur la voiture, au point le plus bas de la section du circuit appelée Fuchsröhre, là où l'on est le plus rapide. De Beaufort ne s'aperçoit pas de la perte, mais bien Hill. Sa BRM percute l'objet virevoltant sur la piste à la vitesse de 230 km/h et, le soubassement de sa voiture éventré par la caméra, dérape sur sa propre huile avant de terminer sa course dans un fossé à l'issue d'un dérapage interminable, triste amas d'acier, d'aluminium et de caoutchouc. Le pilote s'en tire sain et sauf. Un vrai miracle ! Lorsque Hill, emmené par un commissaire de piste, réapparaît dans la zone des stands, il est encore empêtré dans le film de la caméra tel Laocoon assailli par les vipères. Son visage exprime deux choses : une accusation théâtrale, mais aussi un comique de situation feint avec une maîtrise incomparable. Il gagnera la course du dimanche suivant, ainsi que son premier titre de champion du monde à la fin de l'année.

Graham Hill aura dû s'habituer à vivre avec les accidents, qu'il encaisse avec le même stoïcisme qu'un

leaning heavily on crutches. Shortly before the race in Kyalami he threw them away, and then he took sixth place in the private Lotus of his patron Rob Walker.

But at this point Graham was already "over the hill", with a lower-case h, mark you. *The Other Side of the Hill* (with a capital H) was the title of his biography in which his wife Bette marketed her insider knowledge about the popular man with the moustache after his premature death, in order to get through life with her two children Damon and Samantha. Graham and Bette got to know one another in the early 1950s at the London Auriol Rowing Club, whose colors the passionate rower Hill carried on his helmet for old times' sake. He lost the knack of winning after his fifth win in Monaco in 1969. Only once more did he succeed in grand style; at Le Mans in 1972 in a car from the

vviereinhalbstündigen Operation tun die Ärzte, was sie können. Aber sie haben einen Besessenen unter dem Messer. Beim Großen Preis von Südafrika am 7. März 1970 werde er wieder mit von der Partie sein, kündigt Hill an. Im Dezember sitzt er im Rollstuhl. Im Januar stützt er sich schwer auf Krücken. Kurz vor dem Rennen in Kyalami wirft er sie ab und belegt Platz sechs auf dem privaten Lotus seines Gönners Rob Walker.

Zu diesem Zeitpunkt jedoch ist Graham bereits on the other side of the hill, mit klein geschriebenem h, wohlgemerkt. Denn genauso, nur mit großem H, heißt die Biographie, in der seine treue Gattin Bette nach seinem vorzeitigen Ableben ihr Insiderwissen über den populären Schnauzbart vermarkten wird, um sich selbst und ihre beiden Kinder Damon und Samantha durch-zubringen. Man hat sich Anfang der fünfziger Jahre

lycéen un zéro en mathématiques. Watkins Glen début octobre 1969 : sa Lotus freine pour un tronçon appelé The Loop, échappe à son contrôle, percute de plein fouet un remblai de terre et part en d'innombrables tonneaux. Hill est éjecté puisqu'il ne portait pas de ceinture après un arrêt aux stands et il se brise les deux jambes en de complexes fractures. Pour l'opération qui dure quatre heures et demie, les médecins font de leur mieux. Mais c'est un obsédé qu'ils ont sous leur scalpel. Pour le Grand Prix d'Afrique du Sud, le 7 mars 1970, il sera de nouveau au départ, annonce Hill. En décembre, il est assis dans un fauteuil roulant. En janvier, il a du mal à se déplacer avec des béquilles. Mais, peu avant la course de Kyalami, il s'en débarrasse et termine le Grand Prix à la sixième place sur la Lotus privée de son mécène Rob Walker.

French state company Matra, together with local hero Henri Pescarolo. "There's life in the old boy yet", Graham Hill crowed.

The older Hill: hair and beard had become a little unruly, as dictated by the fashion of the time, and he laughed more. His honors tended to be won as ambassador of his sport and elder statesman. His experience in handling the media was evident in the way he could switch his smile and talkativeness on and off with the microphones and the cameras which were thrust into his face. And he was quite capable on occasion of pushing an autograph hunter aside when he felt like it, including children.

His detractors made fun of the ageing hero as "Auntie Hill" after he had lost his bite and simply continued to do what he had always done. When, at the British Grand Prix in 1975, he announced that he would retire, hardly anyone tried to stop him.

His death on 29 November of the same year, at the controls of his Piper Aztec, was all the more shocking. Hill in the meantime had become boss of his own team. It was returning from a test session in Le Castellet, in the south of France. Dense fog lay on the small airport at Elstree, near his home. But Hill did not climb away again to land somewhere else with clear visibility. Instead, the aircraft touched the tips of three trees on Arkley golf course and crashed. Five other people in the plane also died, including the talented young driver Tony Brise, in whom Hill saw a future World Champion.

But Hill the legend survived. When Damon Hill began to make his name, he was still referred to as Graham's son. Today, on the other hand, with Hill Junior having won 21 Grands Prix as opposed to the 14 of Hill Senior, the reverse is the case. Long since, the chroniclers have had to remind a forgetful public that Damon's father had also once been a racing driver, and had even managed to achieve something as double World Champion in Formula 1 and winner in Indianapolis in 1966.

In such a situation Bette Hill always smiles quietly to herself. After all, she knows the other side of the Hill – both of them.

kennengelernt im Londoner Auriol Rowing Club, dessen Farben der passionierte Ruderer Hill am Helm trägt aus alter Verbundenheit. Nach seinem fünften Erfolg in Monaco 1969 hat er das Siegen verlernt. Nur noch einmal klappt es in großem Stil, 1972 in Le Mans in einem Wagen des französischen Staatskonzerns Matra, zusammen mit local hero Henri Pescarolo. »Noch ist Leben in dem alten Knaben«, trumpft Graham Hill auf.

Der späte Hill: Haar und Bart sind ein bißchen ins Kraut geschossen gemäß der Zeitmode, und er lacht auch mehr. Seine Meriten verdient er nun eher als Botschafter seines Sports und elder statesman. Man merkt seine Routine im Umgang mit den Medien, wenn er sein Lächeln und seine Mitteilsamkeit an- und abschaltet mit den Mikrophonen und Kameras, die ihm ins Gesicht gehalten werden. Und er schiebt auch schon einmal einen Autogrammjäger unwirsch zur Seite, selbst Kinder, wenn ihm danach ist.

Spötter schmähen den alternden Helden gar »Auntie Hill«, Tantchen Hill, nachdem er seinen Biß verloren hat und einfach weitermacht, was er immer gemacht hat. Als er beim Grand Prix von England 1975 ankündigt, er werde sich in den Ruhestand zurückziehen, versucht kaum jemand, ihn zurückzuhalten.

Umso tragischer ist sein Tod am 29. November des gleichen Jahres am Steuerknüppel seiner Piper Aztec. Inzwischen ist Hill Chef eines eigenen Teams. Man kehrt zurück von einer Testsitzung im südfranzösischen Le Castellet. Dichter Nebel lagert über dem kleinen Flugplatz von Elstree. Aber Hill startet nicht durch, um vielleicht woanders bei klarer Sicht zu landen. Die Maschine kappt die Spitzen dreier Bäume auf dem Golfplatz von Arkley und stürzt ab. Auch fünf weitere Insassen kommen ums Leben, unter ihnen der begabte junge Fahrer Tony Brise, in dem Hill einen künftigen Champion vermutete.

Der Mythos Hill aber dauert an. Noch als Damon Hill beginnt, sich einen Namen zu machen, spricht man von ihm als Grahams Sohn. Heute indessen, wo Hill junior 21 Grands Prix gewonnen hat gegenüber den 14 des Seniors, ist es umgekehrt. Denn längst müssen die Chronisten ein vergeßliches Publikum darüber aufklären, Damons Vater sei einst auch Rennen gefahren und habe es sogar zu etwas gebracht als Doppelweltmeister in der Formel 1 und Sieger in Indianapolis 1966.

Bette Hill lächelt dann immer still in sich hinein. Immerhin kennt sie the other side of the Hill, und gleich von zweien.

A cette époque, pourtant, Graham est déjà « on the other side of the hill », avec un h minuscule, notez-le bien. C'est en effet, mais avec un H majuscule, exactement le titre de la biographie avec laquelle sa fidèle épouse Bette commercialise ses connaissances d'initiée au sujet du populaire porteur de moustache après son décès prématuré. Elle travaille même comme secrétaire pour arriver à joindre les deux bouts et rembourser les compagnies d'assurance, avec ses deux enfants Damon et Samantha. Bette et Graham se sont connus au début des années cinquante à l'Auriol Rowing Club de Londres, le vieux club dont Graham Hill, passionné d'aviron, arbore les couleurs sur son casque par fidélité. Après son cinquième succès à Monaco en 1969, les victoires se font rares. Il en signe encore une, ultime mais prestigieuse, en 1972 au Mans dans une voiture du groupe public français Matra, coéquipier du régional de l'étape Henri Pescarolo. « Il y a encore du jus dans le vieux bonhomme », déclare Graham Hill triomphant.

Le Hill tardif : les cheveux et la moustache se sont un peu allongés, comme cela était à la mode à cette époque, et il rit aussi un peu plus. Il gagne maintenant plutôt ses mérites comme ambassadeur de son sport et elder statesman. On sent sa routine dans les rapports avec les médias lorsqu'il allume et coupe son sourire et ses bavardages en même temps que les micros et les caméras qu'on lui brandit sous le nez. Et il n'hésite pas non plus à repousser fraîchement un demandeur d'autographe, même si c'est un enfant, quand cela ne lui convient pas.

Ses détracteurs ironisent sur le héros vieillissant en le surnommant « Auntie Hill », tata Hill, lorsque celui-ci a perdu de son mordant et continue tout simplement à faire ce qu'il a toujours fait. Lorsqu'il annonce, au Grand Prix d'Angleterre de 1975, qu'il va prendre sa retraite, pratiquement personne ne cherche à le retenir.

Sa mort est d'autant plus tragique : elle survient le 29 novembre de la même année aux commandes de son Piper Aztec. Entre-temps, Hill a fondé sa propre écurie de Formule 1, Embassy. Il revient d'une séance d'essais sur le circuit du Castellet, sur la Côte d'Azur. Un épais brouillard noie le petit aéroport d'Elstree près de chez lui. Mais Hill ne cherche pas à reprendre son vol pour tenter d'atterrir ailleurs où la vue serait plus claire. L'avion frôle le sommet de trois arbres sur le terrain de golf d'Arkley et s'écrase au sol. Cinq autres passagers meurent avec lui. Parmi eux, un grand talent, le jeune pilote Tony Brise, dans lequel Hill voyait un futur champion du monde.

Mais le mythe de Hill perdure. Même lorsque Damon Hill commence à se faire un nom, on parle encore de lui comme le fils de Graham. Aujourd'hui, par contre, maintenant que Hill junior a gagné 21 Grands Prix, contre quatorze pour Hill senior, il en va inversement. En effet, il y a longtemps que les chroniqueurs doivent expliquer à un public qui a la mémoire courte que le père de Damon avait lui aussi couru jadis et qu'il avait même connu une grande réussite en tant que double champion du monde de Formule 1 et vainqueur d'Indianapolis en 1966.

Bette Hill sourit alors toujours discrètement. Elle connaît en effet the other side of the Hill, et même ses deux côtés.

1966

The 24th Monaco Grand Prix on 22 May 1966 was also the first Grand Prix in the first year of the 3-liter formula. Improvisation was still the order of the day, and only seven of the 16 cars in the starting line-up made use of the new limit of 3,000 cc to the full. The colorful collection of engines came from many different places. There was the V12 of John Surtees' Ferrari with 2,984 cc from the sports car and a V6 with 2,417 cc in the Tipo 246 of his team-mate Lorenzo Bandini, from the collection for the Tasman series. The Repco (Replacement Parts Company) in Jack Brabham's Brabham BT19 had been developed by the Australian engineer Phil Irving from a modest Oldsmobile V8, while the origins of the Ford V8 in the back of Bruce McLaren's McLaren M2B were found in an Indy propulsion unit. They proved quite evenly matched with the smaller engines on the majestic and hilly Monégasque street course: Surtees shared the front row of the grid with Jim Clark's Lotus 33 in pole position, and his Coventry Climax V8 had only 1,970 cc, slightly less than the two BRM P261s for Graham Hill and Jackie Stewart. The Cooper T81s for Jochen Rindt and Richie Ginther, in contrast, were equipped with massive 3-liter 12-cylinder engines from Maserati.

As in 1960, this race turned into a war of attrition, the sole difference being that on this occasion only six cars trundled to the end of the race and towards the points. As the field approached the right-hand bend at Mirabeau in an angry crescendo, an Italian spectator at the Station Hairpin murmured "una macchina rossa, una macchina rossa", beseechingly, as if in prayer. His wish was fulfilled. John Surtees, still convalescing after a serious CanAm accident in the previous year, was in the lead in a Ferrari. Attentively followed by the cameras for John Frankenheimer's Formula 1 film epic *Grand Prix*, the red car with starting number 17 made the running for 14 laps until the transmission gave up the ghost. From that point on Jackie Stewart determined the course of events while Bandini settled down in second position, 26 seconds separating the two at the half-way point. In the meantime, the two racing icons Jim Clark and Graham Hill were fighting for third place. On lap 61, just as the flying Scotsman had wrestled the English moustache out of the way, the Lotus landed roughly in the bales of straw at the gasometer; the rear suspension had broken. Clark had taken a long time to get going at the start because he was stuck in first gear, but he made up for this loss of time with a furious chase until his car was nosing the transmission of Hill's BRM. In the end, the notorious bad luck which was always with him in Monaco, but which left him alone at Spa to balance the scales of justice, had struck again.

In his chase of Stewart, Bandini broke the lap record, but then had to slow down as his front brakes began to fail. The Scot also treated his BRM more carefully after his first gear had left him in the lurch, but he still retained an impressive 40-second lead at the finish.

Der 24. Große Preis von Monaco am 22. Mai 1966 ist zugleich der erste Grand Prix im Gründerjahr der Dreiliterformel. Noch improvisiert man: Nur sieben der 16 Wagen in der Startaufstellung schöpfen das neue Limit von 3000 cm³ voll aus. Das bunte Sammelsurium von Triebwerken stammt aus vielerlei Regalen: aus dem Sportwagen zum Beispiel der V12 des Ferrari von John Surtees mit 2984 cm³, aus dem Repertoire für die Tasman-Serie ein V6 mit 2417 cm³ im Tipo 246 seines Teamgefährten Lorenzo Bandini. Den Repco (Replacement Parts Company) in Jack Brabhams Brabham BT 19 hat der australische Ingenieur Phil Irving aus einem biederen V8 von Oldsmobile sublimiert, während die Ursprünge des Ford V8 im Heck von Bruce McLarens McLaren M2B in einem Indy-Treibsatz zu finden sind. Vor der Majestät des monegassischen Gebirgskurses sind alle gleich: Surtees teilt sich die erste Startreihe mit dem Lotus 33 von Jim Clark in der Pole Position, und dessen V8 von Coventry Climax hat gar nur 1970 cm³, etwas weniger als die beiden BRM P 261 für Graham Hill und Jackie Stewart. Die Cooper T 81 von Jochen Rindt und Richie Ginther hingegen sind bestückt mit klobigen Dreiliter-Zwölfzylindern von Maserati.

Wie 1960 wird das Rennen zum Zermürbungskrieg, nur daß diesmal am Ende nur sechs Autos über die Piste und in die Punkte tröpfeln. Als sich das Feld in wütendem Crescendo zum ersten Mal dem Rechtsknick bei Mirabeau nähert, murmelt ein italienischer Zuschauer an der Bahnhofskurve »una macchina rossa, una macchina rossa« – beschwörend, wie ein Gebet. Es wird ihm erfüllt: John Surtees, immer noch Rekonvaleszent nach einem schweren CanAm-Unfall im Jahr zuvor, führt im Ferrari. Aufmerksam verfolgt von den Kameras für John Frankenheimers Formel-1-Filmepos *Grand Prix,* macht der Rote mit der Startnummer 17 auch 14 Runden lang das Tempo, bis das Getriebe aufgibt. Von da an bestimmt Jackie Stewart den Lauf der Dinge, während sich Bandini auf Rang zwei einnistet. 26 Sekunden trennen die beiden bei Halbzeit. Unterdessen streiten sich die beiden Renn-Ikonen Jim Clark und Graham Hill um den dritten Rang. In der 61. Runde, just hat der fliegende Schotte den englischen Schnauzbart niedergerungen, landet der Lotus am Gasometer unsanft in den Strohballen: Bruch der Hinterradaufhängung. Die Vorgeschichte: Beim Start kommt Clark erst spät in Fahrt, weil der erste Gang klemmt. Er arbeitet seinen Rückstand in einer furiosen Aufholjagd wieder auf, bis daß die Nase seines Wagens am Getriebe von Hills BRM schnüffelt. Schließlich schlägt das notorische Pech wieder zu, das ihm in Monaco immer widerfährt und das ihn etwa in Spa in einem Akt ausgleichender Gerechtigkeit ungeschoren läßt.

Bei seiner Hatz auf Stewart fährt Bandini noch Rundenrekord, muß aber dann zurückstecken mit versagenden Vorderradbremsen. Auch der Schotte geht am Ende behutsamer mit seinem BRM um, nachdem ihn sein erster Gang im Stich gelassen hat. Aber 40 Sekunden Vorsprung sind ja immer noch eindrucksvoll.

Le 24e Grand Prix de Monaco, de mai 1966 est aussi le premier Grand Prix de l'ère de la formule trois litres. On en est encore réduit à l'improvisation : sept seulement des seize voitures sur la grille exploitent à fond la nouvelle limite de trois litres. La collection hétéroclite de moteurs vient des quatre horizons : d'une voiture de sport, par exemple le V12 de la Ferrari de John Surtees de 2984 cm³ ; de la banque d'organes de la série Tasman, un V6 de 2417 cm³ pour la Tipo 246 de son coéquipier Lorenzo Bandini. L'ingénieur Australien Phil Irving a sublimé d'un banal V8 d'Oldsmobile le Repco (contraction de Replacement Parts Company) de la Brabham BT 19 de Jack Brabham tandis le Ford V8 implanté à l'arrière de la McLaren M2B de Bruce McLaren est dérivé d'un moteur d'Indianapolis. Mais tous sont égaux devant la majesté du circuit escarpé de Monaco : Surtees se partage la première ligne de départ avec la Lotus 33 de Jim Clark, qui a signé la pole position, et son V8 Coventry Climax n'a même que 1970 cm³ de cylindrée, un peu moins que les deux BRM P 261 de Graham Hill et Jackie Stewart. Les Cooper T 81 de Jochen Rindt et Richie Ginther par contre, sont propulsées par d'encombrants trois-litres à douze cylindres Maserati.

Comme en 1960, la course se mue en une guerre d'usure à cette différence près que, cette année, six voitures seulement voient le drapeau à damier et engrangent des points. Lorsque le peloton se rapproche pour la première fois du coude droit de Mirabeau en un crescendo hystérique, un spectateur italien au virage de la Gare murmure « una macchina rossa, una macchina rossa » – sur un ton conjurateur, comme récitant une prière. Son vœu est exaucé : John Surtees, encore convalescent après son grave accident de la série CanAm de l'année précédente, déboule en tête avec sa Ferrari. Suivi comme son ombre par les caméras tournant l'épopée cinématographique de John Frankenheimer consacrée à la Formule 1, *Grand Prix,* le bolide rouge au numéro 17 fait la loi en tête pendant quatorze tours avant que la boîte de vitesses ne commence à faire des siennes. Dès lors, Jackie Stewart reprend la conduite des opérations tandis que Bandini s'incruste au deuxième rang, 26 secondes séparant les deux hommes à la mi-temps. Pendant ce temps, les deux icônes de la compétition, Jim Clark et Graham Hill, se battent pour la troisième place. Au 61e tour, alors que l'Ecossais volant vient de battre le barbu anglais, la Lotus percute violemment les bottes de paille au Gazomètre : rupture de la suspension arrière. Au départ, Clark ne s'élance que lentement parce que sa première ne rentre pas. Il comble pourtant son retard au cours d'une remontée effrénée jusqu'à ce que le museau de sa voiture vienne flairer la boîte de vitesses de la BRM de Graham Hill. Finalement, cette malchance notoire qui jamais ne le quitte à Monaco, mais qui l'épargne toujours à Spa, par exemple, en une espèce de justice immanente, frappe de nouveau brutalement.

Dans sa poursuite de Stewart, Bandini bat encore le record du tour, mais doit ensuite freiner ses ardeurs parce que ses freins avant faiblissent. L'Ecossais, lui aussi, doit ménager sa BRM à la fin, car sa première l'a abandonné, mais 40 secondes d'avance constituent une performance remarquable en fin de parcours.

Exchange of views among colleagues: the BRM drivers Stewart and Hill with Jim Clark (center).

Kollegialer Gedankenaustausch: die BRM-Piloten Stewart und Hill mit Jim Clark (Mitte).

Echange de vues entre collègues : les pilotes de BRM Stewart et Hill avec Jim Clark (au centre).

N°	DRIVERS		ENTRANTS	CARS	ENGINES	PRACTICE RESULTS	RACE RESULTS
12	**Jackie Stewart**	**GB**	**Owen Racing Organisation**	**BRM P261**	**BRM V8 1988 cc**	**3rd: 1'30"3**	**1st: 2h33'10"5**
16	Lorenzo Bandini	I	SEFAC Ferrari S.p.A.	Ferrari 246	Ferrari V6 2417 cc	5th: 1'30"5	2nd: 2h33'50"7
11	Graham Hill	GB	Owen Racing Organisation	BRM P261	BRM V8 1988 cc	4th: 1'30"4	3rd: 99 laps
19	Robert Bondurant	USA	Team Chamaco-Collect	BRM P261	BRM V8 1988 cc	16th: 1'37"3	4th: 95 laps
21	Guy Ligier	F	Guy Ligier	Cooper T81	Maserati V12 2989 cc	15th: 1'35"2	NC: 75 laps
18	Joakim Bonnier	S	Anglo-Suisse Racing Team	Cooper T81	Maserati V12 2989 cc	14th: 1'35"0	NC: 73 laps
9	Richie Ginther	USA	Cooper Car Co.	Cooper T81	Maserati V12 2989 cc	9th: 1'32"6	R
4	*Jim Clark*	*GB*	*Team Lotus*	*Lotus 33*	*Climax V8 1974 cc*	*1st: 1'29"9*	R
10	Jochen Rindt	A	Cooper Car Co.	Cooper T81	Maserati V12 2989 cc	7th: 1'32"2	R
14	Joseph Siffert	CH	RRC Walker Racing Team	Brabham BT11	BRM V8 1988 cc	13th: 1'34"4	R
6	Mike Spence	GB	Reg Parnell Racing	Lotus 25	BRM V8 1988 cc	12th: 1'33"5	R
7	Jack Brabham	AUS	Brabham Racing Organisation	Brabham BT19	Repco V8 2995 cc	10th(11): 1'32"8	R
17	John Surtees	GB	SEFAC Ferrari S.p.A.	Ferrari 312	Ferrari V12 2989 cc	2nd: 1'30"1	R
8	Denis Hulme	NZ	Brabham Racing Organisation	Brabham BT22	Climax 4L 2495 cc	6th: 1'31"1	R
2	Bruce McLaren	NZ	Bruce McLaren Motor Racing	McLaren M2B	Ford V8 2995 cc	10th: 1'32"8	R
15	Bob Anderson	GB	DW Racing Enterprises	Brabham BT11	Climax 4L 2695 cc	8th: 1'32"5	R

(1) Fine prospect: a mighty stand rises above the site of the former station. (2) A crowded midfield as the cars snake up to the Casino. (3) Peak time: Stewart at the highest point of the circuit. (4) On their way to positions six and four: Bonnier (Cooper) and Bondurant (BRM). (5) Step in the right direction: second Grand Prix victory for Jackie Stewart.

(1) Beste Aussichtslage: Über dem Grundstück des ehemaligen Bahnhofs erhebt sich eine mächtige Tribüne. (2) Getümmel im Mittelfeld im Geschlängel hinauf zum Casino. (3) Das ist der Gipfel: Stewart am höchsten Punkt des Circuits. (4) Unterwegs zu den Plätzen 6 und 4: Bonnier (Cooper) und Bondurant (BRM). (5) Schritt in die richtige Richtung: zweiter Grand-Prix-Sieg für Jackie Stewart.

(1) Bien placés : à la place de l'ancienne Gare s'élève maintenant une imposante tribune. (2) Le peloton se rue dans la montée serpentée vers le Casino. (3) C'est le sommet : Stewart au point le plus élevé du circuit. (4) En route vers les places six et quatre : Bonnier (Cooper) et Bondurant (BRM). (5) Tout est bon : deuxième victoire en Grand Prix pour Jackie Stewart.

(1) Slow motion: one of the accident victims is removed after the usual rodeo in Formula 3. Originals: (2) the twelve-cylinder engine of Surtees' Ferrari; (3) the H16 of BRM, which, however, is not used. And fakes: (4–6) more rough than ready, Formula 3 cars prepared to look like their Formula 1 counterparts for John Frankenheimer's film epic *Grand Prix*. In (4) Jean Pierre Sarti alias Yves Montand and his fake Ferrari are enjoying friendly attention after their fictional win.

(1) Slow Motion: Nach dem üblichen Rodeo in der Formel 3 wird ein Havarist entfernt. Originale: (2) der Zwölfzylinder von Surtees' Ferrari, (3) der H16 von BRM, der aber nicht zum Einsatz gelangt. Und Fälschungen: (4–6) für das Film-Epos *Grand Prix* von John Frankenheimer mehr schlecht als recht aufbereitete Formel-3-Wagen. In (4) erfahren gerade Jean Pierre Sarti alias Yves Montand und sein falscher Ferrari freundliche Zuwendung nach ihrem fiktiven Sieg.

(1) Ralenti : Evacuation de l'une des nombreuses épaves de Formule 3. Originaux : (2) le douze-cylindres de la Ferrari de Surtees, (3) le H16 de la BRM, qui ne prendra toutefois pas le départ. Et les copies : (4–6) pour l'épopée cinématographique *Grand Prix* de John Frankenheimer avec des voitures de Formule 3 plutôt mal maquillées. (4) Jean Pierre Sarti, alias Yves Montand, et sa fausse Ferrari bénéficient de toutes les attentions après leur victoire fictive.

1967

Oh, oh, oh – accident à la chicane", said the public address commentator during lap 82 of the 25th Monaco Grand Prix. There seemed little concern in his voice, the words spoken almost casually: accidents at this spot are not serious. Alberto Ascari's and Paul Hawkins' descents into the harbor in 1955 and 1965, respectively, had demonstrated that.

But something went terribly wrong for Lorenzo Bandini. For some laps the Italian, tired and yet stirred up by the applause of his demanding compatriots, had shot through the chicane taking a rather curious line. And then it happened: the Ferrari landed on top of the straw bales to the left at the quay wall, turned over to the right and caught fire immediately. It took a long time for the driver to be rescued and, disfigured by terrible burns, he died three days later. People had not rushed to the blaze because something – the left back wheel, in fact – had flown into the harbor, and it was thought to have been the driver again, just like Ascari, like Hawkins.

The second Ferrari 312 was driven by Chris Amon, while John Surtees, who had angrily left the Scuderia after Spa in 1966, started with a lone Honda RA 273, a bulky, screaming, overweight 12-cylinder machine. Bruce McLaren, too, went solo with his own-production M4B. Dan Gurney's was the only Eagle to get as far as the start line-up; his V12, designed by Harry Weslake and his team in the English spa town of Rye, was beautiful but not very powerful. "Black Jack" himself and Denny Hulme were at the wheels of the Brabhams, and the two Cooper-Maseratis were being tamed by Jochen Rindt and Pedro Rodriguez. The Lotus 49, with its Ford DFV engine, would not celebrate its premiere until Zandvoort, so in Monaco the two Lotus 33s had to suffice for Jim Clark and Graham Hill. The blond Johnny Servoz-Gavin was at the wheel of the Matra MS 5, a quick and agile Formula 2 racing car, and BRM, in contrast, arrived with various calibres: a 2-liter V8 for Jackie Stewart, the weighty Type P83 with H16 engine for Mike Spence. The start and finish line had been moved a little forward, which shortened the starting sprint to Sainte Dévote and increased the final spurt from the gasometer bend.

At the beginning, the men on the front row took the lead, with Bandini in front of Brabham. But the Australian arrived at Mirabeau backwards with an exploding engine and liberally sprinkled the track with oil. On this mixture of oil and cement, Jim Clark slid into the emergency exit at the chicane on the second lap, but fought back from 14th position to fourth place until forced to quit on lap 43 after the Tabac bend with a broken suspension; Monaco and the Scot simply could not hit it off.

Stewart led Hulme for a while until the differential of the BRM refused to cooperate any longer, and the Scot started his walk home to the pits in an anti-clockwise direction. From lap 15 onwards, the New Zealander in the seriously oversteering Brabham became unstoppable, with Bandini behind him, closely at first, but then increasingly falling back until the terrible end to his chase. It was Hulme's first Grand Prix victory, but all pleasure had gone for him. What had happened at the chicane on this occasion had cast a shadow over everything else.

Oh, oh, oh – accident à la chicane«, sagt der Streckensprecher während der 82. Runde des 25. Grand Prix de Monaco. Das klingt nur wenig besorgt, fast beiläufig: Unfälle an dieser Stelle gehen glimpflich ab. Die Abflüge von Alberto Ascari 1955 und Paul Hawkins 1965 ins Hafenbecken haben das gezeigt.

Der von Lorenzo Bandini geht schief. Schon seit ein paar Runden durchpfeilt der Italiener, müde und aufgeputscht durch den fordernden Beifall seiner Landsleute, die Schikane auf merkwürdigen Linien. Und dann passiert es: Der Ferrari landet rittlings auf den Strohballen links an der Kaimauer, überschlägt sich nach rechts, fängt augenblicklich Feuer. Erst spät wird der Pilot geborgen. Von schrecklichen Verbrennungen entstellt, stirbt er drei Tage später. Man ließ sich mit der Rettung Zeit, irgendetwas – das linke Hinterrad – flog ja in den Hafen. Da hat wieder einer Glück gehabt, wie Ascari, wie Hawkins.

Den zweiten Ferrari 312 lenkt Chris Amon, während John Surtees, der die Scuderia nach Spa 1966 im Zorn verließ, mit dem einsamen Honda RA 273 antritt, einem klobigen, kreischenden, übergewichtigen Zwölfzylinder. Ebenfalls als Solist spielt Bruce McLaren auf mit seinem M4B aus eigener Fertigung. Nur der Eagle Dan Gurneys dringt bis in die Startaufstellung vor. Sein V12, Copyright Harry Weslake im englischen Seebad Rye, ist schön, aber nicht potent. Am Volant der Brabham sitzen »Black Jack« selbst und Denny Hulme. Die beiden Cooper-Maserati bändigen Jochen Rindt und Pedro Rodriguez. Der Lotus 49 mit seinem Ford DFV-Triebwerk wird erst in Zandvoort Premiere feiern. In Monaco müssen noch die beiden Lotus 33 für Jim Clark und Graham Hill herhalten. Flink und wendig der Matra MS 5, Rennwagen der Formel 2, für den blonden Johnny Servoz-Gavin. BRM hingegen fährt unterschiedliche Kaliber auf: einen Zweiliter V8 für Jackie Stewart, den gewichtigen H16 vom Typ P83 für Mike Spence. Die Start- und Ziellinie hat man ein Stück nach rechts verlegt, was den Anfangssprint nach Sainte Dévote verkürzt und den Schlußspurt aus der Gasometerkurve verlängert.

Anfänglich führen die Männer aus der ersten Reihe, Bandini vor Brabham. Aber in Mirabeau trifft der Australier rückwärts ein, Motorplatzer, benetzt die Piste liberal mit Öl. Auf einer Mischung von Öl und Zement rutscht Jim Clark in der zweiten Runde an der Schikane in den Notausgang, kämpft sich von Position 14 wieder auf Position vier vor, bevor er in Runde 43 hinter der Tabakskurve mit gebrochener Aufhängung ausscheidet. Monaco ist des Schotten Pflaster nicht.

Eine Zeitlang setzt sich Stewart vor Hulme, bis das Differential des BRM in den Ausstand tritt und der Schotte den Heimweg zur Box gegen den Uhrzeigersinn zu Fuß antritt. Vom 15. Durchgang an ist der Neuseeländer im heftig übersteuernden Brabham nicht mehr zu bremsen, hinter ihm Bandini, erst näher, schließlich zurückfallend – bis zum schlimmen Ende seiner Jagd. Es ist Hulmes erster Grand-Prix-Sieg, aber freuen mag er sich nicht. Was zuvor an der Schikane geschah, überschattet alles andere.

Oh, oh, oh – accident à la chicane », s'écrit le speaker au 82e tour du 25e Grand Prix de Monaco. Rien de dramatique ne transparaît dans ses propos, bien au contraire : les accidents à cet endroit ne sont généralement pas graves. Les plongeons dans le port d'Alberto Ascari en 1955 et de Paul Hawkins en 1965 en sont bien la preuve.

Mais celui de Lorenzo Bandini aura un dénouement tragique. Depuis quelques tours déjà, l'Italien, fatigué et comme dopé par les applaudissements frénétiques de ses compatriotes, franchit la chicane selon des trajectoires bizarres. Et finalement arrive ce qui devait arriver : la Ferrari monte à cheval sur les bottes de paille de gauche bordant le mur du quai, part en tonneau vers la droite, et prend immédiatement feu. Il faut un certain temps pour dégager le pilote. Atrocement brûlé, il décédera trois jours plus tard. La foule ne s'est pas ruée sur la voiture en flammes : en effet, un objet – il s'agit en réalité de la roue arrière gauche – a fait un vol plané dans le port, mais chacun pense qu'il s'agit du pilote, comme ce fut le cas d'Ascari et d'Hawkins.

La seconde Ferrari 312 est pilotée par Chris Amon tandis que John Surtees, qui a quitté dans la colère la Scuderia après Spa en 1966, a pris le départ avec une Honda RA 273 bien isolée, une douze-cylindres joufflue, stridente, bien trop lourde. Un autre soliste est Bruce McLaren avec sa M4B fabriquée de ses mains. Seule l'Eagle de Dan Gurney parvient à se qualifier pour la course. Son V12, concocté par Harry Weslake dans la station balnéaire britannique de Rye, est joli, mais pas assez puissant. Au volant des Brabham, on trouve « Black Jack » en personne et Denny Hulme. Jochen Rindt et Pedro Rodriguez s'efforcent de dompter les deux Cooper-Maserati. La Lotus 49 à moteur Ford DFV ne célébrera sa première qu'à Zandvoort. A Monaco, Jim Clark et Graham Hill doivent encore se contenter des deux Lotus 33. Vive et maniable, la Matra MS 5, une voiture de course Formule 2, a été confiée au jeune espoir blond Johnny Servoz-Gavin. BRM, de son côté, n'a pas mis tous ses œufs dans le même panier : un V8 de deux litres pour Jackie Stewart et la lourde H16 type P83 pour Mike Spence. La ligne de départ et d'arrivée a été légèrement avancée, ce qui raccourcit le sprint initial vers Sainte Dévote et rallonge d'autant le sprint final à la sortie du virage du Gazomètre.

Au début, les hommes partis en première ligne restent en tête, Bandini devant Brabham. Mais l'Australien s'engage dans le Mirabeau en marche arrière, moteur éclaté, arrosant généreusement la piste d'huile. Sur un mélange d'huile et de ciment, Jim Clark, au deuxième tour, est contraint de prendre l'échappatoire à la chicane et, parti de la 14e place, remonte jusqu'à la quatrième avant de devoir abandonner au 43e tour, suspension rompue à la sortie du virage du Bureau de tabac. Monaco n'est pas le circuit de prédilection de l'Ecossais.

Pendant un certain temps, Stewart prend le dessus sur Hulme jusqu'à ce que le différentiel de la BRM le laisse en plan et oblige l'Ecossais à rentrer à pied au stand en remontant le circuit à contre-courant. A partir du 15e tour, le Néo-Zélandais est indomptable dans sa Brabham brutalement survireuse, suivi de Bandini, d'abord tout proche, puis de plus en plus lointain – jusqu'à la triste issue de sa chasse. C'est la première victoire d'Hulme au Grand Prix, mais il ne parvient pas à se réjouir. Ce qui s'est passé cette fois à la chicane jette son ombre sur tout le reste.

N°	DRIVERS		ENTRANTS	CARS	ENGINES	PRACTICE RESULTS	RACE RESULTS
9	**Denis Hulme**	**NZ**	**Brabham Racing Organisation**	**Brabham BT20**	**Repco V8 2995 cc**	**4th: 1'28"8**	**1st: 2h34'34"3**
14	Graham Hill	GB	Team Lotus	Lotus 33	BRM V8 2070 cc	8th: 1'29"9	2nd: 99 laps
20	Chris Amon	NZ	SEFAC Ferrari S.p.A.	Ferrari 312	Ferrari V12 2989 cc	14th: 1'30"7	3rd: 98 laps
16	Bruce McLaren	NZ	Bruce McLaren Motor Racing	McLaren M5A	BRM V12 2998 cc	9th(10): 1'30"0	4th: 97 laps
11	Pedro Rodriguez	MEX	Cooper Car Co.	Cooper T81	Maserati V12 2989 cc	16th: 1'32"4	5th: 96 laps
5	Mike Spence	GB	Owen Racing Organisation	BRM P83	BRM H16 2998 cc	12th: 1'30"6	6th: 96 laps
18	Lorenzo Bandini	I	SEFAC Ferrari S.p.A.	Ferrari 312	Ferrari V12 2989 cc	2nd: 1'28"3	R
6	Piers Courage	GB	Owen Racing Organisation	BRM P261	BRM V8 2070 cc	12th(13): 1'30"6	R
12	Jim Clark	GB	Team Lotus	Lotus 33	Climax V8 1998 cc	4th(5): 1'28"8	R
7	John Surtees	GB	Honda Racing	Honda RA 273	Honda V12 2992 cc	3rd: 1'28"4	R
17	Joseph Siffert	CH	RRC Walker & J. Durlacher Racing Team	Cooper T81	Maserati V12 2989 cc	9th: 1'30"0	R
10	Jochen Rindt	A	Cooper Car Co.	Cooper T81	Maserati V12 2989 cc	15th: 1'30"8	R
4	Jackie Stewart	GB	Owen Racing Organisation	BRM P261	BRM V8 2070 cc	6th: 1'29"0	R
23	Dan Gurney	USA	Anglo-American Racers Inc.	Eagle T1G	Weslake V12 2997 cc	7th: 1'29"3	R
2	Johnny Servoz-Gavin	F	Matra Sports	Matra MS5	Cosworth FVA 4L 1598 cc	11th: 1'30"4	R
8	Jack Brabham	AUS	Brabham Racing Organisation	Brabham BT19	Repco V8 2995 cc	1st: 1'27"6	R

Terrible end: on the 82nd lap, Bandini's Ferrari bursts into flames after a driving error at the chicane. The driver dies a few days later of his horrific injuries. A nation mourns.

Ende mit Schrecken: In der 82. Runde geht Bandinis Ferrari nach einem Fahrfehler hinter der Schikane in Rauch und Flammen auf. Der grausam verletzte Fahrer stirbt ein paar Tage später. Eine ganze Nation trauert.

Tout est mal qui finit mal : au 82e tour, la Ferrari de Bandini s'enflamme après une erreur de pilotage à la sortie de la chicane. Grièvement brûlé, le pilote décédera quelques jours plus tard. Toute une nation porte le deuil.

MARCHÉ COMMUN :

la "session marathon" de la négociation Kennedy a débuté hier à Genève

(LIRE NOTRE INFORMATION EN PAGE 7)

LE GENERAL BARRIENTOS
président de la République bolivienne :

" REGIS DEBRAY EST UN AVENTURIER "

(VOIR NOTRE INFORMATION EN PAGE 13)

LE PÈRE DE BRIGITTE BARDOT RENVERSÉ PAR UNE VOITURE

PARIS — Le père de Brigitte Bardot a été renversé par une voiture, hier à Paris. Il n'est que légèrement blessé.

L'accident s'est produit place Pinson (16e arrondissement), non loin du domicile de M. Bardot. Le père de la vedette sortait de chez un fleuriste. Alors qu'il s'engageait sur la chaussée, une camionnette l'a renversé et l'a traîné sur six mètres. M. Bardot a été secouru par des passants. Le conducteur de la camionnette l'a conduit à l'hôpital.

M. Bardot est atteint de nombreuses plaies, notamment aux mains. Il a fallu lui faire 21 points de suture. Après avoir été soigné à l'hôpital, M. Bardot a pu regagner son domicile.

CANNES
XXe FESTIVAL INTERNATIONAL DU FILM

SYLVA KOSCINA DÉBARQUE

TROIS NOUVEAUX ATTENTATS AU PLASTIC A LAUSANNE

PAS DE VICTIMES MAIS DEGATS IMPORTANTS
(Voir en page 14)

Résultat du tiercé

9 8 2

TIGZIRT   LANISTE
BEAUCHALOT
qui rapporte
1 010.70 F dans l'ordre
et
134.70 F dans le désordre

• Nice-Matin • (José Farauti) a donné le tiercé dans l'ordre d'arrivée en sept chevaux.

Notre correspondant parisien, Maurice Bernardet, l'a désigné en désordre en cinq chevaux.

DRAME SUR LE CIRCUIT DE MONACO

Lorenzo BANDINI grièvement brûlé dans son bolide en flammes

L'infortuné pilote n'a pu être secouru qu'avec la plus grande difficulté

Ci-contre : au centre de ce brasier, Bandini, prisonnier de son véhicule qui est retombé, en flammes, roues en l'air après avoir capoté. (Photo Oggero). Dessous : le pilote, atrocement brûlé, est extrait de la voiture noyée de mousse carbonique. (Photo Briano)

(Voir en dernière page l'article de Jean Bomy et le film de l'accident)

L'épreuve a été enlevée par Denis HULME

Une arrivée spectaculaire hier au Festival : celle de la capiteuse vedette italo-yougoslave Sylva Koscina, abondamment fleurie, au moment de son débarquement sur les quais de Cannes. (Traverso)

(LIRE NOS INFORMATIONS EN DERNIÈRE PAGE)

L'ANNIVERSAIRE DE LA VICTOIRE DE 1945 CÉLÉBRÉ AUJOURD'HUI

PARIS. — La victoire de 1945, marquée par la capitulation allemande du 8 mai, il y a 22 ans, sera célébrée ce lundi un peu partout en France par des manifestations commémoratives.

Le président de la République participera à ces cérémonies dans la capitale. Il passera en revue les troupes de la garnison, sur la place de l'Étoile, à 18 h 25, en présence des membres du gouvernement et des personnalités, puis ravivera la flamme du tombeau du soldat inconnu sous l'Arc de Triomphe.

M. Michelet, ministre d'État, présidera dans l'après-midi, devant le Mémorial de la France combattante au mont Valérien, une cérémonie à la mémoire des 4.500 patriotes fusillés par les troupes d'occupation allemandes.

Dans la soirée aura lieu à l'Arc de Triomphe une veillée des anciens de « Rhin et Danube ».

(1) Rodriguez (Cooper) at Mirabeau. Dan Gurney's Eagle on the pavement, parked after five laps due to a fuel blockage. Kiwi firsts: (2, 4) first place in a Grand Prix for the first time for Denny Hulme (Brabham) and (3) first start for Chris Amon in a Ferrari. Victory, however, will always elude this New Zealander.

(1) Rodriguez (Cooper) bei Mirabeau. Auf dem Bürgersteig Dan Gurneys Eagle, nach fünf Runden mangels Benzinzufuhr eingeparkt. Kiwi-Premieren: (2, 4) zum ersten Mal Platz eins in einem Grand Prix für Denny Hulme (Brabham), (3) erster Start für Chris Amon im Ferrari. Für einen Sieg wird es allerdings für den Neuseeländer nie reichen.

(1) Rodriguez (Cooper) à Mirabeau. Sur le trottoir, l'Eagle de Dan Gurney condamnée à abandonner au bout de cinq tours sur panne de pompe à essence. Premières des Kiwis : (2, 4) pour la première fois, première place dans un Grand Prix pour Denny Hulme (Brabham) et (3) premier départ pour Chris Amon sur Ferrari. Ce Néo-Zélandais ne réussira pourtant jamais à remporter une seule victoire.

Limited adhesion: three-way battle
on oil and cement between the
protagonists Hulme, Stewart (BRM)
and Bandini.

Beschränkte Haftung: Dreikampf
auf Öl und Zement mit den
Protagonisten Hulme, Stewart
(BRM) und Bandini.

Adhérence limitée : duel à trois sur
l'huile et le ciment avec comme
protagonistes Hulme, Stewart
(BRM) et Bandini.

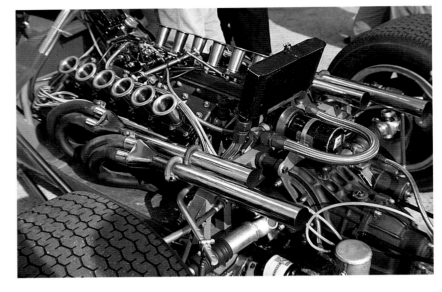

Magic dozen: the twelve-cylinder engines from (1) Weslake,
(2) McLaren BRM and (3) Honda with exhaust pipes snaking down.

Magisches Dutzend: die Zwölfzylinder von (1) Weslake, (2) McLaren
BRM und (3) Honda mit kaskadenartig abfallendem Auspuffgewürm.

La douzaine magique : les douze-cylindres de (1) Weslake,
(2) McLaren BRM et (3) Honda avec leurs pots d'échappement qui
font penser à une assiette de spaghetti.

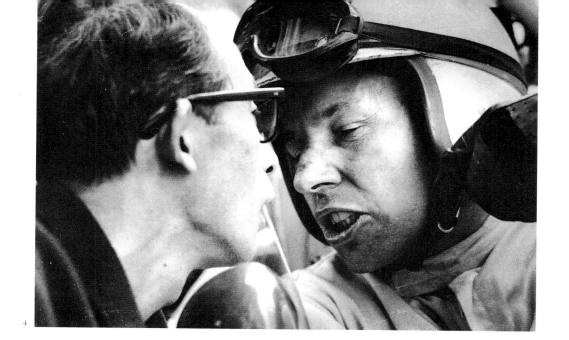

Talking shop: (4) John Surtees in conversation with Honda engineer Yoshio Nakamura. (5) McLaren, (6) Amon, (7) Pedro Rodriguez and (8) Hulme.

Macher und Gestalter: (4) John Surtees im Gespräch mit Honda-Ingenieur Yoshio Nakamura. (5) McLaren, (6) Amon, (7) Pedro Rodriguez und (8) Hulme.

Concepteur et réalisateur : (4) John Surtees s'entretenant avec l'ingénieur de chez Honda Yoshio Nakamura. (5) McLaren, (6) Amon, (7) Pedro Rodriguez et (8) Hulme.

1968

Dark clouds gathered over the 26th edition of the Monaco Grand Prix: a general strike in France cast doubt on whether it would be held at all. As a precaution, the organizers stocked up with 1,150 liters of fuel as iron rations. And after the race there were rumors that this one might have been the last unless income began clearly to exceed expenditure. The chicane now lurked 100 meters further in the direction of the Tabac bend and having been made narrower was more difficult to negotiate, which cost about one second per lap. At the same time the classic on the Riviera had been shortened to 80 laps, turning it into a two-hour affair almost to the minute.

Before Graham Hill, the uncrowned but immensely popular "king of Monaco", climbed his throne for the fourth time, despite a long night spent in the Tip-Top Bar, he had to fight off the charge of the "Nobodies". Hill was driving a Ford Cosworth-powered Lotus 49B, the rear panelling of which rose in a wedge shape in the red, white and gold colors of the team's new sponsor Gold Leaf, while Jackie Oliver, making his debut had to make do with a conventionally shaped Type 49. Jack Brabham had entered a Brabham BT 26 for himself and a BT 24 for Jochen Rindt. Two Cooper-BRM T 86s were available for Ludovico Scarfiotti and Lucien Bianchi. Pedro Rodriguez (with the P 133) and Richard Attwood (in a P 126) took to the track in BRMs. Matra was represented twice, once with the factory 12-cylinder MS 11 for Jean-Pierre Beltoise, and once with an eight-cylinder MS 10 provided by Ken Tyrrell for the long-haired Frenchman Johnny Servoz-Gavin. The two McLaren M7As were driven by the practised duo Bruce McLaren and Denny Hulme, while John Surtees and Dan Gurney started on their own against the rest in a Honda RA 301 and an Eagle TG 1 respectively. Ferrari was missing, after making lame excuses in a telex, and Jackie Stewart attended the event merely as a spectator due to a hairline fracture in the right wrist, which he had acquired in an accident in the Formula 2 race in Jarama.

At the start, Hill wisely allowed Servoz-Gavin to go. The impulsive Frenchman, with his blond mop of hair, was thought bound to make a mistake somewhere. That did indeed happen during the fourth lap when the Matra touched the chicane: a broken half-shaft, defective rear suspension and injured ego. From this point onwards, the Londoner took over the lead, only moderately affected by attacks from the space behind him. First there was John Surtees, until the transmission of the noisy Honda gave up the ghost on lap 17. Later there was Richard Attwood, called "Tatty Atty" by his friends, if only for the rhyme. The BRM came within two seconds of the Lotus and registered a new lap record – in vain. After a quarter of the race only five drivers were left, many of the other 11 having been forced to drop out because of accidents. For on those special Sundays in May road traffic in Monaco is particularly liable to take it out of you.

Über der 26. Edition des Grand Prix de Monaco ballt sich düsteres Gewölk: Ein umfassender Streik in Frankreich bedroht seine Austragung. Vorsichtshalber bunkern die Organisatoren 1150 Liter Treibstoff als eiserne Reserve. Und nach dem Rennen munkelt man, es könnte das letzte gewesen sein, es sei denn, die Einnahmen überstiegen deutlich die Ausgaben. Die Schikane lauert nun 100 Meter später in Richtung Tabakskurve und behindert die Durchfahrt mit größerer Enge, was ungefähr eine Sekunde pro Runde kostet. Zugleich ist der Côte-Klassiker verkürzt worden auf 80 Runden, eine Angelegenheit von zwei Stunden – fast auf die Minute.

Bevor Graham Hill, der ungekrönte, aber immens populäre König von Monaco trotz einer langen Nacht in der Tip-Top-Bar seinen Thron zum vierten Mal erklimmt, muß er den Ansturm der Nobodys abwehren. Hill fährt einen Lotus 49 B mit Ford-Cosworth-Motor, dessen Heckverkleidung sich keilförmig hebt, im Rotweißgold des Sponsors Gold Leaf, während Debütant Jackie Oliver sich mit dem konventionell geformten Typ 49 begnügen muß. Jack Brabham hat einen Brabham BT 26 für sich selbst und einen BT 24 für Jochen Rindt gemeldet. Zwei Cooper-BRM T 86 stehen Ludovico Scarfiotti und Lucien Bianchi zur Verfügung. Auf BRM sind Pedro Rodriguez (mit dem P 133) und Richard Attwood (auf einem P 126) unterwegs. Matra ist zweifach vertreten, mit dem Zwölfzylinder MS 11 des Werks für Jean-Pierre Beltoise und einem Achtzylinder MS 10, eingesetzt von Ken Tyrrell, für den langhaarigen Franzosen Johnny Servoz-Gavin. Die beiden McLaren M7A werden gefahren von dem eingespielten Duo Bruce McLaren und Denny Hulme, wogegen John Surtees mit dem Honda RA 301 und Dan Gurney auf dem Eagle TG 1 jeweils allein gegen alle antreten. Ferrari fehlt, wofür ein Fernschreiben eine fadenscheinige Begründung anbietet. Und Jackie Stewart wohnt der Veranstaltung lediglich als Zuschauer bei, Haarriß im rechten Handgelenk, zugezogen bei einem Unfall beim Formel-2-Lauf in Jarama.

Beim Start läßt Hill Servoz-Gavin weise ziehen. Irgendwo wird der ungestüme Blondschopf schon einen Fehler machen. Der kommt in der Tat in der vierten Runde, als der Matra die Schikane touchiert: gebrochene Halbwelle, defekte Hinterradaufhängung, verletztes Ego. Von nun an führt der Londoner, nur mäßig beeindruckt von Attacken aus der Tiefe des Raumes. Da ist zunächst John Surtees, bis das Getriebe des lärmenden Honda in der 17. Runde den Dienst aufkündigt. Da ist später Richard Attwood, den seine Freunde »Tatty Atty« nennen, wenn auch mehr um des Reimes willen. Der BRM nähert sich dem Lotus bis auf zwei Sekunden und verbucht auch einen neuen Rundenrekord – umsonst. Nach einem Viertel sind nur noch fünf Teilnehmer im Rennen, viele der elf anderen durch Unfälle ausgeschieden. An jenen besonderen Sonntagen im Mai geht nämlich der Straßenverkehr von Monaco immer besonders an die Substanz.

Des nuages sombres s'amassent au-dessus du ciel de la 26ᵉ édition du Grand Prix de Monaco : une grève générale en France menace son organisation. Par précaution, les organisateurs ont fait le stock de 1150 litres de carburant. Et, après la course, on murmure que cela pourrait avoir été la dernière à moins que les recettes n'excèdent nettement les dépenses. La chicane a été déplacée de 100 mètres en direction du virage du Bureau de tabac et elle est plus serrée, ce qui coûte environ une seconde au tour. Simultanément, la longueur de la grande classique de la Côte d'Azur a été ramenée à 80 tours, soit une durée de deux heures – à une minute près.

Avant que Graham Hill, le roi non couronné, mais toujours populaire, de Monaco ne grimpe, malgré une longue nuit passée au Tip-Top-Bar, pour la quatrième fois sur son trône, il doit résister à l'offensive des seconds couteaux. Hill pilote une Lotus 49 B équipée d'un moteur Ford Cosworth au carénage arrière cunéiforme dans la magnifique livrée rouge-blanc-or du nouveau sponsor de l'équipe, le cigaretier Gold Leaf, tandis que le débutant Jackie Oliver doit se contenter de la 49 plus conventionnelle. Jack Brabham a amené une Brabham BT 26 pour lui-même et une BT 24 pour Jochen Rindt. Ludovico Scarfiotti et Lucien Bianchi disposent de deux Cooper-BRM T 86. Pedro Rodriguez, avec une P 133, et Richard Attwood, avec une P 126, sont également au volant d'une BRM. Matra est représentée avec deux voitures, la douze-cylindres MS 11 d'usine pour Jean-Pierre Beltoise et une huit-cylindres MS 10, engagée par Ken Tyrrell, pour un jeune Français aux cheveux longs, Johnny Servoz-Gavin. Les deux McLaren M7A sont pilotées par un duo rompu à la tâche, Bruce McLaren et Denny Hulme, tandis que John Surtees avec sa Honda RA 301 et Dan Gurney avec son Eagle TG 1 sont respectivement seuls contre tous. Ferrari est absente, s'étant excusée par télex sous un prétexte évident. Et Jackie Stewart ne participe à la course qu'en spectateur, victime d'une fêlure au poignet droit subie lors d'un accident en Formule 2 à Jarama.

Après le départ, Hill laisse intelligemment Servoz-Gavin prendre la tête. L'impatient blondinet finira bien par commettre une faute. Et il ne faut pas attendre longtemps puisque la Matra percute la chicane au quatrième tour : demi-arbre brisé, suspension arrière effondrée, ego blessé. Dès lors, le Londonien prend la tête, à peine impressionné par les attaques de ses poursuivants. Ils ont pour noms, tout d'abord, John Surtees jusqu'à ce que la boîte de vitesses de la bruyante Honda ne rende l'âme au 17ᵉ tour. C'est ensuite Richard Attwood, que ses amis surnomment « Tatty Atty », mais plus par amour des rimes. La BRM se rapproche à deux secondes de la Lotus et signe aussi un nouveau record du tour – c'est peine perdue. Après un quart de la course, il n'y a plus que cinq participants sur le circuit, beaucoup des onze autres ayant dû abandonner par suite d'accidents. Ce dimanche particulier de mai, en effet, la circulation routière dans les rues de Monaco prélève toujours un tribut particulier.

Pole position: the other place where ingenious stands such as this one can be seen is Monza.

Bei der Stange geblieben: Individuell gestaltete Tribünen wie die dieses Solisten gibt es sonst vor allem in Monza.

A la barre : il n'y a normalement qu'à Monza que l'on trouve des tribunes aussi originales que celles de ce soliste qui n'a pas le vertige.

N°	DRIVERS		ENTRANTS	CARS	ENGINES	PRACTICE RESULTS	RACE RESULTS
9	**Graham Hill**	**GB**	**Gold Leaf Team Lotus**	**Lotus 49B**	**Cosworth V8 2993 cc**	**Ist: I'28"2**	**Ist: 2h00'32"3**
15	Richard Attwood	GB	Owen Racing Organisation	BRM P126	BRM V12 2998 cc	6th: I'29"6	2nd: 2h34'00"5
7	Lucien Bianchi	B	Cooper Car Co.	Cooper T86B	BRM V12 2998 cc	14th: I'31"9	3rd: 76 laps
6	Ludovico Scarfiotti	I	Cooper Car Co.	Cooper T86B	BRM V12 2998 cc	15th: I'32"9	4th: 76 laps
12	Denis Hulme	NZ	Bruce McLaren Motor Racing	McLaren M7A	Cosworth V8 2993 cc	9th(10): I'30"4	5th: 73 laps
8	John Surtees	GB	Honda Racing	Honda RA 301	Honda V12 2992 cc	4th: I'29"I	R
4	Pedro Rodriguez	MEX	Owen Racing Organisation	BRM P133	BRM V12 2998 cc	9th: I'30"4	R
16	Piers Courage	GB	Reg Parnell Racing	BRM P126	BRM V12 2998 cc	11th: I'30"6	R
I	Jean-Pierre Beltoise	F	Matra Sports	Matra MS II	Matra V12 2993 cc	8th: I'29"7	R
17	Joseph Siffert	CH	RRC Walker & J.Durlacher Racing Team	Lotus 49	Cosworth V8 2993 cc	2nd(3): I'28"8	R
19	Dan Gurney	USA	Anglo-American Racers Inc.	Eagle IG	Eagle V12 2997 cc	15th(16): I'32"9	R
3	Jochen Rindt	A	Brabham Racing Organisation	Brabham BT24	Repco V8 2995 cc	5th: I'29"2	R
2	Jack Brabham	AUS	Brabham Racing Organisation	Brabham BT26	Repco V8 2995 cc	12th: I'31"2	R
II	Johnny Servoz-Gavin	F	Matra International	Matra MS 10	Cosworth V8 2993 cc	2nd: I'28"8	R
10	Jackie Oliver	GB	Gold Leaf Team Lotus	Lotus 49B	Cosworth V8 2993 cc	13th: I'31"7	R
14	Bruce McLaren	NZ	Bruce McLaren Motor Racing	McLaren M7A	Cosworth V8 2993 cc	6th(7): I'29"6	R

(1) On this occasion Graham Hill in his Lotus, decorated in his sponsor's garish colors, has to work hard to defend himself. Directly behind him: Siffert with Rob Walker's Lotus 49 and Surtees in a Honda. (2) Shooting star: Johnny Servoz-Gavin (Matra). (3) Old coachman: Lucien Bianchi (Cooper). (4) Gateway to the sea: virage du Portier. (5) The two BRMs of Attwood and Rodriguez. (6) Warning to Hulme (McLaren): Surtees' Honda is stuck in second gear.

(1) Diesmal muß sich Graham Hill im sponsorbunten Lotus tüchtig seiner Haut wehren. Unmittelbar hinter ihm: Siffert mit Rob Walkers Lotus 49 und Surtees im Honda. (2) Shooting Star: Johnny Servoz-Gavin (Matra). (3) Alter Fuhrmann: Lucien Bianchi (Cooper). (4) Tor zum Meer: Virage du Portier. (5) Die beiden BRM mit Attwood und Rodriguez. (6) Warnung an Hulme (McLaren): Surtees' Honda läuft nur noch im zweiten Gang.

(1) Cette fois-ci, Graham Hill doit chèrement vendre sa peau dans sa Lotus aux couleurs de son sponsor. Juste derrière lui : Siffert au volant de la Lotus 49 de Rob Walker et Surtees sur Honda. (2) Star en un jour : Johnny Servoz-Gavin (Matra). (3) Vieux timonier : Lucien Bianchi (Cooper). (4) Porte ouverte vers la mer : le virage du Portier. (5) Les deux BRM avec Attwood et Rodriguez. (6) Avertissement à Hulme (McLaren) : la Honda de Surtees ne possède plus que sa deuxième vitesse.

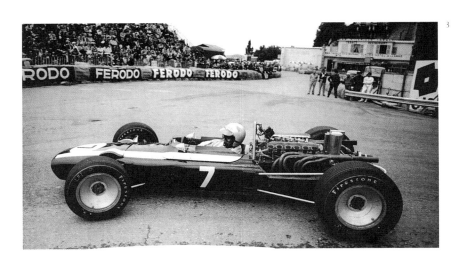

The end for Rodriguez's BRM at Mirabeau after 16 laps. Something,
the Mexican complains, has broken.

Aus für den BRM von Rodriguez bei Mirabeau nach 16 Runden.
Irgendetwas, beschwert sich der Mexikaner, sei gebrochen.

Abandon pour la BRM de Rodriguez à Mirabeau au bout de 16 tours.
Le Mexicain se plaint que quelque chose ait cassé.

Lotus-Ford (Oliver)

Lotus-Ford (Hill)

Repco-Brabham (Rindt)

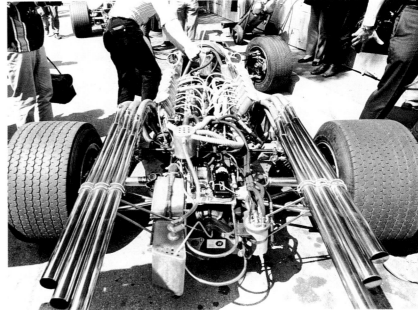

Matra (Beltoise)

(1) King and king-maker: 1968 is a good year for Lotus. Hill (left) becomes Champion, and Colin Chapman (right) wins the Constructor's Championship. (2) That way: McLaren and Louis Chiron. (3) Fast collective: Bonnier, Rindt, Moser and Scarfiotti (from left) on board the transfer bus.

(1) Meister und Meister-Macher: 1968 ist ein gutes Jahr für Lotus. Hill (links) wird Champion, und Colin Chapman (rechts) wird zum Besten unter den Konstrukteuren. (2) Da geht's lang: McLaren und Louis Chiron. (3) Schnelles Kollektiv: Bonnier, Rindt, Moser und Scarfiotti (von links) beim Bus-Transfer.

(1) Le champion et celui qui fait les champions : 1968 est une bonne année pour Lotus. Hill (à gauche) sera sacré champion et Colin Chapman (à droite) remportera le titre des constructeurs. (2) Suivez la bonne direction : McLaren et Louis Chiron. (3) Hommes pressés : Bonnier, Rindt, Moser et Scarfiotti (à partir de la gauche) lors du transfert en bus.

Repco-Brabham (Brabham)

1969

It was Graham Hill who introduced the charm of the large numbers into the results lists of the Monaco Grand Prix: Hill for the fifth time, screamed the headlines on 19 May 1969. The future would show that it was also the last time. And the cool Londoner, whose face remained as impassive as a statue in the two hours of hell of a Grand Prix, had long since ceased simply to leave all the others standing. His victories were those of a consistent and seasoned man, even if some luck was also involved. But luck is precisely what the BRM driver Jackie Oliver did not have during his appearance in the heaving theatre which is Monte Carlo: exit one minute after his debut in 1968, exit after 100 meters during his second attempt in 1969. The reasons were crashes. At Lotus, Richard Attwood replaced Jochen Rindt who had been injured at the Spanish Grand Prix in Barcelona when his car's rear wing collapsed. The same thing happened to Hill at almost the same place, with the difference that he escaped relatively lightly.

The wings, which had begun to sprout and wobble wildly over the front wheels as well, were the topic of the weekend in Monaco. They were to be banned after the training session on the Thursday. Hill's Lotus chassis, the same as in 1968, thus sprouted a metal sheet over the engine as in the previous year. Chris Amon's lonely Ferrari 312/F1 was provided with a similar aid. Curiously, the times recorded without spoilers were faster than those with them; time simply worked differently in Monaco.

Bruce McLaren and Denny Hulme were driving for the McLaren team, Jack Brabham himself and Jacky Ickx for Brabham with the BT26s. Ken Tyrrell utilized two Matra MS80s for Jackie Stewart and Jean-Pierre Beltoise. The Owen Racing Organisation had entrusted Oliver with a BRM P133 while John Surtees drove the P138. This time, too, "Big John" would leave the Principality an unhappy man: troubled by transmission problems, he tangled with Jack Brabham in the tenth lap leaving Portier. The mutilated BRM finally parked on the pavement at the tunnel mouth while the alert Australian continued to drag himself through the badly lit tunnel on three wheels.

At the start, Jackie Stewart took the lead from Amon, creating increasing distance between himself and the fast quartet of Hill, Beltoise, Ickx and Piers Courage driving the privately entered Brabham of his team chief and friend Frank Williams. By the ninth lap Stewart was nine seconds ahead. Could anyone stop the Scot? But then things began to happen as if everything was set up for Hill. Amon had to drop out alongside the Mediterranean shore on lap 17 – his differential had failed. On lap 21 Beltoise was let down by his drive-shaft. On lap 23 Stewart rolled to a halt with the same problem in the emergency exit adjacent to the chicane. On lap 49 a wheel hub on Ickx's Brabham gave way.

Looking back to the previous afternoon, future Grand Prix monuments are often forged in the heat of the Monaco Formula 3 race; the 1969 winner was called Ronnie Peterson.

Graham Hill ist es, der den Charme der großen Zahl in die Ergebnislisten des Grand Prix de Monaco einführt: Hill zum fünften Mal, schmettern die Schlagzeilen am 19. Mai 1969 in alle Welt hinaus. Daß es auch das letzte Mal ist, wird die Zukunft erweisen. Und längst fährt der kühle Londoner, dessen Gesicht in der Zweistundenhölle eines Großen Preises so unbewegt bleibt wie das einer Statue, nicht mehr allen einfach davon. Sein Sieg ist der eines beständigen und gestandenen Mannsbilds, und ein bißchen Glück ist auch im Spiel. Eben dieses hat BRM-Pilot Jackie Oliver bei seinen Auftritten im tosenden Stadttheater von Monte Carlo nicht: Ausfall nach einer Minute beim Debüt 1968, Ausfall nach 100 Metern beim zweiten Anlauf 1969, Grund: Unfälle. Bei Lotus ersetzt Richard Attwood Jochen Rindt, der sich beim Grand Prix von Spanien in Barcelona verletzt hat, als ein Flügel seines Wagens in sich zusammenknickte. Hill widerfuhr Ähnliches an fast der gleichen Stelle, nur daß die Sache vergleichsweise glimpflich abging.

Das inzwischen auch über den Vorderrädern wild wuchernde und wankende Luftleitwerk ist in Monaco Thema des Wochenendes. Nach dem ersten Training am Donnerstag wird es kurzerhand verboten. Also sprießt an Hills Lotus-Chassis, demselben wie 1968, ein über dem Motor sich wölbendes Blech – wie im Jahr zuvor. Auch der einsame Ferrari 312/F1 für Chris Amon wird mit einer ähnlichen Hilfe versehen. Kurios: Die Zeiten ohne Flügel sind schneller als mit Flügeln. In Monaco gehen die Uhren eben anders.

Für McLaren fahren Bruce McLaren und Denny Hulme, für Brabham Jack Brabham selbst und Jacky Ickx mit dem BT26. Ken Tyrrell setzt zwei Matra MS80 für Jackie Stewart und Jean-Pierre Beltoise ein. Die Owen Racing Organisation hat Oliver einen BRM P133 anvertraut, während John Surtees den P138 lenkt. Auch diesmal wird »Big John« das Fürstentum betrübt verlassen: Heimgesucht von Problemen mit dem Getriebe, kommt er sich in der zehnten Runde hinter Portier mit Jack Brabham ins Gehege. Der verstümmelte BRM parkt anschließend vor dem Tunnelmund auf dem Bürgersteig, während sich der wachsame Australier noch auf drei Rädern durch die spärlich illuminierte Röhre schleppt.

Anfänglich führt Jackie Stewart vor Amon, mit einem immer wachsenden Abstand vor dem schnellen Quartett Hill, Beltoise, Ickx und Piers Courage mit dem privaten Brabham seines Teamchefs und Freundes Frank Williams. Im neunten Durchgang hat Stewart neun Sekunden Vorsprung. Wer kann den Schotten stoppen? Doch dann läuft alles wie für Hill inszeniert. In der 17. Runde fällt Amon am Ufer des Mittelmeeres aus, das Differential. In der 21. wird Beltoise von einer Antriebswelle im Stich gelassen. Im 23. Durchgang rollt Stewart mit dem gleichen Schaden im Notausgang neben der Schikane aus. In der 49. Runde macht an Ickx' Brabham eine Radnabe nicht mehr mit.

In der Hitze des Formel-3-Rennens von Monaco werden oft künftige Grand-Prix-Denkmäler geschmiedet. Der Sieger 1969 heißt Ronnie Peterson.

C'est à Graham Hill que l'on doit d'avoir introduit le charme des chiffres prestigieux dans les listes de résultats du Grand Prix de Monaco : Hill pour la cinquième fois, proclament les grands titres des journaux du monde entier le 19 mai 1969. Mais, ce jour-là, personne ne sait encore que ce sera aussi la dernière. Et il y a longtemps que le froid Londonien dont le visage reste aussi imperturbable que celui d'une statue pendant les deux heures d'hostilités d'un Grand Prix ne domine plus de la tête et des épaules. Sa victoire est celle d'un homme qui sait se battre et ne baisse jamais les bras, mais la chance joue aussi un petit rôle. Et c'est justement cette chance qui fait défaut au pilote de BRM Jackie Oliver lors de ses représentations dans le houleux théâtre urbain de Monte-Carlo : abandon au bout d'une minute lors de ses débuts en 1968, abandon au bout de 100 mètres lors de la seconde tentative en 1969, toujours pour la même raison : accident. Chez Lotus, Richard Attwood remplace Jochen Rindt qui s'est blessé lors du Grand Prix d'Espagne à Barcelone lorsque son aileron s'est effondré comme un château de cartes. Hill a été victime de la même mésaventure pratiquement au même endroit, à cette différence près que lui s'en est mieux tiré.

Les ailerons qui prolifèrent et poussent maintenant aussi sur les trains avant sont le thème du week-end à Monaco. A l'issue des essais du jeudi, ils sont inopinément interdits. Ainsi trouve-t-on donc, sur le châssis de la Lotus de Hill, le même qu'en 1968, un carénage dissimulant le moteur — comme l'année précédente. La seule et unique Ferrari 312/F1, pour Chris Amon, possède elle aussi un expédient similaire. Bizarrement, les temps réalisés sans aileron sont meilleurs que ceux couverts avec aileron. A Monaco, les montres ne sont pas à la même heure qu'ailleurs.

Bruce McLaren et Denny Hulme défendent les couleurs de McLaren, Jack Brabham lui-même et Jacky Ickx, sur la BT26, défendant celles de Brabham. Ken Tyrrell a engagé deux Matra MS80 pour Jackie Stewart et Jean-Pierre Beltoise. La Owen Racing Organisation a confié une BRM P133 à Oliver, tandis que John Surtees prend, lui, la P138. Cette année aussi, « Big John » quittera la Principauté de mauvaise humeur : handicapé par des problèmes de boîte de vitesses, il entre en collision avec Jack Brabham, au dixième tour, à la sortie du virage du portier. Il doit alors garer sa BRM endommagée sur le trottoir à l'entrée du tunnel alors que l'Australien parvient encore à se traîner sur trois roues à travers le tube faiblement éclairé.

Au départ, Jackie Stewart est en tête devant Amon, les deux hommes accentuant constamment leur avance sur un quatuor de rapides pilotes — Hill, Beltoise, Ickx et Piers Courage, au volant de la Brabham privée de son chef d'équipe et ami Frank Williams. Au neuvième passage, Stewart a neuf secondes d'avance. Qui pourrait stopper l'Ecossais ? Puis le scénario semble avoir été écrit pour Graham Hill. Au 17e tour, Amon abandonne au bord de la Méditerranée : panne de différentiel. Au 21e tour, Beltoise est réduit à l'impuissance par un arbre de transmission. Au 23e tour, c'est Stewart qui prend l'échappatoire adjacent à la chicane pour le même motif. Au 49e tour, un moyeu de roue se met en grève sur la Brabham de Jackie Ickx.

Dans la chaleur du Grand Prix de Formule 3 de Monaco s'élèvent souvent les monuments des Grands Prix de l'avenir ; le vainqueur de 1969 a pour nom Ronnie Peterson.

Still winged: John Surtees'
BRM. The filigreed rods
inspire little confidence.

Noch beflügelt: der BRM von
John Surtees. Die filigranen
Gestänge wirken wenig
vertrauenerweckend.

Encore avec leurs ailerons :
la BRM de John Surtees.
Cette construction filigrane
n'inspire guère confiance.

N°	DRIVERS		ENTRANTS	CARS	ENGINES	PRACTICE RESULTS	RACE RESULTS
1	**Graham Hill**	GB	**Gold Leaf Team Lotus**	**Lotus 49B**	**Cosworth V8 2993 cc**	**4th: 1'25"8**	**1st: 1h56'59"4**
16	Piers Courage	GB	Frank Williams Racing Cars	Brabham BT26	Cosworth V8 2993 cc	8th(9): 1'26"4	2nd: 1h57'16"7
9	Joseph Siffert	CH	RRC Walker & J. Durlacher Racing Team	Lotus 49	Cosworth V8 2993 cc	5th: 1'26"0	3rd: 1h57'34"0
2	Richard Attwood	GB	Gold Leaf Team Lotus	Lotus 49B	Cosworth V8 2993 cc	10th: 1'26"5	4th: 1h57'52"3
4	Bruce McLaren	NZ	Bruce McLaren Motor Racing	McLaren M7C	Cosworth V8 2993 cc	11th: 1'26"7	5th: 79 laps
3	Denis Hulme	NZ	Bruce McLaren Motor Racing	McLaren M7A	Cosworth V8 2993 cc	12th: 1'26"8	6th: 78 laps
12	Vic Elford	GB	Antique Automobiles	Cooper T86B	Maserati V12 2985 cc	16th: 1'32"8	7th: 74 laps
6	Jacky Ickx	B	Motor Racing Developments	Brabham BT26	Cosworth V8 2993 cc	7th: 1'26"3	R
7	Jackie Stewart	GB	Matra International	Matra MS 80	Cosworth V8 2993 cc	1st: 1'24"6	R
8	Jean-Pierre Beltoise	F	Matra International	Matra MS 80	Cosworth V8 2993 cc	3rd: 1'25"4	R
11	Chris Amon	NZ	SEFAC Ferrari S.p.A.	Ferrari 312	Ferrari V12 2989 cc	2nd: 1'25"0	R
17	Silvio Moser	CH	Silvio Moser Racing Team	Brabham BT24	Cosworth V8 2993 cc	14th(15): 1'30"5	R
10	Pedro Rodriguez	MEX	Tim Parnell Racing	BRM P126	BRM V12 2998 cc	14th: 1'30"5	R
5	Jack Brabham	AUS	Motor Racing Developments	Brabham BT26	Cosworth V8 2993 cc	8th: 1'26"4	R
14	John Surtees	GB	Owen Racing Organisation	BRM P138	BRM V12 2998 cc	5th(6): 1'26"0	R
15	Jackie Oliver	GB	Owen Racing Organisation	BRM P133	BRM V12 2998 cc	13th: 1'28"4	R

Before the ban: wing variations on (1) McLaren's McLaren, (2) Amon's Ferrari and (3) Hill's Lotus. Powerful hearts: the V12s of (4) Amon's Ferrari and (5) Oliver's BRM and (6) the Ford V8 of the Brabham driven by Piers Courage.

Vor dem Verbot: Flügel-Variationen an (1) McLarens McLaren, (2) Amons Ferrari und (3) Hills Lotus. Starke Herzen: die V12 von (4) Amons Ferrari und (5) Olivers BRM sowie (6) der Ford-V8 des Brabham, den Piers Courage fährt.

Avant l'interdiction : Déclinaisons d'ailerons sur la (1) McLaren de McLaren, (2) la Ferrari d'Amon Ferrari et (3) la Lotus de Hill. Cœurs puissants : les V12 de (4) la Ferrari d'Amon et (5) la BRM d'Oliver ainsi que (6) le Ford V8 de la Brabham pilotée par Piers Courage.

(1, 2) Without wings but faster: Bruce McLaren.
(3) Happy atmosphere: Ireland, after falling through his chair. (4) Hill's Lotus has a rounded spoiler, while (5) Attwood's sister car must do without such assistance. (6) Brabham keeps a clear head as he limps out of the darkness of the tunnel on three wheels. Bleak prospects: (7) Jackie Stewart and Colin Chapman as well as (8) the Grimaldis in the royal box.

(1, 2) Unbeflügelt, aber schneller: Bruce McLaren.
(3) Tendenz heiter: Ireland nach seinem Durchbruch durch den Stuhl. (4) Hills Lotus hat ein rundliches Luftleitblech angesetzt, während (5) Attwoods Schwesterfahrzeug ohne eine solche Hilfe auskommen muß. (6) Brabham bewahrt einen klaren Kopf, als er auf drei Rädern aus dem Dunkel des Tunnels humpelt. Ernste Lage: (7) Jackie Stewart und Colin Chapman sowie (8) die Grimaldis in der Fürstenloge.

(1, 2) Sans aileron et pourtant plus rapide : Bruce McLaren. (3) Quand on a de l'humour : Ireland dont le fauteuil vient de s'effondrer sous lui. (4) La Lotus de Hill dotée d'un petit becquet arrondi, alors que la voiture jumelle (5) d'Attwood doit encore se passer d'un tel expédient. (6) Brabham garde son sang froid lorsqu'il sort de l'obscurité du tunnel sur trois roues. La situation est sérieuse : (7) Jackie Stewart et Colin Chapman ainsi que (8) les Grimaldi dans la loge princière.

1970

The 28th Monaco Grand Prix went down in the annals as a classic, as a great advertisement for the sport. With an entry ticket you got a ringside seat for a drama which took on Shakespearean proportions, providing nail-biting tension and surprising twists and turns – it was a drama which marked the ascent of new heroes and the ignominious fall of old ones. For example, the national legend Graham Hill started the race from the last row driving a borrowed factory Lotus (he had destroyed the version belonging to the private team owner Rob Walker in training). This year he never quite managed to make his mark on events. Or Johnny Servoz-Gavin: after failing to qualify, the Frenchman who was in Ken Tyrrell's team with Jackie Stewart announced his retirement from motor racing. Fate held worse things in store for Jack Brabham. The 44-year-old, known as the quiet Australian, had three World Championship titles and 126 major prizes under his belt. But he was destined to have the most painful humiliation of his career in the closing seconds of the race.

It seemed that, once again, the man of the race went by the name of Jackie Stewart. As the holder of the fastest lap time in all three training sessions, the Scot started from pole position, as he had done in the previous year when driving with Chris Amon. Both were sitting in a new model this time – the March 701, the name of which was made up of the initials of Max Mosley, Alan Rees, Graham Coaker and Robin Herd. Amon, who could not rid himself of the reputation of being a permanent "nearly man", was alongside Jo Siffert as factory team driver.

For 22 laps, Brabham's BT33 was on the heels of the two with the fastest qualifying times. Then the Australian overtook Amon. He then unexpectedly took the lead when Stewart headed towards the pits after the twenty-seventh lap. The blue March was crippled by misfiring ignition. Anything less than a workshop repair could not cure the problem, but two laps behind, the Scot took up the chase again, only to retire from the race after the fifty-eighth lap. Meanwhile, at the front, the battle raged between Brabham, Amon and Hulme (in the McLaren M14A).

But Jochen Rindt's hour had come – literally. Drivers starting from the fourth row in Monaco are normally condemned to bringing up the rear. However, the Austrian had other plans and drove the Lotus 49C with the sponsor's striking Gold Leaf emblem like a man possessed. On the thirty-sixth lap, he overtook Henri Pescarolo in the Matra MS120V12 and moved into fourth place, giving Denny Hulme the same treatment in lap 41 to move up into third. Chris Amon escaped his onslaught on lap 61 due to damaged suspension. Now only 13 seconds lay between Rindt and Brabham and they, too, quickly vanished like the morning dew. This was because "Black Jack" was now tired and his brakes were the worse for wear. Disaster struck on the last lap at the final gasometer bend, where Brabham skidded straight into the straw bales. And as the devastated driver headed for the finishing line with a compacted front section, the colorful Lotus darted past – a phantom that came from the deep.

Der 28. Grand Prix de Monaco wird in die Annalen als Klassiker eingehen, als Werbeveranstaltung zum höheren Ruhme des Sports. Im Eintrittspreis enthalten: ein Drama von Shakespeareschen Ausmaßen mit knisternder Spannung und überraschenden Wendungen, dem Aufstieg von neuen Helden und dem schmählichen Absturz von alten. Das Naturdenkmal Graham Hill zum Beispiel geht das Rennen aus der letzten Reihe, mit einem geliehenen Werks-Lotus an, da er das Exemplar des privaten Teambesitzers Rob Walker im Training ramponiert hat. Er vermag sich nie so recht in Szene zu setzen. Oder Johnny Servoz-Gavin: Nachdem er sich nicht qualifizieren konnte, erklärt der Franzose, mit Jackie Stewart zusammen im Aufgebot von Ken Tyrrell, spontan seinen Rücktritt vom Rennsport. Schlimmeres indessen hält das Schicksal für den Jack Brabham bereit, den sie den stillen Australier nennen, 44 Jahre, drei Weltmeisterschaften sowie 126 Große Preise alt. Denn in den letzten Sekunden des Rennens erwartet ihn die schmerzlichste Demütigung seiner Laufbahn.

Der Mann des Meetings – so scheint es – heißt wieder einmal Jackie Stewart. Schnellster in allen drei Trainingssitzungen, startet der Schotte aus der Pole Position, wie im Vorjahr in Gesellschaft von Chris Amon. Die beiden sitzen in einem neuen Fabrikat, dem March 701, in dessen Namen die vier Herren Max Mosley, Alan Rees, Graham Coaker und Robin Herd ihre Initialen verschränkt haben. Amon, dem bereits der Ruf des ewigen Pechvogels anhaftet wie Leim, ist Werkspilot wie auch Jo Siffert.

Den beiden Trainingsschnellsten sitzt 22 Runden lang Brabhams Brabham BT33 im Nacken. Dann schnappt sich der Australier Amon. Aus seiner zweiten Position wird unversehens die Führung, als Stewart nach der 27. Runde die Box anläuft. Der blaue March wird von Fehlzündungen gebeutelt. Ambulante Behandlung reicht da nicht aus: Mit zwei Runden Rückstand geht der Schotte wieder auf die Strecke und scheidet nach der 58. Runde aus. Vorn tobt unterdessen der Dreikampf Brabham, Amon und Hulme (auf dem McLaren M14A).

Da aber hat schon längst die Stunde des Jochen Rindt geschlagen – buchstäblich. Ein Startplatz in der vierten Reihe führt in Monaco gewöhnlich zu einem Dasein als Hinterbänkler. Der Österreicher hat jedoch anderes im Sinn, fährt den Lotus 49C im knalligen Gewand des Sponsors Gold Leaf wie im Rausch. In der 36. Runde hat er Henri Pescarolo mit dem Matra MS120V12 vom vierten Platz verdrängt, in der 41. Denny Hulme vom dritten. Chris Amon entzieht sich seinem Zugriff im 61. Durchgang mit einem Schaden an der Aufhängung von alleine. Da beträgt der Rückstand auf Brabham noch 13 Sekunden, schmilzt indes wie Butter in der Sonne. Denn Black Jack ist müde, und seine Bremsen lassen nach. In der letzten Kurve der letzten Runde passiert es: Der Brabham rutscht am Gasometer geradeaus in die Strohballen. Und während der bestürzte Pilot mit zerdrückter Frontpartie der Ziellinie zustrebt, ist der bunte Lotus des Österreichers vorbeigehuscht – ein Phantom, das aus der Tiefe kam.

Le 28e Grand Prix de Monaco entrera dans les annales comme une grande classique, une représentation médiatique pour la plus grande gloire du sport automobile. Pour le prix d'entrée, on assistera à un drame d'envergure shakespearienne avec un suspense d'une intensité incroyable et des revirements de situation surprenants, l'avènement de nouveaux héros et la décadence humiliante de héros de jadis. Un monument de la course automobile, Graham Hill, par exemple, prend le départ en dernière ligne avec une Lotus officielle d'emprunt, ayant endommagé, aux essais, la voiture du propriétaire d'écurie privé Rob Walker. Il ne parvient jamais vraiment à se mettre en valeur cette année-là. Ou Johnny Servoz-Gavin : n'ayant pu se qualifier, le Français, pourtant coéquipier de Jackie Stewart dans l'écurie de Ken Tyrrell, annonce spontanément sa retraite du sport automobile. Mais le destin sera beaucoup plus cruel avec Jack Brabham, que l'on surnomme l'Australien taciturne, 44 ans, triple champion du monde et avec 126 Grands Prix à son actif. En effet, dans les dernières secondes de la course, il sera victime de la plus grande humiliation de toute sa carrière.

L'homme du week-end – semble-t-il – a, une fois de plus, pour nom Jackie Stewart. Plus rapide lors de chacune des trois séances d'essais, le pilote part de la pole position, comme l'an dernier, en compagnie de Chris Amon. Les deux hommes sont au volant d'une nouvelle voiture, la March 701, dans le nom de laquelle ses quatre créateurs, Max Mosley, Alan Rees, Graham Coaker et Robin Herd, seront immortalisés à travers leurs initiales. Amon, qui a depuis longtemps déjà une réputation d'éternel perdant, est pilote d'usine au même titre que Jo Siffert.

Pendant 22 tours, la Brabham BT33 de Jack Brabham talonne les deux hommes les plus rapides des essais. Puis inopinément l'Australien finit par doubler Amon. Mais sa seconde position se métamorphose inopinément en leadership lorsque Stewart prend la tête aux stands après le 27e tour. La March bleue est victime de ratés d'allumage. Les soins de ses mécaniciens s'avèrent insuffisants : avec deux tours de retard, l'Ecossais reprend la course, mais abandonne après le 58e tour. Aux avant-postes, pendant ce temps, la lutte fait rage entre Brabham, Amon et Hulme (sur sa McLaren M14A).

Mais l'heure de Jochen Rindt va bientôt sonner. A Monaco, partir depuis la quatrième ligne vous condamne en général irrémédiablement à rester englué dans le peloton. Mais ce n'est pas l'avis de l'Autrichien, qui pilote comme transcendé la Lotus 49C à la robe bigarrée de son sponsor Gold Leaf. Au 36e, il dépossède Henri Pescarolo, sur Matra MS120V12, de sa quatrième place et, au 41e tour, Denny Hulme de sa troisième. L'obstacle Chris Amon disparaît de lui-même sur panne de suspension avant qu'il n'ait pu porter son attaque, au 61e tour. 13 secondes seulement séparent Rindt de Brabham, et ce retard fond comme neige au soleil. En effet, « Black Jack » est fatigué et ses freins faiblissent. Dans le dernier virage du dernier tour, l'imprévisible se produit lorsque Brabham fait un tout droit au Gazomètre et percute les bottes de paille. Et, tandis que le pilote, sonné, repart vers la ligne d'arrivée avec la proue de sa voiture défoncée, la Lotus multicolore passe comme un mirage – le fantôme qui venait des profondeurs.

Navel-gazing: the fast and the beautiful always go together in Monaco; in any case, what better place for a Yardley advertisement?

Nabel-Schau: In der Nähe der Schnellen finden sich in Monaco auch immer die Schönen, und eine bessere Stelle für Yardley-Werbung gibt es ohnehin nicht.

Voir et se faire voir : à proximité des stars de la vitesse, on trouve toujours aussi, à Monaco, de beaux félins. Y a-t-il meilleur endroit pour la publicité Yardley ?

N°	DRIVERS		ENTRANTS	CARS	ENGINES	PRACTICE RESULTS	RACE RESULTS
3	**Jochen Rindt**	**A**	**Gold Leaf Team Lotus**	**Lotus 49C**	**Cosworth V8 2993 cc**	**8th: 1'25"9**	**1st: 1h54'36"6**
5	Jack Brabham	AUS	Motor Racing Developments	Brabham BT33	Cosworth V8 2993 cc	4th: 1'25"4	2nd: 1h54'59"7
9	Henri Pescarolo	F	Equipe Matra-Elf	Matra MS120	Matra V12 2993 cc	7th: 1'25"7	3rd: 1h55'28"0
11	Denis Hulme	NZ	Bruce McLaren Motor Racing	McLaren M14A	Cosworth V8 2993 cc	3rd: 1'25"1	4th: 1h56'04"9
1	Graham Hill	GB	Brooke Bond Oxo Racing	Lotus 49C	Cosworth V8 2993 cc	12th(17): 1'26"8	5th: 79 laps
17	Pedro Rodriguez	MEX	Owen Racing Organisation	BRM P153	BRM V12 2998 cc	16th: 1'28"8	6th: 78 laps
23	Ronnie Peterson	S	Antique Automobiles	March 701	Cosworth V8 2993 cc	12th(13): 1'26"8	7th: 78 laps
19	Joseph Siffert	CH	March Engineering	March 701	Cosworth V8 2993 cc	11th: 1'26"2	8th: 76 laps
24	Piers Courage	GB	Frank Williams Racing Cars	De Tomaso 308	Cosworth V8 2993 cc	9th: 1'26"1	NC: 56 laps
28	Chris Amon	NZ	March Engineering	March 701	Cosworth V8 2993 cc	2nd: 1'24"6	R
21	*Jackie Stewart*	*GB*	*Tyrrell Racing Organisation*	*March 701*	*Cosworth V8 2993 cc*	*1st: 1'24"0*	R
16	Jackie Oliver	GB	Owen Racing Organisation	BRM P153	BRM V12 2998 cc	15th: 1'27"5	R
8	Jean-Pierre Beltoise	F	Equipe Matra-Elf	Matra MS120	Matra V12 2993 cc	6th: 1'25"6	R
12	Bruce McLaren	NZ	Bruce McLaren Motor Racing	McLaren M14C	Cosworth V8 2993 cc	9th(10): 1'26"1	R
14	John Surtees	GB	Team Surtees	McLaren M7C	Cosworth V8 2993 cc	14th: 1'27"4	R
26	Jacky Ickx	B	SEFAC Ferrari S.p.A.	Ferrari 312B	Ferrari V12 2991 cc	5th: 1'25"5	R

1

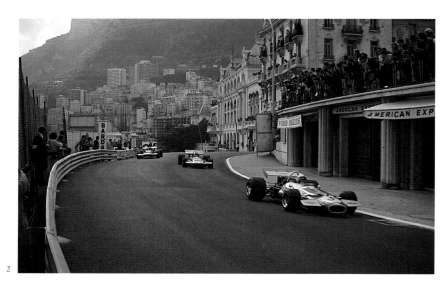

2

3

Battle for Monte Casino: (1) Pescarolo (Matra), (2) Brabham (Brabham) in front of Amon (March),
(3) Rindt (Lotus) with Pescarolo behind and (4) Hulme (McLaren).

Kampf um den Monte Casino: (1) Pescarolo (Matra), (2) Brabham (Brabham) vor Amon (March), (3) Rindt
(Lotus) mit Pescarolo im Schlepptau und (4) Hulme (McLaren).

Lutte pour le Monte Casino : (1) Pescarolo (Matra), (2) Brabham (Brabham) devant Amon (March).
(3) Rindt (Lotus) avec Pescarolo sur ses talons et (4) Hulme (McLaren).

4

(1, 2) "What, only second?" Brabham still can't understand it. Great mood: Jochen Rindt (3) having a joke with Chris Amon and (4) receiving his prize.

(1, 2) »Was, nur zweiter?« Brabham kann es noch nicht fassen. Hoch-Stimmung: Jochen Rindt (3) während einer spaßhaften Spurensuche mit Chris Amon und (4) bei der Siegerehrung.

(1, 2) « Quoi, seulement deuxième ? » Brabham n'arrive pas à le croire. Blagues : Jochen Rindt (3), en train de plaisanter avec Chris Amon (à gauche), à la recherche de traces de pneu, et (4) lors de la remise de la coupe.

1971

On the eve of the 29th year of the race, Jackie Stewart said that Monaco was his favorite racing event. He already had pole position, being over one second faster than Jacky Ickx, who was driving the Ferrari 312 B2. On the following day, the Scot really got a firm grip, achieving a new record for a lap time, leading from start to finish, and picking up nine useful points to help him on the way to his second World Championship. Stewart's victory in the 200th Grand Prix since the beginning of the Formula 1 championship series was the second success enjoyed by his employer Ken Tyrrell, whose new make of car was enjoying its first full season. But one man's meat is another man's poison: it was raining for the first and final qualifying sessions. During the one dry period, the Ferrari driver Mario Andretti became an early casualty and therefore he failed to qualify.

Jo Siffert (BRM P 160) made a lightning start and moved from the second row into second place, but in so doing, he narrowly avoided killing someone since the racing veteran Louis Chiron was actually standing in the way with the starting flag. The two leading men were followed by Ickx, Siffert's team partner Pedro Rodriguez, Ronnie Peterson, in the strangely shaped March 711, and Denny Hulme, in the orange McLaren M 19A. On the second lap, Graham Hill made one of his rare mistakes, squashing the Brabham BT 34 (otherwise known as the lobster claw model) against the wall at the left-hand Tabac bend, damaging two wheels as well as his pride.

Although fumes were making their way into the cockpit of the Tyrrell with the chassis number 003, Stewart was able to move ahead of Siffert, while Ickx gradually disappeared from Siffert's rear-view mirror. However, any fears that the race might turn into a processional drive-past were dissipated by Peterson. Initially, the Swede laid siege to Rodriguez, who seemed equally lacking in any spirit of partnership and cooperation. The Mexican eventually had to yield when a tyre blew while he was braking, shaking both the BRM and its driver to the core.

While many competitors, such as François Cévert, the newcomer of the Tyrrell team, or Ferrari recruit Clay Regazzoni damaged their cars on the pavements, the leaders of the field continued on their way with a level of precision normally only to be found in Swiss watches. Ronnie Peterson, whose speed was reminiscent of that of Jochen Rindt the previous year, continued to be the source of excitement in the race. On the twenty-ninth lap he overtook Ickx, and even made his way past Siffert two laps later — no mean feat. However, the blonde Swede still remained only the second-fastest driver in the field. Jackie Stewart, kept fully aware of the state of affairs by his team at the pit stop, could cope with anything that day and won by a 25-second margin.

The early Seventies were a dangerous time for Formula 1 drivers: two of the main players in Monaco, Jo Siffert and Pedro Rodriguez, did not survive the season — nor had Bruce McLaren, Piers Courage and Jochen Rindt in 1970.

Monaco, sagt Jackie Stewart am Vorabend der 29. Auflage des Rennens, sei seine Lieblingsstrecke. Da geht bereits die Pole Position auf sein Konto, über eine Sekunde schneller als Jacky Ickx auf dem Ferrari 312 B2. Am nächsten Tag sattelt der Schotte drauf, neue Rekordrunde, Start- und Zielführung, nützliche neun Punkte auf dem Weg zu seinem zweiten Championat. Stewarts Sieg im Großen Preis Nummer 200 seit den Anfängen der neueren Formel 1 ist schon der zweite Erfolg für die junge Marke seines Arbeitgebers Ken Tyrrell in ihrer ersten vollen Saison. Des einen Nachtigall, des anderen Eule: Es regnet am ersten und am dritten Trainingstag. Am zweiten bleibt Ferrari-Pilot Mario Andretti frühzeitig auf der Strecke und kann sich daher nicht qualifizieren.

Der Blitzstart von Jo Siffert (BRM P 160) aus Reihe zwei auf Rang zwei muß um ein Haar mit einem Menschenleben erkauft werden, da Rennveteran Louis Chiron mit der Starterflagge eigentlich im Wege steht. Hinter den beiden Männern an der Spitze folgen Ickx, Sifferts Teamgefährte Pedro Rodriguez, Ronnie Peterson auf dem wunderlich geformten March 711 und Denny Hulme im gelben McLaren M 19A. Im zweiten Durchgang macht Graham Hill einen seiner seltenen Fehler, staucht den Brabham BT 34 (Kriegername: die Hummerkralle) in der Tabakskurve rechts gegen die Mauer und beschädigt zwei Räder sowie seine Eitelkeit.

Vorn setzt sich Stewart, obwohl Gase ins Cockpit des Tyrrell mit der Chassisnummer 003 dringen, von Siffert ab, aus dessen Rückspiegel Ickx allmählich verschwindet. Der Verdacht, das Rennen könne sich zu einer Prozession entwickeln, wird allerdings von Peterson entkräftet. Zunächst belagert der Schwede Rodriguez, der gleichwohl den Willen zu partnerschaftlicher Kooperation vermissen läßt. Am Ende muß der Mexikaner einlenken, als ein Bremsplattfuß den BRM und seinen Piloten bis ins Mark erzittern läßt.

Während zahlreiche Konkurrenten wie etwa Tyrrell-Novize François Cévert oder Ferrari-Rekrut Clay Regazzoni ihre Autos an den Bordsteinen beschädigen, ziehen die Spitzenreiter ihre Bahn mit der Präzision, die man Schweizer Uhrwerken nachsagt. Für Unruhe sorgt indessen weiterhin Ronnie Peterson, dessen zügige Fahrt an die von Jochen Rindt im Jahr zuvor erinnert. In der 29. Runde nimmt er Ickx, bremst zwei Durchgänge später gar Siffert aus — kein leichtes Unterfangen. Immer aber bleibt der blonde Schwede der Zweitschnellste auf der Strecke. Jackie Stewart, von seiner Box penibel über die Dinge unterrichtet, weiß auf alles eine Antwort und gewinnt mit 25 Sekunden Vorsprung.

Anfang der Siebziger sind die Zeiten gefährlich für Formel-1-Piloten: Zwei der Protagonisten von Monaco, Jo Siffert und Pedro Rodriguez, werden die Saison nicht überleben — wie 1970 Bruce McLaren, Piers Courage und Jochen Rindt.

Monaco, » déclare Jackie Stewart la veille de la 29ᵉ édition de la course, « est mon circuit préféré. » Il a déjà à son palmarès la pole position, avec plus d'une seconde d'avance sur Jacky Ickx et sa Ferrari 312 B2. Le lendemain, l'Ecossais retourne le couteau dans la plaie : nouveau record de tour, en tête du départ à l'arrivée, et neuf points bien utiles dans la voie de son deuxième titre de champion du monde. La victoire de Stewart au Grand Prix numéro 200 depuis l'instauration des séries de championnat de la Formule 1 est déjà le deuxième succès pour la jeune marque de son employeur, Ken Tyrrell, lors de sa première saison complète. Mais ce qui fait le bonheur des uns fait le malheur des autres : il pleut le premier et le troisième jour des essais. Le jour où le temps est au beau, Mario Andretti, pilote de Ferrari, reste prématurément bloqué sur le circuit et ne peut donc pas se qualifier.

Le départ éclair de Jo Siffert (BRM P 160), qui le catapulte de la deuxième ligne à la deuxième place, manque par la même de coûter une vie humaine : le vétéran de la course, Louis Chiron, était en effet encore sur la piste avec le drapeau du départ à la main. Derrière les deux hommes partis en tête viennent Ickx, le coéquipier de Siffert Pedro Rodriguez, Ronnie Peterson sur March 711 aux formes bizarres et Denny Hulme sur McLaren M 19A orange. Au deuxième tour, Graham Hill commet l'une de ses rares erreurs d'appréciation et frotte sa Brabham BT 34 (surnommée la pince de homard) contre le mur du virage du Bureau de Tabac, ce qui lui coûte deux roues ainsi que sa fierté.

En tête, bien que des gaz pénètrent dans le cockpit de la Tyrrell châssis numéro 003, Stewart accentue son avance sur Siffert, qui voit lui-même disparaître graduellement Ickx de son rétroviseur. Peterson fait vite s'évanouir la crainte que la course ne puisse se muer en une procession ennuyeuse. Le Suédois attaque tout d'abord Rodriguez, qui ne fait pas vraiment preuve d'esprit de coopération. A la fin, le Mexicain doit céder lorsqu'un plat subi au freinage ébranle la BRM et son pilote jusqu'à la moelle.

Tandis que de nombreux concurrents comme François Cévert, le néophyte de chez Tyrrell, ou Clay Regazzoni, la nouvelle recrue de Ferrari, endommagent leurs voitures contre les bordures de trottoir, les hommes de tête continuent à accomplir leurs circonvolutions avec une précision digne de chronomètres suisses. Une régularité que ne cesse de troubler pendant ce temps-là Ronnie Peterson, dont la remontée échevelée n'est pas sans rappeler celle de Jochen Rindt l'année précédente. Au 29ᵉ tour, il double Ickx, et « pique » au freinage Siffert deux tours plus tard – chose pourtant jamais facile avec cet homme. Mais le Suédois aux cheveux blonds reste toujours le deuxième pilote le plus rapide en piste. Jackie Stewart, informé avec précision du cours des choses par son stand, a réponse à tout ce jour-là et gagne avec 25 secondes d'avance.

Au début des années 70, la course est dangereuse pour les pilotes de Formule 1 : deux des protagonistes de Monaco, Jo Siffert et Pedro Rodriguez, ne verront pas la fin de la saison — tout comme Bruce McLaren, Piers Courage et Jochen Rindt en 1970.

Spring on the Riviera: with their position firmly entrenched in the Formula 1 calendar, the organizers of the Monaco Grand Prix also have to make do with the vagaries of the weather at this time of the year.

Frühling an der Côte: Mit ihrem Stammplatz im Terminkalender der Formel 1 haben die Organisatoren des Grand Prix de Monaco die Unwägbarkeiten des Wetters um diese Jahreszeit gleich mitgebucht.

Printemps sur la côte : avec leur date fixe dans le calendrier de la Formule 1, les organisateurs du Grand Prix de Monaco doivent aussi composer avec les aléas de la météo à cette époque de l'année.

N°	DRIVERS		ENTRANTS	CARS	ENGINES	PRACTICE RESULTS	RACE RESULTS
11	Jackie Stewart	GB	Elf Team Tyrrell	Tyrrell 003	Cosworth V8 2993 cc	1st: 1'23"2	1st: 1h52'21"3
17	Ronnie Peterson	S	STP March System Engineering	March 711	Cosworth V8 2993 cc	8th: 1'25"8	2nd: 1h52'46"9
4	Jacky Ickx	B	SEFAC Ferrari S.p.A.	Ferrari 312B2	Ferrari F12 2991 cc	2nd: 1'24"4	3rd: 1h53'14"6
9	Denis Hulme	NZ	Bruce McLaren Motor Racing	McLaren M19A	Cosworth V8 2993 cc	6th: 1'25"3	4th: 1h53'28"0
1	Emerson Fittipaldi	BR	Gold Leaf Team Lotus	Lotus 72D	Cosworth V8 2993 cc	17th: 1'27"7	5th: 79 laps
24	Rolf Stommelen	D	Auto Motor und Sport Eifelland	Surtees TS 9	Cosworth V8 2993 cc	15th(16): 1'27"2	6th: 79 laps
22	John Surtees	GB	Brooke Bond Oxo-Rob Walker-Team Surtees	Surtees TS 9	Cosworth V8 2993 cc	9th(19): 1'26"0	7th: 79 laps
27	Henri Pescarolo	F	Frank Williams Racing Cars	March 711	Cosworth V8 2993 cc	12th(13): 1'26"7	8th: 77 laps
15	Pedro Rodriguez	MEX	Yardley BRM	BRM P160	BRM V12 2998 cc	5th: 1'25"1	9th: 76 laps
8	Tim Schenken	AUS	Motor Racing Developments	Brabham BT33	Cosworth V8 2993 cc	18th: 1'28"3	10th: 76 laps
14	Joseph Siffert	CH	Yardley BRM	BRM P160	BRM V12 2998 cc	3rd: 1'24"8	R
21	Jean-Pierre Beltoise	F	Equipe Matra	Matra MS120B	Matra V12 2993 cc	7th: 1'25"6	R
20	Chris Amon	NZ	Equipe Matra	Matra MS120B	Matra V12 2993 cc	3rd(4): 1'24"8	R
5	Clay Regazzoni	CH	SEFAC Ferrari S.p.A.	Ferrari 312B2	Ferrari F12 2991 cc	11th: 1'26"1	R
10	Peter Gethin	GB	Bruce McLaren Motor Racing	McLaren M14A	Cosworth V8 2993 cc	14th: 1'26"9	R
2	Reine Wisell	S	Gold Leaf Team Lotus	Lotus 72D	Cosworth V8 2993 cc	12th: 1'26"7	R
12	François Cévert	F	Elf Team Tyrrell	Tyrrell 002	Cosworth V8 2993 cc	15th: 1'27"2	R
7	Graham Hill	GB	Motor Racing Developments	Brabham BT34	Cosworth V8 2993 cc	9th: 1'26"0	R

Multitude of species in 1971:
(1) rounded: Hulme's
McLaren. (2) Arrow: the two
Surtees of Stommelen and
Big John himself. (3) Racing
tray: Pescarolo's March (in
front of Gethin's McLaren)
and (4) mobile workbench:
Stewart's Tyrrell.

Arten-Vielfalt 1971: (1) Rund-
ling: der McLaren von Hulme.
(2) Pfeil: die beiden Surtees
von Stommelen und Big John
selbst. (3) Rasendes Servier-
brett: der March von Pescarolo
(vor Gethins McLaren) und
(4) mobile Doppelbank:
Stewarts Tyrrell.

Diversité des espèces en
1971 : (1) tout en rondeurs :
la McLaren de Hulme.
(2) Comme une flèche : les
deux Surtees de Stommelen
et Big John lui-même.
(3) Le plateau le plus rapide
du monde : la March de
Pescarolo (devant la McLaren
de Gethin) et (4) un double
banc mobile : la Tyrrell de
Stewart.

1

2

4

3

Damp pleasures: (1) Wisell (Lotus), (2) Stewart (Tyrrell), (3) Beltoise (Matra), (4) Andretti (Ferrari), who comes to a standstill in front of the Hôtel de Paris on Friday on a dry track with a defective fuel injection and fails to qualify and (5) Stommelen (Surtees). Under these conditions Formula 1 drivers do occasionally ask themselves whether they chose the right profession.

Feuchtes Vergnügen: (1) Wisell (Lotus), (2) Stewart (Tyrrell), (3) Beltoise (Matra), (4) Andretti (Ferrari), der am Freitag bei trockener Strecke mit defekter Einspritzung vor dem Hôtel de Paris stehenbleibt und sich nicht mehr qualifizieren kann, (5) Stommelen (Surtees). Unter diesen Bedingungen stellt sich für den Formel-1-Piloten schon mal die Frage nach der Sinnhaftigkeit seiner Berufswahl.

Driving in the rain : (1) Wisell (Lotus), (2) Stewart (Tyrrell), (3) Beltoise (Matra), (4) Andretti (Ferrari), qui tombera en panne d'injection devant l'Hôtel de Paris le vendredi sur le sec et ne peut pas se qualifier, (5) Stommelen (Surtees). Dans de telles conditions, les pilotes de Formule 1 se demandent parfois ce qu'ils sont venus faire dans cette galère.

Emerson Fittipaldi

Denis Jenkinson

Clay Regazzoni

Mario Andretti

Again and again the magnet which is Monaco attracts the timeless and outstanding figures of the sport such as Nina Rindt, while an army of journalists constantly accompanies the speeding circus, and even, like their doyen Denis Jenkinson, survives several generations of drivers.

Immer wieder zieht der Magnet Monaco zeitlose Größen dieses Sports wie Nina Rindt an, während ein Heer von Journalisten zu den ständigen Begleitern des schnellen Zirkus' zählt oder sogar wie ihr Doyen Denis Jenkinson viele Generationen von Fahrern überlebt.

Monaco attire toujours comme un aimant les célébrités intemporelles de ce sport comme Nina Rindt, tandis qu'une armée de journalistes accompagne en permanence le grand cirque ou a même, comme leur doyen Denis Jenkinson, survécu à de nombreuses générations de pilotes.

Jacky Ickx

Rolf Stommelen

Jackie Stewart

Nina Rindt

Graham Hill

LOOK BACK WITHOUT ANGER

BLICK ZURÜCK OHNE ZORN · REGARD EN ARRIÈRE SANS COLÈRE

In the twelve years between 1960 and 1971, John Surtees belonged to the regulars of the Monaco Grand Prix, in a Lotus, a Cooper, a Lola, a Ferrari, a Honda, a BRM, a McLaren, and finally in the racing cars which "Big John" built himself and which carried his name. His winnings, three fourth places and the fastest lap in 1963, were meagre; but the contribution which the World Champion of 1964 made to the drama which is Monaco is considerable and cannot be measured in figures:

"Actually I preferred tracks with fast bends to those with a stop-and-go rhythm. But that doesn't mean that I did not like Monaco. Of course, I would have liked to have won there.

What annoyed me, first as driver and later as team boss, was all the bureaucracy which surrounded the event. If one wanted a few extra passes that meant a huge fuss. In addition, there were problems in getting about the town during the Grand Prix, or getting to the race track at all. When I was still working for smaller English teams such as Yeoman Credit in the early Sixties, we were sometimes put in tiny garages far outside the town, somewhere towards Nice, and had to drive to the circuit with our racing cars through the ordinary town traffic. With Ferrari it was simpler. It was found accommodation near the start-and-finish before you climb up the hill.

I did not participate in all the to-do which is part of this Grand Prix, or only very reluctantly. There were various reasons for that. On the one hand I was there on business, as it were, and always took the sport pretty seriously. That included going to bed early before the race. On the other hand I did not see myself only as a driver, but also took an intense interest in technical matters. Above all, however, my employers were, as a rule, foreign racing stables, such as Ferrari and Honda. And they did not have the kind of cohesion which existed in the English ones, who were very much into having fun and being sociable, and who liked to run riot on occasion.

The Monaco Grand Prix represented a real challenge to me. I could clearly handle it, but I simply could not transform that into the right result. I could have won at least four times, particularly in 1966, in my last-but-one race for Ferrari. The team had brought along the car which was ideally suited, the Dino 246, which had been used in the Tasman series. On the Modena test track I drove it two seconds faster than the new 3-liter 12-cylinder engine with which I was then presented. That was a real beast, much too big and much too heavy. Lorenzo Bandini was given the Dino, and he promptly took second place with it. Although I succeeded in throwing the fat Tipo 312 round the bends at an astonishing speed – that is clearly visible in the Frankenheimer film *Grand Prix* – in the end things turned out as I had predicted to the Ferrari people: I would lead for a while and then something would break. In this case it was the differential.

These things were part of a political campaign with the purpose of driving a wedge between me and Enzo Ferrari. The string-puller was Mike Parkes, another Englishman with the Scuderia, who was very ambitious and had his finger in every pie. But that did not affect

In den zwölf Jahren zwischen 1960 und 1971 zählt John Surtees zum festen Stamm des Grand Prix de Monaco, im Lotus, im Cooper, im Lola, im Ferrari, im Honda, im BRM, im McLaren, schließlich in den Rennwagen, die »Big John« selber baut und die seinen Namen tragen. Die Ausbeute, drei vierte Plätze und die schnellste Runde 1963, ist mager, beträchtlich hingegen und überhaupt nicht in Zahlen zu messen der Anteil, den der Weltmeister von 1964 zu dem Drama Monaco beigesteuert hat:

»Eigentlich lagen mir Strecken mit schnellen Kurven mehr als solche Pisten mit dem Rhythmus Stop-and-go. Das heißt aber nicht, daß ich Monaco nicht mochte. Natürlich hätte ich gerne mal dort gewonnen.

Was mich immer gestört hat, als Fahrer und später noch mehr als Teamchef, war all die Bürokratie, die diese Veranstaltung umfächelte. Wenn man ein paar Pässe mehr haben wollte, war das stets mit einem Riesentheater verbunden. Außerdem gab es das Problem, sich zur Zeit des Grand Prix in der Stadt zu bewegen oder überhaupt auch nur zur Rennstrecke zu gelangen. Als ich noch für die kleineren englischen Teams fuhr wie Anfang der sechziger Jahre für Yeoman Credit, waren wir manchmal in winzigen Garagen weit außerhalb der Stadt irgendwo in Richtung Nizza untergebracht und mußten dann mit unseren Rennwagen mitten durch den Straßenverkehr zum Circuit fahren. Bei Ferrari hatten wir es einfacher. Für die hatte man eine Unterkunft in der Nähe von Start und Ziel gefunden, noch bevor es den Berg hochgeht.

An dem ganzen Rummel, der mit diesem Grand Prix mitschwimmt, habe ich nicht oder nur sehr ungern teilgenommen. Dafür gab es verschiedene Gründe. Zum einen war ich gewissermaßen geschäftlich da und habe den Sport stets ziemlich ernst genommen. Dazu gehörte, daß ich vor dem Rennen früh zu Bett ging. Zum anderen sah ich mich nicht nur als Fahrer, sondern habe mich auch immer intensiv um technische Aspekte gekümmert. Vor allem jedoch waren meine Arbeitgeber in der Regel ausländische Rennställe wie Ferrari und Honda. Und da gab es nicht diesen Zusammenhalt wie bei den Engländern, die sehr auf Spaß und Geselligkeit bedacht waren und gern mal über die Stränge schlugen.

Für mich bedeutete der Grand Prix de Monaco eine echte Herausforderung. Offenbar konnte ich damit umgehen, nur daß ich das einfach nicht in die richtigen Ergebnisse ummünzen konnte. Mindestens viermal hätte ich der Sieger sein können, vor allem 1966, in meinem vorletzten Rennen für Ferrari. Das Team hatte den Wagen mit, der dafür ideal geeignet war, den Dino 246, den man bei der Tasman-Serie eingesetzt hatte. Auf der Teststrecke in Modena fuhr ich damit zwei Sekunden schneller als mit dem neuen Dreiliter-Zwölfzylinder, den man mir dann in die Hand drückte. Das war ein richtiges Biest, viel zu groß, viel zu schwer. Den Dino bekam Lorenzo Bandini, der denn auch prompt zweiter mit ihm wurde. Zwar gelang es mir, den dicken Tipo 312 erstaunlich schnell um die Ecken zu wirbeln, in dem Frankenheimer-Film *Grand Prix* kann man das gut sehen, aber schließlich traf alles ein, wie ich es den Ferrari-Leuten vorher schon gesagt hatte: Ich würde eine Zeitlang führen, und am Ende würde

De 1960 à 1971, pendant douze ans, John Surtees fait partie de l'*Establishment* du Grand Prix de Monaco, sur Lotus, Cooper, Lola, Ferrari, Honda, BRM, McLaren et, enfin, dans les voitures de course que « Big John » construit lui-même et auxquelles il donne son nom. Le butin est plutôt maigre : trois quatrièmes places et le record du tour à la course de 1963. Le rôle joué par le champion du monde de 1964 dans le drame de Monaco, par contre, est d'une importance considérable et on ne peut pas l'exprimer en chiffres :

« A proprement parler, les pistes aux virages rapides me conviennent mieux que celles où l'on ne fait qu'accélérer et freiner. Mais cela ne veut pas dire pour autant que je n'aimais pas Monaco. Naturellement, j'aurais bien voulu gagner une fois. Ce qui m'a toujours gêné comme pilote et, plus tard, encore plus comme chef d'écurie, c'est toute la bureaucratie qui entourait cette manifestation. Quand on voulait quelques coupe-file de plus, c'était toujours d'une complexité incroyable. En outre, il était extrêmement difficile de se déplacer dans la ville au moment du Grand Prix ou même de parvenir seulement jusqu'au circuit. Alors que je pilotais encore pour de petites écuries britanniques comme, au début des années soixante, pour Yeoman Credit, nous étions parfois cantonnés dans de minuscules garages très loin de la ville, quelque part en direction de Nice, et il nous fallait alors plonger dans la circulation routière avec nos voitures de course pour rejoindre le circuit. Avec Ferrari, c'était déjà plus simple. Pour eux, on avait trouvé un emplacement tout près de la ligne de départ et d'arrivée, avant même que cela commence à grimper.

Je n'ai pas, ou seulement contre mon gré, participé à toute l'animation qui entoure ce Grand Prix. Il y avait de nombreuses raisons à cela. D'abord, j'étais ici en quelque sorte pour mon travail et que j'ai toujours pris le sport comme quelque chose de plutôt sérieux. Ensuite, je me couchais de bonne heure avant la course. De plus, je ne me considérais pas seulement comme un pilote, mais aussi comme quelqu'un qui s'est toujours très préoccupé des aspects techniques. Et, surtout, mes employeurs étaient en règle générale des écuries étrangères comme Ferrari et Honda ; il n'y avait pas cette connivence que l'on rencontre avec les Anglais, qui apprécient toujours le plaisir et la convivialité, dépassant parfois les normes.

Pour moi, le Grand Prix de Monaco était un véritable défi. Apparemment, je n'ai pas eu trop de mal à le relever, sauf que cela ne s'est jamais soldé par une victoire pour moi. J'aurais pu être sacré vainqueur au moins à quatre reprises, notamment en 1966, lors de mon avant-dernière course pour Ferrari. L'écurie avait avec elle la voiture qui me semblait idéale pour cela, la Dino 246, que l'on avait déjà engagée pour la série Tasman. Sur la piste d'essai de Modène, je tournais deux secondes plus vite au tour qu'avec la nouvelle trois-litres de douze cylindres que l'on m'obligea à prendre. C'était une véritable bête, beaucoup trop grosse, beaucoup trop lourde. La Dino fut confiée à Lorenzo Bandini, qui, à son volant, termina d'ailleurs immédiatement deuxième. Certes, j'arrivais à balancer étonnamment vite la grosse Tipo 312 de virage en virage, on le voit d'ailleurs fort bien dans le film de Frankenheimer *Grand Prix*, mais finalement s'est produit tout ce que j'avais déjà annoncé auparavant aux gens de chez Ferrari : je prendrais la tête pendant un

They call him "Big John" and later the "Gray Wolf". John Surtees is honest, grumpy and stubborn to the level of pig-headedness. The old fashioned maxim "my word is my bond" fits him to the present day.

Sie nennen ihn »Big John« und später den »grauen Wolf«. John Surtees ist aufrichtig, grantig und eigensinnig bis hin zur Sturheit. Die altertümliche, aber schöne Maxime »Ein Mann, ein Wort« gilt für ihn bis auf den heutigen Tag.

On le surnomme « Big John » et, plus tard, le « loup gris ». John Surtees est franc, carré et original jusqu'à être parfois têtu. L'antique, mais beau principe « Un homme, une parole » vaut pour lui aujourd'hui encore.

my good relationship with Bandini. On the contrary, when I left Ferrari a few weeks later, after the Belgian Grand Prix, he came to me and told me, with tears in his eyes: "John, please stay." His death a few years later is my worst memory of Monaco.

Of course, I regret the way in which the character of the town has changed over the years, all those beautiful buildings which were torn down to make room for the skyscrapers. That's just how it is: if you can't expand sideways, you have to go upwards.

But there is still sufficient atmosphere left. Monaco is still the Grand Prix of the season, and that is a good thing. The sport simply needs a race track which is completely different to all the others. Things are getting worse all the time. Some person or other sits all by himself somewhere with a computer and works out the shape of the ideal bend, which is then built everywhere. I stick to the view, in any case, that racing cars should be adapted to the circuit and not the other way round. In this respect, too, Monaco is a beautiful exception. In a time of uniformity such alternative thinking is more necessary than ever.

Add to that the splendour and the aura which continue to surround the place. Just think: a Grand Prix in a Principality! There is no better place in the world for a sponsor wanting to get his message across, particularly as practically every spot is covered and illuminated, as it were, by television.

Have I ever thought of making Monaco my second, or even my first, home? God forbid! I measure quality of life by other criteria. I prefer to stay in the lovely old house where I live now. It told me at the time: I need you, rescue me! And that is what I did."

irgendetwas kaputtgehen. Tatsächlich war es dann das Differential.

Diese Dinge waren Teil einer politischen Kampagne, die darauf abzielte, einen Keil zwischen mich und Enzo Ferrari zu treiben. Der Drahtzieher war Mike Parkes, ein gewisser anderer Engländer bei der Scuderia, der sehr ehrgeizig war und überall seine Finger im Spiel hatte. Meinem guten Verhältnis zu Bandini haben sie keinen Abbruch getan, im Gegenteil. Als ich Ferrari ein paar Wochen später verließ, nach dem Großen Preis von Belgien, kam er zu mir und bat mich unter Tränen: »John, bitte bleib.« Sein Tod ein Jahr später ist die schlimmste Erinnerung, die sich für mich mit Monaco verknüpft.

Natürlich bedauere ich, wie die Stadt im Lauf der Jahre ihren Charakter gewandelt hat, all die schönen Häuser, die abgerissen wurden, um Platz zu machen für diese Wolkenkratzer. So ist das eben: Wenn man nicht in die Breite gehen kann, muß man halt in die Höhe ausweichen.

Aber es ist Atmosphäre genug übriggeblieben. Noch immer ist Monaco der Grand Prix der Saison. Und das ist auch gut so. Der Sport braucht einfach eine Rennstrecke, die aus der Norm fällt und völlig anders ist als alle anderen. Das wird doch immer schlimmer. Da sitzen irgendwelche Leute im stillen Kämmerlein am Computer und hecken aus, wie die ideale Kurve auszusehen hat. Und die wird dann überall gebaut. Ich lasse mich ohnehin nicht von der Meinung abbringen, daß Rennwagen den Rennstrecken angepaßt werden sollten und nicht umgekehrt. Auch in dieser Hinsicht fällt Monaco herrlich aus der Rolle. In einer Zeit der Uniformität ist solches Querdenken immer mehr gefragt.

Dazu kommen der Glanz und die Aura, die diesen Platz nach wie vor umgeben. Man bedenke nur: ein Grand Prix in einem Fürstentum! Kein Ort auf der Welt ist besser geeignet für einen Sponsor, der seine Botschaft an den Mann bringen möchte, zumal praktisch jede Stelle durch das Fernsehen erfaßt und gewissermaßen ausgeleuchtet wird.

Ob ich jemals daran gedacht habe, meinen zweiten oder sogar ersten Wohnsitz in Monaco zu beziehen? Gott bewahre! Lebensqualität wird für mich mit anderen Kriterien bemessen. Da bleibe ich lieber in dem schönen alten Haus, in dem ich jetzt wohne. Das hat damals zu mir gesagt: Ich brauche dich, rette mich! Und das habe ich dann getan.«

certain temps et, à la fin, quelque chose se casserait. Et c'est d'ailleurs ce qui s'est produit avec le différentiel.

Cette chose-là faisait partie d'une campagne politique qui avait pour objectif de semer la zizanie entre Enzo Ferrari et moi. L'instigateur en était Mike Parkes, un autre Anglais recruté par la Scuderia, qui était très ambitieux et tirait partout les ficelles. Mais cela n'a pas porté préjudice aux bonnes relations que j'entretenais avec Bandini, bien au contraire. Lorsque j'ai quitté Ferrari quelques semaines plus tard, après le Grand Prix de Belgique, il est venu vers moi et m'a prié, les larmes aux yeux : « John, reste, s'il te plaît ! » Sa mort, un an plus tard, est le pire des souvenirs qui se rattachent pour moi à Monaco.

Naturellement, je regrette la façon dont la ville a changé de caractère au fil des ans, que toutes ces belles maisons aient été rasées pour faire de la place aux gratteciel. Mais comment faire autrement ? Quand on ne peut pas prendre ses aises à l'horizontale, il faut chercher une issue à la verticale.

Mais il est resté suffisamment d'atmosphère. Monaco reste le Grand Prix phare de la saison. Et c'est une bonne chose. Le sport a tout simplement besoin d'un circuit qui ne soit pas conforme à la norme et qui soit complètement différent de tous les autres. Cela va de mal en pis. Il y a toujours des gens quelque part, rivés à leur écran d'ordinateur, qui calculent à quoi doit ressembler le virage idéal. Et ce virage, on le construit alors partout. On ne m'empêchera d'ailleurs pas de penser que ce sont les voitures de course qui doivent s'adapter aux circuits et non pas l'inverse. A ce point de vue, aussi, Monaco fait admirablement bande à part. A une époque d'uniformité, il est bon que certains nagent à contre-courant.

A cela s'ajoutent la gloriole et l'aura qui baignent comme toujours cet endroit. Imaginez-vous : un Grand Prix dans une Principauté! Aucun autre endroit du monde ne se prête mieux pour un sponsor qui veut faire passer son message dans la population, d'autant plus que pratiquement chaque endroit du circuit est constamment sous l'objectif des caméras de télévision qui ne le quittent pas un seul instant.

Est-ce que j'ai pensé un seul jour à installer mon premier ou même mon deuxième domicile à Monaco ? Dieu m'en préserve ! Pour moi, la qualité de la vie se mesure à d'autres critères. Je préfère rester dans la vieille et belle maison où je réside actuellement. Une fois, elle m'a dit : j'ai besoin de toi, sauve-moi ! Et c'est ce que j'ai fait. »

1972

Even the Monaco Grand Prix can become a chore. People take part simply because they have it marked in their diaries; 14 May 1972, for example, was an unforgettable day which all involved wanted to erase from their memories as quickly as possible. It was a grey and colorless day, with icy rain pelting down on the Principality. Streams were created, met to form pools, and the rain flowed down the hills and slopes in torrents.

The pits complex was moved from its traditional site to a traffic island to the right of the final straight at the Quai des Etats-Unis. The old chicane was turned into an access road and the drivers were faced with a new, narrower chicane just in front of the Tabac bend. This arrangement was for safety reasons, unlike another regulation – pushed through by the FIA, being the highest motor sport authority – which authorized 25 cars to go to the starting line. One of the miracles of this weekend was that 18 finished – the same number of cars as had started the race the previous year. Another miracle was the victory drive of Jean-Pierre Beltoise, the only one of this quality in his Grand Prix career. The small Frenchman was by no means seen as one of the elite Formula 1 drivers, and his Marlboro-BRM P 160 B was also considered to have fallen somewhat short of the *crème de la crème*. But if the time and place are right, a man from the reserve bench, driving a less than top-of-the-range car, can sometimes soar to unimagined heights.

Almost symbolically, Beltoise, starting from the second row, was the first to reach the Casino hill and he remained in the lead for the entire 100 minutes that this Grand Prix lasted, while at the same time humiliating such renowned wet-weather driving specialists as Jacky Ickx, in the Ferrari B2. As a minor victory, he also drove the fastest lap – all this to the mischievous pleasure of his shivering compatriots, who had turned out in great numbers.

The Surtees driver Mike Hailwood explained with relief after leaving the race after the fiftieth lap: "I could only follow the tail-lights of the man in front. If he had turned left towards the Grande Corniche, I would have just followed him." Beltoise, of course, alone benefited from the advantages of a clear drive and vision in the opening stages of the race, but he was then forced to thread his way through the army of stragglers with the certainty of a sleepwalker. The regular stars of Formula 1 either failed or drove hesitantly in the wake of the BRM. On the fifth lap, the Ferrari mercenary Clay Regazzoni availed himself of the emergency exit beside the chicane, taking the fastest driver in training, Emerson Fittipaldi (Lotus 72 D), with him. Others, including the McLaren duo Denny Hulme and Brian Redman (M 19 A) met the same fate. Even Jackie Stewart (Tyrrell 004) found himself executing an enormous pirouette at Mirabeau during his fearless, if fruitless, quest for the lead.

Chris Amon went to his pit four times with his Matra MS 120 C to have his visor cleaned. Nevertheless, he managed to claim one more point – one of the unsung records in the history of Formula 1.

Sogar der Grand Prix de Monaco kann zum Pflichtpensum werden. Man bringt es hinter sich, nur weil der Termin-kalender das vorsieht, am 14. Mai 1972 zum Beispiel, einem unvergeßlichen Tag, den alle Beteiligten am liebsten umge-hend aus ihrem Gedächtnis tilgen würden. Grau und eintönig rauscht eisiger Regen auf das Fürstentum nieder, wirft plätschernd winzige Fontänen auf, findet sich zu Lachen zusammen und strömt in Rinnsalen Steigungen und Gefälle herab.

Der Boxenkomplex ist von seinem angestammten Quartier auf einer Verkehrsinsel rechts der Zielgeraden an den Quai des Etats-Unis umgesiedelt worden. Die alte Schikane wurde zur Zufahrt umgewidmet, eine neue, engere Schikane stellt sich den Piloten kurz vor der Tabakskurve entgegen. Dieses Arrangement dient der Sicherheit, im Gegensatz zu einer anderen Regelung: Die oberste Motorsport-Autorität FIA hat durchgesetzt, daß 25 Wagen starten dürfen. Eines der Wunder dieses Wochenendes: 18 davon kommen durch, ebenso viele, wie im Vorjahr das Rennen aufnahmen. Ein anderes: die Siegesfahrt von Jean-Pierre Beltoise, die einzige seiner Karriere. Der kleine Franzose ist ein Mann aus dem zweiten Glied, so wie sein Marlboro-BRM P 160 B als Fahr-zeug der zweiten Garnitur geschmäht wird. Aber am richtigen Ort zur richtigen Zeit können sich ein Mann aus dem zweiten Glied und ein Fahrzeug der zweiten Garnitur zu ungeahnten Höhen emporschwingen.

Gleichsam symbolisch startet Beltoise aus der zweiten Reihe, erreicht den Berg zum Casino als erster und bleibt es über die 100 Minuten dieses Grand Prix, demütigt gefeierte Regenspezialisten wie Jacky Ickx auf dem Ferrari B2. Er markiert als kleine Krönung auch noch die schnellste Runde, all dies zum diebischen Vergnügen seiner zahlreich erschienenen fröstelnden Landsleute.

»Ich habe mich«, berichtet Surtees-Pilot Mike Hailwood nach seinem Ausfall in der 50. Runde erleichtert, »immer nur am Rücklicht meines Vordermannes orientiert. Wäre der irgendwann nach links in Richtung Grande Corniche abgebo-gen, ich wäre einfach hinterhergefahren.« Den Vorzug und damit das Alibi von freier Fahrt und freier Sicht genießt Beltoise nur anfänglich, fädelt sich später mit nachtwand-lerischer Sicherheit durch das Heer der Hinterbänkler. Im Kielwasser des BRM versagen und verzagen unterdessen die Stars der Branche. In der fünften Runde nimmt Ferrari-Söldner Clay Regazzoni den Notausgang neben der Schikane in Anspruch und den Trainingsschnellsten Emerson Fittipaldi (Lotus 72 D) gleich mit. Das gleiche Los ereilt später das McLaren-Duo Denny Hulme und Brian Redman (M 19 A) sowie manchen anderen. Bei seiner fruchtlosen und furcht-losen Jagd auf die Spitze leistet sich selbst Jackie Stewart (Tyrrell 004) eine enorme Pirouette bei Mirabeau.

Chris Amon aber läuft mit seinem Matra MS 120 C viermal seine Box an, um sein Visier reinigen zu lassen. Trotz-dem ergattert er noch einen Punkt – einer der unbesungenen Rekorde in der Chronik der Formel 1.

Le Grand Prix de Monaco lui-même peut parfois n'être qu'une épreuve pénible à accomplir. Une épreuve à laquelle on ne se plie que parce que le calendrier le prévoit. Le 14 mai 1972, par exemple, est un jour que l'on n'oubliera jamais, mais auquel tous les protagonistes préfèrent ne jamais penser. Grise et monotone, une pluie glaciale tombe sur la Principauté en des myriades de fontaines minuscules qui donnent naissance à des flaques d'eau et descendent en torrents le long des rues.

Le complexe des stands a été transféré, quittant son emplacement traditionnel sous les arbres longeant la ligne droite d'arrivée, au quai des Etats-Unis. La vieille chicane a été transformée en une voie d'accès et une nouvelle chicane plus serrée ralentit les pilotes peu avant le virage du Bureau de Tabac. Cette nouvelle disposition a pour but de favoriser la sécurité, contrairement à une autre règle : l'autorité suprême de la compétition automobile, la FIA, a imposé de laisser partir vingt-cinq voitures. L'un des miracles de ce week-end est que dix-huit voient le drapeau à damier, autant qu'il y en avait eu au départ l'année précédente. Autre miracle : la victoire de Jean-Pierre Beltoise, la seule de cette qualité dans sa course au Grand Prix. Le petit Français est un deuxième couteau, au même titre que sa Marlboro-BRM P 160 B est une voiture de deuxième catégorie. Mais, au bon endroit et au bon moment, même un homme de deuxième classe au volant d'une voiture de deuxième catégorie peut parfois se transcender contre toute attente quand les événements s'y prêtent.

Non sans symbolisme, Beltoise est aussi parti de la deuxième ligne, il franchit en tête la montée du Casino et reste aussi en tête pendant les cent minutes de ce Grand Prix, humiliant des spécialistes avérés de la pluie comme Jacky Ickx sur sa Ferrari B2. Cerise sur le gâteau, il signe aussi le tour le plus rapide en course, tout ceci pour le plus grand plaisir de ses nombreux compatriotes frigorifiés dans les tribunes.

« Je me suis toujours orienté exclusivement sur le feu rouge de mon prédécesseur, » confesse, soulagé, Mike Hailwood, pilote de la Surtees, après son abandon au 50e tour. « S'il avait tourné à un moment ou à un autre vers la gauche en direction de la Grande Corniche, je l'aurais suivi aveuglé-ment. » Bien sûr, Beltoise ne bénéficie qu'au début de l'avantage et, donc de l'alibi, de la course en tête et d'une bonne visibilité, mais il se faufile plus tard avec une assurance déconcertante à travers la légion des traînards. Dans le sillage de la BRM périclitent et échouent pendant ce temps nombre de vedettes de Formule 1. Au cinquième tour, Clay Regazzoni, le mercenaire de Ferrari, prend l'échappatoire près de la chicane, emmenant avec lui le plus rapide aux essais, Emerson Fittipaldi (Lotus 72 D). Un destin que partageront plus tard aussi les deux mercenaires de McLaren, Denny Hulme et Brian Redman (M 19 A), ainsi que de nombreux autres pilotes. Lors de sa poursuite effrénée et stérile derrière Beltoise, même Jackie Stewart (Tyrrell 004) se paye le luxe d'une fantastique pirouette à Mirabeau.

Pendant ce temps, Chris Amon se sera rendu quatre fois aux stands avec sa Matra MS 120 C pour y faire essuyer sa visière. Malgré tout, il glane encore un point – encore un record qui sombrera dans l'anonymat de la chronique de la Formule 1.

Of course Jean-Pierre Beltoise feels his best with the victory garland around his neck. However, it only happens to him once, at the Monaco Grand Prix of 1972. He wins, not by profitting from the misfortune of others, but simply by driving the best race of his life.

Natürlich fühlt sich Jean-Pierre Beltoise im Siegerkranz am wohlsten. Das passiert ihm allerdings nur einmal, beim Grand Prix de Monaco 1972. Er profitiert dabei nicht vom Pech anderer, sondern fährt ganz einfach das Rennen seines Lebens.

Naturellement, c'est avec la couronne de lauriers sur les épaules que Jean-Pierre Beltoise préfère poser. Cela ne lui arrivera cependant qu'une seule fois en Formule 1, lors du Grand Prix de Monaco de 1972. Il n'aura alors absolument pas profité du malheur d'autrui, mais signe tout simplement la course de sa vie.

N°	DRIVERS		ENTRANTS	CARS	ENGINES	PRACTICE RESULTS	RACE RESULTS
17	**Jean-Pierre Beltoise**	F	**Marlboro BRM**	**BRM P160B**	**BRM V12 2998 cc**	4th: 1'22"5	1st: 2h26'54"7
6	Jacky Ickx	B	SEFAC Ferrari S.p.A.	Ferrari 312B2	Ferrari F12 2991 cc	2nd: 1'21"6	2nd: 2h27'32"9
8	*Emerson Fittipaldi*	BR	*John Player Team Lotus*	*Lotus 72D*	*Cosworth V8 2993 cc*	*1st: 1'21"4*	*3rd: 79 laps*
1	Jackie Stewart	GB	Elf Team Tyrrell	Tyrrell 004	Cosworth V8 2993 cc	8th: 1'22"9	4th: 78 laps
15	Brian Redman	GB	Bruce McLaren Motor Racing Team Yardley	McLaren M19A	Cosworth V8 2993 cc	10th: 1'23"1	5th: 77 laps
16	Chris Amon	NZ	Equipe Matra	Matra MS120C	Matra V12 2993 cc	5th(6): 1'22"6	6th: 77 laps
12	Andrea de Adamich	I	Ceramica Pagnossin Team Surtees	Surtees TS 9B	Cosworth V8 2993 cc	18th: 1'24"7	7th: 77 laps
26	Helmut Marko	A	Austria Marlboro BRM	BRM P153	BRM V12 2998 cc	17th: 1'24"6	8th: 77 laps
21	Wilson Fittipaldi	BR	Motor Racing Developments	Brabham BT33	Cosworth V8 2993 cc	21st: 1'25"2	9th: 77 laps
27	Rolf Stommelen	D	Team Eifelland Caravan	Eifelland 21 (March 721)	Cosworth V8 2993 cc	25th: 1'29"5	10th: 77 laps
3	Ronnie Peterson	S	STP March System Engineering	March 721X	Cosworth V8 2993 cc	15th: 1'24"1	11th: 76 laps
20	Graham Hill	GB	Motor Racing Developments	Brabham BT37	Cosworth V8 2993 cc	18th(19): 1'24"7	12th 76 laps
5	Mike Beuttler	GB	Clarke-Mordaunt-Guthrie-Durlacher	March 721G	Cosworth V8 2993 cc	23rd: 1'26"5	13th 76 laps
9	Dave Walker	GB	John Player Team Lotus	Lotus 72D	Cosworth V8 2993 cc	14th: 1'24"0	14th:75 laps
14	Denis Hulme	NZ	Bruce McLaren Motor Racing Team Yardley	McLaren M19C	Cosworth V8 2993 cc	7th: 1'22"7	15th: 74 laps
4	Niki Lauda	A	STP March System Engineering	March 721X	Cosworth V8 2993 cc	22nd: 1'25"6	16th: 74 laps
23	Carlos Pace	BR	Frank Williams Motul	March 711	Cosworth V8 2993 cc	24th: 1'26"6	17th: 72 laps
2	François Cévert	F	Elf Team Tyrrell	Tyrrell 002	Cosworth V8 2993 cc	12th: 1'23"8	18th: 70 laps
22	Henri Pescarolo	F	Frank Williams Motul/Politoys	March 721G	Cosworth V8 2993 cc	8th(9): 1'22"9	R
7	Clay Regazzoni	CH	SEFAC Ferrari S.p.A.	Ferrari 312B2	Ferrari F12 2991 cc	3rd: 1'21"9	R
11	Mike Hailwood	GB	Brooke Bond Oxo-Rob Walker-Team Surtees	Surtees TS 9B	Cosworth V8 2993 cc	11th: 1'23"7	R
19	Howden Ganley	NZ	Marlboro BRM	BRM P180	BRM V12 2998 cc	18th(20): 1'24"7	R
10	Tim Schenken	AUS	Brooke Bond Oxo-Rob Walker-Team Surtees	Surtees TS 9B	Cosworth V8 2993 cc	13th: 1'23"9	R
18	Peter Gethin	GB	Marlboro BRM	BRM P160B	BRM V12 2998 cc	5th: 1'22"6	R
28	Reine Wisell	S	Marlboro BRM	BRM P160B	BRM V12 2998 cc	16th: 1'24"4	R

(1) This modest space has been reserved for Team Surtees. Number 12 is driven by Andrea de Adamich. Rain men: (2) Beltoise (BRM), who has the privilege of being able to see, (3) Amon (Matra), (4) Ickx (Ferrari), (5) Stewart (Tyrrell) in front of Gethin (BRM) and (6) Fittipaldi (Lotus).

(1) Diese karge Parzelle ist für Team Surtees reserviert. Nummer 12 wird von Andrea de Adamich gefahren. Rain Men: (2) Beltoise (BRM), der das Privileg freier Sicht genießt, (3) Amon (Matra), (4) Ickx (Ferrari), (5) Stewart (Tyrrell) vor Gethin (BRM) und (6) Fittipaldi (Lotus).

(1) Cette petite place est réservée à l'écurie Surtees. La numéro 12 est pilotée par Andrea de Adamich. Hommes sous la pluie : (2) Beltoise (BRM), qui a le privilège d'avoir la vue libre, (3) Amon (Matra), (4) Ickx (Ferrari), (5) Stewart (Tyrrell) devant Gethin (BRM) et (6) Fittipaldi (Lotus).

Prix des nations: (1) the Swede Peterson (March), (2) the
Frenchman Beltoise, (3) the Brazilian Fittipaldi (Lotus), (4) the
Scotsman Stewart, his wife Helen towering above him, and (5) the
Briton Brian Redman, guest driver for McLaren three times in 1972.

Preis der Nationen: (1) der Schwede Peterson (March), (2) der
Franzose Beltoise, (3) der Brasilianer Fittipaldi (Lotus), (4) der
Schotte Stewart, überragt von Gattin Helen, (5) der Brite Brian
Redman, 1972 insgesamt dreimal Gast bei McLaren.

Prix des Nations : (1) le Suédois Peterson (March), (2) le Français
Beltoise, (3) le Brésilien Fittipaldi (Lotus), (4) l'Écossais Stewart,
dominé par son épouse Helen, (5) le Britannique Brian Redman, qui
pilotera au total trois fois pour McLaren en 1972.

1973

Jackie Stewart set himself two tasks when he arrived for the 31st Monaco Grand Prix on 3 June 1973: to gain his third victory in the Principality, and the twenty-fifth of his career. If he succeeded, then he would overtake Fangio and equal his compatriot Jim Clark in the eternal honors list of Formula 1 legends.

He was to encounter altered terrain – extended by 133 meters to 3,278 meters. Where the old railway station stood there was now the Loews building site which was to give way to one of Monaco's finest hotels. Modifications had allowed some daylight to enter the tunnel from the left, and beyond the Tabac bend an extension of the circuit, won from the sea, passed around the swimming pool. There was a new narrow bend at Rascasse, replacing the gasometer hairpin bend, which had been the source of so much early excitement. There was also a proper pit lane for the first time, which was completely separate from the track.

The Scot approached the task in his characteristically systematic manner and recorded the best time for Tyrrell 006 on both days, securing pole position, as in 1969, 1970 and 1971. Practice had not been without its drama. At one stage, the spoiler from George Follmer's Shadow flew past the Prince's official box. Fortunately, there were no injuries, except that an American, who only wanted to catch a glimpse of fellow American Princess Grace, alias Grace Kelly, was suddenly paler than before.

At the beginning of the race, François Cévert led until the handsome Frenchman's Tyrrell picked up a flat tyre when it nicked the edge of the pavement. Ronnie Peterson darted past with the wedge-shaped Lotus 72 D, while to his rear, the BRM P 160 E of Clay Regazzoni was acting like a mobile chicane, blocking the duel going on behind him between the champions Stewart and Fittipaldi (also in a Lotus 72 D), until his brakes gave out prematurely. The Swede was also having difficulties: his engine was misfiring badly on tight bends. He fell behind the leading duo on the eighth lap, and soon afterwards also found himself behind Niki Lauda's BRM and the Ferrari 312 B 3 of Jacky Ickx, both of whom had set their sights on third place. But their duel was short-lived. On lap 25, the BRM came to a halt with a defective transmission, and on lap 43, a half-shaft terminated the Ferrari's chance of victory. The new race order became Stewart, Emerson Fittipaldi followed by his brother Wilson (Brabham BT 42), Peterson, Cévert and Mike Hailwood. Two things were causing "Mike the Bike" problems: the brakes of his Surtees TS 14 A had malfunctioned and his gear lever had snapped off, cutting his hands to ribbons.

In the closing stages, Stewart's six-second lead quickly dwindled to a couple of car lengths in the last lap, when Fittipaldi set the day's fastest time. When the Brazilian drove alongside the Scot to congratulate him during the lap of honor, the two cars touched and spun wildly, Fittipaldi damaging two of the Lotus' wheels. Sometimes there is only a fine line between a fight and a farce.

Zwei Vorgaben macht sich Jackie Stewart, als er zum 31. Grand Prix de Monaco am 3. Juni 1973 anreist: seinen dritten Sieg im Fürstentum, seinen 25. überhaupt. In der ewigen Bestenliste der Unsterblichen der Formel 1 hätte er dann Fangio überholt und es seinem Landsmann Jim Clark gleichgetan.

Er findet eine veränderte Piste vor, um 133 Meter auf 3278 Meter gewachsen. Da ist die Loews-Baustelle, aus der bald eine der feinsten monegassischen Hoteladressen werden wird, anstelle des alten Bahnhofs. Da dringt von links Tageslicht in den Tunnel. Da windet sich eine Metastase des Circuits, dem Meer abgerungen, um das Schwimmbad. Da ist die enge Kurvenfolge bei Rascasse, wo einmal die Gasometer-Haarnadel für frühe Aufregung sorgte. Da ist eine richtige Boxengasse, von der Strecke abgesondert.

Der Schotte macht sich mit der gewohnten Systematik an die Arbeit: Bestzeit für den Tyrrell 006 am Donnerstag und am Freitag, Pole Position wie schon 1969, 70 und 71. Das Training läuft nicht ohne Dramen ab. Einmal flattert der Flügel von George Follmers Shadow an der Prinzenloge vorüber. Verletzt wird niemand. Nur der Amerikaner, der nur mal vorbeischauen wollte, um die amerikanische Prinzessin Gracia Patricia alias Grace Kelly zu besichtigen, ist noch blasser als sonst.

Am Anfang führt François Cévert, bis sich der Tyrrell des schönen Franzosen an der Bordsteinkante einen Plattfuß einhandelt. Ronnie Peterson mit dem sargschwarzen Lotus 72 D ist im Nu vorbei, während hinter ihm der BRM P 160 E von Clay Regazzoni dem Duell der Champions Stewart und Fittipaldi (ebenfalls Lotus 72 D) gewissermaßen als mobile Schikane vorgeschaltet ist, bis seine Bremsen frühzeitig aufgezehrt sind. Auch der Schwede ist in Not: In engen Kurven stottert das Triebwerk. In der achten Runde muß er das Spitzen-Duo ziehen lassen, bald darauf auch BRM-Pilot Niki Lauda und Jacky Ickx auf dem Ferrari 312 B3. Die beiden haben Position drei im Visier. Aber ihr Zweikampf währt nicht lange. Im 25. Durchgang rollt der BRM mit defektem Getriebe aus, im 43. kündigt am Ferrari eine Halbwelle den Dienst auf. Die neue Ordnung lautet nun Stewart, Emerson Fittipaldi vor seinem Bruder Wilson (Brabham BT 42), Peterson, Cévert und Mike Hailwood. Zwei Dinge machen Mike the Bike zu schaffen: Sein Surtees TS 14 A ist nicht zu bremsen, und ein abgebrochener Ganghebel zerschindet die Hand des Piloten.

In der Schußphase schmilzt Stewarts Vorsprung von sechs Sekunden zügig, welkt bis auf ein paar Wagenlängen im letzten Durchgang, als Fittipaldi die schnellste Zeit des Tages fährt. Als in der Auslaufrunde der Brasilianer neben den Schotten rollt, um ihm zu gratulieren, berühren sich die beiden Wagen. In einem wilden Dreher beschädigt Fittipaldi zwei Räder des Lotus. Vom Fight zur Farce ist manchmal nur ein kurzer Weg.

Jackie Stewart s'est donné deux objectifs lorsqu'il se rend au 31e Grand Prix de Monaco, le 3 juin 1973 : remporter sa troisième victoire dans la Principauté, ce qui serait pour lui la 25e de son palmarès. Au classement éternel des immortels de la Formule 1, il aurait alors doublé Fangio et égalé son compatriote Jim Clark.

Il découvre un circuit modifié, allongé de 133 mètres, à 3278 mètres. Il y a là, par exemple, le chantier du Loews, qui sera bientôt l'un des hôtels les plus prestigieux de Monaco, à la place de l'ancienne gare. De la gauche, la lumière du jour éclaire le tunnel. Viennent ensuite, au-delà du Bureau de Tabac, quelques virages gagnés sur la mer autour de la piscine. Il débouche ensuite sur la série de virages serrés de la Rascasse, où l'épingle à cheveux du Gazomètre a, jadis, causé bien des émotions. Et il y a enfin une véritable voie des stands séparée du circuit.

L'Ecossais se met à l'œuvre avec sa méticulosité coutumière : meilleur temps pour la Tyrrell 006 le jeudi et le vendredi, pole position comme en 1969, 1970 et 1971 déjà. Comme toujours, des incidents ponctuent les essais. L'aileron de la Shadow de George Follmer, par exemple, s'envole au moment où il passe devant la loge princière. Dieu merci, personne n'est blessé, sauf que l'Américain, qui voulait simplement regarder la Princesse américaine Gracia Patricia alias Grace Kelly, est tout à coup plus pâle qu'à son habitude.

Au début de la course, François Cévert mène le bal jusqu'à ce que la Tyrrell du charmant Français aux allures de play-boy ne crève un pneu contre une bordure de trottoir. Ronnie Peterson, au volant de la Lotus 72 D noir et or, ne laisse pas passer l'occasion tandis que, derrière lui, la BRM P 160 E de Clay Regazzoni joue en quelque sorte le rôle de chicane mobile devant les deux champions Stewart et Fittipaldi (également sur Lotus 72 D) impliqués dans un duel à couteaux tirés, jusqu'à ce que ses freins ne le contraignent à un abandon prématuré. Le Suédois, lui aussi, a des problèmes : dans les virages serrés, son moteur s'étouffe. Au huitième tour, il doit laisser passer le duo de tête, dans la foulée duquel s'engagent le pilote BRM Niki Lauda et Jacky Ickx sur Ferrari 312 B3. Les deux hommes se battent pour la troisième place. Mais leur duel ne durera pas longtemps. Au 25e tour, la BRM s'arrête sur panne de boîte de vitesses et, au 43e tour, un demi-arbre contraint la Ferrari à l'abandon. Le nouveau classement voit maintenant Stewart en tête, devant Emerson Fittipaldi et son frère Wilson (Brabham BT 42), Peterson, Cévert et Mike Hailwood. Deux choses préoccupent « Mike the Bike » : les freins de sa Surtees TS 14 A faiblissent et un levier de changement de vitesses brisé déchire la main du pilote.

A la fin de la course, l'avance de Stewart, de six secondes, fond comme neige au soleil, se réduisant à quelques longueurs de voiture au dernier tour lorsque Fittipaldi signe le temps le plus rapide du jour. Lorsque le Brésilien se porte à la hauteur de l'Ecossais pour le féliciter, lors du tour de décélération, les deux voitures se touchent et, dans un brutal tête-à-queue, Fittipaldi endommage deux roues de la Lotus. De la bravoure au burlesque, il n'y a parfois qu'un pas.

New race, different outcome: the end on lap 40 for the previous year's winner, Beltoise, against the barriers at Mirabeau.

Neues Spiel, neues Unglück: Aus in Runde 40 für den Vorjahressieger Beltoise in der Leitplanke bei Mirabeau.

Nouveau jeu, nouvelle malchance : abandon au 40e tour pour le vainqueur de l'année précédente, Beltoise, qui échoue dans les glissières à Mirabeau.

N°	DRIVERS		ENTRANTS	CARS	ENGINES	PRACTICE RESULTS	RACE RESULTS
5	**Jackie Stewart**	**GB**	**Elf Team Tyrrell**	**Tyrrell 006**	**Cosworth V8 2993 cc**	**1st: 1'27"5**	**1st: 1h57'44"3**
1	Emerson Fittipaldi	BR	John Player Team Lotus	Lotus 72D	Cosworth V8 2993 cc	5th: 1'28"1	2nd: 1h57'45"6
2	Ronnie Peterson	S	John Player Team Lotus	Lotus 72D	Cosworth V8 2993 cc	2nd: 1'27"7	3rd: 77 laps
6	François Cévert	F	Elf Team Tyrrell	Tyrrell 006	Cosworth V8 2993 cc	4th: 1'27"9	4th: 77 laps
8	Peter Revson	USA	Yardley Team McLaren	McLaren M23A	Cosworth V8 2993 cc	13th(15): 1'29"4	5th: 76 laps
7	Denis Hulme	NZ	Yardley Team McLaren	McLaren M23A	Cosworth V8 2993 cc	3rd: 1'27"8	6th: 76 laps
9	Andrea de Adamich	I	Ceramica Pagnossin Racing	Brabham BT37	Cosworth V8 2993 cc	26th(NQ): 1'32"1	7th: 75 laps
23	Mike Hailwood	GB	Brooke Bond Oxo-Rob Walker-Team Surtees	Surtees TS14A	Cosworth V8 2993 cc	13th: 1'29"4	8th: 75 laps
27	James Hunt	GB	Hesketh Racing	March 731	Cosworth V8 2993 cc	18th: 1'29"9	9th: 73 laps (R)
17	Jackie Oliver	GB	UOP Shadow Racing Team	Shadow DN1	Cosworth V8 2993 cc	23rd: 1'31"2	10th: 72 laps
11	Wilson Fittipaldi	BR	Motor Racing Developments	Brabham BT42	Cosworth V8 2993 cc	8th(9): 1'28"9	R
14	Jean-Pierre Jarier	F	STP March Racing Team	March 721G	Cosworth V8 2993 cc	13th(14): 1'29"4	R
12	Graham Hill	GB	Embassy Racing	Shadow DN1	Cosworth V8 2993 cc	24th: 1'31"9	R
4	Arturo Merzario	I	SEFAC Ferrari S.p.A.	Ferrari 312B3	Ferrari F12 2991 cc	16th: 1'29"5	R
10	Carlos Reutemann	RA	Ceramica Pagnossin Racing-Team MRD	Brabham BT42	Cosworth V8 2993 cc	19th: 1'30"1	R
3	Jacky Ickx	B	SEFAC Ferrari S.p.A.	Ferrari 312B3	Ferrari F12 2991 cc	7th: 1'28"7	R
25	Howden Ganley	NZ	Frank Williams Racing Cars	Iso IR	Cosworth V8 2993 cc	10th: 1'29"0	R
20	Jean-Pierre Beltoise	F	Marlboro BRM	BRM P160E	BRM V12 2998 cc	10th(11): 1'29"0	R
18	David Purley	GB	LEC Refrigeration Ltd.	March 731	Cosworth V8 2993 cc	24th(25): 1'31"9	R
24	Carlos Pace	BR	Brooke Bond Oxo-Rob Walker-Team Surtees	Surtees TS14A	Cosworth V8 2993 cc	17th: 1'29"6	R
26	Nanni Galli	I	Frank Williams Racing Cars	Iso IR	Cosworth V8 2993 cc	22nd: 1'31"1	R
21	Niki Lauda	A	Marlboro BRM	BRM P160E	BRM V12 2998 cc	6th: 1'28"5	R
22	Chris Amon	NZ	Martini Racing Team	Tecno PA123/6	Tecno F12 2995 cc	12th: 1'29"3	R
19	Clay Regazzoni	I	Marlboro BRM	BRM P160E	BRM V12 2998 cc	8th: 1'28"9	R
15	Mike Beuttler	GB	Clarke-Mordaunt-Guthrie-Durlacher	March 721G	Cosworth V8 2993 cc	21st: 1'31"0	R

3

4

5

6

Strong teams: the Lotus drivers (1) Fittipaldi and (2) Peterson steal points off each other during this season so that (6) Stewart can become Champion for the third time. (4) Tyrrell team-mate Cévert becomes a real rival. But four months later the Frenchman is killed at Watkins Glen. (3) Like a madly racing viper, the snake of pursuers winds up the hill behind Regazzoni (BRM). (5) In second place, for a time, behind his brother Emerson: Wilson Fittipaldi (Brabham).

Starke Teams: Die Lotus-Fahrer (1) Fittipaldi und (2) Peterson stehlen einander in dieser Saison die Punkte, so daß (6) Stewart zum dritten Mal Champion werden kann. Mit (4) Cévert erwächst ihm im Tyrrell-Rennstall ein wirklicher Rivale. Doch vier Monate später kommt der Franzose in Watkins Glen ums Leben. (3) Wie eine rasende Viper windet sich der Stau der Verfolger hinter Regazzoni (BRM) den Berg herauf. (5) Zeitweise zweiter hinter seinem Bruder Emerson: Wilson Fittipaldi (Brabham).

Equipes performantes : les pilotes Lotus, (1) Fittipaldi et (2) Peterson, se chipent mutuellement les points durant cette saison, si bien que (6) Stewart tire les marrons du feu et devient pour la troisième fois champion du monde. Avec (4) Cévert, il a un véritable rival dans l'écurie Tyrrell. Mais le Français se tue quatre mois plus tard à Watkins Glen. (3) Telle une vipère folle, le peloton des poursuivants reste bloqué derrière Regazzoni (BRM) dans la montée. (5) Pour une fois deuxième derrière son frère Emerson : Wilson Fittipaldi (Brabham).

(1) Not interested: sun-bathing beauty in the window.
(2) Relaxed: Mike Hailwood (Surtees). (3) Serene: Graham Hill
(Shadow). (4) Under-powered: Niki Lauda.

(1) Desinteressiert: sonnenbadende Schöne im Fenster. (2) Gelassen:
Mike Hailwood (Surtees). (3) Abgeklärt: Graham Hill (Shadow).
(4) Dürftig motorisiert: Niki Lauda.

(1) Désintéressées : beautés prenant un bain de soleil.
(2) Décontracté : Mike Hailwood (Surtees). (3) A toute épreuve :
Graham Hill (Shadow). (4) Sous-motorisé : Niki Lauda.

1974

The magical name of Monaco conjures up happy memories for Ronnie Peterson. Winner of the Formula 3 race in 1969, seventh place in the 1970 Grand Prix, marking his debut in Formula 1, second place in 1971, third place in 1973, and great performances elsewhere. He was due a victory in 1974, and he was not disappointed.

But matters were not quite so simple – neither for the Swede nor for his Lotus 72, which should already have ended its professional career on the race track. Most of the serious money was placed on cars 11 and 12, the Ferrari B3s of Clay Regazzoni and Niki Lauda, which seemed to stand out from the 23 other competitors, rather like a red-and-white wall on the first row.

The best start on the asphalt leading towards Sainte Dévote was made by Regazzoni. However, Lauda was uncomfortably close, waiting to pounce at the first opportunity, leaving his team colleague in no doubt about his presence for a single moment. The Swiss driver withstood the pressure for 21 laps, but then he made one of his rare blunders, entering the Rascasse much too quickly. Lauda flashed past, with Ronnie Peterson, Jean-Pierre Jarier with the Shadow DN3 and the Tyrrell recruit Jody Scheckter on his tail.

By now, Peterson had already had a very eventful drive, from which the black-and-gold Lotus had not emerged unscathed. A brush with the crash barrier on the fifth lap, a collision with Carlos Reutemann's Brabham BT 44, who was put out of the race, followed by the hunt to catch up from sixth place. When in the lead, Lauda seemed to have the situation under control until the Ferrari's engine ignition died during the thirty-third lap and just failed to get the car back to the pits. Peterson, on the other hand, still had another 45 laps to go before being able to greet his wife Barbro with the victor's crown on his head.

The race was marred by repeated accidents and mishaps. For example, a few seconds after the start there was a mass collision involving seven cars and putting such big Grand Prix names as Denis Hulme (McLaren M23), Jean-Pierre Beltoise (BRM P 201) and Carlos Pace (Surtees TS 16) out of competition. Although the Trojan driven by the Australian Tim Schenken just managed to drag itself back to base, it covered the track with a liberal amount of oil while doing so. This, much to the amusement of the race's organizers, caused rally specialist Vic Elford, in a Porsche Carrera course car, to skid and to execute a complete spin.

Mike Hailwood was lucky on the twelfth lap when his McLaren M23 crashed against the barrier on the Casino hill and, miraculously, he escaped unscathed. Hans-Joachim Stuck was equally fortunate when his March 741 underwent considerable damage in an early jostle with James Hunt's Hesketh on the undulating downhill slope approaching the Mirabeau corner.

One of the stars of the race was the young South African Jody Scheckter, whose second position was a personal best. Another driver, who had long seemed to belong to the fixtures and fittings of the events, gave his final performance in Monaco: Graham Hill. The days of his being able to qualify for the race would end in 1975, the year of his death.

Mit dem magischen Namen Monaco verknüpfen sich für Ronnie Peterson erfreuliche Erinnerungen: Erster im Formel-3-Rennen 1969, Platz sieben im Grand Prix 1970, mit dem Peterson in der Formel 1 debütiert, Rang zwei 1971, Position drei 1973, starke Auftritte auch sonst. Da ist 1974 ein Sieg fällig und stellt sich auch ein.

Aber die Sache ist gar nicht so einfach, für den Schweden nicht und auch nicht für seinem Lotus 72, der eigentlich schon aufs Altenteil abgeschoben werden sollte. Die meisten Jetons liegen nämlich auf den Nummern 11 und 12, den Ferrari B3 von Clay Regazzoni und Niki Lauda, die sich in der ersten Reihe vor den 23 restlichen Konkurrenten wie eine weißrote Wand breitmachen.

Den besten Start radiert Regazzoni in den Asphalt vor Sainte Dévote. Aber hinter ihm lauert Lauda in ungemütlicher Nähe auf seine Chance und läßt den Teamkollegen keinen Augenblick im unklaren über seine Anwesenheit. 21 Runden hält der Schweizer dem Druck stand, bevor er einen seiner seltenen Schnitzer macht und viel zu schnell in Rascasse ankommt. Im Nu ist Lauda vorbei, in seinem Kielwasser Ronnie Peterson, Jean-Pierre Jarier mit dem Shadow DN3 und Tyrrell-Rekrut Jody Scheckter.

Peterson hat zu diesem Zeitpunkt bereits eine ereignisreiche Fahrt hinter sich, die auch für den schwarzgoldenen Lotus nicht ohne Blessuren abging: unsanfter Kontakt mit der Leitplanke in der fünften Runde, Kollision mit Carlos Reutemanns Brabham BT 44, der dabei auf der Strecke bleibt, Aufholjagd aus der sechsten Position. An der Spitze scheint Lauda die Dinge im Griff zu haben, als der Motor des Ferrari in der 33. Runde hinter Rascasse erstirbt. Bis zur Box der Roten ist es da nur ein paar Schritte Fußweg. Peterson hingegen muß weitere 45 Durchgänge abspulen, bevor er seine Frau Barbro mit unter den Siegeskranz nehmen kann.

Unfälle und Ausfälle geben dem Rennen das Gepräge, etwa ein paar Sekunden nach dem Start eine Massenkollision, in die sieben Wagen verstrickt sind und die Grand-Prix-Prominenz wie Denis Hulme (McLaren M23), Jean-Pierre Beltoise (BRM P 201) und Carlos Pace (Surtees TS 16) dahinrafft. Während sich der Trojan des Australiers Tim Schenken noch bis an den Hafen schleppt, benetzt er die Strecke großzügig mit Öl, auf dem Rallye-Spezialist Vic Elford im Porsche Carrera der Rennleitung zur allgemeinen Erheiterung ausgleitet und eine Pirouette vollführt.

Glück hat Mike Hailwood, dessen McLaren M23 in der 12. Runde auf der Steigung zum Casino gegen die Leitplanke schmettert, und auf wundersame Weise ungeschoren kommt auch Hans-Joachim Stuck davon, als sein March 741 bei einer Rempelei mit James Hunts Hesketh auf dem welligen Gefälle Richtung Mirabeau frühzeitig erheblichen Schaden nimmt.

Einer der Stars des Rennens ist der junge Südafrikaner Jody Scheckter mit seiner bislang besten Placierung. Ein anderer, der schon zum lebenden Inventar der Veranstaltung zu gehören scheint, gibt seine Abschiedsvorstellung in Monaco: Graham Hill. 1975, im Jahr seines Todes, wird er sich nicht mehr qualifizieren.

Au nom magique de Monaco, Ronnie Peterson associe des souvenirs réjouissants. Premier lors de la course Formule 3 de 1969, septième au Grand Prix de 1970, où Peterson fait ses débuts en Formule 1, deuxième en 1971, troisième en 1973, et, comme toujours, des prestations brillantes. En 1974, donc, il mériterait la victoire et la Fortune ne lui fait d'ailleurs pas défaut.

Mais tout n'est pas si simple, ni pour le Suédois ni pour sa Lotus 72 qui commence à accuser son âge. La majorité des parieurs auraient en effet placé leurs jetons sur les numéros 11 et 12, les Ferrari B3 de Clay Regazzoni et Niki Lauda qui, en première ligne, s'érigent en une infranchissable muraille rouge et blanche devant les 23 concurrents restants.

C'est Regazzoni qui prend la tête dans l'asphalte de Sainte Dévote. Mais, derrière lui, Lauda, menaçant, le talonne en attendant sa chance et ne laisse aucun instant son coéquipier dans l'incertitude quant à ses intentions. Pendant 21 tours, le Suisse résiste à la pression avant de commettre l'un de ses rares impairs et d'aborder trop rapidement la Rascasse. En un clin d'œil, Lauda est passé, entraînant dans son sillage Ronnie Peterson, Jean-Pierre Jarier avec la Shadow DN3 et la nouvelle recrue de Ken Tyrrell, Jody Scheckter.

A ce moment-là, Peterson a déjà derrière lui une course ponctuée de nombreux incidents qui ont également laissé des traces sur sa Lotus noir et or : contact brutal avec les glissières de sécurité au cinquième tour, collision avec la Brabham BT 44 de Carlos Reutemann, qui doit s'arrêter séance tenante, et remontée depuis la sixième position. En tête, Lauda semble maîtriser la situation lorsque le moteur de la Ferrari se tait derrière la Rascasse, au 33e tour, l'empêchant de regagner les stands. Peterson, quant à lui, doit accomplir encore 45 tours avant de pouvoir prendre son épouse Barbro avec lui sous la couronne de lauriers.

Accidents et abandons marquent la course de leur sceau, par exemple un gigantesque carambolage quelques secondes après le départ qui implique sept voitures et ôte toute chance de victoire à des vedettes des Grands Prix comme Denis Hulme (McLaren M23), Jean-Pierre Beltoise (BRM P 201) et Carlos Pace (Surtees TS 16). Pendant que la Trojan de l'Australien Tim Schenken se traîne encore jusqu'au port, elle répand si généreusement son huile sur la piste que le spécialiste des rallyes Vic Elford, au volant de la Porsche Carrera du directeur de course, part en tête-à-queue dans l'hilarité générale.

La chance est aux côtés de Mike Hailwood, quand sa McLaren M23 s'écrase au 12e tour contre les glissières dans la montée du Casino, car il s'en sort comme par miracle complètement indemne, tout comme Hans-Joachim Stuck dont la March 741 est considérablement endommagée au début de la course dans une collision avec la Hesketh de James Hunt aux abords de la descente de Mirabeau.

L'une des stars de la course est le jeune Sud-Africain Jody Scheckter, qui obtient une deuxième place, son meilleur résultat à ce jour. Un autre, qui fait déjà partie des meubles au Grand Prix, donne sa représentation d'adieu à Monaco : Graham Hill. En 1975, l'année de son accident mortel en avion, il ne parviendra même pas à se qualifier.

Graham Hill catching a lift. The mustachioed Londoner avoids unnecessary walks since his serious crash at Watkins Glen in 1969.

Mitfahrgelegenheit für Graham Hill. Seit seinem schweren Unfall in Watkins Glen 1969 vermeidet der schnauzbärtige Londoner überflüssige Fußwege.

Auto-stop pour Graham Hill. Depuis son grave accident de Watkins Glen, en 1969, le Londonien moustachu évite le plus possible de marcher.

N°	DRIVERS		ENTRANTS	CARS	ENGINES	PRACTICE RESULTS	RACE RESULTS
1	**Ronnie Peterson**	S	**John Player Team Lotus**	**Lotus 72E**	**Cosworth V8 2993 cc**	**3rd: 1'27"1**	**1st: 1h58'03"7**
3	Jody Scheckter	RSA	Elf Team Tyrrell	Tyrrell 007	Cosworth V8 2993 cc	3rd(5): 1'27"1	2nd: 1h58'32"5
17	Jean-Pierre Jarier	F	UOP Shadow Racing Team	Shadow DN3	Cosworth V8 2993 cc	6th: 1'27"5	3rd: 1h58'52"6
11	Clay Regazzoni	CH	SEFAC Ferrari S.p.A.	Ferrari 312B3	Ferrari F12 2991 cc	2nd: 1'26"6	4th: 1h59'06"8
5	Emerson Fittipaldi	BR	Marlboro Team Texaco	McLaren M23	Cosworth V8 2993 cc	12th(13): 1'28"2	5th: 77 laps
28	John Watson	GB	John Goldie Racing	Brabham BT 42	Cosworth V8 2993 cc	21st(23): 1'30"0	6th: 77 laps
26	Graham Hill	GB	Embassy Racing/Graham Hill	Lola T370	Cosworth V8 2993 cc	21st: 1'30"0	7th: 76 laps
27	Guy Edwards	GB	Embassy Racing/Graham Hill	Lola T370	Cosworth V8 2993 cc	NQ(26): 1'30"4	8th: 75 laps
4	Patrick Depailler	F	Elf Team Tyrrell	Tyrrell 006	Cosworth V8 2993 cc	3rd(28): 1'27"1	9th: 74 laps
15	Henri Pescarolo	F	British Racing Motors	BRM P160E	BRM V12 2998 cc	NQ(27): 1'30"7	R
2	Jacky Ickx	B	John Player Team Lotus	Lotus 72E	Cosworth V8 2993 cc	19th: 1'29"4	R
12	*Niki Lauda*	A	*SEFAC Ferrari S.p.A.*	*Ferrari 312B3*	*Ferrari F12 2991 cc*	*1st: 1'26"3*	R
24	James Hunt	GB	Hesketh Racing	Hesketh 308	Cosworth V8 2993 cc	7th: 1'27"8	R
33	Mike Hailwood	GB	Yardley Team McLaren	McLaren M23	Cosworth V8 2993 cc	10th: 1'28"1	R
7	Carlos Reutemann	RA	Motor Racing Developments	Brabham BT 44	Cosworth V8 2993 cc	7th(8): 1'27"8	R
37	François Migault	F	British Racing Motors	BRM P160E	BRM V12 2998 cc	21st(22): 1'30"0	R
22	Vern Schuppan	AUS	Team Ensign	Ensign N174	Cosworth V8 2993 cc	25th: 1'30"3	R
9	Hans Stuck	D	March Engineering	March 741	Cosworth V8 2993 cc	9th: 1'28"0	R
23	Tim Schenken	AUS	Trojan-Tauranac Racing Team	Trojan T103	Cosworth V8 2993 cc	24th: 1'30"2	R
20	Arturo Merzario	I	Frank Williams Racing Cars	Iso FW	Cosworth V8 2993 cc	14th: 1'28"5	R
16	Brian Redman	GB	UOP Shadow Racing Team	Shadow DN3	Cosworth V8 2993 cc	16th: 1'28"8	R
10	Vittorio Brambilla	I	March Engineering	March 741	Cosworth V8 2993 cc	15th: 1'28"7	R
18	Carlos Pace	BR	Bang & Olufsen Team Surtees	Surtees TS16	Cosworth V8 2993 cc	17th(18): 1'29"1	R
14	Jean-Pierre Beltoise	F	British Racing Motors	BRM P201	BRM V12 2998 cc	10th(11): 1'28"1	R
6	Denis Hulme	NZ	Marlboro Team Texaco	McLaren M23	Cosworth V8 2993 cc	12th: 1'28"2	R

Early rush hour on the hill: (1) as in the previous year, Regazzoni (Ferrari) blocks the path of his colleagues at the start like a mobile chicane. (2) Shortly after the start, the pushing and shoving begins between seven cars; Hulme (McLaren) to the left at the front and Beltoise (BRM) next to him on the right are about to tangle. (3) Master and pupil: Hill in front of Edwards (both Lolas). A clear run: (4) Peterson (Lotus), (5) Scheckter (Tyrrell).

Im Frühstau zu Berge: (1) Wie im Jahr zuvor steht Regazzoni (Ferrari) anfänglich seinen Kollegen als mobile Schikane im Wege. (2) Kurz nach dem Start bahnt sich eine Rempelei zwischen sieben Wagen an, links vorn Hulme (McLaren), rechts daneben Beltoise (BRM). (3) Meister und Lehrling: Hill vor Edwards (beide Lola). Freie Fahrt für freie Bürger: (4) Peterson (Lotus), (5) Scheckter (Tyrrell).

A la queue leu leu : (1) comme l'année précédente, Regazzoni (Ferrari) barre tout d'abord le passage à ses collègues, formant ainsi une Chicane mobile. (2) Peu après le départ, un accrochage implique sept voitures, à gauche devant Hulme (McLaren), à droite à côté, Beltoise (BRM). (3) Le maître et son apprenti : Hill devant Edwards (tous les deux sur Lola). La voie est libre : (4) Peterson (Lotus), (5) Scheckter (Tyrrell).

(1) Massage in action: Niki Lauda is being prepared for the Grand Prix. (2) Guided tour: the mature Liz Taylor with current partner Henry Wynberg. (3) Forthcoming: Emerson Fittipaldi. (4) Reserved: Ronnie Peterson.

(1) Massierter Einsatz: Niki Lauda wird für den Grand Prix zubereitet. (2) Treulich geführt: die reife Liz Taylor mit ihrem zeitweisen Lebensgefährten Henry Wynberg. (3) Aufgeschlossen: Emerson Fittipaldi. (4) Zugeknöpft: Ronnie Peterson.

(1) Bien massé : Niki Lauda s'apprête à prendre le départ du Grand Prix. (2) Bien guidée : l'opulente Liz Taylor avec son compagnon d'alors, Henry Wynberg. (3) Souriant : Emerson Fittipaldi. (4) Fermé : Ronnie Peterson.

1975

Twenty years had elapsed since Maurice Trintignant's 1955 victory before another Ferrari racing car driver ascended the steps to the Prince's dais. The man who made this possible was Niki Lauda, particularly since the 312 T (the T standing for *trasversale* – the transmission being mounted transversely) – an outstanding piece of sporting machinery – had been entrusted to him. The Principality was darkened by the memory of another Grand Prix: the Spanish Grand Prix, held at Montjuich in Barcelona 14 days before, which had witnessed Rolf Stommelen's Lola leaving the track and killing five people. Once again, lessons were learned and all possible measures were taken. The chicane was made narrower, only 18 competitors were allowed to enter and the cars were set wider apart at the start.

Lauda had set the fastest times during the practice sessions on both Thursday and Friday, which came as no surprise to anyone. In second place was the shy Welshman Tom Pryce with the black Shadow DN 5, which was indeed a surprise to some. But the Austrian always had everything under control, despite the unpredictability of the weather which, as so often, had assumed the nature of a wild card.

At the beginning, the track was still wet, but the wide tyres soon etched an ideal line on the damp asphalt – at least that was something for the tyres to grip – and the track gradually dried out towards the end of the race. From the twentieth lap onwards, the atmosphere in the pit lane reached fever pitch. Everyone made a pitstop to fit slicks at some point or other, and the good work done by the McLaren crew helped Emerson Fittipaldi with the M 23 to rise from fourth to second place. The jovial Brazilian suddenly seemed to be in a position to threaten Lauda's domination of the sport – a fact which was reinforced when the oil pressure in the Ferrari's 12-cylinder engine began to waver. On lap 75, the pair were separated by just five seconds, but just as the spectators were preparing themselves for a dramatic finale, the Clerk of the Course unfurled the black-and-white chequered flag. The clause which stipulates that a Grand Prix cannot last longer than two hours had come into effect, and the race was over.

Tom Pryce, suffering from intense toothache, had left the race long since due to an accident on lap 39, just like his teammate Jean-Pierre Jarier, who had shared the second row with Ronnie Peterson. His Shadow had scraped against the crash barrier on the first lap when the Frenchman lost no time in foolishly attacking Lauda at Mirabeau; a chaotic half-lap ensued, which ended with a crash at the Tabac bend after extremely close contact with the chicane. Lauda was forced to relinquish his lead briefly on one occasion, during his pit stop on the twenty-fifth lap, when Ronnie Peterson went by with the Lotus 72. The Austrian remained in the pits for half a minute, but a lap later the Swede was at rest for a painful 80 seconds. A wheel nut had rolled under the wheel and had to be located and retrieved. In a sport with such a high technical content as Grand Prix racing, treachery from such a simple object can still be a determining factor in the outcome.

Zwanzig Jahre sind seit dem Sieg von Maurice Trintignant 1955 verstrichen, bevor wieder ein erfolgreicher Ferrari-Pilot die Stufen zur Fürstenloge emporsteigt. Möglich macht das der Mann Niki Lauda, zumal ihm mit dem 312 T (für *trasversale* – das Getriebe ist quer eingebaut) ein hervorragendes Sportgerät an die Hand gegeben wurde. Wieder lastet der Schatten eines anderen Grand Prix auf dem Fürstentum: Beim Großen Preis von Spanien 14 Tage zuvor am Montjuich in Barcelona ist der Lola von Rolf Stommelen von der Strecke abgekommen und hat fünf Menschen erschlagen. Und wieder zieht man im Rahmen des Möglichen die Konsequenzen daraus. Die Schikane wurde verengt, nur noch 18 Konkurrenten sind zugelassen, die Wagen bei der Startaufstellung weiter auseinandergezogen.

Aus den drei Trainingssitzungen Donnerstag und Freitag geht Lauda als Schnellster hervor, was niemanden verwundert. Zweiter ist der scheue Waliser Tom Pryce mit dem schwarzen Shadow DN 5, was manchen in Erstaunen versetzt. Immer aber hat der Österreicher das Heft in der Hand, trotzt auch unbekümmert den Unwägbarkeiten des Wetters, das wie so häufig den Part des Jokers spielt.

Am Anfang ist der Parcours naß, dann gravieren die fetten Räder zumindest eine griffige Ideallinie in den feuchten Asphalt, schließlich trocknet die Strecke ab. Von der 20. Runde an grassiert fieberhafte Hektik im Boxentrakt. Jedermann kehrt ein, um Slicks zu fassen, früher oder später. Gute Arbeit der McLaren-Crew spült Emerson Fittipaldi mit dem M 23 vom vierten auf den zweiten Rang vor. Der joviale Brasilianer scheint plötzlich in der Lage zu sein, Laudas Hegemonie zu bedrohen, zumal der Öldruck des Ferrari-Zwölfzylinders zu schwanken beginnt. Im 75. Durchgang trennen die beiden fünf Sekunden. Aber während sich die Zuschauer an der Strecke auf ein dramatisches Finale einzustimmen beginnen, entrollt der Rennleiter bereits die schwarzweiß karierte Flagge. Die Klausel greift, nach der ein Grand Prix nicht länger als zwei Stunden zu dauern habe. Das Rennen ist zuende.

Da ist Tom Pryce, von heftigen Zahnschmerzen gepeinigt, schon längst durch einen Unfall in der 39. Runde ausgeschieden, ebenso wie sein Teamgefährte Jean-Pierre Jarier, der sich die zweite Reihe mit Ronnie Peterson geteilt hat. Schon in der Startrunde schrammt der Shadow gegen die Leitplanke, als der Franzose Lauda bei Mirabeau unklug attackiert, Beginn einer chaotischen halben Runde, die nach heftiger Tuchfühlung mit der Schikane mit einem Crash an der Tabakskurve endet. Nur einmal mußte Lauda die Führung abgeben. Während seines Boxenstopps in der 25. Runde bleibt Ronnie Peterson mit dem Lotus 72 draußen. Eine halbe Minute verweilt der Österreicher an der Box, qualvolle 80 Sekunden der Schwede gleich darauf: Eine Radmutter ist unter den Wagen gerollt und muß dort erst wieder aufgetrieben werden. In einer technischen Sportart wie Grand-Prix-Rennen kann auch die Tücke des Objekts zum entscheidenden Faktor werden.

Il aura fallu attendre vingt ans depuis la victoire de Maurice Trintignant en 1955 pour voir un pilote de Ferrari monter les marches de la loge princière et ceindre la couronne de laurier. Cet homme, c'est Niki Lauda qui, avec la 312 T (pour *trasversale* – signifiant que la boîte de vitesses est en position transversale), disposait cette année-là d'un bolide à sa mesure. Une fois de plus, l'ombre d'un autre Grand Prix plane sur celui de la Principauté: lors du Grand Prix d'Espagne, quinze jours plus tôt, dans le parc de Montjuich à Barcelone, la Lola de Rolf Stommelen s'est envolée et a tué cinq personnes. Et, de nouveau, on en tire la leçon dans la mesure du possible. A Monaco, la chicane a encore été rétrécie et dix-huit voitures seulement sont admises au départ, les concurrents étant plus éloignés les uns des autres que de coutume sur la grille de départ.

A l'issue des deux journées d'essais, Lauda s'avère le plus rapide, ce qui ne surprend personne. Son dauphin est le timide Gallois Tom Pryce avec sa Shadow DN 5 noire, et cela est déjà plus surprenant. Mais c'est toujours l'Autrichien qui joue le rôle d'un chef d'orchestre que ne troublent même pas les impondérables de la météorologie, lesquels, comme si souvent, se transforment en joker.

Au début, le parcours est encore mouillé, puis les larges roues assèchent peu à peu la trajectoire idéale sur l'asphalte humide et, finalement, tout le circuit est sec. A partir du 20e tour, l'atmosphère devient fébrile aux stands. Chacun s'y précipite pour monter des slicks tôt ou tard. La rapidité des mécaniciens de McLaren permet à Emerson Fittipaldi et à sa M 23 de passer de la quatrième à la deuxième place. Le jovial Brésilien semble soudain en mesure de menacer l'hégémonie de Niki Lauda, d'autant plus que la pression d'huile du douze-cylindres de la Ferrari commence à faire des siennes. Au 75e tour, cinq secondes seulement séparent les deux hommes. Mais, alors que les spectateurs massés le long du circuit s'apprêtent à assister à une finale dramatique, le directeur de course brandit déjà le drapeau à damier. Le règlement prévoit en effet qu'un Grand Prix ne doit pas durer plus de deux heures, et la course est terminée.

Pendant ce temps, Tom Pryce, torturé par de violents maux de dents, a depuis longtemps abandonné après un accident au 39e tour, de même que son coéquipier Jean-Pierre Jarier, qui se partageait la seconde ligne avec Ronnie Peterson. Dès le premier tour, sa Shadow va se frotter contre les glissières de sécurité lorsque le Français attaque peu judicieusement Lauda à Mirabeau ; c'est le début d'un demi-tour chaotique qui, après un nouveau violent contact à la chicane, se terminera par un crash dans le virage du Bureau de Tabac. Niki Lauda n'a dû céder le commandement qu'un court moment. Durant son arrêt au stand, au 25e tour, Ronnie Peterson reste en piste avec sa Lotus 72. L'Autrichien passe trente secondes au stand, mais le Suédois, un tour plus tard, 80 interminables secondes : un écrou est tombé sous la voiture et il faut tout d'abord aller le repêcher. Dans une discipline sportive technique comme les courses de Grand Prix, la malignité des choses peut même faire basculer le destin.

"And how do you manage with an American car on such roads?" Jackie Stewart, in his second year of retirement, interviews Penske driver Mark Donohue.

»Und wie kommt man mit einem amerikanischen Wagen auf solchen Straßen zurecht?« Jackie Stewart, in seinem zweiten Jahr als Pensionär, interviewt Penske-Pilot Mark Donohue.

« Et comment marche une voiture américaine sur de telles routes ? » Jackie Stewart, à la retraite depuis deux ans, interviewant le pilote de Penske, Mark Donohue.

N°	DRIVERS		ENTRANTS	CARS	ENGINES	PRACTICE RESULTS	RACE RESULTS
12	*Niki Lauda*	A	*SEFAC Ferrari S.p.A.*	*Ferrari 312T*	*Ferrari F12 2992 cc*	*1st: 1'26"40*	*1st: 2h01'21"31*
1	Emerson Fittipaldi	BR	Marlboro Team Texaco	McLaren M23	Cosworth V8 2993 cc	9th: 1'27"77	2nd: 2h01'24"09
8	Carlos Pace	BR	Martini Racing	Brabham BT44B	Cosworth V8 2993 cc	8th: 1'27"67	3rd: 2h01'39"12
5	Ronnie Peterson	S	John Player Team Lotus	Lotus 72E	Cosworth V8 2993 cc	4th: 1'27"40	4th: 2h01'59"76
4	Patrick Depailler	F	Elf Team Tyrrell	Tyrrell 007	Cosworth V8 2993 cc	12th: 1'27"95	5th: 2h02'02"17
2	Jochen Mass	D	Marlboro Team Texaco	McLaren M23	Cosworth V8 2993 cc	15th: 1'28"49	6th: 2h02'03"38
3	Jody Scheckter	RSA	Elf Team Tyrrell	Tyrrell 007	Cosworth V8 2993 cc	7th: 1'27"58	7th: 74 laps
6	Jacky Ickx	B	John Player Team Lotus	Lotus 72E	Cosworth V8 2993 cc	14th: 1'28"28	8th: 74 laps
7	Carlos Reutemann	RA	Martini Racing	Brabham BT44B	Cosworth V8 2993 cc	10th: 1'27"93	9th: 73 laps
28	Mark Donohue	USA	First National Citybank Team Penske	Penske PC1	Cosworth V8 2993 cc	16th: 1'28"81	R
24	James Hunt	GB	Hesketh Racing	Hesketh 308	Cosworth V8 2993 cc	11th: 1'27"94	R
26	Alan Jones	AUS	Custom Made Harry Stiller Racing	Hesketh 308	Cosworth V8 2993 cc	18th: 1'29"12	R
9	Vittorio Brambilla	I	Beta Team March	March 751	Cosworth V8 2993 cc	5th: 1'27"50	R
16	Tom Pryce	GB	UOP Shadow Racing Team	Shadow DN5	Cosworth V8 2993 cc	2nd: 1'27"09	R
11	Clay Regazzoni	CH	SEFAC Ferrari S.p.A.	Ferrari 312T	Ferrari F12 2992 cc	6th: 1'27"55	R
18	John Watson	GB	Matchbox-Team Surtees	Surtees TS16	Cosworth V8 2993 cc	17th: 1'28"90	R
27	Mario Andretti	USA	Vel's Parnelli Jones Racing	Parnelli VPJ4	Cosworth V8 2993 cc	13th: 1'28"11	R
17	Jean-Pierre Jarier	F	UOP Shadow Racing Team	Shadow DN5	Cosworth V8 2993 cc	3rd: 1'27"25	R

(1) Arrival at Mirabeau in the first lap. Vittorio Brambilla (March), the "Monza Gorilla", takes an independent route. In step: (2) Emerson Fittipaldi (McLaren), (3) Pace (Brabham), (4) Depailler (Tyrrell) and (5) Peterson (Lotus). (6) Precision work: Jochen Mass (McLaren) takes corrective action.

(1) Ankunft in der ersten Runde bei Mirabeau. Vittorio Brambilla (March), der »Monza-Gorilla«, sucht seinen eigenen Weg. Gleichschritt: (2) Emerson Fittipaldi (McLaren), (3) Pace (Brabham), (4) Depailler (Tyrrell) und (5) Peterson (Lotus). (6) Mass-Arbeit: Jochen Mass (McLaren) korrigiert dagegen einen Quersteher.

(1) Le peloton déboule au premier tour à Mirabeau. Vittorio Brambilla (March), le «gorille de Monza», sur sa trajectoire bien à lui. Tous égaux : (2) Emerson Fittipaldi (McLaren), (3) Pace (Brabham), (4) Depailler (Tyrrell) et (5) Peterson (Lotus). (6) Contre-braquage : Jochen Mass (McLaren) en dehors de la trajectoire.

1

(1) Tunnel-vision: during the early laps, the seaside tunnel offers the benefit of a dry track against the usual disadvantage of reduced visibility. (2) Team Tyrrell: Depailler and Scheckter keep close company. (3) Pace had his Brabham prepared for fine weather – a mistake. (4) A natural stage and backdrop, what better platform for advertising than Monaco?

(1) Tunnel-Vision: In der Anfangsphase bietet die Röhre am Meer den Vorzug einer trockenen Strecke um den üblichen Nachteil verminderter Sicht. (2) Team Tyrrell: Depailler und Scheckter treten gemeinsam auf. (3) Pace hat seinen Brabham für schönes Wetter einstellen lassen – ein Fehler. (4) Von Natur aus Bühne und Kulisse, bietet sich Monaco förmlich an als Forum für Werbebotschaften.

(1) Où est le bout du tunnel ? Au début, le tunnel du bord de mer offre l'avantage d'une piste sèche, mais l'inconvénient d'une moins bonne visibilité. (2) Team Tyrrell : Depailler et Scheckter ne se quittent pas d'une semelle. (3) Pace a fait régler sa Brabham pour une piste sèche – une erreur. (4) Par nature scène et coulisse, Monaco est un endroit idéal pour faire passer des messages publicitaires.

2

(Following double page) On track to pole position: Niki Lauda (Ferrari).

(Folgende Doppelseite) Auf dem Weg zur Pole Position: Niki Lauda (Ferrari).

(Double page suivante) Vers la pole position : Niki Lauda (Ferrari).

(1) Happy news: James Hunt does not charge to carry this message. (2) Assembled experts: Andretti, Lauda and Watson. (3) Taking a seat: McLaren boss Teddy Mayer and Maria-Helena Fittipaldi. (4) Dim prospects: briefing for drivers and unauthorized persons before the race.

(1) Frohe Botschaft: Diesen Slogan trägt James Hunt sogar gratis. (2) Expertenrunde: Andretti, Lauda und Watson. (3) Sitz-Gelegenheit: McLaren-Boß Teddy Mayer und Maria-Helena Fittipaldi. (4) Düstere Aussichten: Briefing für Fahrer und Unbefugte vor dem Rennen.

(1) Bonne nouvelle : ce slogan, James Hunt l'arbore même gratuitement. (2) Entre spécialistes : Andretti, Lauda et Watson. (3) Bien assis : le chef de McLaren, Teddy Mayer, et Maria-Helena Fittipaldi. (4) Ecoutez bien : briefing pour les pilotes et les curieux avant la course.

FACE TO FACE

VON ANGESICHT ZU ANGESICHT · TÊTE-À-TÊTE

Colorful personalities: a very special position is reserved for Nikolaus Lauda in the colorful mosaic of Formula 1 champions.

Farbige Persönlichkeit: Im bunten Mosaik der Formel-1-Champions hat sich Nikolaus Lauda eine ganz besondere Stelle reserviert.

Personnalité scintillante : dans la mosaïque multicolore des champions de Formule 1, Nikolaus Lauda s'est réservé un statut bien à part.

Are grown people responsible for their faces?", Countess Renata wants to know in Hemingway's short novel *Across the River and into the Trees*. "No", is the answer of her interlocutor, Colonel Richard Cantwell. But, "Yes, indeed", is the decisive answer to the same question a few years later in the story *The Fall,* by Albert Camus.

From a literary perspective, Nikolaus Lauda was closer to Hemingway before 1 August 1976. The early Lauda: no freebooter by nature, like his compatriot Jochen Rindt, rather the young man from next door. Studies: Law, medicine, perhaps even theology. Nevertheless, insolent, already lightning quick at that time – an uneducated intellectual who was never short of an answer. Not a person to whom one would take a spontaneous liking: one just needed to hear the way he dealt with journalists he did not like.

But when he sat in his Ferrari again in Monza, six weeks after his flying visit to the flaming hell of the Nürburgring, unafraid but branded for life, he was on the way to becoming a legend. And those were only the first few bars of the Lauda rap: giving up in the rain in Fuji another six weeks later because what had happened at the Ring had left its mark on the soul, then temporary retirement from racing in 1979, a comeback in 1982, his third World Championship in 1984, and final retirement in 1985.

The crazy thing is that this guy is allowed to get away with things which no-one else would be. He never loses face, is brashly disarming, he always manages to find the common denominator for things which are completely incompatible. And as Niki Lauda could always play the media, then as now, television, which can build up or knock down the figures of contemporary history, continues to give us access in exemplary intimacy, so that neither Lauda Air nor the Lauda era, is ever forgotten. Of course, Lauda is responsible for his face. But is that what Camus really meant?

Ob denn ein erwachsener Mensch für sein Gesicht verantwortlich sei, will die Gräfin Renata in Hemingways Kurzroman *Über den Fluß und in die Wälder* wissen. Nein, erwidert ihr Gesprächspartner Oberst Richard Cantwell. Indes: »Sehr wohl«, lautet die entschiedene Antwort auf die gleiche Frage ein paar Jahre später in der Erzählung *Der Fall* von Albert Camus.

Literarisch gesehen, steht Nikolaus Lauda vor dem 1. August 1976 Hemingway näher. Der frühe Lauda: kein Freibeutertyp wie sein Landsmann Jochen Rindt, eher der junge Mann von nebenan, Studium: Juristerei oder Medizin, vielleicht sogar Theologie. Allerdings schon damals rotzfrech, blitzhelle – ein ungebildeter Intellektueller, der gleichwohl nie mit seinem Latein am Ende ist. Kein Mensch, den man spontan ins Herz schließt: Man höre nur, wie er mißliebigen Journalisten übers Maul fährt.

Aber als er sechs Wochen nach seiner Stippvisite in der Flammenhölle des Nürburgrings in Monza wieder im Ferrari sitzt, unerschrocken, aber gebrandmarkt fürs Leben, ist er auf dem Marsch in den Mythos. Dabei sind das nur die ersten Takte des Lauda-Raps: Aufgabe beim Regenrennen in Fuji wieder sechs Wochen später, weil die Sache am Ring eben doch ihre Schmauchspuren an der Seele hinterlassen hat, vorläufiger Rückzug vom Rennsport 1979, Comeback 1982, dritte Weltmeisterschaft 1984, endgültiger Rücktritt 1985. Das Verrückte ist, daß der Kerl Haken schlagen darf, die man keinem sonst nachsehen würde. Das Gesicht verliert er nie, findet stets, schnoddrig entwaffnend, den gemeinsamen Nenner für das völlig Unvereinbare.

Und da Niki Lauda damals wie heute das Medienspiel beherrscht, schafft uns nach wie vor das Fernsehen, das Männer der Zeitgeschichte aufbaut oder vom Sockel kippt, auch diesen in vorgeblicher Intimität heran, auf daß beides nicht in Vergessenheit gerate, Lauda Air und die Ära Lauda. Natürlich kann er etwas für sein Gesicht, der späte Lauda. Aber ob Camus es so gemeint hat?

Un adulte est-il responsable de la tête qu'il a, veut absolument savoir la comtesse Renata dans la nouvelle d'Ernest Hemingway *Au-delà du fleuve et sous les arbres*. Non, lui répond son interlocuteur, le colonel Richard Cantwell. « Absolument » est la réponse sans appel donnée à la même question, quelques années plus tard, dans le roman *La Chute,* d'Albert Camus.

Sur le plan littéraire, Nikolaus Lauda est plus proche d'Hemingway jusqu'au 1er août 1976. Le jeune Lauda : pas le type de baroudeur qu'est son compatriote Jochen Rindt, plutôt le jeune homme bien d'à côté ; études de droit ou de médecine, peut-être même de théologie. Mais, à cette époque déjà, effronté et d'une haute intelligence – un intellectuel pas arrogant, mais qui n'en est, pour autant, jamais au bout de son latin. Ce n'est pas le type d'homme auquel on ouvre spontanément son cœur : il suffit de l'écouter critiquer les journalistes qui ne lui plaisent pas.

Quand, six semaines après avoir failli rôtir dans l'enfer des flammes du Nürburgring, il se glisse de nouveau dans le baquet de sa Ferrari, à Monza, sans peur, mais marqué pour la vie du sceau de la mort, il est en marche vers le mythe. Et ce ne sont pourtant que les premières mesures du rap à la Lauda : abandon lors de la course du Mont Fuji, sous des trombes d'eau, six semaines plus tard, parce que son accident du Nürburgring a tout de même laissé des stigmates dans son âme, puis retrait provisoire de la compétition en 1979, come-back en 1982, troisième titre de champion du monde en 1984 et retraite définitive en 1985.

Ce qui est fou, c'est que ce type peut se permettre des états d'âme que l'on ne pardonnerait à nul autre. Il ne perd jamais la face, trouve toujours, désarmant d'impertinence, le dénominateur commun pour ce qui est totalement inconciliable. Et à cette époque comme aujourd'hui, Niki Lauda joue à la perfection la partition du jeu des médias. La télévision réussit toujours, elle qui élève un monument aux grands hommes de l'histoire contemporaine ou les descend de leur piédestal, parfois en violant une prétendue intimité, à faire en sorte que tous les deux ne sombrent jamais dans l'oubli, ni Lauda Air ni l'ère Lauda. Evidemment qu'il est responsable de son visage, le vieux Lauda. Mais était-ce à quoi Camus avait fait allusion ?

1976

Experts in the field tipped Niki Lauda as being the sure-fire winner of the 34th Monaco Grand Prix. Three factors spoke volumes for the man and his machine: the sarcastic man from Vienna had become the outstanding driver of the mid-Seventies, while the chassis of his Ferrari 312 T2 was balanced to perfection. Its 12 cylinders delivered a tremendous amount of power, tailormade for the undulating terrain of Monaco, which had undergone some minor alterations. Two new chicanes had created an extra 34 meters, bringing the total lap length up to 3,312 meters. One of the chicanes was located at Sainte Dévote, the other followed the double bend at Rascasse. A maximum of 20 cars were allowed to start.

Indeed, as it transpired that weekend, no-one could hold a candle to the Austrian, who had already amassed four Grand Prix wins that season. As holder of pole position, he drove from the starting grid straight to the finishing line with both elegance and precision. His victory began with a comfortable lead being gained at Sainte Dévote, where matters began to get tight and difficult after the start. Here, Ronnie Peterson, with his brand new March 761, pushed himself forward from the second row, past Lauda's team-mate Clay Regazzoni into the red sandwich. To their rear were both of the six-wheeled Tyrrell P34s, whose appearance bordered on the absurd. At first they were being driven side-by-side, but the formerly wild Jody Scheckter had calmed down and he was good enough to allow his colleague Patrick Depailler to take precedence. At a respectful distance behind this quintet, a furious queue was soon trapped behind Emerson Fittipaldi: the Brazilian driver had been one of the favorites for this race, though the odds against him and his home-made B-grade Copersucar were beginning to lengthen. The blocked drivers included James Hunt, destined to become the World Champion in 1976; unsurprisingly, his McLaren M23 proved to be unsuited to the tight corners of the Principality. In addition, this particular 30 May did not seem to be his day: only fourteenth in qualifying, he spun the car repeatedly, coming momentarily to a complete stop on lap 8, and then his Ford Cosworth engine broke on lap 25.

A few minutes later, Peterson's hopes for six points were shattered on the skid pad caused by Hunt's dropped oil. Just before, Regazzoni had also slipped up and fallen behind the two Tyrrells, which swapped places on lap 15. Depailler was plagued by a faulty rear axle and the resulting peculiar handling of the P34. On the sixty-fourth lap the Frenchman fell victim to Regazzoni, whose chase of Scheckter ended in intimate contact with the barrier at Rascasse on the seventy-third lap. Meanwhile, Jacques Laffite, with his Ligier JS 5, Hans-Joachim Stuck, in the March 761, and the McLaren driver Jochen Mass slipped past Fittipaldi, albeit with great difficulty. Laffite's impressive drive ended three laps before the end after a tussle with Mass close to the swimming pool.

Meanwhile, right out in front, Niki Lauda drove on with Olympic ease, and when he later learned of his rivals' problems, they became a source of considerable edification and amusement.

Den 34. Grand Prix de Monaco, verheißen die Auguren der Branche, werde niemand anders als Niki Lauda gewinnen. Drei Faktoren sprechen für Mann und Maschine: Der sarkastische Wiener ist der überragende Fahrer der Mittsiebziger. Das Chassis seines Ferrari 312 T2 ist trefflich austariert. Sein Zwölfzylinder schöpft reichlich Kraft aus der Tiefe, wie maßgeschneidert für die monegassische Berg- und Talbahn. Diese präsentiert sich sanft verändert. Zwei Schikanen haben für einen Zuwachs von 34 Metern auf 3312 Meter Gesamtlänge gesorgt, eine bei Sainte Dévote, die andere hinter der Doppelkurve von Rascasse. Maximal 20 Wagen sind zugelassen.

In der Tat kann an diesem Wochenende keiner dem Österreicher das Wasser reichen, der in der laufenden Saison bereits vier Grand-Prix-Erfolge angehäuft hat: Pole Position, ein mit Eleganz und Präzision herausgefahrener Start-Ziel-Sieg, beginnend mit einem gemütlichen Vorsprung bei Sainte Dévote, wo es nach dem Start eng und haarig wird. Da hat sich Ronnie Peterson mit seinem brandneuen March 761 aus der zweiten Reihe heraus an Laudas Teamgefährten Clay Regazzoni vorbei ins Sandwich der Roten geschoben. Dahinter treffen die beiden absurd anmutenden sechsrädrigen Tyrrell P34 Seite an Seite ein, nur daß der einst so wilde Jody Scheckter vernünftig geworden ist und seinem Kollegen Patrick Depailler artig den Vortritt läßt. In gebührendem Abstand hinter diesem Quintett staut sich hinter Emerson Fittipaldi eine wütende Schlange: Der Pilot ist erste Wahl mit leicht fallender Tendenz, sein Copersucar Handelsklasse B. Einer der Aufgehaltenen: James Hunt, Weltmeister in spe 1976. Sein McLaren M23 zeigt sich für die Ecken und Winkel des Stadtstaats denkbar ungeeignet, und überdies hat er mit diesem 30. Mai einen unglücklichen Tag erwischt: ohnehin nur 14. im Training, Dreher bis zum Stillstand in Runde acht, geplatzter Ford Cosworth nach dem 25. Durchgang.

Auf dem Skidpad seines Öls zerschellt wenige Minuten später Petersons Hoffnung auf sechs Punkte. Kurz zuvor hat sich bereits Regazzoni einen Ausrutscher erlaubt und ist hinter diesem Quintett die beiden Tyrrell zurückgefallen, die in Runde 15 die Plätze getauscht haben: Depailler laboriert an einem Hinterachsschaden und sonderbarem Handling des P34. Im 64. Durchgang schnappt sich der Schweizer den Franzosen. Seine Hatz auf Scheckter endet indes durch einen innigen Kontakt mit der Leitplanke bei Rascasse in der 73. Runde. Inzwischen haben sich Jacques Laffite mit seinem Ligier JS 5, Hans-Joachim Stuck im March 761 und McLaren-Pilot Jochen Mass mit Mühe und Not an Fittipaldi vorbeigequetscht. Laffites rasche Fahrt endet drei Runden vor Schluß nach einer Rempelei mit Mass im Bereich des Schwimmbads.

Ganz vorn jedoch zieht Niki Lauda mit olympischer Gelassenheit seine Bahn. All das dient später nur seiner Unterhaltung und seiner Erheiterung.

Le 34e Grand Prix de Monaco, les augures sont unanimes, nul autre que Niki Lauda ne le gagnera. Trois arguments parlent en faveur de l'homme et de sa machine : le sarcastique Viennois surclasse tous les autres pilotes du milieu des années 70, le châssis de sa Ferrari 312 T2 étant un modèle d'équilibre. Son douze-cylindres dispose d'une cavalerie à profusion dès les bas régimes. Des conditions absolument idéales, donc, pour les montagnes russes de Monaco, dont le circuit a d'ailleurs subi de légères modifications. Deux nouvelles chicanes sont responsables de son allongement de 34 mètres, à 3312 mètres de longueur totale, l'une près de Sainte Dévote, l'autre derrière le double virage de la Rascasse. 20 voitures maximum sont admises au départ.

De fait, ce week-end-là, nul n'arrive à la cheville de l'Autrichien qui, depuis le début de la saison, a déjà remporté quatre Grands Prix : pole position, une course en tête, du départ à l'arrivée, qui se distingue tant par son élégance que par sa précision. Sa voiture s'annonça par une confortable avance à Sainte Dévote où, par tradition, il se produit fréquemment des collisions après le départ. A cet endroit-là, Ronnie Peterson et sa March 761 flambant neuf se sont catapultés de la seconde ligne, se retrouvant en sandwich entre les rouges après avoir doublé Clay Regazzoni, le coéquipier de Niki Lauda. Le duo est talonné par les bizarres Tyrrell P34 aux quatre petites roues avant, mais le jadis si sauvage Jody Scheckter s'est maintenant calmé et a docilement laissé la préséance à son coéquipier Patrick Depailler. A distance respectueuse de ce quintette, Emerson Fittipaldi joue bientôt le rôle de bouchon devant une file de pilotes déchaînés : le Brésilien est l'un des favoris de la course avec une légère tendance à la baisse, mais sa voiture, la Copersucar brésilienne, n'est que de catégorie B. Dans l'embouteillage : James Hunt, le futur champion du monde de 1976. Sa McLaren M23 est tout sauf à sa place sur le circuit urbain sinueux et étroit et, de plus, ce 30 mai n'est vraiment pas son jour de chance : 14e seulement aux essais, tête-à-queue et arrêt au huitième tour, moteur Ford Cosworth explosé après le 25e tour.

Sur la trace de son huile, Ronnie Peterson voit, quelques minutes plus tard, s'évanouir tous ses espoirs de remporter six points. Peu de temps auparavant, Regazzoni s'est payé le luxe d'un dérapage et s'est retrouvé derrière les deux Tyrrell, qui ont échangé leurs places au 15e tour : un élément de fixation de la suspension arrière droite de la Tyrrell a cassé, d'où le comportement bizarre de la P34. Au 64e tour, Regazzoni double à nouveau le Français. Sa poursuite de Scheckter se termine malheureusement par une pirouette à l'issue de laquelle il fracasse l'arrière de sa Ferrari contre les glissières, à la Rascasse, au 73e tour. Entre-temps, Jacques Laffite et sa Ligier JS 5, Hans-Joachim Stuck et sa March 761 ainsi que Jochen Mass et sa McLaren M23 ont finalement réussi à doubler un Fittipaldi en progrès. A trois tours de la fin, une collision avec Mass met un terme à la belle course de Laffite à hauteur de la piscine. Loin devant, Niki Lauda poursuit son chemin avec un calme olympien. Les déboires de ses concurrents provoqueront plus tard son étonnement st son hilarité.

Body language: the messages from his sponsors fuse in a colorful collage on Niki Lauda's overalls. Repetition is deliberate.

Körper-Sprache: Die Mitteilungen seiner Sponsoren finden sich auf Niki Laudas Overall zu einer konfusen Collage zusammen. Auch die Wiederholung ist eingeplant.

Langue gestuelle : sur la combinaison de Niki Lauda, les emblèmes de ses sponsors composent un collage confus. Certains y figurent plutôt deux fois qu'une.

N°	DRIVERS		ENTRANTS	CARS	ENGINES	PRACTICE RESULTS	RACE RESULTS
1	*Niki Lauda*	*A*	*SEFAC Ferrari S.p.A.*	*Ferrari 312T2*	*Ferrari F12 2992 cc*	*1st: 1'29"65*	*1st:1h59'51"47*
3	Jody Scheckter	RSA	Elf Team Tyrrell	Tyrrell P34	Cosworth V8 2993 cc	5th: 1'30"55	2nd: 2h00'02"60"
4	Patrick Depailler	F	Elf Team Tyrrell	Tyrrell P34	Cosworth V8 2993 cc	4th: 1'30"33	3rd: 2h00'56"31
34	Hans Stuck	D	March Racing	March 761	Cosworth V8 2993 cc	6th: 1'30"60	4th: 77 laps
12	Jochen Mass	D	Marlboro Team Texaco	McLaren M23	Cosworth V8 2993 cc	11th: 1'31"67	5th: 77 laps
30	Emerson Fittipaldi	BR	Copersucar Fittipaldi	Copersucar FD04	Cosworth V8 2993 cc	7th: 1'31"39	6th: 77 laps
16	Tom Pryce	GB	Shadow Racing Team	Shadow DN5	Cosworth V8 2993 cc	15th: 1'31"98	7th: 77 laps
17	Jean-Pierre Jarier	F	Shadow Racing Team	Shadow DN5	Cosworth V8 2993 cc	10th: 1'31"65	8th: 76 laps
8	Carlos Pace	BR	Martini Racing	Brabham BT45	Alfa Romeo F12 2995 cc	13th: 1'31"81	9th: 76 laps
28	John Watson	GB	First National Citibank Team Penske	Penske PC3	Cosworth V8 2993 cc	17th: 1'32"14	10th: 76 laps
21	Michel Leclere	F	Walter Wolf Racing	Williams FW05	Cosworth V8 2993 cc	18th: 1'32"17	11th: 76 laps
26	Jacques Laffite	AUS	Equipe Ligier Gitanes	Ligier JS5	Matra V12 2993 cc	8th: 1'31"46	12th: 75 laps (R)
22	Chris Amon	NZ	Team Ensign	Ensign N176	Cosworth V8 2993 cc	12th: 1'31"75	13th: 74 laps
2	Clay Regazzoni	CH	SEFAC Ferrari S.p.A.	Ferrari 312T2	Ferrari F12 2992 cc	2nd: 1'29"91	R
6	Gunnar Nilsson	S	John Player Team Lotus	JPS 12 (Lotus 77)	Cosworth V8 2993 cc	16th: 1'32"10	R
10	Ronnie Peterson	S	Team March	March 761	Cosworth V8 2993 cc	3rd: 1'30"08	R
11	James Hunt	GB	Marlboro Team Texaco	McLaren M23	Cosworth V8 2993 cc	14th: 1'31"89	R
9	Vittorio Brambilla	I	Beta Team March	March 761	Cosworth V8 2993 cc	9th: 1'31"47	R
19	Alan Jones	AUS	Team Surtees	Surtees TS19	Cosworth V8 2993 cc	19th: 1'32"33	R
7	Carlos Reutemann	RA	Martini Racing	Brabham BT45	Alfa Romeo F12 2995 cc	20th: 1'32"43	R

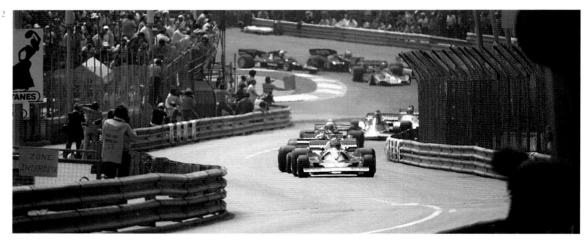

(1–3) There is nothing anyone can do against Lauda and his Ferrari at the 34th Monaco Grand Prix. Six appeal: the six-wheeled Tyrrell P34s of (4) Scheckter and (5) Depailler contribute a great deal to making the race more lively – visually too.

(1–3) Gegen Lauda und seinen Ferrari ist beim 34. Grand Prix de Monaco kein Kraut gewachsen. Six-Appeal: Die sechsrädrigen Tyrrell P34 von (4) Scheckter und (5) Depailler tragen ungemein zur Belebung des Rennens bei – auch visuell.

(1–3) Personne ne peut résister à Lauda et à sa Ferrari lors du 34e Grand Prix de Monaco. Six-Appeal : les Tyrrell P34 à six roues de (4) Scheckter et (5) Depailler contribuent au succès de la course – notamment sur le plan esthétique.

4

5

(1) For days after the Grand Prix, the people of Monaco will still be able to study the ideal line in peace, sitting in traffic jams on the way home. Not a bad day for the Germans: (2) Mass (McLaren) in fifth position, (3) Stuck (March) comes fourth. (4) For their traditional lap before the Grand Prix the royal couple on this occasion entrust themselves to the Mercedes star.

(1) Noch Tage nach dem Grand Prix werden die Monegassen im abendlichen Stau den Verlauf der Ideallinie in aller Ruhe studieren können. Kein schlechter Tag für die Deutschen: (2) Mass (McLaren) landet auf Platz 5, (3) Stuck (March) wird vierter. (4) Bei seiner traditionellen Runde im Vorfeld des Grand Prix vertraut das fürstliche Paar diesmal dem guten Stern auf allen Straßen.

(1) Pendant des jours après le Grand Prix, les Monégasques pourront étudier dans le calme la trajectoire idéale lors des embouteillages de fin d'après-midi. Une journée pas trop mauvaise pour les Allemands : (2) Mass (McLaren) termine cinquième, (3) Stuck (March), quatrième. (4) Lors de son traditionnel tour du circuit juste avant le Grand Prix, le couple princier confie cette fois son destin à la bonne étoile de Mercedes sur toutes les routes.

1977

"Little Red Riding Hood and the Wolf" was the title given to the article about the 35th Monaco Grand Prix in the German specialist magazine *auto motor und sport* of 22 May 1977. Little Red Riding Hood was otherwise known as Niki Lauda, with his striking red helmet in the Ferrari 312 T2. And Jody Scheckter was cast as the wolf, named after the wealthy businessman Walter Wolf, who indulged himself in having his own Formula 1 team as an occasional hobby. Of course, the comparison was misleading in that it was the Austrian who was hunting the South African who himself seemed to be pretty much untouchable: second-best qualifying time, a start-to-finish victory and fastest lap – all this from a brand new car and team, which had won its very first Grand Prix in January in Argentina.

Nevertheless, Scheckter had to fight for every meter, which he did with inimitable precision. At first, things were made extremely uncomfortable for him by John Watson, whose Brabham BT 45 B had been in pole position. His Alfa Romeo engine seemed particularly suited to cope with the properties of the track with its silky smooth power delivery from low revs all the way up – a decisive asset when handling the numerous tight bends of the course. The downside was the added weight and protruding components. Matters for Watson were made worse by transmission problems: on the forty-sixth lap, the bearded Irishman unsuccessfully groped for a gear and was forced to take the emergency exit at the chicane. During the fiftieth lap, all rotation stopped inside his transmission housing, and after an enormous spin, the Brabham came to a standstill in the middle of the track at Sainte Dévote, a rather unpleasant situation given the number of racing cars hurtling past.

Little Red Riding Hood's hunt for the wolf was now in full swing. Lauda, the victor of 1975 and 1976, would like to have made it a magic three in a row, and his dream almost came true. Only 0.89 seconds separated the two drivers at the finishing line. Monaco had never seen the like, and only four seconds separating third and sixth places was another first. Like the leading pair, the others were almost inseparable: Jochen Mass with the McLaren M23 and Mario Andretti in the Lotus 78 in fourth and fifth places, only 0.95 seconds between them after an epic struggle. This year's race had a third curiosity which had never happened before: the first lap took place without any mishap whatsoever. Jostling and confrontation in the early heat of the moment are normally the order of the day on this Sunday in May.

People at Ford and Cosworth were also rubbing their hands in glee – this was Grand Prix victory number 100 for the legendary eight-cylinder DFV engine in its eleventh year of racing. Others could not get over their bad luck and came to the conclusion that there was no justice. James Hunt, for instance, whose McLaren M23 had to be parked in a corner at Sainte Dévote on lap 26 because of a damaged engine. The Briton had finished ninth on his Monaco debut in 1973, but since then he had never crossed the finishing line. It was as if someone had it in for him.

»Rotkäppchen und der Wolf« nennt das Fachblatt *auto motor und sport* seinen Artikel über den 35. Grand Prix de Monaco am 22. Mai 1977. Rotkäppchen – das ist Niki Lauda mit seinem markanten roten Helm im Ferrari 312 T2. Und im Wolf, so genannt nach dem wohlhabenden Geschäftsmann Walter Wolf, der sich zu zeitweiliger Zerstreuung ein eigenes Formel-1-Team gönnt, sitzt Jody Scheckter. Natürlich hinkt der Vergleich auch, denn der Österreicher jagt ja den Südafrikaner, und der zeigt sich ziemlich unnahbar: zweitbeste Zeit im Training, Start-Ziel-Sieg, schnellste Runde, und das in einem brandneuen Auto, das als Hors d'œuvre seinen allerersten Grand Prix gewonnen hat, im Januar in Argentinien.

Gleichwohl muß Scheckter um jeden Meter kämpfen, und er tut dies mit unnachahmlicher Akkuratesse. Zunächst heizt ihm John Watson ein, dessen Brabham BT 45 B in der Pole Position gestanden hat. Sein Alfa-Romeo-Triebwerk geht gewissermaßen bereitwillig auf die Eigenheiten der Strecke ein mit geschmeidiger Kraftentfaltung von unten heraus, ein entschiedenes Plus im Umgang mit den vielen engen Kurven des Kurses. Erkauft wird es mit hohem Gewicht und ausladenden Dimensionen. Dazu gesellt sich Ärger mit dem Getriebe: In der 46. Runde fummelt der bärtige Ire vergeblich nach einem Gang und muß den Notausgang an der Schikane in Anspruch nehmen. Im 50. Durchgang kommt jegliche Rotation im Inneren seines Getriebegehäuses gänzlich zum Erliegen: Nach einem mächtigen Dreher bleibt der Brabham bei Sainte Dévote mitten auf der Straße liegen, ungemütlich umspült von heranpfeilenden Rennwagen.

Da ist die Hatz Rotkäppchens auf den Wolf längst in vollem Gange. Lauda, der Sieger von 1975 und 1976, würde gern die magische Dreizahl vollmachen, und fast gelingt es ihm. Nur 89 Hundertstelsekunden trennen die beiden im Ziel. So etwas gab es noch nie in Monaco, und auch nicht, daß ganze vier Sekunden die Männer auf den Plätzen drei bis sechs trennen. Fast untrennbar vereint ähnlich den beiden Spitzenreitern: Jochen Mass mit dem McLaren M23 und Mario Andretti im Lotus 78 auf den Rängen vier und fünf, nur 95 Hundertstelsekunden voneinander entfernt nach einem epischen Gefecht. Und noch ein drittes ist kurios und noch nicht dagewesen: daß die erste Runde ohne jeglichen Zwischenfall über die Bühne ging. Kontakte und Konfrontationen in der frühen Hitze des Gefechts sind hier ja sonst an der Tagesordnung an jenem Sonntag im Mai.

Auch bei Ford und Cosworth reibt man sich vergnügt die Hände: Das war Grand-Prix-Sieg Nummer einhundert für den legendären Achtzylinder namens DFV in seinem elften Jahr. Andere indessen hadern bekümmert mit ihrem Schicksal und können Gott und die Welt nicht mehr verstehen. So etwa James Hunt, dessen McLaren M23 in der 26. Runde in einer Nische bei Sainte Dévote Zuflucht sucht wegen Motorschadens. Einmal, bei seinem Monaco-Debüt 1973, war der Brite neunter. Seitdem ist er nicht mehr ins Ziel gekommen. Als hätte es jemand auf ihn abgesehen.

Le petit chaperon rouge et le loup » est le titre donné par la revue allemande spécialisée *auto motor und sport* à son article sur le 35e Grand Prix de Monaco, le 22 mai 1977. Le petit chaperon rouge – c'est Niki Lauda avec son spectaculaire casque rouge dans sa Ferrari 312 T2. Et le loup (*Wolf* en allemand) est, d'après le nom de son propriétaire, la voiture du riche homme d'affaires Walter Wolf, qui se paye le luxe d'une propre écurie de Formule 1 par pur plaisir et par passion. Une écurie où le pilote est rien moins que Jody Scheckter. Mais la comparaison est trompeuse, car c'est en réalité l'Autrichien qui pourchassera le Sud-Africain et celui-ci s'avérera pratiquement inattaquable : deuxième meilleur temps aux essais, en tête de bout en bout et record du tour en course tout cela dans une voiture flambant neuf au sein d'une équipe qui a gagné son tout premier Grand Prix, en janvier en Argentine.

Scheckter doit néanmoins se battre sur chaque mètre et il le fait avec son inimitable esprit d'attaquant. Il est tout d'abord attaqué par John Watson, dont la Brabham BT 45 B détenait la pole position. Son moteur Alfa Romeo est absolument idéal pour ce circuit si spécifique, avec sa souplesse et ses reprises dès les bas régimes, un atout déterminant sur ce circuit plus sinueux et étroit que tous les autres. Mais il a le handicap d'un poids élevé et d'un encombrement conséquent. A cela s'ajoutent pour Watson des problèmes de boîte de vitesses : au 46e tour, l'Irlandais barbu cherche en vain à enclencher une vitesse et s'engouffre dans l'échappatoire de la chicane. Au cours du 50e tour, la boîte refuse définitivement tout service et après un impressionnant tête-à-queue, la Brabham reste bloquée au milieu de la piste, à Sainte Dévote, une situation bien inconfortable, vu l'essaim bourdonnant de ses poursuivants qui se rapproche.

Pendant ce temps, le loup pourchasse depuis longtemps le petit chaperon rouge. Lauda, le vainqueur de 1975 et 1976, signerait volontiers un hattrick magique et il y parvient presque. 89 centièmes de seconde seulement séparent les deux adversaires à l'arrivée. On n'a encore jamais vu cela à Monaco, tout comme on n'a encore jamais vu que quatre secondes, en tout et pour tout, séparent les pilotes terminant aux quatre places suivantes. Egalement dans un mouchoir, à l'instar des deux hommes de tête : Jochen Mass avec sa McLaren M23 et Mario Andretti au volant de sa Lotus 78, quatrième et cinquième, séparés seulement par 95 centièmes de seconde à l'issue d'une poursuite épique. Autre curiosité, la troisième, et chose encore inédite : le premier tour s'est déroulé sans le moindre incident. Ici, collisions et confrontations dans la chaleur précoce de la lutte sont normalement à l'ordre du jour de ce dimanche de mai.

Chez Ford et Cosworth aussi, on se frotte les mains : c'est la centième victoire en Grand Prix du légendaire huit-cylindres baptisé DFV au cours de sa onzième année de course. D'autres, en revanche, n'arrivent pas à accepter leur destin et en veulent à Dieu et au monde entier. Par exemple James Hunt, dont la McLaren M23, au 26e tour, doit être poussée hors de la piste à Sainte Dévote suite à une panne de moteur. Une fois, lors de ses débuts à Monaco en 1973, le Britannique a terminé neuvième, mais plus jamais depuis il n'a revu le drapeau à damier. Comme si quelqu'un lui avait jeté un mauvais sort.

"Alors, messieurs…" The
many ceremonies surrounding
the Monaco Grand Prix
include instructions to the
marshals. But this is just the
tip of the iceberg. For
nowhere do the men at the
edge of the track receive a
more thorough training than
here.

»Alors, messieurs…« Zu den
zahlreichen Zeremonien des
Großen Preises von Monaco
gehört die Einweisung der
Helfer. Sie ist aber nur das
Tüpfelchen auf dem i. Denn
nirgendwo erhalten die
Männer am Saum der Strecke
eine gründlichere Schulung
als hier.

« Alors, messieurs… » Parmi
les nombreuses cérémonies
du Grand Prix de Monaco
figure l'instruction des
commissaires de piste. Mais
ce n'est plus que le point sur
le i. En effet, nulle part
ailleurs, les hommes qui
bordent les circuits ne sont
mieux formés qu'ici.

N°	DRIVERS		ENTRANTS	CARS	ENGINES	PRACTICE RESULTS	RACE RESULTS
20	**Jody Scheckter**	**RSA**	**Walter Wolf Racing**	**Wolf WR1**	**Cosworth V8 2993 cc**	**2nd: 1'30"27**	**1st: 1h57'52"77**
11	Niki Lauda	A	SEFAC Ferrari S.p.A.	Ferrari 312T2	Ferrari F12 2992 cc	6th: 1'30"76	2nd: 1h57'53"66
12	Carlos Reutemann	RA	SEFAC Ferrari S.p.A.	Ferrari 312T2	Ferrari F12 2992 cc	3rd: 1'30"44	3rd: 1h58'25"57
2	Jochen Mass	D	Marlboro Team Texaco	McLaren M23	Cosworth V8 2993 cc	9th: 1'31"36	4th: 1h58'27"37
5	Mario Andretti	USA	John Player Team Lotus	JPS 17 (Lotus 78)	Cosworth V8 2993 cc	10th: 1'31"50	5th: 1h58'28"32
17	Alan Jones	AUS	Ambrosio Tabatip Shadow	Shadow DN8	Cosworth V8 2993 cc	11th: 1'32"04	6th: 1h58'29"38
26	Jacques Laffite	F	Equipe Ligier Gitanes	Ligier JS7	Matra V12 2993 cc	16th: 1'32"65	7th: 1h58'57"21
19	Vittorio Brambilla	I	Beta Team Surtees	Surtees TS19	Cosworth V8 2993 cc	14th: 1'32"40	8th: 1h59'01"41
16	Riccardo Patrese	I	Ambrosio Tabatip Shadow	Shadow DN8	Cosworth V8 2993 cc	15th: 1'32"52	9th: 75 laps
22	Jacky Ickx	B	Team Tissot Ensign	Ensign N177	Cosworth V8 2993 cc	17th: 1'33"25	10th: 75 laps
34	Jean-Pierre Jarier	F	ATS Racing	ATS (Penske PC4)	Cosworth V8 2993 cc	12th: 1'32"32	11th: 74 laps
24	Rupert Keegan	GB	Penthouse Rizla Racing	Hesketh 308E	Cosworth V8 2993 cc	18th: 1'33"78	12th 73 laps
6	Gunnar Nilsson	S	John Player Team Lotus	JPS 16 (Lotus 78)	Cosworth V8 2993 cc	13th: 1'32"37	R
7	*John Watson*	*RA*	*Martini Racing*	*Brabham BT45B*	*Alfa Romeo F12 2995 cc*	*1st: 1'29"86*	*R*
4	Patrick Depailler	F	Elf Team Tyrrell	Tyrrell P34	Cosworth V8 2993 cc	8th: 1'31"16	R
18	Hans Binder	A	Durex Team Surtees	Surtees TS19	Cosworth V8 2993 cc	19th: 1'33"49	R
28	Emerson Fittipaldi	BR	Copersucar Fittipaldi	Copersucar FD04	Cosworth V8 2993 cc	18th: 1'33"39	R
1	James Hunt	GB	Marlboro Team Texaco	McLaren M23	Cosworth V8 2993 cc	7th: 1'30"85	R
8	Hans Stuck	D	Martini Racing	Brabham BT45B	Alfa Romeo F12 2995 cc	5th: 1'30"73	R
3	Ronnie Peterson	S	Elf Team Tyrrell	Tyrrell P34	Cosworth V8 2993 cc	4th: 1'30"72	R

1

(1) Jochen Mass (McLaren) and (7) Mario Andretti (Lotus). Their duel is one of the highlights of the race. Red danger (2, 4): Carlos Reutemann (Ferrari) follows Scheckter (Wolf) like a shadow; Niki Lauda (Ferrari), the 1977 World Champion, is unwilling to let anyone put one over on him. (3) Jacques Laffite (Ligier) works his way towards to seventh position, while (5) Hunt (McLaren) has to retire on lap 26 with a defective engine. (6) In the heat of battle Patrese's Shadow receives a bump and has to return to the pits for treatment.

(1) Jochen Mass (McLaren) und (7) Mario Andretti (Lotus). Ihr Duell gehört zu den Highlights des Rennens. (2, 4) Rote Gefahr: Carlos Reutemann (Ferrari) folgt Scheckter (Wolf) bald wie ein Schatten; Niki Lauda (Ferrari), der Weltmeister von 1977, ist nicht gewillt, sich die Butter vom Brot nehmen zu lassen. (3) Jacques Laffite (Ligier) arbeitet sich auf Rang sieben vor, während (5) Hunt (McLaren) in der 26. Runde mit defektem Motor ausscheidet. (6) In der Hitze des Gefechts hat sich Patreses Shadow eine Blessur zugezogen und muß zwecks ambulanter Behandlung an die Box.

(1) Jochen Mass (McLaren) et (7) Mario Andretti (Lotus). Leur duel fera date cette année-là. Le péril rouge (2, 4) : Carlos Reutemann (Ferrari) suit bientôt Scheckter (Wolf) comme son ombre ; Niki Lauda (Ferrari), le champion du monde de 1977, n'est pas disposé à se laisser impressionner. (3) Jacques Laffite (Ligier) remonte jusqu'à la septième place, tandis que (5) Hunt (McLaren) abandonne au 26e tour sur panne de moteur. (6) Dans la chaleur du combat, Patrese a endommagé sa Shadow et doit la faire réparer sommairement aux stands.

2

3

4

5

6

7

4

(1) Poor as a church mouse and yet in the best of moods: Harald Ertl from Zell am See in his Hesketh. Talking to the ladies: (2) Emerson Fittipaldi and (3) Gunnar Nilsson. (4) Jody Scheckter receiving his prize.

(1) Arm wie eine Kirchenmaus und dennoch guter Dinge: Harald Ertl aus Zell am See auf seinem Hesketh. Dialog mit Damen: (2) Emerson Fittipaldi und (3) Gunnar Nilsson. (4) Jody Scheckter bei der Siegerehrung.

(1) Pauvre comme un rat d'église et pourtant toujours de bonne humeur : Harald Ertl, de Zell am See, assis sur sa Hesketh. Bavardage avec dames : (2) Emerson Fittipaldi et (3) Gunnar Nilsson. (4) Jody Scheckter lors de la remise de la coupe.

1978

The received wisdom stated it was extremely improbable to have a winner starting from anywhere but the privileged position of the first two rows. This was a lesson taught by logic and history, said Ken Tyrrell thoughtfully before the 36th Monaco Grand Prix. The experiment of his designer Derek Gardner with the six-wheeled P 34 had come to a dead end. The design of the 008 type could not have been more conventional and the cars were being driven by the Tyrrell recruits Patrick Depailler and Didier Pironi from rows seven and three. The best cars in the best positions had 12-cylinder engines – the Ferrari 312 T3 of Carlos Reutemann and the two Brabham-Alfa BT 46s in which John Watson and Niki Lauda waited for the green light.

But, for the fourth time at Monaco in the history of the F1 World Championship, it was the Marseillaise that was heard at the end; Depailler had proved his boss wrong and made the seemingly impossible happen. A modicum of luck did play a helping hand, for example at the first bend on the first lap, which paved the way for the eventual result. At the top of the incline going up to the little church of Sainte Dévote, the Frenchman moved into second place, while to his rear, the front right spoiler of Lauda's Brabham bore into the rear wheels of Reutemann's Ferrari. James Hunt's hatred for the tiny feudal state was fuelled further when the geometry of his McLaren M 26 moved right out of alignment when he, in the general confusion, crashed into the barrier on the right. However, out at the front, John Watson sped away and was only two and a half seconds behind Depailler, but he put his brakes under too much strain and his car's inherent weight problem was added to at the beginning by having a full petrol tank for his thirsty 12-cylinder engine. On the thirty-ninth lap, he had to take the emergency exit at the chicane, with the result that Depailler and Lauda scuttled past. For seven laps, the little man from Clermont-Ferrand did not have a moment's respite. The man from Vienna exerted pressure mercilessly until he had to stop at his pit for a second time to have two new tyres fitted. This period spent off the track cost him four places, but he redoubled his efforts and went on the attack once again. Driving like a man possessed, Lauda eventually pulled back to second place.

Meanwhile, Watson found himself in the claws of the trio comprising Gilles Villeneuve (Ferrari T3), Jody Scheckter (Wolf WR 1) and Ronnie Peterson (Lotus 78), who were waging a furious battle with one another. The Irishman's problems were partially resolved when transmission damage put the Swede out of the race on lap 57, and an accident, in the tunnel of all places, halted the cool Canadian on lap 64. The thought went through his head as his Ferrari lost a wheel, "Hell, I'm losing valuable World Championship points here."

The Frenchman Jean-Pierre Jabouille, who finished in tenth place, deserved special praise. His Renault RS 01 was as out of place in Monaco as a dolphin on a warm beach: the useful engine speed range of the turbo engine he was using in his first full season was so narrow that he had to change gears 37 times per lap, which meant a total of 2,414 times during the race.

Daß jemand dieses Rennen gewinne, der nicht das Privileg der ersten beiden Startreihen genieße, sei äußerst unwahrscheinlich. Das lehrten die Logik und die Geschichte, sagt Ken Tyrrell vor dem 36. Grand Prix von Monaco nachdenklich. Das Experiment seines Konstrukteurs Derek Gardner mit dem sechsrädrigen P 34 ist in einer Sackgasse geendet, durch und durch konventionell das Design des Typs 008, mit dem die Tyrrell-Rekruten Patrick Depailler und Didier Pironi in Reihe drei und Reihe sieben stehen. Die besten unter den Logenplätzen haben Zwölfzylinder inne, der Ferrari 312 T3 von Carlos Reutemann und die beiden Brabham-Alfa BT 46, in denen John Watson und Niki Lauda auf grünes Licht warten.

Am Ende aber erklingt, in Monaco zum vierten Mal in der Geschichte der neueren Formel 1, die Marseillaise. Depailler hat seinen Chef widerlegt und das schier Unmögliche möglich gemacht. Ein Quentchen Glück war auch dabei, an der ersten Kurve in der ersten Runde zum Beispiel, wo der künftige Ausgang schon ein bißchen vorsortiert wird. Auf der Höhe des Kirchleins Sainte Dévote trifft der Franzose bereits auf Position zwei ein, während hinter ihm der rechte Vorderflügel von Laudas Brabham den linken Hinterreifen von Reutemanns Ferrari anbohrt und James Hunts Haß auf den winzigen Feudalstaat neue Nahrung erhält: Die Geometrie seines McLaren M 26 gerät aus dem Lot, als er im allgemeinen Getümmel und Gefummel die Leitplanke rechts anschrammt. Vorn aber enteilt John Watson, legt bis zu zweieinhalb Sekunden zwischen sich und Depailler, überfordert allerdings die Bremsen seines Wagens, zu dessen natürlichem Übergewicht sich anfänglich das volle Spritreservoir für das durstige Dutzend seiner Zylinder gesellt. In der 39. Runde muß er den Notausgang an der Schikane in Anspruch nehmen, so daß Depailler und Lauda vorbeiwieseln. Sieben Runden lang kommt der kleine Mann aus Clermont-Ferrand nicht zur Ruhe. Denn der Wiener macht gnadenlos Druck, bis er zum zweiten Mal die Box anlaufen muß, um zwei neue Reifen zu fassen. Dieser einstweilige Ruhestand kostet ihn vier Plätze und stachelt seinen Ehrgeiz erneut an: Wie ein Berserker fahrend, landet Lauda auf Rang zwei.

Unterdessen ist Watson in die Klauen des wütend miteinander ringenden Trios Gilles Villeneuve (Ferrari T3), Jody Scheckter (Wolf WR 1) und Ronnie Peterson (Lotus 78) geraten. Zum Teil lösen sich die Probleme des Iren von selbst: Der Schwede fällt in Runde 57 mit Getriebeschaden aus, der unerschrockene Kanadier im 64. Durchgang durch einen Unfall ausgerechnet im Tunnel: »Teufel«, schießt es ihm durch den Kopf, während sein Ferrari ein Rad abstreift, »jetzt gehen mir wertvolle Weltmeisterschaftspunkte verloren.«

Ein besonderes Lob aber gebührt dem Franzosen Jean-Pierre Jabouille auf Rang 10, dessen Renault RS 01 in Monaco fehl am Platze ist wie ein Delphin auf einem heißen Strand: So schmal ist der nutzbare Drehzahlbereich seines Turbo-Triebwerks in seiner ersten vollen Saison, daß er 37 Mal pro Runde schalten muß, 2414 Mal insgesamt.

A Monaco, il est extrêmement improbable que quelqu'un puisse gagner cette course s'il n'a pas le privilège de figurer sur l'une des deux premières lignes de départ. Telles sont les lois de la logique et de l'histoire, déclare Ken Tyrrell, le front soucieux, avant le 36e Grand Prix de Monaco. L'expérience de son constructeur Derek Gardner avec la P 34 à six roues s'est terminée en queue de poisson et sa nouvelle Tyrrell 008 que les deux pilotes français Patrick Depailler et Didier Pironi ont placée en troisième et septième ligne est d'une architecture absolument conventionnelle. Les meilleurs aux places de loge ont sous leur capot un douze-cylindres, la Ferrari 312 T3 de Carlos Reutemann et les deux Brabham-Alfa BT 46 dans lesquelles John Watson et Niki Lauda attendent impatiemment le feu vert.

Mais, à la fin, pour la quatrième fois dans l'histoire du championnat du monde de Formule 1 à Monaco, c'est la Marseillaise que l'on entendra retentir. Contredisant son chef d'écurie, Depailler a rendu possible ce qui semblait absolument impossible. Un peu de chance était aussi de son côté quand, au premier virage du premier tour, par exemple, la future issue de la course commença déjà à prendre forme. A hauteur de la petite chapelle de Sainte Dévote, le Français est déjà deuxième tandis que, derrière lui, l'aileron avant droit de la Brabham de Lauda cisaille le pneu arrière gauche de la Ferrari de Reutemann et que la haine de James Hunt contre le minuscule Etat princier s'aggrave encore : il tord la suspension avant droite de sa McLaren M 26 lorsque, pour échapper au chaos général, il frôle de trop près les glissières de sécurité. Pendant ce temps, en fait, John Watson s'envole et a jusqu'à deux secondes et demie d'avance sur Depailler, mais il en demande trop aux freins de sa voiture, d'autant plus qu'à l'embonpoint naturel de cette dernière s'ajoute, au début, le réservoir d'essence plein à ras bord pour son glouton douze-cylindres. Au 39e tour, il est contraint de prendre l'échappatoire à la chicane, si bien que Depailler et Lauda s'engouffrent dans le passage laissé vide. Pendant sept tours, le petit pilote de Clermont-Ferrand doit se battre comme un lion, car le Viennois ne relâche pas un instant sa pression avant de devoir s'arrêter aux stands pour la deuxième fois afin de monter deux pneus neufs. Cet arrêt forcé lui coûte quatre places et ne fait qu'attiser encore plus son ambition : pilotant le couteau entre les dents, Lauda récupère finalement sa deuxième place.

Entre-temps, Watson s'est retrouvé dans les griffes d'un trio de pilotes déchaînés : Gilles Villeneuve (Ferrari T3), Jody Scheckter (Wolf WR 1) et Ronnie Peterson (Lotus 78). Les problèmes de l'Irlandais se résolvent en partie d'eux-mêmes : au 57e tour, le Suédois doit abandonner sur panne de boîte de vitesses et le Canadien sans peur et sans reproches, au 64e tour, lors d'un accident survenu comme par hasard dans le tunnel : « Bon Dieu », ce sont les mots qui lui traversent l'esprit tandis que sa Ferrari boitille sur trois roues, « encore de précieux points qui s'envolent au championnat du monde. »

Quant au pilote français Jean-Pierre Jabouille, qui termine dixième, il mérite tous les éloges, car sa Renault RS 01 est autant à sa place à Monaco qu'un dauphin le serait sur un banc de sable brûlant : la plage de régime utilisable de son moteur turbo est si mince, durant sa première saison complète, qu'il doit changer de vitesse 37 fois par tour, donc 2414 fois au total.

Everyday life in Monaco: two-way traffic at Mirabeau – which appears strange to anyone who only knows the Principality as a Grand Prix circuit.

Monegassischer Alltag: Gegenverkehr bei Mirabeau – das mutet alle sonderbar an, die das Fürstentum lediglich als Grand-Prix-Piste kennen.

Le quotidien de Monaco : circulation dans les deux sens à Mirabeau – cela étonnera tous ceux qui ne connaissent la Principauté que comme circuit de Grand Prix.

N°	DRIVERS		ENTRANTS	CARS	ENGINES	PRACTICE RESULTS	RACE RESULTS
4	**Patrick Depailler**	**F**	**Elf Team Tyrrell**	**Tyrrell 008**	**Cosworth V8 2993 cc**	**5th: 1'29"14**	**1st:1h55'14"66**
1	Niki Lauda	A	Parmalat Racing Team	Brabham BT46	Alfa Romeo F12 2995 cc	3rd: 1'28"84	2nd:1h55'37"11
20	Jody Scheckter	RSA	Walter Wolf Racing	Wolf WR1	Cosworth V8 2993 cc	9th: 1'29"50	3rd:1h55'46"95
2	John Watson	GB	Parmalat Racing Team	Brabham BT46	Alfa Romeo F12 2995 cc	2nd: 1'28"83	4th:1h55'48"19
3	Didier Pironi	F	Elf Team Tyrrell	Tyrrell 008	Cosworth V8 2993 cc	13th: 1'30"55	5th:1h56'22"72
35	Riccardo Patrese	I	Arrows Racing Team	Arrows FA1	Cosworth V8 2993 cc	14th: 1'30"59	6th:1h56'23"43
8	Patrick Tambay	F	Marlboro Team Texaco	McLaren M26	Cosworth V8 2993 cc	11th: 1'30"8	7th:74 laps
11	*Carlos Reutemann*	A	*SEFAC Ferrari S.p.A.*	*Ferrari 312T3*	*Ferrari F12 2992 cc*	*1st: 1'28"34*	*8th: 74 laps*
14	Emerson Fittipaldi	BR	Fittipaldi Automotive	Fittipaldi F5A	Cosworth V8 2993 cc	20th: 1'31"36	9th: 74 laps
15	Jean-Pierre Jabouille	F	Equipe Renault Elf	Renault RS01	Renault V6 1492 cc + T	12th: 1'30"18	10th:71 laps
5	Mario Andretti	USA	John Player Team Lotus	JPS 17 (Lotus 78)	Cosworth V8 2993 cc	4th: 1'29"10	11th: 69 laps (R)
12	Gilles Villeneuve	CDN	SEFAC Ferrari S.p.A.	Ferrari 312T3	Ferrari F12 2992 cc	8th: 1'29"40	R
6	Ronnie Peterson	S	John Player Team Lotus	JPS 16 (Lotus 78)	Cosworth V8 2993 cc	7th: 1'29"23	R
7	James Hunt	GB	Marlboro Team Texaco	McLaren M26	Cosworth V8 2993 cc	6th: 1'29"22	R
36	Rolf Stommelen	D	Arrows Racing Team	Arrows FA1	Cosworth V8 2993 cc	18th(19): 1'31"31	R
27	Alan Jones	AUS	Williams Grand Prix	Williams FW06	Cosworth V8 2993 cc	10th: 1'29"51	R
22	Jacky Ickx	B	Team Tissot Ensign	Ensign N177	Cosworth V8 2993 cc	16th: 1'30"72	R
16	Hans Stuck	D	Villiger Shadow Racing Team	Shadow DN9	Cosworth V8 2993 cc	17th: 1'31"30	R
26	Jacques Laffite	F	Equipe Ligier Gitanes	Ligier JS9	Matra V12 2993 cc	15th: 1'30"60	R
18	Rupert Keegan	GB	Durex/BAF Team Surtees	Surtees TS19	Cosworth V8 2993 cc	18th: 1'31"31	R

(1) First, despite starting from the third row of the grid: Depailler (Tyrrell). (2) Second, despite problems with a tire: Lauda (Brabham). (3) Third, despite loss of third gear three laps before the end: Scheckter (Wolf). (4) Out of place but still placed: Jabouille in the Renault Turbo. (5) Faster than fast: Villeneuve (Ferrari), who will end the race on three wheels.

(1) Erster trotz Starts aus der dritten Reihe: Depailler (Tyrrell). (2) Zweiter trotz einer Reifenpanne: Lauda (Brabham). (3) Dritter trotz Verlust des dritten Gangs drei Runden vor Schluß: Scheckter (Wolf). (4) Deplaziert und dennoch plaziert: Jabouille im Renault-Turbo. (5) Wildfang: Villeneuve (Ferrari), der das Rennen auf drei Rädern beenden wird.

(1) Premier malgré un départ en troisième ligne : Depailler (Tyrrell). (2) Deuxième malgré une crevaison : Lauda (Brabham). (3) Troisième malgré une troisième vitesse en grève à trois tours du drapeau à damier : Scheckter (Wolf). (4) Déplacé et pourtant placé : Jabouille sur Renault-Turbo. (5) Abîmé : Villeneuve (Ferrari), qui terminera la course sur trois roues.

(1) Showing off: Lamborghini Countach. (2) The red and white colors of Marlboro are the constants of Grand Prix racing, so that even the markings at the edge of the track (4) act as advertising. (3) Jackie Stewart as speeding cameraman. There can be no doubt for whom he is driving.

(1) Zur Schau gestellt: Lamborghini Countach. (2) Das Rotweiß von Marlboro gehört zu den Konstanten im Grand-Prix-Sport, so daß sogar von der Abweiskante Werbewirkung ausgeht (4). (3) Jackie Stewart als rasender Kameramann. Kein Zweifel, für wen er unterwegs ist.

(1) Exposée : Lamborghini Countach. (2) Le rouge et le blanc de Marlboro sont l'une des constantes des courses de Grand Prix, si bien que même (4) le bord de piste a un effet publicitaire. (3) Jackie Stewart en cameraman pressé. Il n'y a pas de doutes quant à son sponsor.

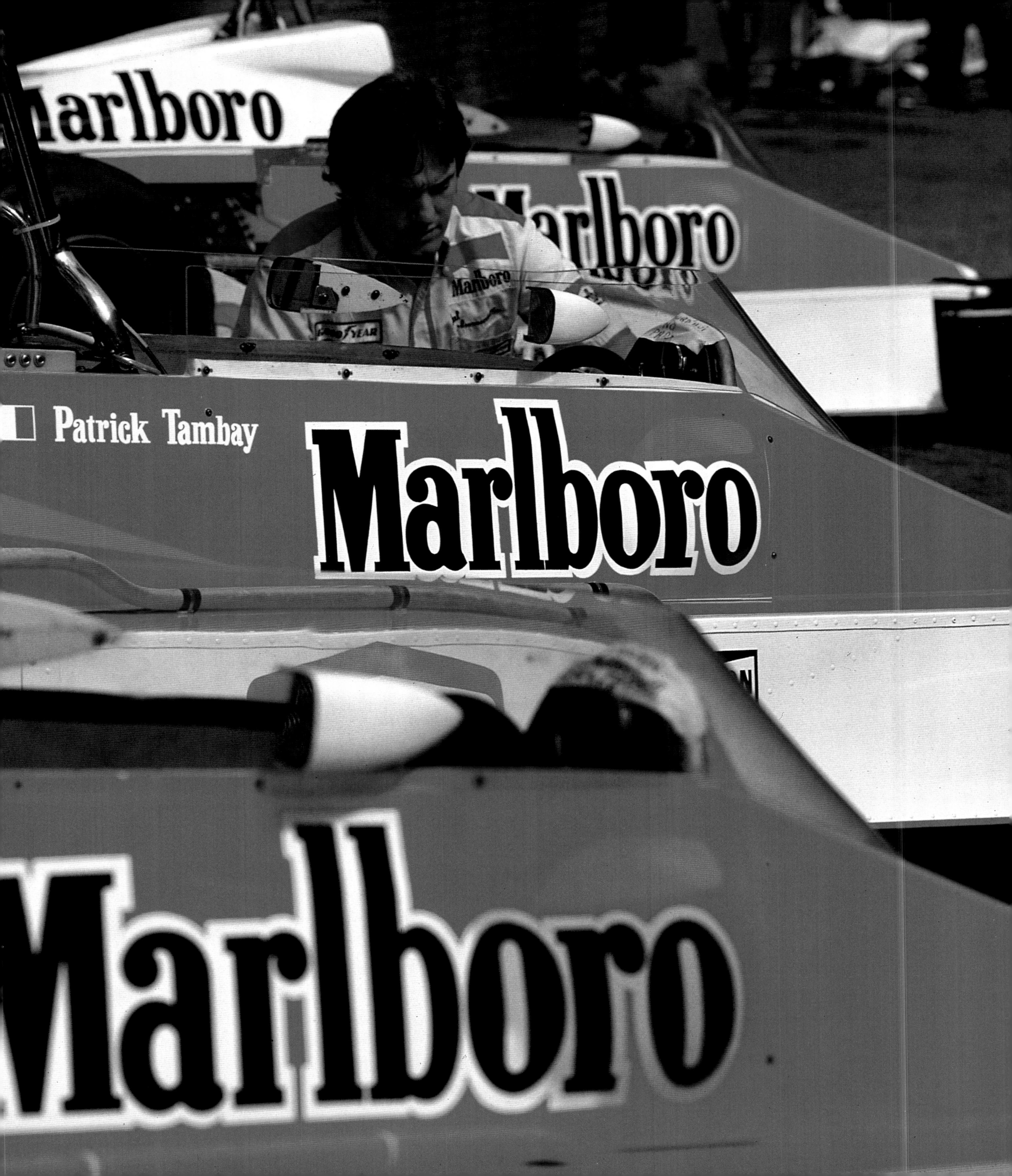
Marlboro
Marlboro
Patrick Tambay
Marlboro
Marlboro

Jody Scheckter

Walter Wolf

Emerson Fittipaldi

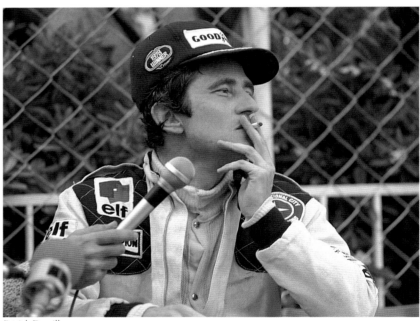

Patrick Depailler

Gilles Villeneuve (left/links/à gauche : Mauro Forghieri)

Niki Lauda

Patrick Depailler collects the first of his two Grand Prix victories in Monaco in 1978. His second occurs in the following season in Jarama. One year after that, in Hockenheim, the popular little Frenchman gives the sport his most valuable possession – his life.

In Monaco holt sich Patrick Depailler 1978 den ersten seiner beiden Grand-Prix-Siege. Der zweite stellt sich in der folgenden Saison in Jarama ein. Wieder ein Jahr später, in Hockenheim, opfert der populäre kleine Franzose seinem Sport das Teuerste, was er hat – sein Leben.

A Monaco, en 1978, Patrick Depailler signe la première de ses deux victoires en Grand Prix. La seconde, il l'obtiendra un an plus tard à Jarama. Et, de nouveau un an plus tard, à Hockenheim, le populaire petit Français offrira à son sport ce qu'il a de plus précieux – sa vie.

1979

In 1979, it was the 50th anniversary of the Monaco Grand Prix, despite the gaps in its history. In the supporting programme there was an historic race reuniting antique cars from half a century of automotive construction. The Mercedes W 125 of the British collector Colin Crabbe filled the Principality's streets with nostalgic echoes and a love of things big, spurred by a reminder of the bizarre noises and exotic smells of the compressor engines of the Thirties. And the indestructible Louis Chiron – with his baseball cap jauntily worn back-to-front – drove the Bugatti 51 as if time had been standing still since 1931.

In the starting line-up for the Grand Prix, the spirit of the new age reappeared, the first row all in red and the last in uniform yellow. This was because the 12-cylinder flat engines of the Ferrari 312 T4s driven by Jody Scheckter and Gilles Villeneuve seemed tailor-made for Monaco, unlike the V6 turbo engines of the Renault RS 10s for René Arnoux and Jean-Pierre Jabouille, which seemed to be completely out of place.

At the start, the Jody and Gilles show, which had been dominating the sport that year, seemed to have taken center stage once again. As had happened so frequently, the small Canadian was hot on the heels of the bear-like South African, giving rise to the suspicion that their team was choreographing the event. The only disruption came in the early stages from Niki Lauda, who threaded his way between the two for the first two laps in his Brabham-Alfa BT 48, which was now 30 kg heavier. He then fell back to the head of the serpentine collection of cars made up of Patrick Depailler and Jacques Laffite in the Ligiers, Didier Pironi in the Tyrrell 009 and Alan Jones with the Williams FW 07. A double victory loomed for Ferrari until Villeneuve left the race in the fifty-fourth lap with a broken drive-shaft.

In the meantime, Pironi turned out to be the villain of the piece: a tussle on lap 19 with Depailler in the full view of the jam-packed Loews hotel balcony cost him ten places, and three laps later an encounter with Lauda at Mirabeau marked the end of the race for the two opponents. Laffite's first setback took the form of a tyre problem, and he had to leave the race on lap 56 with damaged transmission. Then Clay Regazzoni appeared from the back and drew inexorably closer in his Williams. In qualifying, he only managed to make it as far as sixteenth place, but now the man from Lugano was unstoppable, whilst Scheckter, who was in the lead, kept a watchful eye on his tyres. Ten laps from the end, the Williams closed in on the Ferrari, trailing it by only ten seconds, and what had appeared in Scheckter's rear-view mirrors as a tiny dot constantly grew larger. On the last lap, the green-and-white car occasionally edged its nose under the transmission of the Ferrari, but Regazzoni's tricks and ruses were to no avail. The order did not change, although the distance between the first two cars of just 0.44 seconds on the finishing line was the tightest yet. Meanwhile, Gilles Villeneuve received solace for his lost victory in the arms of his wife Joann.

Im Jahr 1979 würdigt man den 50. Geburtstag des Grand Prix de Monaco trotz der Lücken, die in seiner Chronologie klaffen. Ein historisches Rennen im Vorprogramm vereint automobile Zeitzeugen aus einem halben Jahrhundert. So erfüllt der Mercedes W 125 des britischen Sammlers Colin Crabbe die Häuserschluchten des Fürstentums mit dem Geist der Gigantomanie sowie den irrwitzigen Geräuschen und exotischen Gerüchen der Kompressortriebwerke der Dreißiger. Und der schier unverwüstliche Louis Chiron – die Schlägermütze keck nach hinten gekehrt – dreht seine Runden im Bugatti 51, als sei seit 1931 die Uhr stehengeblieben.

In der Startaufstellung zum Großen Preis indessen bildet sich getreulich der Geist der neuen Zeit ab. Die erste Reihe leuchtet ganz in Rot, die letzte einheitlich in Gelb. Denn die Zwölfzylinder-Boxermotoren der Ferrari 312 T4 von Jody Scheckter und Gilles Villeneuve scheinen wie geschaffen für Monaco, die V6-Turbomotoren der Renault RS 10 für René Arnoux und Jean-Pierre Jabouille dagegen gänzlich deplaziert.

Zunächst sieht alles nach der für jenes Jahr typischen Jody-und Gilles-Show aus. Wie so häufig folgt der kleine Kanadier dem bärigen Südafrikaner auf dem Fuße, so daß der Verdacht aufkeimt, hier sei Stallregie im Spiel. Nur für etwas mehr als zwei Runden fädelt sich anfänglich Niki Lauda mit seinem um etwa 30 Kilogramm schwereren Brabham-Alfa BT 48 zwischen den beiden ein und fällt dann zurück an die Spitze einer Verfolgergruppe, in der sich Patrick Depailler und Jacques Laffite auf Ligier, Didier Pironi auf Tyrrell 009 und Alan Jones mit dem Williams FW 07 zusammengefunden haben. Schon zeichnet sich ein Ferrari-Doppelsieg ab, da rollt Villeneuve in der 54. Runde mit gebrochener Antriebswelle aus.

In der Zwischenzeit hat sich Pironi als hemdsärmeliger Schurke dieser Veranstaltung profiliert: Eine Rempelei im 19. Durchgang mit Depailler angesichts der prall gefüllten Balkons des Loews-Hotels kostet diesen zehn Plätze, und drei Runden später bedeutet ein Renkontre mit Lauda bei Mirabeau das Aus für beide Kontrahenten. Laffite wird zunächst von einer Reifenpanne zurückgeworfen und bleibt in Runde 56 mit Getriebeschaden auf der Strecke. Da nähert sich schon unaufhaltsam aus der Tiefe des Raumes Williams-Pilot Clay Regazzoni. Nur zum 16. Rang hat es im Training gereicht. Aber nun ist der Mann aus Lugano nicht zu bremsen, während Scheckter an der Spitze ein wachsames Auge auf seine Reifen behält. Zehn Runden vor Schluß hat sich der Williams dem Ferrari bis auf zehn Sekunden genähert, erscheint in dessen Rückspiegeln bereits als Pünktchen und macht sich immer mehr breit. Im letzten Durchgang schiebt der grünweiße Wagen stellenweise seine Nase unter das Getriebe des roten. Doch Regazzonis Tricks, Finten und Finessen verfangen nicht: Die Reihenfolge der beiden ersten bleibt dieselbe, ihr Abstand von 44 Hundertstelsekunden im Ziel der knappste bislang. Gilles Villeneuve aber tröstet sich im Arm seiner Frau Joann.

En 1979, la Principauté célèbre le cinquantenaire du Grand Prix de Monaco malgré certaines lacunes dans sa chronologie. Une course historique en lever de rideau réunit les témoins de l'automobile d'un demi-siècle. Ainsi la Mercedes W 125 du collectionneur britannique Colin Crabbe fait-elle planer dans les rues de la Principauté l'esprit de la gigantomanie et, à force de réminiscences, les bruits assourdissants et les odeurs exotiques des moteurs à compresseur des années trente. Et l'apparemment inusable Louis Chiron – la visière de sa casquette effrontément glissée sur la nuque – accomplit ses tours en Bugatti 51 comme si le temps s'était arrêté en 1931.

La grille de départ du Grand Prix, par contre, reflète fidèlement l'esprit des temps modernes. La première ligne est tout en rouge comme la dernière est tout en jaune. En effet, les boxers douze-cylindres des Ferrari 312 T4 de Jody Scheckter et Gilles Villeneuve semblent prédestinés pour Monaco alors que les moteurs V6 turbo des Renault RS 10 de René Arnoux et Jean-Pierre Jabouille apparaissent vraiment déplacés.

Au début, tout semble se dérouler selon le scénario typique, cette année-là, du show de Jody et Gilles. Comme si souvent, le petit Canadien suit le taciturne Sud-Africain comme son ombre, à tel point que l'on commence à croire qu'il s'agit d'une stratégie convenue. Pendant les deux premiers tours, Niki Lauda s'insère, au début, entre les deux hommes avec sa Brabham-Alfa BT 48 plus lourde d'une trentaine de kilos avant de se retrouver en tête d'une file de voitures se composant de Patrick Depailler et Jacques Laffite sur Ligier, de Didier Pironi sur Tyrrell 009 et d'Alan Jones sur Williams FW 07. Alors que l'on s'attend déjà à un doublé Ferrari, Villeneuve laisse sa voiture courir sur son erre au 54e tour, demi-arbre de roue brisé.

Entre-temps, Pironi a fait le vide autour de lui : une collision avec Depailler au 19e tour, juste devant les balcons combles de l'hôtel Loews, coûte dix places à ce dernier et, trois tours plus tard, un nouveau contact, cette fois-ci avec Lauda à Mirabeau, signifie l'abandon des deux adversaires. Laffite perd tout d'abord plusieurs places à la suite d'une crevaison avant de devoir garer sa voiture en panne de boîte de vitesses durant le 56e tour. C'est alors que, irrésistible, Clay Regazzoni, sur sa Williams, remonte des profondeurs du classement. Il se trouvait en effet à la seizième place de la grille de départ. Mais, maintenant, rien ne pourrait freiner l'homme de Lugano pendant que Scheckter, en tête, ne quitte pas de l'œil ses pneumatiques. A dix tours de la fin, la Williams s'est rapprochée jusqu'à dix secondes de la Ferrari, petit point blanc dans ses rétroviseurs qui ne cesse de grandir de plus en plus vite. Au dernier tour, la voiture blanche et verte vient même flairer la boîte de vitesses de la rouge. Mais toutes les astuces, attaques et tentatives de Regazzoni restent vaines : le classement des deux premiers hommes ne changera plus même si leur écart d'à peine 44 centièmes de seconde à l'arrivée sera le plus réduit à ce jour. Quant à Gilles Villeneuve, il est allé se consoler dans les bras de sa femme Joann.

Place of pilgrimage for nocturnal revellers, particularly when the Grand Prix is taking place: the Tip-Top bar to the left of the slope down to Mirabeau.

Wallfahrtsort für Nacht-schwärmer, besonders zur Zeit des Grand Prix: die Tip-Top-Bar links vom Gefälle nach Mirabeau.

Pèlerinage pour noctambules, en particulier à l'époque du Grand Prix : « le bar le Tip-Top » à gauche dans la descente vers Mirabeau.

N°	DRIVERS		ENTRANTS	CARS	ENGINES	PRACTICE RESULTS	RACE RESULTS
11	*Jody Scheckter*	*RSA*	*SEFAC Ferrari S.p.A.*	*Ferrari 312T4*	*Ferrari F12 2992 cc*	*1st: 1'26"45*	*1st: 1h55'22"48*
28	Clay Regazzoni	CH	Albilad-Saudia Racing Team	Williams FW07	Cosworth V8 2993 cc	16th: 1'28"48	2nd: 1h55'22"92
2	Carlos Reutemann	RA	Martini Racing Team Lotus	Lotus 79	Cosworth V8 2993 cc	11th: 1'27"99	3rd: 1h55'31"05
7	John Watson	GB	Marlboro Team Texaco	McLaren M28C	Cosworth V8 2993 cc	13th(14): 1'28"23	4th: 1h56'03"79
25	Patrick Depailler	F	Equipe Ligier Gitanes	Ligier JS11	Cosworth V8 2993 cc	3rd: 1'27"11	5th: 74 laps
30	Jochen Mass	D	Warsteiner Arrows Racing Team	Arrows A1	Cosworth V8 2993 cc	8th: 1'27"47	6th: 69 laps (R)
15	Jean-Pierre Jabouille	F	Equipe Renault Elf	Renault RS11	Renault V6 1492 cc + T	20th: 1'28"68	NC: 68 laps
6	Nelson Piquet	BR	Parmalat Racing Team	Brabham BT48	Alfa Romeo F12 2995 cc	18th: 1'28"52	R
26	Jacques Laffite	F	Equipe Ligier Gitanes	Ligier JS11	Cosworth V8 2993 cc	5th: 1'27"26	R
12	Gilles Villeneuve	CDN	SEFAC Ferrari S.p.A.	Ferrari 312T4	Ferrari F12 2992 cc	2nd: 1'26"52	R
27	Alan Jones	AUS	Albilad-Saudia Racing Team	Williams FW07	Cosworth V8 2993 cc	9th: 1'27"67	R
4	Jean-Pierre Jarier	F	Team Tyrrell	Tyrrell 009	Cosworth V8 2993 cc	6th: 1'27"42	R
9	Hans Stuck	D	ATS Wheels	ATS D2	Cosworth V8 2993 cc	12th: 1'28"22	R
5	Niki Lauda	A	Parmalat Racing Team	Brabham BT48	Alfa Romeo F12 2995 cc	4th: 1'27"21	R
3	Didier Pironi	F	Team Tyrrell	Tyrrell 009	Cosworth V8 2993 cc	6th(7): 1'27"42	R
1	Mario Andretti	USA	Martini Racing Team Lotus	Lotus 80	Cosworth V8 2993 cc	13th: 1'28"23	R
14	Emerson Fittipaldi	BR	Fittipaldi Automotive	Fittipaldi F5A	Cosworth V8 2993 cc	17th: 1'28"49	R
16	René Arnoux	F	Equipe Renault Elf	Renault RS10	Renault V6 1492 cc + T	19th: 1'28"57	R
20	James Hunt	GB	Olympus Cameras Wolf Racing	Wolf WR7	Cosworth V8 2993 cc	10th: 1'27"96	R
29	Riccardo Patrese	I	Warsteiner Arrows Racing Team	Arrows A1	Cosworth V8 2993 cc	15th: 1'28"30	R

(1) Left turn at the new Loews Hotel: the Brabham functions so well as a wing car that there is no need for front wings. (2) The driver sits very far forward in the Ferrari 312 T4. (3) Very close at the end: Regazzoni (Williams). (4) Fighting against the vagaries of technology: Laffite (Ligier).

(1) Nach links um die Ecke am neuen Loews-Hotel: So gut funktioniert der Brabham als Wing Car, daß auf die Frontflügel verzichtet werden kann. (2) Ganz weit vorn sitzt der Pilot im Ferrari 312 T4. (3) Am Ende ganz nahe: Regazzoni (Williams). (4) Im Kampf auch gegen die Tücken der Technik: Laffite (Ligier).

(1) A gauche du tournant de l'Hôtel Loews : la Brabham fonctionne si bien comme wing-car qu'elle peut se passer d'aileron avant. (2) Dans la Ferrari 312 T4, le pilote est assis tout à l'avant. (3) A la fin, encore plus près : Regazzoni (Williams). (4) Se bat également contre les mystères de la mécanique : Laffite (Ligier).

Four-second episode: (1–3) the cars tackle the right-hand bend approaching the virage du Portier. (4) Unclassified, since he covered less than 90 percent of the winner's distance: Jean-Pierre Jabouille in the Renault Turbo.

Vier-Sekunden-Spuk: (1–3) die Wagen im Rechtsknick vor der Virage du Portier. (4) Nicht gewertet, denn er hat weniger als 90 Prozent der Distanz des Siegers zurückgelegt: Jean-Pierre Jabouille im Renault-Turbo.

Une affaire de quatre secondes : (1–3) les voitures dans le virage à droite précédant le virage du Portier. (4) Pas classé, car il n'a pas couvert 90 % de la distance du vainqueur : Jean-Pierre Jabouille sur Renault-Turbo.

Bad boy: Pironi emerges unharmed from a fight with Niki Lauda for the same piece of tarmac on lap 22. But his car does not escape unscathed – something which the tight-fisted Ken Tyrrell does not like at all.

Böser Bube: Aus einem Zwist mit Niki Lauda um dasselbe Stück Straße in der 22. Runde geht Pironi unversehrt hervor. Aber sein Auto läßt Federn – etwas, was der knauserige Ken Tyrrell gar nicht liebt.

Mauvais garçon : Didier Pironi sort vainqueur d'un démêlé avec Niki Lauda pour le même morceau de trajectoire au 22e tour. Mais sa voiture y laisse des plumes – ce que l'avare Ken Tyrrell n'aime vraiment pas du tout.

Impressions from behind the lines: (1) still life with (John Watson's) helmet, (2) a wing with a difference: Renault seen from behind, (3) gears in a box, (4, 5) chaos with suitcases, canisters, crash helmets and an overcrowded pit area.

Impressionen von der Etappe: (1) Stilleben mit (John Watsons) Helm, (2) mehr Luftschacht als Flügel: Renault von achtern gesehen. (3, 5) Getriebe an der Box, (4) Chaos mit Koffern, Kanistern und Crashhelmen.

Impressions de l'étape : (1) nature morte avec le casque de John Watson, (2) aileron à étages : la Renault vue de l'arrière. (3) Boîte de vitesses. (4, 5) Chaos de valises, jerricans, casques et des stands bondés.

Candid camera: (1) the Brabham drivers Piquet and Lauda,
(2) Carlos Reutemann, (3) Jochen Mass, (4) Jean-Paul Belmondo,
(5) anonymous beauty at the edge of the track.

Gruppenbilder mit Dame: (1) die Brabham-Piloten Piquet und
Lauda, (2) Carlos Reutemann, (3) Jochen Mass, (4) Jean-Paul
Belmondo, (5) anonyme Schönheit am Rande der Piste.

Photos de groupe avec dame : (1) les pilotes Brabham Piquet et
Lauda, (2) Carlos Reutemann, (3) Jochen Mass, (4) Jean-Paul
Belmondo, (5) beauté anonyme au bord de la piste.

1980

In Monaco, especially in the magic square mile around the Casino, the capricious nature of Lady Luck causes her sometimes to smile, sometimes to sulk. This year, men considered to be outside the premier division had their unexpected chances, while some of the season's heroes fell into oblivion during this weekend in May. In 1980, the favorites were the two Ligier JS 11/15 drivers Didier Pironi and Jacques Laffite. Their driving manner was not particularly aesthetic, but theirs was a brutally utilitarian package that was, quite simply, very fast. The Williams FW 07 Bs of Alan Jones and Carlos Reutemann would also, so it would seem, have something to say. This was a perfect mirror-image of the power relationships of the 1980 season, as was the fact that Jody Scheckter, the 1979 World Champion, was right back on the second-last row with his Ferrari 312 T5. What befell René Arnoux, who, after five races, had been tipped as the lead driver on his arrival in the Principality, was enough to break the pain barrier: he and his Renault RE 24 were in the very last place on the 20-car starting grid.

Seconds after the start, four men in the middle of the track seemed to be sunning themselves in the favor of a guardian angel sent specially for the occasion. When braking for the first time at Sainte Dévote, the Tyrrell of the Irishman Derek Daly was catapulted into the air by the right rear wheel of the Bruno Giacomelli's Alfa Romeo, executed a full pirouette, amputated the rear wing of Alain Prost's McLaren and crashed down on the car of his team-mate Jean-Pierre Jarier. Bits of racing car were strewn everywhere on the track. Ken Tyrrell was less than delighted, because the thrifty Briton did not like it when his cars got damaged. The sponsor Candy, on the other hand, was overjoyed by the additional slow-motion footage which the television devoted to this artistic flight interlude. There were no injuries.

Right at the front, Pironi had to fend off Jones' undivided attention, and Laffite attacked Reutemann, who had an unrelenting hold on third place. The time factor came to the aid of them both: on the twenty-fifth lap the Australian's transmission left him in the lurch, and the transmission also had a hand in Pironi's downfall on the fifty-fifth lap. At Mirabeau, the Frenchman's hand slipped as he fumbled for third gear and he dismembered his Ligier on the crash barrier. This all happened at about the time that a few large raindrops began to fall on the track.

From this moment onwards, Reutemann drove on towards his tenth Grand Prix victory, and nothing and no-one stood in his way. In the meantime, Jacques Laffite's brake pedal started to feel spongy, while the way Riccardo Patrese with his Arrows A3 twice forced René Arnoux into the wall behind the Casino during their battle for ninth place was not an example of how to win friends and influence people.

Despite all this, the results table of the 38th Monaco Grand Prix demonstrated a very pleasing cross-section: the first six places were occupied by six different makes of car.

In Monaco gehen die Uhren manchmal anders. Besonders innerhalb der magischen Quadratmeile rund um das Casino scheint dann die Glücksgöttin launisch zu lächeln oder zu schmollen: Da erhalten Männer aus dem zweiten Glied unvermutet ihre Chance, oder die Helden der Saison stürzen an jenem Wochenende im Mai ins Nichts ab. Favoriten sind 1980 die beiden Ligier JS 11/15 von Didier Pironi und Jacques Laffite, nicht unbedingt schön, aber von brutal verpackter Zweckdienlichkeit und ganz einfach schnell. Die Williams FW 07 B von Alan Jones und Carlos Reutemann werden, so scheint es, ebenfalls ein Wörtchen mitreden. Das spiegelt durchaus die Kräfteverhältnisse des Zyklus von 1980 wider und auch, daß sich Jody Scheckter, der Champion von 1979, mit seinem Ferrari 312 T5 in der vorletzten Reihe findet. Was indessen René Arnoux widerfährt, der nach den fünf Läufen bislang als Spitzenreiter der Wertung ins Fürstentum anreist, verletzt die Schmerzgrenze: Für ihn und seinen Renault RE 24 notiert man den letzten Startplatz.

Der Gunst eines eigens dafür abgestellten Schutzengels indes erfreuen sich offensichtlich vier Männer im Mittelfeld. Beim ersten Anbremsen von Sainte Dévote wird der Tyrrell des Iren Derek Daly vom rechten Hinterrad des Alfa von Bruno Giacomelli wie über eine Rampe in die Luft abgeschossen, vollführt eine komplette Pirouette, amputiert den Heckflügel von Alain Prosts McLaren und geht krachend auf dem Wagen seines Teamgefährten Jean-Pierre Jarier nieder. Rennwagen und Rennwagenpartikel liegen überall in der Fahrrinne herum. Ken Tyrrell ist wenig angetan, denn der sparsame Brite mag es nicht, wenn man seine Autos beschädigt. Der Sponsor Candy hingegen zeigt sich begeistert von den zusätzlichen Zeitlupensekunden, die das Fernsehen dieser Kunstflugeinlage widmet. Verwundet ist niemand.

Ganz vorn aber muß sich Pironi der gesammelten Aufmerksamkeit von Jones erwehren, und Laffite attackiert beharrlich Reutemann in Position drei. Für diese beiden arbeitet die Zeit: In der 25. Runde wird der Australier von seinem Getriebe im Stich gelassen, und das Getriebe spielt auch eine Rolle beim Ausfall Pironis im 55. Durchgang. Da fummelt der Franzose bei Mirabeau vergeblich nach dem dritten Gang und verstümmelt seinen Ligier an der Leitplanke, etwa um die Zeit, als ein paar dicke Regentropfen auf der Strecke verdampfen.

Von diesem Augenblick an fährt Reutemann einem durch nichts und niemanden gefährdeten Sieg entgegen, seinem zehnten insgesamt, während sich Jacques Laffites Bremspedal schwammig anfühlt. Daß Riccardo Patrese mit seinem Arrows A3 René Arnoux beim Kampf um den neunten Platz zweimal hinter dem Casino gegen die Mauer drängt, ist einer Männerfreundschaft keineswegs förderlich.

Die Ergebnisliste des 38. Grand Prix de Monaco zeugt dafür von einer erfreulichen Artenvielfalt: Auf den ersten sechs Plätzen landen sechs verschiedene Marken.

A Monaco, les montres ne fonctionnent pas toujours au même rythme qu'ailleurs. Surtout dans ce quartier magique des environs du Casino, Fortuna, la déesse de la chance, semble parfois sourire à qui bon lui semble parfois aussi bouder : des seconds couteaux se voient alors donner une chance insoupçonnée tandis que certains héros de la saison, ce week-end-là de mai, sont confrontés à leur destin. Les favoris, en 1980, sont les deux Ligier JS 11/15 de Didier Pironi et Jacques Laffite, que l'on ne peut vraiment pas qualifier de beautés, mais d'un fonctionnel brutal et d'une vitesse irrésistible. Les Williams FW 07 B d'Alan Jones et Carlos Reutemann semblent également avoir leur mot à dire. Cela reflète tout à fait le rapport des forces pendant la saison 1980, ce qu'atteste aussi le fait que Jody Scheckter, le champion du monde de 1979, se retrouve en avant-dernière ligne avec sa Ferrari 312 T5. Le sort de René Arnoux, qui arrive dans la Principauté en tête du classement après les cinq premières manches, dépasse le seuil du tolérable : lui et sa Renault RE 24 occupent la toute dernière place sur la grille de départ.

Quelques secondes après le début de la course, quatre hommes du milieu de grille semblent, par contre, avoir amené avec eux leur ange gardien à Monaco. Lors du premier freinage, devant Sainte Dévote, la Tyrrell de l'optimiste Irlandais Derek Daly s'envole sur la roue arrière droite de l'Alfa Romeo de Bruno Giacomelli, effectue un spectaculaire vol plané, arrache l'aileron arrière de la McLaren d'Alain Prost et retombe dans un bruit assourdissant sur la voiture de son coéquipier Jean-Pierre Jarier. Voitures de course et autres ailerons parsèment le virage. Ken Tyrrell n'est guère enchanté, car l'économe Britannique n'aime vraiment pas que l'on abîme ses voitures. Le sponsor, Candy, est ravi de cette publicité bienvenue, car la télévision passe et repasse au ralenti ce spectaculaire incident. Miraculeusement, aucun pilote n'est blessé.

Aux avant-postes, Pironi doit repousser les assauts permanents de Jones et Laffite attaque sans arrêt Reutemann, troisième. Mais le temps travaille pour ces deux hommes : au 25e tour, l'Australien est abandonné par sa boîte de vitesses, organe qui joue également un rôle dans l'abandon de Pironi au 55e tour. Le Français cherche en vain à enclencher la troisième à Mirabeau et, sur la piste glissante, il percute les glissières avec sa Ligier juste au moment où quelques grosses gouttes de pluie humectent la piste.

Dès lors, Reutemann roule vers sa dixième victoire de Grand Prix, que rien ni personne ne pourra plus mettre en danger tandis que Jacques Laffite se bat contre une pédale de frein spongieuse. Le fait que Riccardo Patrese avec son Arrows A3 pousse deux fois de suite René Arnoux contre les glissières du Casino, au cours de leur lutte pour la neuvième place, n'est pas de nature à favoriser une amitié virile entre les deux protagonistes.

La liste de résultats du 38e Grand Prix de Monaco est en revanche le témoignage d'une réjouissante diversité des espèces : aux six premières places, on trouve six marques différentes.

Fast food: in Monaco the Grand Prix atmosphere even rubs off on the speed of the waiters.

Schnelle Bedienung: In Monaco färbt das Ambiente des Grand Prix sogar auf das Tempo der Kellner ab.

Service rapide : à Monaco, l'ambiance du Grand Prix fait même tache d'huile sur la vitesse des serveurs de restaurant.

N°	DRIVERS		ENTRANTS	CARS	ENGINES	PRACTICE RESULTS	RACE RESULTS
28	**Carlos Reutemann**	**RA**	**Albilad-Saudia Racing Team**	**Williams FW07B**	**Cosworth V8 2993 cc**	**2nd: 1'24"882**	**1st: 1h55'34"365**
26	Jacques Laffite	F	Equipe Ligier Gitanes	Ligier JS11/15	Cosworth V8 2993 cc	5th: 1'25'510	2nd: 1h56'47"994
5	Nelson Piquet	BR	Parmalat Racing Team	Brabham BT49	Cosworth V8 2993 cc	4th: 1'25"358	3rd: 1h56'52"091
30	Jochen Mass	D	Warsteiner Arrows Racing Team	Arrows A3	Cosworth V8 2993 cc	15th: 1'26"956	4th: 75 laps
2	Gilles Villeneuve	CDN	SEFAC Ferrari S.p.A.	Ferrari 312T5	Ferrari F12 2992 cc	6th: 1'26"104	5th: 75 laps
20	Emerson Fittipaldi	BR	Skol Fittipaldi Team	Fittipaldi F7	Cosworth V8 2993 cc	18th: 1'27"495	6th: 74 laps
11	Mario Andretti	USA	Team Essex Lotus	Lotus 81	Cosworth V8 2993 cc	19th: 1'27"514	7th: 73 laps
29	Riccardo Patrese	I	Warsteiner Arrows Racing Team	Arrows A3	Cosworth V8 2993 cc	11th: 1'26"828	8th: 73 laps
12	Elio de Angelis	I	Team Essex Lotus	Lotus 81	Cosworth V8 2993 cc	14th: 1'26"930	9th: 68 laps (R)
9	Jan Lammers	NL	ATS Wheels	ATS D4	Cosworth V8 2993 cc	13th: 1'26"883	10th: 64 laps
25	*Didier Pironi*	*F*	*Equipe Ligier Gitanes*	*Ligier JS11/15*	*Cosworth V8 2993 cc*	*1st: 1'24"813*	R
16	René Arnoux	F	Equipe Renault Elf	Renault RE20	Renault V6 1492 cc + T	20th: 1'27"524	R
22	Patrick Depailler	F	Marlboro Team Alfa Romeo	Alfa Romeo 179	Alfa Romeo V12 2995 cc	7th: 1'26"210	R
1	Jody Scheckter	RSA	SEFAC Ferrari S.p.A.	Ferrari 312T5	Ferrari F12 2992 cc	17th: 1'27"182	R
15	Jean-Pierre Jabouille	F	Equipe Renault Elf	Renault RE20	Renault V6 1492 cc + T	16th: 1'27"099	R
27	Alan Jones	AUS	Albilad-Saudia Racing Team	Williams FW07B	Cosworth V8 2993 cc	3rd: 1'25"202	R
23	Bruno Giacomelli	I	Marlboro Team Alfa Romeo	Alfa Romeo 179	Alfa Romeo V12 2995 cc	8th: 1'26"227	R
8	Alain Prost	F	Marlboro Team McLaren	McLaren M29	Cosworth V8 2993 cc	10th: 1'26"826	R
3	Jean-Pierre Jarier	F	Candy Tyrrell Team	Tyrrell 010	Cosworth V8 2993 cc	9th: 1'26"369	R
4	Derek Daly	IRL	Candy Tyrrell Team	Tyrrell 010	Cosworth V8 2993 cc	12th: 1'26"838	R

1

2

(1) Against the grain: the road markings pointing in the wrong direction make the race through the town appear all the more absurd. (2) Applause for the winner: Reutemann (Williams) on his slowing down lap. (3) Losing battle: Scheckter in the Ferrari. (4) Always strongly in the running: Laffite (Ligier). (5) Deprived of victory by bad luck: Pironi (Ligier). (6) Starting from last position: Arnoux (Renault).

(1) Gegen den Strich: Die in die verkehrte Richtung weisenden Verkehrszeichen lassen das Rennen durch die Stadt nur noch absurder erscheinen. (2) Applaus für den Sieger: Reutemann (Williams) in der Auslauf-runde. (3) Auf verlorenem Posten: Scheckter im Ferrari. (4) Immer stark im Rennen: Laffite (Ligier). (5) Vom Pech um den Sieg gebracht: Pironi (Ligier). (6) Vom letzten Platz gestartet: Arnoux (Renault).

(1) A contre-courant : les panneaux de la circulation qui indiquent le sens inverse font paraître encore plus absurde la course à travers la ville. (2) Applaudissements pour le vainqueur : Reute-mann (Williams) dans son tour de décélération. (3) Position sans espoir : Scheckter sur Ferrari. (4) Toujours fort en course : Laffite (Ligier). (5) Privé de la victoire par la malchance : Pironi (Ligier). (6) Parti de la dernière place : Arnoux (Renault).

3

4

(Previous double page) It's raining cars: Derek Daly (Tyrrell) in the final phase of his flying display. He is about to descend on his team colleague Jarier.

(Vorhergehende Doppelseite) Aus der Rolle gefallen: Derek Daly (Tyrrell) in der finalen Phase seiner Flugnummer. Er schickt sich gerade an, auf seinem Teamkollegen Jarier niederzugehen.

(Double page précédente) Saut périlleux : Derek Daly (Tyrrell) durant la phase finale de son envol. Il s'apprête à atterrir sur son coéquipier Jarier.

(1) Beautiful panorama: this is the view of the guests in the Hôtel Loews, who must pay handsomely for it. (2) Jovial: Gilles Villeneuve. (3) Tired: Jarier. (4) Thirsty: Pironi. (5) Injured in a skiing accident: James Hunt. (6) Frustrated: Arnoux. (7) Snappy threesome: Giacomelli, Depailler and girl shouting for joy.

(1) Schönes Panorama: Dieser Blick bietet sich den Gästen des Hôtel Loews und muß fürstlich honoriert werden. (2) Aufgeräumt: Gilles Villeneuve. (3) Müde: Jarier. (4) Durstig: Pironi, (5) Durch Skiunfall verletzt: James Hunt. (6) Frustriert: Arnoux. (7) Flotter Dreier: Giacomelli, Depailler und jauchzendes Mädchen.

(1) Beau panorama : cette vue magnifique est celle dont jouissent les hôtes de l'Hôtel Loews, qui doivent payer pour cela une somme astronomique. (2) Satisfait : Gilles Villeneuve. (3) Fatigué : Jarier. (4) Assoiffé : Pironi. (5) Blessé en faisant du ski : James Hunt. (6) Frustré : Arnoux. (7) Trois boute-en-train : Giacomelli, Depailler et jeunes filles souriantes.

CITY IN TURMOIL

STADT IN AUFRUHR · UNE VILLE EN ÉMOI

Turning a soap opera city into a Grand Prix track is like asking Julius Caesar to carry a laptop. And sticking with Shakespeare: there is method in the madness. The transformation, from tightening the first screw to releasing the last one, takes two months, in which millions of individual moves stack up between April and June each year into the assembly and disassembly of the monument which is the Monaco Grand Prix.

Artificial stands for 20,000 visitors rise up out of the ground in the harbor quarter of La Condamine like sticks of coral or cancers, and 17 miles of robust corrugated iron keep Mansell, Schumacher & Co. in check, household goods, as it were, of the Automobile Club de Monaco, which are stored outside the gates of the city for the rest of the year. About 15,000 square yards of chain-link fence are meant to protect the spectators from small racing car parts whizzing about in the air, cranes in sensitive points, such as Mirabeau or at the swimming baths, are there to lift larger sections from the track if necessary. An army of willing helpers waits everywhere for something which no-one hopes will happen. Lorry park and equipment are without equal.

The perfectly equipped Princess Grace hospital, a stone's throw from the circuit, is placed on emergency level 1 during the race, as if it were expecting a nuclear strike. The risk which remains is still considerable. Coming out of the Virage du Tabac, the cars head directly for stand M for a few seconds, directly behind the following left-hand bend at the swimming baths. Next to the hump at the Casino, where the drivers and their cars throw themselves precipitately down the slope towards Mirabeau, unsuspecting citizens sip their Pernods or Perriers behind a folding screen made of plywood.

All planning and exercises in advance of the Grand Prix would be negated by a super-MCA in the tunnel: imagine a mass pile-up on the first lap, fire, the philatelists meeting one floor above in the Centre de Congrès are roasted by more than 3,000 liters of super fuel. "God forbid", says Pierre Berenguier, press spokesman of the Automobile Club, calling on the law of improbability: "Why should all the risk factors coincide just there?"

The Grand Prix makes the city see red, one way or the other. Those who despise the race book their annual holiday for this time or withdraw indignantly to their chalets in the mountains. On the other hand, it is never more attractive than now, etched by the metal canyons of the three-storey Armco barriers which mercilessly rend the geography of the town asunder to the east of the old town. Between Sanremo and Saint Tropez, even the bathtubs are let out in mid-May. The idea of the Grand Prix becomes a principle from which nothing is immune. In the Hôtel Loews, no youth hostel at the best of times, one would have had to cough up more than £1,500 in 1998 for a double room from the 11th to the 16th of the month – and that is only the room, please note, not including breakfast – if everything had not been fully booked ages ago.

Original variations on the subject of accommodation and travel are also in evidence in the maritime hinter-

Aus einem Seifenoperettenstaat eine Grand-Prix-Piste zu machen, das ist so, als würde man dem Darsteller des Julius Caesar einen Laptop in die Hand drücken. Um gleich bei Shakespeare zu bleiben: Ist es schon Wahnsinn, hat es doch Methode. Der Wandel, vom Befestigen der ersten Schraube bis zum Lösen der letzten, dauert zwei Monate, in denen sich Millionen Handgriffe emporschichten zu Rekonstruktion und Abriß des Denkmals Grand Prix de Monaco, alljährlich zwischen April und Juni.

Da wachsen vor allem im Hafenviertel La Condamine künstliche Tribünen für 20000 Zugereiste wie Korallenstöcke oder Krebsmetastasen aus dem Boden. 27 Kilometer robustes Wellblech verweisen Mansell, Schumacher & Cie in ihre Grenzen, Hausrat sozusagen des Automobile Club de Monaco und für den Rest des Jahres ausgelagert vor den Toren der Stadt. 12500 Quadratmeter Maschendraht sollen die Zuschauer vor umherschwirrenden Rennwagenkleinteilen behüten, Kräne an neuralgischen Punkten wie Mirabeau oder am Schwimmbad unter Umständen größere Brocken von der Strecke klauben. Eine Armee von Hilfswilligen harrt überall der Dinge, die dann hoffentlich doch nicht eintreten. Fuhrpark und Ausrüstung suchen ihresgleichen.

Im mustergültig ausgestatteten Hospital Princess Grace, einen Steinwurf vom Circuit entfernt, herrscht während des Rennens Alarmstufe 1, als sei ein Atomschlag zu befürchten. Das Restrisiko bleibt dennoch beträchtlich. Aus der Virage du Tabac kommend, zielen die Fahrzeuge sekundenlang auf die Tribüne M unmittelbar hinter der folgenden Linkskurve am Schwimmbad. Neben dem Buckel am Casino, an dem sich Fahrer und Wagen kopfüber in den Steilhang Richtung Mirabeau stürzen, süffeln arglose Bürger hinter einer spanischen Wand aus Sperrholz ihre Pernods oder Perriers. Den Rahmen jedes Planspiels im Vorfeld des Grand Prix sprengen würde der Super-Gau im Tunnel: Massenkarambolage in der ersten Runde, Feuer, das Philatelisten-Meeting einen Stock höher im Centre de Congrès flambiert über 3000 Litern Superbenzin. »Da sei Gott vor«, bemüht Pierre Berenguier, Pressemann des Automobile Club, das Gesetz der Unwahrscheinlichkeit: »Warum sollen ausgerechnet da alle ungünstigen Faktoren zusammenkommen?«

Der Grand Prix bringt die Stadt in Harnisch, so oder so. Säuerliche Renn-Verächter buchen um diese Zeit ihren Jahresurlaub oder ziehen sich indigniert in ihre Chalets in den Bergen zurück. Andererseits ist sie nie attraktiver als jetzt, durchfurcht von den Metallschluchten der dreistöckigen Armco-Planken, die überdies die Geographie ostwärts der Altstadt gnadenlos auseinanderreißen. Zwischen San Remo und Saint Tropez ist Mitte Mai jede Badewanne vermietet. Dabei wird der Begriff Grand Prix zum Prinzip, das schlechthin alles durchdringt. Im Loews Hotel, schon in normalen Zeiten keine Jugendherberge, müßte man in diesem Jahr für ein Arrangement vom 11. bis zum 16. des Monats im Doppelzimmer 4700 Mark berappen – nur Übernachtung, kein Frühstück, wohlgemerkt – wenn nicht schon längst alles ausgebucht gewesen wäre.

Aparte Variationen zum Thema Logis und Logistik lassen sich auch dem maritimen Hinterland der Steuer-

Vouloir faire d'un Etat d'opérette le théâtre d'un Grand Prix revient à donner un laptop à Jules César. Théâtre ou cinéma : ce qui semble une entreprise folle a cependant de la méthode. De la première vis serrée au dernier écrou démonté – il faut deux mois durant lesquels des millions de gestes sont faits pour élever puis démonter le monument du Grand Prix de Monaco, comme chaque année, entre avril et juin.

On voit surtout s'élever, dans le quartier du port de la Condamine, des tribunes pour 20000 spectateurs, véritables barrières de corail, voire métastases cancéreuses et 27 kilomètres de solides rails de sécurité jugulent les ardeurs des Mansell, Schumacher & compagnie, rails qui font pour ainsi dire partie des meubles de l'Automobile Club de Monaco et sont stockés, pendant le reste de l'année, devant les portes de la ville. 12500 mètres carrés de grillages ont pour but de protéger les spectateurs de tout projectile lancé par les voitures de course et des grues placées aux endroits névralgiques comme Mirabeau ou la Piscine sont chargées de pêcher en clin d'œil sur la piste les éventuels plus gros morceaux. Une légion d'auxiliaires, les nerfs à vif, montent la garde partout, dans l'attente de choses qui – espèrent-ils – ne se produiront pas. Le parc automobile et les équipements sont sans comparaison.

A l'hôpital Princesse Grace, magnifiquement équipé, à un jet de pierre du circuit, l'alarme rouge règne pendant la course comme si l'on craignait un bombardement nucléaire. Le risque résiduel n'en reste pas moins considérable. Jaillissant du virage du Bureau de Tabac, les voitures visent pendant quelques secondes la tribune M placée immédiatement à la sortie du virage gauche suivant la piscine. Près de la bosse du Casino, où pilotes et voitures se jettent tête baissée et à l'aveuglette dans la descente en direction de Mirabeau, des touristes inconscients dégustent leur Pernod ou leur Perrier derrière un paravent de contreplaqué.

Une méga-catastrophe dans le tunnel dépasserait toutes les précautions prises en vue du Grand Prix : imaginons une seconde un carambolage au premier tour, le feu et la conférence des philatélistes réunis un étage au-dessus, au Centre de Congrès, grillant sur trois mille litres d'essence. « Dieu aura tout prévu », s'empresse d'ajouter Pierre Berenguier, l'attaché de presse de l'Automobile Club, qui se fie à la loi de l'improbabilité : « Pourquoi faudrait-il, comme par hasard, que se conjuguent ici tous les facteurs défavorables ? »

Le Grand Prix met la ville en émoi d'une façon ou d'une autre. Les adversaires dépités de la course planifient leurs congés annuels pour cette période ou se retirent dans la tour d'ivoire de leur chalet dans les montagnes. D'un autre côté, la ville n'a jamais été aussi attrayante que maintenant, sillonnée de la triple rangée de glissières de sécurité Armco qui, telle une cicatrice, dépare sans pitié toute la partie orientale de la Vieille Ville. A la mi-mai, la moindre baignoire est louée à prix d'or entre San Remo et Saint-Tropez. A cette occasion, le Grand Prix devient un principe qui imprègne tout par définition. L'Hôtel Loews, par exemple, qui ne pratique déjà pas des tarifs d'auberge de jeunesse en temps

land of the tax haven. The snow-white fleet of cruisers,
worth millions, in the harbor offers an incalculable
number of beds and bars – preferably for those who for
some reason or other are called the "Beautiful People".
Beware, however, that many a dream of privileged
accommodation in a cabin with a view of the sea ends
in a sleeping bag on the quay, since a stiff swell is often
blown in from the sea, with its well-known effects on
stomach and morale. In this situation, anyone with a
permanent residence in Monaco is definitely better off.
The mini-kingdom of Rainier III is also a popular
retirement place, above all for wealthy Britons seeking
to put as much distance as possible between themselves
and the vagaries of the British weather and the English
cuisine.

High above the Boulevard Albert Ier, for example,
the Grand Prix veteran Roy Salvadori resides in a luxury
apartment with a magnificent view of the start and
finish areas and the port to Cap Martin. As with
everyone who lives adjacently, he is entitled to a certain
number of complementary tickets, and thus his spacious
balcony always turns into an Arthurian round table of
old racing knights, imbibing whisky and Welsh mineral
water as the youngsters below them roll to their
starting positions.

At least ten of these people, too, are currently
registered as resident in Monaco. Nowhere, and that is
certainly a paradox of this profession, do men like Mika
Hakkinen, Ukyo Katayama or Karl Wendlinger have
such a short walk to work as here, at the most
exclusive of all Grands Prix. And nowhere are they so

oase abgewinnen. Die schneeweiße Flotte der
Millionen-Kreuzer im Hafen bietet Betten und Bars in
unbekannter Zahl, vorzugsweise aber denen, die aus
irgendeinem Grund »The Beautiful People« genannt
werden. Allerdings endete schon mancher Traum vom
privilegierten Wohnen in Kajüte mit Meerblick in einem
Schlafsack auf der Mole, da von draußen häufig eine
stramme Dünung hereinsteht, mit den bekannten
Folgen für Magen und Moral. Da ist schon besser dran,
wer in Monaco einen festen Wohnsitz hat. Das kleine
Reich Rainiers des Dritten ist auch eine beliebte
Seniorenresidenz, vor allem für betuchte Briten fern
der Schikanen des englischen Wetters und der
englischen Küche.

Hoch über dem Boulevard Albert Ier haust zum
Beispiel der Grand-Prix-Veteran Roy Salvadori, 72, in
einem Luxusappartement mit herrlichem Blick über den
Start und Ziel-Bereich und den Port bis hin zum Cap
Martin. Wie jedem Anrainer steht ihm ein bestimmtes
Kontingent an Freikarten zu, und so findet sich auf
seinem geräumigen Balkon stets eine Artusrunde der
alten Renn-Ritter bei Whisky und walisischem
Mineralwasser zusammen, wenn da unten die jungen
auf ihre Startplätze rollen. Zehn von denen sind im
Augenblick ebenfalls als in Monaco wohnhaft gemeldet.
Für Männer wie Mika Hakkinen, Ukyo Katayama oder
Karl Wendlinger, und das zählt mit Sicherheit zu den
Paradoxien der Branche, ist der Weg zur Arbeit
nirgends so kurz wie hier, beim exklusivsten aller Grand
Prix. Und nirgends sind sie dem Fan so nah – und doch
so fern. Abseits der Klausur der monegassischen

normal, n'hésitera pas à facturer, en 1998, pour un
arrangement du 11 au 16 du mois en chambre double,
plus de 15 000 francs – rien que pour la nuit, sans petit
déjeuner, cela va de soi ; mais tout risque déjà d'être
loué longtemps à l'avance.

On peut décliner à volonté le thème du logis et de
la logistique, qui se combine à la perfection sur les
vagues de l'oasis fiscale. La flotte immaculée des yachts
de milliardaires dans le port offre un nombre inconnu
de lits et de bars, mais ils sont réservés en général à
ceux que, pour une raison inconnue, on surnomme *the
beautiful people*. Bien des rêves de logement privilégié
dans une couchette avec vue sur la mer se sont,
toutefois, souvent terminés dans un sac de couchage
sur le môle, car il est fréquent qu'une brise fraîche
dresse un clapot escarpé avec ses conséquences bien
connues pour l'estomac et l'esprit. Celui qui, à Monaco,
réside sur le continent, est alors logé à meilleure
enseigne. Le petit royaume de Rainier III est aussi un
lieu de résidence très apprécié des tempes grises,
notamment des Britanniques aisés protégés des
bizarreries du temps anglais et de la cuisine anglaise par
une distance confortable.

La tête dans les nuages au-dessus du Boulevard
Albert Ier, par exemple, Roy Salvadori, vétéran des
Grands Prix âgé de 72 ans, réside dans un somptueux
appartement d'où il a une vue magnifique sur la grille de
départ et le port jusqu'à Cap Martin. Comme chaque
riverain, il a droit à un contingent déterminé de billets
gratuits et c'est ainsi que son spacieux balcon héberge
toujours une nuée de prestigieux chevaliers du volant

near to their fans – and yet so far. Removed from the exclusivity of the Monegasque properties, or the high-security area of the race track, the fans gather in a defensive circle of motorhomes at the Quai Antoine Ier, frozen out and barren. Here they are among their own kind. And if the permanent residents need to withdraw from the sticky grasp of the freaks, they can always take to the sea.

The fans must be content with meagre pickings. They consider themselves lucky if they see the gladiators transferring from the pit area to the harborside paddock, and a thunderous roar rises from the slope below the Grimaldi palaces where thousands and thousands of paupers are clinging to the rock on so-called "pelouses" at welfare prices of approximately 30 dollars, having been fighting like crows over the best spots since midnight. While the names of the stars are chanted almost lovingly, the inevitably sparsely clothed glamour girls in the retinue of the sponsors are slagged off, their innocence being called into question if not denied altogether.

A late feudalism has grown up in the shadow of the Grimaldis: Monaco is a good place for monarchs. The last one, Ayrton Senna, with six victories to his name, was as inaccessible as a van Gogh in private ownership. Since the battle of the opportunistic, populist Alain Prost for the throne petered out after four attempts, his claim must be seen as an interregnum. The first king of Monaco, Graham Hill, was, however, a man of the people despite five wins; he would go for a beer in the Tip-Top Bar 85 yards to the left behind the Casino and immerse himself in the crowd, even on the evening before the race, his cord jacket an appropriate British Racing Green.

Rosie and Jean-Louis Bernard in the Chatham Bar, recently moved from its more familiar location to the left of the lightning fast upward twist approaching Massenet, will willingly chat about those years. She is a friendly relic from the time of the fairy-tale Roman-ticism of towers, bay windows and pillars, where today the cityscape on both sides of the track has been forced into right-angles. The demolition of the modest establishment some years ago was only prevented by an international outcry.

The whole world, then, romps about in the already claustrophobic confinement of the pits – despite the restrictive use of special permits personally supervised by Bernie Ecclestone. In the magical two hours before the start, the vainglorious display their wares while the Grand Prix workers go about their business unmoved, with only the occasional biting remark. Then, real members of the jet set and from showbiz might even be identified, with a Royal here or there, such as King Karl XVI Gustav of Sweden. He is without Silvia and bodyguards, and really is a person like you and me in the face of the majesty of the Monaco Grand Prix.

In the 1970s, Jochen Mass sometimes brought along his neighbour from Cap Ferrat, David Niven, an affable old gentleman, tiny and remarkably unarrogant. Why did he subject himself to this? Well, first of all as a favor to Jochen, and then, the whole thing is quite exciting after all. In 1996, the busty bombshell Brigitte Nielsen appeared as a guest of Benetton, dressed in a small

Eigenheime oder des Hochsicherheitstrakts der Rennstrecke igelt man sich ein in der Wagenburg am Quai Antoine Ier, in der tiefgekühlten und nur von innen transparenten Einöde der Motorhomes. Dort wächst nur zusammen, was ohnehin zusammengehört, und notfalls kann man sich dem klebrigen Zugriff des Freaks auf dem Seewege entziehen.

Deren Erfolgserlebnisse, karg bemessen, finden zum Beispiel statt, wenn die Gladiatoren vom Boxenbereich ins Fahrerlager wechseln. Dann braust ein Ruf wie Donnerhall aus dem Hang unterhalb der Grimaldipaläste, wo Abertausende von Habenichtsen auf den sogenannten »pelouses« zum Sozialtarif von umgerechnet 50 Mark im Fels hängen und sich schon um Mitternacht wie die Krähen um ihre Parzelle zanken. Während Volkes Mund beinahe zärtlich die Vornamen der Stars skandiert, überschüttet er die unvermeidlichen sparsam gewandeten Glamour Girls aus dem Sponsor-Troß zuverlässig mit gallischem und galligem Schmäh, der die Unschuld der Betroffenen in Zweifel zieht oder gänzlich in Abrede stellt. Im Schatten der Grimaldis gedeiht ein später Feudalismus: Monaco ist ein gutes Pflaster für Monarchen. Der letzte, Ayrton Senna mit sechs Siegen in der Personalakte, gab sich zeitgemäß verschlossen wie ein van Gogh im Privat-besitz. Da der Kampf des Gelegenheitspopulisten Alain Prost um den Thron nach vier Anläufen erlahmte, verkümmerte seine Anwartschaft zum Interregnum. Der erste König von Monaco, Graham Hill, war indessen trotz fünf Erfolgen ein Mann des Volks, suchte etwa in der Tip-Top-Bar 80 Meter links hinter dem Casino das Bad im Bier und in der Menge selbst in der Nacht vor dem Rennen, den Cordanzug stilgerecht in britischem Renngrün.

Von jenen Jahren plaudern bereitwillig Rosie und Jean-Louis Bernard in der Chatham Bar links neben dem pfeilschnellen Aufwärtsschlängel vor Massenet. Sie ist ein freundliches Relikt aus der Zeit der Zuckerbäcker-Romantik der Türme, Erker und Säulen, wo heute der rechte Winkel die Stadtlandschaft beiderseits der Piste unter seine Knute gezwungen hat. Daß das bescheidene Etablissement vor ein paar Jahren der Abbruchbirne geopfert werden sollte, unterblieb nach einem Wutschrei aus aller Welt. Alle Welt tummelt sich denn auch in der ohnehin klaustrophobischen Enge des Boxenbereichs – trotz restriktiven und von Bernie Ecclestone persönlich überwachten Umgangs mit Sonderausweisen. In den magischen zwei Stunden vor dem Start brodelt dort der Basar der Eitelkeiten, während die Grand-Prix-Schaffenden ungerührt ihrem Tagewerk nachgehen und nur ab und an am sich beißen. Dann macht man sogar echte Größen von Jet Set und Showbiz aus, vereinzelt selbst Royalty wie den schwedischen Landesvater Karl XVI Gustav, ganz ohne Silvia und Leibwächter und eigentlich ein Mensch wie du und ich angesichts der Majestät des Grand Prix de Monaco.

In den siebziger Jahren brachte Jochen Mass manchmal seinen Nachbarn David Niven aus Cap Ferrat mit, einen leutseligen älteren Herrn, witzig und bemerkenswert unarrogant. Warum er sich das hier antue? Naja, zunächst einmal dem Jochen zu Gefallen, und dann sei die Angelegenheit schon ganz schön

réunis autour de quelques bouteilles de whisky et d'eau minérale du Pays de Galles quand, à leurs pieds, leurs jeunes collègues s'élancent pour prendre leur place au départ.

Dix d'entre eux au moins ont, actuellement, le privilège d'être résidents monégasques. Pour des hommes comme Mika Hakkinen, Ukyo Katayama ou Karl Wendlinger – ce qui est assurément un paradoxe dans leur métier – le chemin pour se rendre au travail n'est nulle part plus court qu'ici, pour le plus exclusif de tous les Grands Prix. Et ils ne sont nulle part jamais aussi proches – et pourtant aussi éloignés – des fans qu'ici. En dehors du huis-clos des appartements monégasques ou de l'aile à haute sécurité du circuit, les protagonistes se réfugient dans le camp fortifié du Quai Antoine Ier, dans la froideur climatisée des motorhomes qui ne laissent passer le regard que depuis l'intérieur. Ici ne cohabitent de toute façon que ceux qui font depuis longtemps déjà partie du sérail et qui, si besoin est, peuvent aussi échapper à la mainmise omniprésente des freaks en prenant l'issue de secours de la voie maritime.

Leur notoriété, qui laisse parfois à désirer, grandit par exemple quand les gladiateurs quittent la zone des stands pour se rendre au parc fermé. Une rumeur déferle alors comme un coup de tonnerre sur le Rocher, au pied du palais des Grimaldi, où des milliers de pauvres hères s'agrippent, sur les flancs de la falaise, à ce que l'on appelle les « pelouses » vendues au tarif démocratique d'environ deux cents francs par personne et où ils se battent déjà, vers minuit, telles des hyènes défendant leur territoire. Alors que la vox populi scande presque avec tendresse les prénoms des stars, les glamour girls toujours à demi dévêtues faisant la publicité d'un quelconque sponsor sont invariablement la cible des quolibets et autres plaisanteries douteuses qui remettent en question ou dénient totalement leur virginité.

Dans l'ombre jetée par le palais des Grimaldi prospère un féodalisme tardif : Monaco est un endroit prédestiné pour les monarques. Le dernier, Ayrton Senna, avec six victoires à son palmarès, se murait dans son silence, aussi inaccessible que le van Gogh d'un collectionneur privé. Le populiste et arriviste Alain Prost ayant mis fin à son combat pour le trône après quatre tentatives, la régence de Senna s'est dégradée en un interrègne. Le premier roi de Monaco, Graham Hill, était en revanche, malgré ses cinq succès, un homme adulé du peuple et qui recherchait, au Tip-Top Bar, à 80 mètres à gauche du virage du Casino, le bain de bière et de foule même durant la nuit précédant la course, vêtu en bon Anglais d'un costume de velours d'une couleur en accord avec l'événement, British Racing Green.

Cette époque fournit matière à confidences à Rosie et Jean-Louis Bernard, les propriétaires du Chatham Bar qui a quitté son cadre traditionnel pour venir s'installer à gauche de l'ultra rapide série de virages précédant Massenet. C'est une touchante relique du rococo avec son accumulation de tourelles, d'échauguettes et de colonnades là où, aujourd'hui, l'angle droit fait régner sa loi des deux côtés de la piste. Quand l'on voulut raser le modeste établissement, il y a quelques années, un tollé s'est élevé dans le monde entier. Et le monde

Vicious circle: over the years the houses have risen higher and the facades become smoother, the yachts and racing cars have travelled faster, and everything has got very much more expensive.

Entwicklungsgebiet: Im Laufe der Jahrzehnte sind die Häuser immer höher, die Fassaden immer glatter, die Yachten und die Rennwagen immer schneller geworden und alles viel, viel teurer.

Cercle vicieux : au fil des années, les immeubles sont devenus de plus en plus hauts, les façades, de plus en plus planes, les yachts et les voitures de course, de plus en plus rapides et tout coûte beaucoup, beaucoup plus cher.

black number which revealed more than it covered, and flirted dutifully with Michael Schumacher. And the familiar cheeky face of Jean Paul Belmondo suddenly appeared in the March pit – backup as it were for his Formula 1 racing driver son Paul, much older than one expects from the films, of course, but still with his cheeky grin. No sooner had the professional charmer made his appearance when the news spread like wildfire that the "Great Greek", Anthony Quinn, was approaching. And, indeed, it was him surrounded by swarms of autograph hunters, much larger and of course also much older than in the films. Still, they all obey the unwritten law of the day, that the real stars – and the only ones – are the Grand Prix drivers.

Others have greater difficulty in obeying that law, those who misuse the area between the Williams pit at one end and the Minardi pit at the other to parade their inflated egos. They include the old gentleman, stiff with arthritis, who last year paraded his very young female friend through the crowd, a sugar daddy and real picture of frustration – truly embarrassing.

"When the flag drops, the bullshit stops", the three-times World Champion Sir Jack Brabham used to say. Since the prominent people also take time to disperse, the whole thing has been over long since – until next year.

aufregend. Vor zwei Jahren kreuzte als Benetton-Gast das Busenwunder Brigitte Nielsen auf, im kleinen Schwarzen, das mehr bloßlegte als verhüllte, und schäkerte pflichtschuldig mit Michael Schumacher. Und in der March-Box zeigte sich plötzlich das vertraute Backpfeifengesicht von Jean Paul Belmondo, als Truppenbetreuung gleichsam für seinen Formel-1-fahrenden Sohn Paul, natürlich viel älter, als man es aus dem Film kennt und trotzdem mit dieser unverschämten Grinse auch in natura. Kaum war der Auftritt dieses Profi-Charmeurs beendet, verbreitete sich wie ein Lauffeuer die Kunde, der »Große Grieche« Anthony Quinn sei im Anmarsch. Und in der Tat, er war's, umschwirrt von Schwärmen von Autogrammjägern, viel größer und natürlich ebenfalls viel älter, als man ihn aus dem Film kennt. Gleichwohl: Man unterwirft sich willig dem ungeschriebenen Gesetz des Tages, die eigentlichen Stars seien die Grand-Prix-Piloten und nur sie.

Anderen fällt das schwerer, jenen, die die Zeile zwischen der Williams-Box und der Minardi-Box am anderen Ende als Laufsteg der aufgeblähten Ichs mißbrauchen. Wie jener Alte, steif von ächzender Arthrose, der im vorigen Jahr seine blutjunge Freundin durch das Getümmel paradierte, ein »sugar daddy«, wie die Engländer sagen, ein Zuckerpapi und wahres Väterchen Frust und eigentlich nur rasend peinlich.

»When the flag drops, the bullshit stops«, pflegt der dreifache Weltmeister Sir Jack Brabham zu sagen – wenn die Flagge fällt, hört das Affentheater auf. Da auch der Prominenten-Abtrieb seine Zeit braucht, ist dann in Monaco längst der ganze Spuk verflogen – bis zum nächsten Jahr.

entier se marche d'ailleurs aussi sur les pieds dans l'étroitesse, propice à la claustrophobie, de la zone des stands – malgré la distribution restrictive de coupe-file de Bernie Ecclestone, qui surveille personnellement les portes d'accès. Durant les deux heures magiques précédant le départ palpite ici le bazar des m'as-tu-vu pendant que les serfs du Grand Prix accomplissent imperturbablement leur pensum de travail quotidien et ne laissent transparaître que de temps à autre leur énervement. On peut même y reconnaître d'authentiques célébrités de la jet set et du show-business, voire, parfois, des têtes couronnées comme le roi de Suède Charles Gustave XVI, pour une fois sans sa Silvia ni gardes du corps et, à proprement dit, un homme comme toi et moi face à la majesté du Grand Prix de Monaco.

Dans les années 70, Jochen Mass faisait parfois venir son voisin David Niven, du Cap Ferrat, un vieil homme convivial, spirituel et absolument pas arrogant. Pourquoi se pliait-il à une telle procédure, lui demanda-t-on un jour. Eh bien, répondit-il, tout d'abord pour faire plaisir à Jochen et puis, tout de même, parce que c'est quelque chose de vraiment excitant. En 1996, la plantureuse Brigitte Nielsen, invitée par l'écurie Benetton, y déambulait, vêtue d'un petit costume noir découvrant plus qu'il ne dissimulait, et bavardait sur un ton de passion feinte avec Michael Schumacher. Et, dans le stand de March, se profila soudain la silhouette bien connue de Jean-Paul Belmondo, espèce de factotum pour son rejeton de pilote de Formule 1, Paul, naturellement beaucoup plus âgé qu'on le connaît du cinéma et, malgré tout, avec sa gouaille irrésistible même en nature. A peine ce charmeur professionnel avait-il mis fin à son intermède que se propagea, comme un feu de poudre, la nouvelle que « Zorba le Grec », alias Anthony Quinn, arrivait. Et, de fait, c'était bien lui, assailli par des chasseurs d'autographes, beaucoup plus grand et, naturellement, lui aussi beaucoup plus âgé qu'on le connaît du cinéma. Et pourtant : chacun se soumet docilement aux lois non écrites du jour, qui veulent que les vedettes proprement dites soient uniquement les pilotes de Grand Prix.

D'autres ont déjà beaucoup plus de mal à s'y plier, notamment ceux qui arpentent la centaine de mètres entre le stand des Williams, d'un côté, et celui de Minardi, à l'autre extrémité, stratagème dont ils abusent comme d'une scène pour leur ego hyper extraverti. Tel ce vieil homme quasi paralysé par une arthrite grinçante qui, l'an dernier, paradait avec sa Lolita dans la foule, « a sugar daddy », comme disent ironiquement les Anglais, papa-gâteau et véritable petit père frustré, plutôt ridicule qu'autre chose.

« When the flag drops, the bullshit stops », avait l'habitude de répondre le triple champion du monde Sir Jack Brabham – lorsque le drapeau est abattu, le cirque est terminé. Mais la transhumance des personnalités demande du temps elle aussi et, à Monaco comme ailleurs, le tapage dure longtemps avant de s'évanouir – jusqu'à l'année prochaine.

1981

An admiring Ken Tyrrell said of him that he would get in his car and say to it, "Right. Now you'll do what I tell you." And, indeed, one could say: Where there is a Villeneuve, there is a way. This was never demonstrated so clearly as in the 39th Grand Prix of Monaco on 31 May 1981. The success of the little man from Quebec was a not insignificant triumph over his Ferrari 126 C. The enormous power delivered by his turbo engine was combined with inadequate suspension. Add Villeneuve's daring and artistic control of his vehicle and there was the perfect recipe for a fascinating, vintage Grand Prix.

That year, Formula 1 was thriving more than ever before and 31 cars were entered. Five failed to clear the hurdle of the pre-qualifying round on the Thursday and in qualifying the six with the worst times were also ejected, including Keke Rosberg in a Fittipaldi. But the flying Finn would not suffer any lasting damage as a result – he became World Champion in 1982 and was the winner in Monaco in 1983.

However, panic spread before the start. Fire broke out in the kitchens in the Loews hotel. The fire was extinguished, but not before water had entered the tunnel, a danger point on the track even under normal circumstances. Would the 20 participants get through the race unscathed with this threat of a sudden loss of traction? Eighteen drivers made it on the first lap, albeit after an hour's delay. Mario Andretti (Alfa Romeo T 179 C) and Andrea de Cesaris (McLaren MP 4/1) had by then already tussled with one another after Sainte Dévote. The high-speed trio at the front initially remained in the order established during the qualifying runs: Nelson Piquet at the wheel of his Brabham BT 49 C, Villeneuve, then Nigel Mansell in the cockpit of the Lotus 87. Mansell was incessantly dogged by Carlos Reutemann until an edge of the front spoiler on the Williams FW 07 C flicked the determined British driver off the track on the fourteenth lap, this incident delivering third place to Reutemann's team colleague, Alan Jones. To move into second place shortly thereafter, the Australian had to work away carefully until he was able to find a way past Villeneuve's wildly drifting Ferrari.

Grim battle was then joined with Piquet, but the Brazilian was only able to hold his own for a short while. On the fifty-fourth lap, the Brabham grazed the Theodore of Patrick Tambay at the Tabac bend and finished up in the crash barrier. But Jones was only able to enjoy his lead for 20 minutes before the Williams was bedevilled by air bubbles in a fuel feed pipe, a pit stop on lap 67 failing to remedy the situation. Returning to the track, Jones then found Villeneuve breathing down his neck, and he overtook the Williams six laps later to the frenetic applause of his fans, the *tifosi,* as they crossed the timing line.

The rest was just a formality: a victory which everyone was hoping for – and, incidentally, the eightieth in the history of Ferrari. Henceforth, the car number 27 took on a special significance.

Der setze sich in sein Auto und befehle: »So, du tust jetzt, was ich von dir verlange«, sagt Ken Tyrrell bewundernd über ihn. Und in der Tat: Wo ein Villeneuve ist, ist auch ein Weg. Nie zeigt sich das deutlicher als beim 39. Großen Preis von Monaco am 31. Mai 1981. Der Erfolg des kleinen Mannes aus Quebec ist nicht zuletzt ein Triumph über seinen Ferrari 126 C. Die Urkraft von seinem Turbo-Triebwerk, gepaart mit einem dürftigen Fahrwerk, dazu Villeneuves Verwegenheit und artistische Fahrzeugkontrolle – das ist genau die richtige Mischung für Grand-Prix-Faszination vom Feinsten.

In jenem Jahr steht die Formel 1 voll im Saft wie nie zuvor. 31 Wagen sind gemeldet. Davon fallen fünf durchs Schüttelrost der Vorqualifikation am Donnerstag. Sechs weitere scheitern im Training am monegassischen Numerus clausus, unter anderem Keke Rosberg auf einem Fittipaldi. Der fliegende Finne wird sich schadlos halten – als Welt-meister 1982 und Monaco-Sieger 1983 zum Beispiel.

Vor dem Start aber geht die Angst um: In den Küchen des Loews-Hotels war Feuer ausgebrochen. Der Brand ist gelöscht, aber Wasser ergoß sich in den Tunnel, ohnehin ein neuralgischer Punkt der Piste. Werden die 20 Teilnehmer bei plötzlicher beschränkter Haftung ungeschoren durch-kommen? 18 tun es, wenn auch mit einer Stunde Verzöge-rung. Mario Andretti (Alfa Romeo T 179 C) und Andrea de Cesaris (McLaren MP 4/1) haben sich bereits hinter Sainte Dévote in die Wolle gekriegt. Die eilige Dreifaltigkeit ganz vorn bleibt zunächst in der Reihenfolge, die im Training ermittelt wurde: Nelson Piquet auf Brabham BT 49 C, Villeneuve, Nigel Mansell mit dem Lotus 87. Dieser wird bald ungestüm bedrängt durch Carlos Reutemann, bis ein Nasenstüber von dessen Williams FW 07 C in der 14. Runde den entschlossenen Briten ins Abseits befördert. Der Zwischenfall beschert Reutemanns Teamkollegen Alan Jones den dritten Rang. Für den zweiten bald darauf muß der Australier so lange arbeiten, bis er einen Weg an Villeneuves wild driftendem Ferrari vorbei gefunden hat.

Seiner unerbittlichen Jagd auf Piquet kann der Brasilianer nur eine Zeitlang widerstehen. Im 54. Durchgang berührt der Brabham den Theodore von Patrick Tambay bei Tabak und landet an der Leitplanke. Jones vermag sich jedoch seiner Führung nur für 20 Minuten zu freuen. Der Williams wird gebeutelt von Blasen in der Benzinzufuhr. Ein Boxenstopp in Runde 67 schafft keine Abhilfe. Als er wieder auf die Strecke geht, sitzt ihm Villeneuve bereits im Nacken und überholt den Williams sechs Runden später unter dem frenetischen Jubel der *tifosi* vor der Zeitnehmerlinie.

Der Rest ist nur noch Formsache, ein Sieg, den alle wollten – übrigens der achtzigste in der Geschichte des Hauses Ferrari. Und die 27 ist von nun an nicht mehr nur irgendeine Zahl.

Il suffisait de s'asseoir dans sa voiture et de lui ordonner : « Bon, tu fais maintenant ce que j'exige de toi », déclare Ken Tyrrell, admirateur, à son sujet. Et, de fait : quand on s'appelle Villeneuve, rien n'est plus simple. Jamais cela n'était paru plus clairement que lors du 39ᵉ Grand Prix de Monaco, le 31 mai 1981. Le succès du petit Québécois est aussi et surtout un triomphe sur sa Ferrari 126 C. La force herculéenne de son moteur turbo alliée à un châssis médiocre, plus la témérité de Villeneuve et sa maîtrise stupéfiante de la voiture – tel est le bon cocktail qui rend les Grands Prix si fascinants.

Cette année-là, la Formule 1 remporte un succès sans précédent. 31 voitures sont inscrites. Cinq tombent à travers le tamis des préqualifications du jeudi tandis que six autres sont victimes du numerus clausus des essais à Monaco, notamment Keke Rosberg sur sa Fittipaldi. Le Finlandais volant n'attendra pas longtemps pour se venger – il sera champion du monde en 1982 et gagnera notamment à Monaco en 1983 !

Dès avant le départ, les pilotes sont nerveux : un incendie a éclaté dans les cuisines de l'Hôtel Loews. Le feu est éteint, mais de l'eau a coulé dans le tunnel, qui est de toute façon l'un des points névralgiques du circuit. Les 20 pilotes le franchiront-ils sains et saufs face à une adhérence soudain aléatoire ? 18 y réussiront au premier tour, mais avec une heure de retard. Mario Andretti (Alfa Romeo T 179 C) et Andrea de Cesaris (McLaren MP 4/1) se sont déjà accrochés à la sortie de Sainte Trinité. La sainte Trinité respecte tout d'abord l'ordre qui s'est cristallisé lors des essais : Nelson Piquet sur Brabham BT 49 C devant Villeneuve sur Ferrari et Nigel Mansell sur Lotus 87. Celui-ci va bientôt être attaqué sans répit par Carlos Reutemann qui, d'un coup de pouce de sa Williams FW 07 C, précipitera au 14ᵉ tour l'ambitieux Britannique dans les glissières. L'incident vaudra à Alan Jones, le coéquipier de Reutemann, de récupérer la troisième place. Mais, pour conquérir la deuxième, l'Australien devra se battre avec acharnement avant de trouver le passage derrière la Ferrari de Villeneuve toujours en sauvages contre-braquages.

Le Brésilien Piquet ne peut résister qu'un certain temps aux attaques acharnées de l'Australien. Au 54ᵉ tour, la Brabham entre en contact avec la Theodore de Patrick Tambay au virage du Bureau de Tabac et atterrit dans les glissières de sécurité. Jones ne pourra cependant se réjouir de son cadeau du ciel que pendant 20 minutes : la Williams est ralentie par des difficultés d'alimentation en essence. Un arrêt au stand au 67ᵉ tour ne permet pas d'y remédier. Lorsqu'il reprend la piste, il ressent déjà l'haleine brûlante de Villeneuve, qui double la Williams six tours plus tard, sous les applaudissements frénétiques des *tifosi,* juste devant la ligne de chronométrage.

Le reste n'est plus qu'une formalité, une victoire que tous voulaient – une victoire qui est la quatre-vingtième dans l'histoire de Ferrari. Dorénavant, le 27 n'est plus un chiffre anonyme.

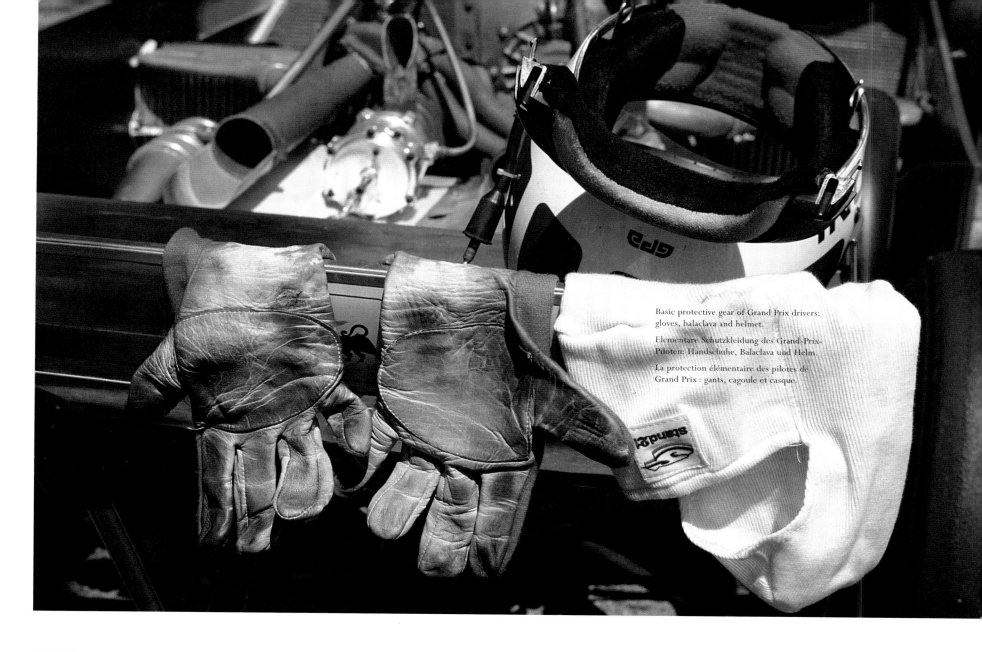

Basic protective gear of Grand Prix drivers:
gloves, balaclava and helmet.

Elementare Schutzkleidung des Grand-Prix-
Piloten: Handschuhe, Balaclava und Helm.

La protection élémentaire des pilotes de
Grand Prix : gants, cagoule et casque.

N°	DRIVERS		ENTRANTS	CARS	ENGINES	PRACTICE RESULTS	RACE RESULTS
27	**Gilles Villeneuve**	**CDN**	**SEFAC Ferrari S.p.A.**	**Ferrari 126CK**	**Ferrari V6 1496 cc + T**	**2nd: 1'25"788**	**1st: 1h54'23"38**
1	Alan Jones	AUS	Albilad-Saudia Racing Team	Williams FW07C	Cosworth V8 2993 cc	7th: 1'26"538	2nd: 1h55'03"29
26	Jacques Laffite	F	Equipe Ligier Gitanes	Ligier JS17	Matra V12 2993 cc	8th: 1'26"704	3rd: 1h55'52"62
28	Didier Pironi	F	SEFAC Ferrari S.p.A.	Ferrari 126CK	Ferrari V6 1496 cc + T	17th: 1'28"266	4th: 75 laps
3	Eddie Cheever	USA	Tyrrell Racing	Tyrrell 010	Cosworth V8 2993 cc	15th: 1'27"594	5th: 74 laps
14	Marc Surer	CH	Ensign Racing	Ensign N180B	Cosworth V8 2993 cc	19th: 1'28"339	6th: 74 laps
33	Patrick Tambay	F	Theodore Racing Team	Theodore TY 01	Cosworth V8 2993 cc	16th: 1'27"939	7th: 72 laps
5	*Nelson Piquet*	*BR*	*Parmalat Racing Team*	*Brabham BT49C*	*Cosworth V8 2993 cc*	*1st: 1'25"710*	R
7	John Watson	GB	McLaren International	McLaren MP4	Cosworth V8 2993 cc	10th: 1'27"058	R
23	Bruno Giacomelli	I	Marlboro Team Alfa Romeo	Alfa Romeo 179C	Alfa Romeo V12 2995 cc	18th: 1'28"323	R
4	Michele Alboreto	I	Tyrrell Racing	Tyrrell 010	Cosworth V8 2993 cc	20th: 1'28"358	R
15	Alain Prost	F	Equipe Renault Elf	Renault RE30	Renault V6 1492 cc + T	9th: 1'26"953	R
2	Carlos Reutemann	RA	Albilad-Saudia Racing Team	Williams FW07C	Cosworth V8 2993 cc	4th: 1'26"010	R
16	René Arnoux	F	Equipe Renault Elf	Renault RE20B	Renault V6 1492 cc + T	13th: 1'27"513	R
11	Elio de Angelis	I	Team Essex Lotus	Lotus 87	Cosworth V8 2993 cc	6th: 1'26"259	R
29	Riccardo Patrese	I	Arrows Racing Team	Arrows A3	Cosworth V8 2993 cc	5th: 1'26"040	R
12	Nigel Mansell	GB	Team Essex Lotus	Lotus 87	Cosworth V8 2993 cc	3rd: 1'25"815	R
30	Siegfried Stohr	I	Arrows Racing Team	Arrows A3	Cosworth V8 2993 cc	14th: 1'27"564	R
22	Mario Andretti	USA	Marlboro Team Alfa Romeo	Alfa Romeo 179C	Alfa Romeo V12 2995 cc	12th: 1'27"512	R
8	Andrea de Cesaris	I	McLaren International	McLaren MP4/1	Cosworth V8 2993 cc	11th: 1'27"122	R

(1) By his arrival at the Loews Hotel on the first lap, Nelson Piquet (Brabham) has already built himself a useful little lead. (2) A stronger presence, but struggling in Monaco: the Renaults, here with Alain Prost.

(1) Bei der Ankunft vor dem Loews-Hotel in der ersten Runde hat sich Nelson Piquet (Brabham) bereits einen nützlichen kleinen Vorsprung herausgefahren. (2) Stärker in Szene, aber noch immer unbehaust in Monaco: die Renault, hier Alain Prost.

(1) Juste devant l'entrée de l'Hôtel Loews, au premier tour, Nelson Piquet (Brabham) a déjà une petite avance qui lui sera bien utile.
(2) Fait meilleure impression, mais pas toujours comme des poissons dans l'eau à Monaco : les Renault, ici Alain Prost.

(1) In the light at the end of the tunnel: Pironi (Ferrari). (2) Impressive Monaco debut for Nigel Mansell (Lotus number 12), here in front of the two Williamses. (3) Disappointing final performance in the Principality for Andretti (Alfa Romeo).

(1) Im Licht am Ende des Tunnels: Pironi (Ferrari). (2) Eindrucksvolles Monaco-Debüt für Nigel Mansell (Lotus Nummer 12), hier vor den beiden Williams. (3) Trauriges Finale im Fürstentum für Andretti (Alfa Romeo).

(1) Lumière au bout du tunnel : Pironi (Ferrari). (2) Impressionnants débuts à Monaco pour Nigel Mansell (Lotus numéro 12), ici devant les deux Williams. (3) Triste finale dans la Principauté pour Andretti (Alfa Romeo).

(1) Short but not sweet: de Cesaris (McLaren number 8) and Andretti only get a few hundred yards.
(2) Retirement: from the 30th lap onwards, Patrese's Arrows is parked opposite the Tip-Top bar, with a faulty engine. (3) Two exits for Arnoux (Renault), one in qualifying and one in the race, and (4) two departures for Pironi, too, both in qualifying on Thursday.

(1) Kurzes Vergnügen: de Cesaris (McLaren Nummer 8) und Andretti kommen nur ein paar hundert Meter weit. (2) Ruhe-Stand: Patreses Arrows parkt seit der 30. Runde schräg gegenüber der Tip-Top-Bar, Motor kaputt. (3) Zwei Abgänge für Arnoux (Renault), einer im Training und einer im Rennen, (4) zwei Abflüge auch für Pironi, beide im Training am Donnerstag.

(1) Le plaisir n'aura pas duré longtemps : de Cesaris (McLaren numéro 8) et Andretti ne couvriront que quelques centaines de mètres. (2) Stationnement : l'Arrows de Patrese est garée en biais en face du bar le Tip-Top depuis le 30ᵉ tour, moteur cassé. (3) Deux sorties de route pour Arnoux (Renault), une aux essais et une en course, (4) deux sorties de route aussi pour Pironi, toutes les deux durant les essais du jeudi.

4

(1) Tiring business: Mario Andretti, at 41 years of age the doyen among the drivers. (2) Calmly waiting: Villeneuve exercises his patience until the Ferrari 126 C has been reassembled. (3) Paddock snack: a Williams mechanic consumes a banana. General scepticism: (4) Carlos Reutemann, (5) Bruno Giacomelli and (6) John Watson.

(1) Altersmüde: Mario Andretti, mit 41 Jahren Nestor unter den Fahrern. (2) Warte-Stand: Villeneuve übt sich in Geduld, bis das Puzzle Ferrari 126 C wieder zusammengesetzt ist. (3) Natur-Snack: Ein Williams-Mechaniker verzehrt eine Banane. Allgemeine Skepsis: (4) Carlos Reutemann, (5) Bruno Giacomelli und (6) John Watson.

(1) Fatigué : Mario Andretti, à 41 ans, le doyen des pilotes. (2) Attente : Villeneuve fait preuve de patience en attendant que soit recomposé le puzzle de sa Ferrari 126 C. (3) Vitamines : un mécanicien de Williams dévore une banane. Scepticisme général : (4) Carlos Reutemann, (5) Bruno Giacomelli et (6) John Watson.

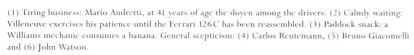

(1) Summit meeting: Jackie Stewart, Juan Manuel Fangio and Stirling Moss framing Helen Stewart. 216 Grands Prix, 67 wins and eight championships are gathered here. James Bond (Sean Connery) is standing in the background. (2) Everblue: Dreyfus' Bugatti, which won in 1930, looks more youthful than its passengers. (3) Raise your glasses: Keke Rosberg knows how to celebrate. (4) United for the last time: Mario Andretti and Alfa designer Carlo Chiti, a legend himself.

(1) Gipfeltreffen: Jackie Stewart, Juan Manuel Fangio und Stirling Moss geben Helen Stewart einen repräsentativen Rahmen. Hier sind 216 Grand Prix, 67 Siege und acht Championate versammelt. James Bond (Sean Connery) hält sich diskret im Hintergrund. (2) Everblue: Der 1930 siegreiche Bugatti von Dreyfus wirkt jugendlicher als seine Passagiere. (3) Hoch die Tassen: Keke Rosberg weiß zu feiern.
(4) Zum letzten Mal vereint: Mario Andretti und Alfa-Konstrukteur Carlo Chiti, auch er eine Legende.

(1) Rencontre au sommet : Jackie Stewart, Juan Manuel Fangio et Stirling Moss composent une galerie vraiment prestigieuse pour Helen Stewart. Ils représentent 216 Grands Prix, 67 victoires et huit titres de champion du monde. James Bond (Sean Connery) se tient discrètement dans l'ombre. (2) Everblue : la Bugatti de Dreyfus, victorieuse en 1930 à Monaco, semble plus en forme que ses passagers. (3) A la vôtre : Keke Rosberg sait comment faire la fête.
(4) Pour la dernière fois réunis : Mario Andretti et l'ingenieur d'Alfa, Carlo Chiti, lui aussi une légende.

1982

The 40th Monaco Grand Prix on 23 May 1982 held everything in store that Formula 1 was capable of delivering in the Principality, the sleep-inducing procession causing many to stifle yawns in the palms of their hands, the hair-tearing cases of bad luck and the exhilarating points on the league table. When the victor crossed the finishing line in this race, he was quite unaware of whether or not he had in fact won. Then, of course, there was the inclement weather, always an unpredictable factor at this time of year, a wild card which exhibited a preference for dispensing good luck to the underdog.

Even the training sessions provided a few surprises. Three of the four turbo-engined cars competing in this event showed their true colors as pike in the goldfish pond of naturally-aspirated engines. Didier Pironi, driving the only Ferrari 126 C2 to enter the race, claimed fifth position on the starting grid, with Alain Prost in the Renault RE 30B in fourth position and his team colleague René Arnoux out in pole position. This seemed like a genuine case of justice being done, because two years previously, the little Frenchman had had to cope with the humiliation of starting from last place on the last row.

This time, he went straight into the lead, while Prost had to content himself with third position until Bruno Giacomelli's Alfa Romeo 182 suffered transmission damage during the fourth lap. Two Renaults out in front — a new and unusual experience in the claustrophobic twists and bends of this urban track. However, the French duel failed to survive beyond the fifteenth lap, when Arnoux went into a spin beside the swimming pool as his engine expired. Alain Prost was now out in front, followed by Riccardo Patrese in his Brabham BT 49D, Pironi's Ferrari and the second Alfa Romeo, with the sometimes erratic Andrea de Cesaris at the wheel. For 59 laps, these four whirled round the track in formation like toy cars on a roundabout — constantly in motion without gaining or losing any ground. That was when the unexpected occurred: a sudden shower of rain mingled with the oil and tyre rubber on the track, turning it into a slippery film.

At this time, Alain Prost had not turned into the cool-headed professor he was to become in later years, and he was the first one to go. A wild skid after the chicane brought him into contact with the barriers lining the track. Patrese was thereforein the lead on lap 74, but then he became the next to go. A spin at the hairpin at Loews and the Ford Cosworth engine stalled. Although the Italian was able to bring it back to life on the following downhill gradient, Pironi shot past and as he passed the timing line he signalled frantically to race official Michel Ferry to stop the event immediately: conditions by then were quite impossible.

He, of course, was the one who stood to benefit most from this, but in the dim light of the tunnel, the Ferrari V6 suddenly lost its voice: a major fault in the electrical system. Even the Alfa Romeo driven by de Cesaris, for whom a first ever Grand Prix win seemed now to be beckoning, failed to get very far. His fuel tank ran completely dry. This left victory to the man laughing to himself from third place — Riccardo Patrese. Mind you, his laughter remained fairly muted for quite a time until he was convinced beyond doubt that he had won.

Der 40. Grand Prix de Monaco am 23. Mai 1982 wartet mit allem auf, was die Formel 1 im Fürstentum zu bieten hat, die einlullende Prozession, bis mancher sein Gähnen hinter der hohlen Hand verbirgt, das haarsträubende Pech und die pfiffige Pointe: Als der Sieger über die Ziellinie fährt, weiß er nicht einmal, daß er gewonnen hat. Und wieder greift das Wetter ein, stets eine Unwägbarkeit um diese Jahreszeit, ein Joker, den das Glück hier gern dem Underdog zuspielt.

Schon das Training sorgt für Überraschungen. Drei der vier anwesenden Turbos erweisen sich als die Hechte im Karpfenteich der Saugmotoren. Didier Pironi steht mit dem einzigen gemeldeten Ferrari 126 C2 auf Position fünf, Alain Prost im Renault RE 30B auf Platz vier, sein Teamkollege René Arnoux gar auf der Pole Position. Das scheint fürwahr ausgleichende Gerechtigkeit, denn zwei Jahre zuvor blieb dem kleinen Franzosen lediglich die Schmach des letzten Rangs in der letzten Reihe.

Diesmal geht er sofort in Führung, während sich Prost an dritter Stelle gedulden muß, bis Bruno Giacomellis Alfa Romeo 182 im vierten Durchgang von einem Getriebeschaden heimgesucht wird. Zwei Renault in Front — das ist neu und ungewöhnlich im klaustrophobischen Kurvengewürm des Kurses durch die Stadt. Das panfranzösische Doppel übersteht indes die 15. Runde nicht: Da dreht sich Arnoux am Schwimmbad, sein Motor verstummt und meldet sich in diesem Rennen nicht mehr zu Wort. Alain Prost ist vorn, gefolgt von Riccardo Patreses Brabham BT 49D, Pironis Ferrari und dem zweiten Alfa Romeo, den der wilde Andrea de Cesaris lenkt. 59 Runden lang zirkulieren diese vier wie die Spielmobile auf einem Karussell — ständig in Bewegung, ohne sich gegeneinander zu verschieben. Dann aber ereignet sich das Unerwartete: Ein Schauer geht nieder, vermischt sich mit Öl und Reifenabrieb rund um die Piste zu einem glitschigen Film.

Noch ist Alain Prost nicht der kühle Professor der späteren Jahre. Ihn erwischt es als ersten: Ausrutscher hinter der Schikane, unsanfter Kontakt mit der Streckenbegrenzung. Patrese führt in Runde 74, doch er ist als nächster dran: Dreher in der Haarnadel bei Loews, abgestorbener Ford Cosworth. Während ihn der Italiener auf dem folgenden Gefälle wieder zum Leben erweckt, passiert Pironi und gibt Rennleiter Michel Ferry durch hektische Handzeichen zu verstehen, er müsse die Veranstaltung umgehend abbrechen, die Bedingungen seien unmöglich.

Vor allem er selbst hätte davon profitiert. Im Halbdunkel des Tunnels verschlägt es dem Ferrari-V6 die Sprache: Schaden an der Elektrik. Und auch der Alfa von de Cesaris, dem plötzlich sein einziger Grand-Prix-Sieg zu winken scheint, kommt nicht mehr weit: staubtrockener Tank. Bleibt als lachender Dritter Riccardo Patrese. Aber sein Gelächter klingt noch einige Zeit verdutzt.

Le 40e Grand Prix de Monaco, le 23 mai 1982, réunit tous les ingrédients que la Formule 1 a coutume d'offrir dans la Principauté: la procession si ennuyeuse que beaucoup ont du mal à dissimuler leurs bâillements derrière la main, la malchance qui vous laisse bouche bée et la surprise la plus inattendue : lorsque le vainqueur franchit la ligne d'arrivée, il ne se doute pas le moins du monde qu'il a gagné. Et, une fois de plus, la météo, toujours imprévisible à cette époque de l'année, vient troubler les règles du jeu, joker que la chance glisse souvent dans les mains de ceux qui restent, sinon, dans un semi-anonymat.

Les essais, déjà, réservent bien des surprises : trois des quatre moteurs turbo jouent les loups dans la bergerie des moteurs atmosphériques. Avec la seule et unique Ferrari inscrite, une 126 C2, Didier Pironi obtient la cinquième place, tandis qu'Alain Prost sur sa Renault RE 30 B est quatrième et son coéquipier René Arnoux détient même la pole position. Ce n'est que justice, car, deux ans auparavant, rien n'avait été épargné au petit Français, pas même l'humiliation de prendre le départ à la place en dernière ligne.

Cette fois-ci, il prend immédiatement le commandement tandis que Prost doit patienter à la troisième place, en attendant que l'Alfa Romeo 182 de Bruno Giacomelli tombe en panne de boîte de vitesses au quatrième tour. Deux Renault en tête — c'est nouveau et pour le moins inhabituel dans les sinuosités qui engendrent la claustrophobie de ce circuit urbain. Le duo franco-français ne verra toutefois pas la fin du 15e tour, lorsqu'Arnoux se met en tête-à-queue à la piscine et cale irrémédiablement son moteur, fin de la représentation. Alain Prost prend la tête, suivi de la Brabham BT 49D de Riccardo Patrese, de la Ferrari de Pironi et de la deuxième Alfa Romeo, pilotée par le bouillant Andrea de Cesaris. Pendant 59 tours, les quatre hommes tournent sagement comme sur un manège — toujours en mouvement, mais sans jamais échanger leurs places. C'est alors que se produit l'inattendu : une averse humidifie la piste, qui, avec le mélange d'huile et de gomme des pneumatiques, se transforme en patinoire.

Alain Prost n'est pas encore le froid professeur qu'il deviendra plus tard. C'est lui la première victime : il avait virtuellement course gagnée quand sa Renault percute très violemment les rails à la sortie de la chicane. Patrese reprend alors la tête au 74e tour, et lui aussi commet alors une faute : tête-à-queue dans l'épingle du Loews, moteur Ford Cosworth calé. Pendant que l'Italien réussit à faire redémarrer son moteur dans la descente, Pironi le double et, en dépassant la ligne de chronométrage, fait comprendre par des signes nerveux au directeur de course, Michel Ferry, qu'il doit interrompre la course, les conditions étant intolérables.

C'est surtout lui, bien sûr, qui en aurait profité. Mais, dans la semi-obscurité du tunnel, le V6 de la Ferrari se tait soudain : défaillance électrique. Et l'Alfa de Cesaris, qui semblait soudain avoir sa première et unique victoire en Grand Prix à portée de la main, n'arrive plus, elle non plus : pénurie d'essence. Rira bien qui rira le dernier. Mais, malgré son rire, le troisième larron Riccardo Patrese restera longtemps encore incrédule, avant d'être enfin persuadé de son incontestable victoire.

Loyalty beyond death: 14 days have passed since Gilles Villeneuve died. But the magic of the small man will live on for a long time.

Treue über den Tod hinaus: Seit 14 Tagen ist Gilles Villeneuve nicht mehr unter den Lebenden. Aber der Zauber, der von dem kleinen Mann ausging, wird noch lange nachwirken.

Fidélité au-delà de la mort : il y a quinze jours que Gilles Villeneuve n'est plus de ce monde. Mais la magie qui émanait de ce petit bonhomme agira encore longtemps.

N°	DRIVERS		ENTRANTS	CARS	ENGINES	PRACTICE RESULTS	RACE RESULTS
2	**Riccardo Patrese**	**I**	**Parmalat Racing Team**	**Brabham BT49D**	**Cosworth V8 2993 cc**	**2nd: 1'23"791**	**1st: 1h54'11"259**
28	Didier Pironi	F	SEFAC Ferrari S.p.A.	Ferrari 126C2	Ferrari V6 1496 cc + T	5th: 1'24"585	2nd: 75 laps (R)
22	Andrea de Cesaris	I	Marlboro Team Alfa Romeo	Alfa Romeo 182	Alfa Romeo V12 2995 cc	7th: 1'24"928	3rd: 75 laps (R)
12	Nigel Mansell	GB	John Player Team Lotus	Lotus 91	Cosworth V8 2993 cc	11th: 1'25"642	4th: 75 laps
11	Elio de Angelis	I	John Player Team Lotus	Lotus 91	Cosworth V8 2993 cc	15th: 1'26"456	5th: 75 laps
5	Derek Daly	IRL	Williams Grand Prix Engineering	Williams FW08	Cosworth V8 2993 cc	8th: 1'25"390	6th: 74 laps (R)
15	Alain Prost	F	Equipe Renault Elf	Renault RE30B	Renault V6 1492 cc + T	4th: 1'24"439	7th: 73 laps (R)
4	Brian Henton	GB	Team Tyrrell	Tyrrell 011	Cosworth V8 2993 cc	17th: 1'26"690	8th: 72 laps
29	Marc Surer	CH	Arrows Racing Team	Arrows A4	Cosworth V8 2993 cc	19th: 1'27"019	9th: 70 laps
3	Michele Alboreto	I	Team Tyrrell	Tyrrell 011	Cosworth V8 2993 cc	9th: 1'25"449	10th: 69 laps (R)
6	Keke Rosberg	SF	Williams Grand Prix Engineering	Williams FW08	Cosworth V8 2993 cc	6th: 1'24"649	R
8	Niki Lauda	A	McLaren International	McLaren MP4B	Cosworth V8 2993 cc	12th: 1'25"838	R
1	Nelson Piquet	BR	Parmalat Racing Team	Brabham BT50	BMW 4L 1499 cc + T	13th: 1'26"075	R
7	John Watson	GB	McLaren International	McLaren MP4B	Cosworth V8 2993 cc	10th: 1'25"583	R
9	Manfred Winkelhock	D	Team ATS	ATS D5	Cosworth V8 2993 cc	14th: 1'26"260	R
26	Jacques Laffite	F	Equipe Talbot Gitanes	Ligier JS19	Matra V12 2993 cc	18th: 1'27"007	R
25	Eddie Cheever	USA	Equipe Talbot Gitanes	Ligier JS19	Matra V12 2993 cc	16th: 1'26"463	R
10	Eliseo Salazar	RCH	Team ATS	ATS D5	Cosworth V8 2993 cc	20th: 1'27"022	R
16	René Arnoux	F	Equipe Renault Elf	Renault RE30B	Renault V6 1492 cc + T	1st: 1'23"281	R
23	Bruno Giacomelli	I	Marlboro Team Alfa Romeo	Alfa Romeo 182	Alfa Romeo V12 2995 cc	3rd: 1'23"939	R

(1) Tire marks fanning out on the ramp after Casino Square show that the ideal line is an individual choice here. Patrese (Brabham) has decided on the middle way. (2) Second in Monaco and moral winner of the 1982 World Championship: Pironi (Ferrari). (3) Wild but apparently indestructible: de Cesaris (Alfa Romeo). (4) Brief luck: two Renaults to the fore, Arnoux in front of Prost.

(1) Strahlenförmig sich auffächernde Radierspuren in der Rampe nach dem Casino-Vorplatz zeigen, daß die Ideallinie hier individuell gewählt wird. Patrese (Brabham) hat sich für den Mittelweg entschieden. (2) Zweiter in Monaco und moralischer Sieger der Weltmeisterschaft 1982: Pironi (Ferrari). (3) Wild, aber offensichtlich unzerstörbar: de Cesaris (Alfa Romeo). (4) Kurzes Glück: zwei Renault vorn, Arnoux vor Prost.

(1) Les diverses traces de freinage après la Place du Casino montrent que chacun recherche ici sa trajectoire personnelle. Patrese (Brabham) a opté pour la voie médiane. (2) Deuxième à Monaco et vainqueur moral du championnat du monde de 1982 : Pironi (Ferrari). (3) Sauvage, mais apparemment indestructible : de Cesaris (Alfa Romeo). (4) Bref bonheur : deux Renault en tête, Arnoux mène devant Prost.

Variations on a theme: (1) V12 from Alfa Romeo in an Alfa Romeo. (2) Turbo-charged in-line four-cylinder engine from BMW in a Brabham. (3) V6 turbo from Renault in a Renault. (4) V8 from Ford in a McLaren.

Thema con variazioni: (1) V12 von Alfa Romeo im Alfa Romeo. (2) Aufgeladener Reihenvierzylinder von BMW im Brabham. (3) V6 Turbo von Renault im Renault. (4) V8 von Ford im McLaren.

Thema con variazioni : (1) V12 Alfa Romeo dans l'Alfa Romeo. (2) Quatre-cylindres en ligne suralimenté de BMW dans la Brabham. (3) V6 Turbo de Renault dans la Renault. (4) V8 Ford dans la McLaren.

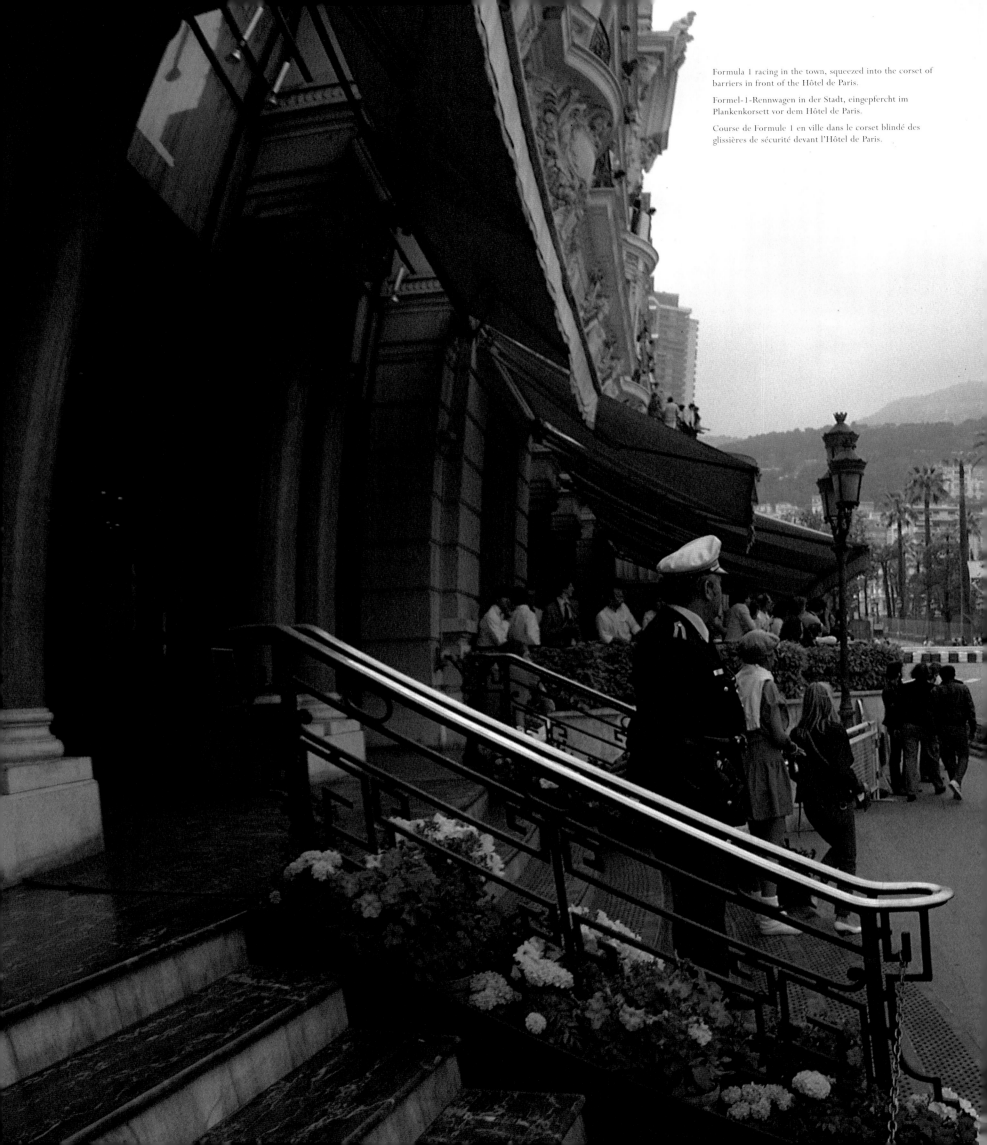

Formula 1 racing in the town, squeezed into the corset of barriers in front of the Hôtel de Paris.

Formel-1-Rennwagen in der Stadt, eingepfercht im Plankenkorsett vor dem Hôtel de Paris.

Course de Formule 1 en ville dans le corset blindé des glissières de sécurité devant l'Hôtel de Paris.

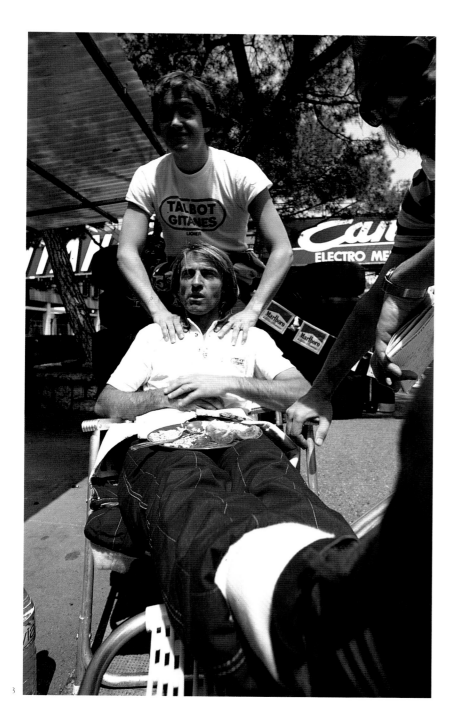

Just having a rest: (1) kitchen staff of the Hôtel de Paris, (2) track staff of the AC de Monaco, (3) driving staff of the Ligier Team, here Jacques Laffite. Dynamic gestures from (4) Jackie Stewart and (5) John Watson. (6) Foolish expression from the surprised winner Patrese.

Einfach mal Pause gemacht: (1) Küchenpersonal des Hôtel de Paris, (2) Streckenpersonal des AC de Monaco, (3) Fahrerpersonal des Ligier-Teams, hier Jacques Laffite. Dynamische Gestik bei (4) Jackie Stewart und (5) John Watson. (6) Tölpelhafte Mimik des überraschten Siegers Patrese.

Une pause sans doute bien méritée : (1) la brigade de la cuisine de l'Hôtel de Paris. (2) Commissaires de piste de l'AC de Monaco. (3) Mercenaires de l'écurie Ligier, ici Jacques Laffite. Discussion animée chez (4) Jackie Stewart et (5) John Watson. (6) Riccardo Patrese est apparemment bien surpris d'apprendre qu'il est le vainqueur.

PERMANENCE AND CHANGE

DAUER IM WECHSEL · PERMANENCE DANS LE CHANGEMENT

The layout of today's circuit is surprisingly similar to the one which that eloquent visionary Antony Noghes planned in October 1928 during his morning walks across the magical mile between the Grimaldi rock and the eastern slope of Monte Carlo. But where "Williams" at that time made do with a speed of 50 mph for his fastest lap, Alain Prost rushed along in his Williams in 1993 at an average speed of 89 mph. That is an increase of 70 percent in speed – and absurdity.

Profound incisions into the anatomy of the course were undertaken three times. In 1932, when the tramlines were levered out of the tarmac, in 1961, when the straw bales were replaced by barriers over large sections of the course, and above all in 1973, when the original course of 2,013 miles had 206 yards added on with a left-right-left passage around the swimming baths, as well as a hook around the Rascasse bar, which replaced the previous gasometer bend.

In 1976, a carefully preserved anachronism disappeared – a sign that the new spirit of the times ruled here too. That year, that Monegasque national monument Louis Chiron, himself a winner in Monaco in 1931, was retired from his role in the start procedure and replaced by a set of light bulbs. For until then the sprightly old man had insisted on lowering the starting flag and facing for one defiant moment the inferno which he had triggered.

Das Layout des heutigen Circuits unterscheidet sich erstaunlich wenig von dem, das sich der beredte Visionär Antony Noghes im Oktober 1928 bei morgendlichen Spaziergängen über die magische Meile zwischen dem Grimaldifelsen und dem Osthang des Monte Carlo zurechtlegte. Wo indes »Williams« damals in seiner schnellsten Runde mit Tempo 85 im Schnitt auskam, beeilte sich Alain Prost auf Williams 1993 mit 143 Stundenkilometern. Das sind 70 Prozent Zuwachs an Geschwindigkeit – und an Absurdität.

Dreimal schnitt man tief in die Anatomie des Kurses ein: 1932, als die Straßenbahnschienen aus dem Makadam gestemmt wurden, 1961, als über weite Abschnitte Leitplanken anstelle der Strohballen traten, und vor allem 1973: Da wurden der Ur-Piste von 3240 Metern Länge 188 Meter angefügt, eine Links-Rechts-Rechts-Links-Passage um das Schwimmbad sowie ein Haken um die Rascasse-Bar anstelle der früheren Gasometerkurve.

1976 verschwand ein sorgsam gehüteter Anachronismus, als Zeichen, nun wehe endgültig der Geist der neuen Zeit, auch hier. Da wurde nämlich das monegassische Nationaldenkmal Louis Chiron, selber Monaco-Sieger 1931, als Bestandteil der Startprozedur durch den üblichen Satz Glühbirnen ersetzt, gewissermaßen im Rahmen der Altersvorsorge. Denn der rüstige Greis ließ es sich bis dahin nicht nehmen, die Startflagge zu senken und sich dann noch trotzig einen Augenblick

Le déroulement du circuit d'aujourd'hui se distingue étonnement peu de celui qu'avait imaginé l'éloquent visionnaire Antony Noghes, en octobre 1928, lors de ses promenades matinales le long des kilomètres magiques entre le rocher des Grimaldi et le versant oriental de Monte-Carlo. Mais, là où « Williams » a couvert son tour le plus rapide à une vitesse moyenne de 85 km/h, Alain Prost, sur sa Williams, en était à 143 km/h en 1993, soit un gain de 70 pour cent en vitesse pure – et en absurdité.

Le circuit a subi une intervention chirurgicale à trois reprises : en 1932, quand on ôta du macadam les rails du tramway ; en 1961, lorsque des rails de sécurité remplacèrent des bottes de paille sur de longues sections, et, surtout, en 1973 : cette année-là, on ajouta en effet à la piste originale de 3 240 mètres 188 mètres supplémentaires, une chicane gauche-droite-droite-gauche autour de la piscine ainsi qu'un crochet autour du restaurant de la Rascasse, à la place de l'ancien virage du Gazomètre.

En 1976 disparaît un anachronisme minutieusement préservé, tel un symbole de l'esprit des temps nouveaux qui soufflent définitivement ici aussi, maintenant. Cette année-là, en effet, le monument national monégasque qu'est Louis Chiron, lui-même vainqueur à Monaco en 1931, qui faisait partie des meubles en tant qu'exécuteur de la procédure de départ, est remplacé par les traditionnels feux rouges et

Once a year Monaco prepares itself and puts on its armor for the Grand Prix. For the rest of the year things carry on as normal, like in the neighboring towns of Nice and Menton, gilded with an ever more sumptuous lifestyle and ever more luxury.

Einmal im Jahr rüstet Monaco auf und panzert sich für seinen Grand Prix. Ansonsten gehen die Dinge ihren Gang wie in den Nachbarstädten Nizza und Menton, vergoldet mit noch mehr Lifestyle und noch mehr Luxus.

Une fois par an, Monaco se transforme en une citadelle pour son Grand Prix. Pour le reste, la vie suit son cours comme dans les villes voisines, Nice et Menton, mais en plaqué or, avec encore plus d'attention accordée aux apparences en encore plus de luxe.

But no element of the track was changed and retouched as frequently as the chicane. This happened mostly if there had been a smash the previous year. Changes were made in 1956, for instance, after Alberto Ascari had ended up in the harbor with his Ferrari in 1955, and in 1968, after Lorenzo Bandini had suffered fatal burns in an accident nearby in 1967.

The section was given its present form in 1986, a compact square which forces the cars into first gear. The previous year, Derek Warwick, for example, had complained that he no longer perceived fixed contours at this spot, but only a wild kaleidoscope of colors. Ascari's exit was copied by the Australian Paul Hawkins ten years later, who also escaped unharmed. The scene has been immortalized in John Frankenheimer's 1966 cult film *Grand Prix*.

The history of the Monaco Grand Prix is full of spectacular crashes, most of which turned out not to be too serious, such as the collision between Nelson Piquet and Riccardo Patrese in a shower of debris, wheels and orange flames at Sainte Dévote in 1985 – perhaps because the little church nearby carries the same name.

dem Inferno entgegenzustellen, das er selbst angerichtet hatte. Kein Element der Strecke wurde indessen so häufig revidiert und retuschiert wie die Schikane, meistens dann, wenn es da im Vorjahr gekracht hatte, 1956 zum Beispiel, weil Alberto Ascari 1955 mit seinem Ferrari im Hafen wasserte, und 1968, nachdem Lorenzo Bandini bei einem Unfall 1967 ganz in der Nähe tödliche Brandverletzungen erlitten hatte. 1986 erhielt der Abschnitt seine gegenwärtige Form, ein kompaktes Karree, das die Wagen auf den ersten Gang zusammenstaucht. Im Jahr zuvor hatte sich etwa Derek Warwick beschwert, an dieser Stelle nehme er nur noch ein irres Kaleidoskop von Farben wahr, aber keine festen Konturen mehr. Die Dublette zu Ascaris Abgang lieferte zehn Jahre später der Australier Paul Hawkins und kam wie dieser für diesmal ungeschoren davon. In John Frankenheimers Kultfilm *Grand Prix* von 1966 ist die Szene verewigt.

Die Chronik der Großen Preise von Monaco ist voll von spektakulären Unfällen, die meistens glimpflich verliefen wie die Kollision von Nelson Piquet und Riccardo Patrese in einem Schauer von Trümmern, Rädern und orangefarbenem Feuer bei Sainte Dévote 1985 – vielleicht weil das Kirchlein ganz in der Nähe so heißt.

verts, en quelque sorte dans une mesure de prévoyance vieillesse. En effet, le vieil homme encore vert ne voulait se priver du plaisir d'abaisser personnellement le drapeau du départ puis de faire face encore, un bref instant, à l'enfer qu'il avait lui-même déclenché. Aucun tronçon du tracé n'a, par contre, été révisé et retouché aussi fréquemment que la chicane, le plus souvent parce qu'il s'y était produit un accident l'année précédente, comme en 1956, par exemple, quand Alberto Ascari avait plongé, en 1955, dans le port avec sa Ferrari, et en 1968, après que Lorenzo Bandini eut été victime d'un accident, en 1967, tout près de là et eut péri par suite de ses brûlures.

Cette section a pris sa forme actuelle en 1986, un carré compact qui oblige les pilotes à rétrograder jusqu'en première. L'année précédente, Derek Warwick s'était par exemple plaint de ne plus percevoir, à cet endroit, qu'un kaléidoscope flou de couleurs, mais plus aucun contour précis. Dix ans après Ascari, l'Australien Paul Hawkins fait un *remake* du plongeon de l'Italien dans le port, et, comme lui, s'en sort sain et sauf cette fois-ci. La scène a été immortalisée dans le film culte de John Frankenheimer, *Grand Prix*, tourné en 1966.

La chronique des Grands Prix de Monaco est émaillée d'accidents spectaculaires qui se sont le plus souvent terminés sans mal pour leurs protagonistes, ainsi la collision entre Nelson Piquet et Riccardo Patrese, qui s'est soldée par un monceau de ruines et de roues balayées par une tornade de feu à Sainte Dévote en 1985 – bénéficiant peut-être, à cette occasion, de la protection de la petite chapelle toute proche.

1983

No matter how firm and unyielding the hierarchies forged in the Darwinian driving project known as Formula 1 may be, all are equal when they face the majesty of the god of weather. This god bestowed his largesse at this, the 41st Monaco Grand Prix, with his customary and untrammelled favoritism, his pampered favorite on this weekend being Keijo Rosberg, known worldwide as Keke. His white Williams FW 08 D bore the starting number 1, gained by winning the previous year's World Championship, and he was first across the finishing line at this Grand Prix.

Others had such awful luck that words simply failed them. For the first practice on the Thursday conditions were dry, but the Michelin tyres on the two McLarens driven by Niki Lauda and John Watson failed to heat up sufficiently to really get to grips with the asphalt down the boulevards and esplanades of Monaco. On Saturday it rained – but too late to make any preparations. As a result, both men failed to qualify – a first for Lauda in his long professional career. The Irishman groaned and the Austrian grumbled. Team boss Ron Dennis was positively fuming.

The only consolation was that he was not faced with difficult decisions on the day of the race. The track was now wet in places, the sky was leaden and rain seemed imminent. Anxious glances at the sky culminated in 12 incorrect decisions: a dozen of the 20 participants took their places on the starting grid with wet-weather tyres, including the two men on the first row, Alain Prost in his Renault RE 40 and René Arnoux in a Ferrari 126 C 2, both with turbo engines behind them. In contrast, the Williams drivers Rosberg (fifth place during qualifying) and Jacques Laffite (eighth on the grid) disregarded the risk and appeared with slicks on their wheels. This paid off well for them. All the way from the convoluted section at Sainte Dévote, the flying Finn was nose-to-tail with Prost and, early on the second lap, he overtook the Frenchman just before the same place, dancing nimbly over the drying track with the acuity of a tightrope artist.

Ten minutes later, the pits became a scene of frenzied activity as everyone pulled in to have slicks fitted. However, the gain in traction is always directly proportional to the loss of irrecoverable time. For example, Alain Prost, already beset by problems with third gear, needed the remainder of the race to work his way back up to third place which, for the management team at Renault, was seen as nothing less than a defeat. Out in front, there was every sign of a double victory taking shape for Williams, with Rosberg leading Laffite until the little man from Paris was forced to leave the race on lap 54 with transmission damage. Nelson Piquet now surged forward in his Brabham BT 52 to take second place, the four-cylinder BMW turbo engine driving him forward like a fist in the small of his back. The Brazilian did everything in his power to further improve his position, but he was still burdened by the valuable seconds he had lost when changing tyres. This meant that the Monaco Grand Prix, the fifth race of the season, had also delivered the fifth winner of the year, and a well-deserved win it was, too.

Die Hierarchien, die sich im darwinistischen Pilot-Projekt Formel 1 ausgebildet haben, mögen noch so streng und festgefügt sein, vor der Majestät des Wettergotts sind alle gleich. Auch beim 41. Großen Preis von Monaco teilt er seine Gunst wieder mit unbekümmerter Willkür zu. Sein verhätschelter Liebling an diesem Wochenende: Keijo Rosberg, von aller Welt Keke genannt, mit der Startnummer eins für die Weltmeisterschaft des Vorjahres auf seinem weißen Williams FW 08 D und am Ende auch die Nummer eins in diesem Großen Preis.

Anderen hingegen geht es so dreckig, daß es ihnen schier die Sprache verschlägt. Beim ersten Zeittraining am Donnerstag ist es trocken. Aber die Michelin-Pneus der beiden McLaren von Niki Lauda und John Watson heizen sich nicht genug auf, als daß sie sich so richtig in den Asphalt der Boulevards und Quais von Monaco krallen könnten. Am Samstag regnet es – zu spät, um noch irgendetwas auszurichten. So qualifizieren sich alle beide nicht, Lauda zum ersten Mal in seiner langen Laufbahn. Der Ire grollt, der Österreicher grantelt, Teamchef Ron Dennis schäumt.

Dafür bleibt ihm am Renntag die Qual der Wahl erspart. Der Parcours ist stellenweise naß, der Himmel bleigrau, weiterer Niederschlag droht. Ängstliche Blicke nach oben münden ein in zwölf Fehlentscheidungen: Ein Dutzend der 20 Teilnehmer steht am Start auf Regenreifen, unter anderen die Männer in der ersten Reihe, Alain Prost auf dem Renault RE 40 und René Arnoux im Ferrari 126 C 2, beide mit Turbo-Triebwerken im Heck. Die Williams-Piloten Rosberg (Rang fünf im Training) und Jacques Laffite (Startplatz acht) jedoch scheuen das Risiko nicht und setzen auf Slicks. Das zahlt sich aus. Schon im Geschlängel von Sainte Dévote sitzt der fliegende Finne Prost im Nacken, und zu Beginn der zweiten Runde hat er den Franzosen vor der gleichen Stelle überholt, seinen Weg mit dem Sensorium eines Seiltänzers über den noch immer feuchten Kurs tastend.

Zehn Minuten später herrscht Hochbetrieb an den Boxen – allüberall zieht man Slicks auf. Der Gewinn von Haftung ist indessen identisch mit dem Verlust von unwiederbringlicher Zeit. Alain Prost zum Beispiel, ohnehin behindert durch Probleme mit dem dritten Gang, benötigt den Rest des Rennens, um sich wieder auf Position drei vorzuarbeiten, aus der Sicht der Régie Renault allemal eine Niederlage. An der Spitze scheint sich unterdes ein doppelter Williams-Sieg anzubahnen, Rosberg vor Laffite, bis der kleine Pariser in Runde 54 ausrollt: Getriebeschaden. Seinen Platz nimmt nun Nelson Piquet auf dem Brabham BT 52 ein, den BMW Vierzylinder-Turbo wie eine starke Faust im Nacken. Der Brasilianer versucht alles, was er kann, aber auch ihm fehlen die kostbaren Sekunden, die der Reifenwechsel gekostet hat.

Und so gibt es beim Grand Prix von Monaco, dem fünften der Saison, auch den fünften Sieger jenes Jahres, und einen würdigen dazu.

Aussi sévères et solides que peuvent s'avérer les hiérarchies qui se concrétisent dans le projet-pilote darwinien de la Formule 1, tous sont égaux devant la majesté du dieu des intempéries. Lors du 41ᵉ Grand Prix de Monaco, aussi, il répartit ses faveurs avec son arbitraire insouciant. Son préféré, ce week-end-là, est manifestement Keijo Rosberg, que le monde entier surnomme Keke et qui arbore le numéro 1 du détenteur du titre de champion du monde de l'année précédente sur sa Williams immaculée FW 08 D. A l'issue de ce Grand Prix, il sera le premier à franchir la ligne d'arrivée.

Envers d'autres, par contre, le destin est si inflexible qu'ils semblent en avoir perdu la parole. Lors des premiers essais, le jeudi, la piste est sèche. Mais les pneus Michelin des deux McLaren de Niki Lauda et John Watson ne montent pas assez vite en température pour leur permettre d'adhérer à l'asphalte des boulevards et des quais de Monaco. Le samedi, il pleut – trop tard pour changer quoi que ce soit à la situation. Ainsi, les deux hommes ne parviennent pas à se qualifier, ce qui est une première pour Lauda au cours de sa longue carrière. L'Irlandais grommelle dans sa colère, l'Autrichien critique et leur chef d'écurie, Ron Dennis, est furieux.

Cela lui épargne l'embarras du choix, le jour de la course. A présent, la piste est mouillée par endroits, le ciel est d'un gris de plomb et un orage menace d'éclater. Les regards soucieux qui scrutent les nuages se traduisent par douze erreurs d'interprétation : 12 des 20 participants choisissent de prendre le départ sur des pneus pluie, parmi eux, les deux hommes en première ligne, Alain Prost sur la Renault RE 40 et René Arnoux sur la Ferrari 126 C 2, tous deux propulsés par des moteurs turbo. Les pilotes Williams, Rosberg (cinquième aux essais) et Jacques Laffite (huitième), n'hésitent pas à courir un risque et optent pour des slicks. Leur audace sera largement récompensée. A la sortie des esses de Sainte Dévote, déjà, le Finlandais volant est dans les pots d'échappement de Prost et, au début du deuxième tour, il double le Français au même endroit, taillant la route avec une adresse de funambule sur la trajectoire encore humide.

Dix minutes plus tard, les stands sont pris d'assaut – sur toutes les voitures, on monte des slicks. Le gain d'adhérence en revanche, est toujours identique à la perte de temps, qui sera irrattrapable. Alain Prost, par exemple, déjà handicapé par des problèmes de boîte de vitesses, a besoin du reste de la course pour remonter à la troisième place, ce qui est un échec aux yeux de la régie Renault. En tête, par contre, un doublé Williams semble s'esquisser, Rosberg devant Laffite, lorsque le petit Parisien abandonne au 54ᵉ tour : panne de boîte de vitesses. Sa place est immédiatement occupée par Nelson Piquet sur sa Brabham BT 52, avec le quatre-cylindres turbo BMW au couple énorme dans le dos. Le Brésilien ne ménage aucun effort, mais lui non plus ne rattrapera pas les précieuses secondes qu'il a perdues lors de son échange de pneumatiques. Et c'est ainsi que le Grand Prix de Monaco, le cinquième de la saison, est remporté par le cinquième vainqueur de cette année-là, une victoire qui, de plus, est bel et bien méritée.

Snack on *Wheels,* the yacht of the German manufacturer Günter Schmid. The hospitality does not suffer either, as the example of Grand Prix reporter Jochen von Osterroth (back left in black shirt) shows.

Kleiner Imbiß zwischendurch auf der Yacht *Wheels* des deutschen Fabrikanten Günter Schmid. Auch das Zwischenmenschliche kommt nicht zu kurz, wie das Beispiel von Grand-Prix-Reporter Jochen von Osterroth (links hinten im schwarzen Hemd) zeigt.

Petit en-cas sur le yacht *Wheels* de l'industriel allemand Günter Schmid. Les relations humaines ne s'en ressentent pas, comme le prouve l'exemple du reporter de Grand Prix Jochen von Osterroth (à gauche au second plan en chemise noire).

N°	DRIVERS		ENTRANTS	CARS	ENGINES	PRACTICE RESULTS	RACE RESULTS
1	**Keke Rosberg**	**SF**	**TAG Williams Team**	**Williams FW08D**	**Cosworth V8 2993 cc**	**5th: 1'26"307**	**1st: 1h56'38"121**
5	Nelson Piquet	BR	Fila Sport Brabham	Brabham BT52	BMW 4L 1499 cc + T	6th: 1'27"273	2nd: 1h56'56"596
15	*Alain Prost*	*F*	*Equipe Renault Elf*	*Renault RE40*	*Renault V6 1492 cc + T*	*1st: 1'24"840*	*3rd: 1h57'09"487*
27	Patrick Tambay	F	SEFAC Ferrari S.p.A.	Ferrari 126C2B	Ferrari V6 1496 cc + T	4th: 1'26"298	4th: 1h57'42"418
4	Danny Sullivan	USA	Benetton Tyrrell Team	Tyrrell 011	Cosworth V8 2993 cc	20th: 1'29"530	5th: 74 laps
23	Mauro Baldi	I	Marlboro Team Alfa Romeo	Alfa Romeo 183T	Alfa Romeo V8 1496 cc + T	13th: 1'28"639	6th: 74 laps
30	Chico Serra	BR	Arrows Racing Team	Arrows A6	Cosworth V8 2993 cc	15th: 1'28"784	7th: 74 laps
6	Riccardo Patrese	I	Fila Sport Brabham	Brabham BT52	BMW 4L 1499 cc + T	17th: 1'29"200	R
2	Jacques Laffite	F	TAG Williams Team	Williams FW08C	Cosworth V8 2993 cc	8th: 1'27"726	R
29	Marc Surer	CH	Arrows Racing Team	Arrows A6	Cosworth V8 2993 cc	12th: 1'28"346	R
35	Derek Warwick	GB	Candy Toleman Motorsport	Toleman TG183B	Hart 4L 1496 cc + T	10th: 1'28"017	R
25	Jean-Pierre Jarier	F	Equipe Ligier Gitanes	Ligier JS21	Cosworth V8 2993 cc	9th: 1'27"906	R
16	Eddie Cheever	USA	Equipe Renault Elf	Renault RE40	Renault V6 1492 cc + T	3rd: 1'26"279	R
22	Andrea de Cesaris	I	Marlboro Team Alfa Romeo	Alfa Romeo 183T	Alfa Romeo V8 1496 cc + T	7th: 1'27"680	R
28	René Arnoux	F	SEFAC Ferrari S.p.A.	Ferrari 126C2	Ferrari V6 1496 cc + T	2nd: 1'25"182	R
9	Manfred Winkelhock	D	Team ATS	ATS D6	BMW 4L 1499 cc + T	16th: 1'28"975	R
26	Raul Boesel	BR	Equipe Ligier Gitanes	Ligier JS21	Cosworth V8 2993 cc	18th: 1'29"222	R
3	Michele Alboreto	I	Benetton Tyrrell Team	Tyrrell 011	Cosworth V8 2993 cc	11th: 1'28"256	R
12	Nigel Mansell	GB	John Player Team Lotus	Lotus 92	Cosworth V8 2993 cc	14th: 1'28"721	R
11	Elio de Angelis	I	John Player Team Lotus	Lotus 93T	Renault V6 1492 cc + T	19th: 1'29"518	R

(1) Red offensive: Cheever (Renault) can barely fend off the Ferrari drivers Tambay and Arnoux. (2) The four-cylinder engine in Piquet's Brabham spews flames. (3) Right on the limit: Patrese in the tunnel. Right choice for the Williamses: (4) Rosberg on slicks in the race, (5) Laffite on wet-weather tires during practice.

(1) Rote Offensive: Kaum kann Cheever (Renault) sich der Ferrari-Piloten Tambay und Arnoux erwehren. (2) Der Vierzylinder in Piquets Brabham speit Flammen. (3) Hart an der Begrenzung: Patrese im Tunnel. Richtige Wahl für die Williams: (4) Rosberg auf Slicks im Rennen und (5) Laffite auf Naßreifen im Training.

(1) L'offensive rouge : Cheever (Renault) n'échappe pas un seul instant aux pilotes de Ferrari, Tambay et Arnoux. (2) Le quatre-cylindres de la Brabham de Piquet crachant des flammes. (3) Flirter avec la limite : Patrese dans le tunnel. Le bon choix pour les Williams : (4) Rosberg sur slicks en course et (5) Laffite sur pneus pluie aux essais.

(1) Living art: the young lady in minimal clothing next to the Ferrari with minimal tires should probably be understood as an integrated work of art. (2) Left out: spectator with a limited view. (3) Brought under cover: Mansell's Lotus is made ready for the start. (4) Grand Prix collage, created by chance.

(1) Living Art: Die junge Dame in Notbekleidung am Ferrari mit Notbereifung versteht sich wohl als Gesamtkunstwerk. (2) Draußen vor der Tür: Zuschauer mit beschränktem Durchblick. (3) Unter die Haube gebracht: Vor dem Start wird Mansells Lotus komplettiert. (4) Grand-Prix-Collage, vom Zufall geschaffen.

(1) Art vivant : la jeune dame peu vêtue près de la Ferrari avec ses pneus galettes se conçoivent sans aucun doute comme une œuvre d'art intégrée. (2) Dehors devant la porte : spectateurs à la vue plutôt limitée. (3) Bien capotée : ultimes opérations sur la Lotus de Mansell avant le départ. (4) Collage de Grand Prix : résultat du hasard.

1

2

(1) Time for reflection: Manfred Winkelhock with latter-day feudal lord Huschke von Hanstein. (2) The Williams drivers Laffite (with two days' worth of stubble) and Rosberg. (3) Race veteran Jacky Ickx. (4) Tennis veteran Björn Borg. (5) René Arnoux after his collision with Laffite on lap seven.

Akteure und Beobachter:
(1) Manfred Winkelhock und Spät-Feudalherr Huschke von Hanstein. (2) Die Williams-Piloten Laffite (mit Zweitagebart) und Rosberg. (3) Renn-Veteran Jacky Ickx. (4) Tennis-Veteran Björn Borg. (5) René Arnoux nach Kollision mit Laffite in Runde sieben.

Acteurs et observateurs :
(1) Manfred Winkelhock et la grande noblesse de la course, le baron Huschke von Hanstein. (2) Les pilotes Williams Laffite (mal rasé) et Rosberg. (3) Le vétéran de la course Jacky Ickx. (4) Le vétéran du tennis Björn Borg. (5) René Arnoux après sa collision avec Laffite au septième tour.

1984

On Sunday, 3 June 1984, the glittering state of Monaco was emanating all the brittle charm of a team shower cubicle. Dark clouds clustered around the tips of the skyscrapers, dumping vast quantities of icy non-stop rain on the streets below. Everyone present agreed that, even back at the horrific Grand Prix of 1972, the Principality had seemed positively benign and welcoming compared with conditions for this event.

By now, the turbo had virtually swept the board in its rise to power, and at teatime, 19 of the 20 cars anxiously awaiting developments on the starting grid were breathing turbocharged air. Only Stefan Bellof, in the black 012 of that loyal Ford client Ken Tyrrell, had made its way to the grid through the qualifying rounds with a naturally-aspirated engine – albeit in last place.

At the front of the grid, Nigel Mansell sat in his Lotus 95 T, powered by a V6 engine from Renault, and second only to Alain Prost in a McLaren MP 4/2. The fact that, in his quest for pole position, Prost had shot around the course faster than anyone had ever achieved before, was of precious little interest to the little Frenchman. The question which occupied his mind was whether – and if so, how effectively – he would be able to navigate his 750 bhp TAG Porsche engine through the wet streets of Monaco for the next two hours. Following a request from the drivers, a firefighting vehicle had sprayed the road surface in the tunnel to ensure that conditions were uniformly treacherous.

Of the planned two hours, only one was now left. While Prost and Mansell effectively made their way on tiptoe through Sainte Dévote, the others were forcing their way almost blind through a dark grey cloud of spray the height of a house. The two Renault drivers Derek Warwick and Patrick Tambay eliminated each other almost straight away, thereby saving themselves a further 60 minutes of agile "reacrobatics" in the no-man's land between existence and eternity. From laps 11 to 15, Mansell led the pack. When Corrado Fabi and his Brabham BT 53 had a big spin at Portier, one of the race marshals rushed selflessly to his assistance, only to be hit by Prost's McLaren, amazingly avoiding injury. The British driver turned this moment to his advantage, only to land in trouble himself ten minutes later: after a massive slide beside the Chatham Bar, on the climb up to the Casino, the Lotus ploughed into the crash barrier – and so ended the day for Mansell.

Prost took over the lead – and he stayed there. However, that day, Formula 1 gave birth to two new stars. One was Ayrton Senna at the wheel of his Toleman TG 184, powered by a Hart engine which was only able to deliver its full power explosively across a narrow engine speed range. The other was Stefan Bellof, whose Tyrrell frolicked in these awful conditions like a fish in water. The Brazilian was catching up four seconds every lap, and the German followed this lead step by step. Then, after 31 laps, race director Jacky Ickx decided that enough was enough. The specified 75 per cent of overall distance had not been reached, so all points would have to be halved. At the end of that season, Alain Prost missed winning the World Championship by just half a point.

Dritter Juni 1984: An diesem Sonntag versprüht der Glitzerstaat Monaco den spröden Charme einer Mannschaftsduschkabine. Düsteres Gewölk stützt sich schwer auf die Spitzen der Wolkenkratzer, entlädt gleichförmig rauschend kalten Dauerregen. Selbst beim Horror-Grand-Prix 1972, darüber sind sich alle einig, mutete das Fürstentum noch relativ anheimelnd an.

Inzwischen hat die totale Machtergreifung der Turbos stattgefunden: 19 der 20 Wagen, die um die Teezeit auf den Start in eine ungewisse Zukunft warten, sind mit zwangs-beatmeten Maschinen ausgerüstet. Nur Stefan Bellof im schwarzen 012 des treuen Ford-Kunden Ken Tyrrell hat sich mit einem Saugmotor den Zugang zu dieser geladenen Gesellschaft erzwungen – an letzter Stelle.

In der ersten Reihe aber stehen Nigel Mansell mit dem Lotus 95 T, im Rücken einen V6 von Renault, und Alain Prost im McLaren MP 4/2. Daß er im Training bei seiner Jagd auf die Pole Position schneller als je jemand zuvor über den Kurs gepfeilt ist, interessiert den kleinen Franzosen herzlich wenig. Die Frage ist, ob und wie er sich in den nächsten zwei Stunden mit den 750 PS seines TAG-Porsche-Triebwerks seinen Weg ungeschoren durch das Feuchtbiotop Monaco bahnen kann. Auf Wunsch der Fahrer hat eine Feuerspritze den Tunnel benetzt, damit die Bedingungen wenigstens einheitlich unerträglich sind.

Von den geplanten zwei Stunden bleibt nur eine. Während Prost und Mansell gewissermaßen auf Zehenspitzen durch Sainte Dévote balancieren, stechen die anderen blindlings in eine haushohe schwarzgraue Spraywolke. Die beiden Renault-Piloten Derek Warwick und Patrick Tambay eliminieren einander umgehend und ersparen sich so 60 Minuten Parterreakrobatik im Niemandsland zwischen Sein und Nichtsein. Zwischen der 11. und der 15. Runde liegt Mansell an der Spitze. Corrado Fabi hat sich mit seinem Brabham BT 53 bei Portier gedreht. Ein Streckenposten eilt unbedacht zu Hilfe und wird von Prosts McLaren berührt, ohne daß er Schaden nimmt. Diesen Augenblick münzt der Brite in seinen Vorteil um. Zehn Minuten später ist er selbst in Not: Nach einem mächtigen Schlenker auf der Höhe der Chatham Bar im Aufstieg zum Casino landet der Lotus in der Leitplanke – das war's.

Prost führt, und das bleibt auch so. Aber hinter ihm werden zwei neue Stars der Formel 1 geboren. Da ist Ayrton Senna mit dem Toleman TG 184, dessen Hart-Maschine ihre volle Leistung nur explosionsartig in einem schmalen Drehzahlbereich herausrückt. Und da ist Bellof, dessen Tyrrell sich in diesen Bedingungen tummelt wie ein Fisch im Wasser. Vier Sekunden je Runde holt der Brasilianer auf, in gleichem Schritt und Tritt folgt der Deutsche. Da befindet Rennleiter Jacky Ickx nach der 31. Runde, nun sei's genug. Die vorgeschriebenen 75 Prozent der Distanz sind nicht erreicht, die Punkte werden halbiert. Am Ende der Saison fehlt Alain Prost ein halber Zähler zur Weltmeisterschaft.

Dimanche 3 juin 1984, Monaco et son cadre merveilleux ont autant de charme que les douches collectives d'un club de football. Le sommet des gratte-ciel disparaît presque dans des nuages sombres d'où se déversent sans discontinuer des trombes d'eau glacée. Même lors du désastreux Grand Prix de 1972 qui restera gravé dans toutes les mémoires – tous sont d'accord à ce sujet – la Principauté était apparue encore relativement accueillante.

Entre-temps, l'hégémonie des turbos est devenue totale et 19 des 20 voitures qui attendent le départ vers un avenir incertain en ce début d'après-midi sont propulsées par des moteurs suralimentés. Seul Stefan Bellof, dans la 012 noire de Ken Tyrrell, le fidèle client de Ford, a conquis de haute lutte une place au sein de cette société triée sur le volet avec son moteur atmosphérique – mais c'est la dernière.

En première ligne, par contre, on découvre Nigel Mansell sur la Lotus 95 T, avec dans le dos un V6 Renault, et Alain Prost sur la McLaren MP 4/2. Le petit Français se moque éperdument d'avoir couvert un tour plus rapidement que tout autre pilote de l'histoire durant les essais, lors de sa chasse à la pole position. Ce qui l'intéresse, c'est de savoir si et comment, au cours des deux prochaines heures, il parviendra à sortir sain et sauf de la piste mouillée de Monaco avec les 750 chevaux de son moteur TAG-Porsche dans le dos. A la demande des pilotes, un camion de pompiers a inondé le tunnel afin que les conditions soient au moins tout aussi insupportables partout.

Des deux heures prévues, il n'en restera qu'une. Alors que Prost et Mansell s'engagent en quelque sorte sur la pointe des pieds dans Sainte Dévote, les autres plongent aveuglément dans un nuage de vapeur d'eau gris foncé aussi haut qu'une maison. Les deux pilotes Renault, Derek Warwick et Patrick Tambay, s'éliminèrent mutuellement dès les premiers mètres et s'épargnent ainsi 60 minutes d'acrobaties périlleuses dans le no man's land entre l'être et le néant. Du 11e au 15e tour, Mansell occupe la tête. Après que Corrado Fabi ait fait un tête-à-queue au virage du Portier avec sa Brabham BT 53, un commissaire de piste cherche à lui venir en aide sans réfléchir et est touché par la McLaren de Prost, qui ne lui cause pas la moindre blessure. Le Britannique profite de cette occasion inespérée, mais, dix minutes plus tard, c'est lui-même qui est à l'agonie : après un imposant écart à hauteur du Chatham Bar, dans la montée du Casino, la Lotus percute les glissières – fermez le ban !

Prost est en tête et il y restera. Mais, derrière lui, naissent deux nouvelles stars de la Formule 1. Le premier est Ayrton Senna au volant de la Toleman TG 184 dont le moteur Hart ne développe toute sa puissance qu'en une véritable explosion sur une mince plage de régime. Le second est Bellof, dont la Tyrrell, dans de telles conditions, se meut comme un poisson dans l'eau. Le Brésilien rattrape quatre secondes au tour, suivi, au même rythme, de l'Allemand. Au bout du 31e tour, le directeur de course, Jacky Ickx, estime que la plaisanterie a assez duré. Les 75 pour cent de la distance prévus ne sont pas atteints et on ne comptera donc que la moitié des points. A la fin de la saison, il manquera un demi-point à Alain Prost pour remporter le championnat du monde.

Alternative program: Monaco on a day like any other, with that blue sky which is the stuff of postcards and the dreams of those who would like to be citizens of the Principality.

Kontrastprogramm: Monaco an einem Tag wie jeder andere, mit jenem Blauhimmel, der die Postkarten und die Träume all derer schmückt, die gerne Bürger des Fürstentums wären.

Contraste : Monaco un jour comme les autres, avec le ciel bleu qui peuple les cartes postales et les rêves de tous ceux qui seraient si volontiers résidents de la Principauté.

(Following double page) Monaco on 3 June 1984, a day like no other. The field is just rolling towards an uncertain future.

(Nächste Doppelseite) Monaco an jenem 3. Juni 1984, einem Tag wie kaum einem anderen. Das Feld rollt gerade einer ungewissen Zukunft entgegen.

(Double page suivante) Monaco le 3 juin 1984, une journée noire à nulle autre pareille. Le peloton s'ébranle vers un avenir incertain.

N°	DRIVERS		ENTRANTS	CARS	ENGINES	PRACTICE RESULTS	RACE RESULTS
7	**Alain Prost**	**F**	**Marlboro McLaren International**	**McLaren MP4/2**	**TAG Porsche V6 1499 cc + T**	**1st: 1'22"661**	**1st: 1h01'07"740**
19	Ayrton Senna	BR	Toleman Group Motorsport	Toleman TG184	Hart 4L 1496 cc + T	13th: 1'25"009	2nd: 1h01'15"186
4	Stefan Bellof	D	Tyrrell Racing Organisation	Tyrrell 012	Cosworth V8 2994 cc	20th: 1'26"117	3rd: 1h01'28"881
28	René Arnoux	F	SEFAC Ferrari S.p.A.	Ferrari 126C4	Ferrari V6 1496 cc + T	3rd: 1'22"935	4th: 1h01'36"817
6	Keke Rosberg	SF	Williams Grand Prix Engineering	Williams FW09	Honda V6 1500 cc + T	10th: 1'24"151	5th: 1h01'42"986
11	Elio de Angelis	I	John Player Team Lotus	Lotus 95T	Renault V6 1492 cc + T	11th: 1'24"426	6th: 1h01'52"179
27	Michele Alboreto	I	SEFAC Ferrari S.p.A.	Ferrari 126C4	Ferrari V6 1496 cc + T	4th: 1'22"937	7th: 30 laps
24	Piercarlo Ghinzani	I	Osella Squadra Corse	Osella FA1F	Alfa Romeo V8 1496 cc + T	19th: 1'25"877	8th: 30 laps
5	Jacques Laffite	F	Williams Grand Prix Engineering	Williams FW09	Honda V6 1500 cc + T	16th: 1'25"719	9th: 30 laps
22	Riccardo Patrese	I	Benetton Team Alfa Romeo	Alfa Romeo 184T	Alfa Romeo V8 1496 cc + T	14th: 1'25"101	R
8	Niki Lauda	A	Marlboro McLaren International	McLaren MP4/2	TAG Porsche V6 1499 cc + T	8th: 1'23"886	R
14	Manfred Winkelhock	D	Team ATS	ATS D7	BMW 4L 1499 cc + T	12th: 1'24"473	R
12	Nigel Mansell	GB	John Player Team Lotus	Lotus 95T	Renault V6 1492 cc + T	2nd: 1'22"752	R
1	Nelson Piquet	BR	MRD International	Brabham BT53	BMW 4L 1499 cc + T	9th: 1'23"918	R
25	François Hesnault	F	Ligier Loto	Ligier JS23	Renault V6 1492 cc + T	17th: 1'25"815	R
2	Corrado Fabi	I	MRD International	Brabham BT53	BMW 4L 1499 cc + T	15th: 1'25"290	R
20	Johnny Cecotto	VEN	Toleman Group Motorsport	Toleman TG184	Hart 4L 1496 cc + T	18th: 1'25"872	R
26	Andrea de Cesaris	I	Ligier Loto	Ligier JS23	Renault V6 1492 cc + T	7th: 1'23"578	R
15	Patrick Tambay	F	Equipe Renault Elf	Renault RE50	Renault V6 1492 cc + T	6th: 1'23"414	R
16	Derek Warwick	GB	Equipe Renault Elf	Renault RE50	Renault V6 1492 cc + T	5th: 1'23"237	R

Mission impossible: (1) de Angelis (Lotus), (2) Tambay (Renault), (3) Senna (Toleman), (4) Bellof (Tyrrell) and (5) Rosberg (Williams). Two new heroes emerge during the saturated hell of those 62 minutes: Senna and Bellof.

Mission impossible: (1) de Angelis (Lotus), (2) Tambay (Renault), (3) Senna (Toleman), (4) Bellof (Tyrrell) und (5) Rosberg (Williams). In der schwärzlichen Hölle dieser 62 Minuten werden zwei neue Helden geschmiedet: Senna und Bellof.

Mission impossible : (1) de Angelis (Lotus), (2) Tambay (Renault), (3) Senna (Toleman), (4) Bellof (Tyrrell) et (5) Rosberg (Williams). Deux nouveaux héros, Senna et Bellof, vont émerger de l'apocalypse noirâtre de ces 62 minutes.

3

4

5

Hands on: Arnoux's Ferrari (1) being transferred from the paddock to the pits, (2) after an incident during qualifying and (3) Winkelhock's ATS. Grand Prix people: (4) Brabham impresario Bernie Ecclestone, (5) Corrado Fabi, representing his brother Teo at Brabham, (6) the Ferrari drivers Alboreto and Arnoux, (7) Nelson Piquet, (8) Nigel Mansell with Lotus designer Gérard Ducarouge, (9) Stefan Bellof.

Hand angelegt: der Ferrari von Arnoux (1) beim Transfer zwischen Fahrerlager und Box, (2) nach einem Ausrutscher während des Trainings und (3) Winkelhocks ATS. Grand-Prix-Schaffende: (4) Brabham-Impresario Bernie Ecclestone, (5) Corrado Fabi, der bei Brabham seinen Bruder Teo vertritt, (6) die Ferrari-Fahrer Alboreto und Arnoux, (7) Nelson Piquet, (8) Nigel Mansell mit Lotus-Konstrukteur Gérard Ducarouge, (9) Stefan Bellof.

A la poussette : la Ferrari d'Arnoux (1) transférée du paddock aux stands, (2) après un dérapage au cours des essais et (3) l'ATS de Winkelhock. Protagonistes du Grand Prix : (4) Bernie Ecclestone, l'imprésario de Brabham. (5) Corrado Fabi, qui remplace chez Brabham son frère Teo. (6) Les pilotes Ferrari Alboreto et Arnoux, (7) Nelson Piquet, (8) Nigel Mansell avec l'ingénieur de Lotus, Gérard Ducarouge, (9) Stefan Bellof.

1985

In the extreme sport of Formula 1, even the bends are awarded superlatives. Tarzan in Zandvoort would certainly be one of the most exciting, while Eau Rouge in Spa is without doubt the most forbidding. Sainte Dévote in Monaco is far and away the most expensive to negotiate, having created scrap costing millions in its time — something which naturally enough leaves painful scars in the memory. Having said that, in terms of personal injury, the proximity of the nearby and eponymous church has worked genuine miracles. To date, thank God, no-one has been seriously hurt there.

Once again in 1985, the series of bends preceding the fast climb towards the Casino had a massive impact on the budgets and work load of a number of race teams. Obvious examples would be Brabham and Benetton: in the center of the field, a high-speed and unpredictable queue had formed, led by Benetton driver Riccardo Patrese, who disobligingly held up traffic. On the seventeenth lap, Brabham mercenary Nelson Piquet lost his patience and tried hard to steal past the Italian down the inside. The latter simply closed the door firmly on his pursuer in a clumsily executed manoeuvre that entwined the protagonists in an awful pile-up, culminating in an inferno of spinning wheels and debris of varying sizes, all enshrouded in orange flames. Further back down the track, Jacques Laffite in the Ligier JS 25 saw the pending obstruction and described a full circle at about 250 kph (155 mph) without even touching an edge. Only the profile of his tyres suffered.

In order to extend the entertainment programme to a full two hours, the Grand Prix had been lengthened to 78 laps. The first eight places on the grid were occupied by no less than seven different marques, all within a second of one another. The token naturally-aspirated participant, Martin Brundle, had managed to push his Tyrrell into the thick of the turbo-dominated action. On the front row, Ayrton Senna (Lotus 97T) and Nigel Mansell (Williams FW10) were waiting for green light, but this Grand Prix was to be given its shape by two men from the second and third rows: Michele Alboreto in the Ferrari 156/85 and Alain Prost in the McLaren MP4/2B. This was because the Renault V6 powering the black-and-gold Lotus number 12, which took off in the lead, smoked its way to the end of its short but hitherto satisfying life on lap 16. Then Mansell, beset by trouble with his brakes, slipped down the field to seventh place — a lion whose claws occasionally proved blunt. Alboreto was then leading the race, but Prost was piling on the pressure. As evidence of the unfriendly encounter between Piquet and Patrese, oil was spread across sections of the track in Sainte Dévote. However, the track marshals failed to warn drivers with the yellow-and-red flag, and the amiable Italian skidded off the track, enabling Prost to flash past. But by the twenty-fourth lap, the Ferrari was back in the lead. Then Alboreto damaged a wheel against the kerb, allowing the small Frenchman to overtake him once again, this time on lap 31.

Throughout the rest of the race, these two kept swapping their initial situation. Alboreto pursued Prost in the way that 15 years earlier Jochen Rindt had given chase to Jack Brabham, with the exception that he never caught his man. Indeed, this time around, the man who was beginning to be called the "professor", was approaching the final part of the race with care and attention. A shower had dampened the track near the Casino, and Prost, who would be World Champion by the end of the year, cautiously drew on the stock of time he had built over Alboreto to secure his victory.

In der Extremsportart Formel 1 werden sogar Kurven mit Superlativen ausgezeichnet. Tarzan in Zandvoort war eine der aufregendsten, Eau Rouge in Spa ist gewiß die unheimlichste, Sainte Dévote in Monaco mit Abstand die kostspieligste. Edelschrott für Millionen – natürlich schmerzt auch das. Was aber Personenschäden anbelangt, wirkt die Nähe der gleichnamigen Kirche wahre Wunder. Noch nie tat sich jemand wirklich weh, Gott sei Dank.

Auch 1985 belastet der Schocker-Schlängel vor der schnellen Steigung empor zum Casino wieder Budgets und Arbeitszeitkonten etlicher Rennställe ungebührlich. Zum Beispiel Brabham und Benetton: Im Mittelfeld hat sich eine rasende und tückisch zuckende Schlange ausgebildet, an ihrem Kopfende Benetton-Pilot Riccardo Patrese, der den Verkehr trotzig aufhält. In der 17. Runde verliert Brabham-Kostgänger Nelson Piquet die Geduld und versucht innen an dem Italiener vorbeizustechen. Der macht entschlossen die Tür zu. Diese unklug eingefädelte Grausamkeit endet in einem Inferno von wirbelnden Rädern und Trümmern unterschiedlichster Größe, umwabert von orangenem Feuer. Dahinter dreht sich Jacques Laffite im Ligier JS 25 bei Tempo 250, ohne irgendwo anzuecken. Nur die Rundung seiner Reifen leidet.

Um auf das volle Unterhaltungsprogramm von zwei Stunden zu kommen, hat man den Grand Prix auf 78 Runden aufgestockt. Auf den ersten acht Startplätzen finden sich sieben verschiedene Marken, alle innerhalb einer Sekunde. Als Alibi-Sauger hat sich diesmal Martin Brundles Tyrrell in die konzertierte Aktion der Turbos gezwängt. In der ersten Reihe warten Ayrton Senna (Lotus 97T) und Nigel Mansell (Williams FW10) auf das grüne Licht. Gestaltet wird dieser Große Preis jedoch von Männern aus dem zweiten und dem dritten Glied: Michele Alboreto auf dem Ferrari 156/85, Alain Prost im McLaren MP4/2B. Denn der Renault-V6 im schwarzgoldenen Lotus Nummer 12, der anfänglich vorn ist, haucht im 16. Durchgang sein kurzes, aber erfülltes Leben aus. Und Mansell, geplagt von Ärger mit den Bremsen, wird bis hinunter zum siebten Rang durchgereicht, ein Löwe, dessen Krallen zeitweise stumpf geworden sind. Alboreto führt, aber Prost macht Druck. Als Altlast der unfreundlichen Begegnung von Piquet und Patrese verschmiert Öl Teile der Piste in Sainte Dévote. Aber die Streckenposten warnen nicht mit der gelbroten Flagge. Da rutscht der freundliche Italiener aus, und Prost ist im Nu vorbei. Im 24. Durchgang liegt der Ferrari wieder in Führung. Dann beschädigt Alboreto ein Rad am Randstein, so daß ihn der kleine Franzose in der 31. Runde erneut passiert.

Während dem Rest des Rennens kehrt sich die anfängliche Situation zwischen diesen beiden um. Alboreto jagt Prost wie 15 Jahre zuvor Jochen Rindt Jack Brabham, nur daß er ihn nicht mehr erreicht. Dabei geht der Mann, den sie den »Professor« zu nennen beginnen, die Sache am Ende behutsam an. Am Casino hat ein Schauer die Fahrbahn befeuchtet, und da zehrt der Champion jenes Jahres lieber von seinem Zeitguthaben.

Dans le sport extrême qu'est la Formule 1, même les virages méritent des superlatifs. Tarzan, à Zandvoort, était l'un des plus excitants ; l'Eau rouge, à Spa, est assurément celui qui demande le plus de courage et Sainte Dévote, à Monaco, est de loin, le plus coûteux. Des épaves s'y accumulent par millions – naturellement, cela, aussi, fait mal. Mais, en ce qui concerne les dommages corporels, la proximité de l'église du même nom semble avoir causé de véritables miracles. Jamais personne à cet endroit ne s'est encore réellement fait mal, Dieu soit loué !

En 1985 aussi, le redoutable esse qui précède la rapide montée du Casino hypothéquera de nouveau lourdement les budgets et les performances de quelques écuries. Par exemple de Brabham et de Benetton : le milieu du peloton consiste en une file de bolides rapides et zigzaguant avec nervosité à la tête de laquelle se trouve le pilote Benetton Riccardo Patrese qui refuse obstinément de se laisser doubler. Au 17e tour, le pilote numéro un de Brabham, Nelson Piquet perd patience et cherche à passer en force à côté de l'Italien. Celui-ci ferme immédiatement la porte. Cette réaction irréfléchie se termine en un enfer de roues et de débris tourbillonnant dans un nuage de feu. Derrière, Jacques Laffite part en tête-à-queue à 250 km/h, avec sa Ligier JS 25, mais sans rien toucher. Seule les sculptures de ses pneus en pâtissent.

Pour que le divertissant programme respecte la durée de deux heures, le Grand Prix a été majoré à 78 tours. Aux huit premières places au départ, on trouve sept marques différentes, toutes regroupées en une seconde. Le seul représentant de la fraction des moteurs atmosphériques est, cette année, la Tyrrell de Martin Brundle, qui a réussi à se joindre à l'action concertée des turbos. En première ligne, Ayrton Senna (Lotus 97T) et Nigel Mansell (Williams FW10) attendent le feu vert. Mais ce sont deux hommes classés en deuxième et en troisième lignes qui marqueront de leur sceau ce Grand Prix : Michele Alboreto sur la Ferrari 156/85 et Alain Prost sur la McLaren MP4/2B. En effet, le Renault-V6 de la Lotus numéro 12 noir et or initialement en tête rend l'âme au 16e tour après une vie brève, mais bien remplie. Et Mansell, handicapé par des freins inconsistants, retombe graduellement jusqu'à la 7e place, lion dont les griffes se sont entre-temps usées. Alboreto est en tête, mais Prost ne relâche pas sa pression. Des restes d'huile témoins de la rencontre inamicale entre Piquet et Patrese souillent une partie de la piste à Sainte Dévote. Mais les commissaires ne préviennent personne et oublient d'agiter les drapeaux jaune et rouge. Surpris, le toujours jovial Italien part en dérapage et Prost le double instantanément. Puis, au 24e tour, la Ferrari est de nouveau en tête. Mais Alboreto endommage une roue contre une bordure de trottoir et doit de nouveau laisser passer le petit Français au 31e tour.

Durant le reste de la course, la situation initiale entre ces deux hommes s'inverse. Alboreto pourchasse Prost comme, 15 ans plus tôt, Jochen Rindt Jack Brabham, à cette nuance près qu'il ne le rattrapera plus jamais. Et pourtant, l'homme que l'on commence à surnommer le « Professeur », tempère son ardeur sur la fin. Au Casino, une ondée a humidifié la piste et Prost qui, fin 1985, allait devenir champion du monde, préfère laisser grignoter quelque dixièmes de secondes de son avance sur Alboreto pour assurer sa victoire.

Ever since she can remember, the Grand Prix has been one of the cyclically recurring events in the life of Princess Caroline Louise Marguerite, here with Stefano Casiraghi, just like Christmas and birthdays.

Seitdem sie denken kann, gehört der Grand Prix für Prinzessin Caroline Louise Marguerite, hier mit Stefano Casiraghi, zu den zyklisch wiederkehrenden Ereignissen in ihrem Leben – wie Weihnachten und Geburtstag.

Au tant qu'elle puisse se le rappeler, le Grand Prix fait partie, pour la princesse Caroline Louise Marguerite, ici avec Stefano Casiraghi, des événements récurrents de sa vie – comme Noël et son anniversaire.

N°	DRIVERS		ENTRANTS	CARS	ENGINES	PRACTICE RESULTS	RACE RESULTS
2	**Alain Prost**	**F**	**Marlboro McLaren International**	**McLaren MP4/2B**	**TAG Porsche V6 1499 cc + T**	5th: 1'20"885	1st: 1h51'58"034
27	Michele Alboreto	I	SEFAC Ferrari S.p.A.	Ferrari 156/85	Ferrari V6 1496 cc + T	3rd: 1'20"563	2nd: 1h52'05"575
11	Elio de Angelis	I	John Player Special Team Lotus	Lotus 97T	Renault V6 1492 cc + T	9th: 1'21"465	3rd: 1h53'25"205
25	Andrea de Cesaris	I	Equipe Ligier	Ligier JS25	Renault V6 1492 cc + T	8th: 1'21"347	4th: 77 laps
16	Derek Warwick	GB	Equipe Renault Elf	Renault RE60	Renault V6 1492 cc + T	10th: 1'21"531	5th: 77 laps
26	Jacques Laffite	F	Equipe Ligier	Ligier JS25	Renault V6 1492 cc + T	16th: 1'22"880	6th: 77 laps
5	Nigel Mansell	GB	Canon Williams Honda Team	Williams FW10	Honda V6 1500 cc	2nd: 1'20"536	7th: 77 laps
6	Keke Rosberg	SF	Canon Williams Honda Team	Williams FW10	Honda V6 1500 cc	7th: 1'21"320	8th: 76 laps
18	Thierry Boutsen	B	Barclay Arrows BMW	Arrows A8	BMW 4L 1499 cc + T	6th: 1'21"302	9th: 76 laps
3	Martin Brundle	GB	Tyrrell Racing Organisation	Tyrrell 012	Cosworth V8 2994 cc	18th: 1'23"827	10th: 74 laps
30	Jonathan Palmer	GB	West Zakspeed Racing	Zakspeed 841	Zakspeed 4L 1495 cc + T	19th: 1'23"840	11th: 74 laps
1	Niki Lauda	A	Marlboro McLaren International	McLaren MP4/2B	TAG Porsche V6 1499 cc + T	14th: 1'21"907	R
19	Teo Fabi	I	Toleman Group Motorsport	Toleman TG185	Alfa Romeo V8 1496 cc + T	20th: 1'23"965	R
22	Riccardo Patrese	I	Benetton Team Alfa Romeo	Alfa Romeo 185T	Alfa Romeo V8 1497 cc + T	12th: 1'21"813	R
7	Nelson Piquet	BR	MRD International	Brabham BT54	BMW 4L 1499 cc + T	13th: 1'21"817	R
12	*Ayrton Senna*	*BR*	*John Player Special Team Lotus*	*Lotus 97T*	*Renault V6 1492 cc + T*	*1st: 1'20"450*	R
23	Eddie Cheever	USA	Benetton Team Alfa Romeo	Alfa Romeo 185T	Alfa Romeo V8 1497 cc + T	4th: 1'20"729	R
28	Stefan Johansson	S	SEFAC Ferrari S.p.A.	Ferrari 156/85	Ferrari V6 1496 cc + T	15th: 1'22"635	R
17	Gerhard Berger	A	Barclay Arrows BMW	Arrows A8	BMW 4L 1499 cc + T	11th: 1'21"665	R
15	Patrick Tambay	F	Equipe Renault Elf	Renault RE60	Renault V6 1492 cc + T	17th: 1'22"912	R

1

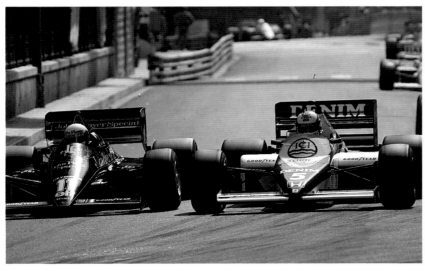

2

3

(1) Minor difference of opinion on lap 17 between Piquet (Brabham) and Patrese (Benetton). On the road: (2) Mansell (Williams) overtakes de Angelis (Lotus). (3) Senna (Lotus), Mansell and Alboreto ahead of Prost (McLaren) and Cheever (Benetton) early in the race. (4) Prost passes Palmer (Zakspeed) in qualifying. (5) Eventful race for Alboreto. (6) Sixth place and one lap behind for Laffite (Ligier).

(1) Kleine Meinungsverschiedenheit in Runde 17 zwischen Piquet (Brabham) und Patrese (Benetton). On the road: (2) Mansell (Williams) überholt de Angelis (Lotus). (3) Senna (Lotus), Mansell und Alboreto vor Prost (McLaren) und Cheever (Benetton) in der Anfangsphase. (4) Prost passiert Palmer (Zakspeed) im Training. (5) Ereignisreiches Rennen für Alboreto. (6) Platz sechs mit einer Runde Rückstand für Laffite (Ligier).

(1) Petite divergence de vues au 17e tour entre Piquet (Brabham) et Patrese (Benetton). Sur la route : (2) Mansell (Williams) double de Angelis (Lotus). (3) Senna (Lotus), Mansell et Alboreto devant Prost (McLaren) et Cheever (Benetton) au début de la course. (4) Prost double Palmer (Zakspeed) aux essais. (5) Course animée pour Alboreto. (6) Sixième place avec un tour de retard pour Laffite (Ligier).

1

2

3

Love's Labors Lost: (1) well-sorted tools and (8) happy optimism before qualifying do not do Erich Zakowski and Jonathan Palmer any good. They fail to qualify after the speeding doctor (3) damages his Zakspeed. (2) Form follows function: Piquet's Brabham BT54 is a thing of bizarre beauty. (4) Belgian national icon: Jacques Bernard Ickx, otherwise known as Jacky. (5) Laughter by Frank Williams after a bon mot from Keke Rosberg. (6) On this occasion row three of the grid and position nine is as far as it goes for his product: BMW engine guru Rosche, otherwise known as Paul the Cam. (7) Stefan Bellof, a sensational third in his Tyrrell the previous year, fails to get onto the grid on this occasion. His boss Ken Tyrrell has to wait for the promised Renault turbos to be able to keep up again.

Vergebliche Liebesmüh: (1) Wohlsortiertes Werkzeug und (8) fröhlicher Optimismus vor dem Training nützen Erich Zakowski und Jonathan Palmer nichts. Man vermag sich nicht zu qualifizieren, zumal der schnelle Doktor (3) seinen Zakspeed beschädigt. (2) Form follows function: Piquets Brabham BT54 ist von bizarrer Schönheit. (4) Belgisches Nationalheiligtum: Jacques Bernard Ickx, genannt Jacky. (5) Frohsinn bei Frank Williams nach einem Bonmot von Keke Rosberg. (6) Diesmal reicht's nur für Reihe drei und Rang neun für sein Produkt: BMW-Motorenguru Rosche, genannt Nocken-Paule. (7) Stefan Bellof, im Vorjahr sensationeller Dritter im Tyrrell, schafft diesmal den Sprung in die Startaufstellung nicht. Man wartet noch auf die verheißenen Turbomaschinen von Renault, um wieder mithalten zu können.

Efforts non récompensés : (1) outils bien triés et (8) optimisme affiché avant les essais ne servent à rien à Erich Zakowski et Jonathan Palmer. Ils ne se qualifieront pas, d'autant plus que le rapide docteur (3) va endommager sa Zakspeed. (2) La forme suit la fonction : la Brabham BT54 de Piquet est d'une beauté bizarre. (4) Monument national belge : Jacques Bernard Ickx, surnommé Jacky. (5) Bonne humeur chez Frank Williams après une blague de Keke Rosberg. (6) Cette fois, il devra se contenter d'une troisième et d'une neuvième place pour son produit : le gourou des moteurs de chez BMW, Paul Rosche, surnommé « Paul la came ». (7) Stefan Bellof, sensationnel troisième sur Tyrrell l'année précédente, ne parviendra pas à se qualifier cette fois-ci. On attend les moteurs turbo promis de Renault pour pouvoir de nouveau jouer les premiers violons.

1986

The superiority of one man, one marque and one engine may give the protagonists concerned a good deal of satisfaction, but it is not a good thing for a Grand Prix. On the second weekend in May 1986, the Principality was ruled by Alain Prost, his McLaren MP4/2C and the TAG Porsche engine – and by boredom. Prost dominated the practice sessions and was awarded pole position. He then drove the fastest lap during the warm-up, and followed suit in the race itself. Prost led the race from start to finish, apart from seven laps around the half-way mark. At this point, his future arch rival, Ayrton Senna, was allowed a brief moment in the lead in his Lotus 98T, but only because the Frenchman had to take to the pit lane for a change of tyres. Moreover, just two weeks previously, Prost had won the Grand Prix in San Marino, and he left Monaco leading the World Championship table and would finish the year as World Champion for the second year in succession.

This year, the track was 16 meters longer than before, the chicane – as an example of genuine chicanery – offering itself to the drivers as a set of right-angled bends once a new section of track had been created above the sea. The bump in Rascasse had been ironed out, and the section following the double bend had been remodelled, enabling the cars to accelerate away in second gear more fiercely than ever before, delivering them straight into the gently banked home run.

A feeling of tension and excitement presided over the entire race, generated by a series of epic moments and dramatic episodes. One example was the vigorous but forlorn chase by Prost's team-mate Keke Rosberg. Monaco was not exactly an ideal stage for his aggressive driving style, and the best he had been able to manage was on this occasion was ninth place on the starting grid. However, by the end of the race, two things had helped to lift him to second position. In the tyre lottery, the Finn had decided in favor of a soft compound, while Prost had favored three hard tyres for the first shift. Rosberg then drove his car with the grim determination which was his personal hallmark.

There was another bout of fisticuffs over sixth position between Nelson Piquet (Williams FW11), Martin Brundle and Patrick Tambay. In the heat of this battle, on lap 68, the Frenchman's Lola went end over end across the Englishman's Tyrrell and landed fairly and squarely astride the crash barrier. Both drivers walked away unscathed, as did two spectators who had been standing just a few centimeters away – one of the many miracles which are considered par for the course in Monaco.

Other drivers also had a black day, in particular the Brabham team. It appeared that designer Gordon Murray had conceived his BT55 with genius: his BMW four-cylinder engine was installed at an angle of 72 degrees, making the car ultra-flat and blessed with a remarkably low center of gravity. Nevertheless, the model proved to be a flop; the transmission caused problems, the oil supply was troublesome and the engine overheated. After lap 31, Brabham driver Elio de Angelis gave up the ghost – his turbocharger had stopped developing any pressure – and seven laps later it was the turn of his colleague Riccardo Patrese, this time with engine damage. Short-termism has never had a place in Formula 1.

Die Überlegenheit eines Mannes, einer Marke und einer Maschine mag den Protagonisten eine Menge Befriedigung geben, einem Grand Prix tut sie nicht gut. Am zweiten Wochenende im Mai 1986 herrschen im Fürstentum Alain Prost, der McLaren MP4/2C, das TAG Porsche Triebwerk – und die Langeweile. Prost dominiert das Training und holt sich die Pole Position. Prost fährt die schnellste Runde im Warmup wie im Rennen. Prost führt vom Start bis ins Ziel, abgesehen von sieben Runden um die Halbzeit. Da darf der künftige Erzrivale Ayrton Senna im Lotus 98T auch mal nach vorn, aber nur, weil der Franzose zum Reifenwechsel die Box anlaufen mußte. Mehr noch: Prost hat bereits vierzehn Tage zuvor den Großen Preis von San Marino gewonnen, führt nach Monaco in der Weltmeisterschaft und wird am Ende Champion wie bereits im Jahr zuvor.

Die Strecke ist um 16 Meter länger geworden: Die Schikane stellt sich nun den Piloten fürwahr schikanös entgegen mit voll ausgeprägten rechten Winkeln, nachdem man ein neues Stück Piste oberhalb des Meeres geschaffen hat. Der Buckel in Rascasse wurde weggebügelt, die Strecke am Ende der Doppelkurve neu modelliert, so daß die Wagen aus dem zweiten Gang beschleunigend noch gieriger durch die sanft gekrümmte Zielpassage hechten.

Einen Hauch von Spannung und Aufregung bezieht das Rennen wie immer aus Bravourstücken einzelner und dramatischen Episoden. Da ist die verwegene Jagd von Prosts Teamgefährten Keke Rosberg. Monaco ist nicht unbedingt ein Tummelplatz für seinen aggressiven Stil, und so bringt er es lediglich auf Startplatz neun. Am Ende aber tragen ihn zwei Dinge auf den zweiten Rang vor. Der Finne setzt im Reifen-Vabanque auf eine weiche Mischung, während Prost bei der ersten Schicht für drei harte Pneus votiert. Und er fährt mit der grimmigen Entschlossenheit, die ihm eigen ist.

Hemdsärmelig geht es auch zu beim Kampf um Position sechs zwischen Nelson Piquet (Williams FW11), Martin Brundle und Patrick Tambay. In der Hitze des Gefechts geschieht es in der 68. Runde, daß die Lola des Franzosen einen Purzelbaum schlägt über den Tyrrell des Engländers und um ein Haar rittlings auf der Leitplanke landet. Beide Fahrer kommen ungeschoren davon, ebenso wie die Zuschauer ein paar Zentimeter weiter – eines der zahlreichen Wunder, die in Monaco zum normalen Ablauf der Dinge gehören.

Einen schwarzen Tag erleben auch andere, besonders aber das Brabham-Team. Den Typ BT55 hat Konstrukteur Gordon Murray, so scheint es, genial ausgedacht: Sein BMW-Vierzylinder ist im Winkel von 72 Grad geneigt eingebaut, das Auto deshalb ultraflach und mit einem besonders tiefen Schwerpunkt gesegnet. Dennoch entpuppt sich das Modell als Flop. Das Getriebe macht Ärger, der Ölhaushalt ist in Unordnung, der Motor überhitzt. Nach Runde 31 gibt Brabham-Pilot Elio de Angelis auf – der Turbolader erzeugt keinen Druck mehr. Sieben Durchgänge später ist Kollege Riccardo Patrese dran: Motorschaden. Kurzarbeit aber war in der Formel 1 noch nie gefragt.

Si la suprématie d'un homme, d'une marque et d'un moteur est, certes, source de satisfaction pour ceux qui en profitent, elle n'est en revanche guère bénéfique pour un Grand Prix. Le second week-end de Mai 1986 règnent dans la Principauté Alain Prost, la McLaren P4/2C, le moteur TAG Porsche – et l'ennui. Prost domine les essais de la tête et des épaules et obtient la pole position. Prost signe le tour le plus rapide tant au warm-up qu'en course. Prost reste en tête du début à la fin, abstraction faite de sept tours à la mi-course. Durant ce bref intermède, l'ennemi héréditaire de Prost, Ayrton Senna, a aussi le plaisir, avec sa Lotus 98T, de couvrir quelques tours en tête, mais seulement parce que le Français doit rallier les stands pour changer de pneus. Plus encore : Prost a déjà gagné le Grand Prix de San Marino quinze jours plus tôt, il quitte Monaco en tête du championnat du monde et, à la fin de la saison, sera sacré champion pour la deuxième année consécutive.

Le circuit s'est allongé de 16 mètres : la chicane mérite maintenant vraiment son nom avec d'authentiques angles droits freinant l'élan des pilotes après que l'on a gagné un nouveau fragment de piste sur la mer. La bosse de la Rascasse a été gommée et les bords de la piste à l'issue de l'épingle à cheveux ont été redessinés, si bien que les voitures, accélérant à fond depuis la seconde, peuvent maintenant attaquer plus sauvagement encore le léger virage de la ligne d'arrivée.

Comme toujours, la course tire sa dose de passion et d'excitation d'une série d'actes de bravoure ou d'épisodes ponctuels et dramatiques. Citons la poursuite effrénée et solitaire du coéquipier d'Alain Prost, Keke Rosberg. Monaco n'est pas absolument une piste à sa mesure pour son style agressif, ce qui explique qu'il n'ait obtenu que la neuvième place au départ. Mais, à la fin, deux facteurs lui rapportent le second rang. Dans le jeu de poker des pneumatiques, le Finlandais misa sur des gommes tendres, tandis que Prost, pour son premier train, opta pour trois pneus durs. Et Rosberg pilote avec la détermination intraitable qui lui est coutumière.

On ne se fait pas de cadeaux non plus dans la lutte pour la sixième place entre Nelson Piquet (Williams FW11), Martin Brundle et Patrick Tambay. Ce qui explique que, dans la chaleur de l'action, au 68e tour, la Lola du Français fasse un bond par-dessus la Tyrrell de l'Anglais et manque de retomber à cheval sur les glissières. Les deux pilotes s'en tirent indemnes, au même titre que les spectateurs éloignés de quelques centimètres seulement – l'un des nombreux miracles qui semblent être à l'ordre du jour à Monaco.

D'autres aussi sont victimes d'une journée à rayer de leur mémoire, ce cas en particulier le cas de l'écurie Brabham. La BT55 de l'ingénieur Gordon Murray, croit-on, est un coup de génie : son quatre-cylindres BMW est monté incliné selon un angle de 72 degrés, raison pour laquelle la voiture est ultraplate et possède un centre de gravité particulièrement bas. Et pourtant, la voiture est un échec. La boîte de vitesses ne cesse de poser problème, le circuit d'huile ne fonctionne pas correctement et le moteur chauffe. Au bout de 31 tours, Elio de Angelis stoppe sa Brabham – le turbocompresseur ne produit plus aucune pression. Puis, sept tours plus tard, son coéquipier Riccardo Patrese abandonne lui aussi : panne de moteur. Le chômage technique n'a encore jamais été très apprécié en Formule 1.

Plants and people come together in a confused symbiotic relationship on the Rocher for three days of the year. Typical spectators here are characterized by lack of wealth and an inner fire verging on fanaticism, and most of their hearts beat for Ferrari.

Auf dem Rocher finden sich an drei Tagen im Jahr Mensch und Pflanze zu einer konfusen Symbiose zusammen. Den typischen Zuschauer hier zeichnen Armut und inneres Feuer bis hin zum Fanatismus aus, und meist schlägt sein Herz für Ferrari.

Sur le Rocher, hommes et plantes se trouvent en symbiose confuse pendant trois jours. Le spectateur typique de cet endroit se distingue par sa pauvreté et son feu sacré qui peut aller jusqu'au fanatisme ; le plus souvent, son cœur bat pour Ferrari.

N°	DRIVERS		ENTRANTS	CARS	ENGINES	PRACTICE RESULTS	RACE RESULTS
1	*Alain Prost*	*F*	*Marlboro McLaren International*	*McLaren MP4/2C*	*TAG Porsche V6 1499 cc + T*	*1st: 1'22"627*	*1st: 1h55'41"060*
2	Keke Rosberg	SF	Marlboro McLaren International	McLaren MP4/2C	TAG Porsche V6 1499 cc + T	9th: 1'24"701	2rd: 1h56'06"082
12	Ayrton Senna	BR	John Player Special Team Lotus	Lotus 98T	Renault V6 1494 cc + T	3rd: 1'23"175	3rd: 1h56'34"706
5	Nigel Mansell	GB	Canon Williams Honda Team	Williams FW11	Honda V6 1499 cc + T	2nd: 1'23"047	4th: 1h56'52"462
25	René Arnoux	F	Equipe Ligier	Ligier JS27	Renault V6 1494 cc + T	12th: 1'25"538	5th: 77 laps
26	Jacques Laffite	F	Equipe Ligier	Ligier JS27	Renault V6 1494 cc + T	7th(21): 1'24"402	6th: 77 laps
6	Nelson Piquet	BR	Canon Williams Honda Team	Williams FW11	Honda V6 1499 cc + T	11th: 1'25"287	7th: 77 laps
18	Thierry Boutsen	B	Barclay Arrows BMW	Arrows A8	BMW 4L 1499 cc + T	14th: 1'25"832	8th: 75 laps
17	Marc Surer	CH	Barclay Arrows BMW	Arrows A8	BMW 4L 1499 cc + T	17th: 1'26"300	9th: 75 laps
28	Stefan Johansson	S	SEFAC Ferrari S.p.A.	Ferrari F1-86	Ferrari V6 1496 cc + T	15th: 1'25"907	10th: 75 laps
4	Philippe Streiff	F	Data General Team Tyrrell	Tyrrell 015	Renault V6 1492 cc + T	13th: 1'25"720	11th: 74 laps
14	Jonathan Palmer	GB	West Zakspeed Racing	Zakspeed 861	Zakspeed 4L 1495 cc + T	19th: 1'26"644	12th:74 laps
3	Martin Brundle	GB	Data General Team Tyrrell	Tyrrell 015	Renault V6 1494 cc + T	10th: 1'24"860	R
16	Patrick Tambay	F	Team Haas (USA) Ltd.	Lola THL-2	Cosworth V6 1497 cc + T	8th: 1'24"686	R
20	Gerhard Berger	A	Benetton Formula Ltd.	Benetton B186	BMW 4L 1499 cc + T	5th: 1'23"960	R
7	Riccardo Patrese	I	Motor Racing Developments	Brabham BT55	BMW 4L 1499 cc + T	6th: 1'24"102	R
27	Michele Alboreto	I	SEFAC Ferrari S.p.A.	Ferrari F1-86	Ferrari V6 1496 cc + T	4th: 1'23"904	R
8	Elio de Angelis	I	Motor Racing Developments	Brabham BT55	BMW 4L 1499 cc + T	20th: 1'27"191	R
19	Teo Fabi	I	Benetton Formula Ltd.	Benetton B186	BMW 4L 1499 cc + T	16th: 1'25"926	R
15	Alan Jones	AUS	Team Haas (USA) Ltd.	Lola THL2	Cosworth V6 1500 cc + T	18th: 1'26"456	R

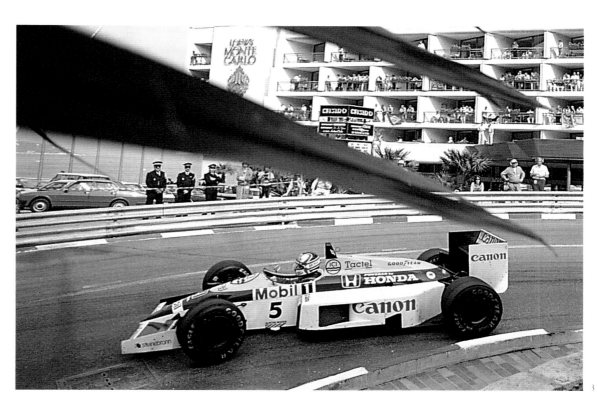

Park and ride: surrounded by the Mediterranean atmosphere of the town on the sea is a beautiful botanical garden. (1) Tambay is about to leap in his Lola as he leads towards Mirabeau, while (2) Surer in the Arrows and (3) Mansell in the Williams are rounding the hairpin in front of Loews.

Park and ride: Umgeben vom mediterranen Ambiente der Stadt am Meer, die auch ein schöner botanischer Garten ist, wird (1) Tambay im Lola gleich Richtung Mirabeau abheben, während (2) Surer im Arrows und (3) Mansell im Williams die Haarnadel vor dem Loews umrunden.

Park and ride : dans l'ambiance méditerranéenne de la ville aux pieds dans l'eau, qui est aussi un magnifique jardin botanique. (1) Tambay sur Lola va bientôt s'envoler en direction de Mirabeau, tandis que (2) Surer sur Arrows et (3) Mansell sur Williams contournent l'épingle du Loews.

(1) Fifth place in his first year after leaving Ferrari: Arnoux (Ligier).
(2) A convincing idea, but not up to Grand Prix reality: the ultra-low
Brabham BT55 of de Angelis. (3) Last row of the grid at the start,
12th place at the finish: Jonathan Palmer's Zakspeed.

(1) Rang fünf im Jahre eins nach seiner Dienstzeit bei Ferrari:
Arnoux (Ligier). (2) Überzeugend ausgedacht, aber der Grand-Prix-
Praxis nicht gewachsen: der Brabham BT55 von de Angelis.
(3) Letzte Reihe am Start, zwölfter Platz im Ziel: der Zakspeed von
Jonathan Palmer.

(1) Cinquième place pour sa première année depuis son départ de
chez Ferrari : Arnoux (Ligier). (2) Bien conçue, mais pas à la hauteur
de la pratique des Grands Prix : la Brabham BT55 de de Angelis.
(3) En dernière ligne au départ, douzième à l'arrivée : la Zakspeed de
Jonathan Palmer.

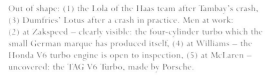

Out of shape: (1) the Lola of the Haas team after Tambay's crash, (3) Dumfries' Lotus after a crash in practice. Men at work: (2) at Zakspeed – clearly visible: the four-cylinder turbo which the small German marque has produced itself, (4) at Williams – the Honda V6 turbo engine is open to inspection, (5) at McLaren – uncovered: the TAG V6 Turbo, made by Porsche.

Aus der Fasson geraten: (1) der Lola des Haas-Teams nach Tambays Unfall, (3) der Lotus von Dumfries nach einem Crash im Training. Men at work: (2) bei Zakspeed – deutlich sichtbar: der Vierzylinder-Turbo, den die kleine deutsche Marke selbst herstellt, (4) bei Williams – gut erkennbar der Honda V6 Turbo, (5) bei McLaren – nicht abgedeckt: der TAG V6 Turbo, made by Porsche.

Boutée endommagée : (1) la Lola de l'écurie Haas après l'accident de Tambay. (3) La Lotus de Dumfries après une collision aux essais. Hommes au travail : (2) chez Zakspeed – nettement visible : le quatre-cylindres turbo que la petite marque allemande fabrique elle-même, (4) chez Williams – bien reconnaissable, le Honda V6 Turbo, (5) chez McLaren – mis à nu : le TAG V6 Turbo, fabriqué par Porsche.

(1) Media man: Jody Scheckter, World Champion in 1979. (2) Beautiful setting: Marc Surer, left his future wife Yolantha. (3) Amused: Alan Jones (center). (4) At home on two wheels since childhood: Jacky Ickx. (5) Not easily shaken: Riccardo Patrese.

(1) Medien-Mann: Jody Scheckter, Weltmeister von 1979. (2) Schöner Rahmen: Marc Surer, links seine künftige Gattin Yolantha. (3) Amüsiert : Alan Jones (Mitte). (4) Von Kindesbeinen an auf zwei Rädern zu Hause: Jacky Ickx. (5) Nicht so leicht zu erschüttern: Riccardo Patrese.

(1) Homme médiatique : Jody Scheckter, champion du monde de 1979. (2) Bien encadré : Marc Surer ; à gauche, sa future épouse Yolantha. (3) Amusé : Alan Jones (au centre). (4) Sur deux roues depuis sa plus tendre enfance : Jacky Ickx. (5) Il en faudrait plus pour lui faire perdre son calme : Riccardo Patrese.

ALAIN AGAINST ALL

ALAIN GEGEN ALLE · ALAIN CONTRE TOUS

Is Alain Prost the greatest? But of course, the figures speak volumes: 51 victories from 199 Grands Prix, a total of 798.5 World Championship points, that is an average of four points per race. These shimmering intarsia of success are embedded in 33 pole positions, 86 starts from the front row of the grid and 41 fastest laps. Alain Prost spent 7,839 miles in the lead, a quarter of the way around the world at Grand Prix speed. That is the annual performance of many a normal driver, peacefully and law-abidingly rolling along.

All of this certainly qualifies the small man with the unmistakable hooked nose for the top seat on the Olympus of the racing gods, which had until then been the preserve in awe-inspiring unapproachability of Juan Manuel Fangio. He could show even more impressive figures if that path were not paved with ifs and buts.

For Alain Prost is allied with luck unusually often, but not always good luck. It was his bad luck, for instance, that it was raining in Monaco on 3 June 1984 – mission impossible. Even before the half-way point, race organizer Jacky Ickx decided that enough was enough and put a merciful end to the Grand Prix. The points were halved, so the winner Prost received only four-and-a-half. Juggling a little with figures and events, others did better out of the weather conditions. The alert Frenchman, who in any case felt uncomfortable on a wet track, was threatened with relegation to second place. If the race had been run over its full length he would have earned himself six points. Less is sometimes more: at the end of the 1984 season, that would have been equal to a one-point lead over his team mate and rival Niki Lauda, and thus would have led to World Championship number five, the same as Fangio, whose record appeared untouchable. And the lifetime performance at the limit by Prost would have stacked up to the round figure of 800 points.

It was also his bad luck that in 1983 the yellow rockets of Régie Renault were characterized not only by brutal speed, but were still suffering from a delicate constitution, despite massive development assistance through Prost himself, who was more sensitive than any other to what is wrong with racing cars. Four victories were not enough; the World Championship was won by Brabham driver Nelson Piquet. It could have been the sixth for Prost, one more than Fangio.

His bad luck, too, that Ayrton Senna shoved him out of the championship race on 21 October 1990 in Suzuka, literally, in a duel in which a McLaren and a Ferrari were used like heavy sabres. Ferrari had engaged Prost as faith healer, as they did Michael Schumacher later on. Things looked good. But then male hatred destroyed the dreams of a whole season. Senna's name, in any case, had long been like a red rag to a bull for Prost from their first year together at McLaren in 1988, when the relationship between the two deteriorated from forced matiness to silence. The fact that the Brazilian was to be his team-mate again at Williams in 1994 finally drove him into early retirement. Alain Prost – World Champion in 1990 in a Ferrari? The red Scuderia had urgent need of it. It would have been most welcome to their star driver. And the monument which was Fangio would finally have been toppled – statistically.

Ist Alain Prost der Größte? Aber klar doch, die Zahlen sprechen ja Bände. 51 Siege in 199 Großen Preisen, 798,5 Punkte insgesamt, das sind im Schnitt vier Punkte pro Rennen. Eingebettet sind diese schimmernden Intarsien des Erfolgs in 33 Pole Positions, 86 Starts aus der ersten Reihe und 41 schnellste Runden. An der Spitze verbringt Alain Prost 12 616 Kilometer, eine Viertelrunde um den Globus im Grand-Prix-Tempo. Auf diese Strecke beläuft sich die Jahresleistung so manches friedfertig und angepaßt dahinrollenden normalen Kraftfahrers.

All das qualifiziert den kleinen Mann mit der unverkennbaren Hakennase durchaus für den Chefsessel im Olymp der Renngötter, auf dem bis zu seinem Erscheinen Juan Manuel Fangio in erhabener Unnahbarkeit thronte. Er könnte sogar noch mehr meßbare Größe vorweisen, wäre nicht der Weg dorthin gepflastert gewesen mit Wenns und Abers.

Denn mit dem Glück im Bunde ist Alain Prost zwar ungewöhnlich oft, aber eben doch nicht immer. Sein Pech zum Beispiel, daß es am 3. Juni 1984 in Monaco regnet, mission impossible. Noch vor Halbzeit befindet Rennleiter Jacky Ickx, nun sei es genug des grausamen Spiels, und setzt dem Grand Prix ein gnädiges Ende. Die Punkte werden halbiert: Als Sieger erhält Prost nur viereinhalb Zähler. Jonglieren wir ein bißchen mit Zahlen und Szenarien: Andere kamen mit den Wetterbedingungen besser zurecht. Dem alerten Franzosen, der sich auf nasser Strecke ohnehin unbehaglich fühlt, drohte der Absturz auf Rang zwei. Wäre das Rennen über die volle Distanz gegangen, hätte er sich sechs Zähler verdient. Weniger ist manchmal mehr: Am Ende der Saison 1984 wäre das gleichbedeutend gewesen mit einem Punkt Vorsprung vor seinem Teamgefährten und Rivalen Niki Lauda und damit Championat Nummer fünf, soviel wie Fangio, dessen Rekord unantastbar schien. Und Prosts Lebensleistung am Limit hätte sich zu der runden Summe von 800 Punkten emporgeschichtet.

Sein Pech auch, daß sich 1983 die gelben Raketen der Régie Renault nicht nur durch brutale Schnelligkeit auszeichnen, sondern noch immer an delikater Konstitution kränkeln – trotz massiver Entwicklungshilfe durch Prost selber, der Rennwagen einfühlsam therapieren kann wie kein Zweiter. Vier Siege reichen nicht aus. Die Meisterschaft gewinnt Brabham-Pilot Nelson Piquet. Es hätte die sechste sein können für Prost, eine mehr als Fangio.

Sein Pech schließlich, daß ihn Ayrton Senna am 21. Oktober 1990 in Suzuka aus dem Rennen um das Championat jenes Jahres schubst, buchstäblich, in einem Duell, in dem ein McLaren und ein Ferrari wie schwere Säbel benutzt werden. Ferrari hat Prost als Wunderheiler engagiert wie später Michael Schumacher. Die Dinge sahen gut aus. Doch dann läßt Männerhaß die Blütenträume einer ganzen Saison platzen. Der Name Senna ist sowieso längst ein Reizwort für Prost, schon im ersten gemeinsamen Jahr bei McLaren 1988, in dem das Verhältnis zwischen den beiden verkommt von gezwungen-lockerer Kollegialität bis hinab zur Sprachlosigkeit. Daß der Brasilianer 1994 wieder sein Teamgefährte bei Williams sein würde, treibt ihn schließlich aufs vorzeitige Altenteil. Alain Prost –

Alain Prost est-il le plus grand ? Mais bien sûr, les chiffres en disent plus long que mille discours. 51 victoires en 199 Grands Prix, un total de 798,5 points de championnat du monde, soit, en moyenne, quatre points par course. Avec, à la clef, dans la marqueterie scintillante du succès, 33 pole positions, 86 départs en première ligne et 41 tours les plus rapides en course. Alain Prost a couvert 12 616 kilomètres en tête, un quart de la circonférence du globe, à un rythme de Grand Prix. Cela équivaut sensiblement au kilométrage couvert en un an par le commun des mortels quand il circule, pacifique et docile, au volant de sa brave voiture.

Tout cela qualifie légitimement le petit homme au nez crochu pour le trône à l'Olympe des dieux de la course que, jusqu'à son apparition, Juan Manuel Fangio occupait dans une inaccessibilité majestueuse. Il pourrait même se prévaloir de plus spectaculaire encore, si le chemin qui l'a mené là-haut n'avait pas été pavé d'un aussi grand nombre de si et de mais.

En effet, Alain Prost s'entend vraiment très souvent comme larron en foire avec la fortune, mais, qui n'est malheureusement pas toujours synonyme de chance. Comme ce 3 juin 1984, où il pleut sur Monaco – mission impossible. Avant même la mi-course, le directeur de course Jacky Ickx estime que la cruelle plaisanterie a suffisamment duré et il a la bonté de mettre fin au Grand Prix. Mais on ne comptera que la moitié des points : vainqueur, Prost ne peut donc inscrire que quatre points et demi à son tableau de chasse. Jonglons un peu avec les chiffres et les hypothèses : d'autres s'en étaient mieux tirés avec les conditions météorologiques. Le rapide petit Français, qui n'a jamais été particulièrement dans son élément sur piste détrempée, menaçait de se faire rattraper. Si la course avait été menée à son terme, il aurait mérité six points. Le mieux est parfois l'ennemi du bien : à la fin de la saison 1984, cela aurait signifié qu'il aurait eu un point d'avance sur son coéquipier et rival Niki Lauda et donc qu'il aurait remporté son cinquième titre de champion du monde, autant que Fangio, dont le record semblait inaccessible. Et le flirt de Prost avec la limite d'adhé-rence lui aurait permis d'arrondir le nombre de points accumulés à la coquette somme de 800 points.

Il n'a pas la baraka non plus lorsque, en 1983, les fusées de la Régie Renault, les fameuses « théières jaunes », se distinguent non seulement par leur rapidité stupéfiante, mais encore et toujours par la délicatesse de leur constitution – malgré une aide au développement tous azimuts par Prost lui-même qui, mieux que tout autre, s'entend à la perfection à guérir avec sensibilité les voitures de course maladives. Quatre victoires ne suffisent pas. C'est Nelson Piquet, sur Brabham, qui gagne le championnat du monde. Cela aurait pu être le sixième pour Prost, un de plus que Fangio.

Et il n'a, enfin, toujours pas la baraka lorsqu'Ayrton Senna, le 21 octobre 1990 à Suzuka – les deux hommes se disputant le titre de champion cette année-là – le sort proprement et brutalement de la piste, dans un duel au cours duquel une McLaren et une Ferrari auront été utilisées comme des armes blanches. Ferrari a engagé Prost comme gourou comme cela sera le cas, plus tard, pour Michael Schumacher. Les choses se présentent bien. Et pourtant, la rivalité entre les deux hommes fait

s'évanouir les rêves de toute une saison. Senna est, depuis longtemps, de toute façon la bête noire de Prost, ce qui a commencé dès leur première année de vie commune, chez McLaren en 1988, au cours de laquelle les rapports entre les deux hommes n'ont cessé de se dégrader, passant d'un esprit d'équipe décontracté, bien que forcé, à une détermination intraitable à ne plus s'adresser la parole. En 1994, le Brésilien aurait de nouveau été son coéquipier chez Williams si cette perspective n'avait pas décidé Prost à prendre prématurément sa retraite. Alain Prost – champion du monde 1990 sur Ferrari ? Et pourtant, Dieu sait si la Scuderia rouge en aurait eu besoin d'urgence. Son pilote vedette aurait été le premier à s'en féliciter. Et le monument Fangio aurait, en fin de compte, réellement été renversé, tout au moins dans les statistiques.

Mais Alain Prost est-il réellement le plus grand ? Absolument pas, critiquent tous ses détracteurs qui donnent la préférence aux vieux chevaux de bataille et anciens bagarreurs que sont Nigel Mansell, Gilles Villeneuve, Ronnie Peterson ou Jochen Rindt, ou qui préfèrent des comètes comme Stefan Bellof, même si leur présence au firmament a duré à peine plus longtemps que le scintillement d'une étoile.

Prost n'est pas une *shooting star*, mais un garçon qui a appris sur le tas. Comment a-t-il fait carrière ? Avec application, étape par étape, mais d'une façon toutefois très française. Il commence avec le karting, gagne en 1975 le prix du Volant Elf pour le meilleur pilote de la promotion de l'école de pilotage Winfield, avec à la clef une monoplace de Formule Renault pour la saison suivante. Il est immédiatement promu en Formule Super Renault en 1977. Deux ans plus tard, en 1979, Prost termine sa deuxième saison en Formule 3 avec un double titre de champion, de France et d'Europe, et avec, comme cerise sur le gâteau, l'honneur de gagner le Grand Prix de Formule 3 de Monaco. En 1980, on le retrouve dans le baquet d'une McLaren. Le bon vieux temps, dit-il, n'a pas toujours été le bon temps, mais les années d'apprentissage des élèves de Formule 1 d'aujourd'hui devraient déjà présenter une certaine similitude avec celles de jadis. Par contre, issus de la Formule 3000, ils croient déjà pouvoir partir à la conquête du monde.

C'est bizarre : il est rare qu'un pilote de course se voie affublé d'un surnom. En son temps, on surnommait le sauvage Belge Mairesse « Willy le kamikaze ». Denis

But is Alain Prost really the greatest? Not at all, say those who prefer to give preference to old war-horses and sometime trouble-makers like Nigel Mansell, Gilles Villeneuve, Ronnie Peterson or Jochen Rindt, or to comets such as Stefan Bellof, even if the time they spent in the firmament is only a short one.

Prost is no whizz-kid, but he learnt his trade from the bottom up. His career has been a careful progression upwards, step by step, even if in a very French way. He started in karts, received the Prix Pilote Elf for the best in his course at the Winfield racing driver school in 1975, and a single-seater to race in Formule Renault the following year. Immediate promotion into Formule Super Renault followed in 1977. In 1979, Prost won the French and European Championships in his second year in Formula 3, to which he added as a special achievement the Formula 3 race in Monaco. In 1980 he sat in a McLaren. The old times were not always the best times, he says, but the apprenticeship years of the Formula 1 learners today should be as they were then. Instead they arrive from Formula 3000 and believe they can conquer the world.

Strangely, racing drivers rarely have nicknames. The wild Belgian, Mairesse, was called "Kamikaze-Willy".

Weltmeister 1990 auf Ferrari. Die rote Scuderia hätte es dringend gebraucht. Ihrem Starpiloten wäre es höchst willkommen gewesen. Und das Monument Fangio wäre am Ende tatsächlich vom Sockel gestürzt, statistisch gesehen.

Ist Alain Prost wirklich der Größte? Keineswegs, nörgeln vor allem die, welche Haudegen, Driftern und Quertreibern vom Schlage eines Nigel Mansell, Gilles Villeneuve, Ronnie Peterson oder Jochen Rindt den Vorzug geben oder Kometen wie Stefan Bellof, auch wenn ihre Verweildauer am Firmament nur kurz bemessen ist. Prost ist kein Senkrechtstarter, sondern lernt sein Handwerk von der Pike auf. Seine Karriere: ein behutsamer Aufstieg Schritt für Schritt, allerdings auf sehr französische Weise. Er beginnt im Kart, erhält 1975 den Pilote Elf-Preis für den Lehrgangsbesten der Winfield-Rennfahrerschule, einen Monoposto für die Formule Renault im folgenden Jahr. Die umgehende Beförderung in die Formule Super Renault folgt 1977. 1979 gewinnt Prost in seinem zweiten Jahr in der Formel 3 die französische und die Europameisterschaft, dazu als Fleißkärtchen der besonderen Art den Formel-3-Lauf in Monaco. 1980 sitzt er im McLaren. Nicht immer, sagt er, sei die alte Zeit die gute Zeit, aber wie

Denis Hulme and Jody Scheckter had "The Bear" as their combat name. Carlos Reutemann was called "The Indian". Alain Prost, on the other hand, was called "The Professor". Perhaps the academic connotations of the name saved him from the incense of fervent worship and everything connected with that: an intellectual and methodical approach with an understanding of how he could use a situation for his benefit; iron control which he exercised over himself; the politics which he mastered in all its nuances between arbitration and intrigue.

In 1996, the third year of his retirement, he worked as a consultant to McLaren-Mercedes, helping with the development of the car, occasionally also showing drivers Mika Hakkinen and David Coulthard a trick or two. He even concerned himself with the personal relations within the team, re-opening with great charm and smooth persuasion avenues of communication which had been closed, a Talleyrand of the race track. Since 1997 Prost has again been among the merry crowd in the pit lane as boss of his own racing stable; he no longer drives but he still has his old fire and ambition.

But there is also life outside racing. His physical constitution is better than in his time as a driver, and he is passionate about his credo of sport as the means to a well-balanced overall personality. Whatever he might do in the future, nothing would prevent him from engaging in sport, even if it meant working 12 hours per day, he has admitted.

Tennis, skiing, jogging and golf have always been part of the fitness programme of Alain Prost. Five years ago he discovered cycling, and he gets up at five o'clock in the morning four days a week in order to train for two hours. In the races, he will always be among the front runners in one of the stages of the Tour de France. Once he pushed forward to 42nd place from a horde of 5,800 starters. That was as much as he could manage, he adds, shrugging his shoulders, the others in front of him were all professionals who spent five hours a day on their bikes. After all, he is not that young anymore. But his results are getting better all the time in the Cyclosport series, five to six runs per year of between 100 and 130 miles each, which sometimes pack a punch. He was not doing that only to stay fit. That was undoubtedly a pleasant by-product. But he also wanted to beat the others.

This Prost has been able to do for three years with cycles from his own production line, machines made to measure. That, too, is part of his philosophy: he has always done other things alongside racing, meeting people, doing business, building something, even if the product was not always successful. That is simply good for the head. For all manner of one-sidedness – and this, too, distinguishes him from his successors in the cockpit – is reprehensible to Alain Prost.

damals sollten die Lehrjahre der Formel-1-Eleven von heute schon beschaffen sein. Die kämen aus der Formel 3000 und glaubten schon, sie könnten die Welt erobern.

Merkwürdig: Rennfahrer haben selten Spitznamen. Den wilden Belgier Mairesse nannten sie »Kamikaze-Willy«. Denis Hulme und Jody Scheckter trugen den Kriegernamen »der Bär«. Carlos Reutemann wurde »der Indianer« genannt. Alain Prost indessen heißt »der Professor«. Vielleicht bewahrt ihn das Brillenhafte dieses Begriffs vor dem Weihrauch inbrünstiger Anbetung und alles, was dahinter steckt: ein intellektueller und methodischer Ansatz, das Wissen darum, wie er eine Situation zu seinem Vorteil ummünzen kann, die eiserne Kontrolle, die er über sich selbst ausübt, das Politische, das er beherrscht in sämtlichen Schattierungen zwischen Schlichtung und Intrige.

Im Jahr drei seines Ruhestands 1996 arbeitet er als Berater für McLaren-Mercedes, hilft beim Entwickeln des Wagens, zeigt den Piloten Mika Hakkinen und David Coulthard auch schon mal, wo es langgeht. Sogar um das Zwischenmenschliche im Team kümmert er sich, legt mit großem Charme und geschmeidiger Beredsamkeit verschüttete Kommunikationswege wieder frei, ein Talleyrand der Pisten. Seit 1997 gehört Prost erneut zu dem bunten Völkchen in der Boxengasse, als Chef seines eigenen Rennstalls zwar nur noch als Fußgänger, aber mit dem alten Feuer und dem alten Ehrgeiz.

Aber es gibt auch ein Leben außerhalb des Rennsports. Seine physische Konstitution ist noch besser als in seiner aktiven Zeit, fast schon leidenschaftlich sein Credo zum Sport als Weg zu einer gut ausgewuchteten Gesamtpersönlichkeit. Was immer er in der Zukunft machen werde, nichts könne ihn davon abhalten, Sport zu betreiben, und wenn er zwölf Stunden am Tag arbeiten müßte, bekennt er. Tennis, Skifahren, Joggen und Golf zählen seit jeher zum Fitneßprogramm des Alain Prost. Vor fünf Jahren hat er den Radsport für sich entdeckt, steht an vier Tagen in der Woche um fünf Uhr früh auf, um anschließend zwei Stunden zu trainieren. Stets wird man ihn bei den Rennen im Vorfeld einer der Etappen der Tour de France antreffen. Einmal stößt er in einer Horde von 5800 Startern auf den 42. Platz vor. Mehr sei für ihn nicht drin gewesen, gibt er achselzuckend zu verstehen, die anderen Burschen vor ihm seien durchweg Profis und ohnehin fünf Stunden täglich mit dem Rad unterwegs. So ganz jung sei er schließlich auch nicht mehr. Aber immer besser werden seine Resultate bei der Cyclosport-Serie, fünf bis sechs Läufe jährlich zwischen 160 und 210 Kilometern, die es manchmal in sich haben. Das tue er nicht nur, um in Form zu bleiben. Das sei zweifellos ein angenehmes Nebenprodukt. Er wolle aber auch die anderen schlagen.

Das kann Prost seit drei Jahren mit Fahrrädern aus eigener Fertigung, Maschinen nach Maß. Auch sowas ist Teil seiner Philosophie: Stets schon habe er irgendetwas ganz anderes nebenher tun müssen, Leute treffen, Geschäfte machen, etwas bauen, auch wenn dem Produkt nicht immer Erfolg beschieden gewesen sei. Sowas sei einfach gut für den Kopf.

Denn alle Einseitigkeit – und auch darin unterscheidet er sich von seinen Nachfahren im Cockpit – ist für Alain Prost verwerflich.

Hulme et Jody Scheckter avaient celui de « l'Ours ». Carlos Reutemann, on l'appelait « l'Indien ». Le surnom d'Alain Prost, en revanche, est « le Professeur ». Peut-être l'évocation d'un porteur de lunettes inhérente à cette notion l'a-t-elle préservé d'être encensé par des adorateurs fanatiques avec tout ce que cela implique : une approche intellectuelle et méthodique, l'art de toujours retourner une situation à son avantage, le contrôle de fer qu'il exerce sur lui-même et ses nerfs, la politique, qu'il maîtrise dans tous les registres, de la modération à l'intrigue.

En l'an III de sa retraite, en 1996, il travaille comme consultant pour McLaren-Mercedes, aide à mettre au point la voiture, montre de temps à autre aux pilotes Mika Hakkinen et David Coulthard comment s'y prendre. Il se charge même des relations humaines au sein de l'écurie, défriche avec son charme irrésistible et son argumentation toujours judicieuse de nouvelles voies de communication oubliées, véritable Talleyrand des circuits. Depuis 1997, Prost fait de nouveau partie de cette peuplade multicolore qui anime la voie des stands : en tant que chef de sa propre écurie, il n'est, certes, plus qu'un piéton, mais toujours animé du feu sacré et guidé par une ambition inextinguible.

Mais il y a aussi une vie en dehors de la compétition automobile. Sa constitution physique est encore meilleure que lorsqu'il était au volant et il récite avec une passion non feinte le credo de la foi dans le sport comme moyen de bien équilibrer sa personnalité générale. Quoi qu'il fasse à l'avenir, dit-il, rien ne pourra l'empêcher de s'adonner au sport, même s'il devra pour cela travailler douze heures par jour.

Tennis, ski, jogging et golf figurent depuis des lustres déjà au programme de culture physique d'Alain Prost. Il y a cinq ans, il a découvert le cyclisme, se lève à cinq heures du matin quatre jours par semaine pour s'échiner ensuite deux heures sur sa petite reine. On ne manquera pas de le rencontrer régulièrement dans le peloton des coureurs amateurs précédant l'une des étapes du Tour de France. Une fois, face à une horde de 5800 concurrents, il termine 42e. C'était tout ce qu'il avait pu faire, dit-il résigné dans un haussement d'épaules, les autres étaient presque tous des pros passant largement cinq heures par jour sur leur vélo. Avant d'ajouter, comme pour s'excuser, qu'il n'était plus tout jeune non plus. Mais ses résultats en cyclisme ne cessent de s'améliorer dans la série où il discute chaque année cinq ou six courses allant de 160 à 210 kilomètres, des courses parfois extrêmement éprouvantes. Il ne le fait que pour garder la forme, dit-il. Cela est sans aucun doute un effet secondaire non négligeable. Mais il veut aussi bel et bien battre ses adversaires.

Et cela, Prost peut le faire depuis trois ans avec des bicyclettes qu'il fait fabriquer lui-même, des vélos réalisés sur mesure. Cela, aussi, fait partie de sa philosophie : il déclare avoir toujours voulu faire quelque chose d'autre à côté, rencontrer des gens, faire des affaires, construire quelque chose, même si le produit ne devait pas toujours être voué au succès. Cela est tout simplement bon pour l'esprit, explique-t-il. En effet, toute forme de monoculture – et, en cela aussi, il se distingue de ses successeurs dans les cockpits – est condamnable au plus haut point pour Alain Prost.

1987

Once again, a Grand Prix field was spread out along the Boulevard Albert I, constituting a boundary separating yesterday from tomorrow – a colorful panoply of what Formula 1 technicians and the FIA legislators in Paris deemed to be feasible and possible. The Williams and Lotus cars were equipped with active suspension and the baritone rumble of the turbo engines mingled once again with the shrill whining of naturally-aspirated engines: 17 of the 24 cars had 1.5-liter turbocharged engines while the rest were powered by 3.5-liter naturally-aspirated units – all supplied by Cosworth under the Ford label. Despite a mild restriction on charge pressure, limiting it to 4 bar, the turbos still dominated. They were able to reserve the first four rows on the starting grid for themselves, and would also take the first four places at the finishing line. However, tyre performance was to play its part in the successful last days of an old model: Monaco demands power at the lower end, rather than the high-performance top-end potency so characteristic of the V6 engines used by Ferrari, Honda and Porsche. Despite this fact, 3.6 seconds separated the leading Honda driver Nigel Mansell in the Williams FW 11 B from Thierry Boutsen in the turbocharged Benetton B 187 in ninth place – light years apart in the rarefied atmosphere of Formula 1.

Thursday turned into a black day for the Ferrari team. During the first practice session, as he hurtled through the fast left-hand bend at Massenet in front of the Casino, Michele Alboreto in the Ferrari F1-87 cannoned into Christian Danner, who was zig-zagging negligently at low speed in order to warm up his tyres just after leaving the pit lane. The ensuing horrendous accident crippled the Ferrari, reducing it to a wreck. No-one was injured, but the German was disqualified with a verdict of "extremely dangerous behaviour". A short while later, Gerhard Berger wrecked the front suspension of the other scarlet car from Maranello when he hit a barrier beside the swimming pool.

Almost one second separated Mansell from the second quickest driver in the qualifying rounds, Ayrton Senna in the Lotus 99 T, and the British driver maintained a similar pace at the start of the race to quickly put the same distance between himself, the Brazilian and the other contenders. Ten laps later, his lead had grown to eight seconds, then to ten by lap 15. But at the end of lap 29, the Williams pit threw in the towel; a turbocharger on Mansell's car had refused to co-operate any longer. This meant that the lead dropped neatly into Senna's lap, safely padded by a 16-second lead over his fellow countryman Nelson Piquet, driving the other Williams ahead of Alboreto and Alain Prost.

The Frenchman proceeded cautiously as his McLaren MP 4/3 was losing oil. Prost waited patiently until Alboreto went in for new tyres, thereby vacating third place. He then carefully reduced turbo pressure and eased his car around the track like a fever-stricken infant, not that this did him any good. Three laps before the chequered flag his engine finally gave up the ghost, while Senna executed his fastest lap, a veritable demonstration of low-level flight which whisked him in exemplary fashion between the maze of crash barriers. By then he was far beyond reach because he had never given Piquet an opportunity to become a serious threat – town race tracks were torture to the man – not that this would stop him from becoming the 1987 World Champion.

Wieder einmal spreizt sich ein Grand-Prix-Feld über dem Boulevard Albert I auf der Grenze zwischen gestern und morgen, eine bunte Messe dessen, was aus der Sicht der Formel-1-Techniker und der Gesetzeshüter der FIA in Paris machbar und möglich ist. Die Williams und die Lotus haben aktive Fahrwerke, und in das baritonale Grollen der Turbomotoren mischt sich erneut das schrille Weinen von nicht zwangsbeatmeten Maschinen: 17 der 24 Wagen haben aufgeladene Maschinen mit 1,5 Litern Hubraum, der Rest Saugmotoren von 3,5 Litern – allesamt Ford Cosworth. Obwohl durch eine Beschränkung des Ladedrucks auf 4 bar zart geschwächt, dominieren noch immer die Turbos: Für sie sind die ersten vier Reihen am Start und die vier ersten Ränge im Ziel reserviert. Damit verdient sich ein Auslaufmodell zugleich das Zeugnis der Reife: Monaco verlangt nach Kraft von unten, und just damit können die obenherum potenten V6 von Ferrari, Honda und Porsche nicht dienen. Dennoch trennen Honda-Pilot Nigel Mansell auf dem Williams FW 11 B von Ford-Fahrer Thierry Boutsen im Benetton B 187 auf Startplatz neun ganze 3,6 Sekunden – das sind Lichtjahre im Biotop der Bleifüßler.

Der Donnerstag wird zum schwarzen Tag für die Roten. Beim ersten Zeittraining trifft Michele Alboreto im Ferrari F1-87 in dem schnellen Linksknick Massenet vor dem Casino in voller Fahrt auf den Zakspeed von Christian Danner, der gerade die Boxengasse verlassen hat und sich in nachlässigem Zickzack die Reifen warmfährt. Der folgende Horrorunfall verkrüppelt den Ferrari zum armen Wrack. Wenig später verstümmelt Gerhard Berger am Schwimmbad einen zweiten Renner aus Maranello. Verletzt wird keiner, Danner indes disqualifiziert, Begründung: »äußerst gefährliches Verhalten«.

Um fast eine Sekunde hat Mansell dem Trainingszweiten Ayrton Senna auf dem Lotus 99 T das Nachsehen gegeben. In diesem Takt setzt sich der Brite auch zu Beginn des Rennens von dem Brasilianer und den anderen ab. Nach zehn Runden ist sein Vorsprung auf acht Sekunden gewachsen, auf fünfzehn auf zehn. Aber am Ende des 29. Durchgangs wirft die Williams-Box das Handtuch: Ein Turbolader an Mansells Wagen macht nicht mehr mit. So fällt die Führung Senna in den Schoß, wattiert mit einem komfortablen Polster von 16 Sekunden gegenüber seinem Landsmann Nelson Piquet auf dem anderen Williams, Alboreto und Alain Prost.

Der Franzose läßt Vorsicht walten. Sein McLaren MP 4/3 verliert Öl. Prost wartet geduldig, bis Alboreto neue Reifen faßt und Platz drei vakant wird, reduziert behutsam den Ladedruck und trägt sein Auto über die Strecke wie einen fiebernden Säugling. Umsonst: Drei Runden vor Schluß läßt ihn sein Triebwerk im Stich, während Senna auf seiner schnellste Runde im Tiefflug schemenhaft durch das Labyrinth der Leitplanken huscht. Im Duell der Brasilianer geht von Piquet nie eine Gefahr aus – Stadtkurse sind ihm ein Greuel. Weltmeister 1987 wird er trotzdem.

Une fois de plus, un plateau de Grand Prix prend son élan sur le Boulevard Albert I, à la frontière entre hier et demain, échantillon représentatif de ce qui est réalisable et possible aux yeux des techniciens de la Formule 1 et des gardiens du Saint-Graal de la FIA à Paris. Les Williams et les Lotus ont des châssis actifs et le hurlement strident de moteurs non suralimentés vient de nouveau troubler les grognements de baryton des moteurs turbo : 17 des 24 voitures sont propulsées par un moteur suralimenté de 1,5 litre de cylindrée, le reste, par un moteur atmosphérique de 3,5 litres – tous des Ford Cosworth. Bien que la pression de suralimentation soit limitée – timidement – à 4 bars, ce sont toujours les turbos qui dominent : ils trustent les quatre premières lignes au départ et occuperont aussi les quatre premières places à l'arrivée. Cependant, la qualité des pneus devait jouer un rôle déterminant pour ce modèle enfin de carrière : Monaco exige des chevaux à bas régime, plutôt que la puissance performante caractéristiques aux V6 de Ferrari, Honda et Porsche. Il n'est donc pas étonnant que 3,6 secondes – des années-lumière dans l'air raréfié du monde de la Formule 1 – séparent Nigel Mansell, en pole position avec sa Williams FW 11 B, du pilote Ford Thierry Boutsen, sur Benetton B 187, au neuvième rang.

Le jeudi est le jour noir des rouges. Lors des premiers essais, Michele Alboreto lancé à fond avec sa Ferrari F1-87, dans le rapide gauche de Massenet précédant le Casino, percute de plein fouet la Zakspeed de Christian Danner qui vient de quitter les stands en faisant des zigzags nonchalants afin d'échauffer ses pneus. L'épouvantable accident qui s'ensuit transforme la Ferrari en une misérable épave. Personne n'est blessé, mais Danner est disqualifié. Motif : « comportement extrêmement dangereux ». Quelques minutes plus tard, Gerhard Berger détruit la suspension avant de l'autre bolide rouge de Maranello en percutant une glissière de sécurité à la hauteur de la piscine.

Mansell a battu de près d'une seconde le deuxième des essais, Ayrton Senna, sur Lotus 99 T. Et c'est aussi à ce même rythme que le bouillant Britannique distance le Brésilien et les autres au début de la course. Au bout de dix tours, son avance s'est élevée à huit secondes, puis à dix au bout de quinze tours. Mais à la fin du 29e tour, les mécaniciens jettent l'éponge dans les stands de Williams : un turbo de la voiture de Mansell refuse tout service. C'est ainsi que Senna hérite inopinément du commandement, avec le confortable oreiller de 16 secondes d'avance sur son compatriote Nelson Piquet, au volant de l'autre Williams, devant Alboreto et Alain Prost.

Le Français est contraint de temporiser : sa McLaren MP 4/3 perd de l'huile. Prost attend patiemment qu'Alboreto doive remplacer ses pneus et laisse vacante la troisième place. Il réduit prudemment la pression de suralimentation et porte sa voiture de virage en virage comme un nourrisson fiévreux. Mais c'est en vain : à trois tours de l'arrivée, son moteur rend l'âme pendant que Senna, couvrant son tour le plus rapide, survole comme un fantôme le labyrinthe des glissières de sécurité. Il est resté jusqu'à présent hors d'atteinte car Piquet ne constituera jamais un danger – il a horreur des circuits en ville. Ce qui ne l'empêchera pas d'être sacré champion du monde en 1987.

The harbor chicane in Monaco might well be described as the mother of all chicanes. Designing and redesigning it has become a kind of art form over the decades. Yet its purpose is fundamentally absurd: to make racing cars slow down.

Die Hafenschikane von Monaco ist gewissermaßen die Mutter aller Schikanen. Ihr Design zu gestalten und umzugestalten wird im Lauf der Jahrzehnte zu einer Art Kunstform. Dennoch ist ihre Bestimmung im Grunde absurd: Rennwagen ihr Tempo zu nehmen.

La Chicane du port de Monaco est en quelque sorte la mère de toutes les chicanes. Au fil des décennies, cela devient une espèce de forme d'art que de la construire et la reconstruire. Et pourtant, dans le fond, son but est absurde : faire ralentir des voitures de course.

N°	DRIVERS		ENTRANTS	CARS	ENGINES	PRACTICE RESULTS	RACE RESULTS
12	**Ayrton Senna**	**BR**	**Camel Team Lotus**	**Lotus 99T**	**Honda V6 1496 cc + T**	**2nd: 1'23"711**	**1st: 1h57'54"085**
6	Nelson Piquet	BR	Williams Grand Prix Engineering	Williams FW11B	Honda V6 1496 cc + T	3rd: 1'24"755	2nd: 1h58'27"297
27	Michele Alboreto	I	SEFAC Ferrari S.p.A.	Ferrari F1-87	Ferrari V6 1496 cc + T	5th: 1'26"102	3rd: 1h59'06"924
28	Gerhard Berger	A	SEFAC Ferrari S.p.A.	Ferrari F1-87	Ferrari V6 1496 cc + T	8th: 1'26"323	4th: 77 laps
3	Jonathan Palmer	GB	Tyrrell Racing Organisation	Tyrrell 016	Cosworth V8 3494 cc	15th: 1'28"088	5th: 76 laps
16	Ivan Capelli	I	March Racing	March 871	Cosworth V8 3494 cc	19th: 1'29"147	6th: 76 laps
9	Martin Brundle	GB	West Zakspeed Racing	Zakspeed 871	Zakspeed 4L 1495 cc + T	14th: 1'27"894	7th: 76 laps
19	Teo Fabi	I	Benetton Formula Ltd.	Benetton B187	Ford V6 1496 cc + T	12th: 1'27"622	8th: 76 laps
1	Alain Prost	F	Marlboro McLaren International	McLaren MP4/3	TAG Porsche V6 1496 cc + T	4th: 1'25"083	9th: 75 laps (R)
11	Satoru Nakajima	J	Camel Team Lotus	Lotus 99T	Honda V6 1496 cc + T	17th: 1'28"890	10th: 75 laps
25	René Arnoux	F	Ligier Sport	Ligier JS29B	BMW 4L 1499 cc + T	22nd: 1'30"000	11th: 74 laps
26	Piercarlo Ghinzani	I	Ligier Sport	Ligier JS29B	BMW 4L 1499 cc + T	20th: 1'29"258	12th: 74 laps
14	Pascal Fabre	F	Equipe El Charro	AGS JH22	Cosworth V8 3494 cc	24th: 1'31"667	13rd: 71 laps
18	Eddie Cheever	USA	Arrows Racing Team	Arrows A10	BMW 4L 1499 cc + T	6th: 1'26"175	R
17	Derek Warwick	GB	Arrows Racing Team	Arrows A10	BMW 4L 1499 cc + T	11th: 1'27"294	R
2	Stefan Johansson	S	Marlboro McLaren International	McLaren MP4/3	TAG Porsche V6 1496 cc + T	7th: 1'26"317	R
30	Philippe Alliot	F	Larrousse et Calmels	Lola LC87	Cosworth V8 3494 cc	18th: 1'29"114	R
7	Riccardo Patrese	I	Motor Racing Developments	Brabham BT56	BMW 4L 1499 cc + T	10th: 1'26"76310	R
21	Alex Caffi	I	Osella Squadra Corse	Osella FA11	Alfa Romeo V8 1497 cc + T	16th: 1'28"233	R
8	Andrea de Cesaris	I	Motor Racing Developments	Brabham BT56	BMW 4L 1499 cc + T	21st: 1'29"827	R
5	*Nigel Mansell*	GB	*Williams Grand Prix Engineering*	*Williams FW11B*	*Honda V6 1496 cc + T*	1st: 1'23"039	R
24	Alessandro Nannini	I	Minardi Team S.p.A.	Minardi M186	Motori Moderni V6 1499 cc + T	13th: 1'27"731	R
4	Philippe Streiff	F	Tyrrell Racing Organisation	Tyrrell 016	Cosworth V8 3494 cc	23rd: 1'30"143	R
20	Thierry Boutsen	B	Benetton Formula Ltd.	Benetton B187	Ford V6 1496 cc + T	9th: 1'26"630	R

3

The two Williamses at the lowest point and approaching the highest point of the track: (1) Piquet leaving Portier and (2) Mansell approaching the Casino. (3, 4) The duel of the Brazilians rages behind Mansell: Senna (Lotus) followed by Piquet; then Alboreto (Ferrari), Prost (McLaren), Cheever (Arrows) and Berger (Ferrari).

Die beiden Williams am tiefsten und vor dem höchsten Punkt der Strecke: (1) Piquet hinter Portier und (2) Mansell vor dem Casino. (3, 4) Hinter Mansell tobt das Duell der Brasilianer: Senna (Lotus) gefolgt von Piquet, dahinter Alboreto (Ferrari), Prost (McLaren), Cheever (Arrows) und Berger (Ferrari).

Les deux Williams au plus bas et au plus haut point du circuit : (1) Piquet à la sortie du virage du Portier et (2) Mansell devant le Casino. (3, 4) Derrière Mansell, le duel des Brésiliens fait rage : Senna (Lotus) suivi par Piquet, derrière lui, Alboreto (Ferrari), Prost (McLaren), Cheever (Arrows) et Berger (Ferrari).

4

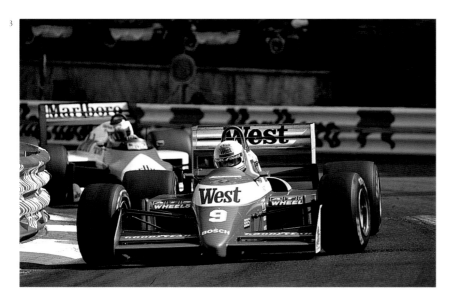

(1) Marching home: sixth place for Capelli's March. (2) Fifth for Palmer (Tyrrell), while (3) Brundle (Zakspeed) comes seventh. (4) The two Ferraris, Alboreto ahead of Berger.

(1) Marching home: Platz 6 für den einsamen March von Capelli. (2) Rang 5 für Palmer (Tyrrell), (3) Brundle (Zakspeed) wird siebter. (4) Die beiden Ferrari, Alboreto vor Berger.

(1) Retour aux stands : sixième place pour la March solitaire de Capelli. (2) Cinquième place pour Palmer (Tyrrell). (3) Brundle (Zakspeed) termine septième. (4) Les deux Ferrari, Alboreto devant Berger.

Meditation: (1) Fabi and (2) Piquet. (3) Serviced and cared for: Prost's McLaren. (4) Satisfied, having qualified for the midfield: Brundle. (5) Eloquent: Mansell. (6) Always reflective: Frank Williams.

Grüblerisch: (1) Fabi und (2) Piquet. (3) Gewartet und gepflegt: Prosts McLaren. (4) Zufrieden, da fürs Mittelfeld qualifiziert: Brundle. (5) Eloquent: Mansell. (6) Immer nachdenklich: Frank Williams.

Pensifs : (1) Fabi et (2) Piquet. (3) Bien entretenue et soignée : la McLaren de Prost. (4) Satisfait d'être qualifié en milieu de peloton : Brundle. (5) Eloquent : Mansell. (6) Toujours pensif : Frank Williams.

1988

Anyone who did not hold shares in the joint venture between McLaren and Honda must have found the world of Formula 1 in 1988 a grim and forbidding place indeed. Moreover, team boss Ron Dennis had promised to make Ayrton Senna and Alain Prost into a dream team, although each was also the other's worst nightmare. When they arrived in Monaco, the two were level-pegging in the Formula 1 drivers' points table: Prost had won in Rio while Senna was the victor at Imola. After Monaco the score was 2 : 1 in favor of Prost, even though Senna had become the superstar. Prost was the victor on this occasion because success – the fourth by the man with the blue, white and red helmet on the bend-ridden coastal course – was really a gift from the man in the yellow helmet, although not one given in the right spirit, in fact one totally lacking in any personal warmth.

It all started with the amazement over the Brazilian's incredibly fast qualifying lap, which had landed him in pole position, one-and-a-half seconds quicker than the Frenchman and two-and-a-half seconds faster than Gerhard Berger in the Ferrari F1-87/88 C in third place. This was, as Prost commented acerbically for the record, a really fantastic time. However, to achieve this, you had to be willing to take an enormous risk, and he indicated that personally he would not be prepared to do this. Moreover, his brakes had overheated and the suspension on his MP 4/4 was not set at its optimum.

That was Saturday, and neither did Sunday appear to be his day. The "Professor" was unable to find second gear at the start of the race and, in the turmoil and confusion, Berger was able to squeeze past – not an easy task at the best of times, and a great accomplishment in Monaco. Seething with rage, Prost peered through the rear spoiler of the Ferrari, an eye witness to the way his team-mate's car was dwindling away to a white-and-red spot until it finally disappeared from view altogether, lapping at least a second per lap faster than anyone else.

By lap 10, Senna's lead over Berger and Prost was almost 14 seconds, extending to 25 seconds by lap 30. By this time, Nigel Mansell, in the Williams FW 12, had caught Prost up and was enjoying an unrestricted panoramic view in his rear-view mirrors of the second Ferrari with Michele Alboreto at the wheel.

On lap 33, the Italian took a fighting inside line beside the swimming pool while the Englishman stuck doggedly to the ideal line. The ensuing hostile contact caused the Williams to spin out of the race. In contrast, Prost took Berger on lap 54 with no problem at all, albeit after a succession of fruitless attempts. At this point, Senna was driving his own race with a lead of almost a mile. The pursuit of his car had withered away to a pointless undertaking. What was worse still – was anyone out there capable of holding a candle to the Brazilian? Yet by the end of lap 67 Alain had become the sole representative of the McLaren camp after Ayrton had wrapped his car into the crash barrier beside Portier. Ron Dennis had just radioed him, counselling him to drive more prudently. He hadn't meant him to fall asleep. But even Senna could occasionally make a mistake – for which all his rivals were duly thankful.

Für jeden, der nicht Teilhaber des Joint Venture von McLaren und Honda ist, sieht die Formel-1-Welt 1988 düster aus. Überdies hat Teamchef Ron Dennis Ayrton Senna und Alain Prost verpflichtet, ein Traumpaar, jeder zugleich ein Alptraum für den anderen. Bei ihrer Ankunft im Fürstentum steht das Match der beiden völlig ausgeglichen: Prost hat in Rio gewonnen, Senna in Imola. Nach Monaco ist der Stand 2 : 1 für Prost. Er ist der Sieger, Senna indes der Superstar. Denn der Erfolg des Mannes mit dem blauweißroten Helm, sein vierter auf dem winkligen Côte-Kurs, ist ein Geschenk des Mannes mit dem gelben Helm, allerdings nicht im rechten Geist und ohne jede Herzenswärme.

Schon die unglaublich schnelle Qualifikationsrunde des Brasilianers für die Pole Position ruft Bestürzung hervor, um anderthalb Sekunden besser als die des Franzosen, um zweieinhalb Sekunden eiliger als die Gerhard Bergers im Ferrari F1-87/88 C. Das sei, gibt Prost säuerlich zu Protokoll, in der Tat eine tolle Zeit. Um sie zu erzielen, müsse man jedoch ein enormes Risiko eingehen, und dazu sei er selbst einfach nicht bereit. Im übrigen hätten seine Bremsen überhitzt, und das Fahrwerk seines MP 4/4 sei keineswegs optimal austariert gewesen.

Das ist am Sonnabend, und auch der Sonntag scheint nicht sein Tag zu sein. Da findet der »Professor« beim Start den zweiten Gang nicht. In der jäh ausbrechenden Konfusion quetscht sich Berger vorbei, schon aus Prinzip schwer zu überholen und in Monaco erst recht. Kochend vor Wut wird Prost beim Blick durch den Heckflügel des Ferrari zum Augenzeugen, wie der Wagen seines Teamgefährten zum weißroten Pünktchen schrumpft und schließlich gänzlich aus dem Blickfeld verschwindet, eine Sekunde pro Runde schneller als der Rest der Welt.

Fast 14 Sekunden mißt sein Vorsprung auf Berger und Prost in Runde 10, mehr als 25 im 30. Durchgang. Inzwischen hat Nigel Mansell im Williams FW 12 aufgeschlossen, in den Rückspiegeln einen ungetrübten Panoramablick auf den zweiten Ferrari mit Michele Alboreto am Lenkrad.

In der 33. Runde geht der Italiener auf eine Kampflinie innen neben dem Schwimmbad, während der Engländer stur auf der Ideallinie bleibt. Die folgende Feindberührung führt zu einem Dreher des Williams und zu seinem Ausscheiden. Prost hingegen nimmt Berger im 54. Durchgang nach vielen vergeblichen Anläufen problemlos. Senna zieht in diesem Augenblick mit anderthalb Kilometern Vorsprung seine Bahn. Die Jagd auf ihn verkümmert zum aussichtslosen Unterfangen. Schlimmer noch: Wer kann dem Brasilianer überhaupt das Wasser reichen? Am Ende des 67. Runde indes hat Alain die Alleinvertretung für McLaren übernommen, Ayrton seinen Wagen bei Portier an der Leitplanke lädiert. Ron Dennis hatte ihn just per Funk zu zurückhaltender Fahrweise ermahnt.

Selbst ein Senna macht gelegentlich Fehler – zum Glück seiner Rivalen.

Le monde de la Formule 1 en 1988 offre des perspectives bien sombres à quiconque n'est pas partie prenante dans le joint venture de McLaren et Honda. En outre, le chef d'écurie Ron Dennis a recruté Ayrton Senna et Alain Prost, un duo de rêve qui est aussi, pour les autres, un cauchemar. Lors de leur arrivée dans la Principauté, le match entre les deux adversaires est à égalité complète : Prost a gagné à Rio, Senna à Imola. Après Monaco, le score est de 2 à 1 à l'avantage de Prost. Il est le vainqueur en l'occurrence, mais c'est Senna qui est en réalité la superstar. En effet, le succès de l'homme au casque bleu blanc rouge, sa quatrième victoire sur le circuit sinueux de la Côte d'Azur, est un cadeau de l'homme au casque jaune, un cadeau qu'il ne lui a toutefois pas fait de son plein gré, sans véritable chaleur humaine.

Le tour apocalyptique qui a valu la pole position au Brésilien, déjà, sème la stupeur générale : il est plus rapide d'une seconde et demie que le Français et de deux secondes et demie que Gerhard Berger dans sa Ferrari F1-87/88 C en troisième position. C'est en effet une sacrée performance, admet Prost non sans amertume face aux journalistes. Pour réaliser un tel temps, dit-il, il faut en revanche courir un risque énorme et lui-même n'est tout simplement pas disposé à le faire. En outre, ses freins auraient chauffé et le châssis de sa MP 4/4 n'aurait absolument pas été réglé à la perfection.

C'est le samedi, et le dimanche non plus ne semble pas être son jour. Au départ, le « professeur » n'arrive pas à enclencher la seconde. Dans la brutale confusion que cela cause, Berger arrive à se faufiler, lui qui, par principe, est déjà difficile à doubler, a fortiori à Monaco. Bouillonnant de fureur, Prost arrive à voir, à travers l'aileron arrière de la Ferrari, comment la voiture de son coéquipier se mue en un petit point blanc et rouge toujours plus minuscule et finit par disparaître totalement de son champ de vision, une seconde plus vite que le reste du monde.

Il a près de 14 secondes d'avance sur Berger et Prost au dixième tour, et plus de 25 au 30ᵉ. Entre-temps, Nigel Mansell au volant de sa Williams FW 12 a rattrapé Prost avec, dans ses rétroviseurs, la menace brûlante de la deuxième Ferrari avec Michele Alboreto au volant.

Au 33ᵉ tour, l'Italien joue le tout pour le tout et cherche à faire l'intérieur à l'Anglais à la piscine. Mais celui-ci reste avec entêtement sur la trajectoire idéale. La touchette des deux protagonistes se solde par un tête-à-queue de la Williams et son abandon. Prost, par contre, double Berger sans difficulté au 54ᵉ tour après d'innombrables et vaines attaques. Pendant ce temps, Senna tourne avec une régularité de métronome et un kilomètre et demi d'avance. Le prendre en chasse semble condamné à l'échec. Pire encore : qui pourrait même bien concurrencer le Brésilien ? A la fin du 67ᵉ tour, pourtant, Alain assume la représentation exclusive de McLaren, Ayrton ayant endommagé sa voiture contre les glissières au virage du Portier. Ron Dennis venait de lui recommander de lever légèrement le pied, mais certainement pas de s'endormir. Même un Senna n'est pas infaillible – ce qui lui valut la gratitude de tous ses concurrents.

Ringed vista: harbor scene with speeding car. On race weekend, there is an astonishing coexistence between lazy idyll and racing haste.

Voller Durchblick: Hafenszene mit Rennwagen. In Monaco kommt es am Rennwochenende zu der erstaunlichen Koexistenz des trägen Idylls mit der rasenden Hast.

Vue générale : scène de port avec voitures de course. A Monaco, le week-end du Grand Prix, on assiste à l'extraordinaire coexistence de l'idylle flottante et du vif argent vibrionnant.

N°	DRIVERS		ENTRANTS	CARS	ENGINES	PRACTICE RESULTS	RACE RESULTS
11	**Alain Prost**	**F**	**Honda Marlboro McLaren**	**McLaren MP4/4**	**Honda V6 1494 cc + T**	**2nd: 1'25"425**	**1st: 1h57'17"077**
28	Gerhard Berger	A	SEFAC Ferrari S.p.A.	Ferrari F1-87/88C	Ferrari V6 1496 cc + T	3rd: 1'26"685	2nd: 1h57'37"530
27	Michele Alboreto	I	SEFAC Ferrari S.p.A.	Ferrari F1-87/88C	Ferrari V6 1496 cc + T	4th: 1'27"297	3rd: 1h57'58"306
17	Derek Warwick	GB	USF&G Arrows Megatron	Arrows A10B	Megatron 4L 1499 cc + T	7th: 1'27"872	4th: 77 laps
3	Jonathan Palmer	GB	Tyrrell Racing Organisation	Tyrrell 017	Cosworth V8 3494 cc	10th: 1'28"358	5th: 77 laps
6	Riccardo Patrese	I	Canon Williams Team	Williams FW12	Judd V8 3498 cc	8th: 1'28"016	6th: 77 laps
29	Yannick Dalmas	F	Larrousse et Calmels	Lola LC88	Cosworth V8 3494 cc	21st: 1'29"601	7th: 77 laps
20	Thierry Boutsen	B	Benetton Formula Ltd.	Benetton B188	Ford V8 3494 cc	16th: 1'28"640	8th: 76 laps
21	Nicola Larini	I	Osella Squadra Corse	Osella FA1L	Alfa Romeo V8 1497 cc + T	25th: 1'30"335	9th: 75 laps
16	Ivan Capelli	I	Leyton House March Racing Team	March 881	Judd V8 3498 cc	22nd: 1'29"603	10th: 72 laps
12	Ayrton Senna	BR	Honda Marlboro McLaren	McLaren MP4/4	Honda V6 1494 cc + T	1st: 1'23"998	R
30	Philippe Alliot	F	Larrousse et Calmels	Lola LC88	Cosworth V8 3494 cc	13th: 1'28"536	R
15	Maurizio Gugelmin	BR	Leyton House March Racing Team	March 881	Judd V8 3498 cc	14th: 1'28"610	R
9	Piercarlo Ghinzani	I	West Zakspeed Racing	Zakspeed 881	Zakspeed 4L 1496 cc	23rd: 1'30"121	R
19	Alessandro Nannini	I	Benetton Formula Ltd.	Benetton B188	Ford V8 3494 cc	6th: 1'27"869	R
24	Luis Perez-Sala	E	Lois Minardi Team S.p.A.	Minardi M188	Cosworth V8 3494 cc	15th: 1'28"625	R
5	Nigel Mansell	GB	Canon Williams Team	Williams FW12	Judd V8 3498 cc	5th: 1'27"665	R
22	Andrea de Cesaris	I	Rial Racing	Rial ARC1	Cosworth V8 3494 cc	19th: 1'29"298	R
25	René Arnoux	F	Ligier Loto	Ligier JS31	Judd V8 3498 cc	20th: 1'29"480 (27)	R
32	Oscar Larrauri	RA	Euro Brun Racing	Euro Brun 188	Cosworth V8 3494 cc	18th: 1'29"093	R
18	Eddie Cheever	USA	USF&G Arrows Megatron	Arrows A10B	Megatron 4L 1499 cc + T	9th: 1'28"227	R
26	Stefan Johansson	S	Ligier Loto	Ligier JS31	Judd V8 3498 cc	26th: 1'30"505	R
31	Gabriele Tarquini	I	Coloni S.p.A.	Coloni FC188	Cosworth V8 3494 cc	24th: 1'30"252	R
1	Nelson Piquet	BR	Camel Team Lotus Honda	Lotus 100T	Honda V6 1494 cc + T	11th: 1'28"403	R
36	Alex Caffi	I	Scuderia Italia	BMS Dallara F188	Cosworth V8 3494 cc	17th: 1'29"075	R
14	Philippe Streiff	F	Automobiles Gonfaronaises Sportives	AGS JH23	Cosworth V8 3494 cc	12th: 1'28"527	R

1

2

3

Separated by a mile: the McLaren drivers (1) Prost at Rascasse and (2) Senna at the exit of Loews. (3) Collage in white and red: McLaren body parts create a grotesque catamaran. (4) Seen through flowers: Alboreto (Ferrari), (5) his team-mate a few yards further on. (6) Qualifying in the rain on Thursday: Patrese (Williams) ahead of Prost.

Eine Meile voneinander entfernt: die McLaren-Piloten (1) Prost bei Rascasse und (2) Senna ausgangs Loews. (3) Collage in Weißbrot: Aus McLaren-Karosserieteilen entsteht ein grotesker Katamaran. (4) Durch die Blume gesehen: Alboreto (Ferrari), (5) sein Teamkollege Berger ein paar Meter weiter. (6) Regentraining am Donnerstag: Patrese (Williams) vor Prost.

A un mile l'un de l'autre : les pilotes McLaren (1) Prost à la Rascasse et (2) Senna à la sortie du Loews. (3) Collage en rouge et blanc : des panneaux de carrosserie de McLaren se transforment en un grotesque catamaran. (4) Vu à travers les fleurs : Alboreto (Ferrari). (5) Son coéquipier Berger quelques mètres plus loin. (6) Qualifications sous la pluie le jeudi : Patrese (Williams) devant Prost.

(1, 2) Collision between Patrese (Williams) and Alliot at Mirabeau on lap 51. While the Lola is disposed of through the emergency exit, the Williams comes sixth. (3–5) Spin by de Cesaris (Rial) at Loews. Prost, Dalmas (Lola), Piquet (Lotus); Nannini (Benetton) and Larini (Osella) squeeze past.

(1, 2) Kollision zwischen Patrese (Williams) und Alliot bei Mirabeau in Runde 51. Während der Lola in den Notausgang entsorgt werden muß, wird der Williams sechster. (3–5) Dreher von de Cesaris (Rial) in Loews. Prost, Dalmas (Lola), Piquet (Lotus) und gleich darauf Nannini (Benetton) und Larini (Osella) quetschen sich vorbei.

(1, 2) Collision entre Patrese (Williams) et Alliot à Mirabeau au 51ᵉ tour. Pendant que l'on évacue la Lola dans l'échappatoire, la Williams termine sixième. (3–5) Tête-à-queue de Cesaris (Rial) au Loews. Prost, Dalmas (Lola), Piquet (Lotus) et, juste derrière, Nannini (Benetton) et Larini (Osella) contournent l'obstacle.

(1) Umbrella man: Piquet. (2, 3) Totally relaxed and deep in meditation: Berger. (4) Still there out of passion: Clay Regazzoni. (5) Out for lack of attention: Senna. (6) Well advised: Prost.

(1) Schirm-Herr: Piquet. (2, 3) Total relaxt und tief in sich gekehrt: Berger. (4) Aus Passion noch immer dabei: Clay Regazzoni. (5) Durch Unachtsamkeit ausgeschieden: Senna. (6) Gut beraten: Prost.

(1) A l'abri : Piquet. (2, 3) Totalement relaxé et profondément introverti : Berger. (4) Toujours là par passion : Clay Regazzoni. (5) Abandon sur faute d'inattention : Senna. (6) Bien conseillé : Prost.

A refuge of the rich at all other times, and clean as a maternity ward, Monaco becomes an amphitheater for the masses on this weekend. (1) Thousands populate the Rocher. (2) If you don't need it anymore – just drop it.

Sonst ein Refugium der Reichen und von der Reinlichkeit einer Entbindungsstation, wird Monaco an diesem Wochenende zum Amphitheater für die Massen. (1) Zigtausende bevölkern allein den Rocher. (2) Was überflüssig geworden ist, läßt man einfach fallen.

Normalement refuge des riches d'une stérilité digne d'une maternité, Monaco est, ce week-end-là, l'amphithéâtre des masses. (1) Des milliers de personnes s'agglutinent rien que sur le Rocher. (2) On laisse tout simplement tomber ce qui ne sert plus.

1

2

TRIUMPHS IN ADVERSITY

TRIUMPHE DES TROTZDEM · LES TRIOMPHES DU DÉFI

The 14 May 1972 was no ordinary Sunday. On this day a black-and-white sequence, as in Françoise Sagan's cult film *Bonjour Tristesse*, was inserted into the colorfully sparkling world of the Monaco Grand Prix, which gave an inkling that hell could also be cold and wet. In greyish green curtains of rain, the 25 drivers, an unusually large number, lost all adhesion. For 147 minutes they faced a wall of spray with the rear lights of the man in front glowing ahead of them like a deceptive glow-worm.

Only one of them, Jean-Pierre Beltoise, who qualified fourth, was untroubled by all of this. At the start, the small Frenchman with the crooked grin aimed for the gap between the fat rear tyres of the people in the first row, Emerson Fittipaldi on the left and Jacky Ickx on the right. This gave him the advantage of clear vision for all of the 80 laps, but he also avoided making any mistakes. This turned out to be his first and only victory and the last one for BRM, the rusting traditional marque from Bourne.

The Monaco boulevard drama created its own heroes, particularly in the rain, and they were not always the same ones as the heroes of the statistics: Ayrton Senna, who won six times, Alain Prost, who made it four times, Graham Hill in between them with his handful of first places in the hilly jumble of bends on the Riviera. But such highlights are ephemeral, the laurel and champagne of yesterday as relevant as last night's cold dinner. At a boat party in the 1980s, the up-and-coming Alessandro Nannini was introduced to Bette Hill, Damon's mother and Graham's widow. "Her husband", someone said, "won five times here." "Is he here as well?" was casual answer.

On 3 June 1984 the most magical square mile in motor sport once again displayed the rough charm of a team shower, even blacker, wetter and colder than in 1972. The fire brigade even hosed the tunnel under Hôtel Loews, in order to create uniform working conditions. The time from the red light to the red flag came to 61 minutes – an hour of such intensity of experience as is otherwise produced only by an artillery barrage. Then, after 31 of 77 planned laps, race organizer Jacky Ickx put an end to the cruel game. The Belgian is fiercely loyal to the House of Porsche, and his decision created something of a stink. He had broken off the race suspiciously early, some whispered, so that Alain Prost with the TAG McLaren-Porsche could win.

For two new stars, Ayrton Senna and Stefan Bellof, had been born that day in the raging pond in which egos were being splashed about like pirhanas, and they were closing relentlessly on the Frenchman. The handling by the Brazilian of the clumsy-looking Toleman, whose Hart engine only produced its full power within a narrow range of engine speeds, was close to wizardry, while Bellof's black Tyrrell, the only car with a naturally aspirated engine, became the shark in the goldfish bowl. The way in which the man from Giessen squeezed past the Ferrari of René Arnoux on the inside at Mirabeau was a model of calculated sang froid, an act committed on a notorious ruffian who fruitlessly attempted to squash his opponent against the wall like a fly.

Calculation, courage and sheer cheek had also been the hallmark of Keke Rosberg's breakneck drive in the

Der 14. Mai 1972 ist kein Sonntag wie jeder andere. Da mogelt sich in die glitzerbunte Welt des Grand Prix de Monaco eine Schwarzweiß-Sequenz wie in Françoise Sagans Kultfilm *Bonjour Tristesse*, eine Ahnung davon, daß die Hölle auch kalt und naß sein könnte. In graugrün niederschleiernden Schwaden mutieren die 25 Piloten, ungewöhnlich viele, zur Gesellschaft mit beschränkter Haftung. 147 Minuten lang rennt man gegen eine Gischtmauer, in der wie ein trügerisches Glühwürmchen das Rücklicht des Vordermanns glimmt.

Einer hat mit all dem keine Last, Jean-Pierre Beltoise, im Training vierter. Beim Start zielt der kleine Franzose mit dem schiefen Grinsen auf die Lücke zwischen den fetten Hinterrädern der Konkurrenten in der ersten Reihe, links Emerson Fittipaldi, rechts Jacky Ickx, genießt anschließend den Vorzug ungetrübter Sicht für alle 80 Runden, macht aber auch nie einen Fehler. Dies wird sein erster Sieg und überdies sein einziger und der letzte für die rostende Traditionsmarke BRM aus Bourne.

Das Boulevard-Stück von Monaco schafft sich seine eigenen Helden, im Regen zumal, und nicht immer sind es die Heroen der Statistik, Ayrton Senna, der sechsmal gewinnt, Alain Prost, der es auf vier Male bringt, mittendrin Graham Hill mit einer Handvoll erster Plätze in dem hügeligen Kurven-Chaos an der Côte. Aber solche Highlights sind vergänglich, Lorbeer und Champagner von gestern aktuell wie ein kaltes Spiegelei: Auf einer Bootsparty in den Achtzigern wird der aufstrebende Alessandro Nannini Bette Hill vorgestellt, Damons Mutter und Grahams Witwe. »Ihr Mann«, sagt jemand, »hat hier fünfmal gewonnen.« »Ist er auch da?« lautet Nanninis unbekümmerte Antwort.

Am 3. Juni 1984 geht von der magischsten Quadrat-meile im Motorsport wiederum der spröde Charme einer Mannschaftsduschkabine aus, noch schwärzer, nässer und kälter als 1972. Feuerwehrleute feuchten sogar den Tunnel unter dem Loews-Hotel an, um einheitliche Arbeitsbedingungen zu schaffen. Von der roten Ampel bis zur roten Flagge vergehen 61 Minuten – eine Stunde von einer Erlebnisdichte, die sonst nur durch Trommelfeuer erzeugt wird. Dann, nach 31 von 77 vorgesehenen Runden, bereitet Rennleiter Jacky Ickx dem grausamen Spiel ein Ende. Der Belgier ist dem Hause Porsche in Treue fest verbunden, und deshalb gibt es Stunk: Er habe, munkeln manche, das Rennen verdächtig früh abgebrochen, damit Alain Prost mit dem TAG-McLaren-Porsche gewinnen konnte.

Denn in dem tosenden Tümpel, in dem sich die Egos tummeln wie Raubfische, sind zwei neue Stars geboren, und sie nähern sich dem Franzosen unerbittlich, Ayrton Senna und Stefan Bellof. Des Brasilianers Umgang mit dem klotzigen Toleman, dessen Hart-Triebwerk seine volle Kraft nur in einem schmalen Drehzahlband herausrückt, grenzt an Hexerei, während Bellofs schwarzer Tyrrell, das einzige Auto mit einem Saugmotor, zum Hecht im Karpfenteich wird: Allein wie sich der Gießener bei Mirabeau innen am Ferrari von René Arnoux vorbeiquetscht, ist ein Modell von kalkulierter Unverfrorenheit, begangen an einem notorischen Raufbold, der vergeblich versucht, den Gegner an der Mauer zu zerdrücken wie eine Mücke.

Le 14 mai 1972 n'est pas un dimanche comme tous les autres. Ce jour-là, au monde de paillettes multicolores du Grand Prix de Monaco se mélange une séquence en noir et blanc comme dans le livre culte de Françoise Sagan, *Bonjour Tristesse*, qui laisse entrevoir que l'enfer peut aussi être froid et détrempé. Dans les nappes de brouillard et de pluie qui masquent la vue, les 25 pilotes – un nombre inhabituellement élevé – se muent en un club d'amateurs de patinage. Pendant 147 minutes, ils vont se battre contre des trombes d'eau dans lesquelles, comme un ver luisant trompeur, brille le feu rouge du pilote qui précède.

L'un d'eux n'en est en rien affecté, Jean-Pierre Beltoise, quatrième aux essais. Au départ, le petit Français au sourire railleur vise la brèche entre les gros pneumatiques noirs des pilotes de première ligne : à gauche, Emerson Fittipaldi et, à droite, Jacky Ickx. Et si, ensuite, il a le privilège d'une visibilité parfaite pendant les 80 tours, il ne commet pas non plus la moindre erreur. Ceci sera sa première victoire, et d'ailleurs la seule, ainsi que la dernière pour la marque tradition-nelle BRM, de Bourne, dont le blason est déjà bien rouillé. La comédie de boulevard de Monaco se donne ses propres héros, surtout par temps de pluie, mais ce ne sont pas toujours les héros des statistiques : ni Ayrton Senna, qui aura gagné six fois, ni Alain Prost, fort de quatre victoires, ni Graham Hill entre eux deux avec une poignée de premières places remportées dans les montagnes russes de la Côte d'Azur. Mais de telles heures de gloire sont éphémères, les lauriers et le champagne d'hier ont autant de charme que des œufs au plat froids : lors d'une réception sur un yacht, dans les années quatre-vingt, l'espoir italien Alessandro Nannini est présenté à Bette Hill, la mère de Damon et la veuve de Graham. « Son mari a gagné cinq fois ici », dit quelqu'un. « Il est là aussi », réplique ingénument Nannini.

Le 3 juin 1984, les quatre kilomètres carrés les plus magiques de la compétition automobile ont, une fois de plus, la séduction irrésistible d'une douche collective d'un club de football, mais en encore plus noir, plus mouillé et plus froid qu'en 1972. Les pompiers inondent même le tunnel sous l'Hôtel Loews afin de créer des conditions de travail uniformes. Du feu rouge au drapeau rouge s'écoulent 61 minutes – une heure d'une densité événementielle que seul un feu roulant est, sinon, en mesure d'engendrer. Mais alors, après 31 des 77 tours prévus, le directeur de course Jacky Ickx met un terme à cette cruelle comédie. Le Belge est étroitement lié à la maison Porsche, raison pour laquelle sa décision semble suspecte à beaucoup : il aurait, déclarent certains, interrompu la course à un moment étrangement prématuré pour qu'Alain Prost, avec sa McLaren TAG Porsche puisse gagner. En effet, dans la mare bouillonnante où les ego surnagent comme des dauphins, deux nouvelles stars sont nées ce jour-là et elles se rapprochent imparablement du Français : Ayrton Senna et Stefan Bellof. L'adresse avec laquelle le Brésilien au volant de son encombrante Toleman, dont le moteur Hart ne délivre sa pleine puissance que sur une très mince plage de régimes, frôle la sorcellerie, tandis que la Tyrrell noire de Bellof, la seule voiture propulsée par un moteur atmosphérique, se sent ici comme un poisson dans l'eau : à elle seule, la façon

Jean-Pierre Beltoise

Williams the previous year. Once again rain was involved, making the choice of tyres a risky matter because of wet patches on the track. The Finn came down in favor of slicks, which meant that he and his car were balanced on a knife-edge during the first laps before he defended his lead tooth and claw against Nelson Piquet's attack. His hands were covered in blisters by the end.

Stirling Moss, now an observer and still unable to tear himself away from Grand Prix racing, told how on one occasion in 1960 he himself had been surprised by a shower and sought the dry patches under the trees because his Lotus had suddenly become almost impossible to drive. During the last four laps the engine had been connected to the chassis by nothing more than a water hose – all the bolts had sheared off.

Moss has been called the greatest driver never to become World Champion, and in Monaco in 1961 he showed why when he held off the full might of the Ferrari team with the dark blue Lotus 18 belonging to the racing stable owner Rob Walker. The Ferrari Tipo 156s had 180 bhp, the Climax engine of his Lotus 151.8 bhp. The balance of 28 bhp was made up by that genius of a driver, Stirling Moss.

These things were recounted and written about widely, but in 1970 television came on the scene, trumpeting the events from the intimacy of the harbor district to all the world and preserving the fascination of the moment for posterity. Jochen Rindt in his red, white and gold Lotus chasing Jack Brabham's blue and yellow Brabham, taking two seconds off the ancient warrior on every lap until the latter slid into the barrier at the last bend and, wounded in car and soul, hobbled past the finishing line in second place.

The Australian, of course, was horribly embarrassed by the whole thing, and since a camera had been

Von Kalkül, Courage und schierer Frechheit zeugt auch Keke Rosbergs rasende Fahrt mit dem Williams im Jahr zuvor. Wieder ist Regen im Spiel, wird wegen nasser Stellen auf der Strecke die Reifenwahl zum Vabanque. Der Finne votiert für Slicks, balanciert die ersten Runden auf dem schmal gewordenen Strich zwischen Sein und Nichtsein und verteidigt dann seine Führung mit Zähnen und Klauen gegen den anstürmenden Nelson Piquet. Am Ende sind seine Hände mit Blasen übersät. Da plaudert Stirling Moss, der als Reporter noch immer nicht von den Grand-Prix-Pisten loskommt, längst aus dem Nähkörbchen: Wie er selbst 1960 von einem Schauer überrascht wurde und die trockenen Flecken unter den Bäumen aufsuchte, da sein Lotus plötzlich kaum zu fahren war. In den letzten vier Runden habe die Verbindung zwischen Motor und Chassis nur noch aus einer Wasserleitung bestanden – alle Bolzen seien abgeschert.

Sie nennen ihn den größten Fahrer, der nie Weltmeister wurde. Und in Monaco zeigt er auch zuverlässig warum, 1961 zum Beispiel, als Moss das erdrückende Ferrari-Aufgebot niederknüppelt, mit dem blauen Lotus 18 des Rennstallbesitzers Rob Walker. 180 PS leisten die Ferrari Tipo 156, die Climax-Maschinen der Lotus 151,8 PS. Den Saldo von 28 PS gleicht das Fahrgenie Stirling Moss aus. Noch erfährt man diese Dinge vom Hörensagen und vom Lesen.

1970 ist schon das Fernsehen dabei, das die Vorgänge aus der Intimität des monegassischen Hafenviertels in alle Welt posaunt und die Faszination des Augenblicks für die Nachwelt bewahrt. Jochen Rindt im rotweißgoldenen Lotus hetzt Jack Brabhams blaugelben Brabham, knöpft dem alten Kämpen pro Runde zwei Sekunden ab, bis der in der letzten Kurve in die Leitplanke rutscht und, blessiert an Auto und Seele, nur als zweiter ins Ziel humpelt. Natürlich ist dem

Jacky Ickx

dont le pilote allemand de Giessen se glisse, à Mirabeau, le long de la Ferrari de René Arnoux à l'intérieur du virage est un modèle d'effronterie calculée commise contre une brute notoire qui cherche en vain à écraser l'adversaire contre le mur comme un moustique gênant.

L'épopée de Keke Rosberg et de sa Williams, l'année précédente, a été aussi un exemple brillant de calcul, de courage et d'impertinence par excellence. Une fois de plus, la pluie vient troubler les cartes, et le choix des pneumatiques équivaut à un coup de poker en raison des portions mouillées du circuit. Le Finlandais opte pour des slicks, lui et sa machine couvrent les premiers tours en pilotant sur le fil du rasoir avant de défendre son leadership bec et ongles contre les assauts répétés de Nelson Piquet. A la fin, ses mains sont couvertes d'ampoules. Pendant ce temps, Stirling Moss, qui ne réussit toujours pas, en tant qu'observateur, à résister à l'attrait des pistes de Grand Prix, confia une fois comment lui-même, en 1960, surpris par une ondée, recherchait des endroits secs sous les arbres parce que sa Lotus ne se laissait soudain plus conduire. Durant les quatre derniers tours, la liaison entre le moteur et le châssis ne consistait plus qu'en une durit d'eau – tous les boulons étaient sectionnés.

Moss fut surnommé le plus grand pilote qui n'est jamais devenu champion du monde. Et, à Monaco, il montre que ce surnom n'est pas le fait du hasard. En 1961, par exemple, lorsqu'il tient la dragée haute à la force concentrée de l'écurie Ferrari avec la Lotus 18 bleu foncé du propriétaire privé Rob Walker. Les Ferrari Tipo 156 développent 180 ch, le moteur Climax de sa Lotus, 151,8 ch exactement. Mais le coup de volant de Stirling Moss compense ce déficit de 28 chevaux. C'est ce qu'on apprend un peu partout par le bouche à oreille ou la presse, mais en 1970, déjà présente, la télévision trahit quelque peu l'intimité du quartier portuaire de Monaco qu'elle propage dans le monde entier et préserve pour la postérité la fascination de l'instantané. Jochen Rindt, dans sa Lotus rouge-blanc-or, comme un chien enragé derrière la Brabham bleue et jaune de Jack Brabham, grignote deux secondes au tour à ce vieux renard de la course jusqu'à ce que celui-ci, dans l'ultime virage, dérape et percute le rail pour, avec une voiture endommagée et

Bette Hill

positioned at precisely that bend, he had, as it were, skidded right into everyone's living room. And so the usually taciturn man of few words explained later that never had he encountered such jams as in this race, that he had not known whether he should pass Piers Courage, who was dawdling along, on the left or right side on the approach to the corner. And to top it all, he had had to give a race marshal, who had fallen on to his car, the opportunity to dismount again before he could drive off to complete the lap. What makes a legend is, after all, also a matter of perspective.

But in the late afternoon of 31 May 1981, nobody was reflecting on such definitions. Then everyone was watching with bated breath the struggle of man against machine, the struggle of the French Canadian Gilles Villeneuve with the Ferrari 126 C, a rough lump of a car

Jochen Rindt

Keke Rosberg

which catapulted its driver brutally and without warning from serious turbo lag into extreme acceleration. On that occasion there was a happy end, a triumph in the face of adversity. Sometimes, perhaps taking advantage of a favorable moment, a talent flares up like a firework in the shadow of Monte Carlo, only to fizzle out again. Take 1968 for example, when the blonde Frenchman Johnny Servoz-Gavin, half monk, half playboy, led for three laps in Ken Tyrrell's Matra, and the balding Briton Dickie Attwood, who came second in a 12-cylinder BRM. Rindt and Villeneuve achieved legendary status. But Attwood and Servoz-Gavin are still alive.

Australier die Sache gräßlich peinlich. Da genau an der Ecke eine Kamera gestanden habe, sei er ja Millionen Zuschauern gleichsam direkt ins Wohnzimmer geschliddert. Und so erklärt er später, sonst wortkarg und maulfaul, noch nie sei er auf solche Staus aufgelaufen wie bei diesem Rennen, habe nicht gewußt, ob er an dem dahintrödelnden Piers Courage vor dieser Kurve rechts oder links vorbei sollte. Und schließlich habe er noch einem Streckenposten die Gelegenheit geben müssen, wieder abzusteigen, da der ihm bei dem Ausritt auf den Wagen gefallen sei. Was eine Legende ist, ist schließlich auch eine Frage der Perspektive.

In den späten Nachmittagsstunden des 31. Mai 1981 jedoch denkt niemand über solche Definitionen nach. Da verfolgt jeder mit angehaltenem Atem den Kampf eines Menschen gegen eine Maschine, des verwegenen Frankokanadiers Gilles Villeneuve gegen den Ferrari 126 C, einen ungehobelten Klotz, der seinen Piloten aus dem Turboloch übergangslos und brutal in eine extreme Beschleunigung reißt. Für diesmal gibt es ein Happy-end, den Triumph des Trotzdem. Manchmal aber, vielleicht durch die Gunst der Stunde genährt, blitzt im Schatten des Monte Carlo ein Talent auf und verglüht wie eine Silvesterrakete. 1968 zum Beispiel, wo der semmelblonde Franzose Johnny Servoz-Gavin, halb Mönch, halb Playboy, in Ken Tyrrells Matra drei Runden lang führt und der kahlköpfige Brite Dickie Attwood zweiter wird im Zwölfzylinder BRM. Rindt und Villeneuve haben ihren festen Platz im Mythos. Aber Attwood und Servoz-Gavin leben noch.

profondément humilié, rejoindre la ligne d'arrivée en boitillant comme deuxième seulement.

Naturellement, l'incident est extrêmement pénible pour l'Australien, et comme une caméra de télévision se trouvait comme par hasard dans ce virage, des millions de téléspectateurs ont pu en être les témoins directs sans quitter leur salon. Et c'est ainsi qu'il explique plus tard, encore moins loquace que de coutume, qu'il n'aurait encore jamais été aussi souvent bloqué que lors de cette course, qu'il n'avait pas su s'il devait doubler Piers Courage traînaillant à droite ou à gauche avant ce virage. Et, enfin, qu'il avait encore dû donner à un commissaire de piste qui était tombé sur sa voiture la possibilité de redescendre avant qu'il puisse prendre le virage à fond. Ce qui est une légende est, finalement aussi, une question de point de vue.

En cette fin d'après-midi du 31 mai 1981, en revanche, personne ne se perd en de telles conjectures. Chacun observe, le souffle court, le combat d'un homme contre sa machine, celui du téméraire Franco-Canadien Gilles Villeneuve contre la Ferrari 126 C, une brute aux mœurs sauvages qui fait passer son pilote, sans prévenir et avec brutalité, d'un dramatique temps mort dû au turbo dans une accélération foudroyante. Pour cette fois-ci, tout se solde par une happy end, le triomphe du défi. Mais parfois, profitant peut-être d'un coup de pouce du destin, un talent scintille dans l'arène de Monte-Carlo et s'éteint comme une fusée de la Saint-Sylvestre. En 1968, par exemple, où le Français à la chevelure blonde Johnny Servoz-Gavin, à moitié moine, à moitié play-boy, mène pendant trois tours au volant de la Matra de Ken Tyrrell et où le Britannique chauve Dickie Attwood termine deuxième avec sa douze-cylindres BRM. Rindt et Villeneuve ont leur place inamovible au Panthéon des pilotes de Formule 1. Mais Attwood et Servoz-Gavin vivent encore.

Dickie Attwood

1989

It almost seemed as if McLaren boss Ron Dennis had taken a two-year lease on two plots on the Boulevard Albert I. Once again the first row of the grid sported the white-and-red colors of Marlboro, the sponsor, and once again the two protagonists were Ayrton Senna and Alain Prost – in that order. However, their always brittle partnership had been aged by the 15 Grands Prix since the 1988 Monaco race and an increasing frostiness was discernible in their relationship. This was despite the fact that with a time difference between them of one second the Brazilian had merely inflicted only a moderate amount of humiliation on his French colleague, whereas in the previous year he had given him a resounding slap.

The turbo nonsense was finished, for this was the first year of the naturally-aspirated 3.5-liter engines. The high-pitched scream of the V10s from Honda and Renault dominated the concerto of engine noise on the race track, but the prize for the most beautiful sound had to be awarded to the V12 of the Ferrari F1-89. However, this engineering marvel, with its 60 valves, was not always reliably matched by the seven-gear semi-automatic transmission attached to it. Gerhard Berger had injured both body and soul at the previous race in Imola, when he left the track at 170 mph at the notorious Tamburello bend, and consequently was only a spectator in Monaco, nursing painful burns. So this year – the first after the death of Enzo Ferrari – the powerful Briton, Nigel Mansell, whom the men from Maranello had signed as their new hope, carried the flag with the prancing horse held high until lap 30 – when his sophisticated transmission failed and halted his Ferrari.

The race was shortened from 78 to 77 laps when the original start had to be aborted because the Ford Cosworth engine of Derek Warwick's Arrows A 11 in row three of the grid died due to capricious electronics. After another parade lap the race eventually got under way ten minutes late and the 26 cars snaked through Sainte Dévote, strung out like a giant necklace, Senna in front of Prost, Thierry Boutsen with the Williams FW 12 C, Mansell, Martin Brundle in a Brabham BT 58 and the others.

This time the Frenchman stayed close behind his Brazilian opponent and followed him like a shadow over more than a fifth of the race. Then the pair encountered the Ligier of René Arnoux, who angrily resisted the received wisdom that ex-Ferrari drivers are past their peak in Formula 1. No car seemed to be wider between the pavements of Monte Carlo than his, yet with his sixth sense of where a gap might open up, Senna swept him aside. Prost, on the other hand, had no option but to study the sponsorship logos on the back wing of the Ligier for what must have appeared to him an endless period of time. As a result, he was almost a minute behind at the end, plagued, in addition, by transmission problems. But the same had been true of Senna. At about half-distance in the race, he lost the use of first gear, and a few laps later his second gear also gave out, two of the most important weapons in the guerrilla warfare round the houses.

Fast scheint es, als hätte McLaren-Chef Ron Dennis die beiden Parzellen auf dem Boulevard Albert I für zwei Jahre gepachtet: Wieder ist die erste Reihe eingekleidet im Weißrot des Sponsors Marlboro. Wieder heißen die Protagonisten Ayrton Senna und Alain Prost – in dieser Reihenfolge. Seit dem Grand Prix de Monaco 1988 ist allerdings ihre immer schon bröckelige Partnerschaft um 15 Große Preise gealtert, und auf dem Zwischenmenschlichen funkeln Eiskristalle. Dabei hat der Brasilianer seinem gallischen Kollegen mit einer Sekunde Abstand lediglich eine mittelschwere Demütigung zugefügt, wo er ihm im Vorjahr noch eine schallende Ohrfeige verpaßte.

Der Turbo-Spuk ist vorbei: Wir schreiben das erste Jahr der atmosphärisch beatmeten 3,5-Liter. Im lärmenden Straßenkonzert dominiert der helle Schrei der V10 von Honda und Renault. Der Preis für den schönsten Sound indessen gebührt dem V12 des Ferrari F1-89. Dieses Wunderwerk der Technik mit 60 Ventilen wird kongenial, aber nicht immer verläßlich unterstützt durch eine Halbautomatik mit sieben Gängen. Gerhard Berger hat sich beim letzten Lauf in Imola bei einem Abflug mit Tempo 280 im berüchtigten Tamburello-Knick an Leib und Seele verletzt und fehlt in Monaco. So hält im Jahre eins nach Enzo der kampfstarke Brite Nigel Mansell, den die Männer zu Maranello als neuen Hoffnungsträger verpflichtet haben, die Fahne mit dem Pferdchen hoch, bis zur 30. Runde – da macht sein raffiniertes Getriebe dem Ferrari den Garaus.

Das Rennen wird mit zehn Minuten Verspätung gestartet und von 78 auf 77 Runden verkürzt: Der Ford Cosworth von Derek Warwicks Arrows A 11 in der dritten Reihe ist auf Grund eines launischen elektronischen Managements erstorben. Dann aber winden sich die 26 wie an einer gigantischen Perlenschnur aufgefädelt durch Sainte Dévote, Senna vor Prost, Thierry Boutsen mit dem Williams FW 12 C, Mansell, Martin Brundle im Brabham BT 58 und den anderen.

Diesmal bleibt der Franzose hart am Gegner, folgt ihm wie ein Schatten über ein Fünftel der Distanz. Dann trifft das Gespann auf René Arnoux. Der stämmige Franzose wehrt sich wütend gegen die Branchenweisheit, ein ausgedienter Ferrari-Pilot habe stets auch seine besten Jahre in der Formel 1 hinter sich. Kein Wagen wird zwischen den Bordsteinen der Operettenstadt breiter als seiner. Dennoch: Senna, mit seinem unheimlichen Sensorium für Lücken, macht mit ihm wenig Federlesens. Prost hingegen bleibt über eine schier endlos lange Zeit nur die aufmerksame Lektüre der Sponsor-Logos auf dem Heckflügel des Ligier. So ist er am Ende um fast eine Minute ins Hintertreffen geraten, überdies behindert von Getriebeproblemen. Wie Senna: Dem hat gegen Halbzeit der erste Gang und ein paar Runden später auch der zweite den Dienst aufgekündigt, die wichtigste Waffe im Guerilla-Kampf um die Häuserecken.

On serait tenté de croire que Ron Dennis, le chef de l'écurie McLaren, détient un bail sur les deux parcelles du Boulevard Albert I pour une durée de deux ans : la première ligne rayonne de nouveau du blanc et rouge du sponsor Marlboro, et une fois de plus, les protagonistes ont pour nom Ayrton Senna et Alain Prost – dans cet ordre. Depuis la course de Monaco 1988, leur mariage de raison a toutefois vieilli de 15 Grands Prix et les relations entre les deux hommes se refroidissent sensiblement de course en course. Et pourtant, avec une avance d'une seconde seulement, le Brésilien a à peine humilié son collègue français alors qu'il lui avait infligé un sévère camouflet, l'année précédente.

Les moteurs suralimentés se sont tus : cette année, nous écrivons le premier chapitre dans la chronologie des moteurs atmosphériques de 3,5 litres. Dans le bruyant concert des gorges de béton, c'est le hurlement strident des V10 Honda et Renault qui prédomine. Mais c'est en revanche au V12 de la Ferrari F1-89 que revient le prix de la plus belle mélodie. Une boîte semi-automatique à sept vitesses apporte à cette merveille mécanique à 60 soupapes son appui génial, mais pas toujours fiable. Lors de la manche précédente, à Imola, au cours d'une effrayante sortie de route à 280 km/h dans le redoutable virage de Tamburello, Gerhard Berger s'est blessé au propre et au figuré encore mal remis de ses brûlures, dut se contenter d'assister à la course en spectateur. Aussi cette année – la première depuis la mort d'Enzo Ferrari – le bouillant Britannique Nigel Mansell, que les hommes de Maranello ont recruté pour exaucer leurs espoirs, brandit contre vents et marées le drapeau du *cavallino rampante* jusqu'au 30e tour – avant que sa boîte de vitesses sophistiquée ne sonne le glas de sa Ferrari.

Les coureurs n'ont plus que 77 tours à couvrir au lieu de 78, après un faux départ dû à la gestion électronique aléatoire du moteur Ford Cosworth de Derek Warwick qui cloue son Arrows A 11 en troisième ligne. Après un nouveau tour d'honneur, la course démarre enfin dix minutes plus tard et les 26 pilotes s'engouffrent dans Sainte Dévote, Senna devant Prost, Thierry Boutsen avec la Williams FW 12 C, Mansell, Martin Brundle sur la Brabham BT 58 et les autres.

Cette fois-ci, le Français talonne le Brésilien, le suit comme son ombre pendant un cinquième de la course. Puis le duo rattrape la Ligier de René Arnoux qui se défend bec et ongles contre une règle d'or de cette branche qui veut qu'un pilote Ferrari à la retraite est toujours considéré, aussi, comme ayant ses meilleures années derrière lui en Formule 1. Aucune voiture ne se fait plus large que la sienne entre les bordures de trottoirs de Monte Carlo. Et pourtant : Senna, avec son célèbre sixième sens pour une faille qui n'existe souvent pas, ne s'en laisse pas compter. Prost, par contre, n'a, pendant une période qui lui semble interminable, d'autre alternative que l'étude attentive des logos du sponsor sur l'aileron arrière de la Ligier. Ainsi accuse-t-il finalement près d'une minute de retard sur son adversaire en étant, qui plus est, handicapé par des difficultés de boîte de vitesses. Comme Senna d'ailleurs : depuis la mi-course, la première lui refuse tout service, ce que fait aussi, quelques tours plus tard, le deuxième rapport, deux armes indispensables dans cette guérilla que l'on se livre aux coins de rues.

Semi-roundabout: the Monaco Grand Prix might be a giant game of roulette. But the participants avoid drawing up in front of the Casino.

Halbkreisverkehr: Der Grand Prix de Monaco mag ein gigantisches Roulette sein. Aber die Teilnehmer vermeiden die direkte Vorfahrt vor dem Casino.

Demi sens giratoire : le Grand Prix de Monaco est peut-être une gigantesque roulette, mais les participants évitent de passer directement devant le Casino.

N°	DRIVERS		ENTRANTS	CARS	ENGINES	PRACTICE RESULTS	RACE RESULTS
1	*Ayrton Senna*	*BR*	*Honda Marlboro McLaren*	*McLaren MP4/5*	*Honda V10 3493 cc*	*1st: 1'22"308*	*1st: 1h53'33"251*
2	Alain Prost	F	Honda Marlboro McLaren	McLaren MP4/5	Honda V10 3493 cc	2nd: 1'23"456	2nd: 1h54'25"780
8	Stefano Modena	I	Brabham Racing Organisation	Brabham BT58	Judd V8 3496 cc	8th: 1'25"086	3rd: 76 laps
21	Alex Caffi	I	Scuderia Italia	BMS Dallara F189	Cosworth V8 3491 cc	9th: 1'25"481	4th: 75 laps
4	Michele Alboreto	I	Tyrrell Racing Organisation	Tyrrell 018	Cosworth V8 3491 cc	12th: 1'26"388	5th: 75 laps
7	Martin Brundle	GB	Brabham Racing Organisation	Brabham BT58	Judd V8 3496 cc	4th: 1'24"580	6th: 75 laps
10	Eddie Cheever	USA	Arrows Racing Ltd.	Arrows A11	Cosworth V8 3491 cc	20th: 1'27"117	7th : 75 laps
19	Alessandro Nannini	I	Benetton Formula Ltd.	Benetton B188	Cosworth V8 3491 cc	15th: 1'26"599	8th: 74 laps
3	Jonathan Palmer	GB	Tyrrell Racing Organisation	Tyrrell 018	Cosworth V8 3491 cc	23rd: 1'27"452	9th: 74 laps
5	Thierry Boutsen	B	Canon Williams Team	Williams FW12C	Renault V10 3500 cc	3rd: 1'24"332	10th: 74 laps
16	Ivan Capelli	I	Leyton House March Racing Team	March 891	Judd V8 3496 cc	22th: 1'27"302	11th: 73 laps (R)
25	René Arnoux	F	Ligier Gitanes	Ligier JS33	Cosworth V8 3491 cc	21st: 1'27"182	12th: 73 laps
22	Andrea de Cesaris	I	Scuderia Italia	BMS Dallara F189	Cosworth V8 3491 cc	10th: 1'25"515	13th: 73 laps
20	Johnny Herbert	GB	Benetton Formula Ltd.	Benetton B188	Cosworth V8 3491 cc	24th: 1'27"706	14th: 73 laps
6	Riccardo Patrese	I	Canon Williams Team	Williams FW12C	Renault V10 3500 cc	7th: 1'25"021(27)	15th: 73 laps
24	Luis Perez-Sala	E	Lois Minardi Team S.p.A.	Minardi M188	Cosworth V8 3491 cc	26th: 1'27"786	R
40	Gabriele Tarquini	I	Equipe AGS	AGS JH25	Cosworth V8 3491 cc	13th: 1'26"422	R
31	Roberto Moreno	BR	Coloni S.p.A.	Coloni CF188B	Cosworth V8 3491 cc	25th: 1'27"721	R
30	Philippe Alliot	F	Larrousse et Calmels	Lola LC89B	Lamborghini V12 3493 cc	17th: 1'26"857	R
15	Maurizio Gugelmin	BR	Leyton House March Racing Team	March 881	Judd V8 3496 cc	14th: 1'26"522(28)	R
11	Nelson Piquet	BR	Camel Team Lotus	Lotus 101	Judd V8 3496 cc	19th: 1'27"046	R
27	Nigel Mansell	GB	SEFAC Ferrari S.p.A.	Ferrari F1/89 (640)	Ferrari V12 3497 cc	5th: 1'24"735	R
32	Pierre-Henri Raphanel	F	Coloni S.p.A.	Coloni CF188B	Cosworth V8 3491 cc	18th: 1'27"011	R
26	Olivier Grouillard	F	Ligier Gitanes	Ligier JS33	Cosworth V8 3491 cc	16th: 1'26"792	R
23	Pierluigi Martini	I	Lois Minardi Team S.p.A.	Minardi M188	Cosworth V8 3491 cc	11th: 1'26"288	R
9	Derek Warwick	GB	USF&G Arrows Megatron	Arrows A11	Cosworth V8 3491 cc	6th: 1'24"791	R

1

2

3

(1) Senna leading Prost (both McLarens). They remain in this order on this occasion. Speeding between barriers: (2) Senna, (3) Alboreto (Tyrrell), (4) Brundle (Brabham). (5) Modena (Brabham) and (6) Caffi (Dallara).

(1) Senna vor Prost (beide McLaren). Bei dieser Reihenfolge bleibt es diesmal. Im Plankenkarussell: (2) Senna, (3) Alboreto (Tyrrell), (4) Brundle (Brabham). (5) Modena (Brabham) und (6) Caffi (Dallara).

(1) Senna devant Prost (tous les deux sur McLaren). Cette fois, ce sera aussi le résultat final. Chasse entre les glissières : (2) Senna, (3) Alboreto (Tyrrell), (4) Brundle (Brabham). (5) Modena (Brabham) et (6) Caffi (Dallara).

(1) Friendly fire: sparks behind a Williams. (2) The end for Schneider (Zakspeed). The German fails to qualify, just like his teammate Suzuki. (3) The leaders have already reached the sea again on the first lap. Warwick (Arrows) leads the pursuers.

(1) Friendly Fire: Funkenflug hinter einem Williams. (2) Aus für Schneider (Zakspeed). Der Deutsche kann sich nicht qualifizieren, ebensowenig wie sein Teamgefährte Suzuki. (3) Die Spitze ist in der ersten Runde schon wieder am Meer angelangt. Warwick (Arrows) führt die Verfolger an.

(1) Feu inoffensif : comète d'étincelles derrière une Williams. (2) Abandon pour Schneider (Zakspeed). L'Allemand ne peut pas se qualifier, de même que son coéquipier Suzuki, d'ailleurs. (3) Les hommes de tête longent de nouveau la mer lors du premier tour. Warwick (Arrows) emmène le peloton.

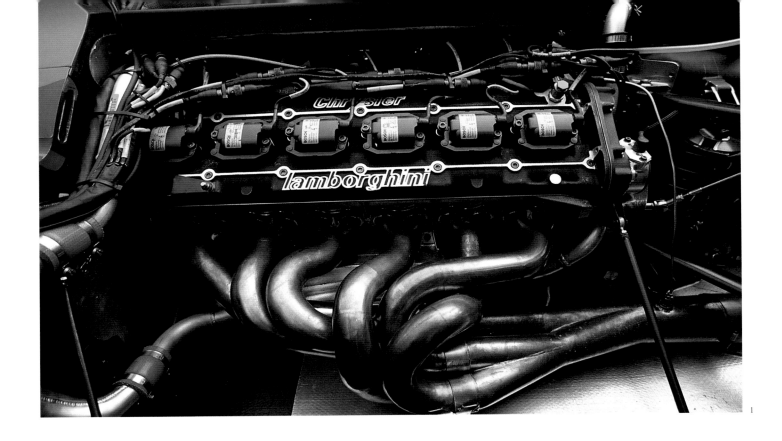

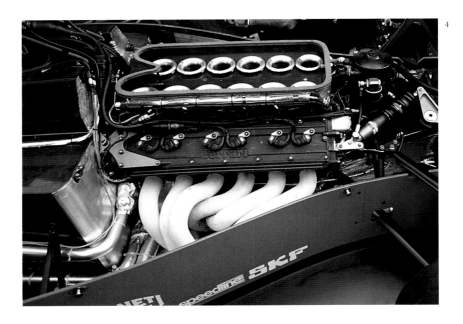

5

6

7

The middle path is the correct one: (3) V10 from Honda, (2) V8 from Ford, the two V12s from (1) Lamborghini and (4) Ferrari. (5) Charmer: Nannini (with Mike Kranefuss). (6) Fun: Mansell and (7) games: Patrese.

Der richtige Weg ist der mittlere: (3) V10 von Honda, (2) V8 von Ford, die beiden V12 von (1) Lamborghini und (4) Ferrari. (5) Charmeur: Nannini (mit Mike Kranefuss), (6) Schalk: Mansell, (7) Schelm: Patrese.

La bonne voie est toujours la voie médiane : (3) V10 de Honda, (2) V8 de Ford, les deux V12 de (1) Lamborghini et (4) Ferrari. (5) Charmeur : Nannini (avec Mike Kranefuss). (6) Farceur : Mansell. (7) Blagueur : Patrese.

1990

As the smoke began to lift from the race track on Saturday, 26 May 1990 at 2 pm, after final qualifying for the 48th Monaco Grand Prix, there was partly surprise and partly that pleasant feeling which comes of having known something all along: Ayrton Senna and Alain Prost were on the first row of the grid for the third time in a row. But something was different. The Frenchman, unwilling to remain in the same team as Senna, had changed sides in annoyance and was now driving for Ferrari, while the Brazilian started as usual in the white-and-red livery of McLaren. Another peculiarity was that, as in the previous year, their Monaco grid positions were the same as they would be at Suzuka, Japan, where once the final round of their battle for the World Championship would be fought with no quarter given.

But the problems at Monaco this time round were caused by others. After the first start, everyone managed to squeeze through Sainte Dévote without incident, but when approaching Mirabeau, Prost was impetuously put under pressure by an impetuous Jean Alesi in his Tyrrell 019. The youthful wild man from Avignon was trembling with impatience to show himself, the world, and above all his fellow Frenchman, what he could do – and he did indeed slip past on the right. Too late, Prost attempted to slam the door shut and rammed Berger in the second McLaren. The track was blocked, the red flag was hung out and everyone returned slowly to the pits to climb into the reserve cars.

Everything went like clockwork at the second attempt, with Senna leading Prost, Alesi, Berger and Thierry Boutsen in the Williams FW 13 B. On the 30th lap Alesi, who was drifting his car everywhere, was rewarded with second place for his hard and consistent work when the Ferrari 641 in front of him was forced to withdraw with a faulty battery. Berger and Patrese in the other Williams were behind him – and Boutsen, who was increasingly being pressured by Nelson Piquet's Benetton. On lap 34, the colorful B 190 spun onto the pavement at Loews, was push-started again by track marshals, only to be told to withdraw from the race by being shown the black flag, for using external assistance. In the meantime, Berger had attached himself to Alesi and was making use of the whole of his vast experience to intimidate the Tyrrell driver – but in vain. Nevertheless, the two had come within one second of Senna at the finish.

Nigel Mansell's endeavours in the second Ferrari also proved in vain. A vehement attack on Boutsen in lap 15 left him ten places further back. Raging at the back of the field like an angry polecat, he finally managed to regain his position breathing down the neck of the Belgian, overtaking him on the 56th lap at the chicane. Ten minutes later fate struck him as it did his team-mate: another faulty battery.

Blissfully unaware of what was going on behind, Ayrton Senna revelled in the magic of the superlatives: he had taken his 45th pole position, had set best time of the day, and it was his third victory in Monaco. Why not more of the same?

Als sich am Samstag, dem 26. Mai 1990, um 14 Uhr nach dem Abschlußtraining zum 48. Grand Prix de Monaco der Pulverdampf über der Piste zu lichten beginnt, herrscht teils Staunen, teils das stets erhebende Gefühl, es vorher schon gewußt zu haben: In der ersten Reihe stehen zum dritten Mal in Folge Ayrton Senna und Alain Prost. Nur: Der Franzose hat vergrätzt die Fraktion gewechselt und fährt nun für Ferrari, während der Brasilianer wie gewohnt im weißrot livrierten McLaren antritt. Auch merkwürdig, daß wie im Vorjahr die Konstellation der beiden die katastrophenträchtige Ausgangslage im japanischen Suzuka vorwegnimmt, aus der heraus der Endkampf um die Weltmeisterschaft jeweils mit schweren Säbeln ausgetragen wird.

Für Ärgernis sorgen diesmal andere. Zwar passiert man nach dem ersten Start Sainte Dévote in innigem Miteinander, jedoch ohne Zwischenfälle. Vor Mirabeau indessen wird Prost ungestüm bedrängt von Jean Alesi im Tyrrell 019. Der junge Wilde aus Avignon bebt vor Ungeduld, es sich selbst, aller Welt, vor allem aber seinem berühmten Landsmann zu zeigen, und schlüpft auch tatsächlich rechts vorbei. Prost versucht noch, die Tür zuzuwerfen – und schon rammt ihn Berger mit dem zweiten McLaren. Die Strecke ist blockiert, die rote Flagge wird herausgehängt, man kehrt im Laufschritt zu den Boxen zurück und steigt in die Reservewagen.

Beim zweiten Mal klappt alles wie am Schnürchen, Senna vor Prost, Alesi, Berger und Thierry Boutsen auf dem Williams FW 13 B. In der 30. Runde wird Alesi, der eigentlich überall driftet, der zweite Platz und damit der Lohn für harte und konsequente Arbeit zuteil, als der Ferrari 641 vor ihm mit defekter Batterie ausfällt. Berger und Patrese im anderen Williams folgen – und Boutsen, unter dessen Getriebe Nelson Piquets Benetton immer häufiger seine Nase schiebt. Im 34. Durchgang dreht sich der bunte B 190 bei Loews auf den Bürgersteig, wird von Kommissaren wieder angeschoben und anschließend mit der schwarzen Flagge aus dem Rennen genommen wegen Inanspruchnahme fremder Hilfe. Unterdessen hat Berger bei Alesi angedockt und spielt sein ganzes Repertoire an Erfahrung aus, um den Tyrrell-Piloten einzuschüchtern – umsonst. Immerhin hat sich das Gespann im Ziel bis auf eine Sekunde an Senna herangearbeitet.

Fruchtlos bleiben auch die Bemühungen von Nigel Mansell im zweiten Ferrari. Eine vehemente Attacke auf Boutsen in Runde 15 kostet ihn den Frontspoiler und zehn Plätze. Im Hinterfeld wütend wie ein Iltis unter Kaninchen, sitzt er dem Belgier schließlich wieder im Nacken und überholt in der 56. Runde an der Schikane. Zehn Minuten später widerfährt ihm das gleiche Schicksal wie seinem Teamkollegen: Batterieschaden.

Von all dem unberührt huldigt Ayrton Senna dem Charme der großen Zahl: 45. Pole Position, beste Zeit des Tages, dritter Sieg in Monaco. Das macht Lust auf mehr.

Quand, le samedi 26 mai 1990, à 14 heures, après les dernières qualifications pour le 48e Grand Prix de Monaco, la poussière du combat commence à se dissiper sur la piste, certains sont frappés d'étonnement et d'autres ont cette sensation gratifiante d'avoir déjà tout su auparavant : la première ligne est, pour la troisième fois consécutive, le butin d'Ayrton Senna et d'Alain Prost. A cette différente près que le Français, peu enclin à rester le coéquipier de Senna, a changé de camp et pilote désormais pour Ferrari alors que le Brésilien arbore comme toujours la casaque blanche et rouge de McLaren. Autre détail étonnant : comme l'année précédente déjà, leurs positions de départ respectives sont les mêmes que bientôt à Suzuka, au Japon, où la dernière bataille, à savoir le championnat du monde, sera disputée sabre au clair.

Cette fois, ce sont d'autres qui se font remarquer par leur indiscipline. Certes, après le premier départ, tout le monde serre les coudes pour passer Sainte Dévote le mieux possible et sans incident notoire. A Mirabeau, par contre, Prost est talonné par l'impétueux Jean Alesi sur sa Tyrrell 019. Le jeune sauvage d'Avignon tremble d'impatience de vouloir montrer à lui-même, au monde entier, mais aussi et surtout à son célèbre compatriote ce dont il est capable et il fait réellement l'intérieur du virage à Prost. Lequel cherche encore à fermer la porte – et, juste à ce moment, Berger le percute avec la seconde McLaren. La piste est bloquée, les drapeaux rouges sont brandis et l'on rentre au pas aux stands pour prendre son éventuel mulet.

Lors du second départ, tout se déroule sans anicroche, Senna mène devant Prost, Alesi, Berger et Thierry Boutsen sur la Williams FW 13 B. Au 30e tour, Alesi, pratiquement à la limite de la sortie de route dans tous les virages, récolte la seconde place et, ainsi, la récompense pour un travail âpre et systématique lorsque la Ferrari 641 qui le devance abandonne sur panne de batterie. Berger et Patrese sur l'autre Williams suivent – et Boutsen dont la Benetton de Nelson Piquet vient de plus en plus souvent renifler la boîte de vitesses. Au 34e tour, la B 190 multicolore atterrit sur le trottoir du Loews après un tête-à-queue, est repoussée sur la piste par les commissaires et ensuite disqualifiée au drapeau noir pour mise à contribution d'une aide extérieure. Pendant ce temps, Berger et Alesi ne font qu'un et l'Autrichien utilise tout son savoir-faire pour intimider le pilote de Tyrrell – mais en vain. Ceci n'empêche pas le duo de se rapprocher jusqu'à une seconde de Senna au moment où celui-ci franchit le drapeau à damiers.

Les efforts de Nigel Mansell, sur la seconde Ferrari, ne seront pas récompensés. Une attaque inconsidérée sur Boutsen, au 15e tour, lui coûtera son capot avant et dix places. Au fin fond du peloton, furieux comme un putois dans un clapier, il est de nouveau dans la nuque du Belge, qu'il double au 56e tour, à la chicane. Dix minutes plus tard, il subit le même destin que son coéquipier : panne de batterie.

Insensible à tout cela, Ayrton Senna déguste le charme des chiffres ronds : 45e pole position, meilleur tour en course, troisième victoire à Monaco. Comme chacun sait, l'appétit vient en mangeant.

Colorful symphony: Nannini's
Benetton blends perfectly
with Monaco's luscious flora.

Symphonie in bunt:
der Benetton von Nannini
harmoniert perfekt mit der
üppigen Flora von Monaco.

Symphonie multicolore :
la Benetton de Nannini
s'inscrit à la perfection dans
la flore luxurieuse de Monaco.

N°	DRIVERS		ENTRANTS	CARS	ENGINES	PRACTICE RESULTS	RACE RESULTS
27	**Ayrton Senna**	**BR**	**Marlboro McLaren Honda**	**McLaren MP4/5B**	**Honda V10 3493 cc**	**1st: 1'21"314**	**1st: 1h52'46"982**
4	Jean Alesi	F	Tyrrell Racing Organisation	Tyrrell 019	Cosworth V8 3494 cc	3rd: 1'21"801	2nd: 1h52'48"069
28	Gerhard Berger	A	Marlboro McLaren Honda	McLaren MP4/5B	Honda V10 3493 cc	5th: 1'22"682	3rd: 1h52'49"055
5	Thierry Boutsen	B	Williams Grand Prix Engineering	Williams FW13B	Renault V10 3500 cc	6th: 1'22"691	4th: 77 laps
10	Alex Caffi	I	Footwork-Arrows Racing Team	Arrows A11B	Cosworth V8 3494 cc	22nd: 1'25"000	5th: 76 laps
29	Eric Bernard	F	Espo Larrousse F1	Lola 90	Lamborghini V12 3493 cc	24th: 1'25"398	6th: 76 laps
35	Gregor Foitek	CH	Onyx Grand Prix Engineering	Onyx Ore 1	Cosworth V8 3494 cc	20th: 1'24"367	7th: 72 laps
11	Derek Warwick	GB	Camel Team Lotus	Lotus 102	Lamborghini V12 3493 cc	13th: 1'23"656	R
2	Nigel Mansell	GB	SEFAC Ferrari S.p.A.	Ferrari 641	Ferrari V12 3495 cc	7th: 1'22"733	R
24	Paolo Barilla	I	Minardi Team S.p.A.	Minardi M190	Cosworth V8 3494 cc	19th: 1'24"334	R
36	J. J. Lehto	SF	Onyx Grand Prix Engineering	Onyx Ore 1	Cosworth V8 3494 cc	26th: 1'25"508	R
26	Philippe Alliot	F	Ligier Sport	Ligier JS33B	Cosworth V8 3494 cc	18th: 1'24"294	R
6	Riccardo Patrese	I	Williams Grand Prix Engineering	Williams FW13B	Renault V10 3500 cc	4th: 1'22"026	R
22	Andrea de Cesaris	I	Scuderia Italia	BMS Dallara F190	Cosworth V8 3494 cc	12th: 1'23"613	R
3	Satoru Nakajima	J	Tyrrell Racing Organisation	Tyrrell 019	Cosworth V8 3494 cc	21st: 1'24"371	R
20	Nelson Piquet	BR	Benetton Formula Ltd.	Benetton B190	Cosworth V8 3494 cc	10th: 1'23"566	disqualified
1	Alain Prost	F	SEFAC Ferrari S.p.A.	Ferrari 641	Ferrari V12 3495 cc	2nd: 1'21"776	R
19	Alessandro Nannini	I	Benetton Formula Ltd.	Benetton B190	Cosworth V8 3494 cc	16th: 1'24"139	R
7	David Brabham	AUS	Motor Racing Development	Brabham BT59	Judd V8 3496 cc	25th: 1'25"420	R
16	Ivan Capelli	I	Leyton House Racing	Leyton House CG901	Judd V8 3496 cc	23rd: 1'25"020	R
25	Nicola Larini	I	Ligier Sport	Ligier JS33B	Cosworth V8 3494 cc	17th: 1'24"206	R
30	Aguri Suzuki	J	Espo Larrousse F1	Lola 90	Lamborghini V12 3493 cc	15th: 1'24"023	R
23	Pierluigi Martini	I	Minardi Team S.p.A.	Minardi M190	Cosworth V8 3494 cc	8th: 1'23"149	R
12	Martin Donnelly	GB	Camel Team Lotus	Lotus 102	Lamborghini V12 3493 cc	11th: 1'23"600	R
8	Stefano Modena	I	Motor Racing Development	Brabham BT59	Judd V8 3496 cc	14th: 1'23"920	R

(1) A man sees red: as early as Sainte Dévote, Alesi in his Tyrrell attacks Prost in his Ferrari with barely constrained aggression, while Senna (McLaren) coolly makes his escape. (2) A McLaren on the drop towards Mirabeau. The yellow flag warns of trouble ahead. (3) Prost prepares to lap a Lola.

(1) Ein Mann sieht rot: Schon bei Sainte Dévote attackiert Alesi im Tyrrell Prost im Ferrari in kaum gebändigter Aggression, während Senna (McLaren) kühl das Weite sucht. (2) Ein McLaren beim Absturz nach Mirabeau. Die gelbe Flagge warnt. (3) Prost schickt sich an, einen Lola zu überrunden.

(1) Un homme voit rouge : à Sainte-Dévote, déjà, Alesi et sa Tyrrell attaquent Prost et sa Ferrari dans une agressivité à peine contrôlée, tandis que Senna (McLaren) garde son sang froid et cherche son salut dans la fuite. (2) Une McLaren plongeant vers Mirabeau. Attention, drapeau jaune. (3) Prost s'apprête à mettre un tour à une Lola.

1

2

(1) The double bend at Rascasse is one of the few places where Formula 1 cars keep to the 30 mph speed limit prescribed in the town; here is Berger (McLaren) in front of Donnelly (Lotus). (2) Out of the race on lap 34: Piquet (Benetton). (3) Faulty electronics after 29 laps: Prost (Ferrari).

(1) Der Doppelknick bei Rascasse gehört zu den wenigen Stellen, wo ein Formel-1-Wagen das in der Stadt vorgeschriebene Tempo 50 fährt, hier Berger (McLaren) vor Donnelly (Lotus). (2) In Runde 34 aus dem Rennen gewinkt: Piquet (Benetton). (3) Nach 29 Runden Schaden an der Elektronik: Prost (Ferrari).

(1) Le double droite de la Rascasse est l'un des rares endroits où une voiture de Formule 1 respecte les 50 km/h prescrits en ville. Ici, Berger (McLaren) devant Donnelly (Lotus). (2) Contraint d'abandonner au 34e tour : Piquet (Benetton). (3) Panne électronique après 29 tours : Prost (Ferrari).

1

3

(1) Rattling the Establishment: Jean Alesi. (2) Intimidated by no one: Ayrton Senna. (3) Number two at Ferrari duelling with number two at McLaren: Mansell attacks Berger. (4) Fourth place in his sights: Boutsen in the Williams. (5) Fourth in 1989, this time fifth: Caffi (Arrows) on his way to his second-best placing.

(1) Rüttelt am Establishment: Jean Alesi. (2) Von niemandem einzuschüchtern: Ayrton Senna. (3) Nummer zwei bei Ferrari im Zweikampf mit Nummer zwei bei McLaren: Mansell greift Berger an. (4) Rang vier im Visier: Boutsen im Williams. (5) 1989 vierter, diesmal fünfter: Caffi (Arrows) unterwegs zu seiner zweitbesten Plazierung.

(1) Vient rompre l'ordre établi : Jean Alesi. (2) Ne se laisse impressionner par personne : Ayrton Senna. (3) Le numéro deux chez Ferrari en duel avec le numéro deux chez McLaren : Mansell attaque Berger. (4) Quatrième place dans son collimateur : Boutsen sur Williams. (5) Quatrième en 1989 et cinquième cette année : Caffi (Arrows) vers le deuxième meilleur résultat de sa carrière.

1

2

3

4

5

6

Mood pictures: (1) Nelson Piquet,
(2) Pierluigi Martini, (3) Alex Caffi,
(4, 5) Ayrton Senna, (6) Jean Alesi,
who has just read an article about
himself – in the language of his
fathers.

Stimmungs-Bilder: (1) Nelson
Piquet, (2) Pierluigi Martini,
(3) Alex Caffi, (4, 5) Ayrton Senna,
(6) Jean Alesi, der gerade einen
Artikel über sich selbst gelesen hat –
in der Sprache seiner Väter.

Ambiance : (1) Nelson Piquet,
(2) Pierluigi Martini, (3) Alex Caffi,
(4, 5) Ayrton Senna, (6) Jean Alesi,
qui vient de lire un article qui lui est
consacré – dans la langue de ses
pères.

EARLY PERFECTION

DER FRÜH VOLLENDETE · LA SYMPHONIE INACHEVÉE

A game of chess without time for reflection is how the racing driver and journalist Richard von Frankenberg used to describe a Grand Prix. In the mid-1990s they have become more: the final phase of a chess game with time for reflection, or, as Clausewitz might have said, a continuation of politics by other means.

In this light, Ayrton Senna turned out to be a double champion, equally blessed as driver and politician. Senna the car driver: no weaknesses, only strengths, as, for example when things became slippery, like in the deluge of rain in Monaco 1984 with the cumbersome Toleman Hart. Or when things became difficult to assess and no-one else had any ideas, such as during the chaotic race in Donington in 1993.

Senna the strategist and tactician: cunning, crafty, aware of all the tricks. That started with psychological warfare in his own team. "He attempts to destroy his team-mates so that they are not even capable of their normal performance", said McLaren boss and Senna expert Ron Dennis. This was done via the tried and tested VIP trick of withdrawing in a sulk, only to be carried on the shoulders of the masses and the media to where he wanted to be in the first place. That is how it happened with Senna's apparent holiday in 1993, and reluctant return to the McLaren cockpit, accompanied by Dennis' courting siren calls as well as written confirmation that it was more than a labor of love. Incidentally, Formula 1 does not release its stars that easily. It ended with him complaining like a fishwife and hitting out, for example at the cheeky novice Eddie Irvine, who calmly attacked him in Suzuka in 1993 and got away with a black eye once again.

Senna, too, was only human after all, and a few weeks later in Adelaide, on his departure from McLaren, there were even tears in his eyes. Senna's tears – the carefully nurtured image of the hard man under the yellow helmet began to melt away. Yet: one should refrain from the lame conciliatory phrase "he really was an incredibly nice person". If that were really the case, then Senna would not have been Senna.

In the end, the sport which made him great claimed him on that fateful 1 May 1994 at Imola. And suddenly, many a person had realized, even among his critics, that there are men who are irreplaceable. Ayrton Senna was one of them.

Schachspiel ohne Bedenkzeit, pflegte der Rennfahrer und Journalist Richard von Frankenberg die Grand Prix zu nennen. In den Mittneunzigern sind sie mehr: eher die finale Phase eines Schachspiels mit Bedenkzeit, oder, frei nach Clausewitz, Fortsetzung der Politik mit anderen Mitteln.

In diesem Licht erweist sich Ayrton Senna als Doppel-Champion, gleichermaßen begnadet als Pilot und als Politiker. Senna der Autofahrer: keine Schwächen, nur Stärken. Immer dann zum Beispiel, wenn es schlüpfrig wird, wie im Regen-Inferno von Monaco 1984 mit dem biestigen Toleman Hart. Oder wenn die Dinge unübersichtlich werden und niemand sonst durchblickt, wie beim Chaos-Rennen in Donington 1993.

Senna, der Stratege und Taktiker: gewieft, durchtrieben, mit allen Wassern gewaschen. Das beginnt mit psychologischer Kriegführung in der eigenen Truppe. »Er versucht, seine Teamgefährten zu zerstören, so daß sie nicht einmal mehr zu ihrer normalen Leistung fähig sind«, weiß McLaren-Chef und Senna-Kenner Ron Dennis. Das geht über die altbewährte Prominenten-Posse, sich in den Schmollwinkel zu verkriechen, um dann auf den Schultern der Massen und der Medien dahin getragen zu werden, wohin man sowieso wollte. So geschehen bei Sennas Schein-Urlaub 1993 und zögerlicher Rückkehr ins McLaren-Cockpit, rezitativisch begleitet von Dennis' buhlenden Sirenenrufen sowie seiner verbrieften Zusage, es gehe nicht nur um Gotteslohn. Im übrigen: So leicht läßt die Formel 1 ihre Stars nicht los. Und das endet damit, daß er schimpft wie ein Rohrspatz und handgreiflich wird, dem kessen Novizen Eddie Irvine zur Beherzigung, der ihn 1993 in Suzuka unverfroren attackiert hat und noch einmal mit einem blauen Auge davonkommt.

Auch er ist schließlich nur ein Mensch, und ein paar Wochen später in Adelaide, beim Abschied von McLaren, bekommt er gar feuchte Augen. Sennas Tränen – da schmilzt manch liebevoll gewartetes und gepflegtes Image von dem harten Mann unter dem gelben Helm. Nur: Die laxe Versöhnlichkeitsfloskel »In Wirklichkeit ist er ein unheimlich netter Kerl« sollte man sich schon verkneifen. Verhielte es sich wirklich so, dann wäre Senna nicht Senna.

Am Ende fordert ihn der Sport, der ihn groß gemacht hat, zum Opfer, an jenem fatalen 1. Mai 1994 in Imola. Und plötzlich wird so manchem klar, selbst unter seinen Kritikern: Es gibt eben doch Männer, die sind unersetzlich. Ayrton Senna ist einer von ihnen.

Jeu d'échecs sans temps de réflexion, c'est ainsi que le pilote de course et journaliste automobile Richard von Frankenberg avait coutume de surnommer les Grands Prix. Au milieu des années 90, ils sont plus que cela : plutôt la phase finale d'un jeu d'échecs avec temps de réflexion ou, librement interprétés d'après Clausewitz, la poursuite de la politique avec d'autres moyens.

Sous un tel éclairage, Ayrton Senna se présente en double champion, aussi doué comme pilote que comme homme politique. Senna l'automobiliste : pas de points faibles, uniquement des points forts. Et à chaque fois, par exemple, que la piste est glissante, comme sous les trombes d'eau de Monaco en 1984 au volant de son encombrante Toleman Hart. Ou lorsque les choses basculent totalement dans le chaos et que personne ne sait plus où l'on en est, comme pour la course d'anthologie de Donington, en 1993.

Senna, le stratège et tacticien : madré, génial, vieux renard de la course. Cela commence avec la guerre psychologique au sein de sa propre écurie. « Il fait tout pour déstabiliser ses coéquipiers, si bien qu'ils ne sont plus capables de livrer de nouveau leurs performances habituelles », déclare Ron Dennis, chef de McLaren et, donc, connaisseur intime de Senna. Cela commence avec la bonne vieille tactique de la vedette, qui consiste à bouder dans son coin avant d'arriver, portée sur les épaules des masses et soutenue par les médias, à la première place, là où l'on voulait de toute façon arriver. C'est ce qui s'est passé lors des vacances fictives de Senna en 1993 et avant son retour hésitant dans le cockpit de la McLaren, lorsqu'il succomba au chant de sirène de Ron Dennis après s'être fait attester noir sur blanc que l'enjeu n'était pas seulement le salaire de la peur. Pour le reste : la Formule 1 ne lâche pas ses vedettes aussi facilement. Et cela se termine par une canonnade de jurons, voire un feu roulant de coups de poing, ce que peut confirmer l'effronté néophyte Eddie Irvine, pour avoir osé l'attaquer sans respect en 1993 à Suzuka, qui s'en tira pour une fois avec un œil au beurre noir.

Lui aussi, finalement, est un être humain et, quelques semaines plus tard à Adelaïde, lors des adieux de McLaren, il a même les larmes aux yeux. Les larmes de Senna – cela fait fondre l'image amoureusement créée et cultivée de l'homme dur sous le casque jaune. Mais il ne faut surtout pas croire au bien-fondé du cliché que l'on prononce en guise de réconciliation : « En réalité, c'est un garçon vraiment gentil ! ». S'il en était véritablement ainsi, Senna ne serait pas Senna.

En fin de compte, le sport qui l'a élevé au firmament prélève son tribut, ce fatal 1er mai 1994 à Imola. Et, soudain, nombreux sont ceux qui prennent conscience, même parmi ses détracteurs, que, malgré tout, certains hommes sont vraiment irremplaçables. Et qu'Ayrton Senna en fait assurément partie.

Ayrton Senna da Silva: in the ten years that he sits in the Grand Prix cockpit, his name becomes synonymous with Formula 1.

Ayrton Senna da Silva: In seinen zehn Jahren im Grand-Prix-Cockpit wird sein Name synonym mit der Formel 1.

Ayrton Senna da Silva : en dix ans passés dans les cockpits de voitures de Grand Prix, son nom devient synonyme de Formule 1.

1991

Senna does it again: thus the happy Formula 1 message went out on the evening of 12 May 1991 in all the languages of the world. The 49th edition of the Monaco Grand Prix turned into a sparkling celebration for the Brazilian, whose authority and efficiency was beginning to weigh heavily on the others – his fourth win in the Principality, four wins from the first four races of the season, with the usual pole position as icing on the cake. The only thing left for Alain Prost, his eternal adversary, whose Grand Prix days with Ferrari were already numbered, was merely the fastest time of the day, a fifth place and a grudge against the god of the race track who gave him Senna as a contemporary.

By this time, both of them had screaming 12-cylinder engines behind them, for Honda, the McLaren supplier, had started to build V12s, even though it was beginning to become clear that a V10 was the better solution for the 3.5-liter formula. The other driver on the front row of the grid, who had produced a sensational performance in qualifying, also had a Honda at his command: Stefano Modena, in the Tyrrell 020, although he maintained a respectful distance of half a second from Senna.

The sensation appeared to be confirmed during the race. At the beginning, the Tyrrell followed the white-and-red car in front of him as if tied by a tow-rope, and less than two seconds separated the two of them after 15 laps. But then Senna rigorously began to use all his ruthlessness and experience in lapping the others, shooting through gaps which did not appear to exist, while the Italian kept losing valuable time. In no time at all, the gap between him and the escaping McLaren MP 4/6 had grown to eight seconds. It grew to half a minute when Emanuele Pirro, in a Ferrari-red Dallara, obstructed him for several laps in the firm belief that he was dealing with the Tyrrell number two, Saturo Nakajima.

At that point, Modena already had Riccardo Patrese's Williams FW 14 filling his rear-view mirrors. But the duel came to an end during the 43rd lap, when the Honda engine exploded at the exit of the tunnel, showering the Williams and its driver with blackened lubricant. Patrese ended up against the barriers like a shamefully fallen figure skater. In the meantime, Senna had created a gap of 43 seconds between himself and Prost. Mansell in the other Williams was running a further ten seconds behind, but rapidly closing on the Ferrari after suffering transmission difficulties in the early stages, and overtaking the Frenchman on lap 43.

Six laps before the finish, the cautious "Professor" voluntarily ceded his third place to his team-mate Jean Alesi when he collected another set of new tyres. Then a stubborn wheel nut prevented his rapid return to the race track, so Roberto Moreno in his Benetton B 191 also managed to flit by into fourth place.

Ayrton Senna, in the meantime, had contributed to the growth of more than his own legendary status, adding also to the glory of the McLaren marque: one of their cars had set the best time in qualifying for the 70th time and scored the team's 90th Grand Prix success. Even approaching the end of the 20th century an individual could still achieve great things.

Wieder Senna, lautet die frohe Formel-1-Botschaft am Abend des 12. Mai 1991 in den Sprachen der Welt. Die 49. Auflage des Großen Preises von Monaco: ein Feuerwerk und Festival für den Brasilianer, dessen Autorität und Kompetenz bleischwer auf den anderen zu lasten beginnt – vierter Erfolg im Fürstentum, vierter Sieg zugleich im vierten Rennen der Saison mit der üblichen Pole Position als Sahnehäubchen. Seinem ewigen Widersacher Alain Prost hingegen, dessen Grand Prix bei Ferrari gezählt sind, bleiben lediglich die schnellste Zeit des Tages, Platz fünf und der dumpfe Groll, daß ihm der Gott der Pisten den Mann Ayrton Senna zum Zeitgenossen gemacht hat.

Beiden sitzen inzwischen kreischende Zwölfzylinder im Nacken. Denn McLaren-Lieferant Honda baut neuerdings V12, obwohl sich die Einsicht zu verfestigen beginnt, in der 3,5-Liter-Formel fahre man am günstigsten mit einem V10. Über einen solchen, ebenfalls von Honda, gebietet auch der andere Fahrer in der ersten Reihe, zugleich Sensation des Trainings: Stefano Modena im Tyrrell 020, gleichwohl im Respektabstand von einer halben Sekunde zu Senna.

Die Sensation scheint sich im Rennen zu bestätigen. Anfänglich folgt der Tyrrell dem weißroten Wagen vor ihm wie an einem Schleppseil gezogen. Weniger als zwei Sekunden trennen das Duo nach 15 Durchgängen. Dann aber spielt Senna rigoros seine ganze Rücksichtslosigkeit und Routine beim Überrunden aus, schießt in Lücken, die gar nicht zu existieren scheinen, während der Italiener überall kostbare Zeit verliert. Im Nu beläuft sich sein Rückstand zu dem fliehenden McLaren MP 4/6 auf acht Sekunden. Er wächst auf eine halbe Minute, als ihn Emanuele Pirro im ferrariroten Dallara rundenlang behindert, im festen Glauben, er habe es mit Tyrrell-Nummer zwei, Saturo Nakajima, zu tun.

Da hat Modena bereits den Williams FW 14 von Riccardo Patrese formatfüllend im Rückspiegel. Das Duell endet durch höhere Gewalt: In der 43. Runde explodiert der Honda-Motor ausgangs des Tunnels und überschüttet den Williams nebst Piloten liberal mit geschwärztem Schmierstoff. Patrese landet wie ein schmählich gestürzter Eiskunstläufer an der Bande. Inzwischen hat Senna 43 Sekunden Distanz zwischen sich und Prost geschaffen. Zehn weitere Sekunden später folgt Mansell im anderen Williams, der nach Schwierigkeiten mit dem Getriebe in der Anfangsphase zügig zum Ferrari aufschließt und den Franzosen in der 43. Runde überholt.

Sechs Runden vor Schluß rückt der vorsichtige »Professor« seinen dritten Platz freiwillig an seinen Teamgefährten Jean Alesi heraus, als er noch einmal frische Reifen faßt. Eine widerspenstige Radmutter vereitelt seine zügige Rückkehr auf die Piste, so daß auch noch Roberto Moreno im Benetton B 191 auf den vierten Platz vorbeihuscht.

Ayrton Senna indessen hat nicht nur seiner eigenen Legende ein Kapitel hinzugefügt, sondern erneut etwas zum höheren Ruhme der Marke McLaren getan: 70. Trainingsbestzeit, 90. Grand-Prix-Erfolg. Auch im ausgehenden 20. Jahrhundert kann ein einzelner noch viel bewegen.

De nouveau Senna, lance le gai message sur la Formule 1 diffusé dans toutes les langues du monde, le soir du 12 mai 1991. La 49ᵉ édition du Grand Prix de Monaco est un feu d'artifices et un festival pour le Brésilien dont l'autorité et la compétence commencent à peser comme une chape de plomb sur les épaules de ses adversaires : son quatrième succès en Principauté, quatrième victoire aussi en quatre courses depuis le début de la saison avec la pole position traditionnelle à la clé. Son adversaire héréditaire, Alain Prost par contre, dont les Grands Prix sont déjà comptés chez Ferrari, doit se contenter du tour le plus rapide en course, de la cinquième place et de la frustration que le dieu des pistes lui ait donné comme compagnon de route Ayrton Senna.

Les deux hommes ont entre-temps des douze-cylindres stridents dans le dos : en effet, Honda, le fournisseur de McLaren, mise dorénavant sur les V12, bien que l'on commence à constater que, en Formule 3,5 litres, c'est avec un V10 qu'on a les meilleurs atouts. C'est d'ailleurs un tel moteur, également signé Honda, que possède l'autre pilote en première ligne, qui est en même temps la sensation des essais : Stefano Modena sur Tyrrell 020, mais avec tout de même un retard respectueux d'une demi-seconde sur Senna.

La sensation semble se confirmer en course. Au début, la Tyrrell suit comme son ombre la voiture blanche et rouge qui la précède et moins de deux secondes séparent le duo après 15 tours, mais c'est alors que Senna abandonne tous égards et profite de sa routine à doubler les concurrents, s'engouffre dans des failles qui semblent ne pas exister, alors que l'Italien perd partout de précieuses fractions de seconde. En un rien de temps, son retard sur la McLaren MP 4/6 en fuite s'élève à huit secondes. Il passe ensuite à une demi-minute lorsque Emanuele Pirro, sur sa Dallara rouge Ferrari, le bloque pendant plusieurs tours, intimement convaincu d'avoir à faire au pilote numéro deux de Tyrrell, Saturo Nakajima.

Modena a alors la Williams FW 14 de Riccardo Patrese plein format dans ses rétroviseurs, mais un cas de force majeure met un terme à ce duel au 43ᵉ tour, lorsque le moteur Honda explose à la sortie du tunnel et asperge la Williams et son pilote de lubrifiant brûlant. Tel un patineur qui a perdu l'équilibre, Patrese percute les glissières. Entre-temps, Senna a pris 43 secondes d'avance sur Prost. Lequel est suivi, à dix secondes, par Mansell sur l'autre Williams, qui, après des difficultés de boîte de vitesses en début de course, rattrape rapidement la Ferrari et double le Français au 43ᵉ tour.

Six tours avant la fin, le prudent « Professeur » cède volontairement sa troisième place à son lieutenant Jean Alesi et va chausser des pneus neufs. A ce moment, un écrou bloqué l'empêche de reprendre rapidement la piste, ce qui permet aussi à Roberto Moreno sur Benetton B 191 de se glisser à la quatrième place.

Pendant ce temps, Ayrton Senna n'a pas seulement ajouté une nouvelle mosaïque à sa propre légende, il a aussi contribué à la célébrité de la marque McLaren : une voiture issue de cette écurie a obtenu le meilleur temps aux essais pour la 70ᵉ fois et remporté la 90ᵉ victoire en Grand Prix. En cette fin de 20ᵉ siècle, un individu peut donc encore déplacer des montagnes.

With a stationary camera the Formula 1 car in front of the Hôtel de Paris becomes an indistinguishable blur passing by.

Bei statischem Blickwinkel wird der Formel-1-Wagen vor dem Hôtel de Paris zum wesenlos huschenden Schemen.

Photo à angle fixe : la Formule 1 longeant l'Hôtel de Paris se mue en un fantôme méconnaissable.

N°	DRIVERS		ENTRANTS	CARS	ENGINES	PRACTICE RESULTS	RACE RESULTS
1	*Ayrton Senna*	*BR*	*Marlboro McLaren Honda*	*McLaren MP4/6*	*Honda V12 3493 cc*	*1st: 1'20"344*	*1st: 1h53'02"334*
5	Nigel Mansell	GB	Williams Grand Prix Engineering	Williams FW14	Renault V10 3500 cc	5th: 1'21"205	2nd: 1h53'20"682
28	Jean Alesi	F	SEFAC Ferrari S.p.A.	Ferrari 642	Ferrari V12 3495 cc	9th: 1'21"910	3rd: 1h53'49"789
19	Roberto Moreno	BR	Benetton Formula Ltd.	Benetton B191	Cosworth V8 3494 cc	8th: 1'21"804	4th: 77 laps
27	Alain Prost	F	SEFAC Ferrari S.p.A.	Ferrari 642	Ferrari V12 3495 cc	7th: 1'21"455	5th: 77 laps
21	Emanuele Pirro	I	Scuderia Italia S.p.A.	BMS Dallara F191	Judd V8 3496 cc	12th: 1'23"022	6th: 77 laps
25	Thierry Boutsen	B	Ligier Sport	Ligier JS35	Lamborghini V12 3493 cc	16th: 1'23"431	7th: 76 laps
32	Bertrand Gachot	F	Jordan Grand Prix	Jordan 191	Cosworth V8 3494 cc	24th: 1'24"208	8th: 76 laps
29	Eric Bernard	F	Larrousse F1	Lola 91	Cosworth V8 3494 cc	21st: 1'24"079	9th: 76 laps
26	Eric Comas	F	Ligier Sport	Ligier JS35	Lamborghini V12 3493 cc	23rd: 1'24"151	10th: 76 laps
22	J. J. Lehto	SF	Scuderia Italia S.p.A.	BMS Dallara F191	Judd V8 3496 cc	13th: 1'23"023	11th: 75 laps
23	Pierluigi Martini	I	Minardi Team S.p.A.	Minardi M191	Ferrari V12 3495 cc	14th: 1'23"064	12th: 72 laps
11	Mika Hakkinen	SF	Team Lotus	Lotus 102B	Judd V8 3496 cc	26th: 1'24"829	R
24	Gianni Morbidelli	I	Minardi Team S.p.A.	Minardi M191	Ferrari V12 3495 cc	17th: 1'23"584	R
15	Maurizio Gugelmin	BR	Leyton House Racing	Leyton House CG911	Ilmor V10 3500 cc	15th: 1'23"394	R
4	Stefano Modena	I	Tyrrell Racing Organisation	Tyrrell 020	Honda V10 3493 cc	2nd: 1'20"809	R
6	Riccardo Patrese	I	Williams Grand Prix Engineering	Williams FW14	Renault V10 3500 cc	3rd: 1'20"973	R
8	Mark Blundell	GB	Motor Racing Development	Brabham BT60	Yamaha V12 3500 cc	22nd: 1'24"109	R
9	Michele Alboreto	I	Footwork Racing Team	Footwork FA12	Porsche V12 3500 cc	25th: 1'24"606	R
3	Satoru Nakajima	J	Tyrrell Racing Organisation	Tyrrell 020	Honda V10 3493 cc	11th: 1'22"972	R
30	Aguri Suzuki	J	Larrousse F1	Lola 91	Cosworth V8 3494 cc	19th: 1'23"898	R
33	Andrea de Cesaris	I	Jordan Grand Prix	Jordan 191	Cosworth V8 3494 cc	10th: 1'22"764	R
16	Ivan Capelli	I	Leyton House Racing	Leyton House CG911	Ilmor V10 3500 cc	18th: 1'23"642	R
17	Gabriele Tarquini	I	AGS Formule 1	AGS JH25B	Cosworth V8 3494 cc	20th: 1'23"909	R
2	Gerhard Berger	A	Marlboro McLaren Honda	McLaren MP4/6	Honda V12 3493 cc	6th: 1'21"222	R
20	Nelson Piquet	BR	Benetton Formula Ltd.	Benetton B191	Cosworth V8 3494 cc	4th: 1'21"159	R

(1) In Monaco, it is often the rebel whose hour has come. Here Modena (Tyrrell) puts pressure on that monument of excellence, Senna (McLaren) after the start. Rail traffic: (2) Prost (Ferrari) and (3) Moreno (Benetton). Corner-cutting: (4) Mansell (Williams) and (5) Pirro (Dallara).

(1) In Monaco schlägt oft die Stunde der Aufständischen. Hier bedrängt Modena (Tyrrell) das Monument Senna (McLaren) nach dem Start. Schienen-Verkehr: (2) Prost (Ferrari) und (3) Moreno (Benetton). Rechts-Ruck: (4) Mansell (Williams) und (5) Pirro (Dallara).

(1) A Monaco, le destin est souvent favorable aux rebelles. Ici, Modena (Tyrrell) ne se laisse pas intimider par le monument qu'est Senna (McLaren) après le départ. Comme sur des rails : (2) Prost (Ferrari) et (3) Moreno (Benetton). A droite toute : (4) Mansell (Williams) et (5) Pirro (Dallara).

(Following double page) Fire at will: Gugelmin's Leyton House sprays sparks in the tunnel like a machine gun on the rampage.

(Nächste Doppelseite) Feuer frei: Im Tunnel versprüht der Leyton House von Gugelmin Funkengarben wie ein irrsinniges Maschinengewehr.

(Double page suivante) Pleins feux : dans le tunnel, la Leyton House de Gugelmin lance une gerbe d'étincelles qui fait penser à une rafale de mitrailleuse.

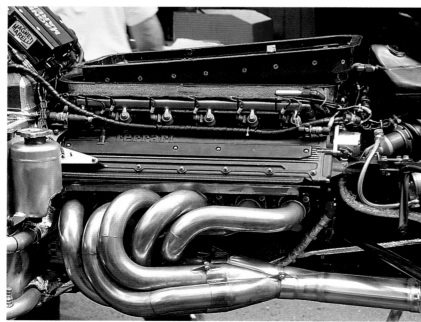

Formula 1 is also the formula for abundance: (1–3) with Ferrari,
(4) Benetton and (5, 6) McLaren.

Formel 1 ist auch die Formel für strotzenden Überfluß: (1–3) bei Ferrari,
(4) bei Benetton und (5, 6) bei McLaren.

La Formule 1 est aussi la formule de la profusion affichée : (1–3) chez
Ferrari, (4) chez Benetton et (5, 6) chez McLaren.

Support troops: (1) helmet bearers with McLaren and (2) employees of the AC de Monaco during the siesta at Rascasse. (3) Assessment of qualifying results by Berger and Senna (McLarens). (4) All in black: Jean Alesi (Ferrari) in his carbon fiber cocoon. (5) For a moment the autograph hunters come very close to their star.

Geschultes Personal: (1) Helm-Träger bei McLaren und (2) Bedienstete des AC de Monaco während der Siesta in Rascasse. (3) Nachbereitung der Trainingsergebnisse durch Berger und Senna (beide McLaren). (4) Ganz in schwarz: Jean Alesi (Ferrari) in seinem Kokon aus Kohlefaser. (5) Für einen Augenblick sind die Autogrammjäger ihrem Star ganz nahe.

Personnel bien formé : (1) porteur de casque chez McLaren et (2) commissaires de piste de l'AC Monaco pendant la sieste à la Rascasse. (3) Etude des résultats des qualifications par Berger et Senna (tous les deux sur McLaren). (4) Tout en noir : Jean Alesi (Ferrari) dans son cocon en fibre de carbone. (5) Pendant un instant, les chasseurs d'autographes peuvent toucher du doigt leur star.

1992

Nineteen ninety-two was without doubt the zenith of Nigel Mansell's career. He was called the "Lion" because of his drive to win and his fighting power. In addition, the Williams team presented itself as an integrated whole. The symbiosis between the compact FW 14 B chassis and the V10 engine from Renault, at 780 bhp the strongest engine in the field and blessed with smooth power development, worked perfectly, as did the semi-automatic transmission and active suspension of the Williams. The first five Grands Prix of the season were won with depressing monotony by Mansell, who arrived sated with success and full of robust confidence at the 50th Monaco Grand Prix on 31 May.

At McLaren, on the other hand, a crisis was brewing. The MP 4/7 was showing weaknesses, and the V12 prestige project by Honda was at full stretch with 770 bhp. The joint venture would be buried at Monza in September and the Japanese would withdraw from Formula 1 completely for a time. Star driver Ayrton Senna, used to being pampered by success, was monosyllabic and grumpy, while team boss Ron Dennis remained brusque and tight-lipped. This time they had entered the "Lion's" lair in Monaco.

The two Williams did indeed stand like a bulwark on the first row of the grid with Mansell and his team-mate Riccardo Patrese. But while the Briton retained the upper hand in the sprint to Sainte Dévote, Senna managed to squeeze past on the inside of the Italian. The same thing was done further back to Gerhard Berger in the other McLaren by Michael Schumacher, in the Benetton B 192, in the battle for fifth place. Jean Alesi, in contrast, initially remained where he had qualified: in fourth place. His Ferrari F 92 A should have won a prize for captivating beauty, but otherwise it was a flop. The Frenchman was put under increasing pressure. Schumacher was pushing impetuously from behind, and once, on lap 11, the two cars even became entangled in front of Hôtel Loews and its champagne-drinking guests. Nevertheless, they resumed their combat in the same order as before until lap 21, when Alesi's transmission gave out. Ten minutes later, the Ferrari also had to drop out. Schumacher worked his way forward until he was behind the second Williams, but then he met his match in Patrese's experience and his much-proven skill in preventing opponents from overtaking.

Right at the front, however, the "Lion" raced through the streets of the mini-state, his sixth win of the season within sight and, it seemed, within reach. But he could not have been more wrong. After lap 70 the Williams raced into the pit. One tyre was leaking air, it was said. Mansell spent the rest of the race in Senna's slipstream, and the latter was well able to keep anyone at bay. The time difference between them at the end was barely a quarter of a second, a tight finish like never before.

When Mansell fell down, exhausted, after crossing the finishing line and climbing out of his car, the Brazilian helped him up again – a gesture of ambivalent symbolism.

Kein Zweifel: 1992 hat Nigel Mansell den Zenit seiner Karriere erreicht. Sie nennen ihn den »Löwen« wegen seines Siegeswillens und seiner Kampfstärke. Überdies präsentiert sich das Williams-Aufgebot wie aus einem Guß. Die Symbiose zwischen dem kompakten Chassis FW 14 B und dem V10 von Renault, mit 780 PS das stärkste Triebwerk im Feld und mit geschmeidiger Kraftentfaltung begnadet, funktioniert perfekt, desgleichen die Halbautomatik und die aktive Aufhängung des Williams. Die ersten fünf Großen Preise der Saison hat Mansell in beklemmender Monotonie gewonnen und trifft erfolgssatt und voller stämmiger Zuversicht zur 50. Edition des Grand Prix de Monaco am 31. Mai ein.

Bei McLaren hingegen knistert und kriselt es. Der MP 4/7 zeigt Schwächen, das Prestigeprojekt V12 von Honda ist mit 770 PS voll ausgereizt. In Monza wird man im September das Joint Venture zu Grabe tragen, und die Japaner werden sich in vorläufiger Endgültigkeit aus der Formel 1 zurückziehen. Starpilot Ayrton Senna, sonst vom Erfolg gehätschelt und getätschelt, gibt sich einsilbig und muffig, Teamchef Ron Dennis schroff und zugeknöpft. In Monaco hat man sich diesmal wohl in die Höhle des »Löwen« begeben.

In der Tat stehen die beiden Williams wie ein Bollwerk in der ersten Reihe, Mansell und sein Teamkollege Riccardo Patrese. Während der Brite beim Sprint hin zu Sainte Dévote die Oberhand behält, quetscht sich allerdings Senna ganz innen an dem Italiener vorbei. Ähnliches widerfährt weiter hinten beim Kampf um den fünften Platz Gerhard Berger im anderen McLaren durch Michael Schumacher im Benetton B 192. Jean Alesi hingegen bleibt zunächst da, wo er sich qualifiziert hat: auf Rang vier. Seinem Ferrari F 92 A gebührt ein Preis für bestechende Schönheit, im übrigen ist er ein Flop. Immer mehr gerät der Franzose unter Druck: Schumacher drängt ungestüm von hinten, und einmal, in der elften Runde, verhaken sich die beiden Wagen sogar vor dem Hôtel Loews und seiner champagnertrinkenden Klientel. Gleichwohl nehmen sie ihr Gefecht von neuem auf in der vorherigen Reihenfolge, bis zum 21. Durchgang, als Alesi von seinem Getriebe im Stich gelassen wird. Zehn Minuten später fällt der Ferrari aus. Noch bis ans Heck des zweiten Williams arbeitet sich Schumacher vor, scheitert aber dann an der Routine Patreses und an dessen vielfach bewährter Kunst, Konkurrenten am Überholen zu hindern.

Ganz vorn jedoch tobt der »Löwe« durch die Straßen des Zwergstaats, den sechsten Saisonsieg vor Augen und, so scheint es, auch schon in der Tasche. Doch weit gefehlt: Nach der 70. Runde prescht der Williams an die Box. Ein Reifen ließ Luft, so heißt es. Den Rest des Rennens verbringt Mansell im Windschatten Sennas, und auch der vermag sich Leute vom Leibe zu halten. Knapp eine Viertelsekunde beträgt ihr Abstand am Ende, so wenig wie noch nie.

Als sich Mansell nach der Zieldurchfahrt erschöpft auf den Boden wirft, hilft ihm der Brasilianer wieder auf die Beine – eine Geste von schillernder Symbolik.

Il n'y a pas de doute : en 1992 Nigel Mansell a atteint le zénith de sa carrière. Les fans le surnomment « le Lion » en raison de sa soif de victoires et de son ardeur au combat. De plus, le cocktail concocté par Williams n'a aucun défaut. La symbiose du compact châssis FW14B et du V10 Renault, le plus puissant du plateau avec 780 ch et l'atout supplémentaire d'une montée en puissance souveraine, fonctionne à la perfection, ce qui est aussi le cas de la boîte semi-automatique et de la suspension active de la Williams. Mansell a remporté avec une monotonie lassante les cinq premiers Grands Prix de la saison et s'aligne pour le départ de la 50e édition du Grand Prix de Monaco, le 31 mai, saturé de succès, mais empreint d'une confiance indéfectible.

Chez McLaren, par contre, la crise est latente. La MP 4/7 a de nombreuses maladies de jeunesse et le projet de prestige, le V12 Honda, est au bout du rouleau avec ses 770 ch. En septembre à Monza, la Formule 1 va réserver au joint-venture un enterrement de première classe et les Japonais se retireront « définitivement-provisoirement » de la Formule 1. La super-star Ayrton Senna, elle-même comblée de succès, ne répond aux questions que d'un ton monocorde et las, comme son chef d'écurie Ron Dennis, de mauvaise humeur et peu bavard. A Monaco, ils se sont cette fois-ci bel et bien jetés dans la gueule du « Lion ».

Et, de fait, les deux Williams occupent comme un rempart la première ligne, Mansell devant son coéquipier, Riccardo Patrese. Alors que le Britannique conserve le dessus lors du sprint jusqu'à Sainte Dévote, Senna réussit toutefois à doubler l'Italien en se glissant entre lui et les glissières. Un destin qui sera aussi, loin derrière, dans la bagarre pour la cinquième place, celui de Gerhard Berger sur l'autre McLaren face à Michael Schumacher au volant de la Benetton B 192. Jean Alesi, quant à lui, conserve tout d'abord la place à laquelle il s'est qualifié : la quatrième. Sa Ferrari F 92 A mériterait d'être sacrée reine de beauté à Monaco, mais, pour le reste, c'est un échec. Le Français est de plus en plus sous pression : Schumacher fait des pieds et des mains pour le doubler et, une fois, au onzième tour, les deux voitures s'accrochent même devant l'Hôtel Loews et son gratin d'amateurs de champagne. Cela ne les empêche pas de repartir à l'attaque dans le même ordre jusqu'au 21e tour, lorsque Alesi se voit abandonné par sa boîte de vitesses. Dix minutes plus tard, le pilote Ferrari doit, lui aussi, jeter l'éponge. Schumacher arrive encore à rattraper la seconde Williams, mais achoppe sur la routine de Patrese et son art proverbial d'empêcher les concurrents de le doubler.

Aux avant-postes, pendant ce temps, « le Lion » rugit dans les rues de l'Etat d'opérette, sa sixième victoire de la saison à portée de la main et, semble-t-il, aussi déjà en poche. Mais il ne faut pas vendre la peau de l'ours avant de l'avoir tué : à l'issue du 70e tour, la Williams s'engouffre dans les stands. Crevaison lente. Le reste de la course, Mansell le passe dans le sillage de Senna et lui aussi s'y entend à repousser les attaques de ses adversaires. A peine un quart de seconde sépare les deux hommes à la fin de la course, l'arrivée la plus serrée connue à ce jour.

Lorsque, après avoir franchi le drapeau à damiers, Mansell, épuisé, se laisse tomber au sol, le Brésilien l'aide à se relever – un geste qui ne manque pas de symbolisme.

Flag signal: even the more affluent among the visitors to the 1992 Grand Prix do not hide their support for the "Lion".

Flaggen-Zeichen: Auch die Wohlhabenderen unter den Besuchern des Grand Prix 1992 machen aus ihrer Sympathie für den »Löwen« kein Hehl.

La langue des drapeaux : même les nantis parmi les visiteurs du Grand Prix de 1992 ne cachent pas leur sympathie pour le « Lion ».

N°	DRIVERS		ENTRANTS	CARS	ENGINES	PRACTICE RESULTS	RACE RESULTS
1	**Ayrton Senna**	**BR**	**Marlboro McLaren Honda**	**McLaren MP4/7**	**Honda V12 3493 cc**	**3rd: 1'20"608**	**1st: 1h50'59"372**
5	*Nigel Mansell*	*GB*	*Williams Grand Prix Engineering*	*Williams FW14B*	*Renault V10 3500 cc*	*1st: 1'19"495*	*2nd: 1h50'29"587*
6	Riccardo Patrese	I	Williams Grand Prix Engineering	Williams FW14B	Renault V10 3500 cc	2nd: 1'20"368	3rd: 1h51'31"215
19	Michael Schumacher	D	Benetton Formula Ltd.	Benetton B192	Cosworth V8 3494 cc	6th: 1'21"831	4th: 1h51'38"666
20	Martin Brundle	GB	Benetton Formula Ltd.	Benetton B192	Cosworth V8 3494 cc	7th: 1'22"068	5th: 1h52'20"719
29	Bertrand Gachot	F	Larrousse F1	Venturi LC92	Lamborghini V12 3493 cc	15th: 1'23"122	6th: 77 laps
9	Michele Alboreto	I	Footwork Grand Prix International	Footwork FA13	Mugen-Honda V10 3493 cc	11th: 1'22"671	7th: 77 laps
23	Christian Fittipaldi	BR	Minardi Team S.p.A.	Minardi M192	Lamborghini V12 3493 cc	17th: 1'23"487	8th: 77 laps
21	J. J. Lehto	SF	Scuderia Italia	BMS Dallara F192	Ferrari V12 3495 cc	20th: 1'23"862	9th: 76 laps
26	Eric Comas	F	Ligier Sport	Ligier JS37	Renault V10 3500 cc	23rd: 1'23"974	10th: 76 laps
10	Aguri Suzuki	J	Footwork Grand Prix International	Footwork FA13	Mugen-Honda V10 3493 cc	19th: 1'23"641	11th: 76 laps
25	Thierry Boutsen	B	Ligier Sport	Ligier JS37	Renault V10 3500 cc	22nd: 1'23"909	12th: 75 laps
28	Ivan Capelli	I	SEFAC Ferrari S.p.A.	Ferrari F92A	Ferrari V12 3495 cc	8th: 1'22"119	R
2	Gerhard Berger	A	Marlboro McLaren Honda	McLaren MP4/7	Honda V12 3493 cc	5th: 1'21"224	R
11	Mika Hakkinen	SF	Team Lotus	Lotus 107	Cosworth V8 3494 cc	14th: 1'22"886	R
27	Jean Alesi	F	SEFAC Ferrari S.p.A.	Ferrari F92A	Ferrari V12 3495 cc	4th: 1'20"895	R
33	Maurizio Gugelmin	BR	Jordan Grand Prix	Jordan 192	Yamaha V12 3500 cc	13th: 1'22""863	R
12	Johnny Herbert	GB	Team Lotus	Lotus 107	Cosworth V8 3494 cc	9th: 1'22"579	R
34	Roberto Moreno	BR	Andrea Moda Formula	Andrea Moda S921	Judd V10 3500 cc	26th: 1'24"945	R
4	Andrea de Cesaris	I	Tyrrell Racing Organisation	Tyrrell 020B	Ilmor V10 3500 cc	10th: 1'22"647	R
15	Gabriele Tarquini	I	Fondmetal F1 S.p.A.	Fondmetal GR 01	Cosworth V8 3494 cc	25th: 1'24"479	R
32	Stefano Modena	I	Jordan Grand Prix	Jordan 192	Yamaha V12 3500 cc	21st: 1'23"890	R
3	Olivier Grouillard	F	Tyrrell Racing Organisation	Tyrrell 020B	Ilmor V10 3500 cc	24th: 1'23"990	R
16	Karl Wendlinger	A	March	March CG 911B	Ilmor V10 3500 cc	16th: 1'23"264	R
24	Gianni Morbidelli	I	Minardi Team S.p.A.	Minardi M192	Lamborghini V12 3493 cc	12th: 1'22"733	R
22	Pierluigi Martini	I	Scuderia Italia	BMS Dallara F192	Ferrari V12 3495 cc	18th: 1'23"508	R

(1, 2) 1992 is the year when the Williams driver Mansell turns the red five into a legend. (3) Nevertheless, the winner in Monaco is Ayrton Senna (McLaren), who has success presented to him on a plate on this occasion.

(1, 2) 1992 ist das Jahr, in dem Williams-Pilot Mansell die rote Fünf zum Mythos macht. (3) Der Sieger in Monaco heißt gleichwohl Ayrton Senna (McLaren), dem der Erfolg diesmal gewissermaßen als Geschenk überreicht wird.

(1, 2) 1992 est l'année durant laquelle le pilote de chez Williams, Nigel Mansell, élève le cinq rouge au rang de mythe. (3) Le vainqueur de Monaco cette année-là est néanmoins Ayrton Senna (McLaren), qui remporte cette fois-ci une victoire inespérée.

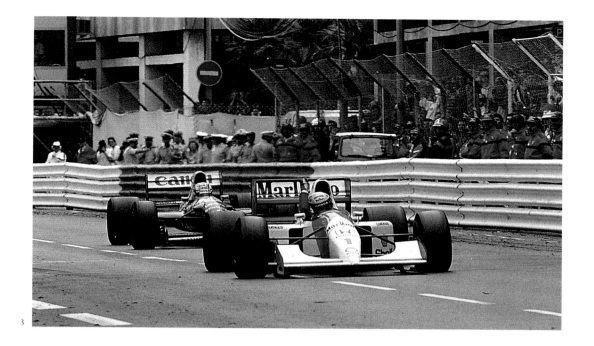

3

(1) Convincing appearance in the Williams: Patrese.
(2) Close encounters of the rough kind: Schumacher (Benetton) tangles with Alesi at Loews. (3) The Frenchman's damaged Ferrari only makes it to lap 28: gearbox trouble. (4, 5) Invincible in the armor of his self-confidence, Senna keeps Mansell at bay – even on the lap of honor.

(1) Überzeugender Auftritt im Williams: Patrese.
(2) Begegnung der ruppigen Art: Schumacher (Benetton) kommt sich bei Loews mit Alesi ins Gehege. (3) Die Fahrt des Franzosen im lädierten Ferrari dauert bis Runde 28: Getriebeschaden. (4, 5) Schier unverletzlich im Panzer seines Selbstvertrauens hält sich Senna Mansell vom Leibe – sogar während der Ehrenrunde.

(1) Démonstration convaincante sur Williams : Patrese.
(2) Corps à corps : Schumacher (Benetton) entre en contact avec Alesi au Loews. (3) La course du Français avec la Ferrari blessée s'achèvera au 28ᵉ tour : panne de boîte de vitesses. (4, 5) Apparemment invulnérable dans l'armure de sa confiance en soi : Senna repousse toutes les attaques de Mansell – même pendant le tour d'honneur.

5

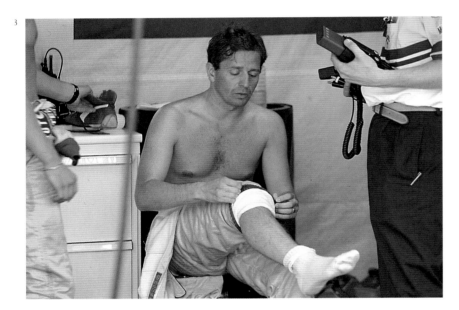

(1) Hand signal: this 31 May is not a good day for Berger. (2) Man down: Mansell is on the ground. Patrese looks on amused. (3) Calm before the storm: Martin Brundle. (4) Both hands full: Mansell has won the first five Grands Prix of the season, but Senna wins his fifth Grand Prix de Monaco.

(1) Hand-Zeichen: Berger hat mit diesem 31. Mai keinen guten Tag erwischt. (2) Mansell am Boden: Patrese schaut amüsiert zu. (3) Ruhe vor dem Sturm: Martin Brundle. (4) Zwei Hände voll: Mansell hat die ersten fünf Grands Prix der Saison gewonnen, Senna gewinnt seinen fünften Großen Preis von Monaco.

(1) Signe de la main : ce 31 mai ne porte pas bonheur à Berger. (2) Mansell sur le sol. Patrese le regarde d'un air amusé. (3) Le calme avant la tempête : Martin Brundle. (4) A pleines mains : Mansell a remporté les cinq premiers Grands Prix de la saison, mais Senna gagne son cinquième Grand Prix de Monaco.

LIONHEART

LÖWENHERZ · CŒUR DE LION

In the past 45 years we lost an empire, but instead we won the Falklands war and Nigel Mansell", an English colleague commented at the start of the 1990s, with that reflective sarcasm which always contains a grain of truth. In the last quarter of this period, Mansell blossomed from an extra into the darling of the statisticians.

Before the majesty of his 31 Grand Prix wins, that other British icon of motor sport history, Stirling Moss, pales into insignificance. As a freelance working for the American publication *Road & Track,* Stirling, ironically, had for a time to report to his readers on the implosion of his own legend, that of being the greatest driver never to have won a World Championship. Until 1992 – then Mansell became Champion and the status quo returned.

And there is something else which puts Mansell ahead of his cool compatriot Moss. He is a gifted self-publicist, straight from the libretto of a 19th century opera, who plays the whole gamut from joy to frustration. "A man of the people", the Fleet Street press celebrates him. English patriots claim him for their own as "Our Nige". And Italian fans were still giving him his combat name "Il Leone" (the Lion) two years after his time with Ferrari.

Is Nigel Mansell a nice person? "Rubbish", answers Mansell's former boss Frank Williams. "Mister Nice Guy does not get very far in this field. Prost, Senna, Mansell – they are here to win. To do this they are capable of anything." Mansell the fighter: in Silverstone 1987, his team-mate Nelson Piquet was leading until just before the end of the race. Pushed far behind by a pit stop, Mansell then humiliated the Brazilian with one record lap after another, finally to push past him unstoppably. But Piquet became World Champion that year.

Later, another Brazilian brought out the beast in Mansell: Ayrton Senna. In Monaco in 1992, the Briton had to go into the pits again. Then his Williams clung to the back of Senna's McLaren as if attached by a towrope. Mansell called on all his skills while the other countered them with everything he knew until they raced past the finishing line. Maleficence at 150 mph.

Driven by compulsion at the wheel, Mansell is not averse to a man-to-man fight, either. The whole of him then turns into a physically uncoordinated problem area. In Barcelona in 1991, he hit out at Gerhard Berger. Without harmful intent, he had knocked against the ankle which Mansell had twisted two days before in a football match against journalists. And in Spa in 1987, he grabbed his arch enemy Senna by the lapels after the two had clashed during the second lap.

Mansell the man of sorrows: in Adelaide in 1986 a rear tyre of the Williams blew at 180 miles per hour. For half an eternity the driver and his car were suspended in the no-man's land between existence and non-existence. Hours later, Mansell's sorrowful face still bore the expression of someone who had been deeply wounded by the tricks of fate. Alain Prost became World Champion.

Without restraint, Mansell gave the magma of his emotions free reign in Monaco in 1992 after he had crossed the finishing line, documented audio-visually in 300 million households: "Il Leone", supported by a bull-

In den vergangenen 45 Jahren haben wir ein Weltreich verloren, dafür aber den Falkland-Krieg und Nigel Mansell«, sagt Anfang der Neunziger ein englischer Kollege über ihn, mit jenem nachdenklichen Sarkasmus, in dem immer auch ein Fünkchen Ernst steckt. Im letzten Viertel dieser Zeitspanne hat sich Mansell vom Statisten zum Hätschelkind der Statistiker gemausert.

Vor der Majestät seiner 31 gewonnenen Grand Prix verblaßt ein anderer britischer Heiliger der Motorsport-Historie zur wurmstichigen Ikone: Stirling Moss. Als freier Mitarbeiter der amerikanischen Publikation *Road & Track* muß er eine Zeitlang seinen Lesern ironischerweise von der Implosion seines eigenen Mythos berichten: der größte Fahrer zu sein, der niemals eine Weltmeisterschaft gewann. Bis 1992 – da wird Mansell Champion, und der Status quo ist wieder hergestellt.

Und noch eines hat Mansell seinem kühlen Landsmann Moss voraus. Er ist ein begnadeter Selbstdarsteller, wie einem italienischen Opernlibretto des 19. Jahrhunderts entsprungen, bespielt die ganze Bandbreite zwischen Lust und Frust total, von himmelhoch jauchzend bis zu Tode betrübt, ohne indessen den Namen Goethe auch nur buchstabieren zu können. »Ein Mann des Volkes« frohlockt die Fleet-Street-Presse. Als »Our Nige« vereinnahmen ihn englische Patrioten. Und mit dem Kriegernamen »Il Leone« (der Löwe) schmücken ihn die italienischen Fans noch zwei Jahre nach seiner Zeit bei Ferrari.

Ist Nigel Mansell ein angenehmer Mensch? »Schnickschnack«, antwortet Mansells Chef Frank Williams. »Mister Nice Guy bringt es nicht weit in dieser Branche. Prost, Senna, Mansell – sie sind hier, um zu gewinnen. Dafür sind sie zu allem fähig.« Mansell der Fighter: In Silverstone 1987 führt Teamkollege Nelson Piquet bis kurz vor Schluß des Rennens. Durch einen Boxenstopp weit zurückgeworfen, demütigt Mansell den schönen Brasilianer mit einer Rekordrunde nach der anderen und zieht schließlich unwiderstehlich vorbei. Weltmeister wird dennoch Piquet.

Später bringt ein anderer Brasilianer das Biest in Mansell heraus: Ayrton Senna. Auch in Monaco 1992 muß der Brite an die Box. Anschließend hängt der Williams wie durch ein Abschleppseil gezerrt am Heck von Sennas McLaren. Mansell bietet alles auf, was er kann, der andere hält mit allem dagegen, was er weiß, bis ins Ziel, Malefiz bei Tempo 250.

Ein Triebtäter am Lenkrad, geht Modellathlet Mansell auch einer Keilerei von Mensch zu Mensch nicht aus dem Weg. Der ganze Mann wird dann zur motorisch unkoordinierten Problemzone. In Barcelona 1991 setzt es Hiebe für Gerhard Berger. Der hat arglostäppisch gegen den Knöchel gepocht, den sich Mansell zwei Tage zuvor bei einem Fußballspiel gegen Journalisten verstaucht hat. Und in Spa 1987 nimmt er Erzfeind Senna beim Schlafittchen, nachdem die beiden in einer Rempelei in der zweiten Runde aneinandergeraten sind.

Mansell der Schmerzensmann: In Adelaide 1986 detoniert bei 300 Stundenkilometern ein Hinterreifen des Williams. Eine halbe Ewigkeit torkeln Fahrer und Wagen im Niemandsland zwischen Sein und Nichtsein. Aber über Mansells wehem Antlitz lagert noch Stunden

Ces 45 dernières années, nous avons perdu un empire, mais, en revanche, gagné la guerre des Malouines et Nigel Mansell », déclare à son sujet, au début des années 90, un collègue anglais avec ce sarcasme à double sens dans lequel réside toujours aussi une petite pointe de sérieux. Durant le dernier quart de cette période, Mansell s'est métamorphosé de pâle figurant en coqueluche des fanas de la course et des spécialistes de la statistique.

Devant la majesté de ses trente et une victoires en Grand Prix, un autre saint britannique de l'histoire de la compétition automobile ne fait plus figure que d'icône piquée par les vers : Stirling Moss. En tant que collaborateur *free-lance* de la revue spécialisée américaine *Road & Track,* il doit, pendant un certain temps, ironiquement consacrer, pour ses lecteurs, des reportages à l'implosion de son propre mythe : avoir été le plus grand pilote qui n'aura jamais remporté un championnat du monde. Mais cela ne dure que jusqu'en 1992 – car, cette année-là, Mansell coiffe la couronne et rétablit le statu quo.

Et il y a encore une chose par laquelle Mansell a l'avantage sur son froid compatriote Moss. Il sait se mettre en scène de façon inimitable, comme dans le livret d'un opéra italien du 19e siècle, décline toutes les variations des états d'âme de l'homme, de l'allégresse à la frustration, un jour criant sa joie au ciel pour arborer une mine d'enterrement le lendemain, sans même pouvoir épeler correctement le nom de Goethe. « Un homme du peuple », titrent gaiement les tabloïds de Fleet Street. Sous le nom de « Our Nige », les patriotes anglais le font rouler pour eux. Et avec le surnom de guerre « Il Leone » (le Lion), les *tifosi* italiens le célèbrent encore, deux ans après son départ de chez Ferrari.

Nigel Mansell est-il un homme de bon rapport ? « Ce n'est pas là la question », répète Frank Williams, l'ancien chef de Mansell. « Mister Nice Guy, celui qui n'est pas un battant, n'ira pas loin dans cette branche. Prost, Senna, Mansell – ils sont ici pour gagner. Et, pour cela, ils sont capables de tout. » Mansell *the Fighter* : à Silverstone, en 1987, son coéquipier Nelson Piquet est en tête à quelques encablures de l'arrivée. Rejeté loin en arrière par suite d'un arrêt aux stands, Mansell humilie ensuite le Brésilien en signant un record du tour après l'autre et il finit par le doubler imparablement. Mais le champion du monde cette année, ce sera Piquet.

Plus tard, un autre Brésilien fait se réveiller la bête qui sommeille en Mansell : Ayrton Senna. A Monaco aussi, en 1992, le Britannique doit rentrer aux stands. Ensuite, la Williams reste collée à la boîte de vitesses de la McLaren de Senna. Mansell tire toutes les flèches de son carquois, l'autre réplique avec toutes les astuces qu'il a dans sa boîte à malices, jusqu'à l'arrivée, véritable danse sur le volcan à plus de 250 km/h.

Obsessionnel au volant, l'athlète modèle qu'est Mansell ne recule non plus devant aucun combat au corps à corps. Sa motricité échappant à tout contrôle, l'homme entier devient alors une zone à problèmes. A Barcelone en 1991, Gerhard Berger s'en tire avec quelques coups de poing. Ingénu et empoté, celui-ci l'avait frappé involontairement juste contre la cheville que Mansell s'était foulée deux jours plus tôt lors d'un match de football contre des journalistes. Et, à Spa en

necked official like a feverish infant, shaking and swaying. Shock or show – he probably did not know himself. In Montreal 14 days later he attacked Senna at a spot where this is simply not done, skidded off the track and landed back on it at right-angles to an approaching wave of racing cars. For one-and-a-half minutes he remained in the car, frozen into a symbol of silent reproach under his crash helmet and flameproof overalls. But it was a demonstration which backfired on him: "Unforced error", is the cold analysis of the ex-McLaren driver and former Eurosport reporter John Watson, an awful boob.

Mansell happy: always after a win, of course, but above all at Silverstone, the holy of holies of English motor racing. There are few people in the Grand Prix circus who are less restrained in their happiness than "Our Nige". And more likeable – everyone at Williams

später das Stigma dessen, den die Schikanen des Schicksals bis ins Mark getroffen haben. Weltmeister wird Alain Prost.

Ungehemmt läßt Mansell dem Magma seiner Emotionen 1992 in Monaco nach der Zieldurchfahrt freien Lauf, audiovisuell dokumentiert in 300 Millionen Haushalten: »Il Leone« im Arm eines stiernackigen Offiziellen wie ein fiebernder Säugling, zitternd und wankend. Schock oder Show – vermutlich weiß er's selber nicht. In Montreal 14 Tage später attackiert er Senna an einer Stelle, wo man so etwas einfach nicht tut, rutscht von der Strecke, strandet wieder auf ihr, quer zum anbrandenden Rennwagenverkehr. Anderthalb Minuten bleibt er im Wagen, unter Sturzhelm und zündelsicherem Overall ganz zum stummen Vorwurf erstarrt. Dabei demonstriert er nur gegen sich selbst: »Unforced error«, analysiert Ex-

1987, il en vient aux mains avec son ennemi intime Ayrton Senna après que les deux hommes sont entrés en collision au cours du cinquième tour.

Mansell, l'expression même de la douleur : à Adelaïde en 1986, le pneu arrière gauche de sa Williams se désintègre à 300 km/h. Pendant ce qui semble une éternité, le pilote et son bolide serpentent dans le no man's land entre l'être et le ne pas être. Et, des heures plus tard, le faciès de Mansell affiche encore les stigmates de celui que la dureté du destin a touché jusqu'au plus profond de la moelle épinière. Une saison entière bascule en une fraction de seconde et Alain Prost est sacré champion du monde.

Sans scrupules, Mansell laisse éclater au grand jour le magma en fusion de ses émotions, en 1992 à Monaco, après avoir franchi l'arrivée, documenté en direct sur 300 millions d'écrans de télévision :

is first of all given a short handshake, a few nice words, a brief embrace. In the meantime, the Ferrari people from next door applaud "Il Leone" although he has not been one of theirs for a long time. A nice person after all, and particularly when he is in a good mood, as a hobby policeman, for instance, on the Isle of Man, where he lived for a few years, calling on traffic offenders to drive defensively. Or in a game of golf with the world class player Greg Norman, his friend, for whom he can provide some serious opposition with a handicap of 4 and falling.

Nigel Mansell in 1992: the best there ever was, trained to the tips of his toes with gymnastics, jogging on a sloping track, then gymnastics again for three hours per day. At the end he jumps into the water several times with weights and dives until there is no breath left in his body. His yacht is called *Lionheart* – here Nigel Mansell is without doubt flirting with Nigel Mansell.

However: towards the end of that Championship season, frost began to appear on the relationship between employer Frank Williams and his impulsive star. In a fit of pique, Mansell emigrated to the United States, sought his fortune in the IndyCar series, won the Championship at his first attempt in 1993 – phenomenal. After Senna's death at Imola, in 1994, a seat in the Williams cockpit became vacant for the rest of the season. Agreement was reached for several races, half sulkingly, half grudgingly. But Frank Williams was plotting, putting his faith in new names. In 1995, the Scot David Coulthard was to drive for him next to Damon Hill. This was the beginning of the rapidly approaching end for Mansell in Formula 1. With two lacklustre Grands Prix in the McLaren, Mansell wrote a sad epilogue to his unprecedented success story.

He will never understand that even lions grow old.

McLaren-Pilot und Eurosport-Reporter John Watson kalt, ein grober Schnitzer.

Mansell im Glück: immer nach Siegen natürlich, vor allem in Silverstone, dem Allerheiligsten des englischen Motorsports. Kaum jemand im Grand-Prix-Zirkus freut sich unbändiger als »Our Nige«. Und sympathischer – jeder bei Williams bekommt erst einmal einen kurzen Händedruck, ein gutes Wort, eine flüchtige Umarmung. Unterdessen applaudieren die Ferrari-Leute von nebenan, obwohl der »Löwe« längst nicht mehr einer der ihren ist. Ein netter Mensch eben doch, und erst recht, wenn er gut drauf ist, als Hobby-Marshal der Polizei auf dem heimischen Eiland Isle of Man zum Beispiel, der Verkehrssünder zu defensivem Fahrverhalten auffordert. Oder beim Golfspielen gegen den Weltklassemann Greg Norman, seinen Freund, dem er mit Handicap 4 durchaus ein ernsthafter Gegner sein kann.

Nigel Mansell 1992: der beste, den es je gab, austrainiert bis in die Spitzen seines Schnäuzers, mit Gymnastik, Joggen auf einem schrägen Laufband, wieder Gymnastik, täglich drei Stunden. Am Ende springt er mehrmals mit Gewichten ins Wasser und taucht, bis ihm die Puste wegbleibt. Seine Yacht heißt *Lionheart*, Löwenherz – da kokettiert Nigel Mansell ohne Zweifel mit Nigel Mansell.

Indes: Spätestens gegen Ende der Saison glitzert Rauhreif auf dem Verhältnis zwischen Arbeitgeber Frank Williams und seinem impulsiven Star. Mansell wandert pikiert in die Vereinigten Staaten aus, sucht sein Glück im IndyCar, gewinnt auf Anhieb die Meisterschaft 1993 – phänomenal. Nach Sennas Tod in Imola 1994 ist für den Rest der Saison ein Sitz im Williams-Cockpit vakant. Man einigt sich halb schmollend und grollend für den Rest der Saison. Aber Frank Williams brütet Verrat, setzt auf neue Namen. 1995 soll neben Damon Hill der Schotte David Coulthard für ihn fahren. Von nun an geht's bergab, und zwar rapide. Mit zwei lustlosen Grands Prix im McLaren schreibt Mansell einen tristen Epilog unter seine beispiellose Erfolgsstory.

Daß selbst Löwen altern, wird er nie verstehen.

« il Leone » tombe dans les bras d'un officiel à la nuque de taureau tel un nourrisson frappé par la fièvre, tremblant et chancelant. Choc ou show – sans doute ne le sait-il même pas lui-même. A Montréal, quinze jours plus tard, il attaque Senna à un endroit où cela équivaut au suicide, quitte la piste, revient sur celle-ci en dérapage, en travers de la meute de voitures de course qui déboulent vers lui. Pendant une minute et demie, il reste dans sa voiture, paralysé en un reproche muet sous son casque et dans sa combinaison ininflammable. Ce faisant, il ne manifeste que contre lui-même : « unforced error », analyse froidement John Watson, expilote de McLaren et ancien commentateur pour la chaîne de télévision Eurosport. Erreur impardonnable.

Mansell comblé de bonheur : après chaque victoire, naturellement, en particulier à Silverstone, le saint des saints de la compétition automobile britannique. Pratiquement personne dans le cirque des Grands Prix ne se réjouit de façon plus extravertie que « Our Nige ». Ni avec plus de sympathie – chacun, chez Williams, se voit tout d'abord donner une brève poignée de main, entend prononcer un mot de reconnaissance, se voit pris furtivement dans les bras. Pendant ce temps, les gens de chez Ferrari, à côté, applaudissent, bien que « le Lion » ait depuis longtemps cessé d'être des leurs. C'est tout simplement un type sympa, a fortiori lorsqu'il est en forme, en tant que marshal amateur de la police de l'Ile de Man, où il a momentanément élu domicile et éduque les chauffards à adopter un style de conduite défensif. Ou bien quand il joue au golf contre « le Requin » Greg Norman, son ami, l'un des meilleurs joueurs professionnels du monde, pour lequel, avec un handicap de 4, Mansell pourrait fort bien s'avérer un adversaire redoutable.

Nigel Mansell en 1992 : le meilleur crû que l'on n'ait jamais connu, en forme jusqu'à la pointe de sa moustache, qui s'adonne à la gymnastique, au jogging sur un tapis roulant incliné, de nouveau à la gymnastique, et ce au rythme de trois heures par jour. A la fin, il saute plusieurs fois dans l'eau avec des poids et reste sous la surface jusqu'au moment où ses poumons menacent d'éclater. Il a baptisé son yacht *Lionheart*, cœur de lion – non sans humour, Nigel Mansell citant Nigel Mansell.

Et pourtant, au plus tard vers la fin de cette saison de championnat, le torchon commence à brûler entre son employeur Frank Williams et sa vedette impulsive. Vexé, Mansell émigre aux Etats-Unis, tente sa chance en IndyCar et remporte d'emblée le championnat de 1993 – un phénomène ! Après la mort de Senna, à Imola en 1994, un siège devient vacant dans le cockpit d'une Williams pour le reste de la saison. Bon gré mal gré, les deux hommes se mettent d'accord plusieurs courses. Mais Frank Williams craint d'être trahi, il mise sur de nouveaux noms. En 1995, il veut que l'Ecossais David Coulthard le rejoigne comme coéquipier de Damon Hill. Dès lors, c'est le début de fin de carrière en Formule 1 pour Mansell. Après deux Grands Prix accomplis sans enthousiasme, Mansell met un point final, avec un triste épilogue, à sa si brillante « success story ».

Il n'admettra sans doute jamais que même les lions vieillissent.

His opponents accuse him of being unnecessarily tough. Yet Mansell is a classic racing driver, still a public attraction and money-spinner not only in the United Kingdom, as well as being friendly and sociable on a personal level.

Seine Gegner kreiden ihm unnötige Härte an. Dabei ist Mansell der Rennfahrer, wie er im Buche steht, ein Publikumsmagnet und Kassenfüller nicht nur auf der Insel und darüberhinaus freundlich und umgänglich in der persönlichen Begegnung.

Ses adversaires lui reprochent une dureté non nécessaire. Or Mansell est le pilote de course par excellence, adulé du public, il fait sonner le tiroir-caisse des organisateurs non seulement en Angleterre et, en outre, il est convivial et de bon rapport.

1993

"The king is dead, long live the king" is the formula of shifting allegiances. The old king of Monaco was Graham Hill, with five wins, who had been killed in a plane crash on 29 November 1975. The new king was Ayrton Senna. As early as 1992 he staked his claim to the vacant throne when he achieved Hill's record. On 23 May 1993 the enigmatic Brazilian added another win and became the undisputed ruler. Nevertheless, the victories no longer came quite as easily. The qualifying results show that clearly enough: from 1988 to 1991 he started from the front row of the grid, from 1989 in pole position; in 1992 and 1993 this became the second row, where third place was reserved for him.

But even in third place on the grid Senna could afford to smile at a job well done, for the McLaren stable, previously so full of confidence in white and red, had for some time been plunging towards the second-rate. Team boss Ron Dennis had lost out in the gamble for the strongest engines and had had to make do with an off-the-peg Ford V8, around which designer Neil Oatley had designed the compact MP 4/8 chassis. Whereas Senna, the genius of the open throttle, was good for one second per lap, his partner Michael Andretti, struggling to come to terms with Formula 1, would finish the race in eighth position, two laps behind. That said it all.

The people who really made this Grand Prix, however, were the men of the first rank. Alain Prost stood in pole position, returned from his one-year early retirement and destined to become World Champion once more with his Williams FW 15. Michael Schumacher lurked beside him in a Benetton B 193, the new rising star in the racing driver firmament. Shortly before the lights turned to green, the Frenchman made a rare error. The Williams crept forward and had to be stopped before then making a perfect start. That would return to haunt him. On the tenth lap Prost was ordered into the pits to serve a time penalty. The usual ten seconds were supplemented by a further 20 when the Renault V10 died on him and resolutely refused to start again for a time. When Prost shot back onto the race track, fuming with anger, he had fallen back to 22nd place, one lap behind.

Michael Schumacher was in the lead and, driving like a man possessed, had already taken 20 seconds off Senna. The twilight of the gods seemed to be beckoning to the Brazilian when the German stopped in front of Hôtel Loews on lap 33 with defective transmission hydraulics. A small fire was smouldering, but was quickly extinguished. At that point Alain Prost had just reached eighth place, he was in points position again by lap 37, and came fourth in the end. Perseverance pays.

But Senna held on to his lead, even with a final pit-stop. It was his last Monaco Grand Prix. Long live the king, as the saying goes. Ayrton Senna da Silva, however, was to remain among us only until the 1994 San Marino Grand Prix; after that, the blazing Grand Prix microcosm was to lose a little of its brilliance.

Der König ist tot, es lebe der König, lautet die Formel des schnöden Vergessens. Der alte König von Monaco: Graham Hill, fünf Siege, mit dem Flugzeug abgestürzt am 29. November 1975. Der neue: Ayrton Senna. Schon 1992 macht er seinen Anspruch auf den vakanten Thron geltend, als er Hills Rekord einstellt. Am 23. Mai 1993 sattelt der enigmatische Brasilianer noch einmal drauf und herrscht nun unumschränkt. Allerdings geht ihm das Siegen nicht mehr ganz so leicht von der Hand. Die Resultate im Training bilden das getreulich ab: Zwischen 1988 und 1991 startete er aus der ersten Reihe, ab 1989 aus der Pole Position, 1992 und 1993 aus der zweiten, wo Rang drei für ihn reserviert ist.

Und so ist der lachende Erste zugleich der lachende Dritte. Denn sein McLaren-Rennstall, früher ganz Zuversicht in Weißrot, stürzt längst im freien Fall in die Zweitrangigkeit ab. Im Poker um die stärksten Maschinen hat Teamchef Ron Dennis diesmal verloren und muß sich mit einem Ford V8 von der Stange begnügen, um den herum Konstrukteur Neil Oatley das kompakte Chassis MP 4/8 entworfen hat. Wo der Vollgas-Genius Senna für eine Sekunde je Runde gut ist, landet sein Partner Michael Andretti auf Platz acht – zwei Runden zurück. Das sagt alles.

Eigentlich gestaltet aber wird dieser Grand Prix von den Männern aus dem ersten Glied. Auf Startplatz eins steht Alain Prost, aus einjähriger Frührente zurückgekehrt, um mit dem Williams FW 15 noch einmal Champion zu werden. Neben ihm lauert im Benetton B 193 Michael Schumacher, der neue Komet am Rennfahrerhimmel. Kurz bevor die Ampel auf Grün geschaltet wird, macht der Franzose einen seiner seltenen Schnitzer. Der Williams kriecht, muß erst wieder zum Stillstand gebracht werden, ehe er einen perfekten Start hinlegt. Das soll sich bitter rächen: In der zehnten Runde wird Prost zum Abbüßen einer Zeitstrafe in die Box bestellt. Zu den üblichen zehn Sekunden kommen zwanzig weitere, weil der Renault V10 abstirbt und eine Zeitlang hartnäckig den Dienst verweigert. Als Prost schäumend vor Wut wieder auf die Strecke schießt, ist er auf die 22. Position zurückgefallen, eine Runde im Rückstand.

Michael Schumacher führt, wie entfesselt fahrend, hat Senna bereits 20 Sekunden abgeknöpft. Am Horizont scheint die Götterdämmerung für den Brasilianer zu grauen, da hält der Deutsche in Runde 33 mit defekter Getriebehydraulik vor dem Hôtel Loews. Ein Feuerchen kokelt, ist aber rasch erstickt. Alain Prost ist just wieder auf Platz acht angelangt, findet sich in Runde 37 erneut in den Punkterängen und wird am Ende vierter. Denn Hartnäckigkeit zahlt sich aus.

Senna jedoch braucht seine Führung nicht einmal mehr beim letzten Boxenstopp abzugeben. Es ist sein letzter Grand Prix de Monaco. Es lebe der König, so heißt es. Ayrton Senna da Silva indes ist nur noch bis zum 1. Mai 1994 unter uns, bis zu jenem Großen Preis von San Marino, nach dem der gleißende Mikrokosmos Grand Prix ein wenig dunkler sein wird.

Le roi est mort, vive le roi ! proclame la formule dédiée à l'oubli du commun des mortels. Le vieux roi de Monaco, c'est Graham Hill, avec cinq victoires à son palmarès, dont l'avion s'est écrasé le 29 novembre 1975. Le nouveau, c'est Ayrton Senna. Dès 1992 il revendique le trône vacant en égalant le record de Graham Hill. Le 23 mai 1993, l'énigmatique Brésilien bat ce record et est désormais le souverain incontesté. Il n'aligne toutefois plus les victoires avec autant de facilité que jadis. Les résultats des essais en sont le reflet fidèle : de 1988 à 1991, il prend le départ en première ligne ; à partir de 1989 depuis la pole position, mais, en 1992 et 1993, de la deuxième ligne où la troisième place lui est réservée.

Mais, même en étant troisième au départ, Senna peut être vraiment content de sa performance. En effet, son écurie McLaren, jadis l'expression de la confiance même avec ses fières couleurs blanc et rouge est en chute libre dans l'anonymat. Dans la partie de poker pour les moteurs les plus puissants, le chef d'écurie Ron Dennis a perdu cette fois-ci et doit se contenter d'un Ford V8 client autour duquel son ingénieur Neil Oatley a conçu le châssis compact MP 4/8. Alors que Senna, le génie de l'accélérateur, gagne une bonne seconde par tour, son coéquipier, Michael Andretti, ayant toutes les peines du monde à mater sa Formule 1, se retrouve huitième, à deux tours du Brésilien. C'est tout dire.

Ce sont en réalité les hommes du premier peloton qui dicteront ce Grand Prix. La pole position est occupée par Alain Prost, de retour d'une retraite prématurée d'un an, qui veut devenir une nouvelle fois champion du monde avec la Williams FW 15. A côté de lui se tapit, dans la Benetton B 193, Michael Schumacher, la nouvelle comète au firmament des pilotes de course. Juste avant que le feu ne passe au vert, le Français commet l'une de ses rares erreurs. Sa Williams frémit imperceptiblement et doit de nouveau s'arrêter avant de signer un départ parfait. La facture ne se fait pas attendre, et elle est lourde : au dixième tour, Prost est arrêté aux stands pour une pénalité de dix secondes. A ces dix secondes normales s'en ajoutent vingt autres parce que le Renault V10 s'étouffe et refuse avec entêtement de redémarrer. Lorsque Prost reprend la piste, écumant de fureur, il est retombé à la 22ᵉ place et accuse un tour de retard.

Déchaîné, Michael Schumacher emmène la meute et a déjà vingt secondes d'avance sur Senna. Le crépuscule des dieux semble se profiler à l'horizon quand l'Allemand, au 33ᵉ tour, est contraint à s'arrêter devant l'Hôtel Loews sur panne d'hydraulique de boîte de vitesses. Une petite flamme s'allume, mais est elle éteinte immédiatement. Pendant ce temps, Alain Prost poursuit sa remontée et est alors huitième ; au 37ᵉ tour, il est de nouveau dans les points et termine quatrième. Ne jamais jeter l'éponge porte toujours ses fruits.

Mais Senna n'a même pas à craindre de perdre son leadership lors de son dernier arrêt aux stands. Ce sera son dernier Grand Prix de Monaco. Vive le roi ! dit-on. Ayrton Senna da Silva ne sera plus des nôtres que jusqu'au 1ᵉʳ mai 1994, jusqu'à ce funeste Grand Prix de San Marino, à Imola, après lequel le microcosme scintillant des Grands Prix sera devenu un peu plus sombre.

Quiet withdrawal: like his compatriot Berger, the Austrian Karl Wendlinger can draw renewed strength from a few minutes of relaxation.

Rückzug in die Ruhe: Mit seinem Landsmann Berger teilt der Österreicher Karl Wendlinger die Fähigkeit, aus ein paar Minuten Entspannung neue Kraft zu schöpfen.

Sieste : avec son compatriote Berger, l'Autrichien Karl Wendlinger partage la capacité à tirer une énergie nouvelle de quelques minutes de détente.

N°	DRIVERS		ENTRANTS	CARS	ENGINES	PRACTICE RESULTS	RACE RESULTS
8	**Ayrton Senna**	**BR**	**McLaren International**	**McLaren MP4/8**	**Ford V8 3500 cc**	**3rd: 1'21"552**	**1st: 1h52'10"947**
0	Damon Hill	GB	Williams Grand Prix Engineering	Williams FW15	Renault V10 3500 cc	4th: 1'21"825	2nd: 1h53'03"165
27	Jean Alesi	F	SEFAC Ferrari S.p.A.	Ferrari F93A	Ferrari V12 3495 cc	5th: 1'21"948	3rd: 1h53'14"309
2	*Alain Prost*	*F*	*Williams Grand Prix Engineering*	*Williams FW15*	*Renault V10 3500 cc*	*1st: 1'20"557*	*4th: 77 laps*
23	Christian Fittipaldi	BR	Minardi Team S.p.A.	Minardi M193	Ford V8 3500 cc	17th: 1'24"298	5th: 76 laps
25	Martin Brundle	GB	Ligier Sports	Ligier JS39	Renault V10 3500 cc	13th: 1'23"786	6th: 76 laps
11	Alessandro Zanardi	I	Lotus Team International	Lotus 107B	Ford V8 3500 cc	20th: 1'24"888	7th: 76 laps
7	Michael Andretti	USA	McLaren International	McLaren MP4/8	Ford V8 3500 cc	9th: 1'22"994	8th: 76 laps
14	Rubens Barrichello	BR	Jordan Grand Prix	Jordan 193	Hart V10 3500 cc	16th: 1'24"086	9th: 76 laps
4	Andrea de Cesaris	I	Tyrrell Racing Organisation	Tyrrell 020C	Yamaha V10 3500 cc	19th: 1'24"544	10th: 76 laps
24	Fabrizio Barbazza	I	Minardi Team S.p.A.	Minardi M193	Ford V8 3500 cc	25th: 1'26"582	11th: 75 laps
19	Philippe Alliot	F	Larrousse F1	Larrousse LH93	Lamborghini V12 3493 cc	15th: 1'23"907	12th: 75 laps
29	Karl Wendlinger	A	Team P. P. Sauber	Sauber C12	Ilmor V10 3500 cc	8th: 1'22"477	13th 74 laps
28	Gerhard Berger	A	SEFAC Ferrari S.p.A.	Ferrari F93A	Ferrari V12 3495 cc	7th: 1'22"394	14th 70 laps (R)
12	Johnny Herbert	GB	Lotus Team International	Lotus 107B	Ford V8 3500 cc	14th: 1'23"812	R
6	Riccardo Patrese	I	Benetton Formula Ltd.	Benetton B193B	Ford V8 3500 cc	6th: 1'22"117	R
20	Eric Comas	F	Larrousse F1	Larrousse LH93	Lamborghini V12 3493 cc	10th: 1'23"246	R
10	Aguri Suzuki	J	Footwork Racing	Footwork FA14	Mugen-Honda V10 3493 cc	18th: 1'24"524	R
9	Derek Warwick	GB	Footwork Racing	Footwork FA14	Mugen-Honda V10 3493 cc	12th: 1'23"749	R
5	Michael Schumacher	D	Benetton Formula Ltd.	Benetton B193B	Ford V8 3500 cc	2nd: 1'21"190	R
3	Ukyo Katayama	J	Tyrrell Racing Organisation	Tyrrell 020C	Yamaha V10 3500 cc	22th: 1'25"236	R
21	Michele Alboreto	I	Scuderia Italia	Lola-BMS T93/30	Ferrari V12 3495 cc	24th: 1'26"444	R
30	J. J. Lehto	SF	Team P. P. Sauber	Sauber C12	Ilmor V10 3500 cc	11th: 1'23"715	R
15	Thierry Boutsen	B	Jordan Grand Prix	Jordan 193	Hart V10 3500 cc	23rd: 1'25"267	R
26	Mark Blundell	GB	Ligier Sports	Ligier JS39	Renault V10 3500 cc	21st: 1'24"972	R

(1) First arrival at Sainte Dévote: Prost (Williams) is just ahead of Schumacher (Benetton), while Damon Hill in the second Williams cannot fight off Senna's (McLaren) attack. (2) Zero lap: Hill on his way to fourth place on the starting grid. (3) Slight understeer: Schumacher. (4) Winner's fist: Senna. (5) Fifth in qualifying, third in the race, dissatisfied: Alesi (Ferrari). (6) Second start in Monaco, fifth at the finish: Christian Fittipaldi (Minardi).

(1) Erste Ankunft bei Sainte Dévote: Prost (Williams) führt knapp vor Schumacher (Benetton), während dahinter Damon Hill im zweiten Williams den Angriff Sennas (McLaren) nicht abwehren kann. (2) Null-Runde: Hill auf seinem Weg zu Startplatz vier. (3) Leicht untersteuernd: Schumacher, (4) Die Faust des Siegers: Senna. (5) Fünfter im Training, dritter im Rennen, nicht zufrieden: Alesi (Ferrari). (6) Zweiter Start in Monaco, Rang fünf: Christian Fittipaldi (Minardi).

(1) Première arrivée à Sainte-Dévote : Prost (Williams) en tête talonné par Schumacher (Benetton) tandis que, derrière, Damon Hill, sur la deuxième Williams, ne parvient pas à repousser l'attaque de Senna (McLaren). (2) Un tour pour rien : Hill se dirigeant vers sa quatrième place sur la grille. (3) Léger sous-virage : Schumacher. (4) Le poing du vainqueur : Senna. (5) Cinquième aux essais, troisième en course, pas satisfait : Alesi (Ferrari). (6) Deuxième départ à Monaco, cinquième place : Christian Fittipaldi (Minardi).

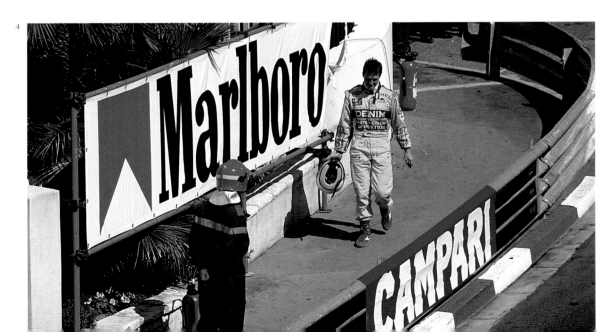

(1) Rain break: Hill in qualifying. (2) On rain tires: the two Ferraris. (3) While the color from Schumacher's Benetton disappears under the foam, (4) the driver returns on foot to the pits. (5) Hanging on: Berger's Ferrari is recovered after a collision with Hill. (6) Concept by Mercedes-Benz: Ilmor engine in the Sauber. (7) Concept by Ferrari: V12 in Berger's F93A.

(1) Regen-Pause: Hill im Training (2) Auf Regenreifen: die beiden Ferrari. (3) Während Schumachers Benetton unter Löschmitteln die Farben verliert, (4) kehrt der Pilot heim zur Box. (5) Hänge-Partie: nach einer Kollision mit Hill wird Bergers Ferrari geborgen. (6) Concept by Mercedes-Benz: Ilmor-Triebwerk im Sauber. (7) Concept by Ferrari: V12 in Bergers F93A.

(1) Interruption sous la pluie : Hill aux essais. (2) Sur pneus pluie : les deux Ferrari. (3) Tandis que la Benetton de Schumacher pâlit sous la poudre des extincteurs, (4) son pilote rentre à pied aux stands. (5) Ballet des grues : après une collision avec Hill, la Ferrari de Berger est évacuée de la piste. (6) Concept by Mercedes-Benz : le moteur Ilmor de la Sauber. (7) Concept by Ferrari : le V12 de la F93A de Berger.

1

2

3

4

With their thinking caps on: (1) Fittipaldi, (2) Wendlinger, (3) Prost. (4) Composition of names, colors, forms and objects. Three hours in the life of Ayrton Senna: (5) before the race (with Berger), (6) sitting in the racing car and (7) after the race.

Verkappte Talente: (1) Fittipaldi, (2) Wendlinger, (3) Prost. (4) Komposition aus Namen, Farben, Formen und Objekten. Drei Stunden im Leben des Ayrton Senna: (5) vor dem Rennen (mit Berger), (6) im Rennwagen sitzend und (7) nach dem Rennen.

Talents méconnus : (1) Fittipaldi, (2) Wendlinger, (3) Prost. (4) Composition de noms, de couleurs, de formes et d'objets. Trois heures de la vie d'Ayrton Senna : (5) avant la course (avec Berger), (6) assis au volant et (7) après la course.

1994

No name was mentioned more often in Monaco on this third weekend in May 1994 than that of Ayrton Senna. But the pole position, where he would most likely have stood with his Williams, remained empty in tribute to the deceased, as did the position beside it: the great Brazilian and his buddy Roland Ratzenberger had been killed two weeks earlier in Imola. A memorial service was held in Monaco cathedral on the Wednesday before the Grand Prix. The many demonstrative gestures also included a minute of silent reflection before the start. The Grand Prix world, magically spared tragedies for such a long time, was beginning to lose its reputation.

Neither was an end to the nightmare in sight. A few minutes before the end of the first qualifying session on Thursday, the Austrian Karl Wendlinger had a serious accident at the chicane in his black Sauber. He suffered head injuries and fell into a coma. For a long time his recovery was in doubt. There was a need to do something, and at a press conference on the Friday, Max Mosley and Bernie Ecclestone, the boss and deputy boss of motor sport's legislative body FISA (Fédération Internationale du Sport Automobile), spoke about the future of Formula 1. Yet no sooner had it escaped from their lips than the concept of safety turned into an empty phrase. For from this season onwards refuelling was announced with thousands of gallons of fuel stored in the pits.

At the same time the change of guard of the mid-1990s was in full swing. Senna was no more, and Alain Prost and Nigel Mansell had retired. Already a new Grand Prix deity was being worshipped: Michael Schumacher. The run of successes by the German on the way to achieving his first World Championship was breathtaking. He had already won the first three races of the 1994 season and cheerfully continued in this fashion in Monaco; best time in qualifying, in the lead from start to finish, fastest lap in the race as early as the 35th lap – an indication that he was never put under pressure in the second half either.

Possible challengers, kept at bay during qualifying with a time difference of at least a second, eliminated one another after a few hundred yards. Damon Hill in his Williams FW 16, carrying the absurd start number 0, pushed Mika Hakkinen's McLaren MP 4/9 into the barriers on the left at Sainte Dévote. While the wounded Williams still managed to drag itself to the climb to the Casino, only to expire there, the white-and-red car was immediately hoisted into the air with bent suspension and broken nose by the crane waiting for its prey at this point. The 52nd Monaco Grand Prix thus turned into little more than a procession. Two-thirds of the way through the race and the final points positions were already clear. Only Martin Brundle in the second McLaren and Ferrari driver Gerhard Berger remained on the same lap as the victor, who leapt at the Benetton team boss like a happy kid after crossing the finishing line.

Kein Name wird an diesem dritten Wochenende im Mai 1994 in Monaco häufiger genannt als Ayrton Senna. Aber die Pole Position, auf der er mit seinem Williams wohl gestanden hätte, bleibt leer als Verneigung vor einem Toten, ebenso wie der Platz daneben: Der große Brasilianer und sein Kamerad Roland Ratzenberger kamen 14 Tage zuvor in Imola ums Leben. Am Mittwoch vor dem Grand Prix gibt es einen Gedächtnisgottesdienst in der Kathedrale von Monaco. Zu den zahlreichen demonstrativen Gesten zählt auch eine Minute des stillen Gedenkens vor dem Start. Die Welt der Grands Prix, so lange wundersam von Tragödien verschont, ist ins Gerede gekommen.

Und der Alptraum dauert an. Ein paar Minuten vor dem Ende des ersten Trainings am Donnerstag hat der Österreicher Karl Wendlinger in seinem schwarzen Sauber einen schweren Unfall an der Schikane. Er trägt Kopfverletzungen davon und fällt ins Koma. An seiner Genesung wird zunächst gezweifelt. Rechtfertigungsnotstand besteht, und auf einer Pressekonferenz am Freitag erteilen Max Mosley und Bernie Ecclestone, Boß und Vizechef der Motorsport-Legislative FISA (Fédération Internationale du Sport Automobile), Auskunft darüber, wie es weitergehen soll mit der Formel 1. Gleichwohl zerbröckelt der Begriff Sicherheit in ihrem Mund zur Leerformel. Denn von dieser Saison an ist wieder Nachtanken angesagt, und Tausende von Litern Treibstoff lagern in den Boxen.

Im übrigen ist der Wachwechsel der Mittneunziger in vollem Gange. Senna ist nicht mehr, Alain Prost und Nigel Mansell haben sich aufs Altenteil zurückgezogen. Und schon beginnt man einer neuen Grand-Prix-Gottheit zu huldigen: Michael Schumacher. Die Erfolgsserie des Deutschen auf dem Weg zu seiner ersten Weltmeisterschaft verschlägt einem schier den Atem. Die ersten drei Läufe des Zyklus 1994 hat er bereits gewonnen, und in diesem Stil fährt er in Monaco munter fort: Bestzeit in der Qualifikation, Start-Ziel-Sieg, schnellste Runde auch im Rennen, und zwar bereits im 35. Durchgang als Indiz dafür, daß er auch in der zweiten Halbzeit nie in Bedrängnis gerät.

Mögliche Konkurrenten, im Training schon mindestens eine Sekunde auf Distanz gehalten, eliminieren einander nach ein paar hundert Metern. Da schubst Damon Hill im Williams FW 16 mit der absurden Startnummer 0 den McLaren MP 4/9 von Mika Hakkinen bei Sainte Dévote links in die Leitplanke. Während sich der Williams noch waidwund bis zu dem Gefälle hinter dem Casino schleppt und dort verendet, baumelt der weißrote Wagen im Nu mit gekrümmter Aufhängung und geborstener Nase an dem Kran, der an dieser Stelle auf Beute lauert. Der 52. Grand Prix de Monaco verkümmert somit zur Prozession. Schon nach zwei Dritteln sind die endgültigen Positionen für die Vergabe der Punkte bezogen. Nur Martin Brundle im zweiten McLaren und Ferrari-Fahrer Gerhard Berger bleiben in der gleichen Runde wie der Sieger, der nach der Zieldurchfahrt den Benetton-Teamchef anspringt wie ein vergnügter Bub.

Ce troisième week-end de mai 1994 à Monaco, aucun autre nom n'est cité aussi souvent que celui d'Ayrton Senna. Mais la pole position, là où il se serait sans aucun doute tenu avec sa Williams, reste vide par déférence envers un disparu, au même titre que la place à côté de lui : le grand Brésilien et son camarade Roland Ratzenberger ont trouvé la mort deux semaines plus tôt à Imola. Le mercredi précédant le Grand Prix, un service religieux est organisé en leur souvenir à la Cathédrale de Monaco. Parmi les nombreux gestes démonstratifs figure aussi une minute de silence avant le départ. Le monde des Grands Prix, si longtemps épargné comme par miracle par la tragédie, suscite de nouveau la critique.

Et le cauchemar perdure. Quelques minutes avant la fin de la première séance de qualification du jeudi, l'Autrichien Karl Wendlinger est victime d'un grave accident à la chicane, au volant de sa Sauber noire. Blessé à la tête, il est emmené à l'hôpital dans le coma. Pendant longtemps, on doute qu'il survive. Les instances officielles doivent se justifier et, lors d'une conférence de presse organisée le vendredi, Max Mosley et Bernie Ecclestone, président et vice-président de la FISA, l'organe de tutelle de la compétition automobile, font part de leurs intentions sur l'avenir de la Formule 1. Simultanément, le terme sécurité perd tout son sens sur leurs lèvres. En effet, depuis le début de cette saison, les ravitaillements en course sont de nouveau autorisés et des milliers de litres de carburant sont stockés dans les stands.

Pour le reste, la relève de la garde du milieu des années 90 bat son plein. Senna a disparu, Alain Prost et Nigel Mansell sont partis à la retraite. Et l'on commence d'ores et déjà à adorer une nouvelle divinité des Grands Prix : Michael Schumacher. La série de succès qui ponctuent le cheminement de l'Allemand vers son premier titre de champion du monde coupe tout simplement le souffle. Il a déjà gagné les trois premières manches de la saison 1994 et poursuit effrontément dans ce style à Monaco : meilleur temps en qualification, en tête du départ à l'arrivée, meilleur tour en course également et ce, dès le 35e tour, preuve, s'il en était, qu'il n'a jamais été poussé dans ses derniers retranchements durant la seconde moitié de la course non plus.

Ses rivaux possibles, déjà maintenus à une distance d'au minimum une seconde aux essais, s'éliminent les uns les autres au bout de quelques mètres. Damon Hill, avec sa Williams FW 16, portant l'absurde numéro de départ 0, percute par exemple la McLaren MP 4/9 de Mika Hakkinen à Sainte Dévote et l'envoie dans les glissières de gauche. Alors que la Williams agonise encore jusque dans la descente du Casino, où elle meurt, la voiture rouge et blanche est instantanément, avec son nez cabossé, prise aux crochets d'une grue qui attend son butin à cet endroit là. Le 52e Grand Prix de Monaco se mue ainsi en une ennuyeuse procession. Dès les deux tiers de la course, les positions sont définitivement octroyées pour la distribution des points. Seul Martin Brundle, dans la deuxième McLaren, et le pilote Ferrari Gerhard Berger restent dans le même tour que le vainqueur, qui, après avoir franchi la ligne d'arrivée, saute comme un collégien farceur dans les bras de Flavio Briatore, le chef de l'écurie Benetton.

N°	DRIVERS		ENTRANTS	CARS	ENGINES	PRACTICE RESULTS	RACE RESULTS
5	Michael Schumacher	D	Benetton Formula Ltd.	Benetton B194	Ford V8 3500 cc	1st : 1'18"560	1st : 1h49'55"372
8	Martin Brundle	GB	McLaren International	McLaren MP4/9	Peugeot V10 3500 cc	8th : 1'21"222	2nd : 1h50'32"650
28	Gerhard Berger	A	SEFAC Ferrari S.p.A.	Ferrari 412T1	Ferrari V12 3495 cc	3rd : 1'19"958	3rd : 1h51'12"196
15	Andrea de Cesaris	I	Jordan Grand Prix	Jordan 194	Hart V10 3500 cc	14th : 1'22"2651	4th : 77 laps
27	Jean Alesi	F	SEFAC Ferrari S.p.A.	Ferrari 412T1	Ferrari V12 3495 cc	5th : 1'20"452	5th : 77 laps
24	Michele Alboreto	I	Minardi Team S.p.A.	Minardi M194	Ford V8 3500 cc	12th : 1'21"793	6th : 77 laps
6	J. J. Lehto	SF	Benetton Formula Ltd.	Benetton B194	Ford V8 3500 cc	17th : 1'22"679	7th : 77 laps
19	Olivier Beretta	F	Larrousse F1	Larrousse LH94	Ford V8 3500 cc	18th : 1'23"025	8th : 76 laps
26	Olivier Panis	F	Ligier Sports	Ligier JS39	Renault V10 3500 cc	20th : 1'24"131	9th : 76 laps
20	Eric Comas	F	Larrousse F1	Larrousse LH94	Ford V8 3500 cc	13th : 1'22"211	10th : 75 laps
11	Pedro Lamy	P	Lotus Team International	Lotus 107C	Mugen-Honda V10 3493 cc	19th : 1'23"858	11th : 73 laps
12	Johnny Herbert	GB	Lotus Team International	Lotus 107C	Mugen-Honda V10 3493 cc	16th : 1'22"375	R
33	Paul Belmondo	F	Pacific Grand Prix	Pacific PR01	Ilmor V10 3500 cc	24th : 1'29"984	R
34	Bertrand Gachot	F	Pacific Grand Prix	Pacific PR01	Ilmor V10 3500 cc	23rd : 1'26"082	R
9	Christian Fittipaldi	BR	Arrows Racing	Arrows FA15	Ford V8 3500 cc	6th : 1'21"053	R
31	David Brabham	AUS	Simtek Grand Prix	Simtek S941	Ford V8 3500 cc	22nd : 1'24"656	R
4	Mark Blundell	GB	Tyrrell Racing Organisation	Tyrrell 022	Yamaha V10 3500 cc	10th : 1'21"614	R
3	Ukyo Katayama	J	Tyrrell Racing Organisation	Tyrrell 022	Yamaha V10 3500 cc	11th : 1'21"731	R
25	Eric Bernard	F	Ligier Sports	Ligier JS39	Renault V10 3500 cc	21st : 1'24"377	R
14	Rubens Barrichello	BR	Jordan Grand Prix	Jordan 194	Hart V10 3500 cc	15th : 1'22"359	R
23	Pierluigi Martini	I	Minardi Team S.p.A.	Minardi M194	Ford V8 3500 cc	9th : 1'21"288	R
0	Damon Hill	GB	Williams Grand Prix Engineering	Williams FW16	Renault V10 3500 cc	4th : 1'20"079	R
10	Gianni Morbidelli	BR	Arrows Racing	Arrows FA15	Ford V8 3500 cc	7th : 1'21"189	R
7	Mika Hakkinen	SF	McLaren International	McLaren MP4/9	Peugeot V10 3500 cc	2nd : 1'19"488	R

(1) Call of the wild: the screaming V12 of the Ferrari behind him, Gerhard Berger shoots off down the hill. (2) Arrival of the midfield at Mirabeau, led by Alboreto (Minardi) ahead of Comas (Larrousse) and Barrichello (Jordan).

(1) Schrei der Wildnis: Den kreischenden V12 des Ferrari im Nacken, schießt Gerhard Berger zu Tale. (2) Eintreffen des Mittelfeldes bei Mirabeau, an der Spitze Alboreto (Minardi) vor Comas (Larrousse) und Barrichello (Jordan).

(1) Hurlements sauvages : les feulements du V12 Ferrari dans le dos, Gerhard Berger plonge dans la descente. (2) Arrivée du peloton à Mirabeau avec, en tête, Alboreto (Minardi) devant Comas (Larrousse) et Barrichello (Jordan).

(Following double page) A multiplicity of windows, bays, balconies and terraces provides grandiose panoramas unmatched by the expensive spectator seats.

(Nächste Doppelseite) Eine Vielzahl von Fenstern, Erkern, Balkonen und Terrassen eröffnet grandiose Panoramen wie keiner der teuer bezahlten Zuschauerplätze.

(Double page suivante) Une multitude de fenêtres, encorbellements, balcons et terrasses ouvrent de grandioses perspectives comme aucune des places de spectateurs payées à un prix astronomique.

Martin Brundle (McLaren)

Michael Schumacher (Benetton)

Jean Alesi (Ferrari)

Mika Hakkinen (McLaren)

Jyrki Lehto (Benetton)

Johnny Herbert (Lotus)

1

2

The black weekend of Imola is still on everyone's mind and Formula 1 is in the news again (3) due to Karl Wendlinger's serious accident on Thursday at the chicane. This time the story has a happy ending. (1, 2) Quickest to heal are the scratches on the safety cage of the city track. The show must go on.

Das schwarze Wochenende von Imola ist noch in aller Munde, da macht die Formel 1 schon wieder von sich reden (3) durch den schweren Unfall Karl Wendlingers am Donnerstag an der Schikane. Die Sache geht gut aus, wie sich zeigen wird. (1, 2) Am schnellsten verheilt sind die Schrammen am Sicherheitskäfig der Stadtstrecke. The show must go on.

Le sombre week-end d'Imola est encore présent dans tous les esprits quand la Formule 1 fait de nouveau parler d'elle : (3) à cause du grave accident de Karl Wendlinger, le jeudi, à la chicane. Tout se terminera finalement mieux qu'on ne l'avait craint. (1, 2) Ce sont les égratignures du dispositif de sécurité du circuit urbain qui guérissent le plus vite. The show must go on.

3

Away from the battlefield, the 3-D puzzles which are Formula 1 racing cars are constantly taken apart and put together again, both in the big teams (1, 2) Benetton, (3, 4) Ferrari and (5, 6) Williams, and the others. (7) Michael Schumacher shows his pleasure in an unrestrained way. And Flavio Briatore is not easily toppled by anything.

Wenn kein Kampfeinsatz angesagt ist, wird das 3-D-Puzzle Formel-1-Rennwagen im Grunde ständig auseinandergenommen und wieder zusammengesetzt, bei den großen Teams (1, 2) Benetton, (3, 4) Ferrari und (5, 6) Williams wie bei den anderen. (7) Michael Schumacher zeigt seine Freude auf ein unmittelbare und elementare Weise. Und Flavio Briatore wirft so leicht nichts um.

Durant les interruptions des hostilités, le puzzle en trois dimensions qu'est une voiture de Formule 1 est en permanence démonté et remonté. Chez les top teams (1, 2) Benetton, (3, 4) Ferrari et (5, 6) Williams comme chez tous les autres. (7) Michael Schumacher laisse éclater sa joie. Mais il en faudrait plus pour renverser un Flavio Briatore.

1995

The introduction of refuelling stops changed Grand Prix racing, hitherto the domain of the lone man in his monoposto, into a team sport. Races were no longer decided solely by the duel at close quarters on the race track, but also in the duelling at one remove by the tacticians in the pits, in the whirling yet strictly disciplined ballet of the 20 specialists who changed the wheels and topped up the fuel. Michael Schumacher and the Benetton team were masters of both, the solo performance on stage and the clever management behind the scenes.

Five races had already passed in this first season since the rebirth of the 3-liter engines. Schumacher in the Benetton B 195 and Damon Hill with his Williams FW 17 had won two each, both of them propelled by Renault engines. Now, only one point separated them, the German having come third in Buenos Aires and the Briton fourth in Barcelona. In the rush-hour of the second qualifying session for the 53rd Monaco Grand Prix, Schumacher lost; his opponent was in pole position.

Both of them managed to get away unhurt from the chaos which occurred at Sainte Dévote after the first start. David Coulthard, in the second Williams, and Ferrari driver Gerhard Berger mounted an impressive display of acrobatics. After a half-pirouette, Coulthard landed with a crash in the middle of the track, only to be faced with oncoming race traffic. Berger came uncomfortably to a halt beside him and violent hand signals ensued which spoke volumes of their mutual displeasure with the turn of events as, a few dozen yards behind, a further five cars piled into one another.

Fortunately, everything went precisely as planned at the second start, and the screaming pack snaked its way through the narrow twisting streets before the climb to the Casino like beads on a string, Hill in front as before. From that point on the team managers took over. Schumacher had to wait until lap 35 before he was ordered into the pits; Hill, in contrast, was ordered in twice, once after the 24th and then in the 52nd lap.

This double-stop strategy turned out to be ill-conceived. After his first stop the Briton became hopelessly caught up in the stragglers and had already lost the battle. Schumacher relinquished his lead for only one lap during his own pit stop. Jean Alesi in his Ferrari 412 T2 was allowed to the front for a glorious moment and drove the fastest lap of the race in 1 minute, 24.621 seconds before having to come in for his own car to be serviced. From that point onwards things went downhill for him: he was seven seconds behind Schumacher when he rejoined the track, and he spun into the barriers on lap 41 when Ligier driver Martin Brundle lost control in front of him.

But Michael Schumacher achieved his 13th Grand Prix victory on this 28 May, at the same time presenting Renault with its first success in the Principality after 16 attempts. In Monaco, as we know, things often do not quite happen as expected.

Mit der Einführung des Tankstopps mutiert der Grand Prix, sonst die Domäne des Mannes in der absoluten Einsamkeit des Monoposto, zum Mannschaftssport. Rennen werden nicht nur im Nahkampf draußen auf der Piste entschieden, sondern auch im Fernduell der Taktiker an der Box, im wirbelnden und dennoch strikt disziplinierten Ballett der 20 Spezialisten, die die Räder wechseln und den Treibstoff nachfüllen. Michael Schumacher und das Benetton-Team beherrschen beides, den Solopart auf der Bühne und die kluge Inszenierung hinter den Kulissen.

Fünf Rennen ist die Saison im Jahre eins der Wiedergeburt der Dreiliter bereits alt. Je zwei haben Schumacher im Benetton B 195 und Damon Hill mit dem Williams FW 17 gewonnen, beide mit Renault-Maschinen im Nacken. Einen Punkt liegen sie auseinander: in Buenos Aires war der Deutsche Dritter, in Barcelona der Brite Vierter. In der Rush-hour der zweiten Qualifikation für den 53. Großen Preis von Monaco unterliegt Schumacher. Auf der Pole Position steht sein Kontrahent.

Nach dem ersten Start entrinnen beide ungeschoren dem Chaos, das bei Sainte Dévote ausbricht. David Coulthard im zweiten Williams und Ferrari-Fahrer Gerhard Berger glänzen mit akrobatischen Flugeinlagen. Coulthard landet nach einer halben Pirouette krachend mitten in der Fahrspur und findet sich Angesicht zu Angesicht mit Gegenverkehr im Renntempo. Berger kommt in ungemütlichem Zusammensein neben ihm zum Stehen. Mit heftigen Handbewegungen macht man seinem Verdruß über den Verlauf der Dinge Luft. Ein paar Dutzend Meter dahinter verkeilen sich fünf weitere Wagen ineinander.

Beim zweiten Start klappt alles wie am Schnürchen, und wie an einer Schnur gezogen windet sich die heulende Meute durch den engen Schlängel vor dem Anstieg Richtung Casino, Hill allen voran wie beim ersten Mal. Von da an regiert die Regie: Schumacher wird nur nach der Runde 35 an die Box bestellt, Hill dagegen zweimal, im Anschluß an den 24. und den 52. Durchgang.

Diese Doppel-Strategie erweist sich als falsch. Nach seinem ersten Halt verheddert sich der Engländer hoffnungslos im dichten Verkehr der Nachzügler und hat schon verloren. Nur noch für eine einzige Runde gibt Schumacher die Führung bei seinem eigenen Boxenstopp ab. Da darf Jean Alesi mit dem Ferrari 412 T2 für glorreiche Augenblicke an die Spitze und fährt mit einer Minute, 24 Sekunden und 621 Tausendsteln auch rasch die schnellste Runde des Rennens, bevor er selbst zum Service hereinkommt. Von da an geht's bergab: Sieben Sekunden hinter Schumacher geht er wieder auf die Strecke, dreht sich indes in Runde 41 knirschend in die Leitplanke, als Ligier-Pilot Martin Brundle vor ihm ins Kreiseln gerät.

Michael Schumacher jedoch erzielt an diesem 28. Mai seinen 13. Grand-Prix-Sieg insgesamt und beschert Renault zugleich in 16 Anläufen den ersten Erfolg im monegassischen Fürstentum. Dort laufen die Dinge, wie man weiß, häufig ein bißchen anders.

L'introduction des ravitaillements métamorphose la course du Grand Prix, jusque-là domaine de l'homme dans l'isolation absolue de sa monoplace, en un sport d'équipe. L'issue de la course n'est plus uniquement scellée sur la piste dans un duel à couteaux tirés, mais aussi par un duel télécommandé par les tacticiens des stands et le ballet strictement orchestré des vingt spécialistes qui changent les roues et remplissent le carburant. Michael Schumacher et l'écurie Benetton sont des virtuoses dans ces deux registres : la performance en solitaire sur la piste et la mise en scène intelligente dans les coulisses.

La première saison de la renaissance des trois-litres compte déjà cinq courses. Schumacher sur la Benetton B 195 et Damon Hill sur la Williams FW 17 en ont gagné deux chacun, tous les deux avec des moteurs Renault dans le dos. A présent, un seul point les sépare : l'Allemand ayant terminé troisième à Buenos Aires, et le Britannique, à Barcelone, quatrième. Schumacher doit s'avouer vaincu dans le rush des secondes de qualification pour le 53e Grand Prix de Monaco. Son adversaire s'est abrogé la pole position.

Après le premier départ, tous les deux échappent sains et saufs au chaos qui éclate à Sainte Dévote. David Coulthard, dans la seconde Williams, et le pilote Ferrari Gerhard Berger se distinguent par leur envol acrobatique. Après une demi-pirouette, Coulthard atterrit avec fracas en plein milieu de la trajectoire et se trouve confronté à ses collègues arrivant à bride abattue. Berger se retrouve à côté de lui en une coexistence peu enviable, puis des mouvements frénétiques de la main s'ensuivent, qui en disent long sur leur mécontentement mutuel quant à la tournure des évènements. Quelques dizaines de mètres plus loin, cinq autres voitures se télescopent aussi.

Heureusement, lors du second départ, tout marche comme sur des roulettes et la meute hurlante partie sur les chapeaux de roue s'engouffre dans le chas d'aiguille qui ouvre la montée en direction du Casino. Avec Hill de nouveau en tête, comme la première fois. A partir de là, ce sont les stratèges qui dirigent les opérations : Schumacher n'est rappelé aux stands qu'au 35e tour ; Hill, par contre, deux fois, à la fin du 24e et du 52e.

Cette stratégie des deux arrêts s'avère être une erreur. Après son premier arrêt, l'Anglais reste désespérément englué parmi les traînards de la fin du peloton et a déjà perdu la bataille. Schumacher ne cède le commandement que pendant un tour, lors de son propre arrêt de ravitaillement. Pendant quelques instants de gloire, Jean Alesi a alors l'honneur de caracoler en tête avec sa Ferrari 412 T2, ce qu'il fait pendant une minute 24 secondes et 621 millièmes en signant rapidement, à l'occasion, le tour le plus rapide en course avant de devoir ravitailler lui-même sa propre machine. A partir de là, le beau scénario s'effondre : il reprend la piste sept secondes derrière Schumacher, mais part en tête-à-queue dans les glissières au 41e tour en voulant éviter le pilote Ligier Martin Brundle, lui-même parti en dérapage devant lui.

Ce 28 mai-là, Michael Schumacher remporte en revanche sa treizième victoire en Grand Prix et donne par la même occasion à Renault le premier succès dans la Principauté monégasque après pas moins de seize tentatives. Ici, comme il est de notoriété publique, les choses ne prennent pas toujours la tournure que l'on escompte.

Always a question of perspective: Damon Hill and Michael Schumacher as garden gnomes in front of a select harbor panorama.

Alles eine Frage der Perspektive: Damon Hill und Michael Schumacher als Gartenzwerge vor ausgesuchtem Hafenpanorama.

Tout est une question de perspective : Damon Hill et Michael Schumacher jouent les mascottes devant le panorama du port.

N°	DRIVERS		ENTRANTS	CARS	ENGINES	PRACTICE RESULTS	RACE RESULTS
1	**Michael Schumacher**	**D**	**Benetton Formula Ltd.**	**Benetton B195**	**Renault V10 2998 cc**	**2nd: 1'22"742**	**1st: 1h53'11"258**
5	*Damon Hill*	*GB*	*Williams Grand Prix Engineering*	*Williams FW17*	*Renault V10 2998 cc*	*1st: 1'21"952*	*2nd: 1h53'46"075*
28	Gerhard Berger	A	SEFAC Ferrari S.p.A.	Ferrari 412T2	Ferrari V10 2998 cc	4th: 1'23"220	3rd: 1h54'22"705
2	Johnny Herbert	GB	Benetton Formula Ltd.	Benetton B195	Renault V10 2998 cc	7th: 1'23"885	4th: 77 laps
7	Mark Blundell	GB	McLaren International	McLaren MP4/10B	Mercedes V10 2998 cc	10th: 1'24"933	5th: 77 laps
30	Heinz-Harald Frentzen	D	Team P. P. Sauber	Sauber C14	Ford V8 2998 cc	14th: 1'25"661	6th: 76 laps
23	Pierluigi Martini	I	Minardi Team S.p.A.	Minardi M195	Cosworth V8 2998 cc	18th: 1'26"913	7th: 76 laps
29	Jean-Christophe Bouillon	F	Team P. P. Sauber	Sauber C14	Ford V8 2998 cc	19th: 1'27"145	8th: 74 laps (R)
9	Gianni Morbidelli	BR	Arrows Grand Prix International	Arrows FA16	Hart V8 2996 cc	13th: 1'25"447	9th: 74 laps
21	Pedro Diniz	BR	Parmalat Forti Ford	Forti FG01/95	Cosworth V8 2998 cc	22th: 1'29"244	10th: 72 laps
24	Luca Badoer	I	Minardi Team S.p.A.	Minardi M195	Cosworth V8 2998 cc	16th: 1'25"969	R
26	Olivier Panis	F	Ligier F1	Ligier JS41	Mugen-Honda V10 2998 cc	12th: 1'25"125	R
4	Mika Juhani Salo	SF	Tyrrell Racing Organisation	Tyrrell 023	Yamaha V10 2996 cc	17th: 1'26"473	R
14	Rubens Barrichello	BR	Jordan Grand Prix	Jordan 195	Peugeot V10 2998 cc	11th: 1'25"081	R
16	Bertrand Gachot	F	Pacific-Team Lotus Grand Prix	Pacific PR02	Cosworth V8 2998 cc	21st: 1'29"039	R
27	Jean Alesi	F	SEFAC Ferrari S.p.A.	Ferrari 412T2	Ferrari V10 2998 cc	5th: 1'23"754	R
25	Martin Brundle	GB	Ligier F1	Ligier JS41	Mugen-Honda V10 2998 cc	8th: 1'24"447	R
10	Taki Inoue	J	Arrows Grand Prix International	Arrows FA16	Hart V8 2996 cc	26th: 1'31"542	R
3	Ukyo Katayama	J	Tyrrell Racing Organisation	Tyrrell 023	Yamaha V10 2996 cc	15th: 1'25"808	R
15	Eddie Irvine	GB	Jordan Grand Prix	Jordan 195	Peugeot V10 2998 cc	9th: 1'24"857	R
6	David Coulthard	GB	Williams Grand Prix Engineering	Williams FW17	Renault V10 2998 cc	3rd: 1'23"109	R
22	Roberto Moreno	BR	Parmalat Forti Ford	Forti FG01/95	Cosworth V8 2998 cc	24th: 1'29"608	R
8	Mika Hakkinen	SF	McLaren International	McLaren MP4/10B	Mercedes V10 2998 cc	6th: 1'23"857	R
12	Jos Verstappen	NL	Simtek Grand Prix	Simtek S951	Cosworth V8 2998 cc	23rd: 1'29"391	R
17	Andrea Montermini	I	Pacific-Team Lotus Grand Prix	Pacific PR02	Cosworth V8 2998 cc	25th: 1'30"149	disqualified
11	Domenico Schiattarella	I	Simtek Grand Prix	Simtek S951	Cosworth V8 2998 cc	20th: 1'28"337	R

Blessings from on high: after the start, Coulthard (Williams) and Berger (Ferrari) demonstrate that driving in the intended direction and with full adhesion are just two of the options from a large Formula 1 driving repertoire.

Alles Gute kommt von oben: Nach dem Start demonstrieren Coulthard (Williams) und Berger (Ferrari), daß die Reise in Fahrtrichtung und mit voller Bodenhaftung nur zwei Möglichkeiten aus dem großen Repertoire der Formel 1 sind.

Tout ce qui est bon vient du ciel : après le départ, Coulthard (Williams) et Berger (Ferrari) prouvent que rouler dans le bon sens et avec une totale adhérence ne sont que deux possibilités du riche répertoire de la Formule 1.

(1) Large stage: the arrangement of the seating, the course of the circuit and the ideal line etched into the track all reflect the amphitheater which is Monaco. A handful of actors with their props: (2) Schumacher (Benetton), (3) Hill (Williams), (4) Blundell (McLaren), (5) Herbert (Benetton) and (6) Alesi (Ferrari).

(1) Große Bühne: In der Anordnung der Zuschauertribünen, dem Verlauf der Piste und der in die Fahrbahn eingebrannten Ideallinie bildet sich das Amphitheater Monaco noch einmal ab. Eine Handvoll Darsteller und ihre Requisiten: (2) Schumacher (Benetton), (3) Hill (Williams), (4) Blundell (McLaren), (5) Herbert (Benetton) und (6) Alesi (Ferrari).

(1) Scène de théâtre: Monaco l'amphithéâtre se reflète dans l'agence-ment des tribunes pour les spectateurs, dans le déroulement du circuit et dans la trajectoire idéale gravée sur la piste. Une poignée d'acteurs et leurs instruments : (2) Schumacher (Benetton), (3) Hill (Williams), (4) Blundell (McLaren), (5) Herbert (Benetton) et (6) Alesi (Ferrari).

1

2

3

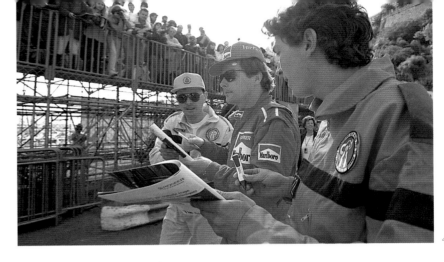

4

5

6

7

8

10

9

11

The aura of men like (4) Gerhard Berger and (6) Michael Schumacher and their machines is felt in Monaco more than anywhere else: (1) Benetton, (2) Ferrari and (3) McLaren. The hardcore of racing tourists includes (5) the travelling fan club, which, in this case, has come from neighboring Italy. (7) Eddie Irvine, who returned on foot after 22 laps in the Jordan, also enjoys the general acclamation. People involved with the Grand Prix: (8) timekeeper, (10) cameraman and (11) camerawoman, (9) restaurant guests at Tabac. (12) Bubbly or mineral water? Flavio Briatore generously offers Hill champagne, while Schumacher prefers something more modest.

Mehr als irgendwo sonst wird in Monaco die Aura spürbar, die ausgeht von Männern wie (4) Gerhard Berger und (6) Michael Schumacher und ihren Maschinen: (1) Benetton, (2) Ferrari und (3) McLaren. Zum harten Kern unter den Renn-Touristen zählt (5) der reisende Fanclub, der vom benachbarten Italien herübergekommen ist. Auch (7) Eddie Irvine, der nach 22 Runden im Jordan zu Fuß zurückkehrt, genießt die allgemeine Akklamation. Leute im Umfeld des Grand Prix: (8) Zeitnehmer, (10) Kameramann und (11) -frau, (9) Restaurantgäste bei Tabac. (12) Sekt oder Selters? Flavio Briatore offeriert Hill hochherzig Champagner, während Schumacher mit schlichterem Getränk vorliebnimmt.

A Monaco plus qu'ailleurs, on peut palper le charisme qui émane d'hommes comme (4) Gerhard Berger et (6) Michael Schumacher et de leurs machines : (1) Benetton, (2) Ferrari et (3) McLaren. Au noyau dur des touristes de la course figure (5) le fan club itinérant qui, cette fois-ci, est venu de l'Italie toute proche. (7) Eddie Irvine, aussi, qui rentre à pied après 22 tours en Jordan, reçoit les acclamations du public. Acteurs anonymes du Grand Prix : (8) chronométreurs, (10) cameraman et (11) photographe, (9) hôtes de restaurant au virage du Bureau de Tabac. (12) Champagne ou Vichy ? Flavio Briatore tend généreusement une bouteille de champagne à Hill tandis que Schumacher préfère une boisson moins alcoolisée.

12

1996

The 54th Monaco Grand Prix on 19 May 1996 turned into a Grand Prix of inconsistencies and oddities, of things which had not happened before or only a long time in the past.

This began with the time set for the start. By hallowed custom it had been set at 3.30 pm in order not to disturb the siesta of the Grimaldis; but, bowing to almighty television, it had been moved forward by an hour. Once again the spring heavens opened like sluice gates and the track took some time to dry out. The result of that was a quarter-hour-long qualifying session for orientation purposes towards midday, and the reduction of the race to 75 laps so that the limit of two hours could be maintained.

That affected Michael Schumacher's role, who in the meantime had been signed up by Ferrari as a doer of great deeds. During qualifying he did indeed fully meet the tremendous expectations placed in him: pole position for the F 310, the first here for a red racer from Maranello for 17 years. When the German subsequently received the applause of the *tifosi,* when travelling at a leisurely pace at the approach to the chicane, Benetton driver Gerhard Berger burst out of the tunnel at full speed and went into frightening pirouettes in an attempt to avoid the obstacle.

Worse was to happen on Sunday. Schumacher, one of the best on a wet track, and the rain hero of Barcelona two weeks later, left the straight and narrow as early as the first lap at Portier, crumpling the nose and other exposed parts of the red car as he bounced like a ping-pong ball against the barriers. It had been his own fault and he was sorry, as he said later for the record. And Ferrari team boss Jean Todt responded in kind by saying that so much honesty and self-criticism did honor to his star.

That also applied not least to the surprise victor, Olivier Panis, in his Ligier JS 43, the young Frenchman having started the race on the seventh row of the grid. But without wishing to belittle his success, the leaders first had to fall by the wayside before the path was cleared for him. Williams driver Damon Hill was leading by half a minute in front of Jean Alesi in the second Benetton when his engine expired in the tunnel on lap 41. This was the first sudden death for one of the robust V10s from Renault since a similar thing had happened to Alain Prost in Monza in 1993. Alesi now appeared to be driving towards certain success, but during the 60th lap the roadholding of his car suddenly became spongy. The driver suspected that air might be escaping from a rear tyre, only to be informed from the pits that his rear suspension had collapsed.

A festive mood, in the meantime, had invaded the Ligier-Gauloises Blondes team. Success had truly become a rare event for them, the last victory of the marque having been dated 27 September 1981, when Jacques Laffite won the Canadian Grand Prix in Montreal.

A further parallel also had to be sought in the semi-darkness of history: the last time a mere four drivers were flagged down by the black-and-white chequered flag in Monaco had been in 1966.

Der 54. Große Preis von Monaco am 19. Mai 1996 gerät zum Grand Prix der Ungereimtheiten, des Absonderlichen, des noch nie oder schon lange nicht mehr Dagewesenen.

Das beginnt mit der Uhrzeit für den Start: nach geheiligtem Brauch mit Rücksicht auf die fürstliche Siesta der Grimaldis bislang um halb vier, neuerdings als Reverenz vor der Allmacht des Fernsehens 60 Minuten früher angesetzt. Wieder einmal hat der Frühlingshimmel seine Schleusen geöffnet, nur allmählich wird die Strecke abtrocknen. Konsequenzen daraus sind ein viertelstündiges Orientierungstraining gegen Mittag und die Verkürzung des Rennens auf 75 Runden, damit das Limit von zwei Stunden eingehalten werden kann.

Das betrifft die Rolle Michael Schumachers, der inzwischen als Garant für große Taten von Ferrari engagiert worden ist. In der Qualifikation wird er den hochgespannten Erwartungen durchaus gerecht: Pole Position für den F 310, die erste hier für einen roten Renner aus Maranello seit 17 Jahren. Als der Deutsche anschließend in gemächlichem Tempo vor der Schikane die Ovationen der *tifosi* in Empfang nimmt, birst Benetton-Pilot Gerhard Berger in voller Fahrt aus der Finsternis des Tunnels und vollführt furchterregende Pirouetten bei dem Versuch, dem Hindernis auszuweichen.

Schlimmeres folgt am Sonntag: Da kommt Schumacher, auf nasser Piste einer der Besten und der Regenheld von Barcelona 14 Tage später, schon in der ersten Runde in Portier vom rechten Pfade ab und zerknautscht die Nase sowie weitere exponierte Teile des Roten im Pingpong gegen die Streckenbegrenzung. Sein Fehler sei das gewesen, die Sache tue ihm leid, gibt er nachher zu Protokoll. Und Ferrari-Rennleiter Jean Todt erwidert artig, soviel unverblümte Offenheit und Selbstkritik gereiche seinem Star zur Ehre.

Das gilt nicht zuletzt für den Sieger Olivier Panis in seinem Ligier JS 43. Der junge Franzose geht das Rennen aus der siebten Reihe an. Ohne sein Verdienst schmälern zu wollen: Ehe der Weg für ihn frei ist, bleiben erst einmal die bisherigen Spitzenreiter auf der Strecke. Williams-Mann Damon Hill führt eine halbe Minute vor Jean Alesi im zweiten Benetton, da platzt in der 41. Runde sein Triebwerk im Tunnel. Dies ist der erste Todesfall für einen der robusten V10 der Régie Renault, seitdem Alain Prost 1993 in Monza Ähnliches widerfuhr. Dann scheint Alesi einem sicheren Erfolg entgegenzufahren. Im 60. Durchgang wird die Straßenlage seines Autos jedoch plötzlich teigig. Der Pilot argwöhnt, aus einem Hinterreifen sei die Luft entwichen. An der Box belehrt man ihn indessen, die Hinterradaufhängung sei kollabiert.

Hochstimmung kommt indessen am Ende beim Team Ligier-Gauloises Blondes auf. Man ist des Erfolgs wahrlich entwöhnt. Der letzte Sieg der Marke datiert auf den 27. September 1981 zurück. Da gewann Jacques Laffite den Grand Prix von Kanada in Montreal.

Nach einer weiteren Parallele muß man ebenfalls im Halbdunkel der Historie suchen: Das letzte Mal geschah es 1966, daß in Monaco lediglich vier Piloten mit der schwarzweiß karierten Zielflagge abgewinkt wurden.

Le 54ᵉ Grand Prix de Monaco, le 19 mai 1996, est le Grand Prix de l'absurde, du bizarre, de ce qui ne s'est encore jamais produit ou plus produit depuis longtemps.

Tout commence avec l'heure du départ : fixée jusqu'ici à trois heures et demie selon une coutume sacrée qui prenait en considération l'auguste sieste princière des Grimaldi, elle est désormais avancée d'une heure par égard envers la toute-puissance de la télévision. Une fois de plus, le ciel printanier a ouvert ses écluses et la piste ne commence à sécher que timidement. La conséquence en est un quart d'heure d'essai de reconnaissance vers midi et le raccourcissement de la course à 75 tours pour respecter la limite de deux heures au maximum.

Cela concerne le rôle de Michael Schumacher, qui a entre-temps été recruté par Ferrari comme garantie de faits héroïques. En qualification, il satisfait tout à fait aux espoirs ambitieux mis en lui : pole position pour la F 310, la première ici pour un bolide rouge de Maranello depuis 17 ans. Lorsque l'Allemand se rapproche ensuite à basse vitesse de la chicane pour répondre aux ovations des *tifosi,* le pilote Benetton Gerhard Berger jaillit à pleine vitesse de l'obscurité du tunnel et exécute d'épouvantables pirouettes dans la tentative d'éviter l'obstacle.

Mais le pire ne se produira que le dimanche : Schumacher, l'un des meilleurs pilotes sur le mouillé et héros de Barcelone 14 jours plus tard, quitte le bon chemin au virage du Portier dès le premier tour et écrase le nez ainsi que d'autres pièces sensibles de sa voiture en faisant du ping-pong entre les glissières. Il admet son erreur et cela lui est infiniment pénible, déclarera-t-il plus tard en guise de commentaire. Et le directeur du service course de Ferrari, Jean Todt, répliquera élégamment, de son côté, que tant de franchise non dissimulée et d'autocritique est tout à l'honneur de sa vedette.

Cela vaut aussi et surtout pour le vainqueur inattendu, Olivier Panis, et sa Ligier JS 43. Le jeune Français prend le départ de la course depuis la septième ligne. Sans vouloir minimiser ses mérites : avant que la voie ne soit libre pour lui, il faut tout d'abord que les leaders successifs jettent l'éponge. Le mercenaire de Williams, Damon Hill, est en tête avec une demi-minute d'avance sur Jean Alesi avec la seconde Benetton lorsque son moteur rend l'âme dans le tunnel au 41ᵉ tour. C'est le premier cas de mort subite pour l'un des robustes V10 de la régie Renault depuis qu'Alain Prost a subi le même destin à Monza en 1993. Alesi semble alors rouler vers une victoire promise. Au 60ᵉ tour, la tenue de route de sa voiture commence pourtant soudain à se dégrader. Le pilote pense que de l'air s'échappe de l'un des pneus arrière. Arrivé aux stands, on lui apprend en revanche que c'est la suspension arrière qui s'affaisse.

L'allégresse règne pendant ce temps dans l'écurie Ligier Gauloises Blondes. Celle-ci est en effet depuis longtemps privée de succès, la dernière victoire de la marque remontant au 27 septembre 1981 : ce jour-là, Jacques Laffite avait gagné le Grand Prix du Canada à Montréal.

Pour trouver d'autres similitudes, il faut également remonter loin dans la semi-obscurité de l'histoire : la derrière fois où cela s'était produit, c'était en 1966, lorsque quatre pilotes seulement avaient vu brandir le drapeau à damier devant leurs roues.

All weathers: The large Ferrari umbrella offers protection for intimacy à trois.

Alle Wetter: Der große Ferrari-Schirm bietet Schutz für intime Dreisamkeit.

Satanée météo : le grand parapluie Ferrari offre une protection à trois intime.

N°	DRIVERS		ENTRANTS	CARS	ENGINES	PRACTICE RESULTS	RACE RESULTS
9	**Olivier Panis**	**F**	**Ligier F1**	**Ligier JS43**	**Mugen-Honda V10 2998 cc**	**14th: 1'22"358**	**1st: 2h00'45"629**
8	David Coulthard	GB	McLaren International	McLaren MP4/11	Mercedes V10 2998 cc	5th: 1'21"460	2nd: 2h00'50"457
14	Johnny Herbert	GB	P. P. Sauber International	Sauber C15	Ford V10 2998 cc	13th: 1'22"346	3rd: 2h01'23"132
15	Heinz-Harald Frentzen	D	P. P. Sauber International	Sauber C15	Ford V10 2998 cc	9th: 1'21"929	4th: 74 laps
19	Mika Juhani Salo	SF	Tyrrell Racing Organisation	Tyrrell 024	Yamaha V10 2996 cc	11th: 1'22"235	5th: 70 laps (R)
7	Mika Hakkinen	SF	McLaren International	McLaren MP4/11	Mercedes V10 2998 cc	8th: 1'21"688	6th: 70 laps (R)
2	Eddie Irvine	GB	SEFAC Ferrari S.p.A.	Ferrari F310	Ferrari V10 2998 cc	7th: 1'21"542	7th: 68 laps (R)
6	Jacques Villeneuve	CDN	Williams Grand Prix Engineering	Williams FW18	Renault V10 2998 cc	10th: 1'21"963	R
3	Jean Alesi	F	Benetton Formula Ltd.	Benetton B196	Renault V10 2998 cc	3rd: 1'20"918	R
22	Luca Badoer	I	Forti Corse	Forti FG03/96	Ford V8 2998 cc	21st: 1'25"059	R
5	Damon Hill	GB	Williams Grand Prix Engineering	Williams FW18	Renault V10 2998 cc	2nd: 1'20"888	R
12	Martin Brundle	GB	Jordan Grand Prix	Jordan 196	Peugeot V10 2998 cc	16th: 1'22"519	R
4	Gerhard Berger	A	Benetton Formula Ltd.	Benetton B196	Renault V10 2998 cc	4th: 1'21"067	R
10	Pedro Diniz	BR	Ligier F1	Ligier JS43	Mugen-Honda V10 2998 cc	17th: 1'22"68217	R
16	Ricardo Rosset	BR	Arrows Grand Prix International	Arrows FA17	Hart V8 2996 cc	20th: 1'24"976	R
18	Ukyo Katayama	J	Tyrrell Racing Organisation	Tyrrell 024	Yamaha V10 2996 cc	15th: 1'22"460	R
11	Rubens Barrichello	BR	Jordan Grand Prix	Jordan 196	Peugeot V10 2998 cc	6th: 1'21"504	R
1	*Michael Schumacher*	*D*	*SEFAC Ferrari S.p.A.*	*Ferrari F310*	*Ferrari V10 2998 cc*	*1st: 1'20"356*	*R*
20	Pedro Lamy	P	Minardi Team S.p.A.	Minardi M195B	Ford V8 2998 cc	19th: 1'23"350	R
21	Giancarlo Fisichella	I	Minardi Team S.p.A.	Minardi M195B	Ford V8 2998 cc	18th: 1'22"684	R
17	Jos Verstappen	NL	Arrows Grand Prix International	Arrows FA17	Hart V8 2996 cc	12th: 1'22"327	R

(1) Pussy-footing it: the field feels its way through Sainte Dévote for the first time. Hill (Williams) is already on the hill, Schumacher (Ferrari) follows, the two Benettons breathing down his neck.
(2) Victory after starting from row seven of the grid: Panis (Ligier), (3) third place after also starting from row seven of the grid: Herbert (Sauber). (4) Just a minute: Schumacher.

(1) Eiertanz: Zum erstenmal tastet sich das Feld durch Sainte Dévote. Hill (Williams) ist schon am Berg, Schumacher (Ferrari) folgt, die beiden Benetton im Nacken. (2) Sieg nach Start aus Reihe sieben: Panis (Ligier), (3) Platz drei nach Start aus Reihe sieben: Herbert (Sauber). (4) Minuten-Brenner: Schumacher.

(1) Comme sur des oeufs : pour la première fois, le peloton aborde prudemment Sainte Dévote. Hill (Williams) est déjà dans la montée, suivi par Schumacher (Ferrari), avec les deux Benetton sur ses talons. (2) Victoire après un départ en septième ligne : Panis (Ligier). (3) Troisième place après un départ en septième ligne : Herbert (Sauber). (4) N'a pas fait long feu : Schumacher.

(1) Gloves off: Panis against Irvine (Ferrari) at Loews. (2) Frentzen's Sauber emerges slightly damaged from his duel with Irvine's Ferrari (3) after contact at Sainte Dévote. Caught between the poles of aerodynamics and traction, cars become increasingly similar: (4) Brundle (Jordan), (5) Coulthard (McLaren), (6) Alesi (Benetton).

(1) Mit harten Bandagen: Panis gegen Irvine (Ferrari) bei Loews. (2) Aus dem Gefecht mit Irvines Ferrari geht Frentzens Sauber (3) nach einem Kontakt bei Sainte Dévote leicht lädiert hervor. Im Spannungsfeld zwischen den Polen Aerodynamik und Traktion werden die Wagen immer ähnlicher: (4) Brundle (Jordan), (5) Coulthard (McLaren), (6) Alesi (Benetton).

(1) Pas de cadeaux : Panis contre Irvine (Ferrari) au Loews. (2) Après le duel avec la Ferrari d'Irvine, la Sauber de Frentzen (3) porte les traces de leur contact à Sainte Dévote. En voulant concilier l'inconciliable, aérodynamique et motricité, les voitures se ressemblent de plus en plus : (4) Brundle (Jordan), (5) Coulthard (McLaren), (6) Alesi (Benetton).

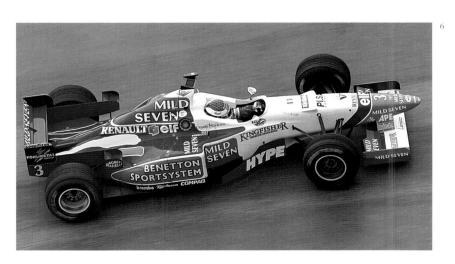

Monaco in the rain claims its victims: (1) Fisichella (Minardi) and (3) Schumacher exit in the first lap, (2) Katayama (Tyrrell) after the second. (4) 81 mph (130 kph) for Coulthard's McLaren at Massenet, (5) 130 mph (210 kph) for Hill's Williams approaching the swimming pool.

Das Wagnis Monaco im Regen fordert seine Opfer: (1) Fisichella (Minardi) und (3) Schumacher: Abgang in der ersten Runde, (2) Katayama (Tyrrell): Abgang nach zwei Runden. (4) Tempo 130 für Coulthards McLaren in Massenet, (5) Tempo 210 für Hills Williams vor dem Schwimmbad.

Sous la pluie, la patinoire de Monaco prélève son tribut : (1) Fisichella (Minardi) et (3) Schumacher : abandon au premier tour. (2) Katayama (Tyrrell) : abandon au bout de deux tours. (4) A 130 km/h : la McLaren de Coulthard à Massenet, (5) à 210 km/h, la Williams de Hill devant la Piscine.

1

2

5

Mixed doubles: (1) Niki Lauda with an official, (2) Ferrari designer Gustav Brunner with his former employer Günter Schmid, (3) René Arnoux with open-hearted friend. (4) All alone: Schumacher on the long march back to the pits. (6) Trop de bruit: guardsmen surprised and shocked by the noise. (7) Mixed reactions: Panis and Coulthard appear not to be satisfied with their placings, but Herbert (right) is cheerfully relaxed. (5) The big picture: this mighty screen keeps spectators up to date.

Gemischte Doppel: (1) Niki Lauda mit Offiziellem, (2) Ferrari-Konstrukteur Gustav Brunner mit seinem früheren Arbeitgeber Günter Schmid, (3) René Arnoux mit offenherziger Freundin. (4) Mutterseelenallein: Schumacher auf dem langen Marsch zurück ins Fahrerlager. (6) Trop de bruit: vom Lärm überraschte und geschockte Gardisten. (7) Hiobsbotschaft: Panis und Coulthard scheinen mit ihren Plazierungen nicht einverstanden zu sein, während Herbert (rechts) heitere Gelassenheit an den Tag legt. (5) Tafel-Freuden: Dieser mächtige Bildschirm hält die Zuschauer immer auf dem laufenden.

Double mixte : (1) Niki Lauda avec un officiel, (2) l'ingénieur Ferrari Gustav Brunner avec son ancien employeur Günter Schmid, (3) René Arnoux avec une amie au grand cœur. (4) Désespérément seul : Schumacher regagnant à pied le paddock. (6) Trop de bruit : des agents de police en uniforme se protègent les tympans. (7) Que penser ? Panis et Coulthard n'ont pas l'air satisfaits leur résultat tandis que Herbert (à droite) ne peut dissimuler sa satisfaction. (5) Nouveauté : grâce à cet écran vidéo géant, les spectateurs sont toujours parfaitement informés.

3

4

BRIEF APPEARANCE

KURZER AUFTRITT · BRÈVE APPARITION

Schumacher?", the man with the sparse black hair asks hesitatingly, almost beseechingly, with the emphasis on the third syllable. "Schumacher!" the sonorous choir returns. Thumbs up in confirmation. The mantra triggers an understanding between Germans and Italians in the jam-packed compartment which transcends national frontiers, Schumania and Ferrari-fever have coalesced into a dual delirium ever since Imola. There is certainly no doubt which racing stable to support: everyone wears the uniform of their obsession with the almost sacred emblem of the marque from Maranello, at a minimum the red cap with the adored logo of the prancing horse and golden Schumi lettering.

For the race days, Monaco has turned into the Lourdes of motor sport, except that the cavallino has replaced the Cross, and the primadonna, Michael Schumacher, the real Madonna. Indeed, any reference to the holy spring is completely out of place – in Formula 1, holy they are not. As the special trains from Cannes and Ventimiglia come and go, the invasion of the *tifosi* is decanted downwards towards the harbor district, La Condamine, flooding the boulevards and avenues, branching into smaller side roads and lanes, dripping into the stands, seeping along the rows and running into the hard seats which had been booked the previous year – just in case. These people are really out of place: Monaco, this aloof beauty, has elitist tastes, as everyone knows. The money is welcome, but the guests less so, particularly when they come in crowds. The tiny street-cleaning machines flit between ambling legs, followed by appropriately attired road cleaners with long-handled scoops, who pick up every cigarette butt with an expression of distaste, as if they were using a pooper scooper.

In the meantime, all hell has broken loose on the Autoroute La Provençale and the Austostrada dei Fiori. At the Bordighera junction, a horde of Ferraris, all of them red, go roaring westwards, where the holy of holies beckons, as did Imola in the east two weeks previously. Half a dozen Fiat Barchettas and Alfa Spiders are being driven along in their slipstream. All of them, after all, are part of the same family, in spirit at least, and even a classic 275 GTB has to show its paces. The Grand Prix is being rehearsed as the cars, in close proximity, scream into tunnels of which the drivers

Schumacher?« fragt der mit den schütteren schwarzen Haaren zögernd, beschwörend fast, mit Betonung auf der dritten Silbe. »Schumacher!« tönt es in sonorem Chor zurück. Daumen werden zur Bestätigung nach oben gereckt. Die Losung löst im proppenvollen Abteil länderumspannendes Einvernehmen zwischen Deutschen und Italienern aus, Schumania und Ferrari-Fieber addieren sich seit Imola zum Doppel-Delirium. Welchem Rennstall man die Stange hält, darüber besteht sowieso kein Zweifel: Alle tragen ja die Uniform der Leidenschaft mit den fast schon sakralen Emblemen der Marke aus Maranello, zumindest aber eine rote Mütze auf der Seele, mit dem geliebten Pferdchen-Logo und goldenem Schumi-Schriftzug.

In diesen Tagen wird Monaco zum Lourdes des Motorsports, nur daß das Cavallino an die Stelle des Kreuzes tritt und die Primadonna Michael Schumacher an die Stelle der Madonna Maria. Die wunderkräftige Heilquelle ist gar gänzlich entbehrlich – in der Formel 1 sind sowieso alle mit allen Wassern gewaschen. Im Rhythmus der Züge und Sonderzüge aus Richtung Cannes und Ventimiglia ergießt sich die Invasion der *tifosi* abwärts in Richtung auf das Hafenviertel La Condamine, flutet über Boulevards und Avenuen, verästelt sich in Gassen und Gäßchen, tröpfelt in die Tribünen, sickert in lange Reihen, verliert sich auf den harten Sitzen, die man vorsichtshalber schon letztes Jahr gebucht hat. Die Leute sind eigentlich fehl am Platze: Monaco, diese spröde Schöne, hat bekanntlich einen elitären Geschmack. Das Geld ist willkommen, die Gäste weniger, vor allem wenn sie in Scharen auftreten. Und so flitzen winzige Reinigungsmaschinen wieselflink zwischen wandernden Beinen, gefolgt von proper gewandeten Straßenkehrern, die mit Schäufelchen an langen Stielen jede Kippe aufnehmen, als sei es Hundedreck.

Unterdessen ist auf der Autoroute La Provençale und auf der Austostrada dei Fiori die Hölle los. Aus der Einfahrt Bordighera driftet eine Horde Ferrari, alle rot, röhrt gen Westen, wo an diesem Tag das Allerheiligste lockt wie 14 Tage zuvor Imola im Osten. Im Windschatten flattert ein halbes Dutzend Fiat Barchetta und Alfa Spider. Alle kommen schließlich aus einer großen Familie, im Geiste sowieso, und auch der Klassiker 275 GTB wird nicht geschont. Man probt gewissermaßen den Grand Prix, heult Rad an Rad in Tunnel,

Schumacher », demande l'homme à la chevelure noire éclaircie sur un ton hésitant, presque conjurateur, en mettant l'accent sur la troisième syllabe. « Schumacher », renvoie l'écho de ses compagnons. Qui pointent le pouce vers le haut en signe d'admiration. Dans le compartiment plein à craquer, il suffit de prononcer ce nom pour déclencher un consensus international entre Allemands et Italiens et, depuis Imola, Schumania et fièvre de Ferrari s'additionnent pour donner naissance à un délire à la puissance deux. De quelle écurie sont-ils fanatiques ? La question est superflue : tous portent l'uniforme de la passion avec les emblèmes déjà cultuels de la marque de Maranello, ou tout au moins une casquette rouge dans le cœur avec la silhouette du petit cheval cabré adoré et le nom Schumacher brodé en lettres d'or.

Ces jours-là, Monaco est devenu le Lourdes de la compétition automobile, à cette différence près que le cavallino remplace la croix et la Primadonna Michael Schumacher, la madone Sainte-Marie. L'effet thérapeutique de la source miraculeuse n'est même pas nécessaire – en Formule 1, tous nagent de toute façon en eaux troubles. Au rythme des trains réguliers et spéciaux arrivant de Cannes et de Vintimille, le raz-de-marée des *tifosi* se déverse en direction du quartier du port de la Condamine, débordant sur les boulevards et les avenues, s'infiltrant dans les rues et ruelles pour remplir goutte-à-goutte les tribunes, défilant en rangées interminables qui se répartissent sur des sièges inconfortables que l'on a déjà réservés l'année dernière par mesure de prudence. Tous ces gens-là ne sont, à proprement parler, pas à leur place ici : Monaco, cette beauté inaccessible, a, de notoriété publique, un goût élitaire. L'argent est bienvenu, les hôtes, un peu moins, surtout quand ils déboulent en hordes. De minuscules nettoyeuses virevoltent comme des feux follets entre les jambes des promeneurs, suivies de balayeurs en uniforme d'une propreté irréprochable qui, avec une petite pelle au bout d'un long manche, ramassent le moindre mégot de cigarette comme s'il s'agissait de crottes de chien.

Pendant ce temps, c'est l'enfer sur l'autoroute la Provençale et sur l'Austostrada dei Fiori. A l'entrée de Bordighera, une horde de Ferrari piaffantes, toutes en rouge, rugit en direction de l'Ouest où, ce jour-là, le saint des saints attire ses fidèles comme Imola, à l'Est, quinze jours plus tôt. Dans leur sillage bourdonne une demi-douzaine de Fiat Barchetta et d'Alfa Spider. Tous viennent finalement d'une grande famille, par l'esprit de toute façon, et même une vénérable classique comme la 275 GTB n'est pas épargnée non plus. On s'entraîne en quelque sorte pour le Grand Prix, hurlant roue à roue dans les tunnels, bien que l'on ne puisse pas voir la lumière du jour à leur extrémité, à fond de sixième comme le complexe du Loews, un cauchemar où le grand-père de Savone avec sa Cinquecento qui, ce dimanche matin-là, voulait seulement aller entretenir la tombe familiale à Mortola-Inferiore. Derrière les pare-brise fortement inclinés, des lèvres murmurent le mot Schumacher, en mettant l'accent sur la troisième syllabe. Sa pole position conquise la veille leur a donné à tous encore une fois une poussée d'adrénaline supplémentaire. La toute-puissance du gigantesque

Stronghold: this balcony, too, changed its function to become a Ferrari enclave. No doubt about the name of the person in whom all hope is vested.

Hoch-Burg: Auch dieser Balkon wurde zur Ferrari-Enklave umfunktioniert. Kein Zweifel wie der Hoffnungsträger heißt.

Bastion : ce balcon aussi s'est mué en une enclave de Ferrari. Il n'y a pas de doute quant à celui qui porte leurs espoirs.

cannot see the light at the other end, as if they are under the Loews complex in sixth gear – a nightmare for the grandpa from Savona in his Cinquecento, who simply wants to visit the family grave in Mortola-Inferiore this Sunday morning. Behind steeply raked windscreens mouths form the word Schumacher, again with emphasis on the third syllable. The fight for pole position yesterday gave everyone a real kick. Nevertheless, the huge traffic jam at the toll booths and the border crossing point at Menton, which takes no account of class, reunites Testarossa and Punto: the onward journey, at a snail's pace to the destination of the pilgrimage, is undertaken in enforced fraternity.

But this democracy has disappeared again by the time we get to the cheap places on the steep slope below the Grimaldi palace and the cathedral, which appear from a distance like a rhapsody in Ferrari red. The common language of communication is Italian. The motto of the dispossesed, "We down here, you up there" has – literally – been stood on its head. We up here: the fan pure and simple – strong, tough and equipped with a facility which is otherwise only displayed by mountain goats: to spend long periods on extremely steep hillsides without complaint. This species only has one natural enemy, the well-armoured flora such as the local cacti *opuntia* or Ceree (*cactoidea*). You down below: a truly large contingent of VIPs, called by the British for some odd reason the "beautiful people", although many have passed their prime, like withered hydrangeas in October, and equipped with the most blue of special passes. The Germans among them, too, often have their places of permanent residence just around the corner, attractive owner-occupied properties in the neighbouring communes of Cap-Martin or Beaulieu; or they appear as boat people with snow-white luxury liners filled to the brim with Moët et Chandon, Malossol caviar and Red Bull, bobbing up and down in the gentle swell of the Port de Monaco. Even the density of reporters is above average. The carefully staged RTL interview with Michael Schumacher suddenly turns into a pilgrimage. The lines begin to wobble, fighting breaks out at the back, complete strangers shout inexcusable insults at one another.

The start is at 2.30 pm, the tension rises until it becomes unbearable. "Schumacher?" the man with the sparse black hair asks hesitatingly, almost beseechingly, with emphasis on the third syllable. But he was eliminated after just 45 seconds, a driving error. He will never appear at the swimming baths, where our friend has taken up position.

obwohl man das Licht an deren Ende nicht sehen kann, sechster Gang voll wie unter dem Loews-Komplex, ein Alptraum für den Opa aus Savona mit seinem Cinque-cento, der an diesem Sonntagmorgen nur mal eben das Familiengrab in Mortola-Inferiore besuchen wollte. Hinter stark geneigten Windschutzscheiben formen Münder das Wort Schumacher, mit Betonung auf der dritten Silbe. Die Pole Position gestern hat allen noch einmal den richtigen Kick gegeben. Die klassen-übergreifende Allmacht des Riesenstaus vor der Zahlstation und dem Grenzübergang bei Menton führt indessen Testarossa und Punto wieder zusammen: Die Weiterreise im Schrittempo zu den Stätten der Sehnsucht tritt man brüderlich zwangsvereint an.

Weit weniger demokratisch geht es auf den billigen Plätzen am Steilhang unterhalb von Grimaldi-Palast und Kathedrale zu, von weitem eine Rhapsodie in Ferrari-rot. Verkehrssprache ist italienisch. Dort hat man das Motto der Mißgunst »Wir hier unten, ihr da oben« gewissermaßen auf den Kopf gestellt, buchstäblich. Wir hier oben: der Fan pur, überdies stark und zäh und mit einer faszinierenden Fähigkeit ausgestattet, die sonst nur Gamsböcke aufweisen: lange und bedürfnislos auf extremen Schrägen zu verweilen. Diese Spezies fürchtet eigentlich nur einen natürlichen Gegner, wehr-hafte Flora wie die ortsansässigen Kakteen Opuntie (*opuntioidea*) oder Ceree (*cactoidea*). Ihr da unten: ein wahrer Massenauftrieb von Promis, all jene, die die Engländer aus irgendeinem Grunde »the beautiful ones« nennen, obwohl viele abgeblüht sind wie Hortensien im Oktober, gleichwohl ausgestattet mit den edelsten Sonderausweisen. Auch die Deutschen unter ihnen haben häufig feste Wohnsitze just um die Ecke, schmucke Eigenheime in den Nachbargemeinden Cap-Martin oder Beaulieu, oder treten als Boat People mit schneeweißen Luxuslinern randvoll mit Moët & Chandon, Malossol-Kaviar und Red Bull auf, die in der sanften Dünung des Port de Monaco dümpeln. Selbst die Dichte an Berichterstattern ist hoch wie nirgends sonst: Beim sorgfältig inszenierten RTL-Interview mit Michael Schumacher wird die Szene plötzlich zur Walstatt. Die Reihen geraten ins Wanken. In den hinteren Rängen bricht eine Rangelei aus, Wildfremde teilen einander Nichtwiedergutzumachendes mit.

Start ist um halb drei, die Spannung schier uner-träglich. »Schumacher?« fragt der mit den schütteren schwarzen Haaren zögernd, fast beschwörend, mit Betonung auf der dritten Silbe. Aber der ist nach 45 Sekunden ausgeschieden, ein Fahrfehler. Am Schwimm-bad, wo unser Freund seinen Platz bezogen hat, wird Michael Schumacher nie vorbeikommen.

embouteillage devant la station de péage et à la douane de Menton, qui réunissent dans leur giron toutes les classes de la société, fait malgré tout se réunir à nouveau Testarossa et Punto : de force, on entame dans la fraternité la poursuite du mariage à pas comptés vers les lieux du culte de la nostalgie.

En revanche, les choses se passent beaucoup moins démocratiquement aux places bon marché du Rocher, au pied du palais des Grimaldi et de la cathédrale. Vu de loin, une rapsodie en rouge Ferrari. La langue officielle est l'italien. Là, l'on a en quelque sorte inversé, mais littéralement, la devise de l'envie. Nous, ici en haut : le fan à l'état pur, et qui plus est fort et endurant et doté d'une aptitude fascinante que ne possèdent, sinon, que les chamois : séjourner sur des pentes extrêmes pendant longtemps et sans manifester le moindre besoin. Cette espèce ne craint à proprement parler qu'un ennemi naturel, une flore qui sait se défendre comme les cactus autochtones Opuntie (*opuntioidea*) ou Ceree (*cactoidea*). Vous, là en bas : un véritable raz-de-marée de vedettes et VIP, tous ceux que les Anglais, pour des raisons insondables, surnomment « the beautiful people » bien que beaucoup soient déjà fanés comme les hortensias en octobre, malgré tout dotés des coupe-file les plus prestigieux. Parmi eux, les Allemands ont fréquemment aussi un domicile à quelques pas de là, de magnifiques villas dans les communes voisines de Cap-Martin ou de Beaulieu, ou se produisent tels des *boat people* sur de magnifiques yachts immaculés de grand luxe débordant de Moët et Chandon, de caviar Malossol et de Red Bull, qui se laissent bercer par les douces vagues du port de Monaco. Même la densité de reporters est plus élevée que partout ailleurs : lors de l'interview de Michael Schumacher mis en scène par RTL comme une grande production, l'intermède se mue soudain en lieu de pèlerinage. La foule frémit. Une bagarre éclate parmi ceux qui sont trop loin du feu de l'action, des inconnus se jettent mutuellement des mots qu'ils ne pourront plus jamais se pardonner.

Le départ est prévu pour deux heures et demie, la tension semble insupportable. « Schumacher », demande l'homme à la chevelure noire éclaircie sur un ton hésitant, presque conjurateur, en mettant l'accent sur la troisième syllabe. Mais le brave Schumacher a abandonné au bout de 45 secondes seulement, erreur de pilotage. A la Piscine, là où notre ami a pris place, il ne verra jamais passer Michael Schumacher.

ROSIE'S MEMORIES

ROSIES ERINNERUNGEN · LES SOUVENIRS DE ROSIE

When the Chatham Bar was closed in September 1996, this ill-tempered administrative act provoked a world-wide reaction which was not restricted to the establishment's sporting friends. Two hundred meters to the left, behind Sainte Dévote at the edge of the track, it appeared to be part of the fixtures and fittings of the Monaco Grand Prix, a friendly fossil which had seen better days. And yet today, the memories of the former lessee, Rosie Bernard, turns into praise of the good old times:

"My father, Eugène Balbo, opened the Bar in 1946 and called it after the Chatham naval base, in southern England. The English were also our most frequent visitors after the locals. In 1950 I watched daddy for a few months to see how it was done and then became boss in 1951, when I was just twenty. Soon everyone was calling the pub Rosie's Bar. During the Grand Prix, in particular, it became a magnet for everybody who was anybody. People wanted to have fun, and they took the time to have it. They arrived a whole week in advance of the race and stayed, if at all possible, for at least another few days afterwards.

Stirling Moss came as long ago as the early fifties, at that time still a very young fellow with a great deal of hair and always accompanied by his mother and father. Peter Collins came and so did Mike Hawthorn, and sometimes Fangio and even Enzo Ferrari, a real aristocrat and gentleman who, like Rob Walker, in those days maintained a successful private team. Those three drivers were very serious like, later, Jim Clark and Gilles Villeneuve would be, yet they were good with people, approachable and not at all snobbish.

One of my most faithful customers was Graham Hill, who often came with his wife Bette, Damon's mother. He almost always wore this funny hat, with a peak at the front and back, and he was immensely popular. Obviously he never forgot that he had once been a mechanic himself, he had a kind word and a joke for everyone, and usually he invited the whole BRM team for a drink. On those occasions it might well happen that beer flowed in streams on the floor. Or Champagne: some people thought it a great joke to fire the corks across the road at passing cars. My husband, Jean-Louis, sang in accompaniment and played the guitar, a real artist. In those times it was about fun, friendship, comradeship, not just money, money and more money, as it is today.

Once they carried the complete stock of the bar on to the race track, put a fence around the whole lot and declared it private property. No-one minded – especially not if they were invited for a drink! Finally the police came, a friendly lot at that time still, and asked us to call it a day. Another time the Lotus people, under their boss Colin Chapman, built a Formula 1 car from things in the bar, with beer barrels for wheels.

By the way, the terrace in front of the bar was the best spectator platform you could imagine. Before the barriers were raised, a few straw bales at most lay about and there was nowhere in the world where you were closer to the cars and drivers than where we were. No-one bothered about the danger. The last person able to celebrate such boisterous parties was Keke Rosberg. At the end they were all shouting "Keke,

Als die Chatham Bar im September 1996 geschlossen wird, löst dieser unwirsche Verwaltungsakt nicht nur unter den Freunden des Sports weltweit eine kleine Betroffenheit aus. 200 Meter links hinter Sainte Dévote am Rande der Piste, scheint sie zum Inventar des Grand Prix de Monaco zu gehören, ein freundliches Fossil aus besseren Tagen. Und so geraten die Erinnerungen ihrer früheren Pächterin Rosie Bernard unversehens zum Lob der guten alten Zeit:

»Mein Vater Eugène Balbo eröffnete die Bar 1946 und nannte sie nach dem Kriegshafen Chatham in Südengland. Engländer waren denn auch neben den Einheimischen unsere häufigsten Besucher. 1950 schaute ich Papa ein paar Monate zu, wie man sowas macht, und wurde 1951 selbst Chefin, gerade mal zwanzig Jahre alt. Bald hieß das Lokal bei jedermann Rosie's Bar. Vor allem während des Grand Prix wurde es zum Magneten für alles, was Rang und Namen hatte. Die Leute wollten Spaß haben und nahmen sich die Zeit dafür: Man traf schon eine ganze Woche vor dem Rennen ein und blieb, wenn sich das machen ließ, noch mindestens eine halbe Woche danach. Stirling Moss kam schon Anfang der Fünfziger, damals noch ein blutjunger Bursche, mit vielen Haaren auf dem Kopf, stets in Begleitung seiner Mutter und seines Vaters. Peter Collins kam und Mike Hawthorn, und manchmal Fangio und sogar Enzo Ferrari, ein richtiger Aristokrat und Gentleman, ähnlich Rob Walker, der ein erfolgreiches privates Team unterhielt. Diese drei waren sehr ernsthaft, ebenso wie später Jim Clark und Gilles Villeneuve. Und dennoch hatten sie ein gutes Händchen mit den Menschen, waren ansprechbar und überhaupt nicht hochnäsig.

Einer meiner treuesten Kunden war Graham Hill, oft zusammen mit seiner Frau Bette, Damons Mutter. Er hatte fast immer diese witzige Mütze auf, mit je einem Schirm vorn und hinten, und war immens populär. Er hat offenbar nie vergessen, daß er selbst einst Mechaniker gewesen war, hatte ein gutes Wort und einen Scherz für jedermann und lud gewöhnlich das ganze BRM-Team zu einem Umtrunk ein. Da konnte es schon mal vorkommen, daß Bier in Strömen über den Boden floß. Oder Champagner: Manche Leute machten sich einen Jux daraus, die Korken über die Straße und gegen vorbeifahrende Autos zu schießen. Mein Mann Jean-Louis sang dazu und spielte die Gitarre, ein richtiger Künstler. Damals waren Fun, Freundschaft und Kameradschaft angesagt, nicht nur Geld, Geld und nochmals Geld wie heute.

Einmal haben sie das komplette Inventar der Bar hinausgeschleppt auf die Piste, das Ganze umzäunt und als Privatgrundstück deklariert. Niemand nahm das übel, vor allem, wenn er zu einem Drink eingeladen wurde. Schließlich kam die Polizei, die damals noch freundlich war, und bat uns, wir möchten allmählich Schluß machen. Ein anderes Mal haben die Lotus-Leute unter ihrem Chef Colin Chapman einen Formel-1-Wagen aus Requisiten des Lokals gebaut, mit Bierfässern als Rädern. Übrigens stellte die Terrasse vor der Bar den schönsten Zuschauerplatz dar, den man sich vorstellen kann. Bevor die Leitplanken hochgezogen wurden und höchstens ein paar Strohballen

Lorsque le Chatham Bar ferme ses portes, en septembre 1996, cette décision administrative arbitraire déclenche une vague d'indignation parmi les amoureux de la course du monde entier et pas seulement parmi eux. A 200 mètres à gauche derrière Sainte Dévote, juste au bord de la piste, il semble faire partie de l'inventaire du Grand Prix de Monaco, fossile accueillant qui a déjà vu des jours meilleurs. Et c'est ainsi que les souvenirs de son ancienne gérante, Rosie Bernard, sont pratiquement un éloge au bon vieux temps :

« Mon père Eugène Balbo a ouvert le bar en 1946 et l'a baptisé d'après le port de guerre de Chatham, dans le sud de l'Angleterre. Avec les Monégasques, les Anglais étaient en effet nos meilleurs clients. En 1950, j'ai regardé pendant quelques mois par-dessus l'épaule de papa pour apprendre, puis je suis moi-même devenue la patronne en 1951, alors que j'avais tout juste vingt ans. Bientôt, l'établissement fut pour tout le monde le Rosie's Bar. Durant le Grand Prix, notamment, il devint le lieu de passage obligé pour toutes les célébrités. Les gens voulaient s'amuser et ils en prenaient le temps : certains arrivaient même une semaine avant la course et, dans la mesure du possible, restaient encore trois ou quatre jours après. Stirling Moss est venu dès le début des années cinquante, encore tout jeune à cette époque, avec beaucoup de cheveux sur la tête, toujours accompagné de sa mère et de son père. Peter Collins venait, Mike Hawthorn aussi, parfois Fangio et même Enzo Ferrari, un authentique aristocrate et gentleman, tout comme Rob Walker, qui entretenait avec succès une écurie privée. Ces trois derniers pilotes étaient très sérieux, tout comme, plus tard, Jim Clark et Gilles Villeneuve. Et, pourtant, ils avaient un bon contact avec les gens, on pouvait leur adresser la parole et ils n'étaient pas du tout arrogants.

L'un de mes clients les plus fidèles était Graham Hill, qui venait souvent avec sa femme Bette, la mère de Damon. Il avait presque toujours cette amusante casquette à la Sherlock Holmes et jouissait d'une immense popularité. Sans doute n'avait-il jamais oublié qu'il avait lui-même commencé comme mécanicien : il avait toujours un mot gentil et une bonne blague pour chacun et offrait souvent une tournée à toute l'écurie BRM. Il arrivait parfois que la bière coule à flots sur le plancher. Ou le champagne : certains prenaient un malin plaisir à faire sauter les bouchons dans la rue pour canarder les voitures qui circulaient. Mon mari Jean-Louis chantait et les accompagnait à la guitare, un véritable artiste. A cette époque-là, plaisir, amitié et camaraderie n'étaient pas encore de vains mots et on ne pensait pas seulement à l'argent, à l'argent et encore à l'argent comme aujourd'hui.

Une fois, ils ont tout transporté sur la piste l'inventaire au grand complet du bar, clôturé le tout et l'ont déclaré propriété privée. Personne n'en a été vexé, surtout quand on l'invitait à prendre un verre. Finalement, la police est arrivée – elle était encore conciliante à cette époque – et elle nous a priés de bien vouloir mettre de l'ordre petit à petit. Une autre fois, les gens de chez Lotus et leur chef Colin Chapman ont construit une Formule 1 avec les accessoires du café, avec des fûts de bière à la place des roues. La terrasse devant le bar

Keke" and they even made Kekes into the common currency, instead of the usual francs!

In the eighties everything changed, as did the topics of conversation. Previously people talked about everything under the sun, but from then on they spoke about nothing but technical matters – and money, of course. That spelled the end of Rosie's Bar. The building belonged to the government, and the world-famous hospital for heart diseases behind it was given permission to build an extension on our piece of land – which, by the way, has still not happened. When Bette Hill heard about it she said spontaneously: "It would be a pity if something nice like that were to be lost to posterity." She founded a society and shipped the whole pub, with all the details like the windows and pictures on the walls, to England. There it is to be rebuilt at Silverstone, but Bernie Ecclestone is demanding a lot of money for it.

As long ago as the autumn of 1987, BMW built an accurate copy of Rosie's Bar at the Racing Car Show in Earls Court, with me as landlady of course, and invited journalists to a press conference in it. When the pub was closed, the drivers gave me a crocheted cloth with the portraits of all the previous Grand Prix winners. I found that very touching. At the same time I turned over a new leaf in the book of my life and am very happy with it. Today I own a small souvenir shop in the heart of the old town of Monte Carlo, in the Rue Comte Félix Gastaldi, surrounded by lots of nice people. Its name: Rosie's Memories.

1998 will be the first time in fifty years that I will not be in town during the Grand Prix because a niece is getting married. But that doesn't matter because there's a time for everything."

herumlagen, war man Wagen und Fahrern nirgendwo auf der ganzen Welt näher als bei uns. Um die Gefahr hat sich niemand geschert. Der letzte, der solche ausgelassenen Feste feiern konnte, war Keke Rosberg. Am Ende haben sie alle »Keke, Keke« gebrüllt und sogar Kekes zur gängigen Münze gemacht anstatt der üblichen Francs.

In den achtziger Jahren wurde alles anders, so wie sich auch die Gesprächsthemen änderten: Früher redete man über Gott und die Welt, und plötzlich drehte sich alles nur noch um Technik und, natürlich, ums liebe Geld. Da waren die Tage von Rosie's Bar bereits gezählt: Das Gebäude gehörte der Regierung, und die weltberühmte Klinik für Herzkrankheiten dahinter erhielt die Erlaubnis, auf unserem Grundstück einen Anbau hochzuziehen, was allerdings bis heute noch nicht geschehen ist. Als Bette Hill davon hörte, sagte sie spontan: »Es wäre ein Jammer, wenn so etwas Schönes der Nachwelt verlorenginge.« Sie gründete eine Gesellschaft und verfrachtete das komplette Lokal mit sämtlichen Einzelheiten wie den Fenstern und den Bildern an der Wand nach England. Dort soll es in Silverstone wieder erstehen, aber Bernie Ecclestone verlangt sehr viel Geld dafür. Schon im Herbst 1987 hatte BMW auf der Rennwagenshow in Earls Court eine getreue Kopie von Rosie's Bar aufgebaut, selbstver-ständlich mit mir selbst als Wirtin, und die Journalisten dort zu einer Pressekonferenz eingeladen. Zur Schließung des Lokals bekam ich von den Fahrern ein gehäkeltes Deckchen mit den Portraits der früheren Sieger der Grands Prix. Das hat mich sehr gerührt. Zugleich habe ich ein neues Blatt im Buch meines Lebens aufgeschlagen und bin sehr glücklich damit. Ich besitze heute einen kleinen Souvenirladen im Herzen der Altstadt von Monte Carlo, umgeben von lauter netten Leuten, in der Rue Comte Félix Gastaldi. Sein Name: Rosie's Memories.

1998 werde ich zum ersten Mal seit fünfzig Jahren während des Großen Preises nicht in der Stadt sein, weil eine Nichte heiratet. Das macht aber gar nichts, denn alles hat seine Zeit.«

était d'ailleurs le plus bel endroit que l'on puisse imaginer pour les spectateurs. Avant que l'on installe les glissières, il n'y avait que quelques bottes de paille ici et là, nulle part ailleurs dans le monde on n'était aussi près des voitures et des pilotes que chez nous. Et personne n'a jamais eu la moindre pensée pour le risque. Le dernier qui a pu faire de telles fêtes aussi débridées a été Keke Rosberg. A la fin, tout le monde a hurlé « Keke, Keke » et les « Kekes » sont même devenus monnaie de payement à la place des francs officiels.

Dans les années quatre-vingt, tout a commencé à changer, comme ont aussi commencé à changer les thèmes des discussions : autrefois, on parlait de tout et de rien et, soudain, on n'a plus parlé que de la technique et, naturellement, de l'argent qui dicte tout. Dès lors, les jours du Rosie's Bar étaient déjà comptés : l'immeuble appartenait au gouvernement, et la clinique pour les maladies cardiaques qui se trouvait derrière chez nous, de réputation mondiale, obtint l'autorisation de construire un bâtiment sur notre terrain, ce qui ne s'est toutefois toujours pas fait jusqu'à aujourd'hui. Lorsque Bette Hill en entendit parler, elle déclara spontanément : « Ce serait tout de même dommage que quelque chose d'aussi beau soit perdu pour la postérité. » Elle fonda une société et transporta en Angleterre l'établissement au grand complet avec tout son aménagement comme les fenêtres et les tableaux accrochés aux murs. Son idée était de le reconstruire à Silverstone, mais Bernie Ecclestone exigeait énormé-ment d'argent pour cela. A l'automne 1987, au Salon de la voiture de course d'Earls Court, déjà, BMW avait reconstruit sur son stand une copie fidèle du Rosie's Bar, bien évidemment avec moi-même comme patronne, et y avait invité les journalistes à une con-férence de presse. Pour la fermeture de l'établissement, les pilotes m'ont offert un napperon au crochet avec les portraits des anciens vainqueurs des Grands Prix. J'ai été profondément émue. Mais j'avais déjà ouvert un nouveau chapitre dans le livre de ma vie et j'en suis très heureuse. Je possède aujourd'hui un petit magasin de souvenirs au cœur de la Vieille Ville de Monte Carlo, suis entourée de gens tous plus gentils les uns que les autres, dans la rue du Comte Félix de Gastaldi. Son nom : Rosie's Memories.

En 1998, je ne serai pas en ville pendant le Grand Prix pour la première fois depuis cinquante ans parce que l'une de mes nièces se marie. Mais ça ne fait rien, car il y a un temps pour tout. »

1997

The mood in the pit lane always develops in the same way. First there is tense expectation among everyone before the start; this is followed by a sparkling mood in one camp and downcast expressions in the others after the cars have crossed the finishing line. Only the protagonists change.

Pure joy reigned at Ferrari after the 55th edition of the Monaco Grand Prix. "Prince rainier of Monaco" was the punning headline of the British specialist magazine *Autosport* above its report. The rain prince was Michael Schumacher, who, in his F 310 B, had delivered another example of his unmatched skills when adhesion is at its minimum, a veritable kingpin of success.

While thousandths of a second had still counted in the struggle for pole position, the German had moved up the heavy guns for the race, and the courage and morale of his opponents crumbled under their heavy fire. The Ferrari shot through the light barrier of the timing line with a lead of 6.5 seconds after the first lap, with a lead of 12 seconds after the second, with half a minute after the tenth, and with almost a whole minute at the end of lap 62, when the Grand Prix was prematurely called off because the two-hour barrier was threatening once again.

A short detour into the emergency exit at Sainte Dévote on lap 53 did not cause any stress: stop, turn the car, return to the hilly part of the course, and a mere eight seconds lost. Nobody is perfect – not even Michael Schumacher.

Unrestrained Scottish happiness was also in evidence at Stewart Grand Prix. The Brazilian Rubens Barrichello had come second, scoring the first points in the fifth race since the birth of the company. Never had he been so moved, team founder and three-times World Champion Jackie Stewart told the cameras and microphones in a voice choked with emotion, never in his whole career as a racing driver.

There were long faces amongst the other big names, however, who railed against their fate. Williams was badly advised to send both its FW 19s into combat on slick tyres. "I was quite confused and thought, do they know something that I don't?", Michael Schumacher commented later. In such a situation even the best qualifying times were of little use to Heinz-Harald Frentzen. He crashed into the harbor chicane after 39 laps, while Jacques Villeneuve absented himself after the 16th lap having smashed into the barrier at Sainte Dévote. No Williams, incidentally, had won in Monaco since 1983.

Despondency also for Benetton. The team was labouring with an old problem associated with the B 197 – that the car's tyres did not heat up sufficiently. Lap times and placings even during qualifying had been miserable, and during the ninth lap Gerhard Berger dented his car in Mirabeau and dawdled along without enthusiasm. On lap 16 Jean Alesi spun in Portier and stalled the engine – and that was it. At McLaren, any discussion about the wrong choice of tyres became academic anyway. During the second lap, David Coulthard (on "intermediates") set off a chain reaction in front of the chicane and took his team-mate Mika Hakkinen (on slicks) with him out of the race.

Die Stimmung in der Boxengasse entwickelt sich immer gleich: Gespannte Erwartung bei allen vor dem Start, nach der Zieldurchfahrt Champagnerlaune bei den einen und betretene Mienen bei den anderen. Nur die Protagonisten wechseln.

Eitel Freude herrscht nach der 55. Edition des monegassischen Grand Prix bei Ferrari. »Prince rainier of Monaco« titelt das englische Fachmagazin *Autosport* seinen Bericht in listigem Doppelsinn. Der Regenprinz: Michael Schumacher, der mit dem F 310 B eine neue Probe seiner ans Unwirkliche grenzenden Kunst bei beschränkter Haftung abgeliefert hat, ein veritabler Hecht im Karpfenteich.

Wurde beim Ringen um die Pole Position noch nach tausendstel Sekunden abgerechnet, fährt der Deutsche im Rennen gröberes Geschütz auf. In dessen Kugelhagel zerbröckeln Mut und Moral der Konkurrenten: Mit sechseinhalb Sekunden Vorsprung gischtet der Ferrari nach der ersten Runde durch die Lichtschranke der Zeitnahme, mit zwölf nach der zweiten, mit einer halben Minute nach der zehnten, mit fast einer ganzen am Ende der 62., als der Grand Prix vorzeitig abgewunken wird. Denn die Zwei-Stunden-Barriere droht, wieder einmal.

Ein kurzer Abstecher in den Notausgang bei Sainte Dévote im 53. Durchgang wird dabei locker weggesteckt: Rallyewende, Rückkehr auf den gebirgigen Teil des Kurses, acht Sekunden Verlust. »Nobody is perfect«, nicht einmal dieser Michael Schumacher.

Schottisch-moderater Frohsinn auch bei der Stewart Grand Prix Limited: Der Brasilianer Rubens Barrichello wird zweiter, erste Punkte im fünften Rennen seit der Geburt der Firma. Nie sei er emotional so bewegt gewesen, äußert sich Gründervater und Dreifach-Champion Jackie Stewart vor Kameras und Mikrophonen mit erstickter Stimme, nicht einmal in seiner eigenen aktiven Karriere.

Bei den anderen Großen hingegen gibt es lange Gesichter bis hin zu dumpfem Hadern mit dem Schicksal. Bei Williams ist man übel beraten, als man beide FW 19 auf Slicks ins Gefecht schickt. »Ich war ganz verwirrt und dachte, die wissen etwas, was ich nicht weiß«, höhnt Michael Schumacher später. Da nützt Heinz-Harald Frentzen auch die beste Trainingszeit nichts: Er eckt nach 39 Runden massiv in der Hafenschikane an, Jacques Villeneuve hat sich schon im Anschluß an die 16. nach heftigem Kontakt mit der Leitplanke bei Sainte Dévote verabschiedet. Übrigens: Seit 1983 hat kein Williams mehr gewonnen in Monaco.

Trauerfall zwei: Benetton. Man laboriert an einem alten Problem des B 197 – die Reifen heizen sich nicht genügend auf. Schon Werte und Plazierungen in der Qualifikation sind miserabel. Im neunten Durchgang ramponiert Gerhard Berger sein Auto in Mirabeau und trödelt lustlos weiter, in Runde 16 rotiert Jean Alesi in Portier und würgt den Motor ab – das war's. Bei McLaren indes erübrigt sich jegliche Diskussion über die verfehlte Reifenwahl von ganz allein. In der zweiten Runde löst David Coulthard (auf Intermediates) vor der Schikane eine Kettenraktion aus und nimmt seinen Teamkollegen Mika Hakkinen (auf Slicks) gleich mit aus dem Rennen.

L'ambiance dans la voie des stands est toujours la même : une tension qui met les nerfs de tous à vif avant le départ, mais, après l'arrivée bouchons de champagne qui sautent chez les uns et visages déçus chez les autres. Il n'y a que les protagonistes qui changent.

Après la 55ᵉ édition du Grand Prix de Monaco, l'allégresse est totale chez Ferrari. « Prince rainier of Monaco », affiche en titre la revue spécialisée britannique *Autosport* en un jeu de mots réussi entre Rainier et pluie (*rain* en anglais). Le prince de la pluie est Michael Schumacher qui, avec sa F 310 B a donné un nouvel échantillon de son don d'équilibriste surnaturel dans des conditions d'adhérence minimum, véritable loup dans la bergerie – ou doit-on plutôt dire poisson dans l'eau ?

Si, pour conquérir la pole position, on se bat encore à coups de millièmes de seconde, en course, l'Allemand utilise des arguments plus frappants. Sous ses coups répétés s'effritent le courage et le moral de ses concurrents : à l'issue du premier tour, la Ferrari franchit les cellules photos électriques du chronométrage avec six secondes et demie d'avance, puis avec douze au deuxième tour, une demi-minute après le dixième et presque une minute à la fin du 62ᵉ, lorsque le Grand Prix est arrêté prématurément. En effet, une fois de plus, l'épée de Damoclès de la limite des deux heures pend au-dessus de la tête des pilotes.

Le pilote allemand fait une brève excursion dans l'échappatoire à Sainte Dévote, au 53ᵉ tour, comme si cela n'était qu'une anecdote : arrêt, demi-tour sur place et retour dans la partie escarpée du circuit, ayant perdu en cours de route huit secondes. « Nobody is perfect », pas même ce Michael Schumacher.

Une joie débridée à l'écossaise éclate au grand jour lors du Grand Prix Stewart : le Brésilien Rubens Barrichello termine deuxième, marquant les premiers points lors de la cinquième course depuis la naissance de la firme. Jamais il n'a été aussi ému, déclare d'une voix étouffée, devant caméras et microphones, le fondateur de l'écurie et triple champion du monde Jackie Stewart, pas même au cours de sa propre carrière de pilote.

Chez les autres Grands, par contre, les visages se sont allongés et beaucoup ont du mal à accepter leur destin. Chez Williams, on a perdu toute chance en décidant d'envoyer les deux FW 19 au combat sur slicks. « J'étais abasourdi, expliquera plus tard Michael Schumacher ironique, je pensais qu'ils savaient quelque chose que je ne savais pas ». Même le meilleur temps aux essais réalisé par Heinz-Harald Frentzen ne lui sera d'aucune utilité : il percute brutalement la glissière à la chicane du port au 39ᵉ tour et Jacques Villeneuve a déjà abandonné, à l'issue du 16ᵉ, après être entré violemment en contact avec le rail à Sainte Dévote. Un détail : depuis 1983, plus aucune Williams n'a gagné à Monaco.

Deuxième coup du destin une fois de plus pour Benetton. On ne réussit pas à résoudre un vieux problème de la B 197 – les pneus ne s'échauffent pas assez. Les temps de parcours et les emplacements sur la grille de départ, déjà, sont misérables. Au 9ᵉ tour, Gerhard Berger endommage sa voiture à Mirabeau et repart sans grande envie – au 16ᵉ tour, Jean Alesi fait un tête-à-queue au virage du Portier et étouffe son moteur : terminé ! Chez McLaren, par contre, toute discussion est vaine sur le mauvais choix de pneus. Au second tour, David Coulthard (sur pneus « intermédiaires ») déclenche une réaction en chaîne devant la chicane et accroche irrémédiablement son coéquipier Mika Hakkinen (sur slicks) qui est contraint à l'abandon.

Approaching lensmen: the photographers Paul-Henri Cahier and Terry Griffin on their way to work.

Aufmarsch der Lichtbildner: die Fotografen Paul-Henri Cahier und Terry Griffin auf dem Weg zur Arbeit.

Arrivée des reporters : les photographes Paul-Henri Cahier et Terry Griffin se rendant au travail.

N°	DRIVERS		ENTRANTS	CARS	ENGINES	PRACTICE RESULTS	RACE RESULTS
5	**Michael Schumacher**	**D**	**SEFAC Ferrari S.p.A.**	**Ferrari F310B**	**Ferrari V10 2998 cc**	**2nd: 1'18"235**	**1st: 2h00'05"654**
22	Rubens Barrichello	BR	Stewart Grand Prix Ltd.	Stewart SF-1	Ford V10 2998 cc	10th: 1'19"295	2nd: 2h00'58"960
6	Eddie Irvine	GB	SEFAC Ferrari S.p.A.	Ferrari F310B	Ferrari V10 2998 cc	15th: 1'19"723	3rd: 2h01'27"762
14	Olivier Panis	F	Prost Grand Prix	Prost JS45	Mugen-Honda V10 2998 cc	12th: 1'19"626	4th: 2h01'50"056
19	Mika Juhani Salo	SF	Tyrrell Racing Organisation	Tyrrell 025	Ford V8 2998 cc	14th: 1'19"694	5th: 61 Laps
12	Giancarlo Fisichella	I	Jordan Grand Prix	Jordan 197	Peugeot V10 2998 cc	4th: 1'18"665	6th: 61 Laps
23	Jan Magnussen	DK	Stewart Grand Prix Ltd.	Stewart SF-1	Ford V10 2998 cc	19th: 1'20"516	7th: 61 Laps
18	Jos Verstappen	NL	Tyrrell Racing Organisation	Tyrrell 025	Ford V8 2998 cc	22nd: 1'21"290	8th: 60 Laps
8	Gerhard Berger	A	Benetton Formula Ltd.	Benetton B197	Renault V10 2998 cc	17th: 1'20"199	9th: 60 Laps
20	Ukyo Katayama	J	Minardi Team S.p.A.	Minardi M197	Hart V8 2996 cc	20th: 1'20"606	10th: 60 Laps
4	*Heinz-Harald Frentzen*	*D*	*Williams Grand Prix Engineering*	*Williams FW19*	*Renault V10 2998 cc*	*1st: 1'18"216*	*R*
3	Jacques Villeneuve	CDN	Williams Grand Prix Engineering	Williams FW19	Renault V10 2998 cc	3rd: 1'18"583	R
10	David Coulthard	GB	McLaren International	McLaren MP4/12	Mercedes V10 2998 cc	5th: 1'18"779	R
11	Ralf Schumacher	D	Jordan Grand Prix	Jordan 197	Peugeot V10 2998 cc	6th: 1'18"943	R
16	Johnny Herbert	GB	Team Sauber Formel 1	Sauber C16	Petronas V10 2998 cc	7th: 1'19"105	R
9	Mika Hakkinen	SF	McLaren International	McLaren MP4/12	Mercedes V10 2998 cc	8th: 1'19"119	R
7	Jean Alesi	F	Benetton Formula Ltd.	Benetton B197	Renault V10 2998 cc	9th: 1'19"263	R
17	Nicola Larini	I	Team Sauber Formel 1	Sauber C16	Petronas V10 2998 cc	11th: 1'19"468	R
1	Damon Hill	GB	Arrows Grand Prix International	Arrows FA18	Yamaha V10 2996 cc	13th: 1'19"674	R
2	Pedro Diniz	BR	Arrows Grand Prix International	Arrows FA18	Yamaha V10 2996 cc	16th: 1'19"860	R
21	Jarno Trulli	I	Minardi Team S.p.A.	Minardi M197	Hart V8 2996 cc	18th: 1'20"349	R
15	Shinji Nakano	J	Prost Grand Prix	Prost JS45	Mugen-Honda V10 2998 cc	21st: 1'20"961	R

(1) The undoing of Hakkinen's McLaren. (2) Real Rubens: Barrichello in the Stewart. (3) Without wings: Berger's Benetton (ahead of Herbert's Sauber). (4) Quick turn: Schumacher in the Ferrari. (5) Quick Finn: Salo in the Tyrrell. (6) Earning a podium place for the third time in a row: Irvine (Ferrari).

(1) Phase der Desintegration an Hakkinens McLaren. (2) Echter Rubens: Barrichello im Stewart. (3) Unbeflügelt: Bergers Benetton (vor Herberts Sauber). (4) Kurze Drehung: Schumacher im Ferrari. (5) Finn-Jet: Salo im Tyrrell. (6) Verdient sich sein drittes Podium im dritten Rennen: Irvine (Ferrari).

(1) Phase de désintégration sur la McLaren de Hakkinen. (2) Un véritable Rubens : Barrichello sur Stewart. (3) Sans aileron : la Benetton de Berger (précédant la Sauber de Herbert). (4) Un petit tour et puis s'en va : Schumacher sur Ferrari. (5) Finn-Jet : Salo sur Tyrrell. (6) Signe son troisième podium en trois courses : Irvine (Ferrari).

1

3

2

(1) Fine performance by Nakano in the Prost before his crash on the hill on lap 36. (2) Modest wave: Schumacher during his lap of honor. (3) Hype-notic: graceful decoration for Villeneuve's Williams. (4) Tense wait to spring into action: fire fighter. (5) Fun-Car: the race management circulates in a Renault Spider on this occasion.

(1) Passable Vorstellung von Nakano im Prost bis zu seinem Crash am Berg in Runde 36. (2) Abgewinkt: Schumacher bei der Ehrenrunde. (3) Hype-nose: anmutige Dekoration für Villeneuves Williams. (4) Gespanntes Warten auf den Einsatz: Feuerwehrmann. (5) Fun-Car: Die Rennleitung zirkuliert diesmal im Renault Spider.

(1) Prestation satisfaisante de Nakano sur Prost jusqu'à sa collision dans la montée, au 36ᵉ tour. (2) Sous les drapeaux : Schumacher lors du tour d'honneur. (3) Hype-nose : charmante décoration pour la Williams de Villeneuve. (4) Toujours prêt à intervenir : pompier. (5) Fun-Car : la direction de la course circule cette année-là en Renault Spider.

Bright to overcast: (1) Eddie Irvine, (2) the Schumacher brothers, (3) Heinz-Harald Frentzen, (4) Rubens Barrichello, (5) the threesome on the podium.

Heiter bis wolkig: (1) Eddie Irvine, (2) die Gebrüder Schumacher, (3) Heinz-Harald Frentzen, (4) Rubens Barrichello, (5) das Dreigestirn auf dem Podium.

Mines plus ou moins réjouies : (1) Eddie Irvine, (2) les frères Schumacher, (3) Heinz-Harald Frentzen, (4) Rubens Barrichello, (5) les trois premiers sur le podium.

MISTER FERRARI

MISTER FERRARI · MISTER FERRARI

Michael Schumacher did not arrive, he was suddenly there. The 1991 Belgian Grand Prix, when he appeared on the Formula 1 scene and the worldwide TV screens for the first time, introduced a new era in the sport, and as these lines are being written we are in year seven Anno Schumacher. This new era applies above all to the traditionally barren Formula 1 territory of Germany. During the 42 years leading up to the first victory of the Rhinelander at Spa-Francorchamps in 1992, German drivers had managed only three victories from 516 Grands Prix. Under such circumstances there was not much risk of the organizing club having to use its recording of the German national anthem.

Count von Trips, the leading contender for the 1961 World Championship, undoubtedly profited from the overwhelming superiority of Ferrari in claiming two wins that year prior to his fatal accident at Monza. Rolf Stommelen, Jochen Mass (the only other GP winner from Germany) and Hans-Joachim Stuck all did decent jobs, but mainly in mid-field. Stefan Bellof, whom Ken Tyrrell still considers to be one of the most talented drivers who has ever emerged in this particular line of work, gambled away his young life and a possibly brilliant future in a rash overtaking manoeuvre during a sports car race at Spa in 1985.

Michael Schumacher, on the other hand, quickly set the standard for others. Attentive observers may surmise that even the late Ayrton Senna was not the equal of the early Schumacher. The Brazilian's growing awareness of this might also explain his noticeable irritation and touchiness as regards the German, as well as the mistakes which he suddenly began to make. Drivers learn things about one another out there in the absolute solitude of their cockpits which are better not talked about.

From 1992 onwards, the simple question: "Where on the grid is Schumacher?" became the benchmark by which all the others measured themselves, a kind of Formula 1 DIN standard. Your worst enemy is your team-mate, according to a well-worn truism of motor racing. From this perspective Michael Schumacher was a veritable scourge for all who had to serve at his side – Nelson Piquet, Martin Brundle, Riccardo Patrese, Jos Verstappen, Johnny Herbert and Eddie Irvine, all of them talented drivers in their own right. The question is, how do you handle that kind of situation? In morose resignation like Piquet, or with impish charm like Irvine, who moreover managed the odd miracle?

Things took a peculiar turn when Schumacher changed from Benetton to Ferrari in 1996 and thus slipped into a role to which he was not accustomed – that of the professional loser who is, nevertheless, considered to be capable of achieving everything. At the same time the Ferrari image and his own melded into one: everyone wanted to see them both win, the man and the marque. The whole business was, of course, a lucrative one. The fee which the Scuderia and its financial backers paid the saviour from the North to close the performance gap which separated it from the leading teams like Williams or Benetton would require any normal wage-earner to work for a thousand years.

No sooner done, and a new facet sparkled on Michael Schumacher, the diamond gradually polished to

Michael Schumacher kommt nicht, er ist schlagartig da. Mit dem Großen Preis von Belgien 1991, als er zum ersten Mal auf der Bildfläche und auf dem Bildschirm erscheint, beginnt zugleich eine neue Zeitrechnung im Grand-Prix-Sport: Diese Zeilen entstehen im Jahre sieben nach Schumacher. Das gilt vor allem für das traditionelle Formel-1-Notstandsgebiet Deutschland: In den 42 Jahren vor dem ersten Erfolg des Rheinländers 1992 in Spa tragen Piloten aus dem Land der Dichter und Denker bei 516 Großen Preisen gerade mal drei Siege davon. Da konnte der veranstaltende Club die Platte mit der deutschen Nationalhymne fast risikolos zu Hause liegenlassen.

Graf Trips, Anwärter auf die Weltmeisterschaft 1961, profitierte zweifellos auch von der erdrückenden Ferrari-Überlegenheit jenes Jahres, indem er zwei Siege erzielte, bevor er in Monza tödlich verunglückte. Rolf Stommelen, Jochen Mass (der einzige weitere GP-Gewinner aus Deutschland) und Hans-Joachim Stuck verrichteten manierliche Jobs im Mittelfeld. Stefan Bellof, den Ken Tyrrell noch heute für eines der größten Talente hält, das die Branche je hervorgebracht hat, verspielte sein junges Leben und eine möglicherweise glanzvolle Zukunft 1985 in einem kopflosen und unsinnigen Überholmanöver – bei einem Sportwagenrennen in Spa.

Michael Schumacher indessen, der Messias vom Kerpener Kreuz, wird umgehend zum Maß aller Dinge. Der aufmerksame Beobachter gewinnt den Eindruck, daß selbst der späte Senna dem frühen Schumacher nicht mehr gewachsen ist. Daß sich das Bewußtsein davon bei dem großen Brasilianer einzuschleichen beginnt, erklärt vielleicht sogar seine auffällige Irritation und Gereiztheit gegenüber dem Deutschen und die Fehler, die er plötzlich macht. In der absoluten Einsamkeit des Monoposto da draußen erfährt man Dinge übereinander, die besser nie zur Sprache kommen.

Mit der einfachen Frage: »Wo steht Schumacher?« wird seit 1992 der Standard ermittelt, an dem sich alle anderen orientieren, eine Art DIN-Norm in der Formel 1. Der schlimmste Feind, heißt eine abgedroschene Binsenweisheit aus dem Katechismus des Bleifuß-Business, sei der eigene Teamgefährte. Unter diesem Blickwinkel gesehen, wird Michael Schumacher zur wahren Geißel Gottes für alle, die an seiner Seite Dienst tun müssen, für Nelson Piquet, für Martin Brundle, für Riccardo Patrese, für Jos Verstappen, für Johnny Herbert, für Eddie Irvine. Die Frage ist, wie man damit umgeht, in verdrießlicher Resignation, wie Piquet, oder mit lausbübischem Charme, wie Irvine, der darüberhinaus auch noch manch kleines Wunder bewirkt.

Eine aparte Wendung der Dinge stellt sich ein, als Schumacher 1996 von Benetton zu Ferrari wechselt und damit in eine ungewohnte Rolle schlüpft – in die des Berufs-Unterlegenen, dem man gleichwohl alles zutraut. Zugleich fließen das Ferrari-Image und sein eigenes ineinander: Alle möchten beide siegen sehen, den Mann und die Marke. Natürlich ist die Angelegenheit lukrativ. Für das Honorar, das die Scuderia und ihre finanziellen Helfershelfer dem Heilsbringer aus dem Norden zahlen, um die Sekundenlücke zu führenden Produkten wie Williams oder Benetton zu schließen, müßte ein Normalverdiener 1000 Jahre arbeiten. Und schon funkelt eine neue Facette an dem Diamanten

Michael Schumacher n'arrive pas, il est là d'un seul coup. Avec son arrivée sur la piste et sur l'écran, au Grand Prix de Belgique de 1991, débute simultanément une ère nouvelle dans l'histoire des Grands Prix : ces lignes sont écrites en l'an sept de l'époque Schumacher. Cela vaut surtout pour l'Allemagne, par tradition le parent pauvre de la Formule 1 : durant les 42 années qui ont précédé le premier succès du pilote allemand, en 1992 à Spa-Francorchamps, les représentants du pays des poètes et des philosophes ont remporté en tout et pour tout trois victoires en pas moins de 516 Grands Prix. Les clubs organisateurs de Grands Prix pouvaient sans grand risque laisser l'hymne national allemand dans le placard. Le comte Wolfgang von Trips, candidat au titre de champion du monde 1961, a sans aucun doute profité aussi de l'étouffante suprématie de Ferrari cette année-là, assurant deux victoires avant son accident fatal à Monza. Rolf Stommelen, Jochen Mass, le seul autre champion allemand de Grands Prix, et Hans-Joachim Stuck ont fait leur travail consciencieusement, mais uniquement dans les milieux de peloton. Stefan Bellof, que Ken Tyrrell considère aujourd'hui encore comme l'un des plus grands talents que la Formule 1 ait jamais vu, a sacrifié sa jeune vie et un avenir sans aucun doute extrêmement brillant, en 1985, lors d'une course à Spa, dans une tentative de dépassement irréfléchie et a priori vouée à l'échec.

Michael Schumacher, en revanche, se pose immédiatement en référence absolue. L'observateur attentif aura eu l'impression que même le Ayrton Senna des dernières années ne pouvait plus résister au jeune Schumacher. Le fait que le doute ait peut-être commencé à s'infiltrer dans le grand Brésilien explique même peut-être sa nervosité et son irritabilité soudaines vis-à-vis de l'Allemand ainsi que les erreurs qu'il commet tout d'un coup. Dans la solitude absolue du cockpit, dehors sur la piste, on apprend les uns au sujet des autres des choses qu'il est préférable de ne pas évoquer.

Avec la question concise : « Où est Schumacher ? », on fixe, depuis 1992, le standard vers lequel s'orientent tous les autres, une espèce de norme DIN de la Formule 1. Comme le veut une formule usée jusqu'à la corde qui figure dans le catéchisme des écraseurs d'accélérateur, l'adversaire le plus redoutable est toujours son propre coéquipier. Vu sous cet angle, Michael Schumacher est un véritable fléau de Dieu pour tous ceux qui ont dû piloter à ses côtés, pour Nelson Piquet, Martin Brundle, Riccardo Patrese, Jos Verstappen, Johnny Herbert et Eddie Irvine. La question est : quelle réaction adopter ? Sombrer dans une résignation sans issue, comme Piquet, ou réagir avec un charme de gamin farceur, comme Irvine, lequel est malgré tout capable de réaliser bien des miracles.

La situation s'inverse brutalement lorsque, en 1996, Schumacher quitte Benetton pour Ferrari et endosse par la même occasion un rôle auquel il ne nous a pas habitués : celui du battu d'avance que l'on croit, malgré tout, capable de tout. Par la même occasion, l'image de Ferrari et sa propre image se fondent l'une dans l'autre : chacun souhaite que tous les deux gagnent, l'homme et la marque. Naturellement, le transfert est

Master and manager: Willi Weber keeps Michael Schumacher's back covered – for a suitable fee – so that the latter can accelerate without hindrance.

Meister und Manager: Damit Michael Schumacher unbeschwert gasgeben kann, hält ihm Willi Weber den Rücken frei – gegen anständige Bezahlung.

Maître à danser et manager : pour que Michael Schumacher puisse accélérer sans arrière-pensée, Willi Weber s'occupe de tout – contre une rémunération princière.

perfection by his ability to manage people in an effective way. The German star imposed his northern standards on the red racing stable in a way which only Niki Lauda or John Surtees had done before him, with the difference that back in the 1960s the Ferrari team manager Eugenio Dragoni had from the beginning been in conflict with the self-assured Briton. Schumacher, on the other hand, was literally enveloped in a sea of loyalty – one for all and all for one. By this time the celebrity of Formula 1 had turned the boy from the one-horse town of Manheim, in the Cologne catchment area, into a charismatic figure, every inch the king. The Schumania fan syndrome was spreading like the flu, and it turned out to be just as infectious.

It is undoubtedly true that this represented the ideal marketing opportunity. And here, too, the Schumacher phenomenon put everything which preceded him into the shade, loyally guided by men who were gifted with a highly-developed instinct as to where the money and its equivalent values were to be found. With blanket coverage as an irresistible money-spinner, his logo decorated such apparently incompatible products as salami, champagne and pen holders. Schumi-writings began to sprout like mushrooms after a summer shower. A hour with the star cost a fortune.

But anyone who spoke the name Michael Schumacher released emotions which were not just positive ones. In September 1994 – does anyone still remember? – the governing body of motor sport imposed a one-month ban on him. The Benetton team, it appeared, had exploited the half-light of the Formula

Michael Schumacher, dem das Leben allmählich den letzten Schliff verpaßt: die Fähigkeit zu zeitgemäßer Menschenführung. Der deutsche Star nordet den roten Rennstall auf sich ein, wie es vor ihm allenfalls Niki Lauda getan hat oder John Surtees, mit dem Unterschied, daß sein damaliger Ferrari-Rennleiter Eugenio Dragoni von Anbeginn an das Kriegsbeil gegen den störrischen Briten ausgegraben hat. Schumacher hingegen badet förmlich in einem Meer von Loyalität, einer für alle, alle für einen. Da hat der Glitzer-Sport Formel 1 den Jungen aus dem Kaff Manheim, im Einzugsbereich von Köln, bereits zu einer charismatischen Figur gemacht, jeder Zoll ein König. Das Fan-Syndrom Schumania grassiert wie eine Grippewelle und erweist sich als genauso ansteckend.

Sowas läßt sich zweifellos trefflich vermarkten. Und auch hier stellt das Phänomen Schumacher alles in den Schatten, was vorher gewesen ist, treulich geführt von Männern, die begnadet sind mit einem hochsensiblen Gespür für Geld und Geldeswert. Flächendeckend, spartenübergreifend und unwiderstehlich gewinn-trächtig schmückt sein Logo scheinbar Unvereinbares wie Salami, Sekt und Federmäppchen. Schumi-Schrift-tum sprießt aus dem Boden wie Champignons nach einem milden Sommerregen. Eine Stunde mit dem Star kostet ein Vermögen. Wer auch immer den Namen Michael Schumacher ausspricht, löst Emotionen aus, und nicht nur positive. Im September 1994 – wer entsinnt sich noch? – verhängt die Motorsport-Legislative ein einmonatiges Berufsverbot über ihn. Zumindest das Benetton-Team hat da ein bißchen im trüben gefischt, im Halbschatten, den das Regelwerk für

lucratif. Pour les honoraires que la Scuderia et ses sponsors versent au Messie venu du Nord pour combler les secondes avec les bolides qui font la course en tête comme Williams ou Benetton, un salarié moyen devrait travailler pendant mille ans. Et l'on voit déjà briller une nouvelle facette du diamant qu'est Michael Schumacher, auquel la vie finit par donner la dernière touche : son aptitude à prendre les gens par les sentiments. La star allemande fait retrouver son latin à l'écurie aux bolides rouges comme l'ont fait auparavant, tout au plus, Niki Lauda ou John Surtees, à cette différence près qu'Eugenio Dragoni, le directeur de course de Ferrari, avait été, dans les années soixante, en conflit avec le Britannique têtu. Schumacher, par contre, baigne littéralement dans une mer de loyauté : un pour tous, tous pour un. La Formule 1 avec son superficiel scintillant a déjà fait du jeune homme du patelin de Manheim, dans la grande banlieue de Cologne, une figure charismatique, tel un roi avec un casque comme couronne. Le syndrome de la Schumania sévit parmi les fans aussi irrésistiblement qu'une épidémie de grippe et s'avère tout aussi contagieux.

Un tel homme est une bénédiction de Dieu pour un spécialiste du marketing. Et, ici aussi, le phénomène Schumacher surclasse tout ce que l'on n'a jamais vu auparavant, géré en toute loyauté par des hommes ayant plus qu'un sixième sens pour l'argent et la valeur de l'argent. Dans tous les pays, dans toutes les catégories et de façon incroyablement lucrative, son emblème et sa signature décorent notamment des objets qui ont aussi peu en commun qu'un salami, une bouteille de mousseux et des trousses d'écoliers. Le

1 rules. Did Schumi know about it? Whether he did or did not is irrelevant – he still became World Champion. Nevertheless, the outcome of the contest had to be settled in a few seconds by means of a collision with rival Damon Hill in the final race of the season in Adelaide. In October 1997 in Jerez he once again turned physical, using his Ferrari in an attempt to shove his rival Jacques Villeneuve out of the race. But the manoeuvre backfired – and the Canadian became World Champion. Schumacher had been stripped of his magic, and his critics and those jealous of his success rejoiced, as if such a Grand Prix was an event organized by the YMCA. Yet by the 1998 Argentine Grand Prix, at the latest, Schumacher had passed the vital test of public approval once again, rather like the modified Mercedes-Benz A-Class.

In any case, the hard core of the Schumacher club had remained unaffected by such suspicions and inconvenient facts: on the day after the Jerez fiasco, two young rascals were chasing one another across the playground of a German secondary school, outsized Schumi caps pulled down over their ears. Had the shine on their hero not been tarnished just a little bit, they were asked? The answer was disarming and direct: "Never!"

die Formel 1 wirft. Weiß Schumi davon? Wie auch immer, es macht nichts – Weltmeister wird er dieses Jahr trotzdem. Allerdings müssen vermittels einer Kollision mit dem Rivalen Damon Hill beim Saisonfinale in Adelaide dem Schlachtenglück ein paar Sekunden Nachhilfeunterricht erteilt werden. Im Oktober 1997 wird er im spanischen Jerez mit dem Ferrari erneut handgreiflich, um seinen Rivalen Jacques Villeneuve aus dem Rennen zu boxen. Der Schuß geht nach hinten los – Weltmeister wird der Kanadier, und dieser Schumacher sei nun ganz und gar entzaubert, frohlocken die Neider und die Kritiker, als sei so ein Grand Prix eine Veranstaltung des Christlichen Vereins Junger Männer. Spätestens mit seinem Sieg beim Großen Preis von Argentinien 1998 indes hat Schumacher den Elch-Test in der Publikumsgunst bestanden wie die überarbeitete A-Klasse von Mercedes-Benz.

Dem harten Kern der Schumacher-Gemeinde vermögen dergleichen Verdächtigungen und ärgerliche Fakten ohnehin nichts anzuhaben: Am Tage nach dem Fiasko von Jerez toben zwei Bengels über den Schulhof eines deutschen Gymnasiums, schätzungsweise Klasse sechs, die viel zu großen Schumi-Kappen weit über die Ohren gezogen. Ob denn nun der Lack ihres Helden nicht ein bißchen angekratzt sei, lautet die Frage. Die Antwort kommt entwaffnend und wie aus der Pistole geschossen: »Nö!«

graphisme de Schumacher se propage comme les champignons après une tiède pluie d'été. Une heure avec la star coûte une fortune. Mais quiconque prononce le nom de Michael Schumacher, déclenche des émotions, et pas seulement positives. En septembre 1994 – qui s'en souvient encore ? – les fonctionnaires de la FIA lui infligent une interdiction de piloter d'un mois. L'écurie Benetton, à tout le moins, a un peu dépassé ses prérogatives, opérant dans le flou que les règlements de la Formule 1 ont toujours laissé. Schumacher en était-il au courant? Quoi qu'il en soit, cela ne change rien – il est tout de même sacré champion du monde. Il lui faut toutefois le coup de pouce d'une collision avec son rival Damon Hill, lors de la finale à Adélaïde, pour ceindre la couronne. En octobre 1997, à Jerez, au Grand Prix d'Europe, il se sert de nouveau de sa Ferrari comme d'une arme pour tenter de catapulter de la piste son rival Jacques Villeneuve. Mais cela se retourne contre lui : c'est en effet le Canadien qui est champion du monde. Et ce Schumacher a maintenant perdu toute sa magie, s'empressent de clamer les envieux et les détracteurs, comme si un Grand Prix était une manifestation de la Jeunesse ouvrière catholique. Au Grand Prix d'Argentine de 1998, Schumacher aura passé, de nouveau, avec succès le test capital dans les faveurs du public, comme la renversante Classe A retravaillée de Mercedes-Benz.

Le noyau dur des adorateurs de Schumacher est de toute façon insensible à de tels soupçons et à de telles péripéties, aussi gênantes soient-elles : le lendemain du fiasco de Jerez, deux gamins s'ébattent dans la cour d'un lycée allemand, âgés peut-être de douze à treize ans, avec des casquettes de Schumacher beaucoup trop grandes pour eux qui leur descendent sous les oreilles. Leur héros n'a-t-il pas perdu un peu de son prestige ? leur a-t-on demandé. Désarmants de franchise, ils ont répondu du tac au tac : « Vous blaguez, non ?»

Raised fist: even after thirty Grand Prix wins, Michael Schumacher has not lost the basic joy of winning.

Faust gezeigt: Selbst nach dreißig gewonnenen Grands Prix ist Michael Schumacher die elementare Freude am Siegen nicht vergangen.

Débordement de joie : même après avoir gagné trente Grands Prix, Michael Schumacher est loin d'être blasé après une nouvelle victoire.

1998

Perseverance and the unshakeable belief in oneself do eventually pay off in the Formula One competitive world – even if they do have to withstand the wear and tear of half a decade. Not once had Mika Hakkinen even got as far as the finishing line in the town in which he lives. But on this occasion, in 1998, the flying Finn, as he likes to call himself, did so literally streets ahead of the others. The only one to exert serious pressure on him was his team-mate at McLaren, David Coulthard – in training, in the ding-dong for pole position and in the race – but only until the 18th lap when a connecting rod in the Mercedes engine of the Scot's car gave up the ghost at 16,000 rpm. Monaco is the sixth Grand Prix of the season and there is still much to fight for. "We both drove on the limit for as long as David was breathing down my neck. When he went faster, I responded. It was uncomfortable, all the same, for this is a long race," Hakkinen said later.

Behind him, things sorted themselves out almost by themselves. Monaco requires a genius like Michael Schumacher – that was the general opinion among the journalists talking shop in advance of this Grand Prix. He would be able to tame the McLarens. But the threat from the German never really materialized. To add to his annoyance, he had to miss the qualifying session on Saturday morning as a half-shaft failed and stranded his car. In the race, he became involved in the skirmish of the day and the resulting headlines, ably assisted by the Benetton novice, Alexander Wurz. The Austrian had reached second place when he was caught by the Ferrari star on the approach to Loews bend. Before the following right-hand bend, Wurz insolently hit back; then dirt and shredded bits of tyre caused him to leave the ideal line at Portier. Schumacher attempted to take advantage of this situation, but their two cars became momentarily interlocked. In ten seconds they had overtaken each other three times and touched seven times, as Wurz later so precisely recalled. Their heavy bash at the end led to serious consequences, first for Schumacher, who limped into the pits with a bent rear track rod. For 230 bitter seconds he had to wait while his car received a replacement rod. He had already undone his seatbelts, believing his race was over, and was about to get out when he received the order to continue from Ferrari boss Ross Brawn, which he did.

Wurz, on the other hand, continued the race sitting on a time-bomb. Five laps after the scrap with Schumacher it somehow exploded. The driver miraculously emerged unscathed from the crash at 150 mph which started in the tunnel, in the course of which the Benetton lost both its front wheels, finally to strike the soft padding at the chicane like a spear. He had plenty of time to be afraid.

Unnoticed, his stablemate Giancarlo Fisichella had in the meantime consolidated himself in second place, having built a comfortable gap between himself and Eddie Irvine's Ferrari. He even had time for a quick spin at Rascasse without changing the order.

Beharrlichkeit und ein unerschütterlicher Glaube an sich selbst zahlen sich aus in der Leistungs-Gesellschaft Formel 1 – selbst wenn sie dem Verschleiß durch ein halbes Jahrzehnt trotzen müssen. Nie ist Mika Hakkinen auch nur ins Ziel gekommen in der Stadt, in der er wohnt. Diesmal aber siegt der fliegende Finne 1998, wie er sich selber nennt, und zwar eine Straße weiter als alle anderen. Mächtig Druck wird ihm lediglich durch seinen Teamgefährten bei McLaren David Coulthard gemacht, im Training im Pingpong um die Pole Position und im Rennen – jedoch nur bis in die 18. Runde, als bei 16 000/min im Mercedes-Motor des Schotten ein Pleuel kündigt. Monaco ist der sechste Grand Prix der Saison: Da gibt es noch keine Stallregie. »So lange mir David im Nacken saß, fuhren wir beide voll. Wenn er schneller wurde, schlug ich zurück. Unangenehm war es trotzdem, denn das hier ist ein langes Rennen«, gibt Hakkinen später zu Protokoll.

Hinter ihm regeln sich die Dinge gewissermaßen von alleine. Monaco verlange nach einem Genius wie Michael Schumacher, ist der Tenor bei Fachsimpeleien unter den Journalisten im Vorfeld dieses Großen Preises. Der werde die McLaren schon in den Griff bekommen. Aber nie wird der Deutsche zur echten Bedrohung. Zu allem Überdruß muß er die Trainingssitzung am Samstagmorgen aussitzen, als in seiner ersten Runde eine Halbwelle nicht mehr mitmacht und seinen Wagen aus dem Verkehr zieht. Im Rennen sorgt er gleichwohl für das Scharmützel des Tages und die darauffolgenden Schlagzeilen, kongenial unterstützt durch den Benetton-Novizen Alexander Wurz. Der Österreicher ist auf Position zwei angelangt, als ihn sich der Ferrari-Star vor der Loews-Kurve schnappt. In dem folgenden Rechtsknick schlägt Wurz unverfroren zurück und kommt in Portier auf Dreck und zerschredderten Reifenteilen von der Ideallinie ab. Schumacher versucht aus dieser Situation seinen Vorteil zu ziehen. Aber dann verhaken sich die beiden Wagen. In zehn Sekunden hat man einander dreimal überholt und siebenmal berührt, wie Wurz später penibel aufzählt.

Der heftige Kontakt am Ende zeitigt üble Folgen. Zunächst für Schumacher: Mit geknickter hinterer Spurstange hinkt er an die Box. 230 bittere Sekunden dauert die stationäre Behandlung. Als er schon die Gurte gelöst hat und in dem Glauben, das Rennen sei für ihn vorbei, aussteigen will, erhält er von Ferrari-Konstrukteur Ross Brawn die Order weiterzumachen und tut's auch.

Wurz hingegen reist auf einer Zeitbombe weiter. Fünf Runden nach dem Gerangel mit Schumacher geht sie irgendwie hoch. Aus einem Unfall mit Tempo 250, der im Tunnel beginnt, in dessen Verlauf die Benetton die beiden Vorderräder abstreift und schließlich wie ein Speer in die weiche Polsterung an der Schikane einschlägt, geht der Pilot auf wundersame Weise ungeschoren hervor. Er hatte reichlich Muße, sich zu ängstigen.

In aller Stille hat sich unterdessen sein Stallkollege Giancarlo Fisichella auf Rang zwei eingenistet, mit einem kommoden Abstand zu Eddie Irvines Ferrari. Sogar ein schneller Dreher bei Rascasse tut dem keinen Abbruch.

Persévérance et foi inébranlable en soi-même portent toujours leurs fruits dans la concurrence acharnée que se livre la Formule 1 – même si l'on doit résister à l'usure de cinq longues années. Jamais Mika Hakkinen n'est parvenu à franchir la ligne d'arrivée dans la ville où il réside. Mais, cette fois-ci, en 1998, le Finlandais volant, comme il se surnomme lui-même, gagne, et ce, avec une rue d'avance sur tous les autres. Seul son coéquipier de chez McLaren, David Coulthard, fait peser la pression sur ses épaules, lors du ping-pong pour la pole position durant les essais qualificatifs et pendant la course – jusqu'au 18e tour, lorsque le moteur Mercedes de l'Ecossais rend l'âme à 16 000 tr/mn, bielle coulée. Monaco est le 6e Grand Prix de la saison et de nombreux duels attendent encore les deux hommes. « Tant que David m'a talonné, nous avons roulé tous les deux à la limite. Lorsqu'il était plus rapide que moi, je répliquais immédiatement. Ceci est d'autant plus désagréable, parce que cette course ici est longue », déclare plus tard Hakkinen en guise de commentaire.

Derrière lui, tout se règle en quelque sorte tout seul. Monaco a impérativement besoin d'un génie comme Schumacher, sont unanimes à déclarer les journalistes bavardant entre eux la veille de ce Grand Prix. Il saura bien monter aux McLaren qui est le maître de céans. Mais l'Allemand ne sera jamais une véritable menace. Qui plus est, il doit regarder se dérouler sans lui la séance d'essais qualificatifs du samedi matin lorsque, dès son premier tour, se rompt un demi-arbre. En course, il n'en signe pas moins le plus beau duel du jour et fait les grands titres des journaux, génialement assisté en cela par le néophyte de chez Benetton, Alexander Wurz. L'Autrichien est en seconde position lorsque la star de chez Ferrari tente de le doubler dans le virage du Loews. Dans le droite suivant, Wurz réplique du tac au tac mais, au virage du Portier, se retrouve dans la poussière et des débris de pneus qui le font dévier de la trajectoire idéale. Schumacher tente de profiter de cette situation. Mais les deux voitures s'accrochent alors. En dix secondes, les deux protagonistes se sont doublés trois fois et touchés sept fois, comme Wurz l'aura compté avec précision.

Le brutal contact à la fin de cette joute a des conséquences fatales. Tout d'abord pour Schumacher : avec son bras de convergence arrière tordu, il doit rejoindre les stands. La réparation sur place dure 230 interminables secondes. Alors qu'il a déjà décroché son harnais et veut sortir de voiture, l'ingénieur de Ferrari Ross Brawn lui intime de repartir et il s'exécute.

Wurz, par contre, chevauche une bombe à retardement. Cinq tours après la passe d'armes avec Schumacher, celle-ci finit par éclater. De façon miraculeuse, le pilote se sort indemne d'un accident qui se produit à 250 km/h, commence dans le tunnel, au cours duquel la Benetton perd ses deux roues avant et percute enfin comme un javelot le rembourrage de pneumatiques à la chicane. Le temps ne lui a pas manqué pour analyser sa peur.

Dans le plus grand silence, son coéquipier, Giancarlo Fisichella s'est, quant à lui, incrusté à la deuxième place avec une avance confortable sur la Ferrari d'Eddie Irvine. Et ce n'est pas son tête-à-queue éclair à la Rascasse qui lui fait perdre cette place.

Love parade: the drivers are displayed to the spectators on a mobile platform before the race.

Love-Parade: Vor dem Rennen werden die Piloten dem Publikum auf einer mobilen Plattform gezeigt.

Love-Parade : avant la course, les pilotes sont présentés au public sur une plate-forme mobile.

N°	DRIVERS		ENTRANTS	CARS	ENGINES	PRACTICE RESULTS	RACE RESULTS
8	*Mika Hakkinen*	*SF*	*McLaren International*	*McLaren MP4/13*	*Mercedes V10 2998 cc*	*1st: 1'19"798*	*1st: 1h51'23"595*
5	Giancarlo Fisichella	I	Benetton Formula 1 Ltd.	Benetton B198	Mecachrome V10 2998 cc	3rd: 1'20"368	2nd: 1h51'35"070
4	Eddie Irvine	GB	SEFAC Ferrari S.p.A.	Ferrari F300	Ferrari V10 2997 cc	7th: 1'21"712	3rd: 1h51'64"973
17	Mika Juhani Salo	SF	Arrows Grand Prix International	Arrows FA19	Arrows V10 2998 cc	8th: 1'22"144	4th: 1h52'23"958
1	Jacques Villeneuve	CDN	Williams Grand Prix Engineering	Williams FW20	Mecachrome V10 2998 cc	13th: 1'22"468	5th: 77 laps
16	Pedro Diniz	BR	Arrows Grand Prix International	Arrows FA19	Arrows V10 2998 cc	12th: 1'22"355	6th: 77 laps
15	Johnny Herbert	GB	Team Sauber Formula 1	Sauber C17	Petronas V10 2998 cc	9th: 1'22"157	7th: 77 laps
9	Damon Hill	GB	Jordan Grand Prix	Jordan 198	Mugen-Honda V10 2998 cc	15th: 1'23"151	8th: 76 laps
22	Shinji Nakano	J	Minardi Team S.p.A.	Minardi M198	Ford V10 2998 cc	19th: 1'23"957	9th: 76 laps
3	Michael Schumacher	D	SEFAC Ferrari S.p.A.	Ferrari F300	Ferrari V10 2997 cc	4th: 1'20"702	10th: 76 laps
21	Toranosuke Takagi	J	Tyrrell Racing Organisation	Tyrrell 026	Ford V10 2998 cc	20th: 1'24"024	11th: 76 laps
14	Jean Alesi	F	Team Sauber Formula 1	Sauber C17	Petronas V10 2998 cc	11th: 1'22"257	12th: 73 laps (R)
2	Heinz-Harald Frentzen	D	Williams Grand Prix Engineering	Williams FW20	Mecachrome V10 2998 cc	5th: 1'20"729	R
6	Alexander Wurz	A	Benetton Formula 1 Ltd.	Benetton B198	Mecachrome V10 2998 cc	6th: 1'20"955	R
7	David Coulthard	GB	McLaren International	McLaren MP4/13	Mercedes V10 2998 cc	2nd: 1'20"137	R
10	Ralf Schumacher	D	Jordan Grand Prix	Jordan 198	Mugen-Honda V10 2998 cc	16th: 1'23"283	R
11	Olivier Panis	F	Prost Grand Prix	Prost AP01	Peugeot V10 2998 cc	18th: 1'23"536	R
12	Jarno Trulli	I	Prost Grand Prix	Prost AP01	Peugeot V10 2998 cc	10th: 1'22"238	R
18	Rubens Barrichello	BR	Stewart Grand Prix Ltd.	Stewart SF-2	Ford V10 2998 cc	14th: 1'22"540	R
19	Jan Magnussen	DK	Stewart Grand Prix Ltd.	Stewart SF-2	Ford V10 2998 cc	17th: 1'23"411	R
23	Esteban Tuero	RA	Minardi Team S.p.A.	Minardi M198	Ford V10 2998 cc	21st: 1'24"031	R

1

2

3

4

(1) What Michael Schumacher did not want to see: after the start, Sainte Dévote is blocked by a silver wall of McLarens. (2) Up the hill: Damon Hill (Jordan) at the entry to Massenet. (3) Black knight: Salo in the very competitive Arrows. (4) Grand prix: the three-day arrangement for the floating accommodation in the background costs $4,500.

(1) Was Michael Schumacher nicht sehen mochte: Nach dem Start wird Saint Dévote von einer silbernen McLaren-Wand zugemauert. (2) Up the hill: Damon Hill (Jordan) eingangs Massenet. (3) Schwarzer Ritter: Salo im gut eingestellten Arrows. (4) Grand prix: Das Drei-Tage-Arrangement auf der schwimmenden Unterkunft im Hintergrund kostet 8000 Mark.

(1) Ce que Michael Schumacher ne voulait pas voir : après le départ, Sainte Dévote est muré par un barrage argenté de McLaren. (2) En haut de la côte : Damon Hill (Jordan) à l'entrée de Massenet. (3) Le cavalier noir : Salo dans son Arrows bien réglée. (4) Grand prix : l'arrangement de trois jours sur les hôtels flottants à l'arrière-plan coûte 28 000 francs.

Wheel dilemma: (1, 2) partial amputation of Irvine's Ferrari in the warm-up. (3) First and second: Hakkinen's McLaren and Fisichella's Benetton on the slowing down lap. (4) Build-up to trouble: Wurz (Benetton) and Schumacher (Ferrari) shortly before becoming physical. (5) Nose in the air: Schumacher's car loses important aerodynamic aids after contact with the enemy in the last lap.

Hier herrscht Radlosigkeit: (1, 2) Teilamputation von Irvines Ferrari im Warmup. (3) Gut beieinander: Hakkinens McLaren und Fisichellas Benetton in der Auslaufrunde. (4) Unheilträchtige Konstellation: Wurz (Benetton) und Schumacher (Ferrari) kurz bevor es zu Handgreiflichkeiten kommt. (5) Hochnäsig: Beim Feindkontakt in der letzten Runde hat Schumachers Wagen wichtige aerodynamische Hilfen verloren.

La roue tourne : (1, 2) amputation partielle de la Ferrari d'Irvine au tour de chauffe. (3) Les deux font la paire : la McLaren de Hakkinen et la Benetton de Fisichella lors du tour de décélération. (4) Constellation fatale : Wurz (Benetton) et Schumacher (Ferrari) juste avant leur échauffourée. (5) Le nez en l'air : lors du contact avec un adversaire au dernier tour, la voiture de Schumacher a perdu d'importants expédients aérodynamiques.

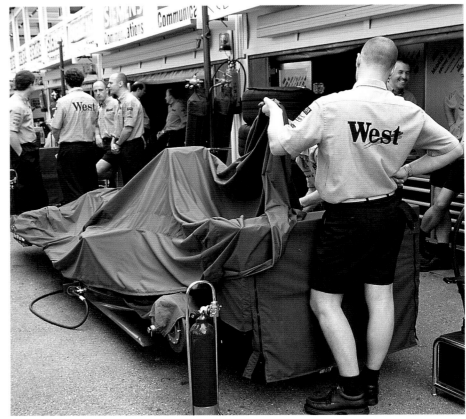

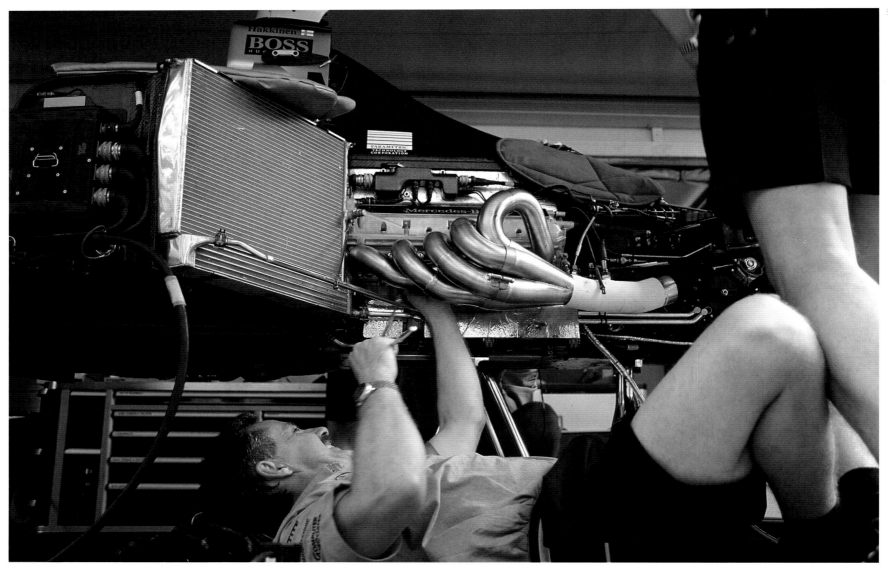

Wrap-up artists: while (1, 2) McLaren makes use of traditional methods and chastely covers all of the MP4/13, Ferrari (4, 5) places value in appropriate and figure-hugging design and leaves parts of the car in the nude. This makes life more difficult for the spies in the pits. (3) Running smoothly from 3,200 to 17,000 rpm: Mercedes engine.

Verpackungskünstler: Während (1, 2) McLaren auf altertümliche Methoden zurückgreift und den MP4/13 keusch in seiner Gänze verhüllt, legt man bei (4, 5) Ferrari Wert auf angemessenes und figurbetonendes Design und läßt Teile des Wagens nackt. So wird den Spionen der Boxengasse das Leben erschwert. (3) Runder Lauf von 3200 bis 17 000/min: Mercedes-Triebwerk.

Christo plagié : tandis que (1, 2) McLaren recourt à des méthodes traditionnelles pour préserver la virginité de sa MP4/13, chez (4, 5) Ferrari, on attache de l'importance à un design adéquat qui souligne les lignes et l'on laisse nues certaines parties de la voiture. Un moyen comme un autre de compliquer l'entrée aux stands aux espions. (3) Tourne rond de 3200 à 17 000 tr/mn : le moteur de Mercedes.

Monaco microcosm: (1) Bernie Ecclestone, (2) Hugh Grant with model Liz Hurley, (3) Jacques Villeneuve and physiotherapist Erwin Göllner, (4) Sylvester Stallone searching for material for his Grand Prix film, (5) Ion Tiriac, (6) Daimler-Benz boss Schrempp, (7) Willie Brown, mayor of San Francisco with Pasquale Lattuneddu, representative of the Formula 1 Administration, (8) the Formula 1 senior citizens Maria-Teresa de Filippis and Paul Frère, (9) Daimler-Benz board member Hubbert and motor sport boss Norbert Haug.

Mikrokosmos Monaco: (1) Bernie Ecclestone, (2) Hugh Grant mit Model Liz Hurley, (3) Jacques Villeneuve und Physiotherapeut Erwin Göllner, (4) Sylvester Stallone auf der Suche nach Stoff für seinen Grand-Prix-Film, (5) Ion Tiriac, (6) Daimler-Benz-Chef Schrempp, (7) Willie Brown, Oberbürgermeister von San Francisco, mit Pasquale Lattuneddu, Repräsentant der Formula 1 Administration, (8) die Formel-1-Senioren Maria-Teresa de Filippis und Paul Frère, (9) Daimler-Benz-Vorstandsmitglied Hubbert und Motorsport-Boß Norbert Haug.

Le microcosme de Monaco : (1) Bernie Ecclestone, (2) Hugh Grant avec le modèle Liz Hurley, (3) Jacques Villeneuve et le physio-thérapeute Erwin Göllner, (4) Sylvester Stallone en quête d'inspiration pour son film sur les Grands Prix, (5) Ion Tiriac, (6) le P.D.G. de Daimler-Benz, Jürgen Schrempp, (7) Willie Brown, le maire de San Francisco, avec Pasquale Lattuneddu, le représentant de la Formula 1 Administration, (8) les doyens de Grand Prix Maria-Teresa de Filippis et Paul Frère, (9) le membre du Directoire de Daimler-Benz, Hubbert, et le chef de la compétition du groupe, Norbert Haug.

(10) Mika Hakkinen, (11) pit beauty between
Eddie Irvine and Corinna Schumacher, (12) Bette
Hill, (13) toilet attendant behind the stands,
(14) reflection of the photographers Rainer
W. Schlegelmilch and Jad Sherif, (15) marshal with
reading material appropriate to the Grand Prix,
(16) the victorious three in feudal company.

(10) Mika Hakkinen, (11) Boxen-Beauty zwischen
Eddie Irvine und Corinna Schumacher, (12) Bette
Hill, (13) Toilettenwärter hinter den Tribünen,
(14) die Fotografen Rainer W. Schlegelmilch und
Jad Sherif im Spiegel-Bild, (15) Streckenposten
bei auf den Grand Prix abgestimmter Lektüre,
(16) die siegreichen Drei in feudalem Umfeld.

(10) Mika Hakkinen, (11) égérie des stands entre
Eddie Irvine et Corinna Schumacher, (12) Bette
Hill, (13) homme-pipi derrière les tribunes,
(14) les photographes Rainer W. Schlegelmilch et
Jad Sherif dans une visière de casque de pompier,
(15) commissaire de piste plongé dans sa lecture
sur le Grand Prix, (16) les trois vainqueurs en
compagnie princière.

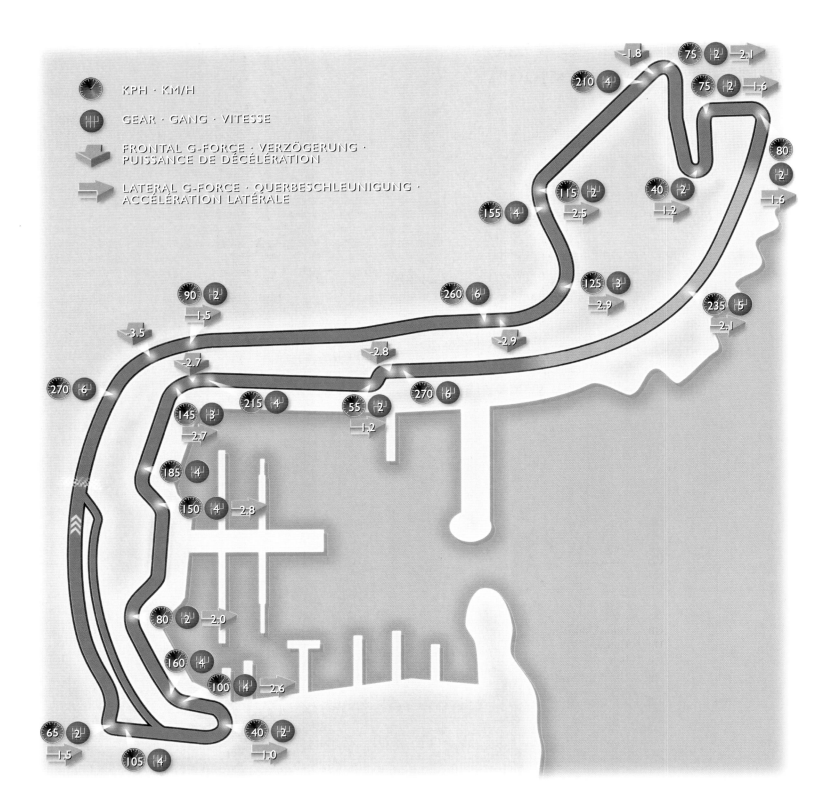

KPH · KM/H

GEAR · GANG · VITESSE

FRONTAL G-FORCE · VERZÖGERUNG ·
PUISSANCE DE DÉCÉLÉRATION

LATERAL G-FORCE · QUERBESCHLEUNIGUNG ·
ACCÉLÉRATION LATÉRALE

The Monaco Grand Prix is pure acrobatics, a helicopter ride through your living room, as Nelson Piquet once put it. Telemetry allows us to measure the adventure, transforms amazement into figures and vastly increases our admiration for the artistes.

Der Grand Prix de Monaco ist Akrobatik pur, ein Flug mit dem Hubschrauber durchs Wohnzimmer, wie es Nelson Piquet einmal formuliert hat. Die Telemetrie macht das Abenteuer meßbar, setzt das Staunen in Zahlen um und steigert die Bewunderung für die Artisten ins Unermeßliche.

Le Grand Prix de Monaco est un véritable numéro d'acrobatie, un vol en hélicoptère à travers son salon, comme l'a dit un jour Nelson Piquet. La télémétrie rend l'aventure mesurable, transpose en chiffres l'étonnement et accroît de façon incommensurable l'admiration que l'on ressent pour les artistes.

KEY TO THE TABLES
ERKLÄRUNG DER TABELLEN · EXPLICATION DES TABLEAUX

N°	DRIVERS		ENTRANTS	CARS	ENGINES	PRACTICE RESULTS	RACE RESULTS
5	Michael Schumacher	D	SEFAC Ferrari S.p.A.	Ferrari F310B	Ferrari V10 2998 cc	2nd: 1'18"235	1st: 2h00'05"654
22	Rubens Barrichello	BR	Stewart Grand Prix Ltd.	Stewart SF-1	Ford V10 2998 cc	10th: 1'19"295	2nd: 2h00'58"960
6	Eddie Irvine	GB	SEFAC Ferrari S.p.A.	Ferrari F310B	Ferrari V10 2998 cc	15th: 1'19"723	3rd: 2h01'27"762
14	Olivier Panis	F	Prost Grand Prix	Prost JS45	Mugen-Honda V10 2998 cc	12th: 1'19"626	4th: 2h01'50"056
19	Mika Juhani Salo	SF	Tyrrell Racing Organisation	Tyrrell 025	Ford V8 2998 cc	14th: 1'19"694	5th: 61 Laps
12	Giancarlo Fisichella	I	Jordan Grand Prix	Jordan 197	Peugeot V10 2998 cc	4th: 1'18"665	6th: 61 Laps
23	Jan Magnussen	DK	Stewart Grand Prix Ltd.	Stewart SF-1	Ford V10 2998 cc	19th: 1'20"516	7th: 61 Laps
18	Jos Verstappen	NL	Tyrrell Racing Organisation	Tyrrell 025	Ford V8 2998 cc	22nd: 1'21"290	8th: 60 Laps
8	Gerhard Berger	A	Benetton Formula	Benetton B197	Renault V10 2998 cc	17th: 1'20"199	9th: 60 Laps
20	Ukyo Katayama	J	Minardi Team S.p.A.	Minardi M197	Hart V8 2996 cc	20th: 1'20"606	10th: 60 Laps
4	Heinz-Harald Frentzen	D	Williams Grand Prix Engineering	Williams FW19	Renault V10 2998 cc	1st: 1'18"216	R

R: Retired
Number
Driver's name
Driver's nationality:

A	Austria
AUS	Australia
B	Belgium
BR	Brazil
CDN	Canada
CH	Switzerland
D	Germany
DK	Denmark
E	Spain
F	France
GB	United Kingdom
H	Hungary
I	Italy
IRL	Ireland
J	Japan
MEX	Mexico
NL	Netherlands
NZ	New Zealand
P	Portugal
PL	Poland
RA	Argentina
RCH	Chile
RSA	South Africa
S	Sweden
SF	Finland
THA	Thailand
USA	United States
VEN	Venezuela
YU	Yugoslavia

R: Ausgeschieden
Startnummer
Name des Fahrers
Nationalität des Fahrers:

A	Österreich
AUS	Australien
B	Belgien
BR	Brasilien
CDN	Kanada
CH	Schweiz
D	Deutschland
DK	Dänemark
E	Spanien
F	Frankreich
GB	Großbritannien
H	Ungarn
I	Italien
IRL	Irland
J	Japan
MEX	Mexiko
NL	Niederlande
NZ	Neuseeland
P	Portugal
PL	Polen
RA	Argentinien
RCH	Chile
RSA	Südafrika
S	Schweden
SF	Finnland
THA	Thailand
USA	Vereinigte Staaten
VEN	Venezuela
YU	Jugoslawien

R: Abandon
Numéro
Nom du pilote
Nationalité du pilote :

A	Autriche
AUS	Australie
B	Belgique
BR	Brésil
CDN	Canada
CH	Suisse
D	Allemagne
DK	Danemark
E	Espagne
F	France
GB	Royaume-Uni
H	Hongrie
I	Italie
IRL	Irlande
J	Japon
MEX	Mexique
NL	Pays-Bas
NZ	Nouvelle-Zélande
P	Portugal
PL	Pologne
RA	Argentine
RCH	Chili
RSA	Afrique du Sud
S	Suède
SF	Finlande
THA	Thaïlande
USA	Etats-Unis
VEN	Venezuela
YU	Yougoslavie

Name of team
Model
Engine manufacturer, number and configuration of cylinders (L: in line, F: flat, V: V-shaped, H: H-shaped); capacity; + C: compressor, + T: turbocharged
Position and fastest lap in qualifying. Pole time in *italics*
Ranking and total time of all laps. Fastest in **bold**

Name des Teams
Modell
Motorhersteller, Zylinderzahl und -anordnung (L: in Reihe, F: Boxer, V: V-förmig, H: H-förmig); Hubraum; + C: mit Kompressor, + T: mit Turbolader
Plazierung und bestes Ergebnis im Training. Schnellster *kursiv*
Plazierung und Gesamtzeit im Rennen. Schnellster **fett**

Nom de l'écurie
Désignation de la voiture
Fabricant du moteur, nombre et disposition des cylindres (L: en ligne, F: boxer, V/H: en forme de V/H) ; cylindrée ; + C: avec compresseur, + T: avec turbocompresseur
Classement et temps de la qualification. Pole position en *italique*
Classement et temps de la course. Vainqueur en **gras**

BIBLIOGRAPHY
BIBLIOGRAPHIE

Auto-Jahr 1953–1997, Edita

Blunsden, J. and A. Brinton: *Motor Racing Year 1960–1977,* Motor Racing Publications Ltd.

Cutter, R. and B. Fendell: *Encyclopedia of Auto Racing Greats,* Prentice-Hall Inc. 1973

Deschenaux, J.: *Marlboro Grand Prix Guide 1950–1997,* Charles Stewart and Company Ltd.

Edler, K.-H. and W. Roediger: *Die deutschen Rennfahrzeuge,* VEB Fachbuchverlag Leipzig 1956

Gill, B.: *John Player Motorsport Yearbooks 1972–1976*

Hewett, M., C. Brown and L. Newman: *Monaco Grand Prix, Portrait of a Pageant,* Motor Racing Publications 1989

Incandela, S.: *The Anatomy and Development of the Formula One Racing Car from 1975,* Haynes 1990

Moity, C., G. Flocon et C. Montariol: *Grand Prix Automobile de Monaco,* Editions d'Art J.P. Barthélémy 1997

Naquin, Yves: *Le Grand Prix Automobile de Monaco, Story of a Legend 1929–1960,* Editions Automobilia

Setright, L.J.K.: *The Grand Prix 1906–1972,* Nelson 1973

Small, S.: *The Guinness Complete Grand Prix Who's Who,* Guinness Publishing 1996

auto motor und sport

Autosport

PHOTOGRAPHIC CREDITS
BILDNACHWEIS · CRÉDITS PHOTOGRAPHIQUES

KEY TO THE TABLES
ERKLÄRUNG DER TABELLEN · EXPLICATION DES TABLEAUX

N°	DRIVERS		ENTRANTS	CARS	ENGINES	PRACTICE RESULTS	RACE RESULTS
5	Michael Schumacher	D	SEFAC Ferrari S.p.A.	Ferrari F310B	Ferrari V10 2998 cc	2nd: 1'18"235	1st: 2h00'05"654
22	Rubens Barrichello	BR	Stewart Grand Prix Ltd.	Stewart SF-1	Ford V10 2998 cc	10th: 1'19"295	2nd: 2h00'58"960
6	Eddie Irvine	GB	SEFAC Ferrari S.p.A.	Ferrari F310B	Ferrari V10 2998 cc	15th: 1'19"723	3rd: 2h01'27"762
14	Olivier Panis	F	Prost Grand Prix	Prost JS45	Mugen-Honda V10 2998 cc	12th: 1'19"626	4th: 2h01'50"056
19	Mika Juhani Salo	SF	Tyrrell Racing Organisation	Tyrrell 025	Ford V8 2998 cc	14th: 1'19"694	5th: 61 Laps
12	Giancarlo Fisichella	I	Jordan Grand Prix	Jordan 197	Peugeot V10 2998 cc	4th: 1'18"665	6th: 61 Laps
23	Jan Magnussen	DK	Stewart Grand Prix Ltd.	Stewart SF-1	Ford V10 2998 cc	19th: 1'20"516	7th: 61 Laps
18	Jos Verstappen	NL	Tyrrell Racing Organisation	Tyrrell 025	Ford V8 2998 cc	22nd: 1'21"290	8th: 60 Laps
8	Gerhard Berger	A	Benetton Formula	Benetton B197	Renault V10 2998 cc	17th: 1'20"199	9th: 60 Laps
20	Ukyo Katayama	J	Minardi Team S.p.A.	Minardi M197	Hart V8 2996 cc	20th: 1'20"606	10th: 60 Laps
4	Heinz-Harald Frentzen	D	Williams Grand Prix Engineering	Williams FW19	Renault V10 2998 cc	1st: 1'18"216	R

R: Retired
Number
Driver's name
Driver's nationality:

A	Austria
AUS	Australia
B	Belgium
BR	Brazil
CDN	Canada
CH	Switzerland
D	Germany
DK	Denmark
E	Spain
F	France
GB	United Kingdom
H	Hungary
I	Italy
IRL	Ireland
J	Japan
MEX	Mexico
NL	Netherlands
NZ	New Zealand
P	Portugal
PL	Poland
RA	Argentina
RCH	Chile
RSA	South Africa
S	Sweden
SF	Finland
THA	Thailand
USA	United States
VEN	Venezuela
YU	Yugoslavia

Name of team
Model
Engine manufacturer, number and configuration of cylinders (L: in line, F: flat, V: V-shaped, H: H-shaped); capacity; + C: compressor, + T: turbocharged
Position and fastest lap in qualifying. Pole time in *italics*
Ranking and total time of all laps. Fastest in **bold**

R: Ausgeschieden
Startnummer
Name des Fahrers
Nationalität des Fahrers:

A	Österreich
AUS	Australien
B	Belgien
BR	Brasilien
CDN	Kanada
CH	Schweiz
D	Deutschland
DK	Dänemark
E	Spanien
F	Frankreich
GB	Großbritannien
H	Ungarn
I	Italien
IRL	Irland
J	Japan
MEX	Mexiko
NL	Niederlande
NZ	Neuseeland
P	Portugal
PL	Polen
RA	Argentinien
RCH	Chile
RSA	Südafrika
S	Schweden
SF	Finnland
THA	Thailand
USA	Vereinigte Staaten
VEN	Venezuela
YU	Jugoslawien

Name des Teams
Modell
Motorhersteller, Zylinderzahl und -anordnung (L: in Reihe, F: Boxer, V: V-förmig, H: H-förmig); Hubraum; + C: mit Kompressor, + T: mit Turbolader
Plazierung und bestes Ergebnis im Training. Schnellster *kursiv*
Plazierung und Gesamtzeit im Rennen. Schnellster **fett**

R: Abandon
Numéro
Nom du pilote
Nationalité du pilote :

A	Autriche
AUS	Australie
B	Belgique
BR	Brésil
CDN	Canada
CH	Suisse
D	Allemagne
DK	Danemark
E	Espagne
F	France
GB	Royaume-Uni
H	Hongrie
I	Italie
IRL	Irlande
J	Japon
MEX	Mexique
NL	Pays-Bas
NZ	Nouvelle-Zélande
P	Portugal
PL	Pologne
RA	Argentine
RCH	Chili
RSA	Afrique du Sud
S	Suède
SF	Finlande
THA	Thaïlande
USA	Etats-Unis
VEN	Venezuela
YU	Yougoslavie

Nom de l'écurie
Désignation de la voiture
Fabricant du moteur, nombre et disposition des cylindres (L : en ligne, F : boxer, V/H : en forme de V/H) ; cylindrée ; + C : avec compresseur, + T : avec turbocompresseur
Classement et temps de la qualification. Pole position en *italique*
Classement et temps de la course. Vainqueur en **gras**

BIBLIOGRAPHY
BIBLIOGRAPHIE

Auto-Jahr 1953–1997, Edita

Blunsden, J. and A. Brinton: *Motor Racing Year 1960–1977,* Motor Racing Publications Ltd.

Cutter, R. and B. Fendell: *Encyclopedia of Auto Racing Greats,* Prentice-Hall Inc. 1973

Deschenaux, J.: *Marlboro Grand Prix Guide 1950–1997,* Charles Stewart and Company Ltd.

Edler, K.-H. and W. Roediger: *Die deutschen Rennfahrzeuge,* VEB Fachbuchverlag Leipzig 1956

Gill, B.: *John Player Motorsport Yearbooks 1972–1976*

Hewett, M., C. Brown and L. Newman: *Monaco Grand Prix, Portrait of a Pageant,* Motor Racing Publications 1989

Incandela, S.: *The Anatomy and Development of the Formula One Racing Car from 1975,* Haynes 1990

Moity, C., G. Flocon et C. Montariol: *Grand Prix Automobile de Monaco,* Editions d'Art J.P. Barthélémy 1997

Naquin, Yves: *Le Grand Prix Automobile de Monaco, Story of a Legend 1929–1960,* Editions Automobilia

Setright, L.J.K.: *The Grand Prix 1906–1972,* Nelson 1973

Small, S.: *The Guinness Complete Grand Prix Who's Who,* Guinness Publishing 1996

auto motor und sport

Autosport

PHOTOGRAPHIC CREDITS
BILDNACHWEIS · CRÉDITS PHOTOGRAPHIQUES

All photographs by Rainer W. Schlegelmilch except

© Photo Archives A.C.M.: 2, 10/11 (ills. 1, 2), 12/13 (ills. 1, 2, 4, 5), 15, 16/17 (ills. 2–6), 18/19, 22/23, 25, 26/27 (ills. 1, 3–5), 28/29, 32/33 (ill.1, 2), 34, 37, 38/39 (ills. 1, 2, 4, 5), 40/41 (ills. 1, 5), 43, 44/45 (ills. 1, 3, 4, 7), 46/47, 50/51 (ills. 1, 3, 4), 55, 56/57 (ills.1, 2, 4), 58/59, 64/65 (ills. 1–3, 5, 6), 67, 68/69, 71, 72/73, 74 (ills. 1, 2, 4), 76

© Bernard Asset: 270/271, 277, 284/285 (ill.4), 288/289 (ill.1), 320/321 (ill. 1), 345, 388/389 (ill. 2), 398/399 (ill. 1), 415, 420/421 (ills. 8, 10), 438/439 (ills. 3, 4), 442 (ill. 2), 448/449 (ill. 4), 452/453 (ill. 4)

Jean-Pierre Bompuget – Ph. Vidal: 79, 80/81 (ills. 1, 2, 5)

© Bernard Cahier: 74 (ill. 3), 85, 86/87 (ills. 2, 5), 95, 96/97 (ill. 5), 98/99 (ill. 2), 101, 102/103 (2, 4, 5), 104/105 (ill. 2, 3), 109 (ill. 2), 114/115 (ill. 2), 116, 118, 122/123 (ills. 1, 3), 142/143 (ills. 1, 4), 150/151 (ill. 5), 154/155 (ills. 1, 2), 156 (ill. 1), 164/165 (ill. 4), 170/171 (ill. 2), 178/179 (ill. 5), 181 (bottom), 183 (ill. 3), 207

© Paul-Henri Cahier: 326/327 (ill. 1), 338/339 (ill. 4), 358/359 (ill. 1), 360/361 (ill. 1), 380/381, 388/389 (ill. 1), 390/391 (ill. 4), 402/403 (ill. 7), 406/407 (ill. 1), 420/421 (ill. 12), 442 (ill. 4)

© Daimler-Benz Classic Archiv: 16/17 (ill. 1), 21, 49, 50/51 (ills. 2, 5), 52/53 (ills. 1, 5), 56/57 (ill. 3), 61, 63, 64/65 (ill. 4), 86/87 (ill. 4), 88/89 (ills.2, 4)
© Diethelm Doll: 35

Froidevaux Sport Fotos: 410/411 (ill. 3)

Oliver Hessmann: 6, 458

© Michael Hewett Collection: 44/45 (ill. 5), 80/81 (ill. 3), 128/129 (ills. 1, 4), 172/173, 188/189 (ill. 6), 194/195 (ills. 3, 4), 203 (right), 226/227 (ill. 1), 244/245 (ill. 4), 275, 357, 360/361 (ill. 3), 408/409, 435

The Klemantaski Collection: 86/87 (ill. 1: Alan R. Smith), 91 (Louis Klemantaski), 92/93 (ills. 3–5: Louis Klemantaski), 96/97 (ills. 1, 2: Louis Klemantaski), 98/99 (ills. 1, 3: Louis Klemantaski, 4: Edward Eves, 5: Louis Klemantaski), 110/111 (ills. 3–4: Edward Eves), 113 (Louis Klemantaski), 114/115 (ill. 3: Robert Daly, ill. 4: Louis Klementaski, ill. 5: Robert Daly), 124/125 (ills 1–3: Louis Klemantaski), 127 (Robert Daley), 128/129 (ills. 2, 3, 5–7: Robert Daley), 136/137 (ill. 1: Robert Daley), 141 (Robert Daley), 162/163 (ills.2, 5: Robert Daley), 168/169 (ill. 4: Robert Daley)

© Ferdi Kräling: 412/413 (ill. 7), 456/457 (ill. 16)

Ludvigsen Library: 52/53 (ill. 2)

Rodolfo Mailander/Ludvigsen Library: 80/81 (ill. 6), 82/83 (ills. 1–10)

Collection Maniago: 12/13 (ill. 3), 26/27 (ill. 2), 31, 32/33 (ill. 3), 38/39 (ill. 3), 40/41 (ills. 2–4), 44/45 (ills. 2, 6), 52/53 (ills. 3, 4, 6, 7), 56/57 (ill. 5), 80/81 (ill. 4), 86/87 (ill. 3), 88/89 (ills. 1, 3), 102/103 (ill. 3), 122/123 (ills. 4, 5), 124/125 (ills. 5, 6), 168/169 (ills. 2, 3)

Günter Molter: 92/93 (ills. 1, 2), 96/97 (ills. 3, 4), 102/103 (ill. 1), 104/105 (ill. 1), 107, 108, 110/111 (ill. 5), 114/115 (ill. 1), 121, 122/123 (ill. 2), 124/125 (ill. 4)

Photo van Bever: 109 (ill. 1), 110/111 (ills. 1, 2)

Reuters/Tom Boland: 438/439 (ill. 1)

© Ing. Alois H. Rottensteiner: 228/229 (ill. 1), 242/243 (ill. 1), 255, 260 (three images left), 262/263, 264/265 (ill. 1), 268/269 (ill. 1), 279, 280/281 (ill.2), 284/285 (ill.1), 296/297, 306/307 (ill. 2), 320/321 (ill. 4), 365, 366/367 (ill. 1), 392 (ills. 2, 4), 418/419 (ills. 1, 6), 420/421 (ill. 9), 428/429 (ill. 1), 430/431 (ills. 6, 7), 442 (ill. 5)

All photographs on the fold-out page by Rainer W. Schlegelmilch except: D. Amaduzzi (1995 first place, 1995 third place and 1983 fifth place); © Ferdi Kräling (1988 fourth place); © Pan Images Photo Jad Sherif (1984 fifth place)

1993	**1992**	**1991**	**1990**

1 Ayrton Senna
McLaren International
McLaren MP4/8

1 Ayrton Senna
Marlboro McLaren Honda
McLaren MP4/7

1 Ayrton Senna
Marlboro McLaren Honda
McLaren MP4/6

1 Ayrton Senna
Marlboro McLaren Honda
McLaren MP4/5B

2 Damon Hill
Williams Grand Prix Engineering
Williams FW15

2 Nigel Mansell
Williams Grand Prix Engineering
Williams FW14B

2 Nigel Mansell
Williams Grand Prix Engineering
Williams FW14

2 Jean Alesi
Tyrrell Racing Organisation
Tyrrell 019

3 Jean Alesi
SEFAC Ferrari S.p.A.
Ferrari F93A

3 Riccardo Patrese
Williams Grand Prix Engineering
Williams FW14B

3 Jean Alesi
SEFAC Ferrari S.p.A.
Ferrari 642

3 Gerhard Berger
Marlboro McLaren Honda
McLaren MP4/5B

4 Alain Prost
Williams Grand Prix Engineering
Williams FW15

4 Michael Schumacher
Benetton Formula Ltd.
Benetton B192

4 Roberto Moreno
Benetton Formula Ltd.
Benetton B191

4 Thierry Boutsen
Williams Grand Prix Engineering
Williams FW13B

5 Christian Fittipaldi
Minardi Team S.p.A.
Minardi M193

5 Martin Brundle
Benetton Formula Ltd.
Benetton B192

5 Alain Prost
SEFAC Ferrari S.p.A.
Ferrari 642

5 Alex Caffi
Footwork-Arrows Racing Team
Arrows A11B

6 Martin Brundle
Ligier Sports
Ligier JS39

6 Bertrand Gachot
Larrousse F1
Venturi LC92

6 Emanuele Pirro
Scuderia Italia S.p.A.
BMS Dallara F191

6 Eric Bernard
Espo Larrousse F1
Lola 90

1989

1 Ayrton Senna
Honda Marlboro McLaren
McLaren MP4/5

2 Alain Prost
Honda Marlboro McLaren
McLaren MP4/5

3 Stefano Modena
Brabham Racing Organisation
Brabham BT58

4 Alex Caffi
Scuderia Italia
BMS Dallara F189

5 Michele Alboreto
Tyrrell Racing Organisation
Tyrrell 018

6 Martin Brundle
Brabham Racing Organisation
Brabham BT58

1988

1 Alain Prost
Honda Marlboro McLaren
McLaren MP4/4

2 Gerhard Berger
SEFAC Ferrari S.p.A.
Ferrari F1-87/88C

3 Michele Alboreto
SEFAC Ferrari S.p.A.
Ferrari F1-87/88C

4 Derek Warwick
USF&G Arrows Megatron
Arrows A10B

5 Jonathan Palmer
Tyrrell Racing Organisation
Tyrrell 017

6 Riccardo Patrese
Canon Williams Team
Williams FW12

1987

1 Ayrton Senna
Camel Team Lotus
Lotus 99T

2 Nelson Piquet
Williams Grand Prix Engineering
Williams FW11B

3 Michele Alboreto
SEFAC Ferrari S.p.A.
Ferrari F1-87

4 Gerhard Berger
SEFAC Ferrari S.p.A.
Ferrari F1-87

5 Jonathan Palmer
Tyrrell Racing Organisation
Tyrrell 016

6 Ivan Capelli
March Racing
March 871

1986

1 Alain Prost
Marlboro McLaren International
McLaren MP4/2C

2 Keke Rosberg
Marlboro McLaren International
McLaren MP4/2C

3 Ayrton Senna
John Player Special Team Lotus
Lotus 98T

4 Nigel Mansell
Canon Williams Honda Team
Williams FW11

5 René Arnoux
Equipe Ligier
Ligier JS27

6 Jacques Laffite
Equipe Ligier
Ligier JS27

1985

1 Alain Prost
Marlboro McLaren
McLaren MP4/2B

2 Michele Alboreto
SEFAC Ferrari S.p.
Ferrari 156/85

3 Elio de Angelis
John Player Special
Lotus 97T

4 Andrea de Cesaris
Equipe Ligier
Ligier JS25

5 Derek Warwick
Equipe Renault Elf
Renault RE60

6 Jacques Laffite
Equipe Ligier
Ligier JS25

| **1984** | **1983** | **1982** | **1981** |

International

1 Alain Prost
Marlboro McLaren International
McLaren MP4/2

1 Keke Rosberg
TAG Williams Team
Williams FW08D

1 Riccardo Patrese
Parmalat Racing Team
Brabham BT49D

1 Gilles Villeneuve
SEFAC Ferrari S.p.A.
Ferrari 126CK

2 Ayrton Senna
Toleman Group Motorsport
Toleman TG184

2 Nelson Piquet
Fila Sport Brabham
Brabham BT52

2 Didier Pironi
SEFAC Ferrari S.p.A.
Ferrari 126C2

2 Alan Jones
Albilad-Saudia Racing Team
Williams FW07C

Team Lotus

3 Stefan Bellof
Tyrrell Racing Organisation
Tyrrell 012

3 Alain Prost
Equipe Renault Elf
Renault RE40

3 Andrea de Cesaris
Marlboro Team Alfa Romeo
Alfa Romeo 182

3 Jacques Laffite
Equipe Ligier Gitanes
Ligier JS17

4 René Arnoux
SEFAC Ferrari S.p.A.
Ferrari 126C4

4 Patrick Tambay
SEFAC Ferrari S.p.A.
Ferrari 126C2B

4 Nigel Mansell
John Player Team Lotus
Lotus 91

4 Didier Pironi
SEFAC Ferrari S.p.A.
Ferrari 126CK

5 Keke Rosberg
Williams Grand Prix Engineering
Williams FW09

5 Danny Sullivan
Benetton Tyrrell Team
Tyrrell 011

5 Elio de Angelis
John Player Team Lotus
Lotus 91

5 Eddie Cheever
Tyrrell Racing
Tyrrell 010

6 Elio de Angelis
John Player Team Lotus
Lotus 95T

6 Mauro Baldi
Marlboro Team Alfa Romeo
Alfa Romeo 183T

6 Derek Daly
Williams Grand Prix Engineering
Williams FW08

6 Marc Surer
Ensign Racing
Ensign N180B

1998	1997	1996	1995	1994

1 Mika Hakkinen
McLaren International
McLaren MP4/13

1 Michael Schumacher
SEFAC Ferrari S.p.A.
Ferrari F310B

1 Olivier Panis
Ligier F1
Ligier JS43

1 Michael Schumacher
Benetton Formula Ltd.
Benetton B195

1 Michael Schumacher
Benetton Formula Ltd.
Benetton B194

2 Giancarlo Fisichella
Benetton Formula 1 Ltd.
Benetton B198

2 Rubens Barrichello
Stewart Grand Prix Ltd.
Stewart SF-1

2 David Coulthard
McLaren International
McLaren MP4/11

2 Damon Hill
Williams Grand Prix Engineering
Williams FW17

2 Martin Brundle
McLaren International
McLaren MP4/9

3 Eddie Irvine
SEFAC Ferrari S.p.A.
Ferrari F300

3 Eddie Irvine
SEFAC Ferrari S.p.A.
Ferrari F310B

3 Johnny Herbert
P. P. Sauber International
Sauber C15

3 Gerhard Berger
SEFAC Ferrari S.p.A.
Ferrari 412T2

3 Gerhard Berger
SEFAC Ferrari S.p.A.
Ferrari 412T1

4 Mika Juhani Salo
Arrows Grand Prix International
Arrows FA19

4 Olivier Panis
Prost Grand Prix
Prost JS45

4 Heinz-Harald Frentzen
P. P. Sauber International
Sauber C15

4 Johnny Herbert
Benetton Formula Ltd.
Benetton B195

4 Andrea de Cesaris
Jordan Grand Prix
Jordan 194

5 Jacques Villeneuve
Williams Grand Prix Engineering
Williams FW20

5 Mika Juhani Salo
Tyrrell Racing Organisation
Tyrrell 025

5 Mika Juhani Salo
Tyrrell Racing Organisation
Tyrrell 024

5 Mark Blundell
McLaren International
McLaren MP4/10B

5 Jean Alesi
SEFAC Ferrari S.p.A.
Ferrari 412T1

6 Pedro Diniz
Arrows Grand Prix International
Arrows FA19

6 Giancarlo Fisichella
Jordan Grand Prix
Jordan 197

6 Mika Hakkinen
McLaren International
McLaren MP4/11

6 Heinz-Harald Frentzen
Team P. P. Sauber
Sauber C14

6 Michele Alboreto
Minardi Team S.p.A.
Minardi M194